I0810186

L'Esprit Manouche

A Comprehensive Study of Gypsy Jazz Guitar

Romane &
Derek Sébastian

English translation by Vincent Michael

Online Audio

www.melbay.com/20014BCDEB

Audio Contents

1	Swing for Nadine	10	Dans le Regard De Laura
2	Pour Trois Pas	11	Arc-en-Ciel (Rainbow)
3	Jo's Remake	12	Gypsy Fire
4	Jo's Remake	13	Valse à Django
5	Jo's Remake	14	Manège
6	Valse á Patrimonio	15	Manège
7	Monticello	16	Ombre
8	Destinée	17	Ombre
9	Dans le Regard de Laura	18	Chessés Croisés

See page 319 for a complete list of M.I.D.I. files.

WWW.MELBAY.COM

L'ESPRIT MANOUCHE intends to take you through an adventure in gypsy jazz guitar. It is actually more of a complete guide, that took a lot of work to accomplish. Such a book has never been published for Gypsy jazz music, up to this day. We sincerely believe we have created a major pedagogic and cultural work.

The audio, which is included with this book, has an abundance of audio excerpts as well as MIDI files. The disc includes all the examples, exercises and complete scores, and you can change speeds so that you can practice along with the rhythm track.

It took us a long time to finish this work and we would like to thank in particular the Carisch/Musicom Publishers and also Jo Behar and Regis Brauchli for the excellent reception and attention they have given us, as well as for their impeccable professionalism. We also thank all of those people who were closely, or remotely involved with this project, and those who have contributed to its result.

Editor's Note: L'Esprit Manouche was originally written in French. While this book has been translated into English, care was taken not to take away its original feel and style. The chord indicators have not been changed. The European standard is to write a "sharp 9" as (9♯), with the accidental following the number. Please read the glossary if there are any unrecognized terms and enjoy your journey in Gypsy Jazz.

LESPRIT MANOUCHE

A Comprehensive Study of Gypsy Jazz Guitar

INTRODUCTION

L'Esprit Manouche consists of 36 chapters, containing 6 to 8 pages each. The degree of difficulty increases progressively. You can expect to finish each chapter in about one to two weeks, depending on your speed of study.

Each chapter is divided into three sections.

PART A

In section A you will develop your guitar technique with the aid of exercises, specific chord progressions/diagrams and illustrations of fingerboard positions.

Practice these exercises and the melodies for about 30 minutes. Then, while going through each chapter, put them together with the other exercises given in this book.

This way, rather than doing the same thing 200 times, you get into the habit to put all your exercises and melodies together, thus ending up with one single melody that can last as long as you want.

PART B

1) Section B1 should, reasonably, take approximately 45 minutes. Here we will study the theory of various chord progressions and how to use these most of the time, such as the II - V - I major and minor progressions, the anatole, etc. In other words, we will study harmony.

While doing this, you should never forget to learn these chord progressions well, so that you can develop your own improvisations and compositions. For instance, you can learn many ways how to use various triads, arpeggios and scales with the V7-Im progression.

With this in mind, I strongly suggest that you first record the rhythm guitar track (while using a metronome!) so that you can practice with it. This way you will, ideally, learn to keep good time.

2) Section B2 should take about 15 to 45 minutes to finish. Here we will include the proper leads, in the style of Manouche, and look at its harmony. This is done with the use of chord diagrams. This section lets you automatically master the indispensable style of Manouche.

PART C

In the third part, we will practice solos. Here we will put together and apply the actual harmonic structure of a given theme. This will include technical diagrams, note embellishments, typical melodies, speed effects, virtuosity exercises, keeping in time, etc.

The study of this part takes between 1 to 4 hours. It will mainly consist of guitar solos taken from the original compositions that you can find on my CDs. These are shown, note-for-note, in the traditional music notation and in tablature. These solos come complete with harmonic symbols that coincide with the improvised melodies.

TEST

In the last chapter, you are given the opportunity to test yourself by taking a comprehensive test (answers located in the back of the book). Here you can test your newly acquired skills. We hope that you can correct any hidden mistakes that may appear while playing. Remember it doesn't matter at which level you play, mistakes will always be a handicap.

Derek Sebastian and I encourage you to study, and wish you great success.

ROMANE

DISCOGRAPHY - LIBRARY

In order to help you with your Jazz adventure, you can use these recorded pieces and educational books, which I have previously prepared. Some of these were done while collaborating with Derek.

CD RECORDINGS

Traces de Loups (Wolf Tracks)
Romane Quintet
Romane Ombre (Romane's Shadow)
(France) (Samois on the Seine)
(New Quintet of France's Hot Club)
(Odd and Waltz)

These albums are available in all the FNAC, VIRGIN and other record stores.

VIDEOS

Virtuosity and Harmony of Jazz Guitar in the style of Manouche.
PDG / Connection Publishing -+33 (0)1.4.42.50.09.87

STUDY MATERIAL
La Guitare Manouche (Manouch style Guitar) Salabert Editions -+33 (0)1.48.24.55.60
Gypsy Jazz Paul Beuscher/Arpege -+33 (0)1.44.54.36.00
(La Pump) (the drive) Henry Lemoine Editions -+33 (0)1.56.68.86.65

You can buy these items in all stores that sell music books.

• GLOSSARY • CONVENTIONAL SYMBOLS • GENERAL INFORMATION •

> = **ACCENT.** If placed above a note, that note should be played louder.

ANACRUSIS = Pickup or lead-in at the beginning of a tune or phrase.

ANATOLE (TURNAROUND) = An anatole is a harmonic progression done by linking together the III (or I) - VI - II - V degrees. For example, an anatole in the key of C major is initially made up with the Em (or C) -Am-Dm-G, chords. See harmonization (of a major scale). Also called a turnaround.

𝅘𝅥𝅮 = This is a **GRACE NOTE**, or "a small note". Its musical effect is to play a very short note right before the main note, as a decoration.

KEY SIGNATURE = This is a group of accidentals exclusively in either sharps or flats that are placed after the clef (𝄞), and is used to show in which key the piece is played. The sharp accidentals are placed on the staff in the following order: F - C - G - A - E - B (ascending circle of fifths). The flats are placed on the staff in the following order: B - E - A - E - B (descending circle of fifths). If the key signature uses sharps, we can find out which (major) key is used by looking at the last sharp placed in that signature: You will find the key 1/2 tone higher than that sharp. For example, if we look at a key signature that has the F♯ - C♯ - G♯ accidentals, the key is one 1/2 tone higher than the G♯, which is A major. If the key signature uses flats, we can find the (major) key, which is indicated by the next to the last flat placed in the key signature. For example, a key signature with Bb - Eb - Ab is in the key of Eb, because Eb is the next to the last flat. A key signature with only one Bb is in the key of F major. All minor keys are located 1 -1/2 tones lower than the major key - for example, the key of D minor is located 1 1/2 tones lower than F (it is called the relative minor of F major). We find it by counting 1-1/2 tones backwards, from F to D.

BEND (+ 1/2) = If this symbol is placed above a note, it shows that you should bend the string to make it sound a 1/2 tone higher.

CADENCE = This is a synonym for a chord progression. For example, the II - V - I cadence.

CHRISTOPHE (PLAGAL CADENCE) = This is a harmonic progression constructed by linking the IV - IVm (or IV dim7) - I degrees together. For example, a Christophe in the key of C major is initially composed with the F - Fm - (or Fdim7) - C chords. Look at harmonization (of a major scale). (The progression called "Christophe" is named after the "Christopher Columbus" theme that used it).

CHROMATIC = This means to proceed from half tone to half tone, from half step to half step. On the guitar, this will be from one fret to the next, which is a "chromatic scale".

⊕ = **CODA.** If this (+) symbol is shown, it indicates that the section of the piece is added at the end of the last measure, and is used as a conclusion.

D. C. = Da Capo. This means to go back to the entire beginning of the score and repeat it. See the example below. A total of sixteen measures should be played:

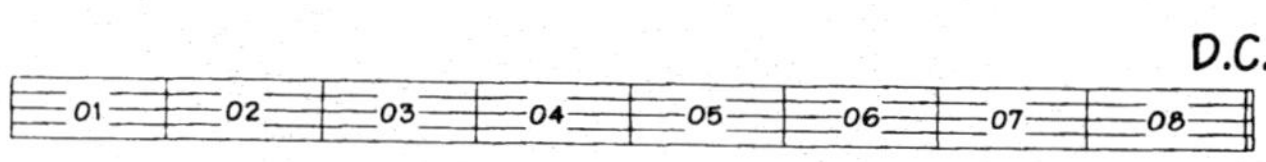

(×) = this indicates a **DEAD NOTE.** A note without a determined pitch, where its character is essentially rhythmic / dynamic in nature.

FUNDAMENTAL (or ROOT NOTE) = The fundamental of a chord is that note from which the chord originates. For example, for the C minor chord, the C note is its fundamental.

GLISS. = Glissando. This means to connect two notes by sliding fast over all the notes in between, either ascending or descending:

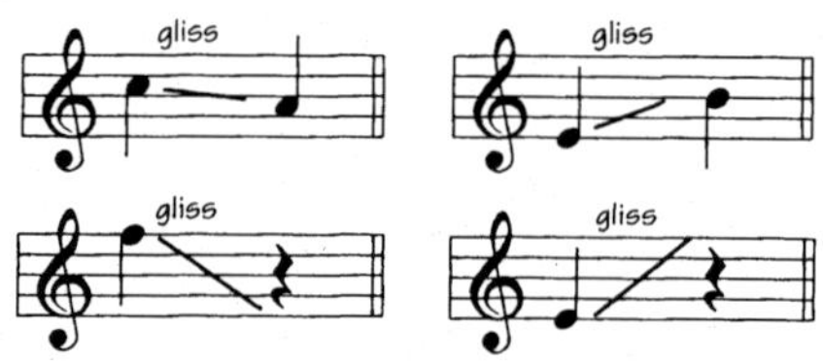

H = abbreviation of Hammer on. It is a technique done by simply playing a note while "hammering" a finger of the left hand on the string, without picking the note. As a matter of fact, it is a "hammered on" tie, we can play two or more ascending or descending notes on a single string with a single attack.

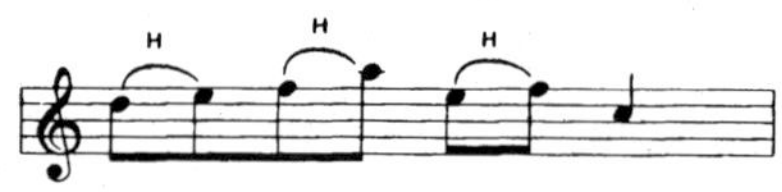

◇ = **HARM.** A harmonic is a note that is produced in a particular way on the fingerboard of the guitar. For example, we can get a harmonic of an octave by striking any of the six open strings, while slightly touching that string above the 12th fret, followed by lifting the finger immediately afterwards.

8va = This means to play the part one octave higher.

8vb = This means to play the part one octave lower.

HARMONIZATION = Harmonization (of the major scale) takes place when we take a major scale and stack a minimum of two intervals of thirds (major = 2 steps, minor = 1 1/2 steps) above any of the 7 notes. This means that one group of seven chords enters into a special relationship with each other. These seven chords are conveniently called "degrees" and are indicated with roman numerals. For example, the harmonization with four tones of the C and D major scales give us the following:

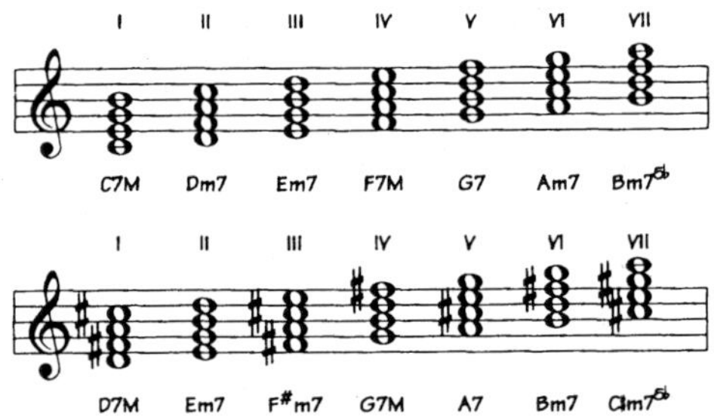

—— = This is a graphic symbol joining and indicating that the set of these notes must be played smoothly and that only the first note is struck.

LOCO = This means to undo the 8va and 8vb symbols.

BRIDGE = This is a synonym for the "B" section of a piece, which is globally recognized.

P = This means Pull- Off. This application works as a tie. The first note is struck only and the second or more notes (lower) is/are produced by pulling off the string without re-striking it. As matter of fact, we can play two or more descending notes on a single string with only a single attack:

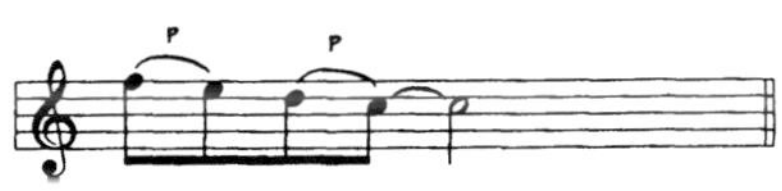

RALL = This is rallentando. If placed above a section it means to gradually slow the speed of that section while playing it.

% = This is the repeat symbol. You must replay the immediate preceding measure, or if this **%%** symbol is shown, you must repeat the immediate preceding two measures (or more if so indicated).

‖: :‖ = This is a repeat sign for a section. You must repeat the music between these two double dotted, double bars once (or more if so specified).

Rub. = This means RUBATO. This indicates to play without paying strict attention to the speed of execution (fluctuations of the metronome).

• = **STACCATTO** or "shortened note": This symbol indicates, that when it is placed above a note (or eventually below a note), you are to cut its regular duration, generally in half.

SUBSTITUTION = This is the replacement of a chord having four tones with that of another that has a similar function than the one replaced. The substitution is made possible thanks to the notes these chord have in common, which makes it possible to join certain chords with certain others. We distinguish two main types of chord substitutions:

1) The so-called "diatonic" substitution, which by itself uses only one and the same key. Thus the chord of the I degree could be replaced with a chord of the III or VI degree, and visa versa. For example, check out the great similarities that appear between the following chords (I, III and VI degree) in the key of C major:

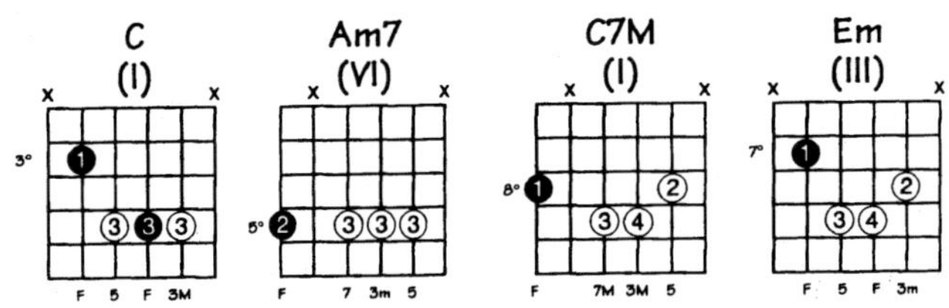

2) The so-called "Tritone" substitution (based on the interval of three tones, called a tritone), that only has to do with the V7 chord (constructed with the 5th degree of the major scale harmonized with 4 tones). This makes it possible for us to go from one "A" key to a "Z" key instantly (that is to say, it is very far fetched). Thus the G7 chord, for example, (the V7 in the key of C major) could be replaced with a Db7 (or a potential V7 in the key of Gb major), thanks to the following similarities.

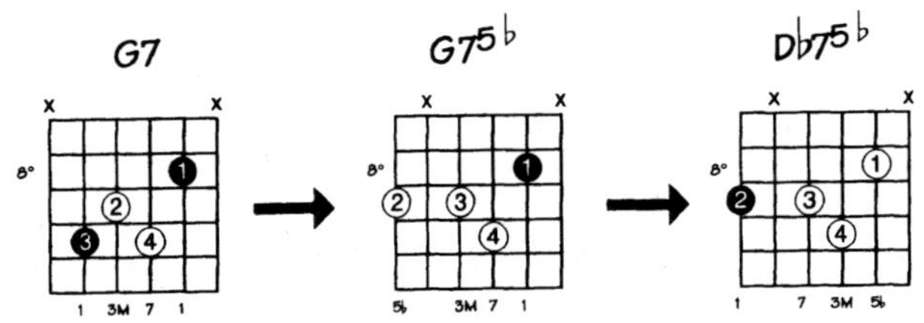

SWEEP = This is used in the area of improvising melodies. It means that we rapidly sweep (strike) the pick over the strings with one single stroke. (⊓ = down stroke; V = up stroke, also known as a return stroke).

TREMELO = Extremely fast repetition of a note (or when it is done with a chord, we call it "rolling").

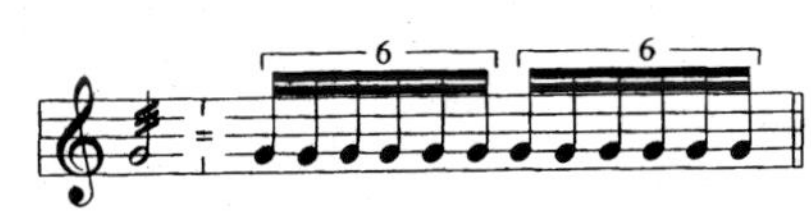

TRIAD = A group of three distinct notes.

• HOW TO READ CHORD DIAGRAMS AND HARMONIC PATTERNS •

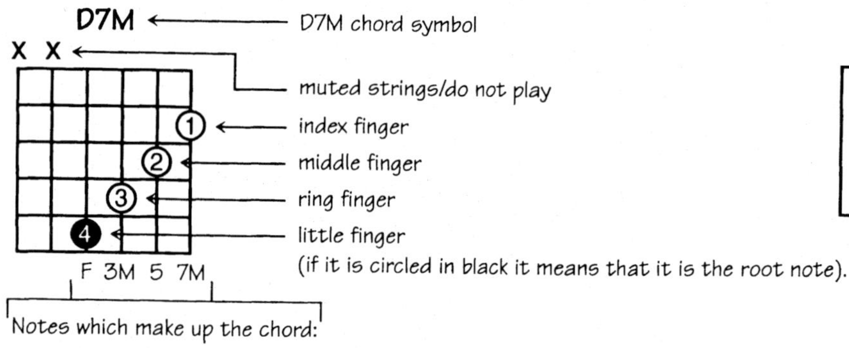

international terminology used to indicate the name of the notes or chords

A	B	C	D	E	F	G
=	=	=	=	=	=	=
la	si	do	re	mi	fa	sol

F = root note → ex. : C
9b = minor ninth → ex. : Db
9 = major ninth → ex. : D
9# = augmented ninth → ex. : D#
3m = minor third → ex. : Eb
3M = major third → ex. : E

4 = perfect fourth → ex. : F
11 = perfect eleventh → ex. : F
11# = augmented eleventh → ex. : F#
5b = diminished fifth → ex. : Gb
5# = augmented fifth → ex. : G#
13b = minor thirteenth → ex. : Ab

6 = major sixth → ex. : A
13 = major thirteenth → ex. : A
7b = seventh diminished → ex. : Bbb
7 = (minor) seventh → ex. : Bb
7M = major seventh → ex. : B

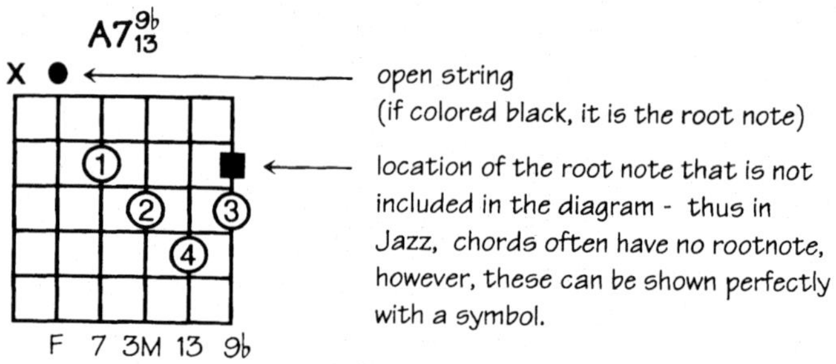

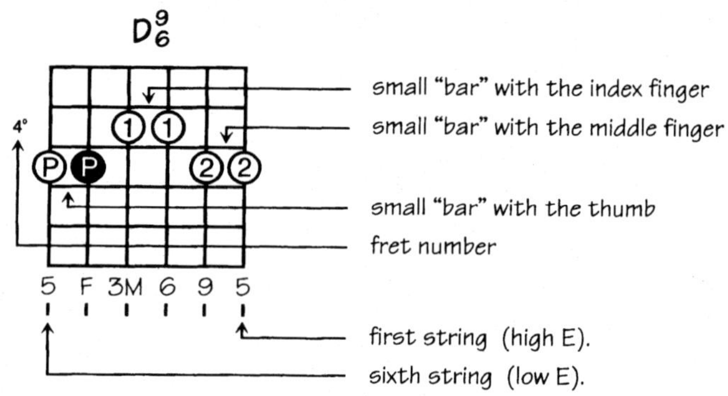

The way to divide the counts / chords is shown with partitions of a block diagram (as it is usually done).

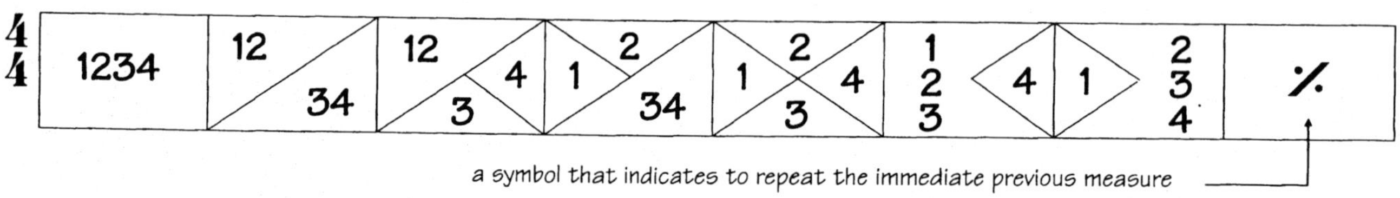

• HOW TO READ SCALE AND ARPEGGIOS DIAGRAMS •

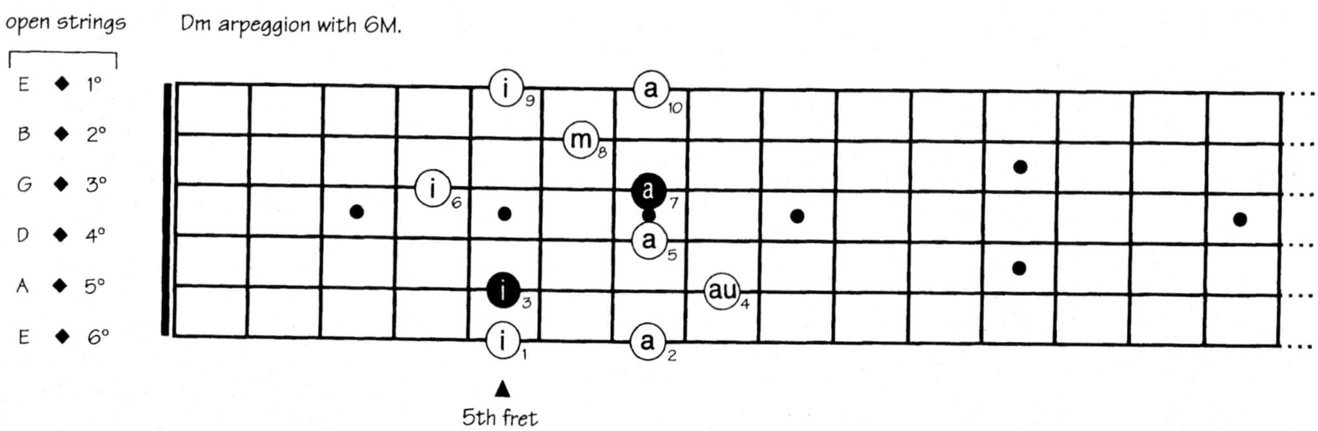

(i) = index finger
(m) = middle finger
(a) = ring finger
(au) = little finger

(i) = index finger (root note)
(m) = middle finger (root note)
(a) = ring finger (root note)
(au) = little finger (root note)

1,2,3,... 10, 9, 8 etc. = this shows the order to play the notes (ascending or descending phrase).

PART A

In the beginning of our adventure we will look into the style of Manouche and, unavoidably, into the world of minor music. We suggest that you practice exercises based on minor triads. All the exercises in the chapters to come will have music notation, chord diagrams and visual chord positions on the fingerboard. By systematically going over a measure or chord positions you will, in principle, develop confidence while improvising leads during a solo!

All the exercises that you find in part A are to be done in eighth notes, unless otherwise indicated. You should practice with a metronome while going up and down the fingerboard. You should use alternating up and down strokes with the pick. If you can, we encourage you to sing the notes at the same time while playing. This develops your musical ear, which is a major element in preparing to improvise.

Exercise 1 and 2 - minor triads 'many forms'

Play the notes following the numbers in the ascending order, then in the descending order (1,2,3. . .).

#1 **Am arpeggio (A minor)**

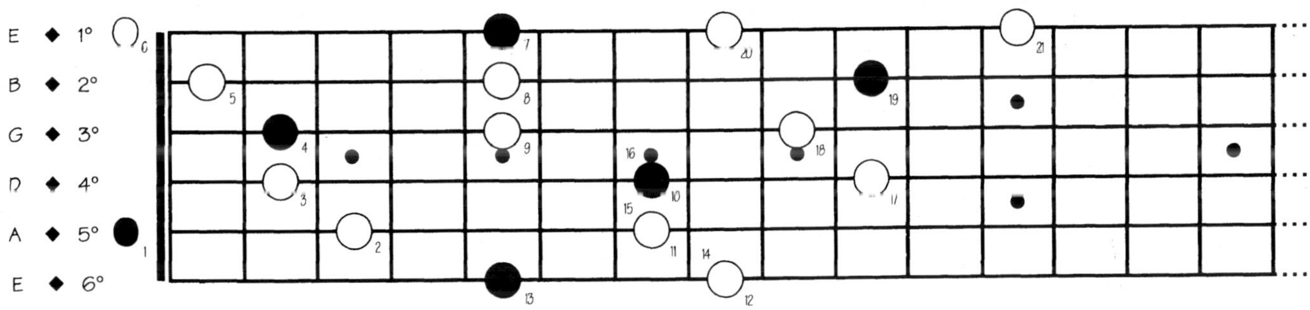

#2 **Dm Arpeggio (D minor)**

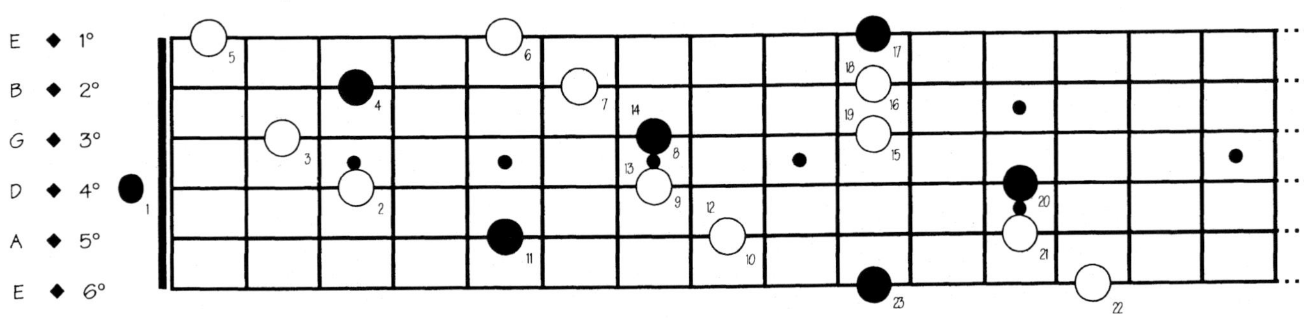

Exercise 3 / diminished seventh arpeggio

This arpeggio consists of a strict progression of minor third intervals (1 1/2 steps). The following diagram is based on the diminished arpeggio.

Note that this diagram only uses two notes per string, and it is shown as some type of an almost regular "scale", with the exception of the third and second strings (we are jumping ahead a step!).

#3

Dim7 arpeggio (Fdim7, or A♭ dim7, or Bdim7, or Ddim7).

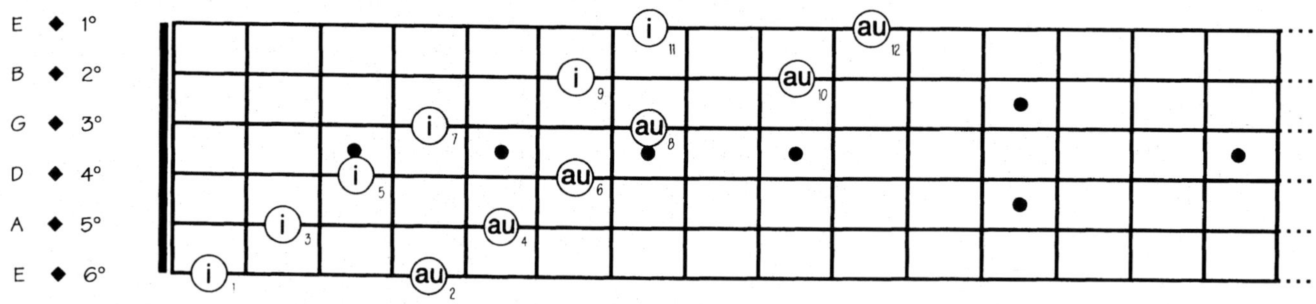

Exercise 4 / diminished seventh arpeggio

Memorize the following diagram. While playing in the style of Manouche, it is often used as an option when you improvise with any type V7 chord that has its root note on the sixth string.

The diagram below uses the A7 chord, starting with the root note (A). Of course, you can use the same diagram for the G7 if you start two frets lower (from the third fret). This it's simply a case of transposing.

#4

A dim7 arpeggio with A7.

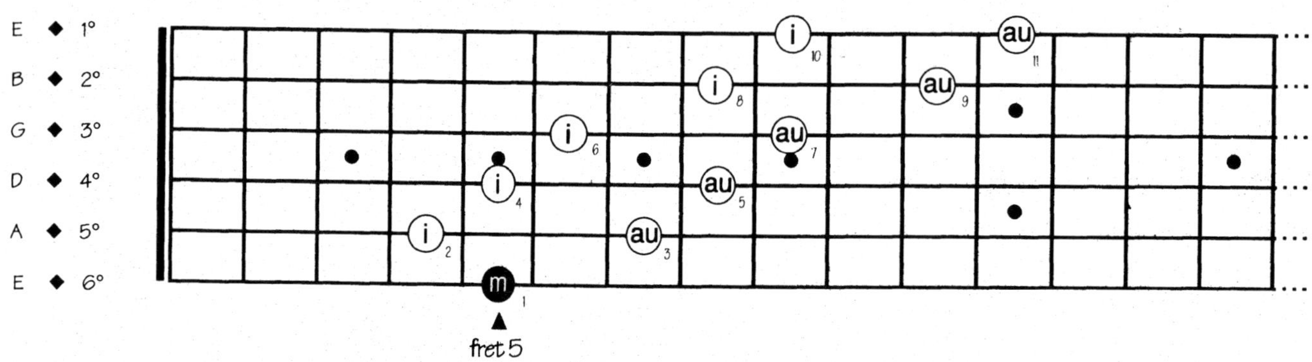

PART B1

We are now reaching the point of looking into the harmony while studying our first diagram with its various aspects. It is in the style of Manouche. We will use the chords from the song "Swing for Ninine".

You can listen to "Swing for Ninine" on the Romane and Romane Quintet albums.

The harmonic structure of this piece is as follows:

Swing For Ninine

structure = 32 measures AABA

♩= 208

A	Am	%	B♭6	%	E7	%	Am (stop chorus)	%
A				8 %%				
B	Dm	%	Am	%	B♭6	%	E7	%
A				8 %%				

This is a "standard" diagram in the sense that it has 32 measures, 4 sections of 8 measures each - where the "A" forms the main theme and "B" the secondary part, which is usually, called a "bridge". This type of structure is often used in songs.

Knowing this structure is essential in Jazz because, from a rhythmic point of view, it lets you avoid the pitfall of guessing where you are while playing a solo. In other words, through memorizing this form, and playing in time, you should always know where you are.

We embellish the structures with its under-structures and its various procedures freely. For example, by listening to "Swing for Ninine", you can hear an eight measure "intro", intended to set the tempo. It is also a "stop chorus", in which the soloist will continue to play alone. The stop chorus plays the role of a "melodic springboard", which serves to give the whole melody a boost, improvised or not. Finally, don't forget the "coda" which historically, always enter at the end of the piece.

Now we will look at how to play the chords of this diagram.

Below, you will see subtle harmonic changes of the symbols that are written on the previous page. For instance: Am6 is used instead of Am. The reason for these changes is simply that Jazz is improvised music, which includes its accompaniment.

This way it is easier to understand the harmonic structure of a song, so that you can improvise over it easily. We usually simplify the name of the chords in the block diagram (basic diagram), even if the chords are sometimes really more complex in nature.

Section A :

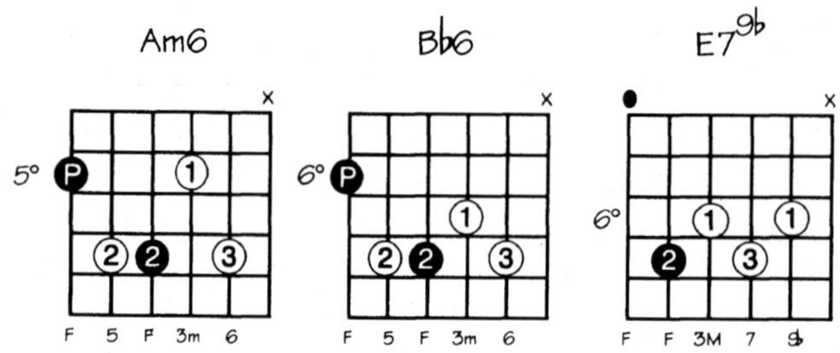

Section B :

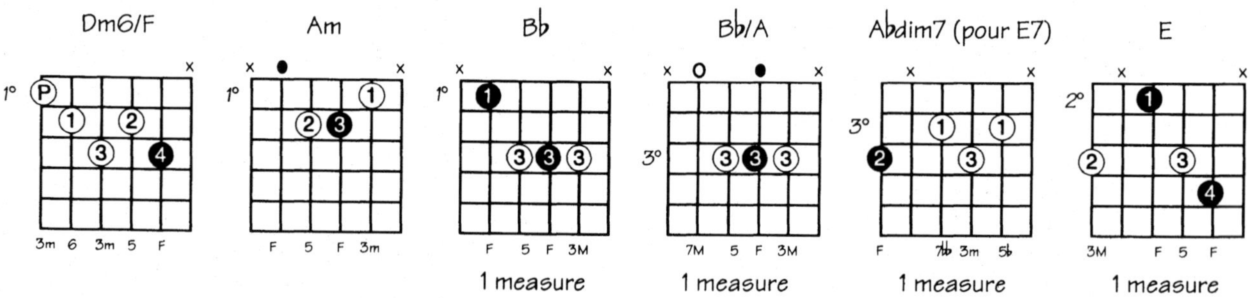

Here are the chords and chord diagrams as they are actually played in the introduction of "Swing for Ninine" (the Romane Quintet version on the CD).

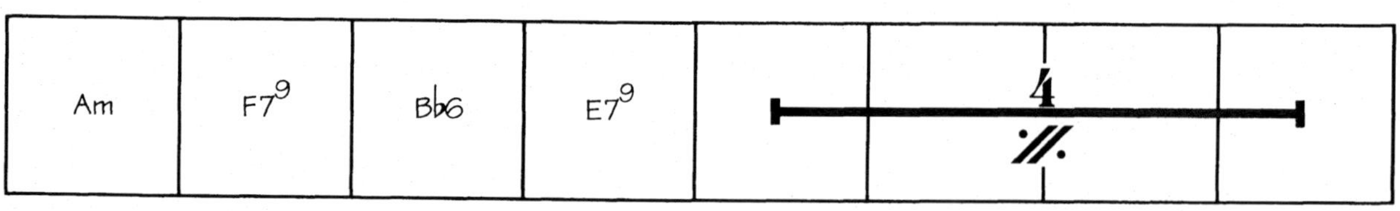

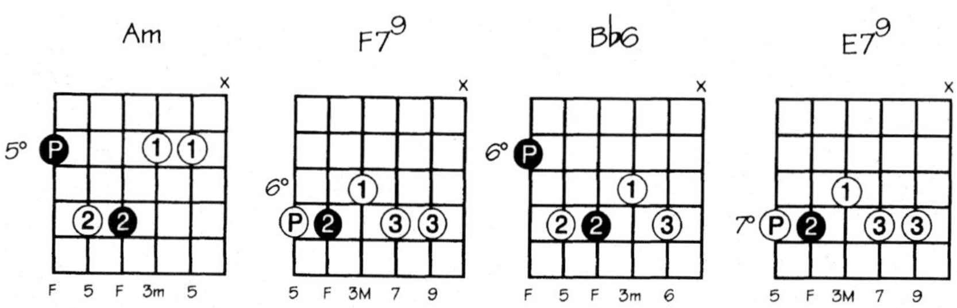

For practicing the solos shown above, record these chord diagrams (while using a metronome!).

PART B2

This section is set apart for studying the leads and intros of "Swing for Ninine" as the Manouche typically play it.

Of course, in this style, the construction of the melodies play a major role in visualizing the fingerboard. The leads and intros of the melody in question will always rely on the principle of the diagrams evolved from these chords that "cross" their diagrams and their fret positions. This uses the identical principle as the one we used to memorize technique exercises, in part A.

"Swing for Ninine" (measures 19, and 25) lead and diagram #1

This lead, which makes up the first four notes of the song, is called a "sweep" in today's musical jargon (see glossary). For several years, it was called a "rest stroke". The fact that the four notes go up makes it an ascending sweep. This applies to the first voice (Guitar 1) as well as to the second (Guitar 2). The two are played together with a single down stroke of the pick (indicated by " ⊓ ").
Nothing is simpler than when these diagrams are based on these sweeps:

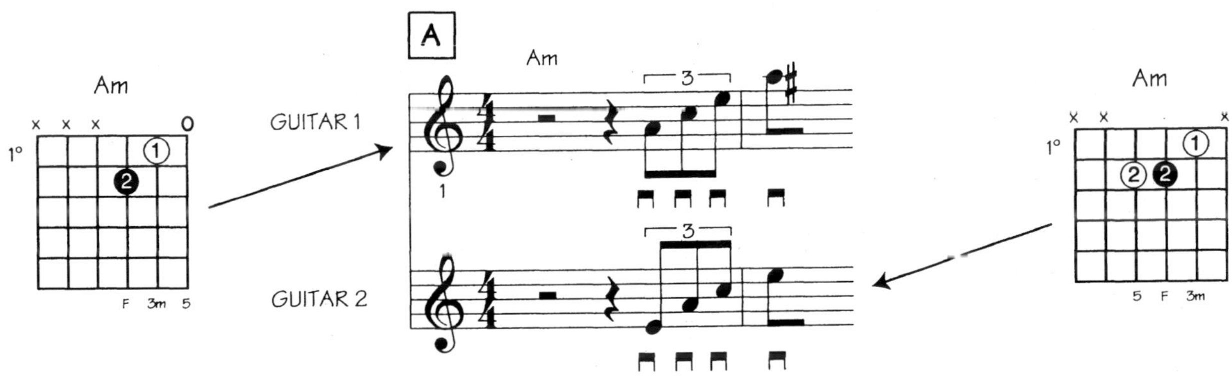

"Swing for Ninine" (measure 17) lead and diagram #2

In the first measure of the bridge, you will find the same ascending sweeps done with the minor chord (Dm). Look at the similarities of these diagrams and their exercises given with multi- forms of minor triads (Part A of this chapter). Once more, be sure to use the up stroke for the note of the triplet.

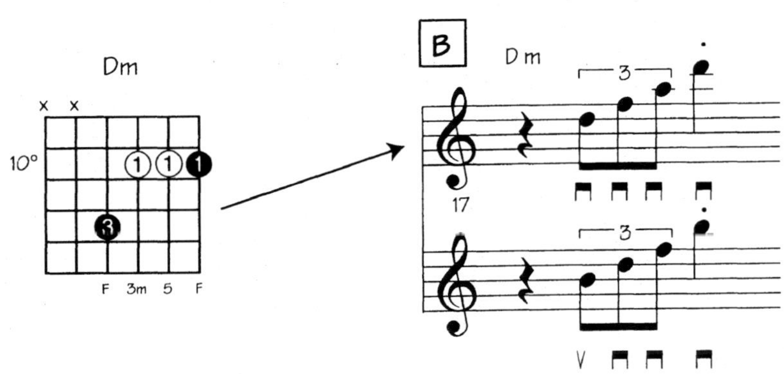

We still use ascending sweeps, but with a different harmonic color, because it is in a major key. It still has a second voice. Be sure to use the up stroke of the first note.

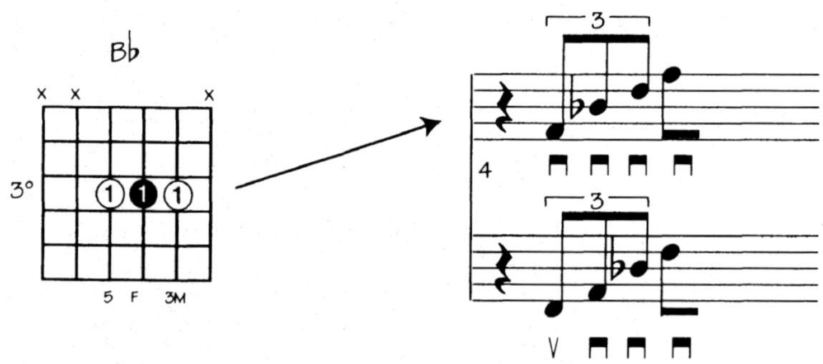

"Swing for Ninine" (measures 7 and 8) lead and diagram #4

This one is more complex; it is an ascending quadruple sweep based on the dim7 chord, which works here as an E7 chord. This gives it a certain virtuosity effect, only because we use triplets with sixteenth notes.

It is important to keep good time here, but to make things easy, you have an excellent reference point for the beat (eighth note): except in the first entire sweep. Notice that all the upstrokes (V) are done exactly on the heavy beats of the measure, including the whole last (quarter) note.

As far as the diagrams are concerned, they are founded on the harmonic properties of the dim7 chord that reproduces the same notes, systematically separated with minor thirds. All you have to do is move the same diagram three frets (a minor third).

Finally, pay attention to which fingers you place behind the frets while following the diagram. The success to play this lead like Manouche depends on this.

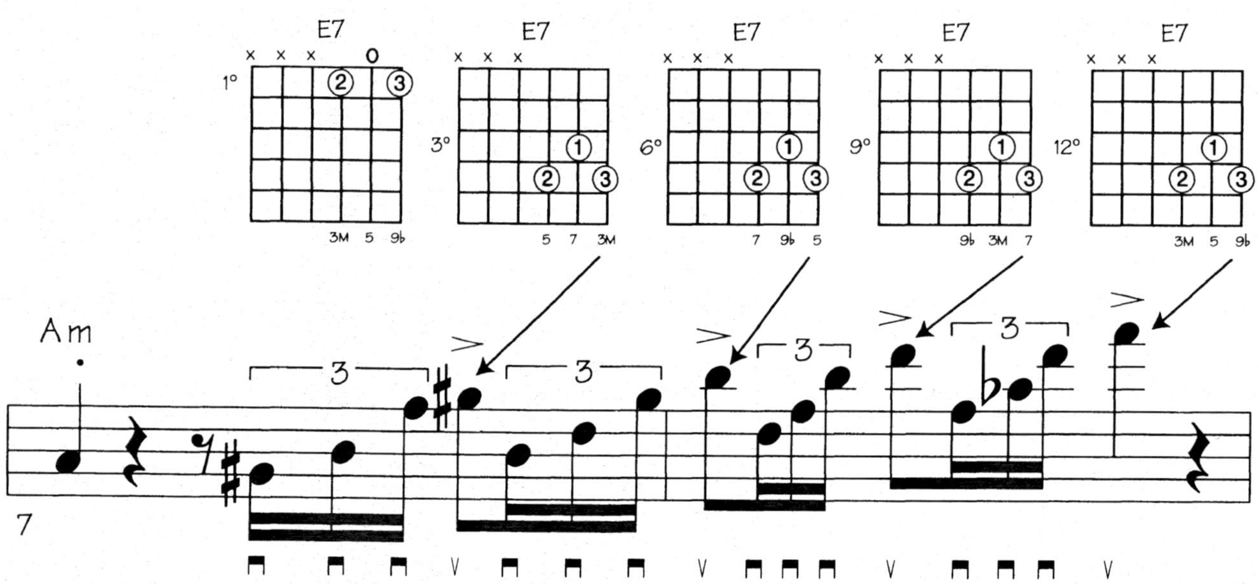

PART C

In this first chapter we are going to study the first measures of the "Swing for Ninine" song (which is continued and finished in chapter 2).

This version is taken from the Romane Quintet album. It has a second voice, played with a violin, but nothing prevents you from playing it on guitar.

Notice that the notes are played in a compound way, as indicated. Swing the eighth notes.

#5

Swing For Ninine

music by ROMANE

♩=208

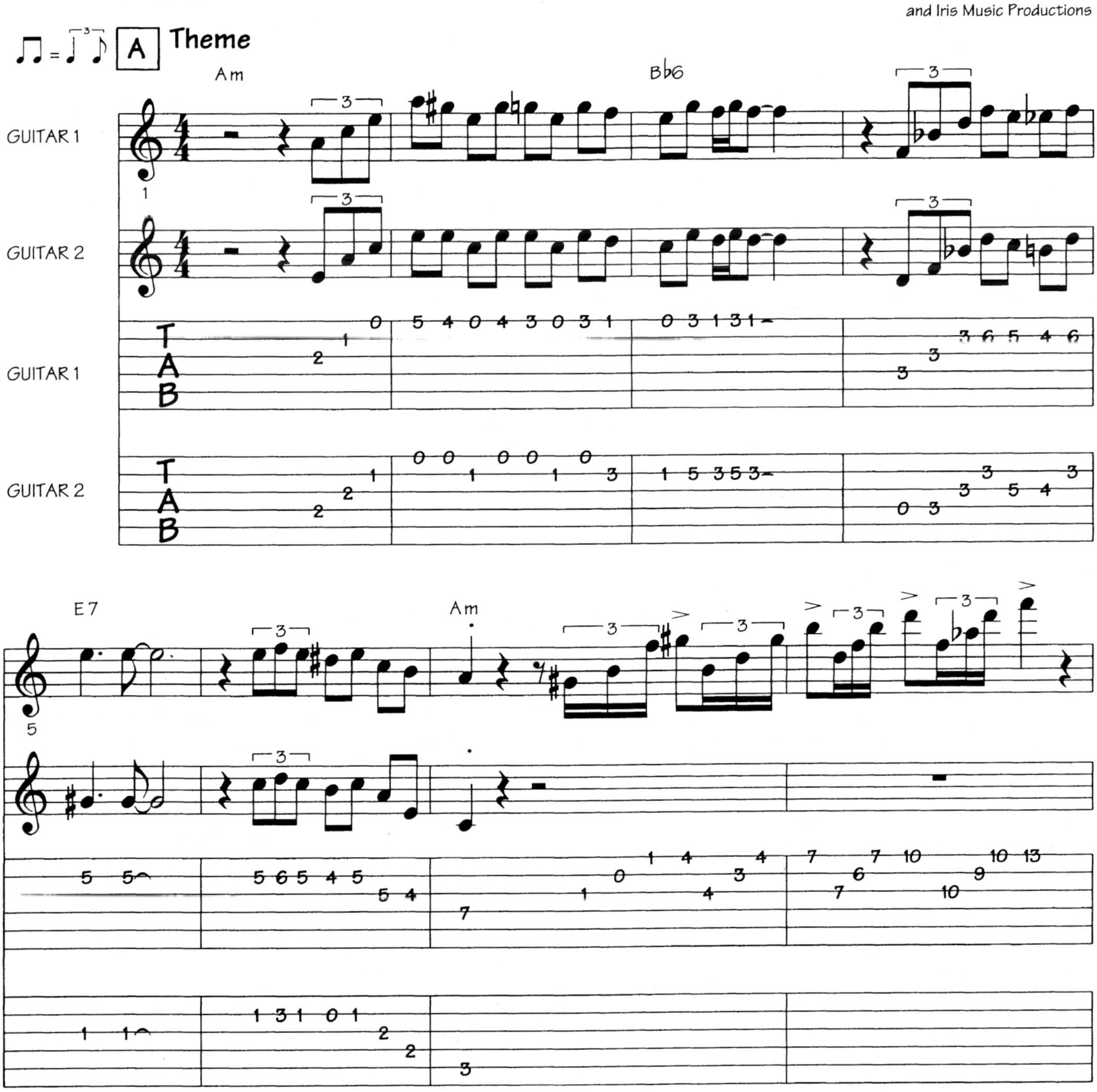

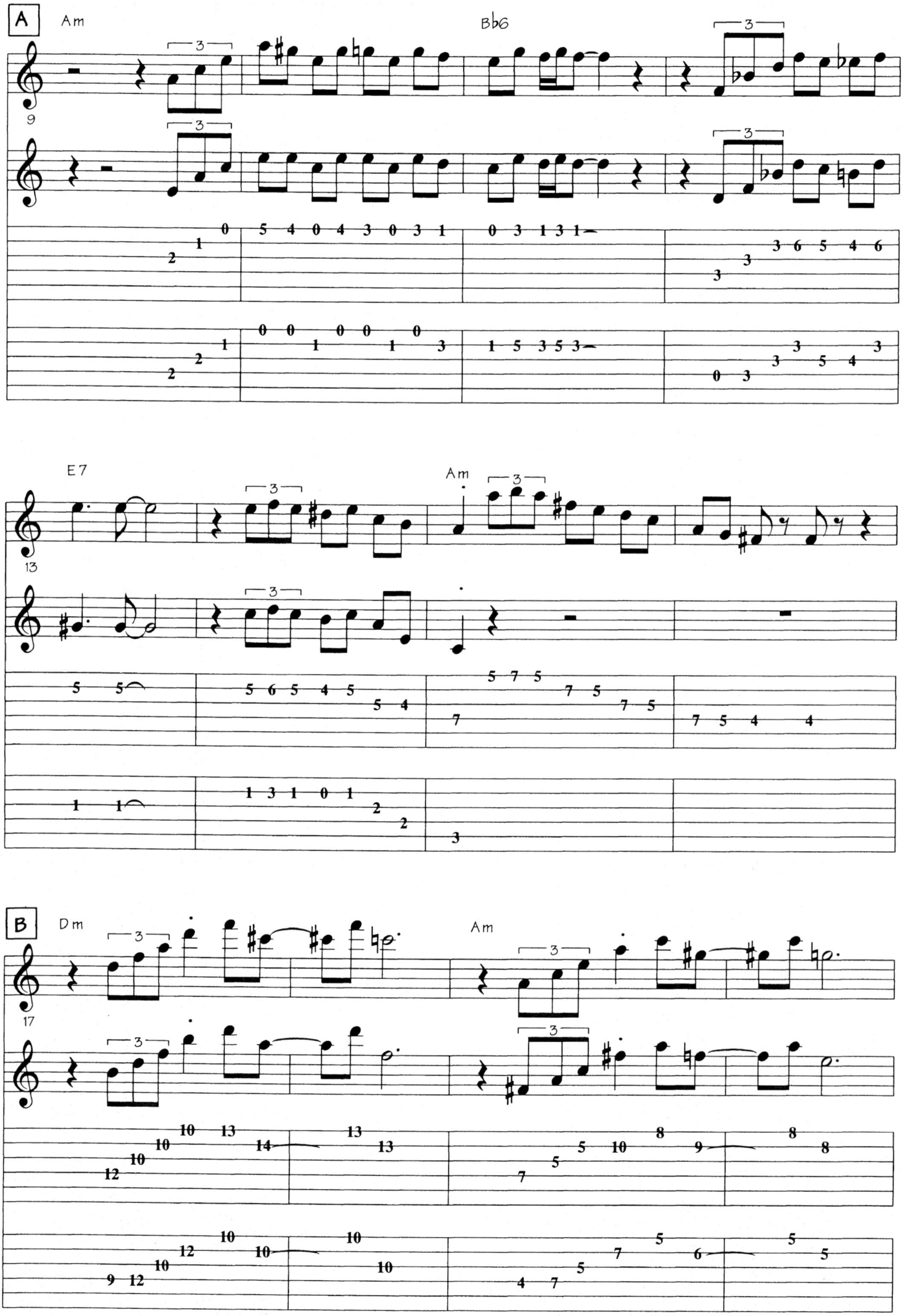
A
Am
Bb6
E7
Am
B
Dm
Am

PART A

Here we are going to study exercises based on major triads.

As always, practice with a metronome while using eighth notes, with an ascending and descending phase, using down and up strokes of the pick, and don't forget to transpose these into other keys. Also, remember to sing the notes as you play.

Exercise 10 and 11 - minor triad with major second

Play the notes in the order of increasing numbers (1.2.3...), then in the decreasing order.

Notice: We will leave the fingering up to you, when the diagram uses many octaves.

#6

B♭ major arpeggio

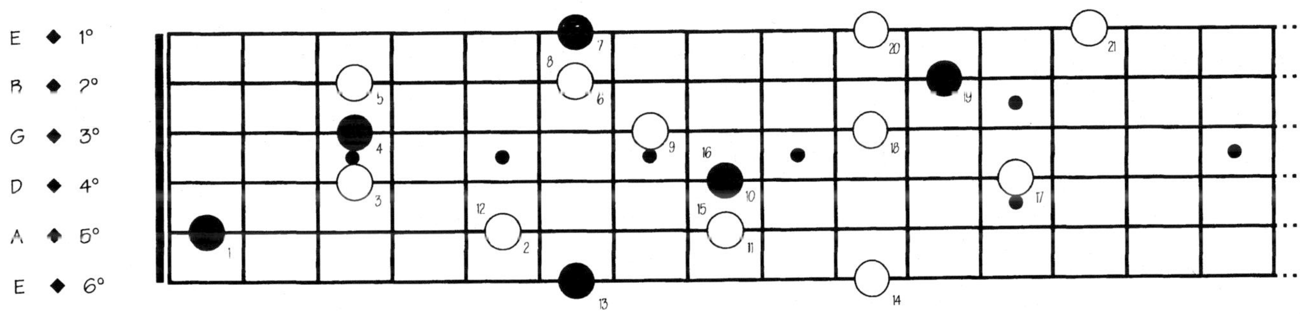

#7

E major arpeggio

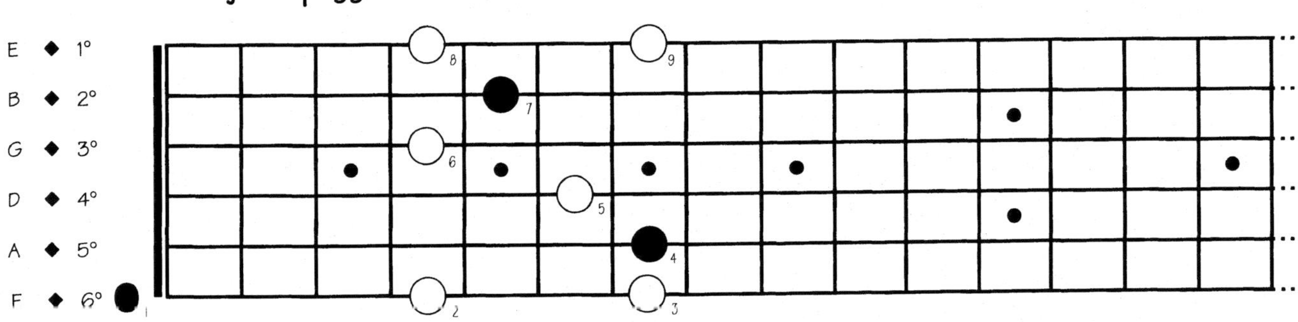

Next we continue with a very common scale, styled after the way Manouche plays it. When improvising in a minor key they use the harmonic minor scale.

Here we show two forms, one form is known as 'in position', the other one as 'reaching over'. You have to know the two perfectly.

Exercise 7 and 7bis - harmonic minor scale

Play the notes in increasing numerical order (1,2,3...), then in decreasing numerical order.

#8

A harmonic minor scale (position).

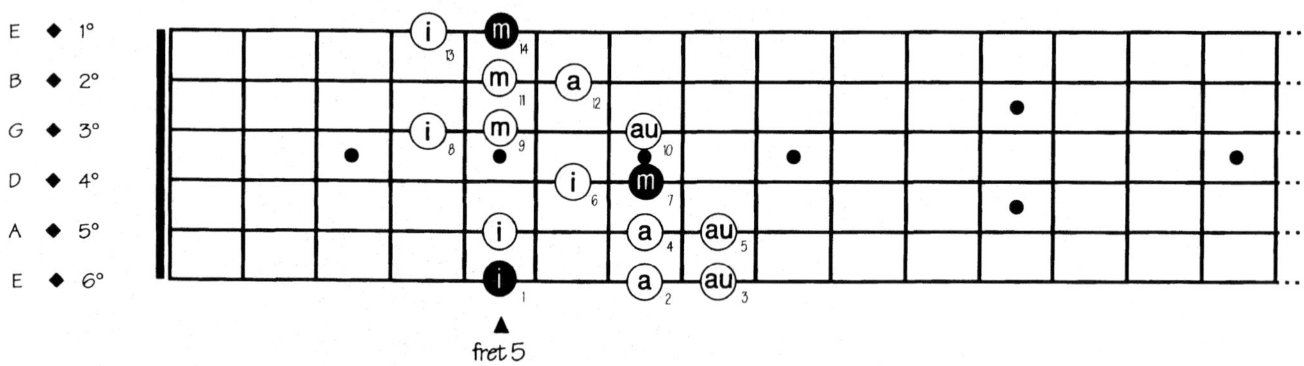

#9

A harmonic minor scale (overreaching).

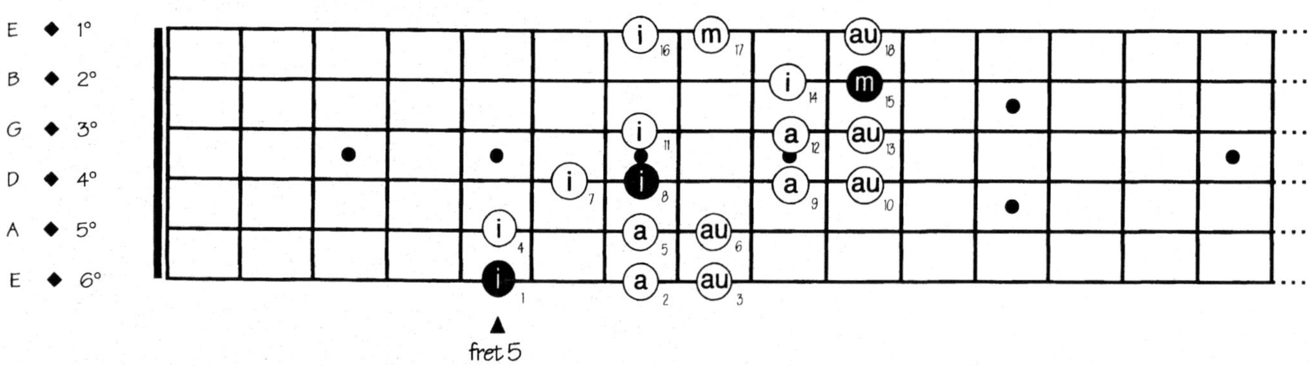

Although it shows the simplest harmonic minor scale (by naming the notes in succession) that starts from the A note. You will eventually have to start this scale from other root note centers as well. In other words, you have to transpose.

PART B1

We will still be using the minor harmonic scale to explore its theoretical aspects, namely, to show you how to use of the chords the same way as Manouche does.

The structure of the minor harmonic scale is as follows (A - harmonic minor, shown below):

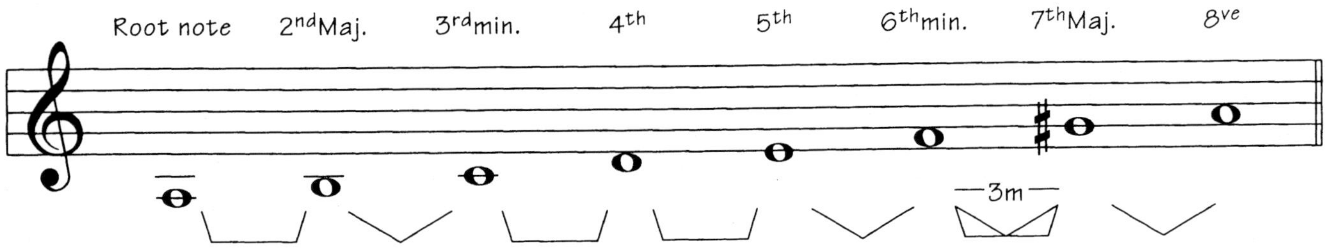

Note: Notice that the G♯ - which is the only change - is not placed in the key signature! You do not always have to do this.

Now, let's see what type of chords we can produce with this scale when we harmonize it. That is to say, when we place thirds above each (M or m) of the seven notes. We are now going to stack up three thirds, and will get chords with four distinct notes:

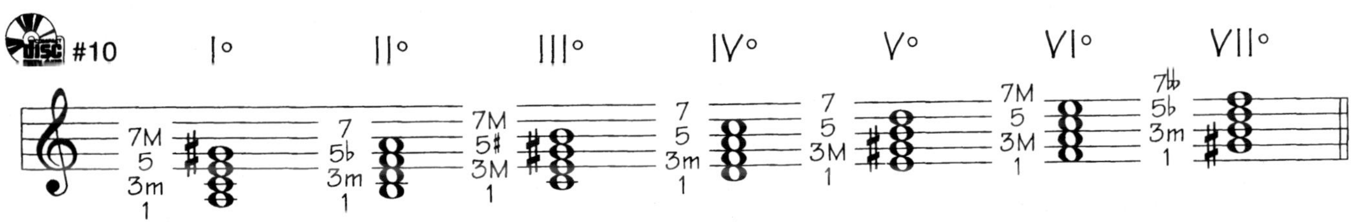

harmonic symbols with 3 notes :	Am	Bdim	C +	Dm	E	F	G♯dim
harmonic symbols with 4 notes :	Am7M	Bm7$^{5♭}$	C7M$^{5♯}$	Dm7	E7	F7M	G♯dim7

One thing should be cleared up with this basic harmonization, before we do anything else. With its fifth degree (V7), the minor harmonic scale develops a "dominant seventh" type chord. That is to say, when we go from low to high, we will get, as you can see, the root note, a major third, a perfect fifth and a minor seventh. All this can be summarized up as "1 - 3 - 5 -7" (in this case we get: E - G♯ - B - D = the E7 chord).

In reality, as far as the development of melodies in a minor harmonic context is concerned, the harmonic minor scale is mainly, and freely, used with the V7 chord that comes before the central Im (for example, in the key of A minor, E7 comes before the Am). This chord is "colored" more often than not, by raising it with a minor ninth (♭9). This is done for the good and simple reason that this ♭9 appears with the V7 of the harmonic minor scale, when we continue to harmonize it.

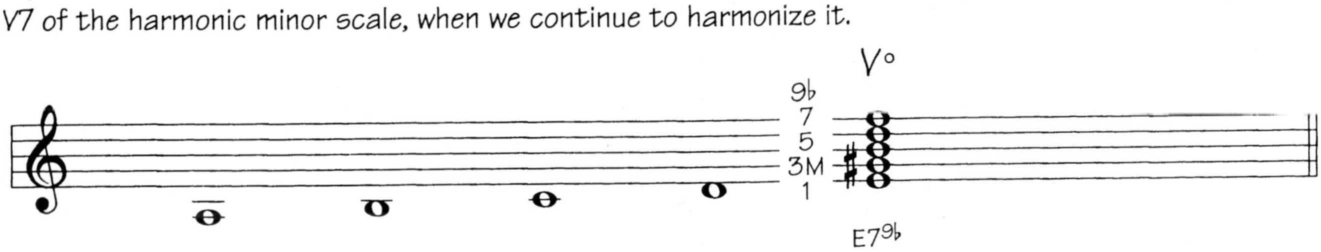

Besides, this plays an important role in the way Manouche plays - this V7(♭9) chord has very close ties with the dim7 chord, as we will see.

Of course, everything is logical with harmony. The V7(♭9) chord is related to the dim7 chord in the measure where this last one also appears by itself during the harmonization of the harmonic minor scale - in this case with the seventh degree (VIIdim7).

The small difference is because the V7(9♭) is a chord with only five tones, while the VIIdim7 has only four.

But what happens if you hide the root note of the V7(9♭) chord?

Well, we simply end up with the VIIdim7 chord!... a "sleight of hand" which we call "making a substitution": the two chords are closely related because they share common notes. That's why it is always possible to replace one with the other or, to be more exact, consider a VIIdim7 in place of the other V7(♭9).

Whatever the case is with the dim7 chord, the substitutions can go much farther because it can have not only two, but eight combinations.

It has a very particular structure that is produced with an exclusive succession of minor thirds. Thus, the "dim7" chord has the ability to let you use exactly the same harmonic symbols to start from each of its composed notes.

#11

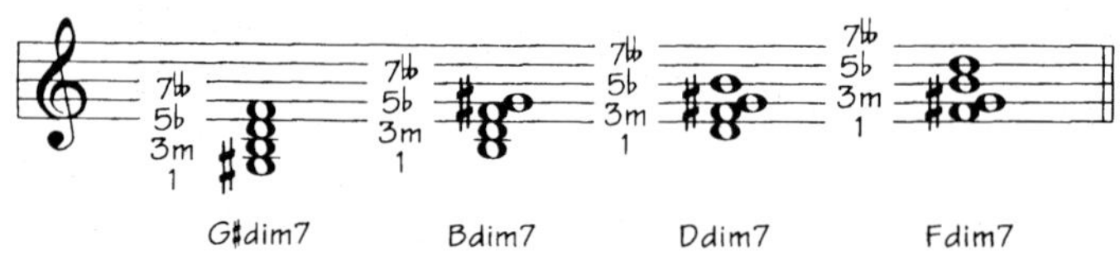

And since the entire "dim7" chord has ties with the 7(♭9) chord, the total substitutions amount to well over eight chords, each having its own distinct names. Except for the symbols, where the same can be done with good sense... particularly with those that will suit you best, according to the harmonic context in which you will be:

#11

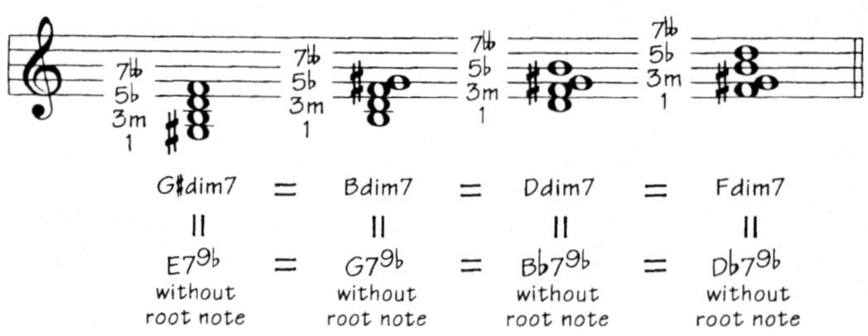

Of course, by just knowing this part of the theory by itself won't do you any good if you don't take the trouble to experiment with it during practice when you hear the notes. Also, take a moment to let the lower E of the guitar ring, and now place a "dim 7" chord over it, while moving it three whole frets:

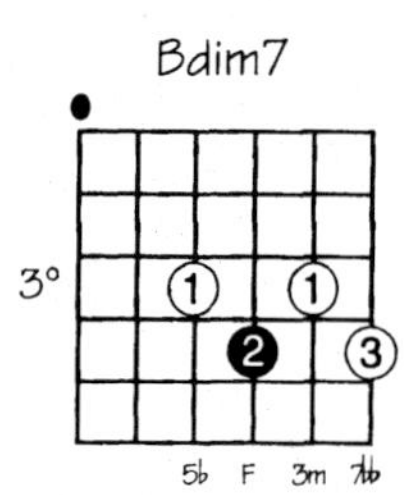

Do you recognize the sound of the #4 lead (chapter 1, page 6)?

PART B2

We are now going to check out the leads in the style of Manouche. We will use the end of the song and the beginning of the chorus from "Swing for Ninine".

Notice: What we call a "chorus" is an improvisation that takes place in the complete harmonic cycle of the piece. In the case of "Swing for Ninine", 1 chorus = 32 measures.

But, of course, in other pieces the chorus doesn't always last 32 measures. As a result you can have a solo which will last 1, 2, 3... or 30 measures per chorus.

"Swing for Ninine" (measures 23 - 24) lead and diagram #5

This is a true illustration of the harmonic minor scale with the V7 (E7), that precedes the Im (Am).

Notice the use of triplets that serves to underline the notes - keys of the harmony while easing the linear aspect, by turning the phrase into a "scale". The diagram uses the: harmonic minor scale, exercise 7.

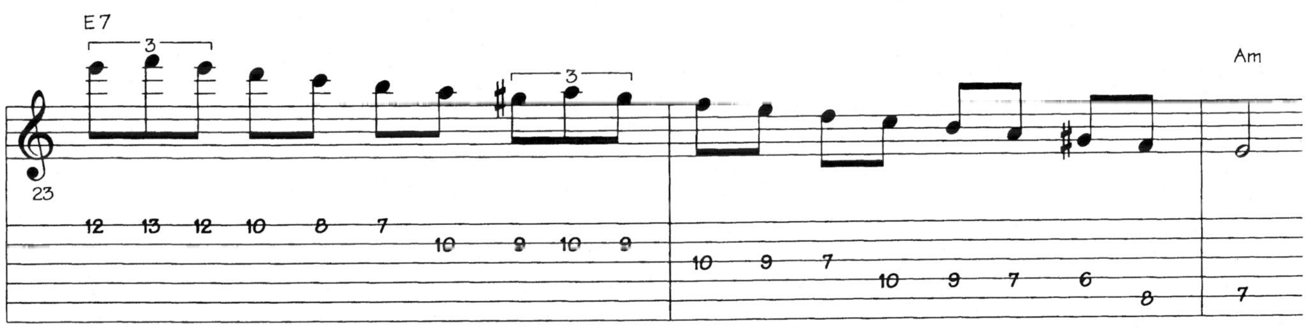

"Swing for Ninine" (measures 42 - 43) lead and diagram #6

Here, according to the diagram, the phrase goes through the chord position, as shown below:

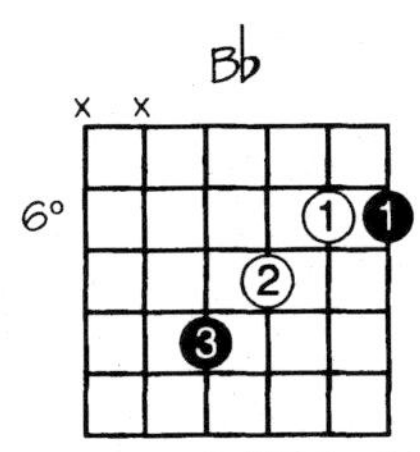

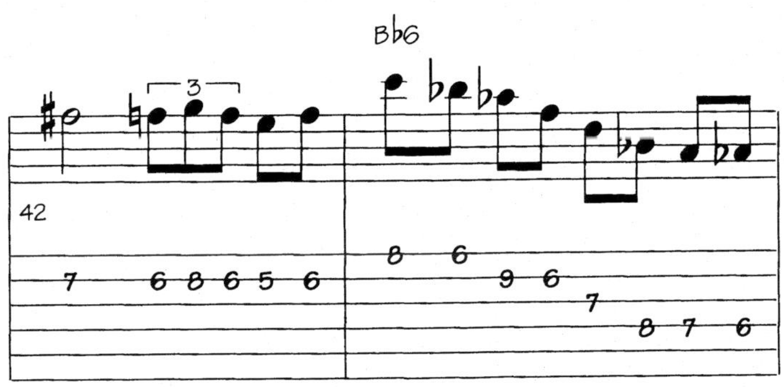

"Swing for Ninine" (measures 45 - 47) lead and fingerboard diagram #7

Here we use one form that is a by-product of the "dim7" arpeggio with the V7 chord (E7), by starting with the major third, on the fourth string. (Exercise 4, chapter 1).

We then go up chromatically, which is very characteristic of Manouche's delivery. This will result in a very natural ending, using the root note of the "resolution" chord, the Im (Am).

Finally, the re-descent, as shown in the diagram and musical notation, is done with a minor triad (Exercise 1 – 2, Chapter 1).

Dim7 arpeggio with E7

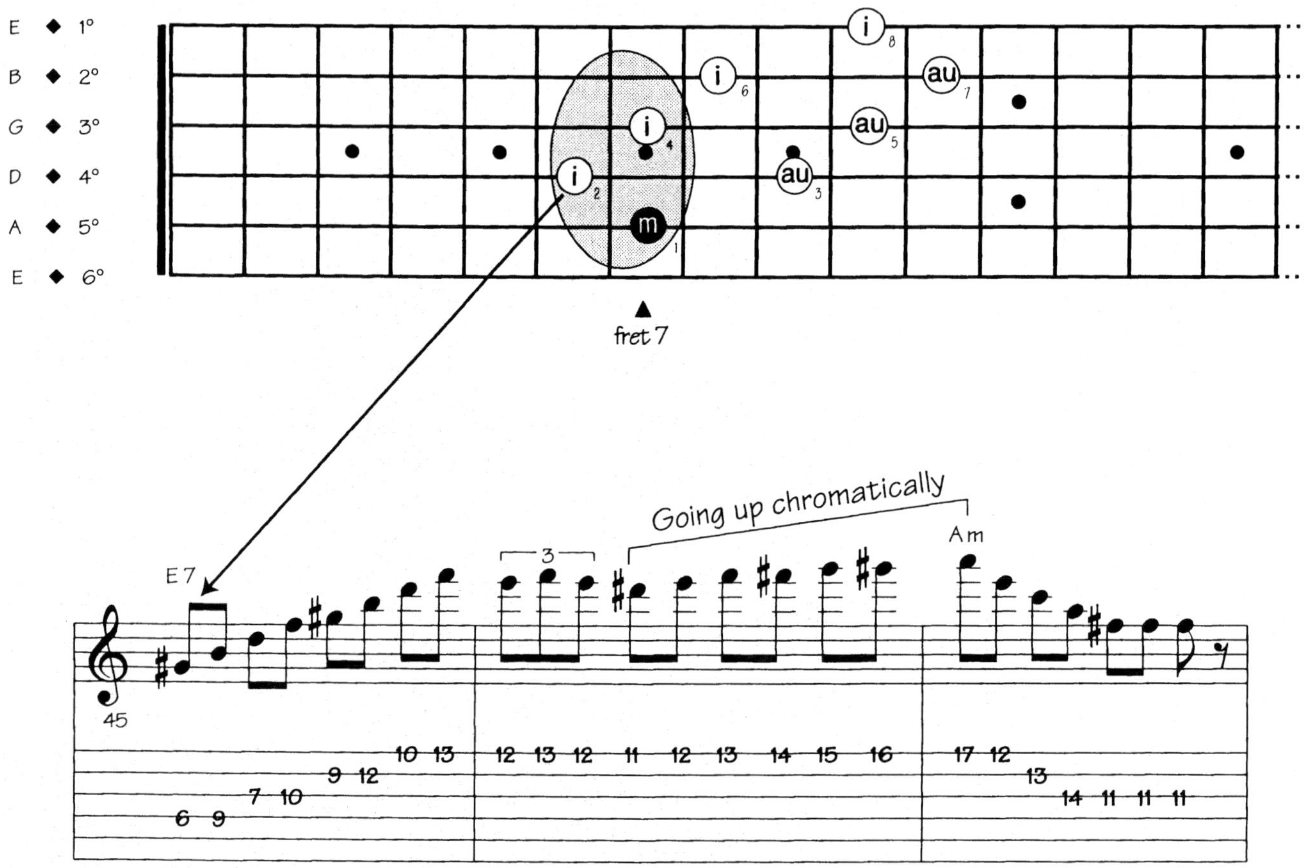

PART C

Continuation of "Swing for Ninine".

Although we only talked about it, you nevertheless will notice the spirit "solo" in certain passages (measures 21-24 and, of course, the measures which form the starting point of the actual solo, beginning with measure 33).

Do not forget to "pick" the staccato notes correctly - listen to the CD to understand the interpretation of these quarter notes.

In measure 44 look for the "bend" of a half-tone. Finally, watch out for all the eighth note triplets, those are a very important rhythmic elements like Manouche used to play it.

#5

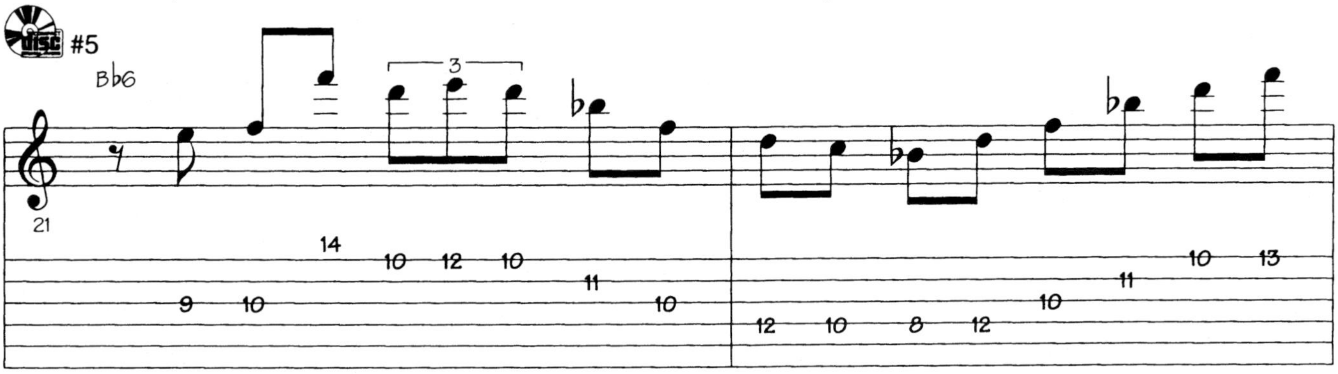

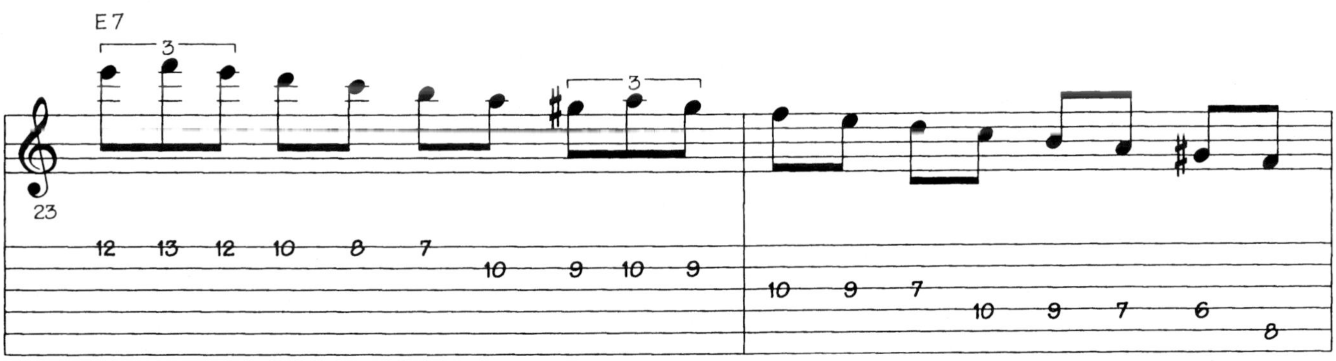

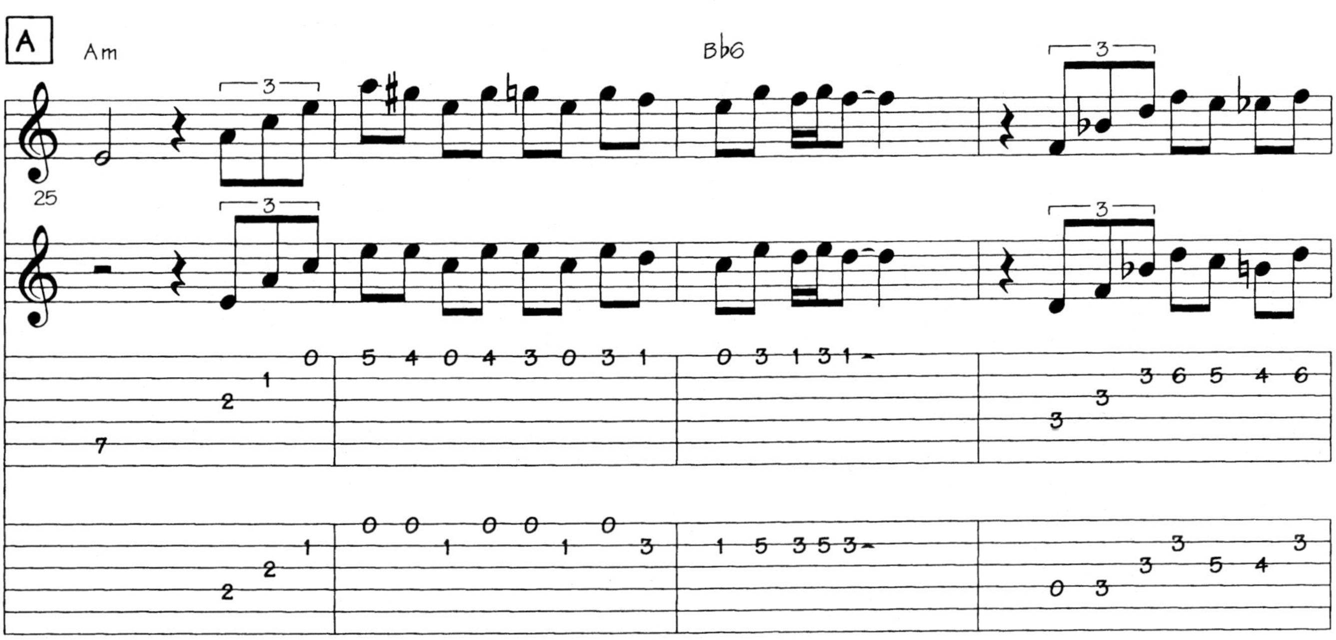

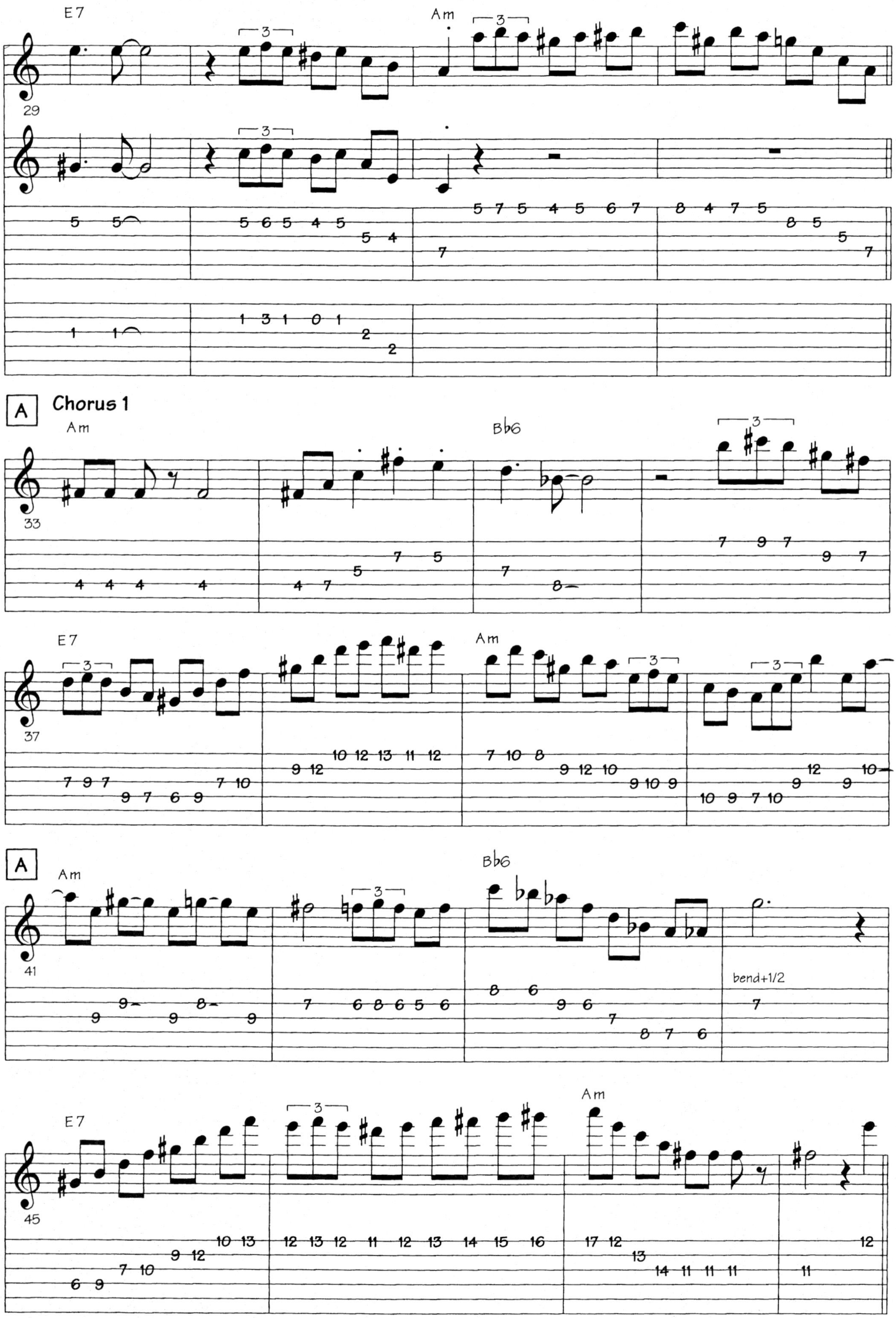
E7
Am
A
Chorus 1
Am
B♭6
E7
Am
A
Am
B♭6
bend+1/2
E7
Am

PART A

The exercises in this third step introduce colorations with minor triads.

In the first place, we are going to enrich the A minor triad with a major sixth (M6), a very typical coloration in the manner that Manouche plays it, in context of the tonal minor.

Exercise 8 and 9 - Minor triad with major sixth

Play the notes following the numbers in an increasing order, then in a decreasing order. The first position starts with the root note of the minor chord: the second with its perfect fifth.

#12

A minor arpeggio with M6 (Am6 chord) – position 1.

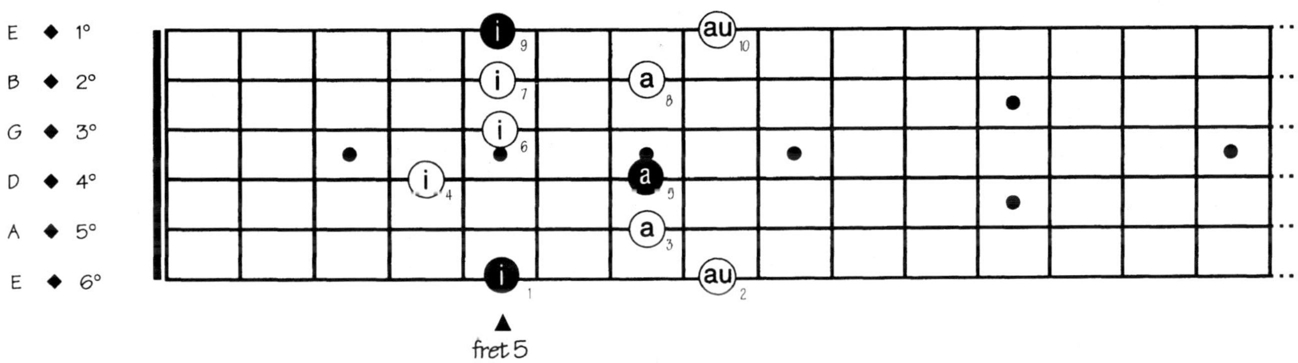

#13

A minor arpeggio with M6 (Am6 chord) – position 2.

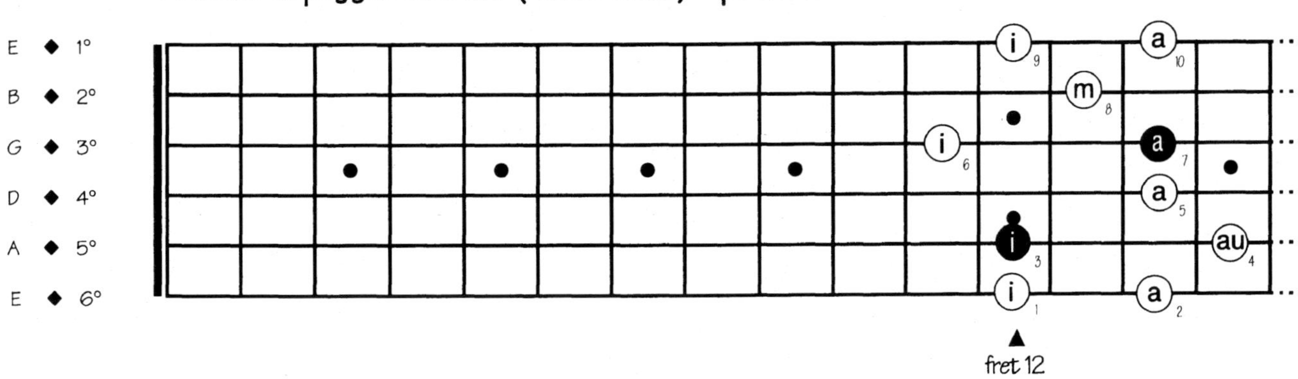

Chapter 3 / page 2

Now we are going to color the A minor triad with a major second (M2 or M9), which decorates it just as interestingly as the one we saw before, with the minor chord.

Exercise 10 and 11 - minor triad with major second

Play the notes in increasing numerical order. The two positions start with the root note of the chord, but with different chords.

#14

Am arpeggio with M2 (Am9 chord) – position 1

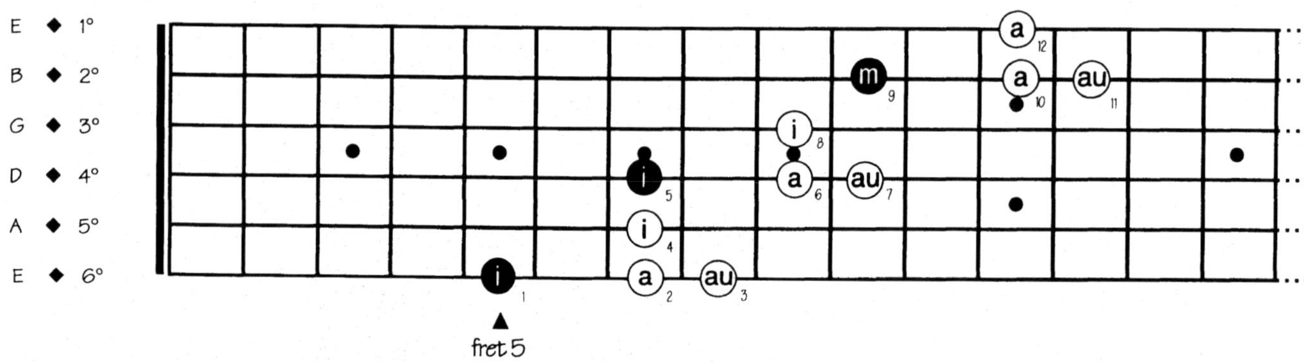

#15

Am arpeggio with M2 (Am9 chord) – position 2

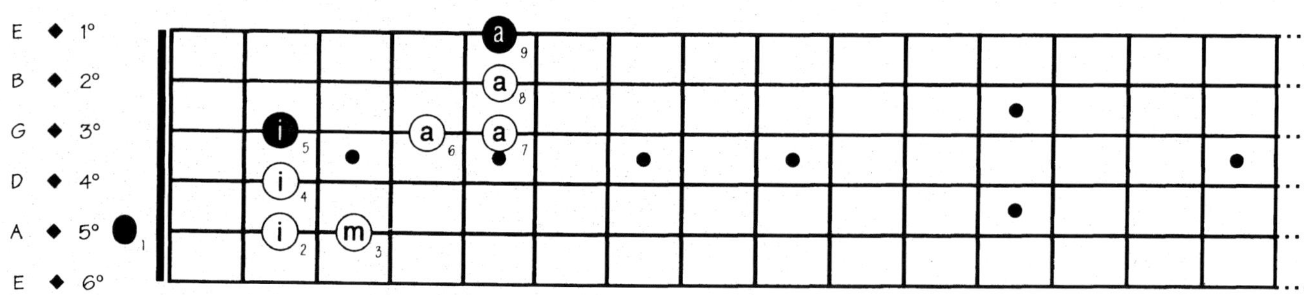

PART B1

Finally, we begin to see that triads, as well as arpeggios, can be emphasized with the help of certain notes. It is not necessary to deduct some of these colorations that must be expressed with the rhythm chords.

Indeed, there is a strong reason that this accompaniment is placed after a chorus, you have to understand that the integration of these colorations often produces the opposite effect of the expected result: this density takes away the soloist's total freedom of his expression at will (don't forget that it is HIS solo!) as well as the colorations in question with the chords based on the diagram... this is evidently very regretful for the dynamics of the whole orchestra all together.

On the contrary, the accompanist who knows how to choose simple chords and how to make it more sophisticated if he wants, plays like Manouche. This enables him to keep all the "drive" and the power of the beat. This in turn helps him to keep time. It creates an ideal platform for the soloist that lets him play a convincing melody, where he can create a surprise with each measure... in short, he can do his solo!

Of course, you now have to have in your bag of tricks that, what it takes to accomplish this. You must not only know the "basic" chords and rhythms, but also make the right choices within the proper context of a given accompaniment. This must include the way Manouche plays it.

Thus here are, by looking at the "Swing For Ninine" diagram, some possibilities which you can try out for your own benefit.

Immediately, while listening to the CD, observe how the accompaniment is done with the rhythm, because of what we call "to drive it". That is to say, we regularly mark the four beats per measure, by systematically accenting the 2nd and 4th beat, as shown here:

drive like Manouche "straight": all beats are played staccato.

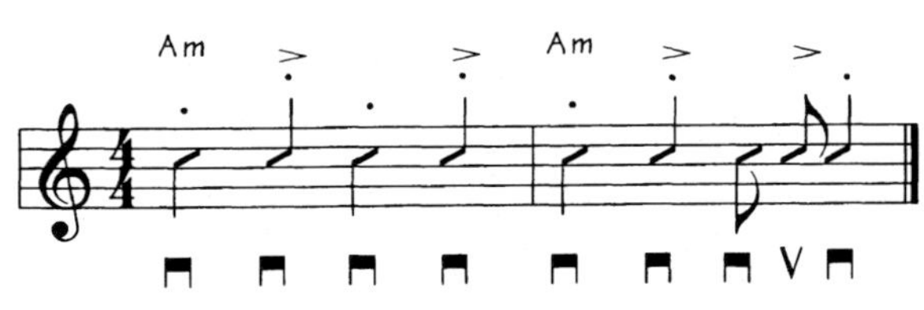

drive like Manouche "swing": the 1st and 3rd beat are played sustained (in contrast with staccato).

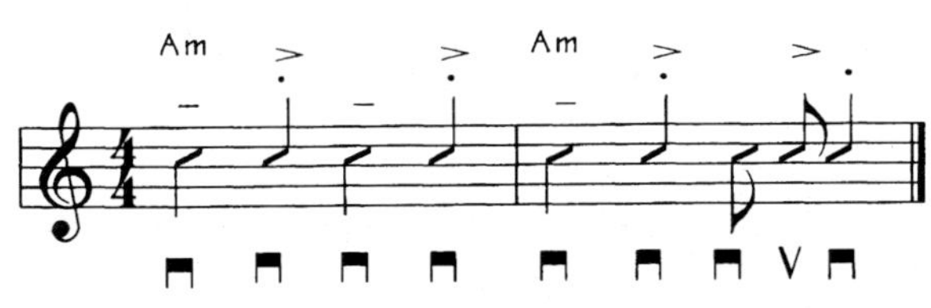

drive like Manouche "swing": A variation.

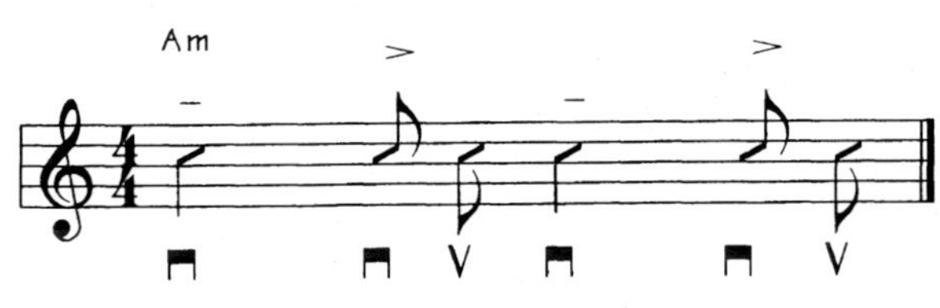

You can use the following chord positions with the chorus of "Swing for Ninine", like we did with the rhythm chords. We do this by completing those that we already gave you for the accompaniment of the theme (Chapter 1, page 4):

Sections A :

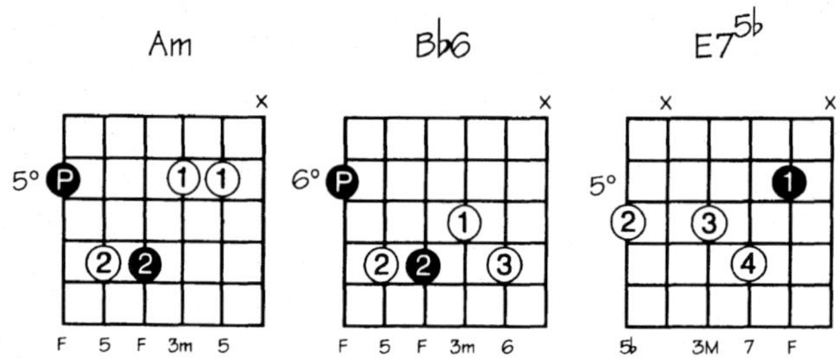

Sections B :

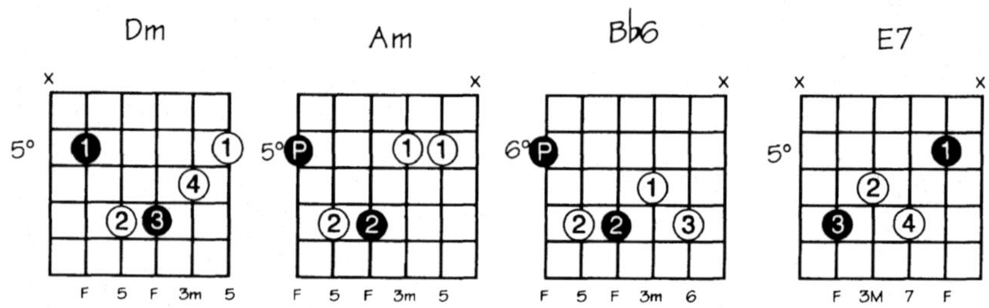

We used accompaniments with simple chords that can be decorated with particular colorations in certain areas of the harmony.

Thus this is shown in section B of your "Swing for Ninine" choruses, where you can hear the following chords, that are heightened with an effect called "rolling of the pick" (tremolo). This by itself is much more typical of the Manouche style.

"the rolling of the pick" - will be done with all the chords of the bridge and the B section

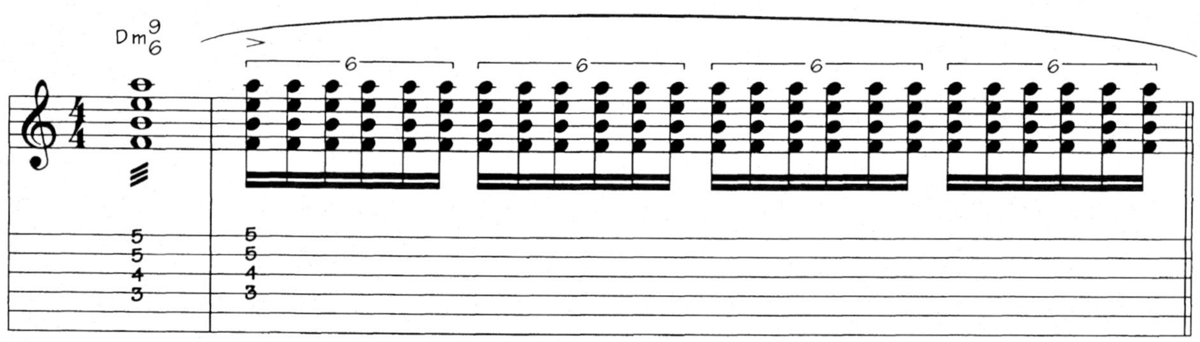

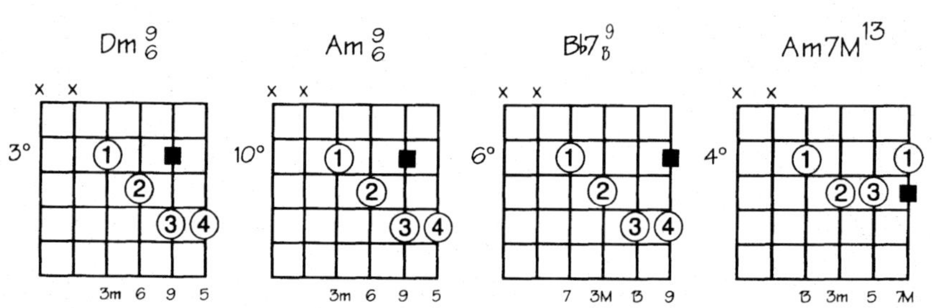

(for Dm) (for Am) (for Bb6) (for the first chord last one A)

Here is the way the tremolo is played: slide from one chord to the other while keeping the fingers on the strings, accenting the first beat in groups of two measures / chords.

PART B2

We are now going to tackle the leads (after measure 48), while continuing with the first chorus of "Swing for Ninine."

"Swing for Ninine" (measures 55 - 58) lead and music #8

The measures at the end of the second A (the beginning of the bridge), where the harmony shows a V7 cadence → Im (E7 → Am), are rich in phrases that are characteristic in the gypsy jazz guitar style.

We immediately see the influence of these six notes. This is done using chromatic notes, where the only objective is to viguorously push the next ascending phrase forward. This is based entirely on how the pick is used, and we suggest that you concentrate on developing it. This is very important. The whole dynamic effect depends on it.

Next we start with the root note of the E7 chord, and go up with a dim 7 arpeggio (see diagram #7, chapter 2, page 4) that is finishished with an (Am) chord resolution, using a chromatic descent of "broken" notes (★) with interrupted triplets… and is finished by using a half tone "bend".

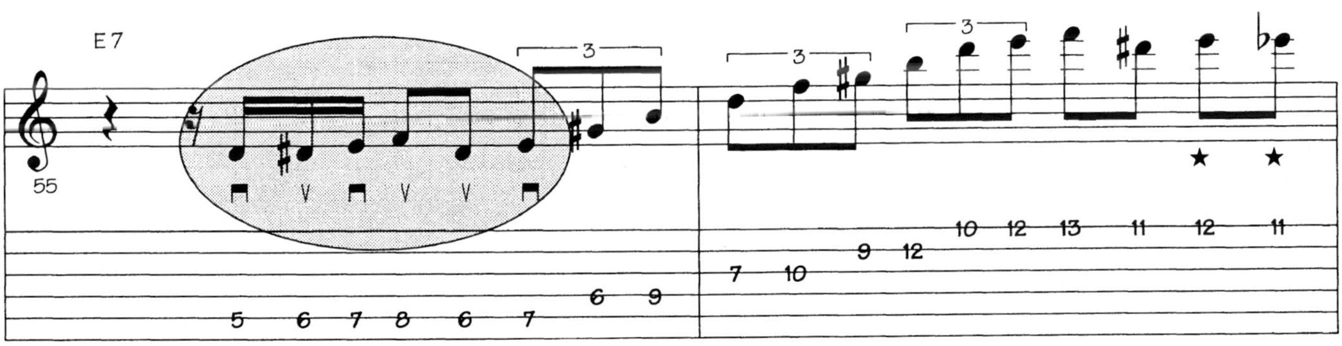

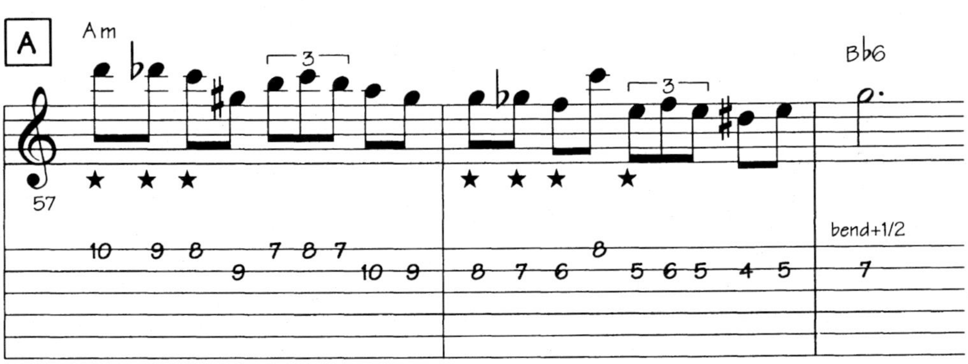

"Swing for Ninine" (measure 66) lead and diagram #9

Measure 64 has a very fast, forceful sweep using the Am chord. So fast even, although it's done with a chord arpeggio, that this type of lead is usually marked simply as a "≀" sign... which is much easier to read than if it is written with quadruple eighth notes!

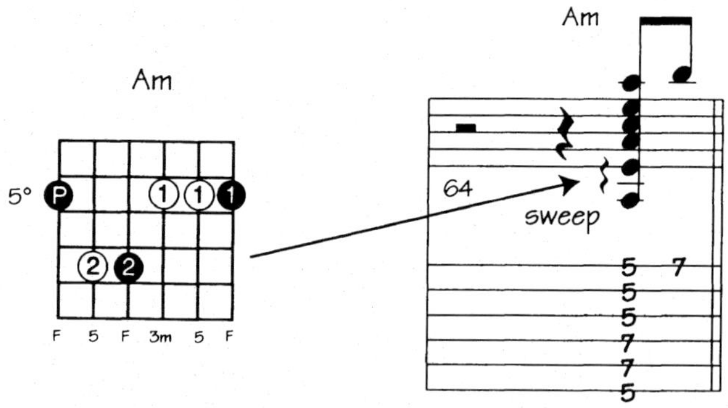

"Swing for Ninine" (measure 66) lead and diagram #10

This is an illustration of the minor triad colored with a major second (notes ★) – compare with exercises 10 and 11, page 2 of this chapter.

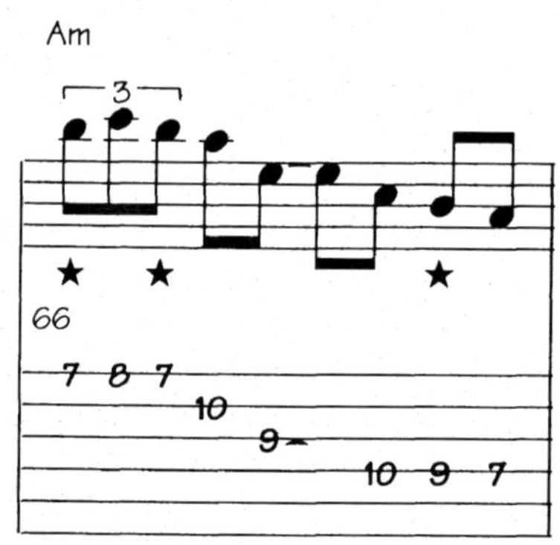

"Swing for Ninine" (measure 67) lead and diagram #11

We have a new and very fast sweep, this time using the Bb6/9 chord. Notice how it intervenes very little after the first beat (Am). This shows evidence of the aesthetic principle of the "question and answer" method that is very current and very efficient, in the area of improvising. The question is – sweeping through Am – and the answer is – sweeping through Bb6/9.

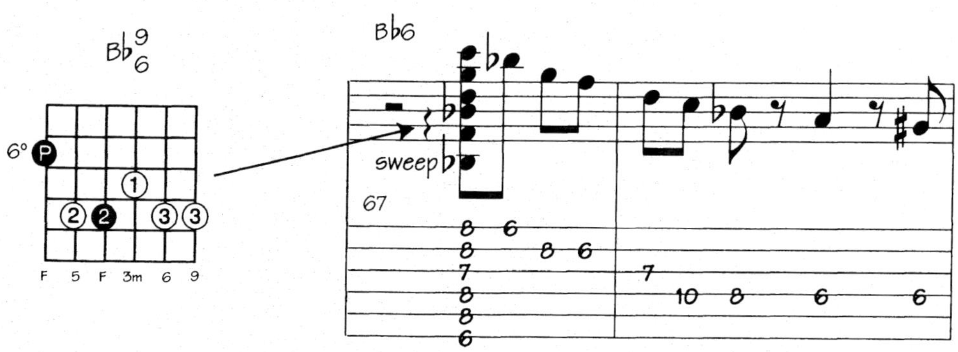

PART C

Now we continue with of the first chorus of "Swing for Ninine" and the first A section of the second chorus.

As always, watch the triplets, there are many here. Watch the staccato notes as well (measures 70-72). Pay attention while listening to the CD and try to understand the refinement of the interpretations of the "dead notes" (x), (measure 52), the bends (measures 59-60), and the slides (measures 52 and 54).

#5

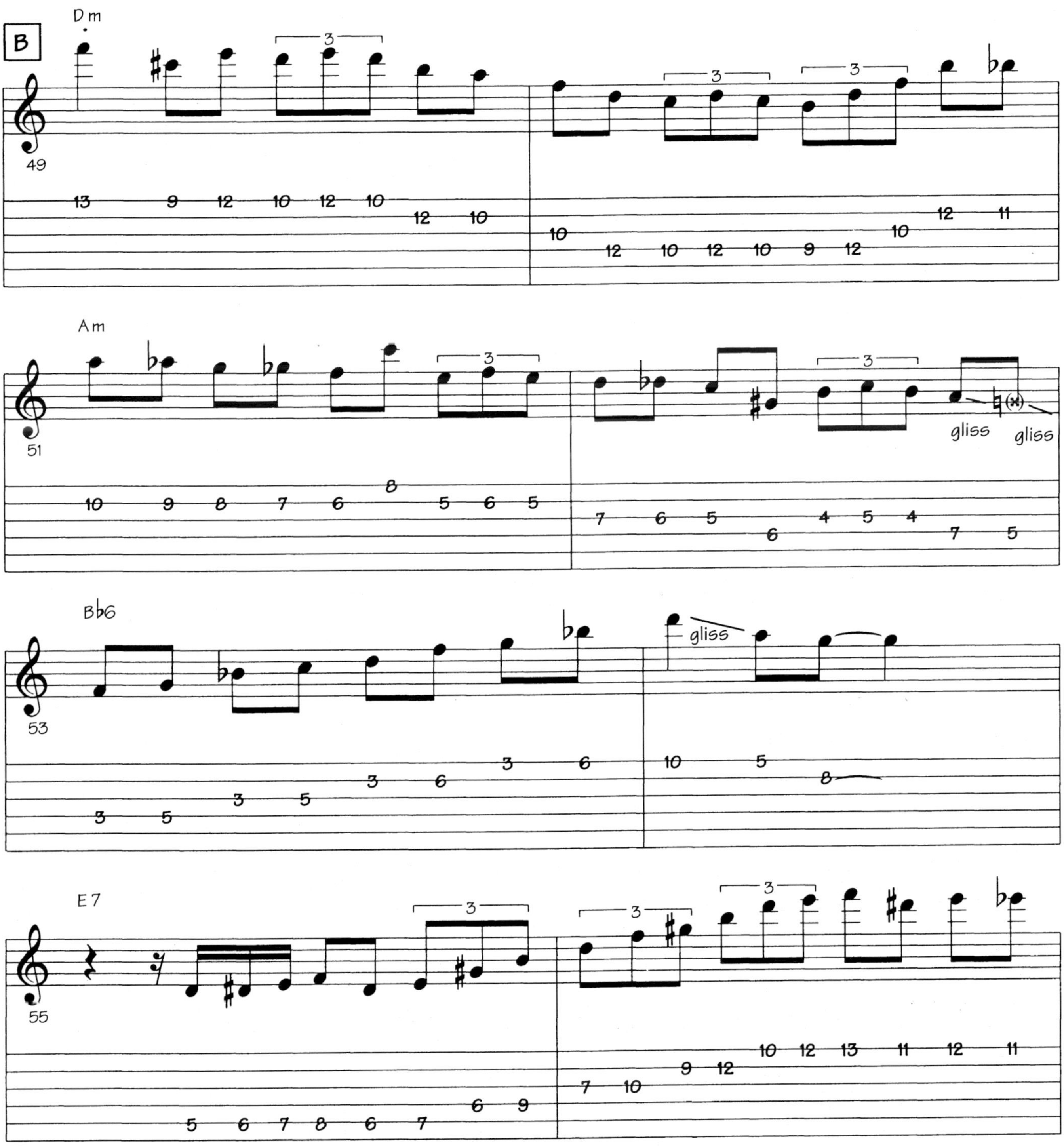

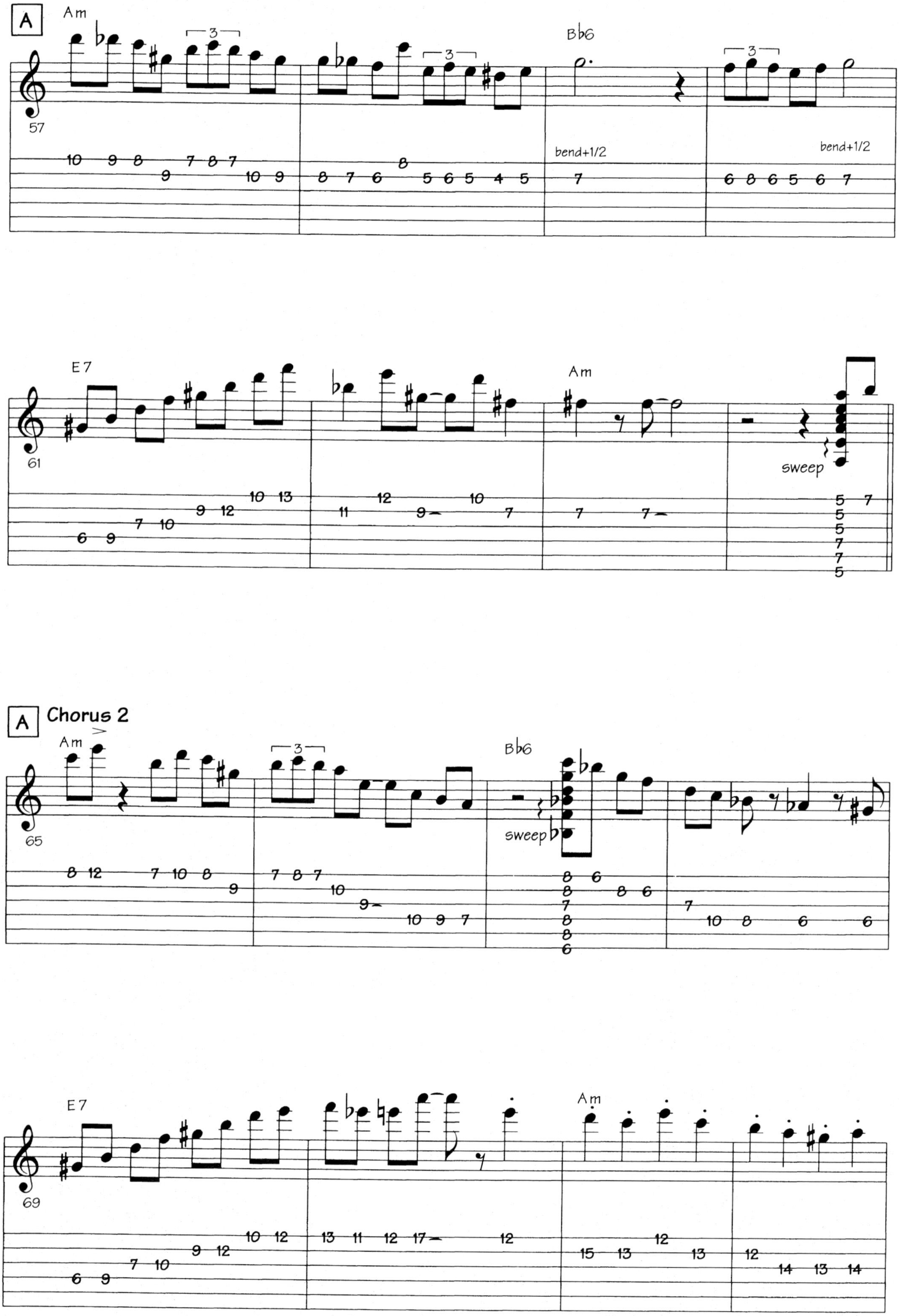
A
Am
B♭6
bend+1/2
bend+1/2
E7
Am
sweep
A
Chorus 2
Am
B♭6
sweep
E7
Am

PART A

Here are two exercises that are aimed at developing the speed of gypsy jazz guitar. It will let you practice the articulation / synchronization with the right and left hand, which is a major point.

Practice the exercises with the two first chords, as indicated, while carefully and mentally visualizing the diagram that goes with the harmony (the chord position). Do not forget to play this exercise in all the keys.

Train yourself to practice the exercises using eighth note triplets with the six notes shown in the diagram, - 12 notes (4 times 3) in a 4/4 measure. Also practice to get into a habit of correctly playing the notes while keeping the beat. Practice these exercises with a metronome, while progressively speeding it up.

You can hear the real execution of one of these exercises in measures 81- 82 of "Swing for Ninine", of section B in the second chorus.

Exercise 12 - speed on two strings (1)

The first exercise is based on the position of the Am6/9 chord. By following the numbers, play the six "enclosed" notes (repeat those many times over and over again).

#16

Speed with Am6/9.

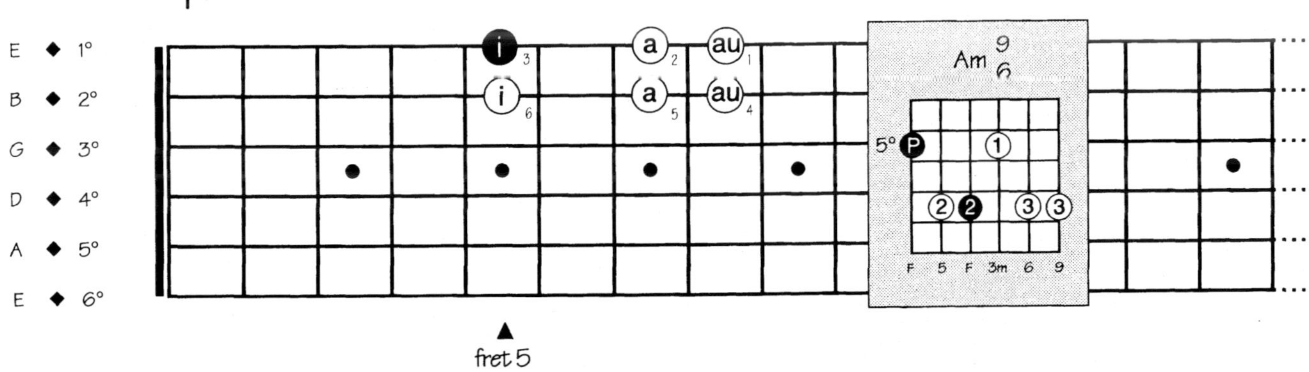

Exercise 13 - speed on two strings (2)

The second exercise is based on the position of the G6/9 chord.

#17

Speed with G6/9.

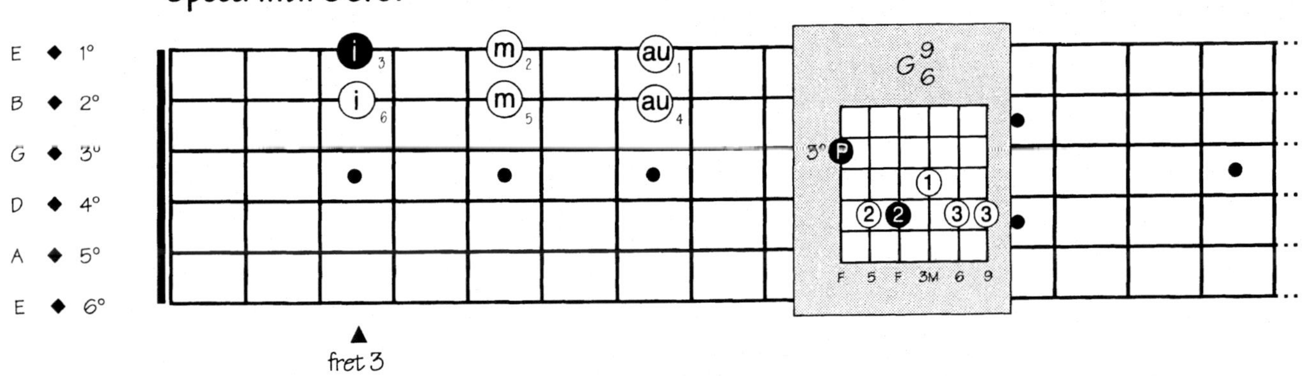

This is another type of exercise to develop speed. It should not be neglected. This one uses the chromatic scale.

When this scale was used in a chorus, Django Reinhardt, the master, used open strings. And to be honest, the use of those last ones let you play a very convincing lead. It is very impressive when you play some type of "rolling" notes, as a virtuoso, at a very convenient speed, and with an irreproachable articulation.

Exercise 14 - chromatic scale (1)

Play the notes in the order of the increasing numbers. Practice with eighths but also with eighth note triplets (use the metronome!). The whole exercise is played while assigning a distinct finger per fret on the fingerboard. But pay attention: on the third string, that you don't put your little finger on the fourth fret, since it would be for the B note, which is effectively played with the open 2nd string.

#18

Chromatic scale with open strings.

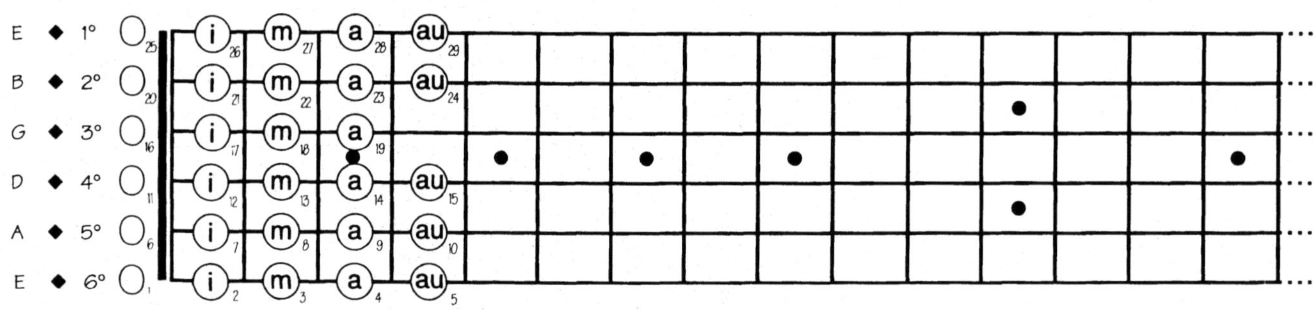

PART B1

Since we are using the chromatic scale, this gives us an occasion to speak about its relationship with the harmony.

This scale uses all 12 possible notes, it is theoretically acceptable to leave out that unimportant note or chord placed within the time structure... without having to worry. Therefore, we intend to improvise by using the milestones, that are given to us by the influence of the harmony.

This is conceivable, but when doing it, this "casual" use doesn't make it any easier to find a solution other than with the other scales or arpeggios. This is an external question of "tensions" and melodic - "resolutions", or, if you prefer, the art and manner to elegantly start and end the phrases.

When using the chromatic scale it is possible to begin or finish a phrase anywhere we like. The laws (of tensions /resolutions) that governs the total execution of the melody are not clear on this.

You should certainly be able to hear how gypsy jazz guitar improvises the melody. It freely uses the chromatics. It doesn't limit itself to use it "loosely" in the higher end. It also uses the chromatic scale while accounting for the harmony, by following the diagram of these chord positions on the fingerboard. For example:

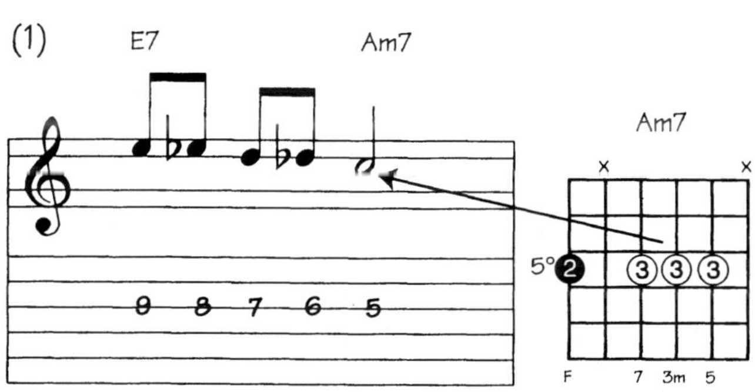

(1) begin with the root note of E7;
until the minor third of Am.

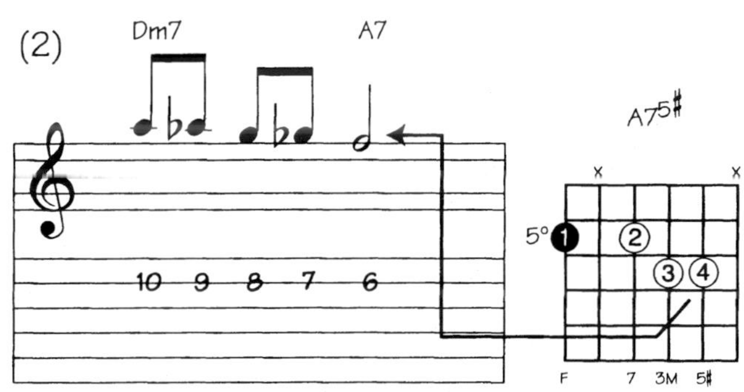

(2) begin with the fifth of Dm,
until the augmented fifth of A7.

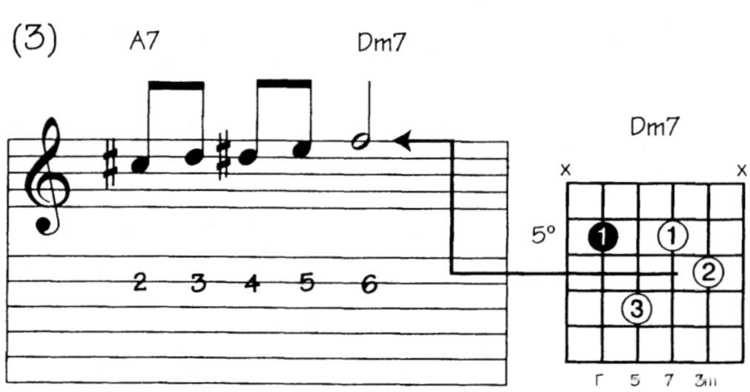

(3) begin with the major third of A7;
until the minor third of Dm.

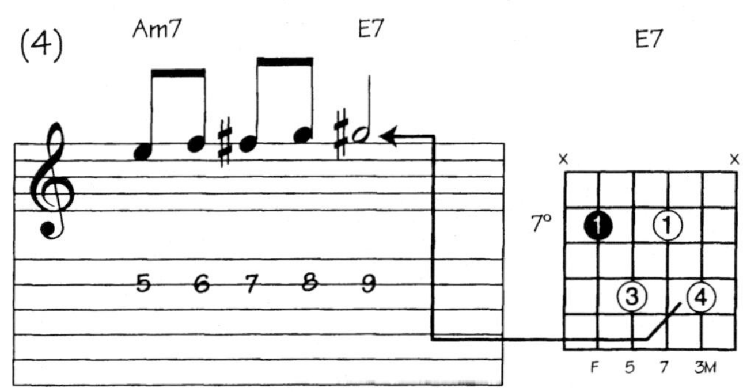

(4) begin with the fifth of Am;
until the major third of E7.

Look in these examples at how the beginnings and endings of the notes that make up the chords are done.

Certainly, the augmented fifth isn't part of the second chord in example (2), which is constructed with a perfect fifth. Nevertheless, this type of occurrence is harmonically allowed –and is even welcome - with the whole V7 chord (A7 = V7) in context with the tonal minor (Dm7 – Im).

In the case of examples (1) and (3), these notes are "resolution" type notes. Be well aware that, by looking at the rhythm, these take place on the strong beat of the measure. It is very important for us to understand the manner of how a coherent melody is constructed, by using the correct "syntax".

It is to delicate to speak of "resolution", when we check out the beginning notes in example (2) and (4), where the final harmony is finished with a non-resolute (type V7 chord). We will discuss it later.

These are of course, worked out with chromatic successions, just as with the "tension" notes of these four examples. This was shown in example (1) of the E♭, D, D♭ notes. Here you will notice in the passage, that the D is a note from the E7 chord (D = the minor seventh of E7), which comes on the accented beat of the measure.

There are many ways to improvise chromatically, with respect to the harmony. We now encourage you to check out these possibilities, and keeping up the spirit by following these simple points:

- start with a note from the chord,
- finish with a note of the chord, (resolution),
- start on an accented beat of the measure.

Note: you could start out with a mellow beat, since a good finish always leaves a much better impression than a good introduction.

For example, with this in mind, practice by relying on various chromatic ways to play. For instance, use ascending and descending leads, eighth notes, triplets, start from a root note, or use a root note, the third, etc. Practice with the chords of the "Am7 - D7" chord progression, keeping in mind that these chords are made up with the following notes:

Am7	D7
G = 7	C = 7
E = 5	A = 5
C = 3m	F♯ = 3M
A = 1	D = 1

PART B2

Now let's look at the continuation and end of the second chorus of "Swing for Ninine", by showing the leads and diagrams that you can use to improvise with.

"Swing for Ninine" (measures 76 - 77)

We have already seen these two measures of the bridge with its diagrams (in chapter 2). The one using the major triad– with the B♭ chord – and the one using the dim7 arpeggio, that starts with the major third of the (E7) chord.

The only difference exists here in the fact that the harmonic progression is not identical. With this suggestion in mind, it is easy to show that the chromatic progression (B♭6 – E7), or the two root notes of the two chords, are in a "tritonic" relationship with each other (three separated pitches). This gives birth to an interesting concept when we look at its construction from the global point of view.

Indeed, this tritonic relationship allows you to magnify the melody while creating another "space", a supplementary tension in the middle of the melody. And this tritonism is a principle that we will often see at the end of the chapters during this adventure.

Whatever it may be, the notes of the measures 76 -77 follow exactly the same diagram as the ones used in measures 43, followed by 45. Therefore, we simply take the ones shown to you in chapter 2 (pages 5 and 6) and use it to study the present passage.

"Swing for Ninine" (measures 87 - 89)

Measure 87 offers a new method of using the dim7 arpeggio with the E7 chord. This time start with a low root note, on the open 6th string, and develop a three octave arpeggio. This creates a very typical phrase in the style of Manouche:

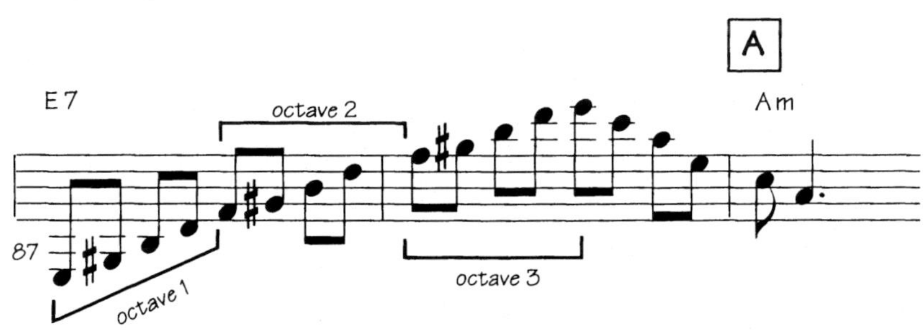

Remember that the dim7 arpeggio and its diagram are in exercises 3 and 4 (chapter 1).

The end of the present lead, starting from the E note, is based on the music of exercise 2 that uses the minor triad (chapter 1)

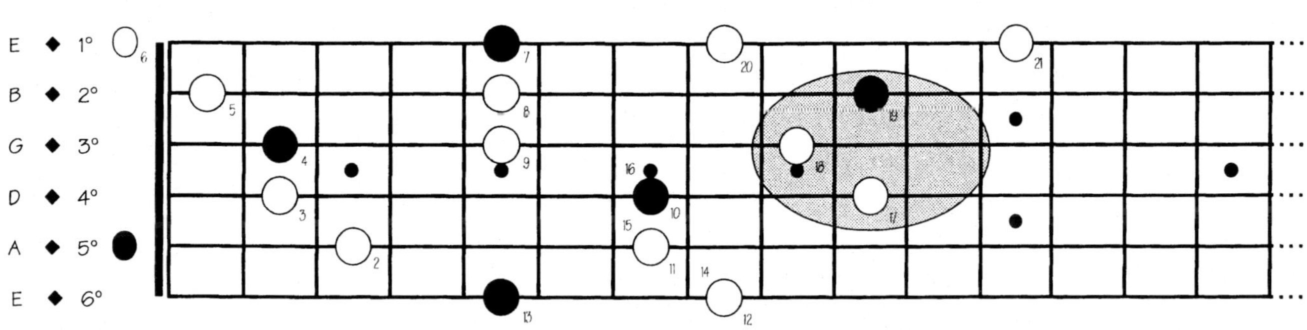

Chapter 4 / page 6

"Swing for Ninine" (measures 91 - 92) lead and diagram #12 and 13

Measure 91 shows a coloration in the diagram of the major triad (chapter 2, exercise 5). With the present B♭6 chord, this coloration is the A note, which corresponds with the major seventh chord. Some improvisers consider this major seventh like a composing note of the major chord that creates a global type "7M" arpeggio (four notes). Whatever the case may be, to play in the style of Manouche, we prefer to consider this major seventh as a simple coloration (★ notes), not as a component note, so that we can recognize it again under the same name. We have, for example, the minor triad colored with a major sixth or a major ninth (compare with chapter 3, pages 1 and 2).

Here is the passage in question and its corresponding diagram:

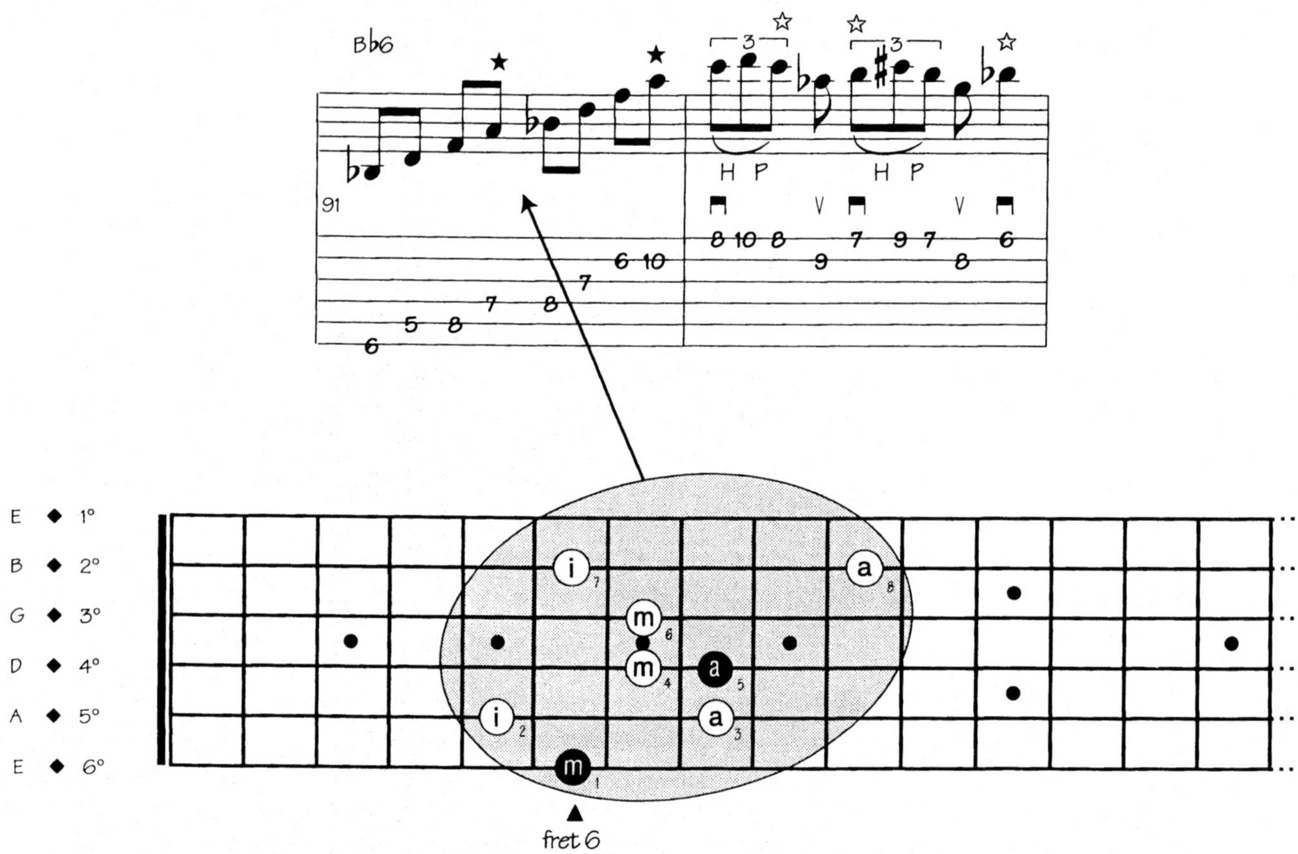

As for measure 92, it shows a lead that relies on the chromaticism of "broken" (notes ★) that designates the root note of the chord: in the last beat of the measure.

We also start a combination of techniques "hammer-ons"/(H) "pull-offs"/(P) done in time with the metronome; each triplet ought to be played very smoothly.

Finally, look at the unusual placement of the second group of the triplets that are placed on the heavy beat "on horseback". This rhythmic difference creates an interesting asymmetry, which makes the lead stand out... and gives it a realistic "structure". It is a standard phrase, that is freely used with jazz improvisations, and not only by guitarists.

PART C

Here is the continuation and end of the second chorus of "Swing for Ninine": second A, bridge and the last A.

To play the quarter note triplets while keeping in time (measure 73), think: "use three regular attacks in the place of two (of a half note)." Listen to the passage on the CD.

Finally, pay special attention on how you place your fingers on the frets!

#5

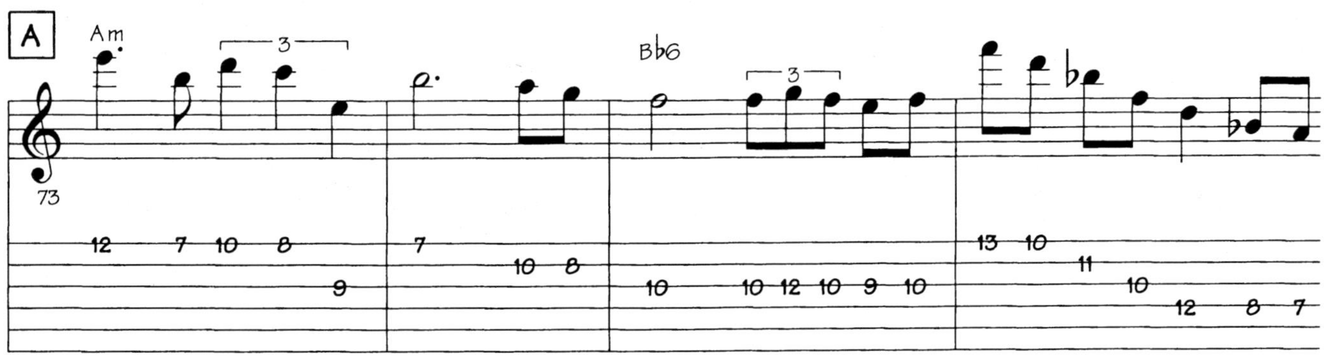

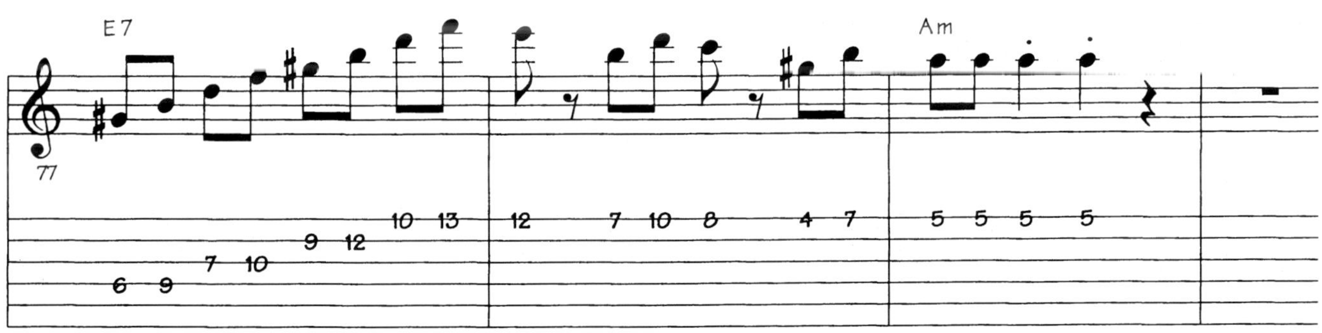

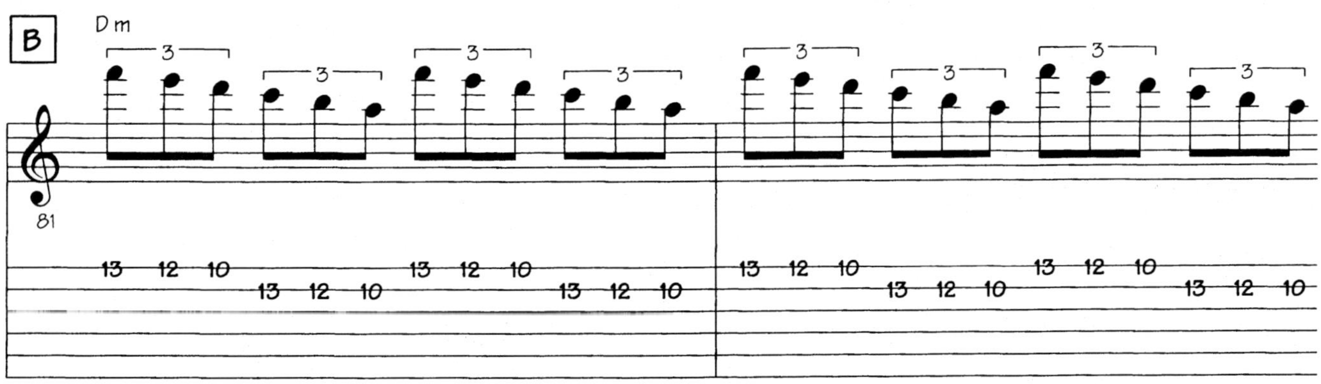

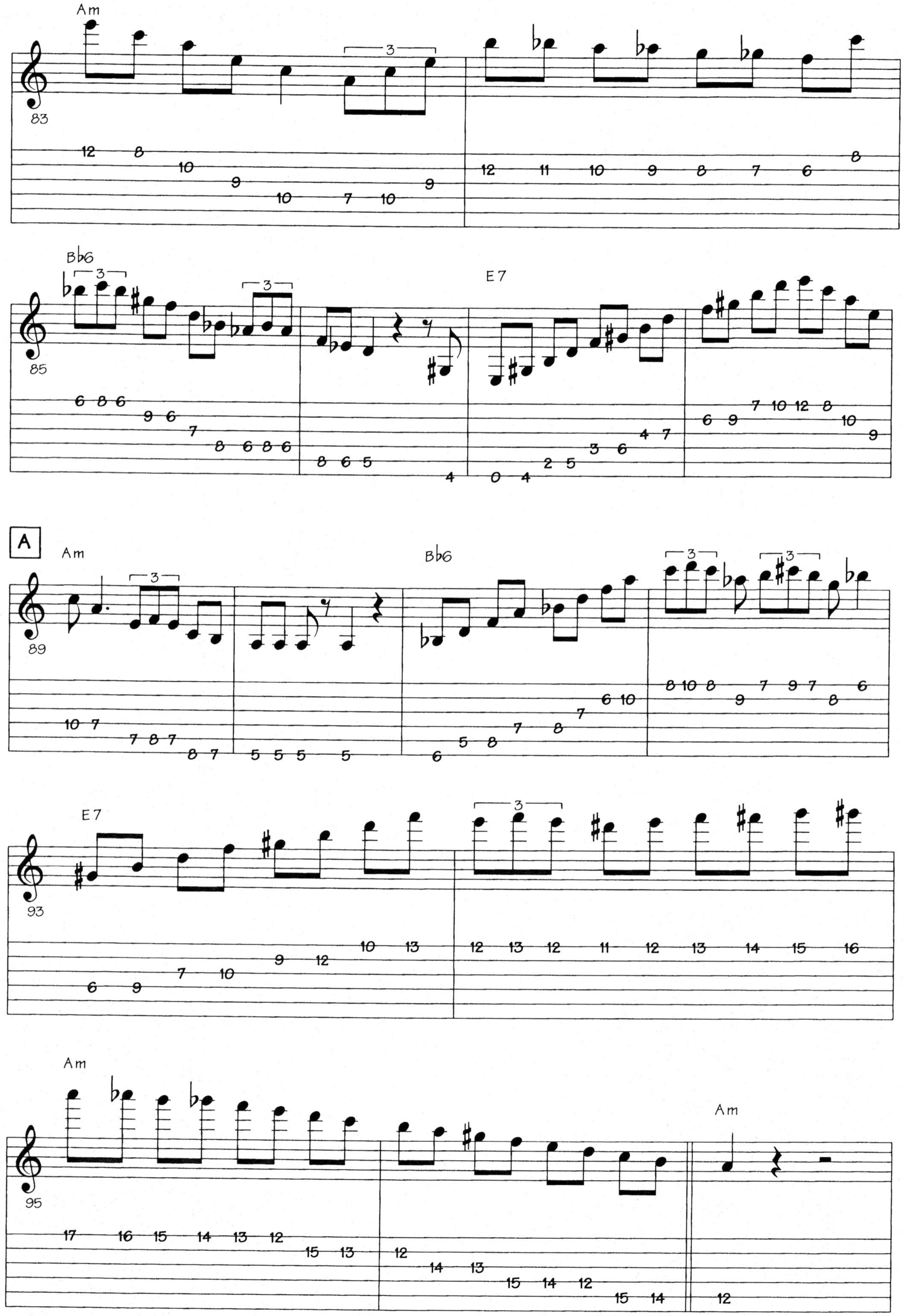
Am
Bb6
E7
A
Am
Bb6
E7
Am
Am

PART A

To start this chapter, we will begin with another phase of the dim7 arpeggio, since the basic diagram has already been shown in chapter 1 (Exercise 3).

Here we will discuss basic permutations: we modify the order of the notes that make up the initial diagram. We do it in such a way that it creates a longer phrase within the time structure, but is unchanged from a harmonic point of view.

Exercise 15 - 'broken' seventh diminished arpeggio (1)

Play the notes in increasing numerical order (ascending arpeggio), then in a decreasing order (descending arpeggio). Pay attention to the change of one fret on the 2nd and 3rd strings.

disc #19

Fdim7 arpeggio (or Ab, dim7, or Bdim7, or Ddim7).

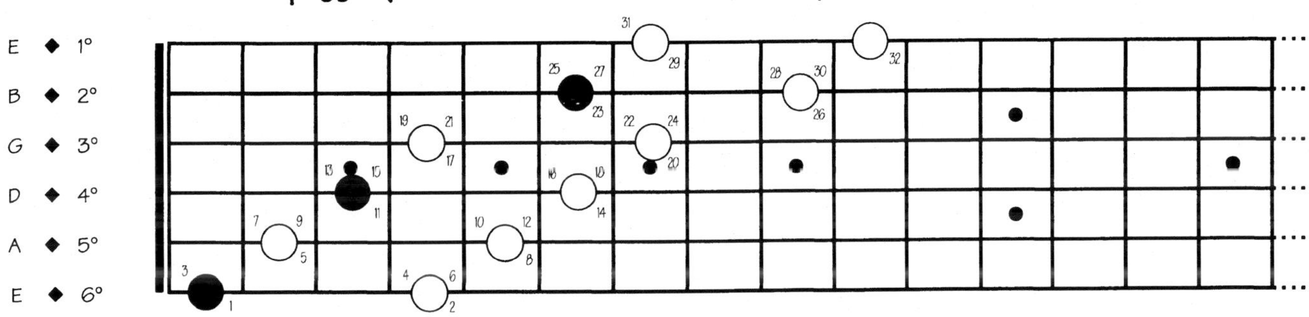

This "broken" dim 7 arpeggio is written as:

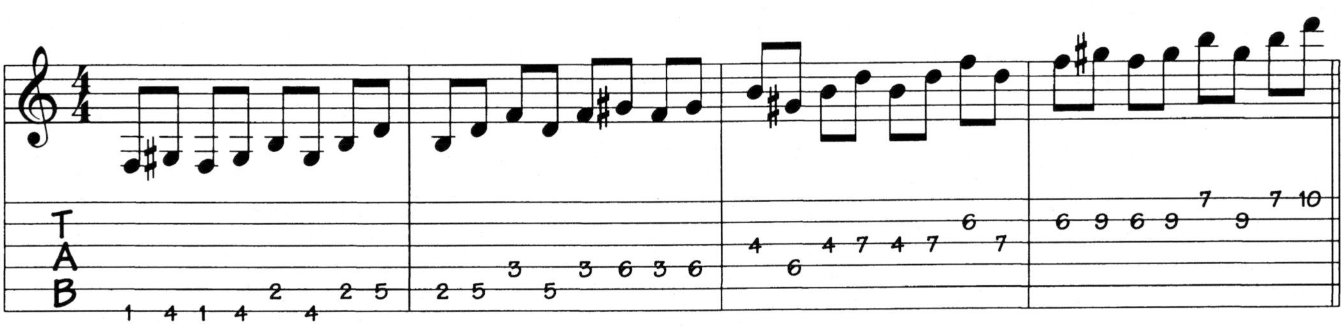

Of course, for reasons discussed in chapter 2, page 4, this Fdim7 arpeggio works also with the Abdim7, E7 (9b), Bb7 (9b) and Db7 (9b).

We will continue with arpeggios and show you some music notation that is frequently used in jazz. You already have had a short overview of it, while studying colorations of the perfect major arpeggio (lead of "Swing for Ninine", Step 4, page 6).

Exercise 16 - major seventh arpeggio

Here is a three octave G7M arpeggio. It is played by using two unique notes per string.

Play the notes in the increasing numerical order, then in the decreasing numerical order.

You should know the diagram of the first four notes well: later you will see that these are identically reproduced on the remaining strings.

Once more, pay attention to the shift between the 2nd and 3rd strings.

#20

G7M arpeggio.

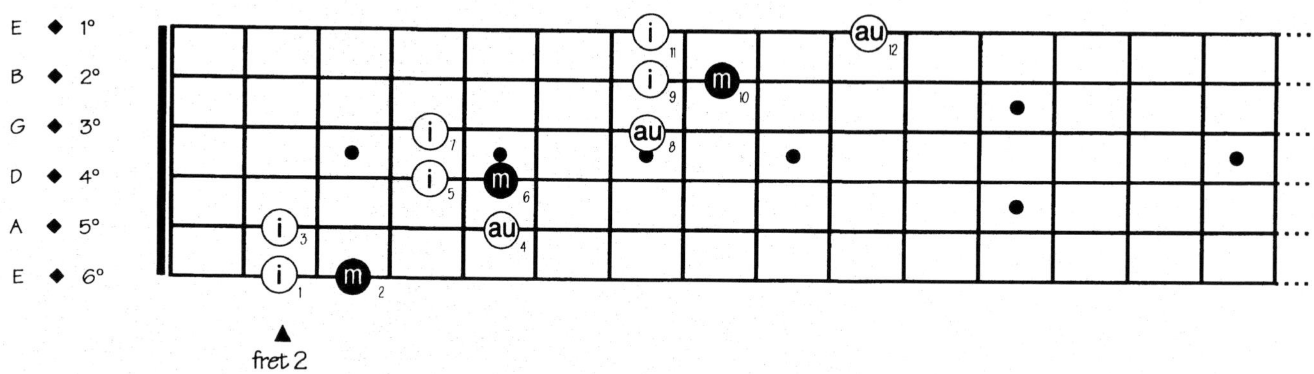

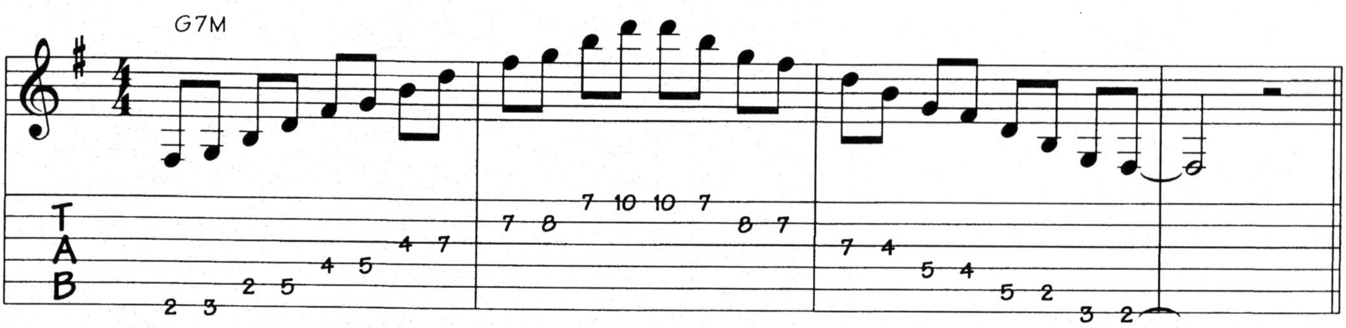

PART B1

Let's study a new harmonic diagram in the style of Manouche. In this case we will use one of the "Pour Trois Pas" songs. You can hear it on the "Romane" CD.

Here are the featured chords of this piece.

Pour Trois Pas

(With Three Steps)

Structure = 40 measures AA'B – integrated structure = 13 measures AA'B / AA'B / AA "(coda)" $\frac{3}{4}$ ♩= 196

A	‖: Am	Dm	Am	%	Dm	%	Am	%
A'	1st A B7	%	E7	% :‖	2nd A B7	E7	Am	%
B	Ebm7	Ab7	Db7M	Bb7$^{5\#}$	Ebm7^{5b}	Ab7$^{5\#}$	Dbm7	%
	Bm7	E7	C#m7	F#7	Cm7	F7	Bm7	E7
A" (coda)	Am	Dm / G7	C	C#dim7	rall... Dm	E7	F	%
	Bb	E7	𝄐 A					

As the time signature indicates, "Pour Trois Pas" is a waltz (3/4 beats per measure). It is different than in "Swing for Ninine". Each section of the diagram counts three beats. In the second measure of the coda (section A) we divide the chords up as follows:

-Dm has 2 beats
-G7 has 1 beat.

Also be aware that this song has longer parts and deviates somewhat from the usual "standard" form: when we count the A sections of this piece, we not only get 8, but 12 measures.

Here are the chords for "Pour Trois Pas".

Sections A and Coda :

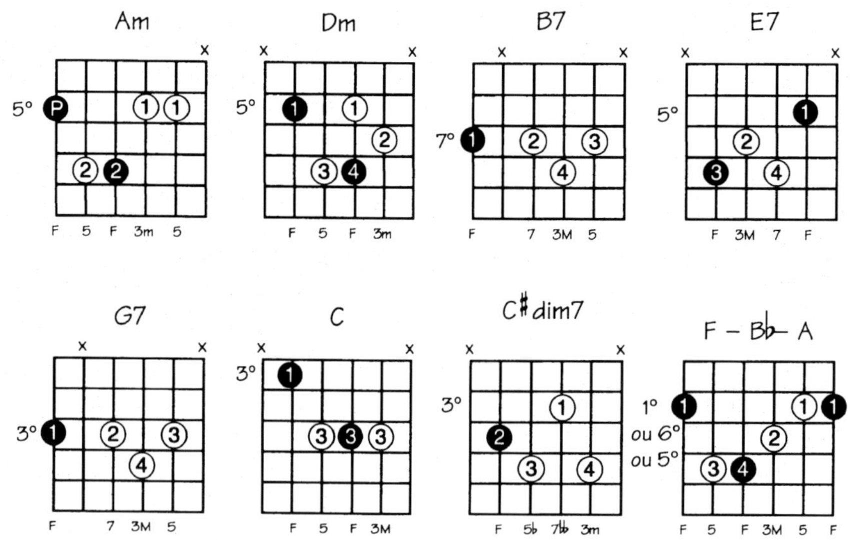

Section B :

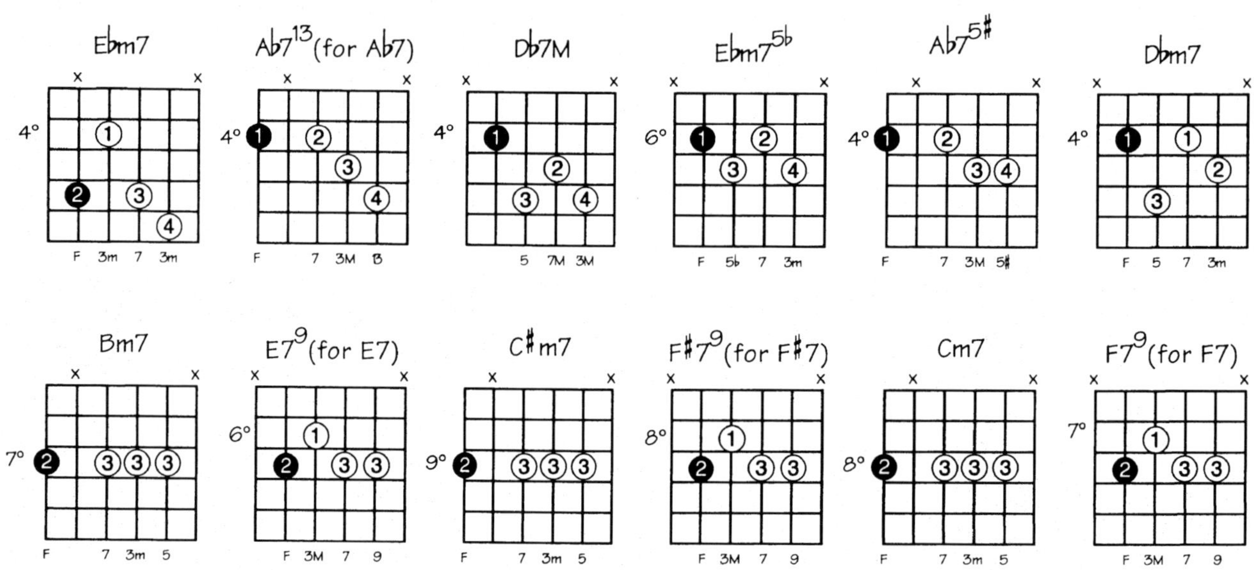

Notice that certain chords have slightly modified symbols, as shown in the initial diagram. These are modified here for same reasons as the ones shown in chapter 1, page 4 (chords for "Swing for Ninine").

On the other hand, we know, that jazz is improvised music, where the "variations" play a major role - for the harmony as well as the melody and rhythm. These "voicings" represents only one simple choice of possibilities out of many.

PART B2

Let's look at the music and leads relative to section A of "Pour Trois Pas".

Pour Trois Pas (measure 1 - lead and diagram #1)

In the first place, you should know that this melody starts with a pickup measure. The true beginning of the song starts after the first notes (pickup notes).

Thus many jazz songs (this is also true of other styles of music) start with a pickup measure. More often than not, the pickup measure of has two simple notes (called pickup notes). It would be wrong to say the pickup measure is part of the introduction.

With the "Pour Pas Trois", we are going to play a strong pickup since it fills almost the whole measure! In measure 1 we once again see our first diagram that is based on the Am chord. Or better yet, the diagram of the Am triad arpeggio, colored with a second major (chapter 3, page 2):

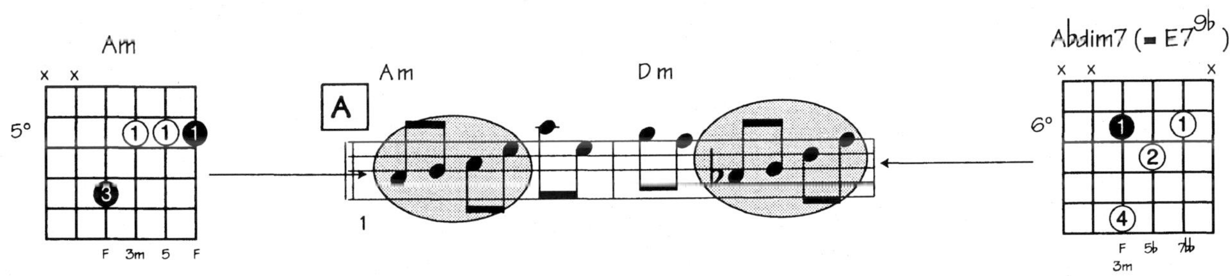

Pour Trois Pas (measure 2 - lead and diagram #2)

In measure 2 we see a diagram of the dim7 chord where the root note is Ab. This chord, Abdim7, may be considered to be the same as an E7b9. And although the harmony of this measure will be in Dm, this E7 chord perfectly works itself in, since it comes back as a V7, with the A minor chord in measure 3.

Pour Trois Pas (measure 7 - 8) lead and diagram #3

Measure 5 offers another exploitation of permutations of the dim7 chord. This Ddim7 chord (notes ★), belongs to the close family of E7... and as a consequence there is nothing more logical than to go back to the Am, in measure 7.

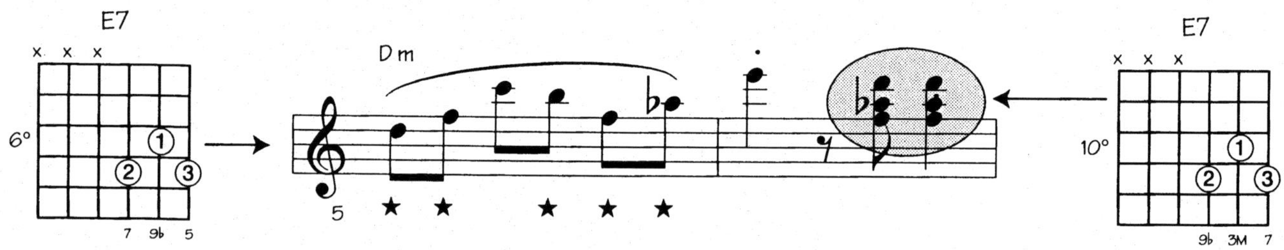

Pour Trois Pas (measure 7 - 8) lead and diagram #4

Finally, in measures 7 and 8, the melody uses the two minor chord diagrams, with A as its root note.

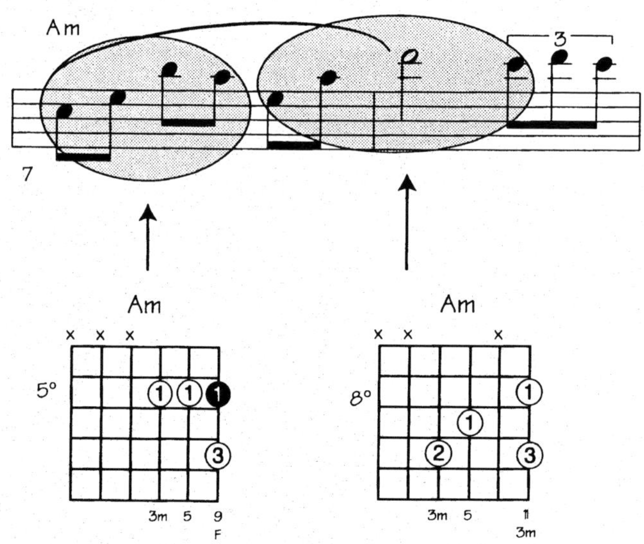

PART C

To finish this chapter, we suggest that you learn the first 24 measures of the waltz "Pour Trois Pas" (whose continuation and end are worked out in chapters 6 and 7).

Of course, this is a waltz and we recommend that you study it well, as well as the lyrics in the phrase!

disc #21

Pour Trois Pas

music by ROMANE

♩=196

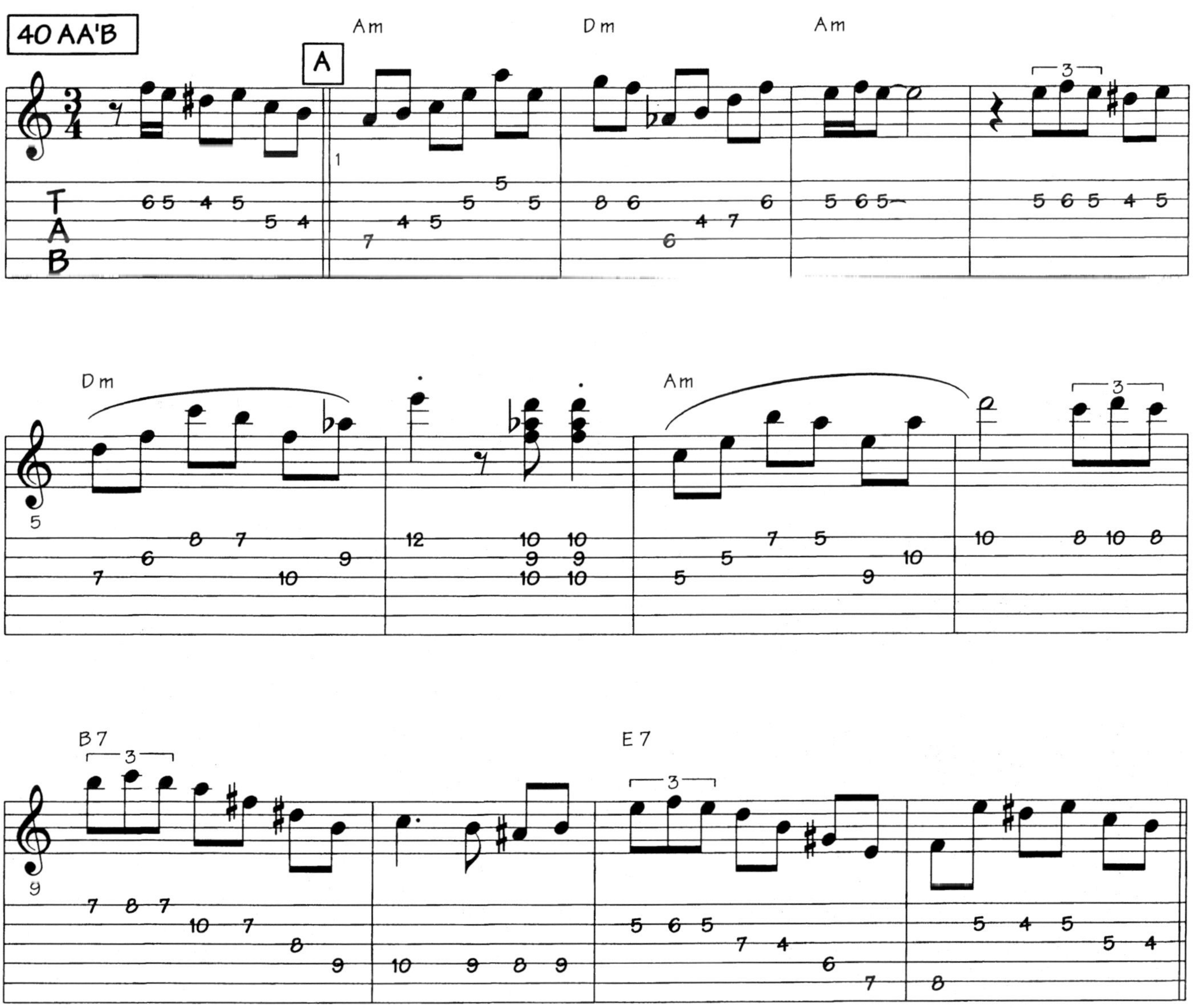

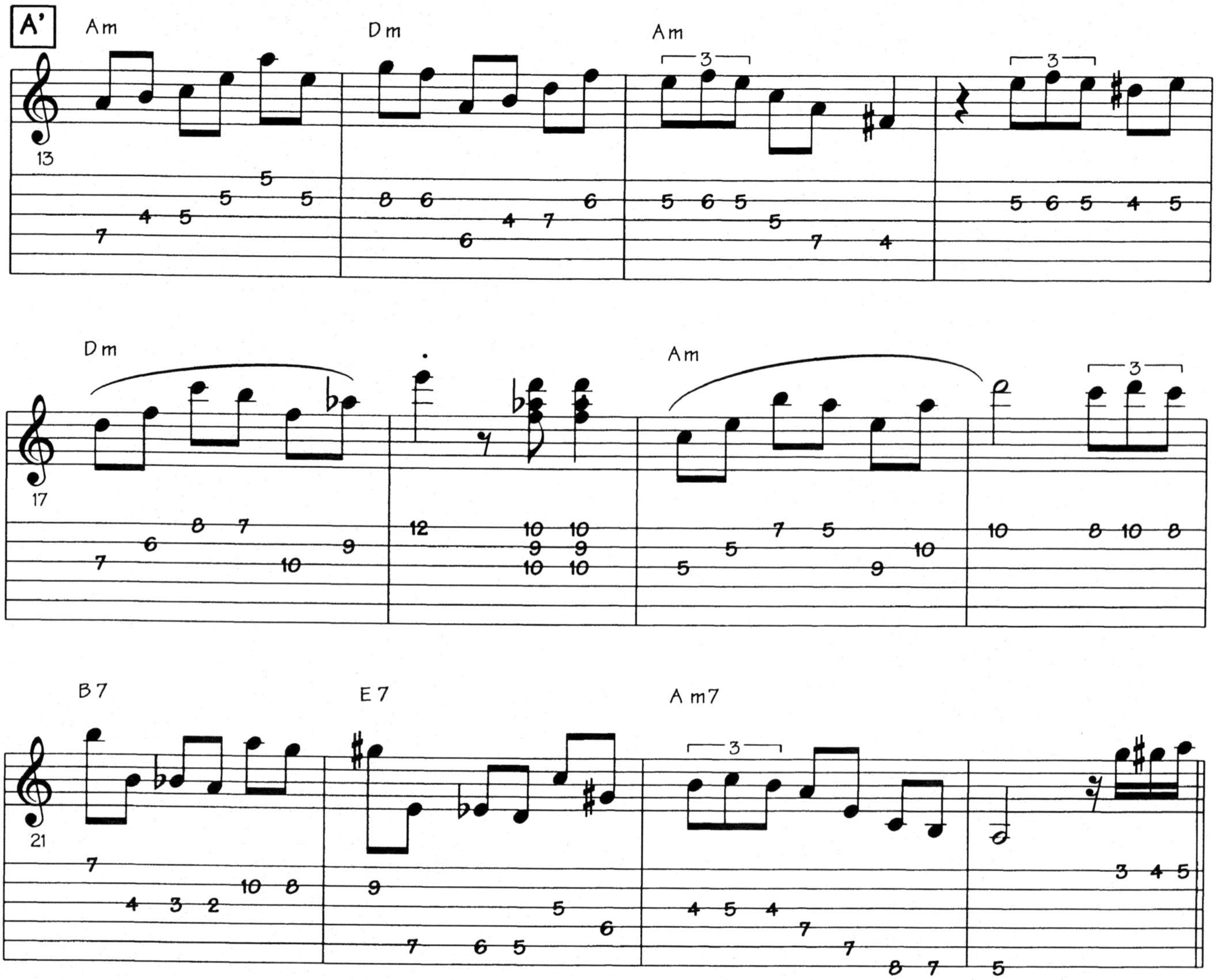

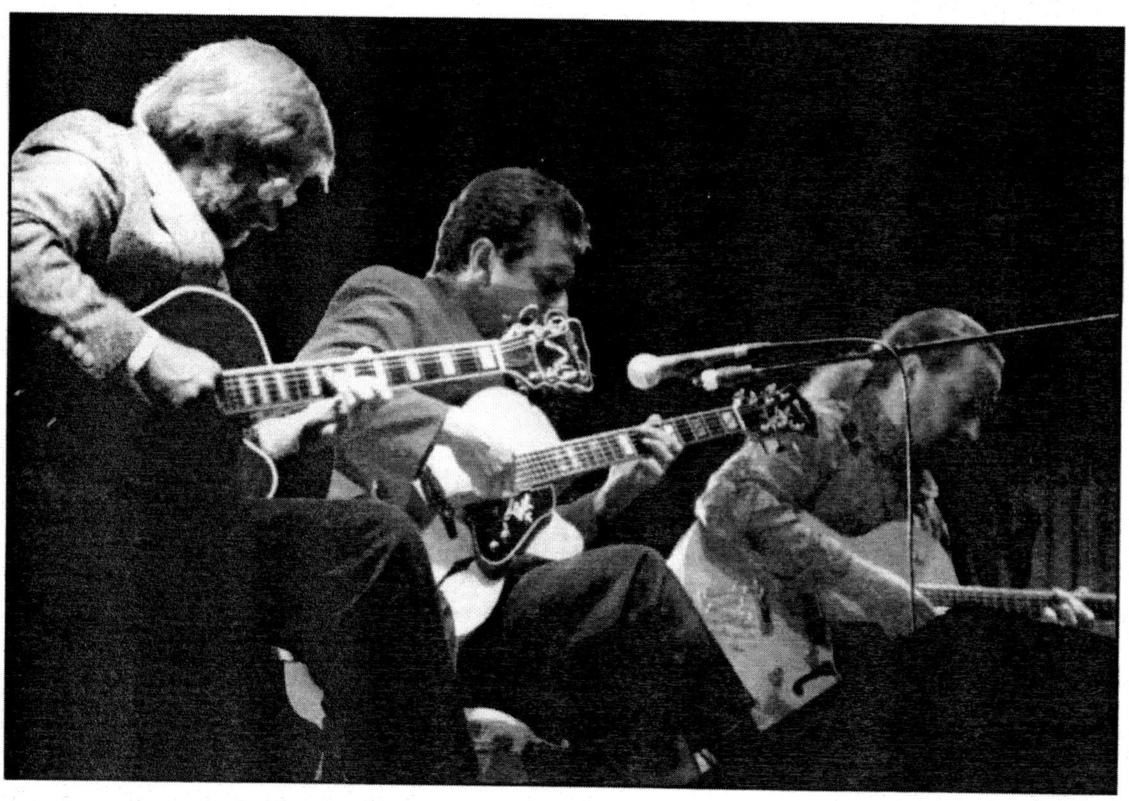

Jim Nichols, Romane, and Martin Taylor

PART C

Let's start this chapter with two exercises illustrating sweeps using the right hand.

Exercise 17 - sweep with the major seventh arpeggio

Here is a short arpeggio using a sweep with the G7M chord. Play the notes in the increasing order, then in the decreasing order. Pay attention to how you use the pick.

Sweep with the G7M arpeggio.

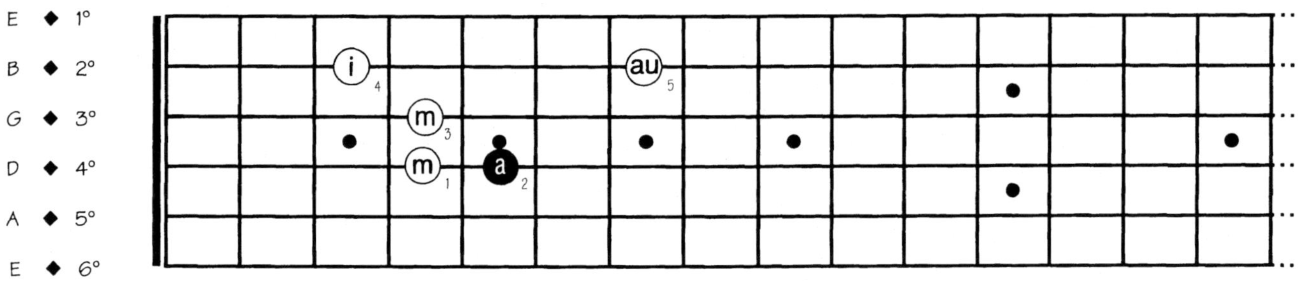

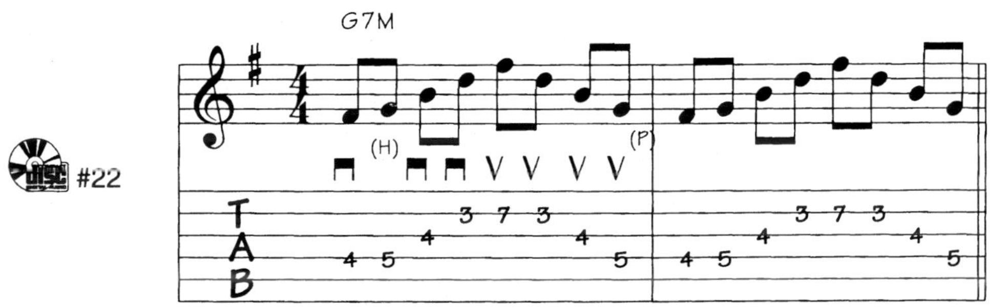

Exercise 18 - sweep with the minor seventh arpeggio

Here is another very similar sweep of one octave, using the Am7 chord. Play the notes in increasing order, then in decreasing order.

Sweep with the Am7 arpeggio.

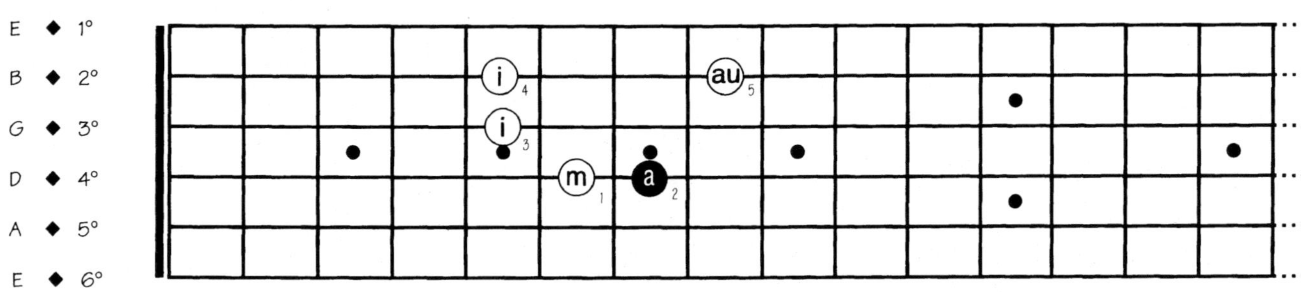

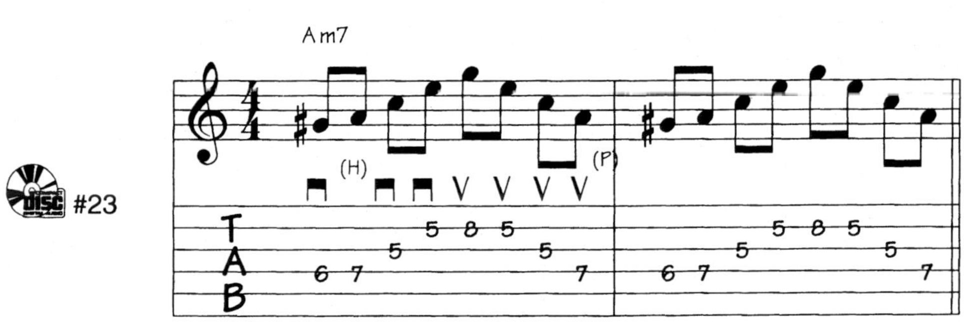

Notice how the sweeps in exercises 17 and 18 can be joined together to form an interesting lead. This lead determines a "diatonic" group made up of the degrees of the G major key: the sweep of G7M = degree I, the sweep of Am7 = degree II. And you can go as high as the IV degree of this key by copying the same diagram,:

-----1 → sweep with G7M (degree I),
-----2 → sweep with Am7 (degree II)
-----3 → sweep with Bm7 (degree III) = sweep with Am7 is moved up two frets,
-----4 → sweep with C7M (degreeIV) = sweep with G7M is moved up five frets.

Exercise 19 - diagram with designated notes using the major sixth chord

This diagram – which Django played using only his index and middle finger – relies on the four notes that make up the C6 chord. These notes (★) are "designated" in the measure where they systematiccally follow the lower half-tone note, which gives us a chromatic tension that finds its resolution in one of the other designated notes.

Notice that this principle of the chromatic approach with the lower half-tone can be used with a great number of three-or four-note arpeggios, and even with five notes. To be honest, this procedure will always work superbly in the measure, or when it relies on the V7 (tension) principle → I (resolution), with the chromatic note that "fits in" with one of the designated notes.

For example, in the case shown below, the B note designates the C note, this B "appreciates" C – or, if you prefer, B is the major third of the G7 chord (V7, tension), which is driven by the C6 chord (I, resolution).

Play the notes in increasing order, then in decreasing order. Don't forget to transpose.

disc #24

Diagram with designated notes of the C6 chord.

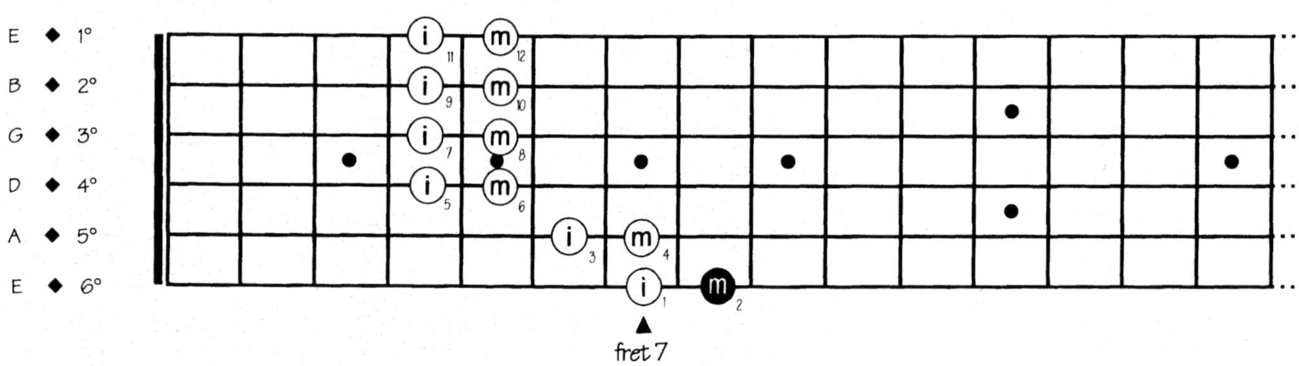

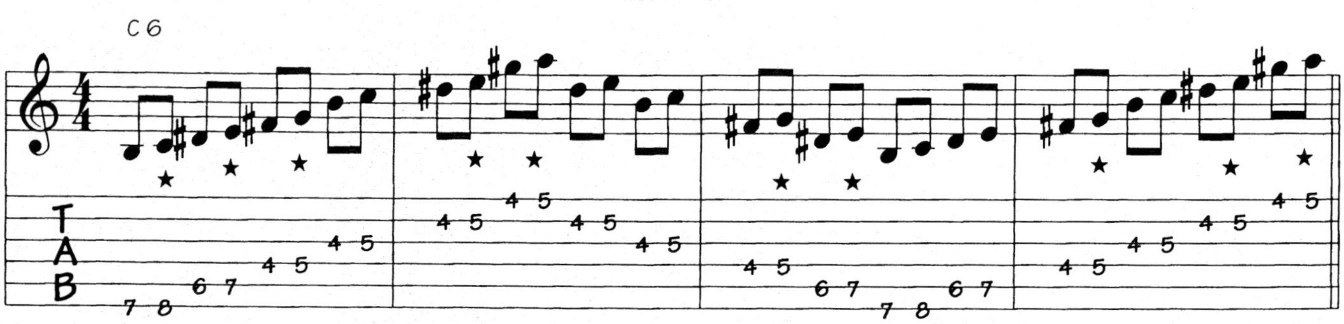

▪ PART B1

We are now going to dig deeper into a few things in regards to the harmony, while still using the diagram and chords of "Pour Trois Pas" (chapter 5). We are going to analyze the structure of the harmony of "Pour Trois Pas" in such a way, that we will show you the principles of its construction. It will be very useful for you to know these general principles if you want to compose.

Here are diagrams of the A sections:

Key : Am

A	(I) Am	(IV) Dm	Am	⁒	Dm	⁒	Am	⁒
A'	1st A (II7) B7	⁒	(V) E7	⁒	2nd A B7	E7	Am	⁒

This group of chords determines the general key, which is A minor: other than the fact that the Am chord systematically takes the place in the uneven measures (measures 1, 3, 7 and 11). Above all, this key is determined by the presence of an E7 (V7 of Am). Let us remember that the "tension" → "resolution" principle is eminently characterized by the V → I ("dominant → root note") progression. This is an absolute principle of music that is in the tonal minor as well as in the tonal major context .

Now you may ask, isn't it true that the Am will always accompany an E7??... Surely, many times the Am comes before the IV degree, which is the case in measures 2-3. But to be honest, this IV degree hides behind an extremely often used harmonic progression: the II-V progression which, in the key of Am, is composed with the Bm7b5 - E7 chords.

However, if you look closely at the positions of the Dm and Bm7b5 chords, as shown below, you will realize that the two chords have three notes in common... and because of this fact it will let you see the Dm as a Bm7b5. As for the V degree (E7), followed in lieu of the II degree, it is represented in the melody (measure 2), by using an Abdim7 arpeggio, which is none other than the E7b9! – See chapter 5.

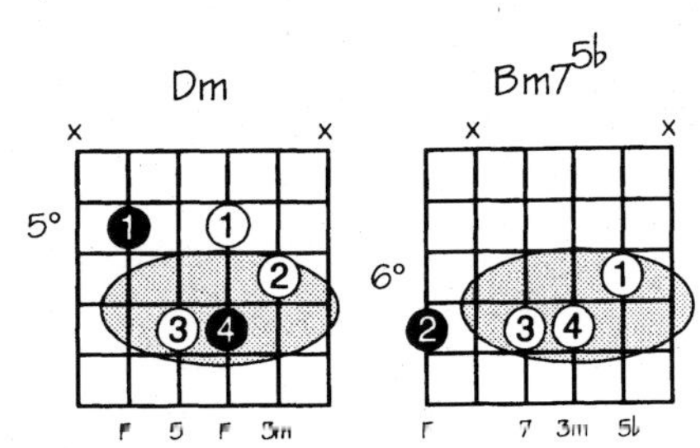

The A sections are finished with II-V (B7 - E7), here the II is "domineering" (transformed into a seventh chord - II7) to make the melody more powerful. Finally, in the case of the second A, also notice the reduction of the harmonic flow, so that it can finish the section with an Am... which is significant here becasue we are modulating.

Let's look at what happens in section B:

B

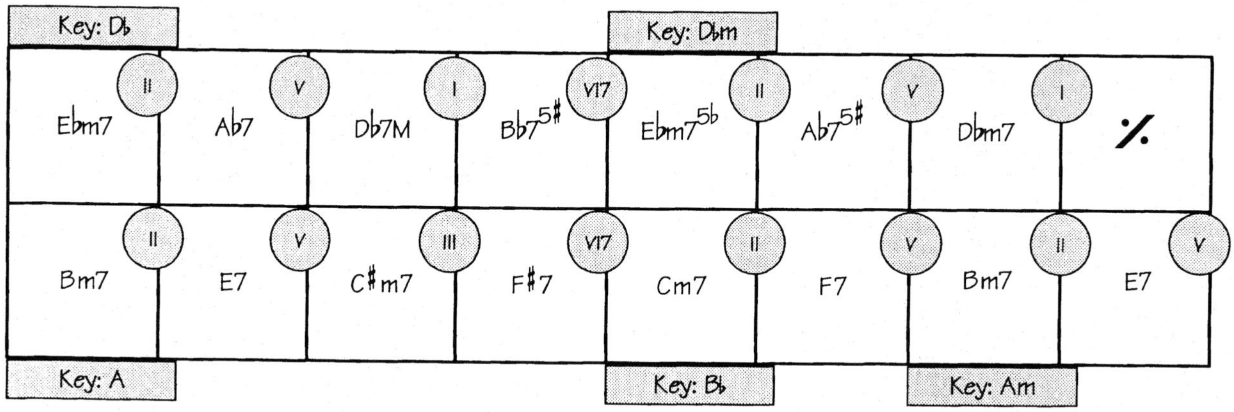

The first eight measures show two keys that have the same central root note, one being a major key, the other a minor key. In both cases the I degree is systematically introduced by its II-V.

In measure 4, the use of Bb7 (VI7) favors the arrival of Ebm7b5... in the measure where Bb7 is the (temporary) V of Ebm7b5. The connection between the two keys (Db major and Db minor) is used to make it go smoothly.

This gives us the opportunity to tell you about the importance of the following harmonic principle:

"All major, minor or dominant chords (Type V7) can be brought in with a dominant chord where the root note is located a perfect fifth (three and a half notes) higher".

The second part of the bridge has three new modulations: A major, Bb major and finally A minor. Look at the intensive use of the II-V progression. If these do not resolve (that's to say they are not followed in order of their degree), it will not take away any of the so-called known keys.

With all the harmonies of "Pour Trois Pas" notice that it uncovers a harmonic construction with a major/minor " mirror effect": the key of A minor and A major, D major and D minor – a procedure in an aesthetic order (between others) that's importance must not be neglected.

What can we get out of this harmonic analysis?

This information is very useful if you want to improvise. It will let you practice with the chords of this diagram. Indeed, thanks to the analysis of the keys, it will give you many progressions.The improvisor will have the freedom to manuver easier than the one who has to think how to play his lead over each unique chord in the measure. In one word, these "packages" of keys permit you to stand back and be relaxed when you think of its creative benefit.

Thus, in the case of "Pour Trois Pas", all the A sections are in A minor. In section B there are four measures in D major, four in D minor, four in A major, two in Bb major, and finally two in A minor.

PART B2

We are now going to look into the leads that are played in the style of Manouche, while studying the rest of the theme of "Pour Trois Pas". We have already seen the first two A sections in chapter 5.

Pour Trois Pas (measures 36 and 38) lead #5

This is done with a thrusting pickup produced very precisely with the pick. It is important to use a down stroke with the first and last notes of the lead (⊓); this has the advantage to give "weight" to this pickup. Also look at the use of sixteenth notes and of chromaticism.

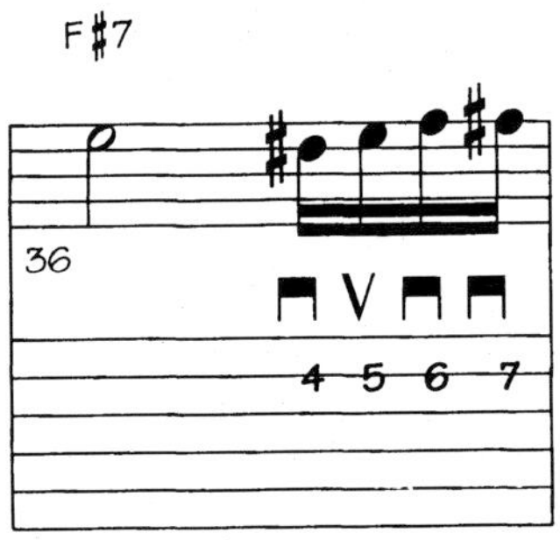

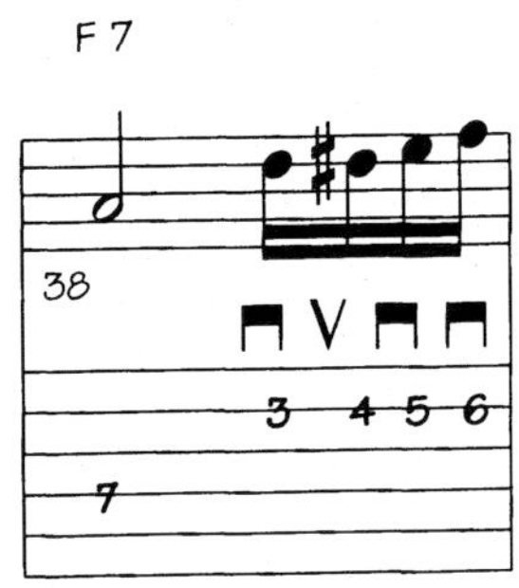

Pour Trois Pas (measures 43 and 55) the harmony explained

Look at the coloration of the Am chord with a major sixth (Am6). This is very much the way Manouche plays the harmony. This coloration is done the same way as in measure 15 (Chapter 5)

Pour Trois Pas (measure 49) the melody explained

Measure 49 (as well as measure 9- chapter 5) is melodically constructed with the dim7 arpeggio (D#dim7): another signature of Manouche. Remember that the whole dim7 arpeggio may be placed in relation with a dominant (V7) chord colored with a b9 – here it is B7b9.

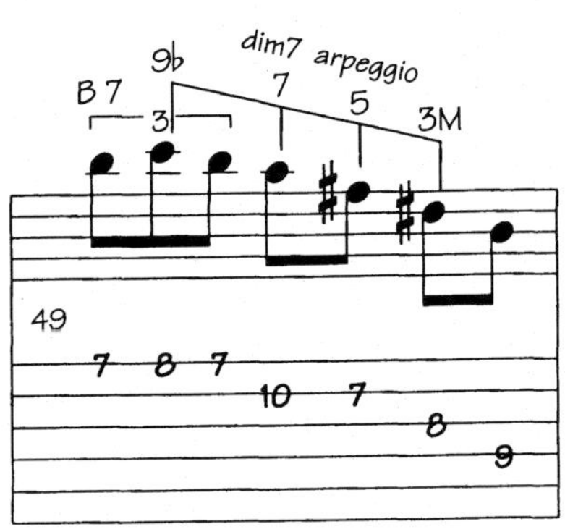

Pour Trois Pas (measure 51) the melody explained

By following the example of measure 49, we see the new application of the dim7 arpeggio with a dominant seventh chord. The difference here is that the arpeggio is one half tone lower (D#dim7 → Ddim7)... although the harmony itself is a fifth lower (B7 → E7). No matter what it is the lead remains perfectly convincing and shines some light on the following principle:

"A progression with descending fifths of two - or more - dominant chords (Type V7) can, from a melodic point of view (improvisation, composition), be treated by means of dim7 arpeggios linked with descending chromaticisms."

The secret of this sleight of hand is evidently in the structure of the dim7 chord: exclusively stacked up with minor thirds. Of course, you can also treat the use of dim7 arpeggios strictly in parrallel with chord progressions, that's to say, with descending fifths. But the melody that results from it, or better yet, that you can play comfortably (visualizing the fingerboard) will be much less convincing in this case.

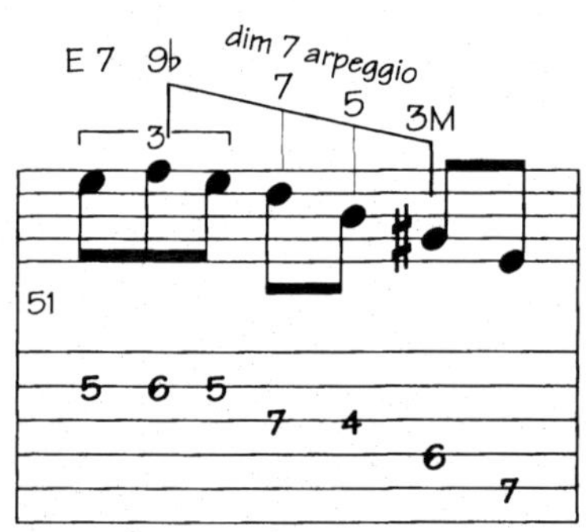

Pour Trois Pas (measures 61 - 62) the melody explained

Measures 61 and 62 (the same for measures 21 and 22 - chapter 5) illustrate three things that you have to remember:
– use skipping intervals (octave and tenths),
– insert chromaticisms, used to decorate the phrase,
– use the "question/ answer" principle: measure 61 = the question; measure 62 (analog phrase) = the response.

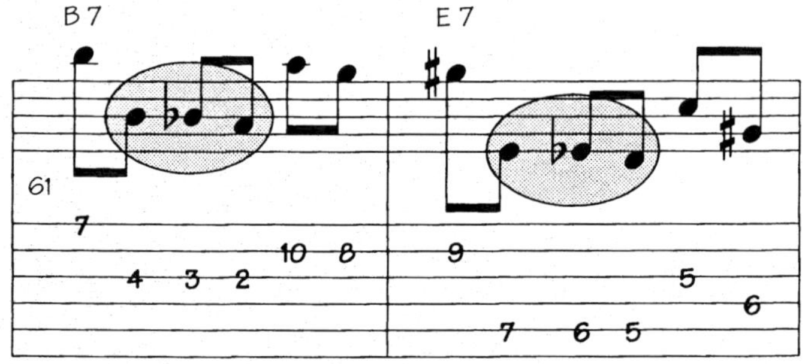

PART C

We'll continue with the song "Pour Trois Pas", this time let's look at the bridge.

To hear the quarter note triplets in measure 27, listen to the CD.

The mystery of the double flats in measure 29 and 30 will be reviewed in chapter 7.

#21

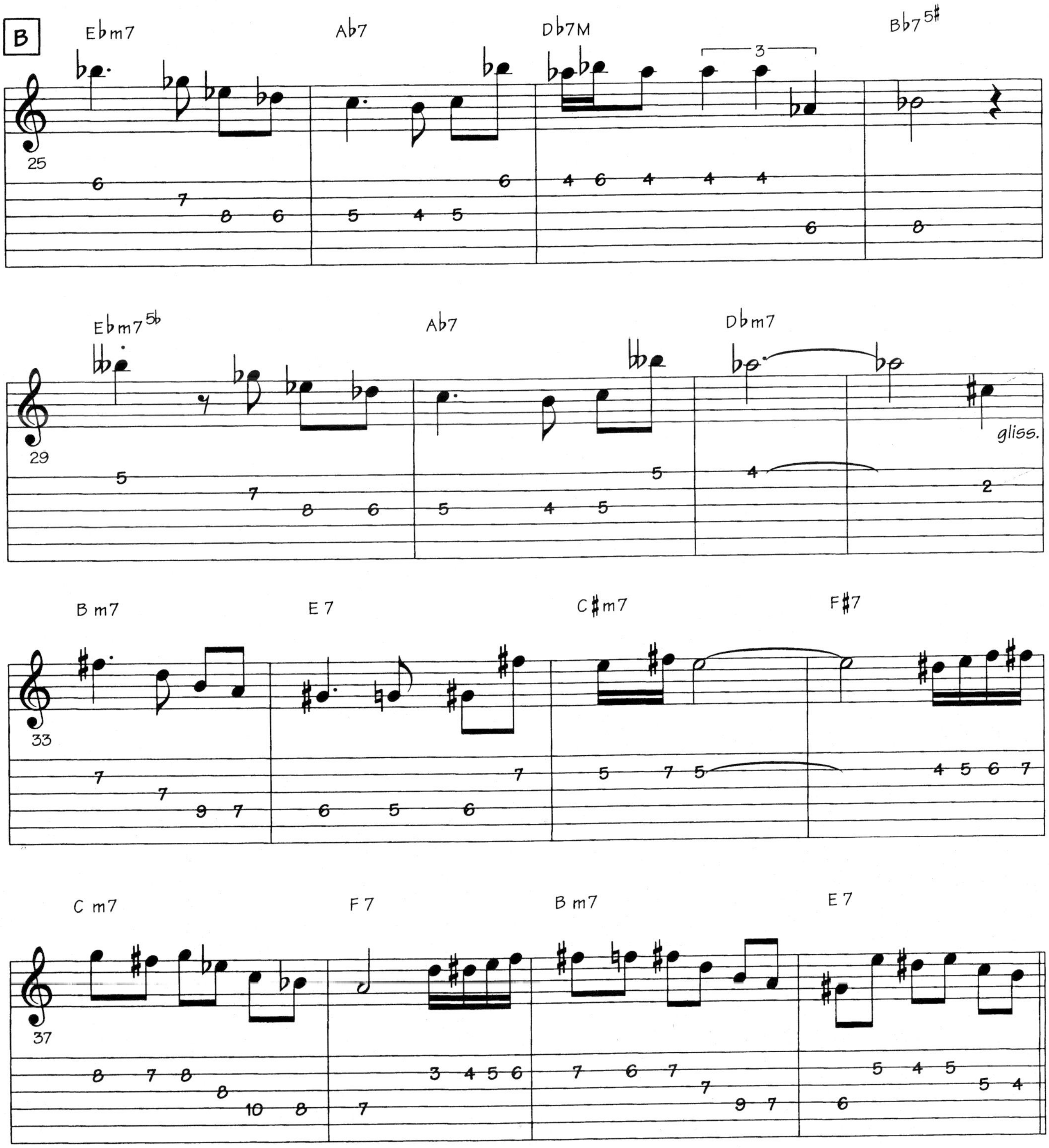

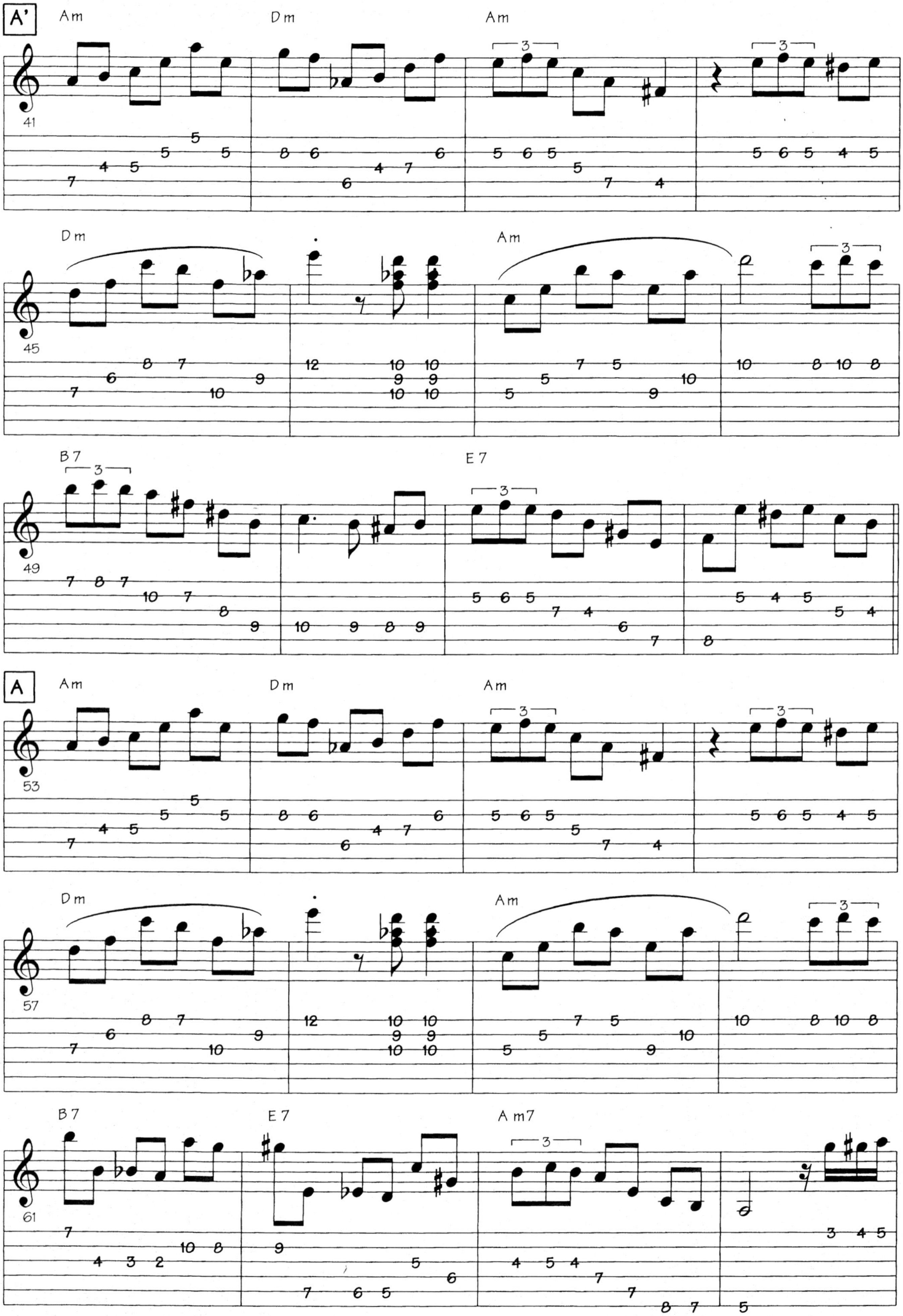
A'
Am
Dm
Am
Dm
Am
B7
E7
A
Am
Dm
Am
Dm
Am
B7
E7
Am7

PART A

The exercises that start this seventh chapter are dedicated to the whole tone scale.

The whole tone scale is a melodic scale with six notes, which is very easy to remember: it is uniquely built with major second intervals.

We use the whole tone scale exclusively with dominant type (V7) chords.

Being given that it is only made up with whole tones, it carries the same name - the whole tone scale, – and it can start with each of its composed notes:

C whole tone (which starts with the C note) = whole tone D, E, F#, G# or A#.

Besides that, within the power of its particular structure, there are only two copies of the whole tone scale with disctinct notes, that relativley have twelve possible tranpositions:

C whole tone = C D E F# G# A# and Db whole tone = Db Eb F G A B.

This property - technically named "A Limited Transposition" - makes the whole tone scale a family member of the dim7 chord, which itself is also a "A Limited Transposition". It is evident that its practical applications are similar.

Exercise 20 - whole tone scale: diagram with descending steps

In the Manouche playing style, we mainly use the whole tone scale in the form of the diagram below " in steps", which is extremely visual.

Here is the diagram in descending steps. To start off, play the eighth notes in the increasing numerical order then in the decreasing numerical order. Use eighths notes (as shown in the diagram below). Then play eighth note triplets (12 notes per measure at 4/4).

disc #25 **Whole tone Scale (of B and all its composing notes) going down in 'steps'.**

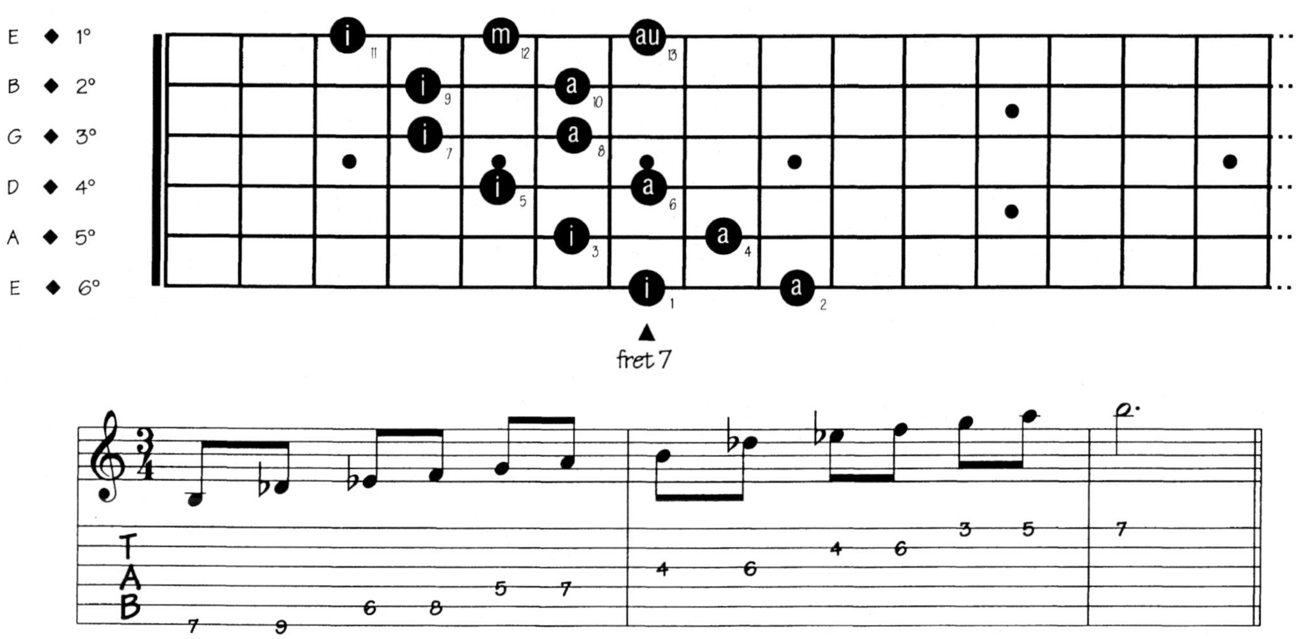

Exercise 21 - whole tone scale: diagram in ascending steps

Here is the diagram in ascending steps. It is different from the descending scale, because this diagram uses three notes per string.

Play the notes in the inceasing numerical order, then in the decreasing numerical order.

First use eighth notes (as indicated below).

Next in eighth note triplets (12 notes per measure at 4/4).
Once more, pay attention to the shift of the frets between the 2nd and 3rd strings.

Whole tone scale (of G and all its components) done in ascending steps.

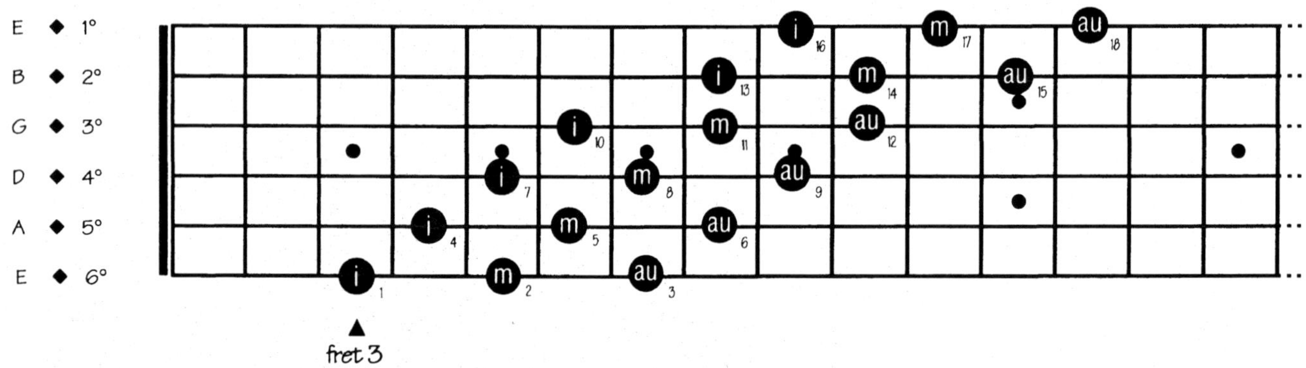

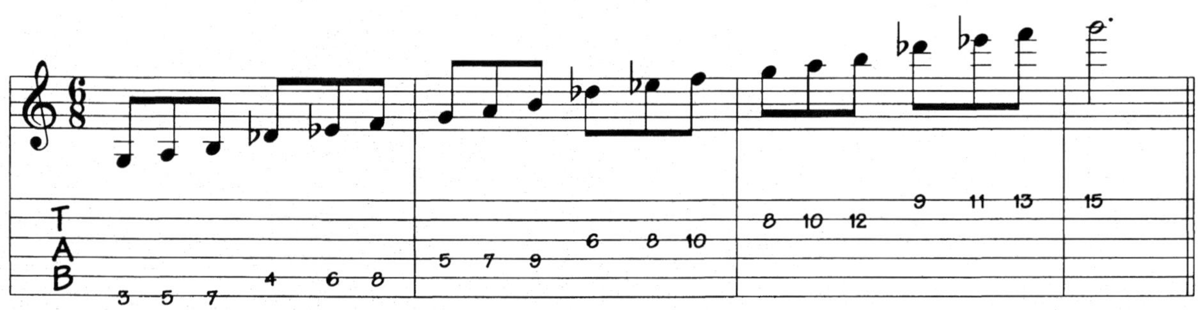

To finish this exercise, practice by playing the following chords for the two diagrams above, in the specified order, or one that you like (record a rhythm track on an audio cassette, or on a computer,etc. Or you can ask a friend who plays guitar to accompany you).

||: F7 | A7 | D♭7 || B7 | E♭ 7 | G7 :||

PART B1

We will now complete the study by using the diagram of "Pour Trois Pas" (chapter 6) and give a harmonic analysis of the last A section (coda).

Harmonic analysis of the coda:

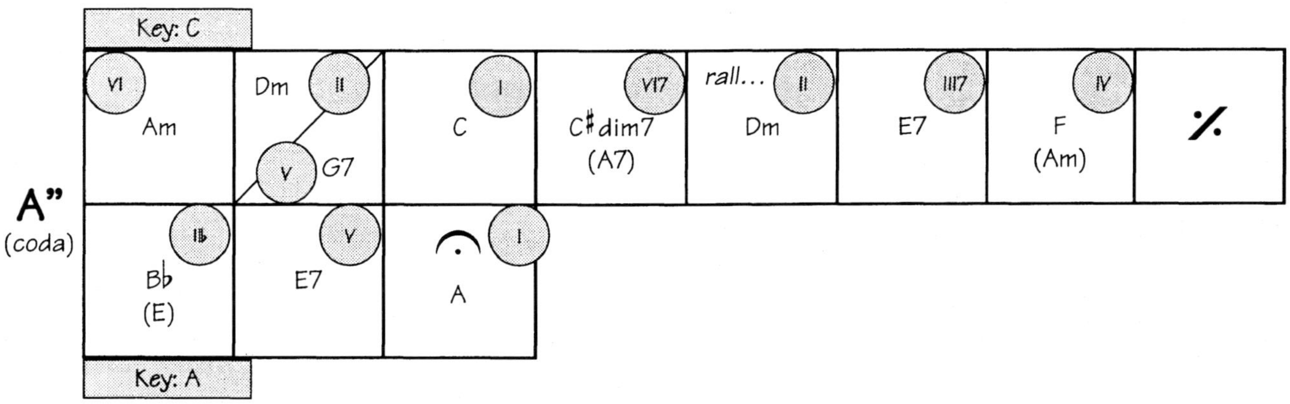

We use two separate keys here.

The first (C major) comes very close to the initial (A minor) key that controls the other A sections. We will now look at what is called the "relative" keys: The C scale uses exactly the same notes as the (natural) Am scale.

Observe how the C chord is used: it comes after the Am (I in the key of A minor, and also the VI in the key of C major) followed by the Dm (the IV in A minor, also the II in C major) followed by a G7 (the V in C major). All of these form a harmonic progression which is exceptionally useful - shown as the 'VI-II-V" which is also called an "ANATOLE" (turnaround).

MEASURES 4-5: This is a VI7 degree (disguished as a I#dim7 in order to squeeze out, with precision, the ascending movement of the C, C#, D, E and F root notes), which moves the Dm a fifth down in one movement (A → D).

MEASURES 5-6: a "domineering" III degree (the E7 = III7 – normaly the III in the key of C major is Em) it is the way to introduce the IV chord (F), which is a chord close to the VI of the (Am), in a sense that the IV and VI share common notes... which explains the presence of the III7 (E7), that is the V7 of Am.

MEASURES 9-11: the goal is to reach the final key of A major. We let the E7 get ahead of the A (substitution), and this E7 by a Bb... which is only the "tritonic" expression of the same E7 (substitution). For right now, simply use this tritonic action for what it is. We will come back to this in more detail.

To finish, look at the choice of the second key of this coda: A major. This is where we could logically expect to hear what will be an A minor, like in the other A sections... this simply means: in music it is not unusual to be surprised!

Chapter 7 / page 4

Since we are speaking about "keys", the moment has come to shed the light on the mysterious double B flats, which you will certainly notice. These are diliberately used in measures 29 and 30 (section B of the song "Pour Trois Pas" – look at the score on page 7, chapter 6).

Why the Bbb note? Wouldn't it have been easier to write A?

Easier? Yes. More correct? No.

Because in the context where we have this Bbb, we are in the Db minor key, and the (natural) minor scale determines that that key effectively brings with it a Bbb:

D natural minor scale:

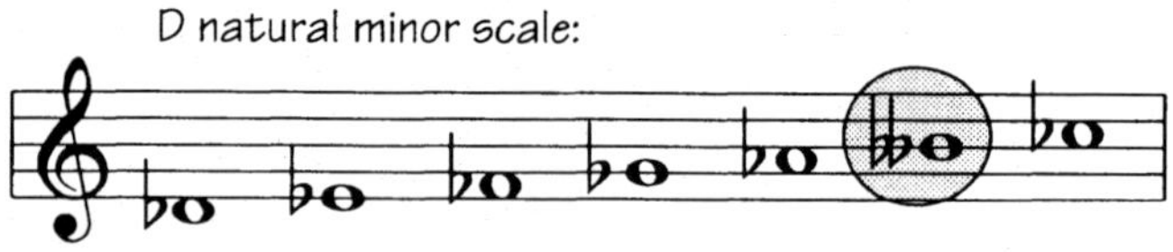

C# natural minor scale

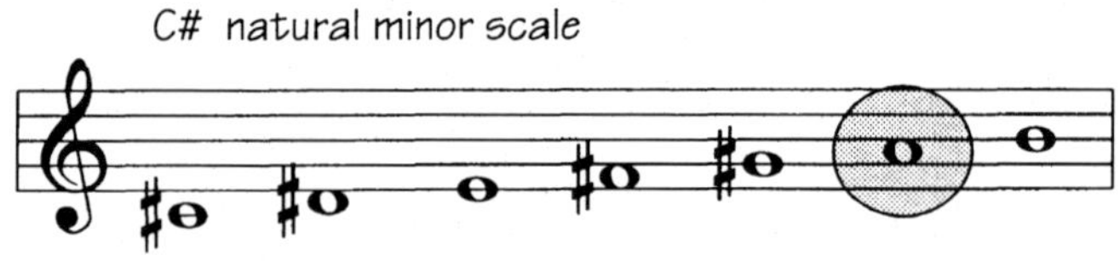

Maybe you will object since you could avoid the Bbb by using the C# minor key, the "enharmonic" equivalent of the Db minor (that sounds the same, but has a different name). Calling it C# minor will be much easier.

Yes, the C# minor makes it all possible... under the condition that it must not make a small trip beforehand, in the key of Db major – that is precisely what is happening here! Because the lead of this passage would have become:

Ebm7	Ab7	Db7M	Bb7$^{5\#}$?	D#m7^{5b}	G#7$^{5\#}$	C#m7	%

This could cause a problem with logical transitions, the clarity of the harmonic line between the Bb7#5 and D#7b5: the movement of descending fifths (the Bb → Eb = principle V → I, (even if this is a provisional "I") stops being obvious.

There, now you know how and why this is Bbb.

This is an extreme case - which is less and less used in jazz.

PART B2

We are now going to look at the continuation and the end of "Pour Trois Pas".

Pour Trois Pas (measures 70 - 71) lead and diagram #6

Measure 70 shows us a particular area of the whole tone scale, using the augmented chord (triplet). This chord is created with the whole tone scale (among other scales) and, of course, it possesses with it the a Limited Transposition.

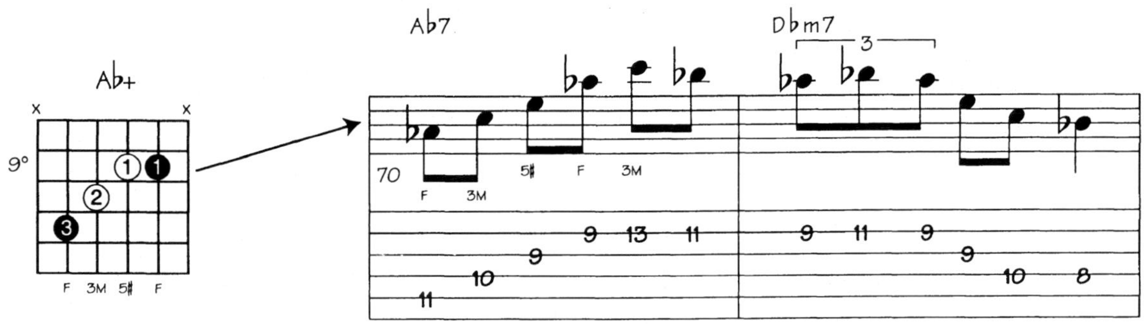

Pour Trois Pas (measures 73 and 75) lead and diagram #7

These phrases are constructed with a diagram of the minor chord, transposed with succesive spaces of one tone in strict parallelism with the harmonic movement.

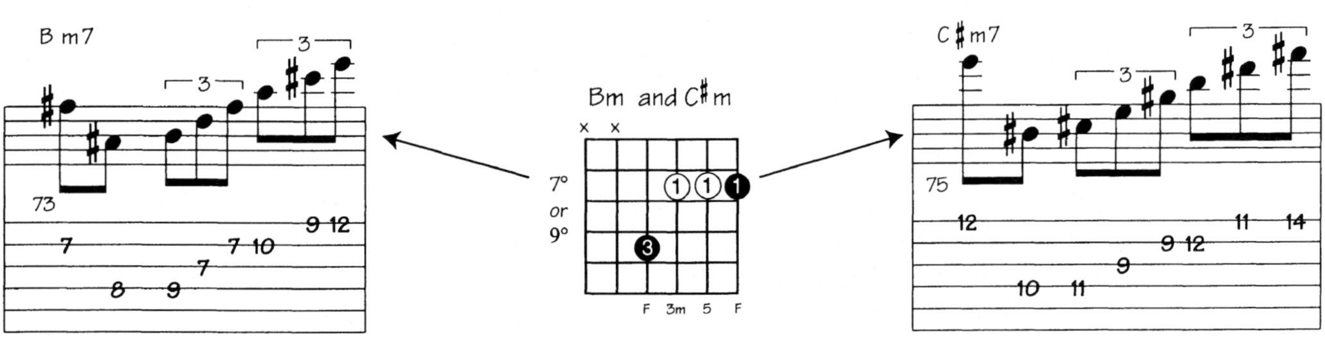

Pour Trois Pas (measures 74 and 76) lead and diagram #8

We are still using an arpeggio, in the major key this time... one which apparently does not correspond with the harmony. In measure 74, the Bb major arpeggio with the E7 and in measure 76 the C major arpeggio with F#7. Is this a mistake?

Evidentally not. It only seems so. In reality, we find it to be among one of the most used and efficient processes to improvise with... It is known as the " tritone substitution".

For now this is something new, just take it as it is and simply be pleased. Play this passage, while listening to it. Later we will comeback to this passage.

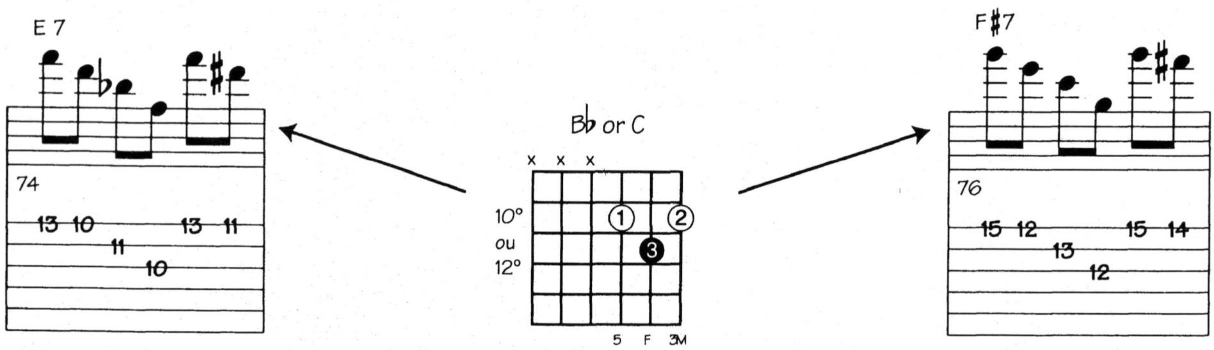

Pour Trois Pas (measures 82 and 83) lead and diagram #9

For the last part we will return to our good old dim7 arpeggio, which used to be a V7 chord (this is the E7, which re-introduces the Am). Notice how this is counted: we have triplets in eighths, whose outcome is the (Am) root note of the chord that we are using here, which is placed on a heavy beat of the measure.

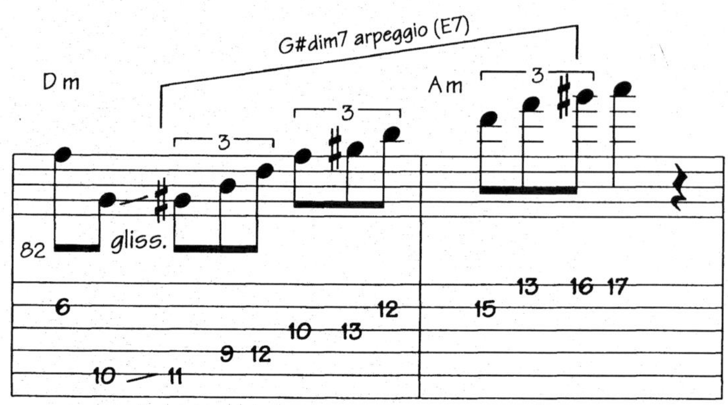

PART C

Continuation and the end of "Pour Trois Pas": bridge (solo), the last A and coda.

Pay attention to the unusual counpound set up of measure 69 (a reversed formula). Listen to the passage on the CD.

Finally, be well aware of what happens when you slow down the beat (rall ...measure 97), it sets the mood for the ending of the piece.

#21

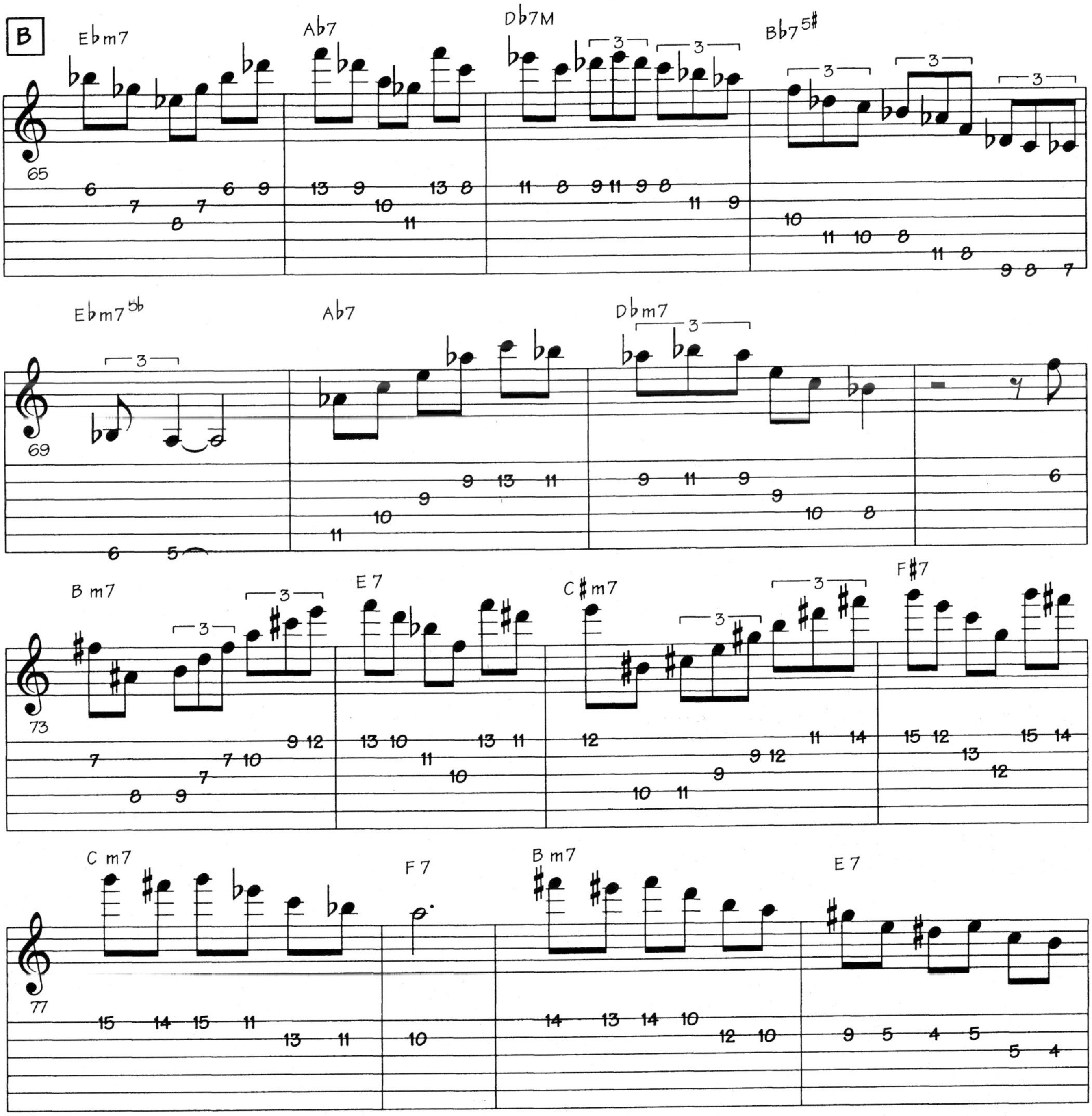

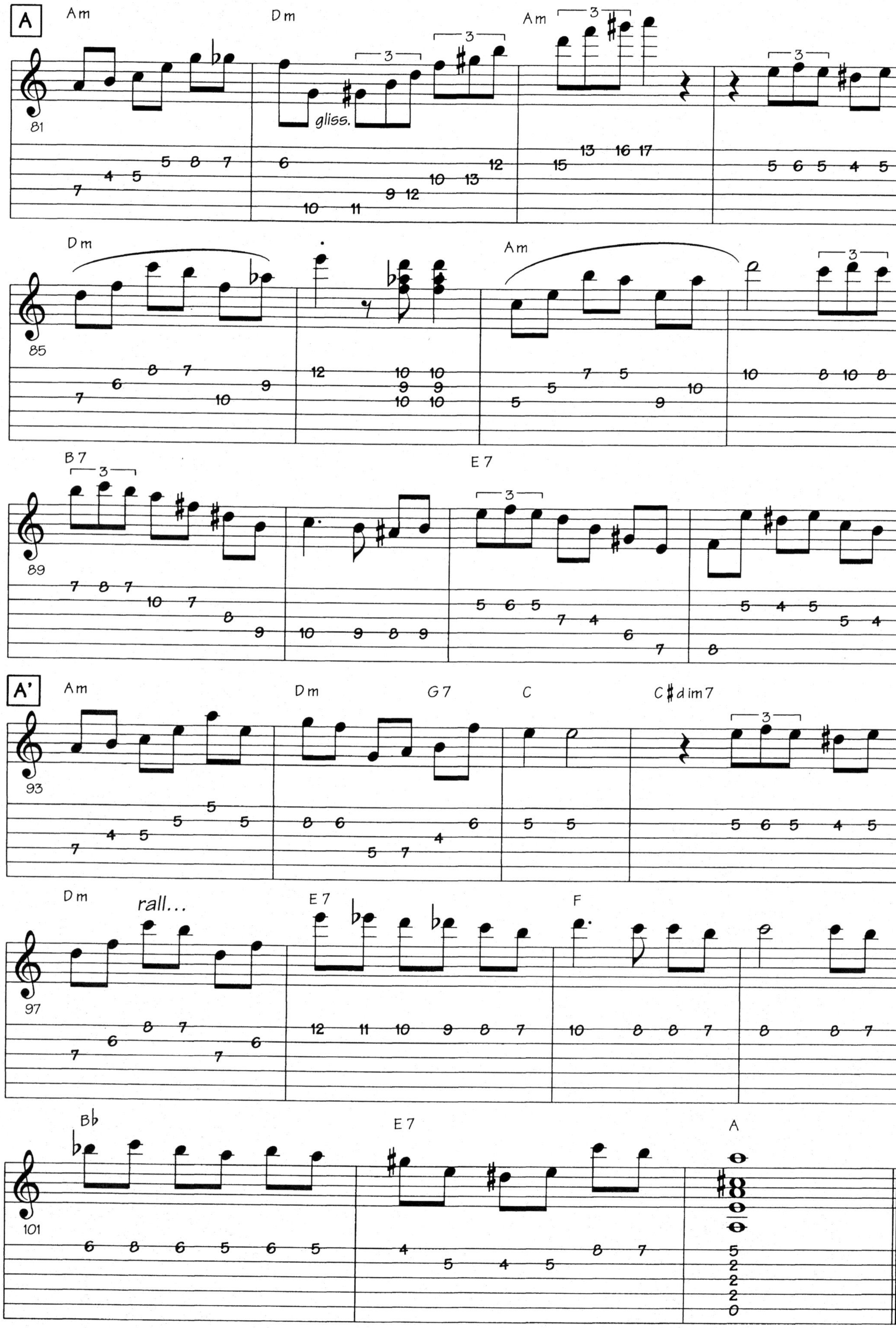
A
Am
Dm
Am
gliss.
Dm
Am
B7
E7
A'
Am
Dm
G7
C
C♯dim7
Dm
rall...
E7
F
B♭
E7
A

PART A

We are going to study a diagram that is often used when playing in the Manouche style. It is a close parent of one that we have already looked at for the minor chord in chapter 3 (exercise 10).

Exercise 22 - major triad with a major second

Play the notes following the increasing numerical order.

#27 **G major arpeggio with 9M (Gmajor9).**

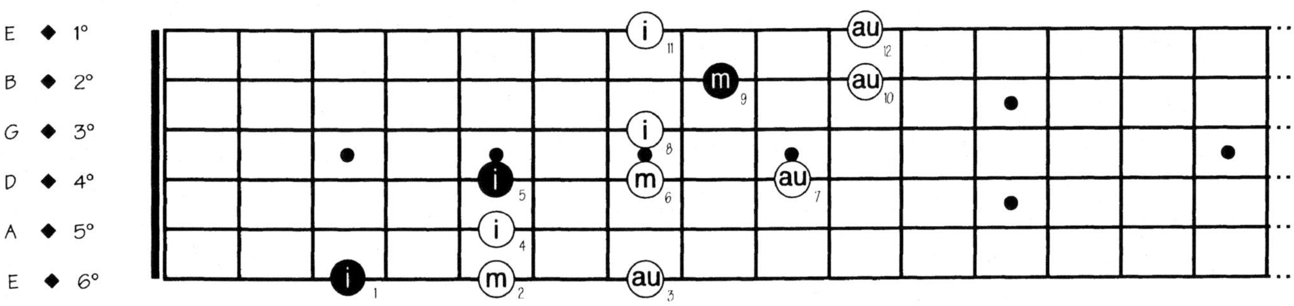

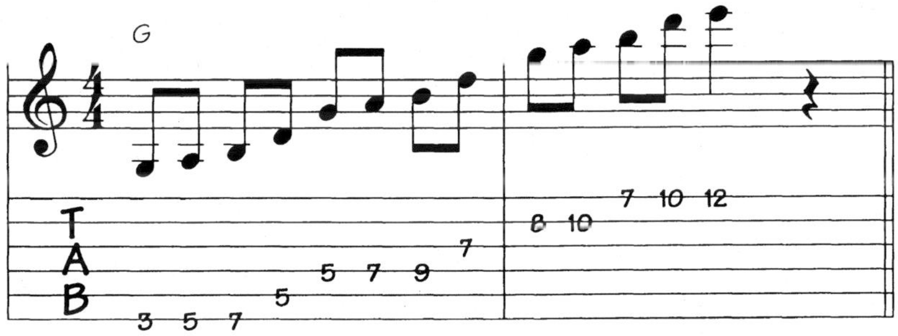

Exercise 23 - Dim7 arpeggio and diminished scale

The following exercise is what is called a "structured melody": a vocabulary phrase that we will be able to use within the real context of improvisation. With this structure we can use the D7 chord and make use of the dim7 arpeggio (ascending phase) and the diminished scale (descending phase).

Look at the beginning. We have the "driving" eighth note triplet that is preceded by a syncopated eighth, this rhythm is used often in jazz.

#28

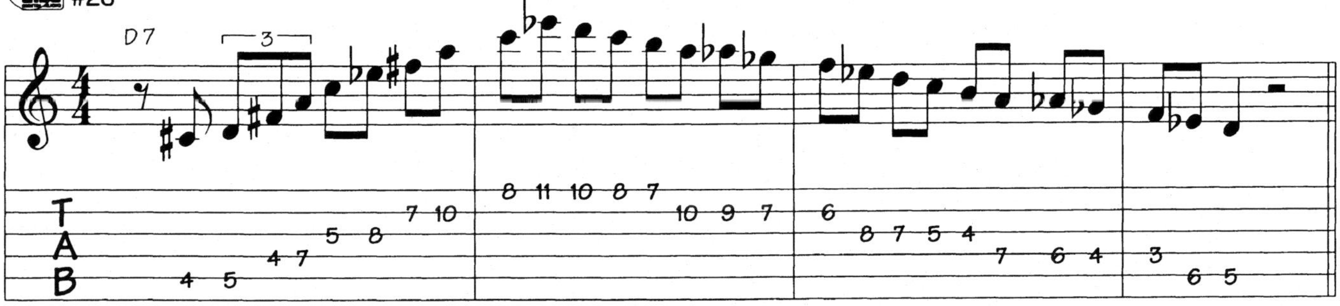

Exercise 24 - continuing the G major arpeggio

Here is another melody that uses the chords (degrees) of the G major key.

It is called a "diatonic" progression, because of the way the root notes of the chords are linked together in the order of the notes of the scale (G, A, B...). The G/B chord (a G major and a B bass), can also be considerd as a Bm7.

Of course, this is all done with alternating sweeps of the pick (down – up)

#29

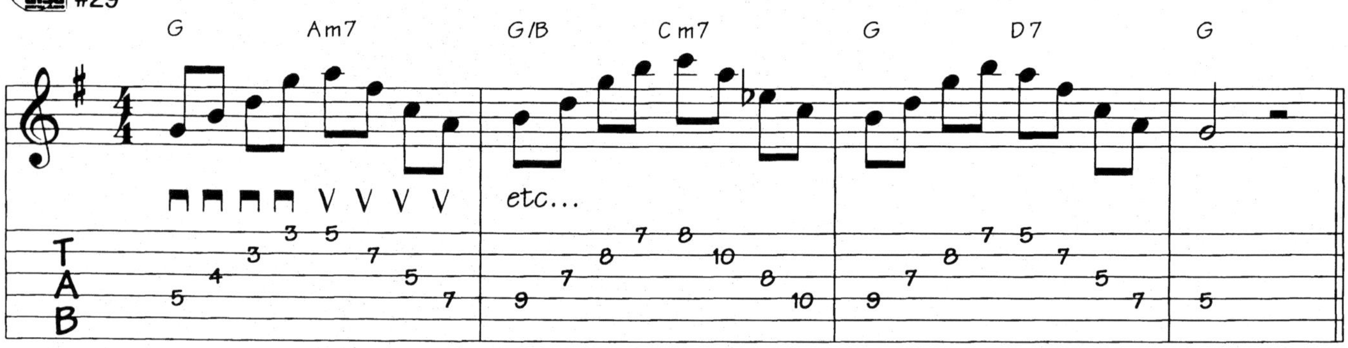

Exercise 25 - diminished scale with a G major cadence

This rhytmic motive is identical with the one of Exercise 23 (a triplet preceded by a syncopated eighth) and has a similar phrase using the diminished scale of the dominant seventh chord (D7).

Notice the time placement: the last note of the lead is resolved with the major third note of the G chord.

#30

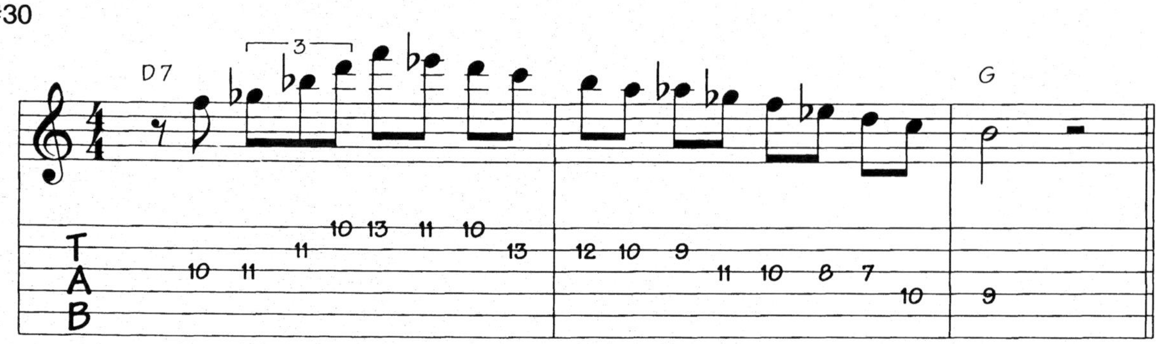

Exercise 26 - a phrase with G7

Here is another melody composed with chromatics (with the goal to stall the beat) and interval skipping that gives us an excellent opportunity to work with the pick while switching strings. The entire lead relies on the basic diagram of G major.

#31

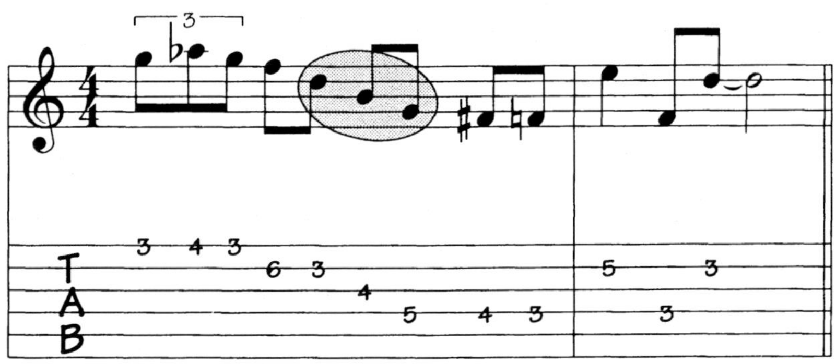

Exercise 27 - diagram with G7sus4 (Dm7)

Here is still another illustration of a typical visual fingerboard diagram in the style of Manouche.

It's done here with one sweep (strike) per note per string, with a two fret gap between them, which works with the G7sus4 chord, colored by a major second.

The "7sus4" type chord is a chord that lacks the third, and is built up with a root note, a fourth, a fifth plus the minor seventh. These are the G, C, D, F notes of the G7sus4 chord. In this diagram here, the root note is partially replaced by the major second (the A note). This type of chord could also be considered as an "m7(11)" G7sus4 = Dm7(11); this is the case with a substitution.

Play the notes in the increasing order, then in the decreasing order.

G7sus4 diagram using a sweep.

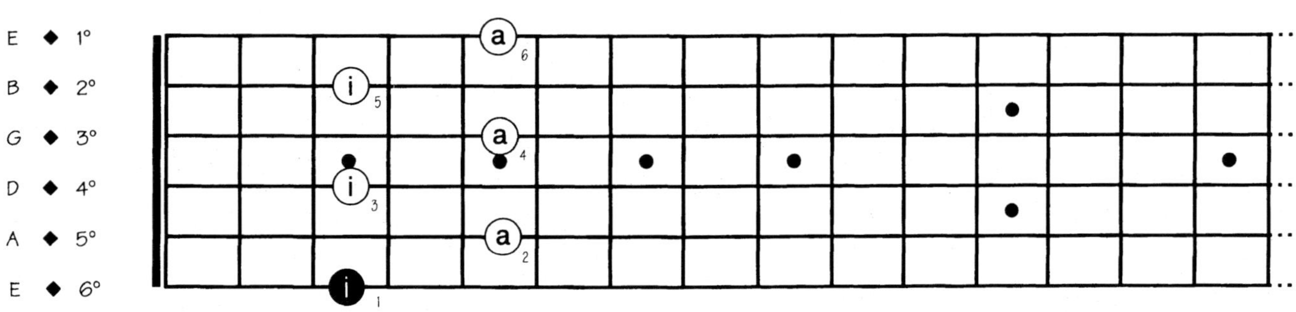

#32

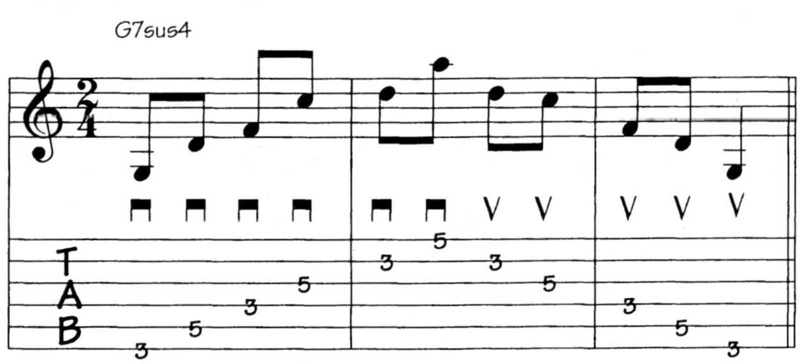

▪ PART B1

We will now look at the chord diagram for "Jo's Remake". You can hear it on the "Romane Ombre" CD.

Here is the block diagram of this piece that we will use to study the guitar choruses on page 8 of this chapter:

Jo's Remake

Structure = 32 measures ABA'C

♩= 290

A	G7M	G7M / A♭dim7	Am7	D7	𝄎		G7M	𝄎
B	B7M	B7M / Cdim7	C♯m7	F♯7	𝄎		B7M	D7
A'	6 𝄎 (measures 1–6)						B7	𝄎
C	C7M	C♯dim7	G6/D	E7	A7	D7	G6	D7

And here are the possible chord positions:

Sections A, B and A'

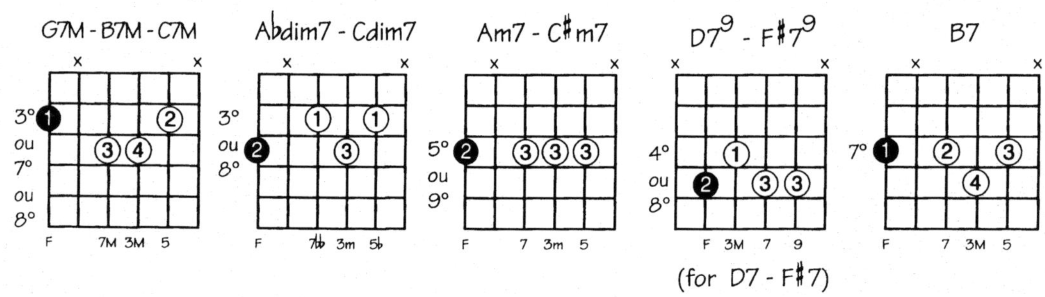

Section C

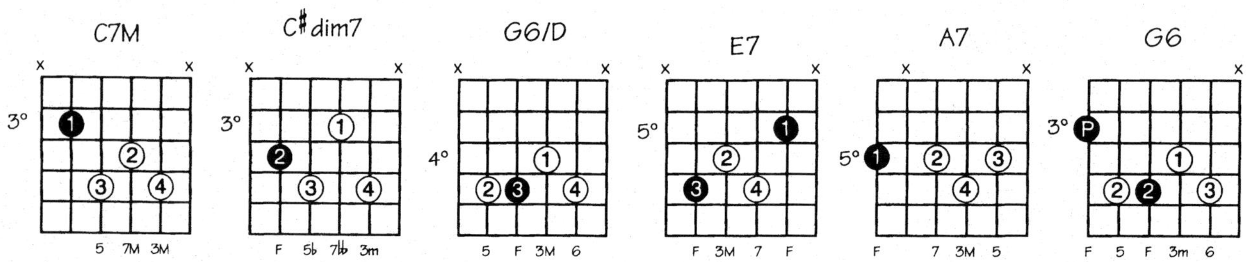

We are going to dedicate the following two pages to study certain aspects of harmony. This knowledge will enable you to gain extremely precious time, and give you so much of the rhythm structure that it enables you to improvise.

This will show you how to structure chord progressions (particularly in jazz), as well as giving you the reason for these progressions.

THE DESCENDING QUINT CIRCLE

You probably have already seen our previous occassional analyses of the harmony, and the chords that are used to form the diagrams of the groups that determine the keys. The root notes of these chords are frequently separated by the same type of intervals: descending fifths (or, with ascending fourths, done the same way).

Thus you can construct a diagram by following the chords of a given key (such as the C major key, shown below).

#33

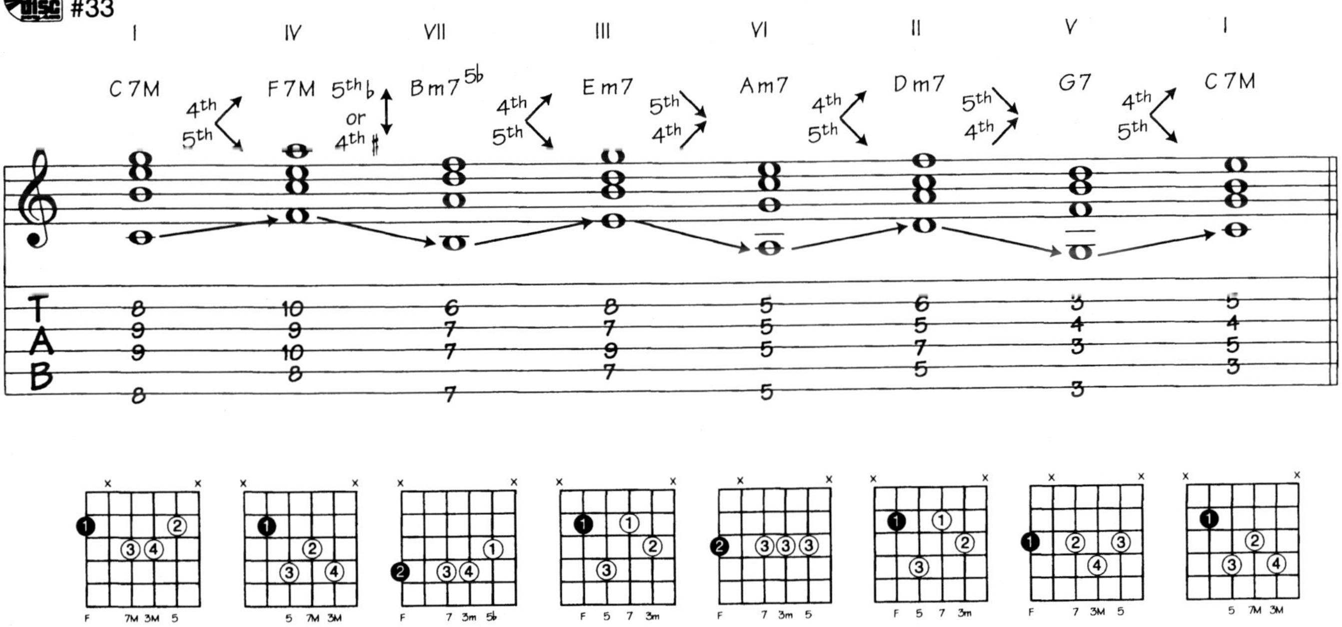

Since you already know the correct way of how to place the accidentals in the key signature to show in what key the piece is played (see glossary), you are certainly familiar with this descending group of fifths. Indeed, it is the cycle that shows you where to place the flats:

B E A D G C F (B♭ E♭ A♭ D♭ G♭)...

Whatever the case is, be sure to memorize it, so that you can make the chord progressions. Be able to recognize the formation of the degrees (I - IV - VII - III - VI - II - V - I). You will see this over and over again.

To help you memorize it, here is a table of all the tones (keys) that puts the seven degrees of the major scale linked by descending fifths as a group.

It is useless to learn this table by heart. Simply look at it when you need to. For example, if you want to do an analyses of any lead by yourself.

	I°	IV°	VII°	III°	VI°	II°	V°	I°
C	C7M	F7M	Bm7$^{5\flat}$	Em7	Am7	Dm7	G7	C7M

Keys with ♯	I°	IV°	VII°	III°	VI°	II°	V°	I°
G	G7M	C7M	F♯m7$^{5\flat}$	Bm7	Em7	Am7	D7	G7M
D	D7M	G7M	C♯m7$^{5\flat}$	F♯m7	Bm7	Em7	A7	D7M
A	A7M	D7M	G♯m7$^{5\flat}$	C♯m7	F♯m7	Bm7	E7	A7M
E	E7M	A7M	D♯m7$^{5\flat}$	G♯m7	C♯m7	F♯m7	B7	E7M
B	B7M	E7M	A♯m7$^{5\flat}$	D♯m7	G♯m7	C♯m7	F♯7	B7M
F♯	F♯7M	B7M	E♯m7$^{5\flat}$	A♯m7	D♯m7	G♯m7	C♯7	F♯7M

Keys with ♭	I°	IV°	VII°	III°	VI°	II°	V°	I°
F	F7M	B♭7M	Em7$^{5\flat}$	Am7	Dm7	Gm7	C7	F7M
B♭	B♭7M	E♭7M	Am7$^{5\flat}$	Dm7	Gm7	Cm7	F7	B♭7M
E♭	E♭7M	A♭7M	Dm7$^{5\flat}$	Gm7	Cm7	Fm7	B♭7	E♭7M
A♭	A♭7M	D♭7M	Gm7$^{5\flat}$	Cm7	Fm7	B♭m7	E♭7	A♭7M
D♭	D♭7M	G♭7M	Cm7$^{5\flat}$	Fm7	B♭m7	E♭m7	A♭7	D♭7M
G♭	G♭7M	C♭7M	Fm7$^{5\flat}$	B♭m7	E♭m7	A♭m7	D♭7	G♭7M

PART B2

We are now going to study diagrams and leads from the first guitar chorus of "Jo's Remake".

Jo's Remake (measures 1 and 2) the melody explained

This solo starts with a spiritual lead which could be played on a trumpet: using very high notes, with some staccatto notes. Using inspiration from a wind instrument to create a guitar solo is never a bad idea. It is even recommanded, and it has the advantage to lighten the discourse by being able to breath in between notes... which guitarists too often neglect - and for a reason!

Jo's Remake (measures 6 and 7) lead and diagram #1

A worked out phrase with a major sixth chord diagram... and done with the major pentatonic scale (no,no, this is not from the blues!).

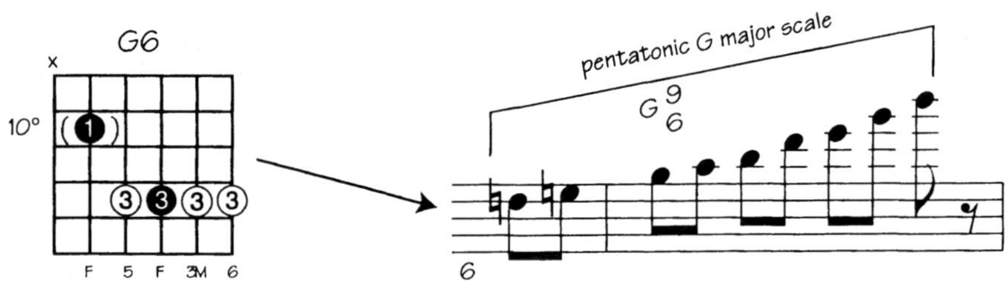

Jo's Remake (measure 9) lead and diagram #2

This is another phrase with another chord diagram: the a "7M" type:

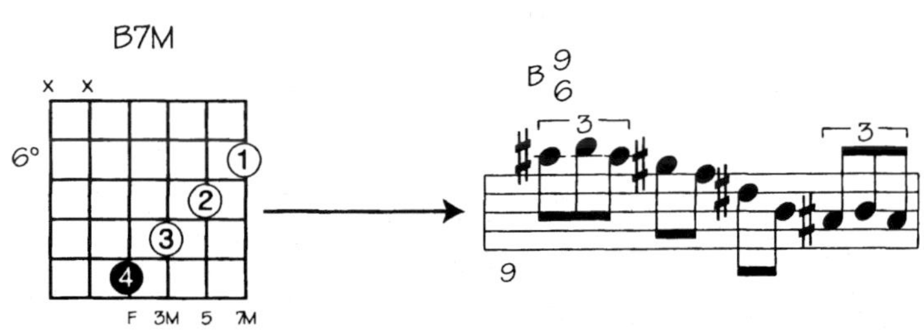

Jo's Remake (measures 11 and 12) the melody explained

Here we see triplets, staccato notes and resolvent chromaticism with the root note of the chord: there are as many essential ingredients in the vain of jazz that you might need when you want to improvise a melody!

Jo's Remake (measure 16) lead and diagram #3

Here again is a lead that uses the diagram of the minor chord (compare it with the one in "Swing for Ninine").

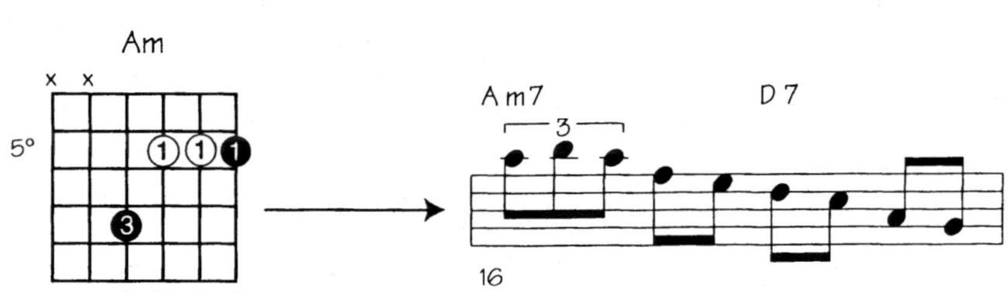

PART C

Here are the first 16 measures of the chorus to"Jo's Remake".

This solo is played very fast, but take your time. Listen carefully to the CD.

#35

Jo's Remake

music by ROMANE

♫ = ♩♪ ♩=290

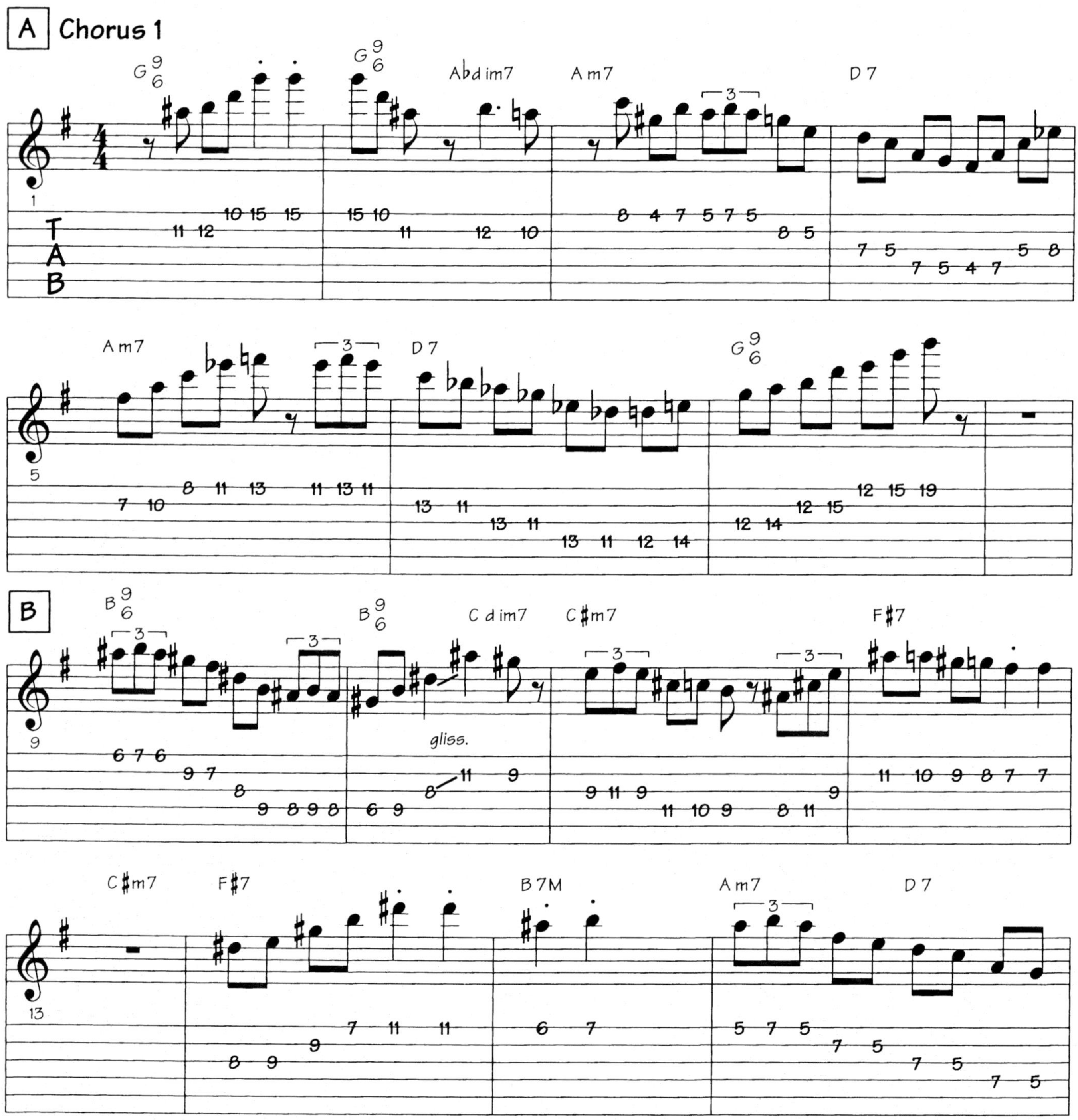

PART A

How well do you know the fingerboard of your guitar? After these first eight chapters, we hope you know it more in depth. Nevertheless, it is our intention to assist those of you who still do not know it perfectly, and cannot find the notes fast. Here then are some simple strategies that can help you close the gap.

If you want to play in the style of Manouche, you will primarely be interested in where the notes on the 5th and 6th strings are. And, of course, how to find the notes by relying on the fingerboard diagram .

LOCATION THE NOTES - ANATOLE (TURNAROUND) DIAGRAM

Since the root note of a chord of the I degree is located on the 5th string, you could find the root notes of three other chords in the middle of diagram 1, as shown below: C(I) - A(VI) - D (II) - G (V) - C (I). Play the notes in increasing numerical order.

Location of the notes: root notes of the anatole.

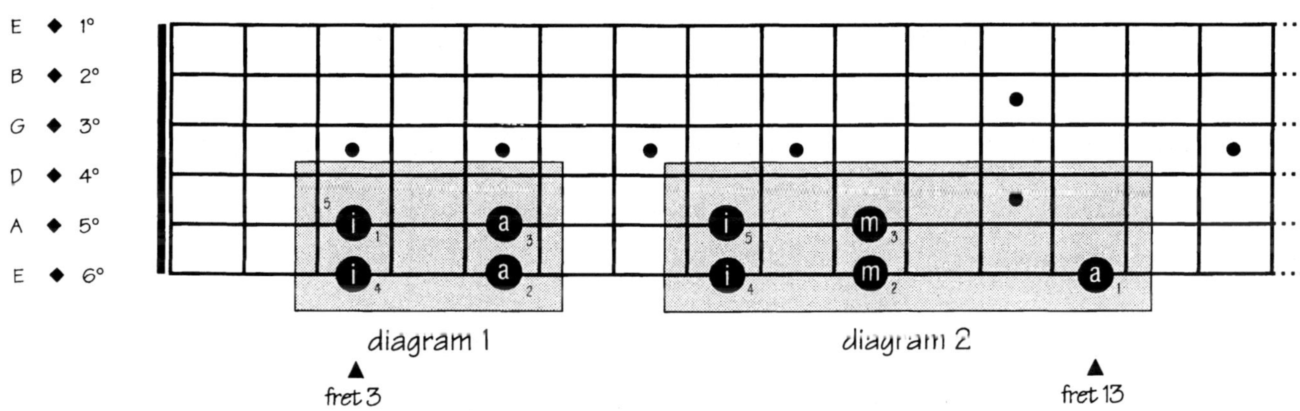

LOCATION OF THE NOTES -THE CIRCLE OF FIFTHS (quint circle).

Of course, it is possible to sweep through all the (12) notes of the descending circle of fifths (a complete octave) by joining one or the others of these diagrams together, and by knowing that each of the groups with five notes also forms an (III- VI - II –V – I) anatole (turnaround). Play the notes in increasing numerical order.

Location of the notes: descending circle of fifths.

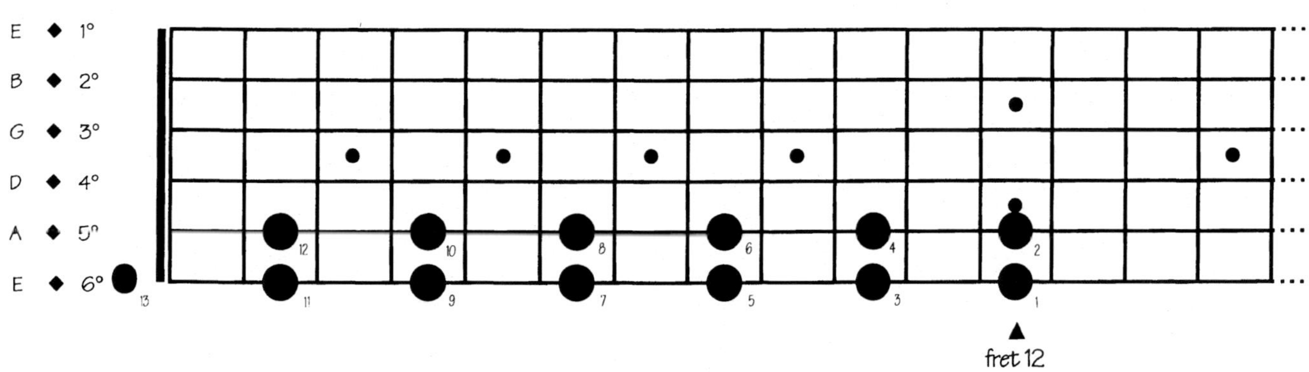

LOCATION OF THE NOTES - THE "TRITONE"

Now, we have another diagram that should not be negelcted and must be memorized: this is the one where the intervals are three notes apart, and are called a "tritone". Without doubt you have seen this while working with the diminished and whole tone scales, such as with the dim7 arpeggio – melodic "tri-tonic" scale, at its best.

Besides that, Being able to visualize the "tritone" makes it easier for you to understand a very important harmonic concept. - It is the concept of the Tritone Substitution, which we will discuss soon.

In the following diagram, all the notes are separated by an interval of a diminished fifth (or augmented fourth) with three tones, also known as a "tritone". This is absolutely true and makes sense... by considering that by dividing an octave into two equal parts will be the same as six half-tones, or three tones.

Play the notes in inceasing numerical order, then decreasing numerical order.

Location of the notes: the triton.

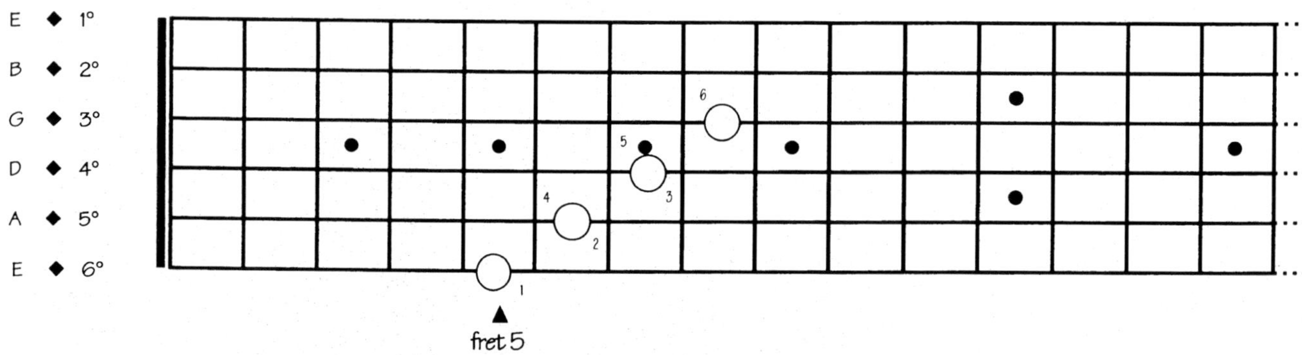

Exercise 28 - whole tone scale with A7

Here is a way to form a whole tone scale by showing the tritone interval. Play eighth note triplets (the first and last notes fall on an accented beat), following the increasing numerical order. Of course, it is important here to know how to use the pick (three notes using the upstroke ⊓ and three notes using the down stroke V).

#36 **Whole tone scale in tritones: A7 chord.**

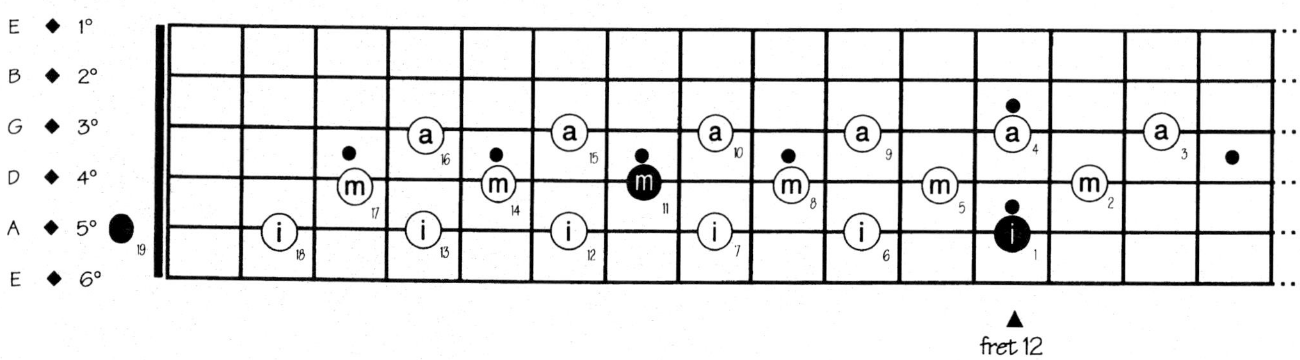

Exercise 29 - fingerboard diagram and sweep with the G7b5 chord

Since we are using the tritone, we want to show you a typical Manouche lead. This very clearly shows the diagram of the tritone on the fingerboard.

While alternating the direction of the pick, play the notes in increasing numerical order, then in decreasing numerical order.

Sweep of G7(5♭).

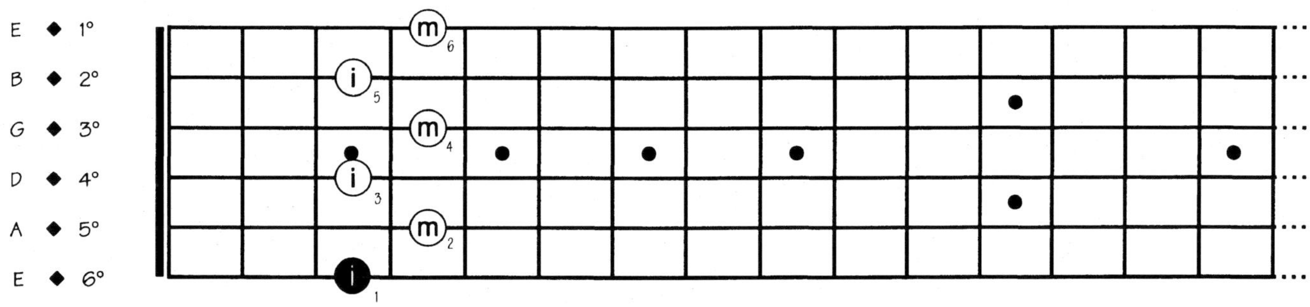

#37

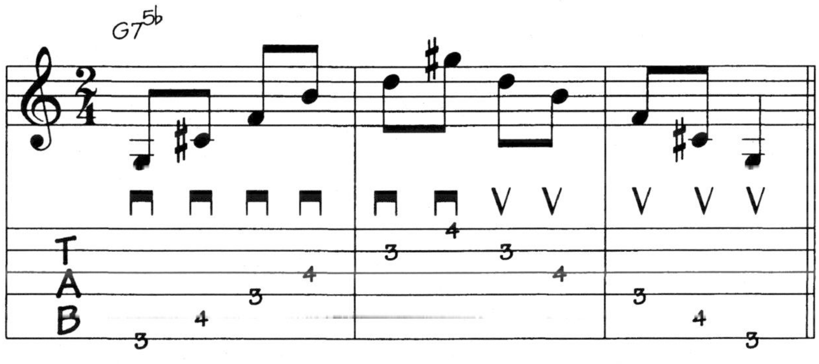

Exercise 30 - diagram and sweep with the Dm chord

We are going to finish up the present series of exercises with a new sweep that uses the diagram of the perfect minor chord. This lead has two colorations (notes ★) that you can use with this chord - these are the seventh major (7M) and the seventh minor (7m), in succession.

Although these colorations will not be joined together, notice that they are done with descending chromaticisms and with the same type of a melody line.

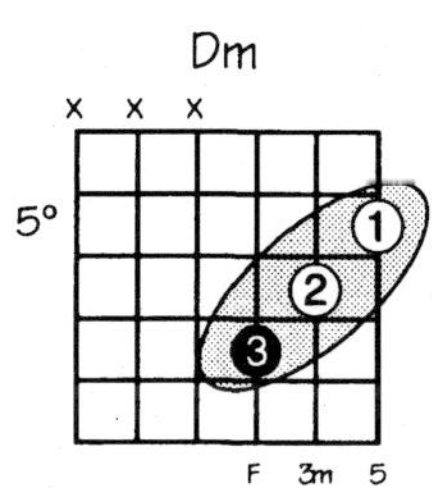

#38

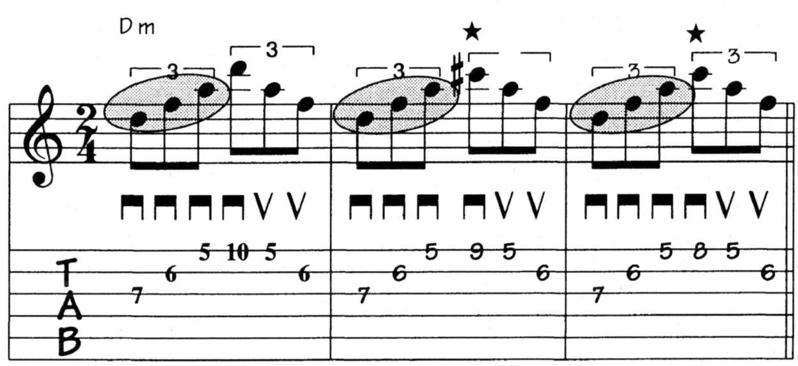

PART B1

Let's look at some harmony theory .

THE ANATOLE (TURNAROUND) PROGRESSION

This harmonic progression is the real "iron spear" of the jazz sound - and not only in jazz. In other words, if you understand the anatole you are capable of playing most parts in the standard swing and the Manouche style, and not just rhythm.

Do not only summarize it by knowing what makes up the progression with the I - VI - V - I degrees of the scale in a major key, in order to understand the anatole. Certain aspects of the anatole will, without any doubt, still be obscure at this point of your adventure, despite your "know-how" that you by now most likely have acquired. Let's clear it up!

1- The (major) "perfect" anatole is in really like this: "III - VI - II - V – I". We find this in the measure where we intervene exclusively with the descending quint circle. In the key of D major, the anatole will thus consist of the Em7 - Am7 - Dm7 - G7 - C7M.

2- It is currently correct to call it degree "I" instead the degree "III", and visa versa. We find this in the measure where these two chords have notes in common... and as a consequence are known as a diatonic "substitution" chords (diatonic substitution = replacement of chords which only works in one and the same key). For instance:

(A)

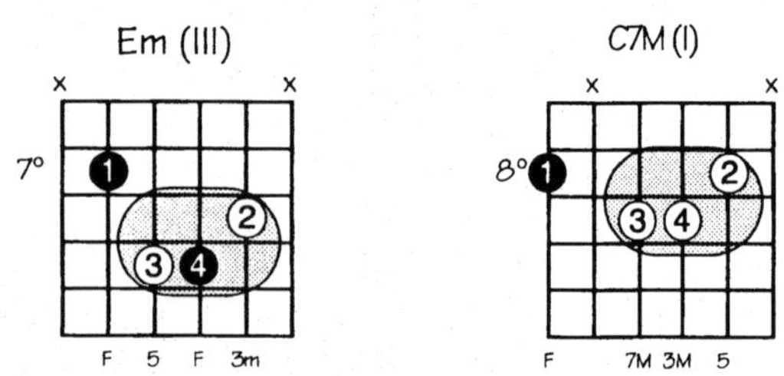

(B)

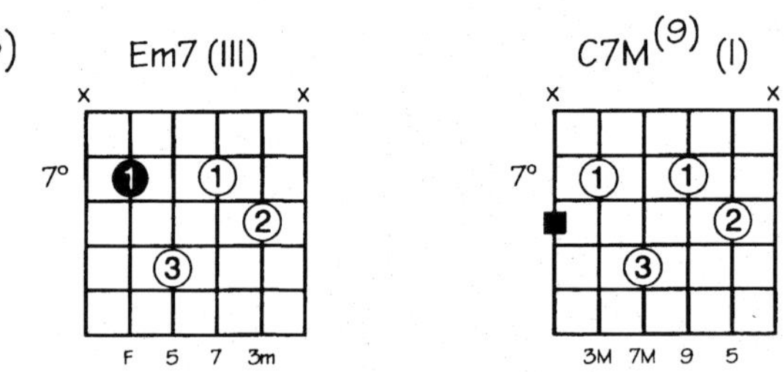

Example (B) shows a sleight of hand - substitution! - This is very characteristic in jazz. It consists of looking at a chord in relation to various root notes (that are often lacking in the chord), with the goal to establish the corresponding ones. These are the inter-chord ties that form the basis of numerous applications: decorations of a lead, enrichments of chords, reharmonizations, ideas for improvising the melody, etc.

3. The (major) "altered" anatole is "III - VI7 - II - V - I". For instance, when we look at the key of D major, the chords are Em7 - A7 - Dm7 - G7 - C7M:

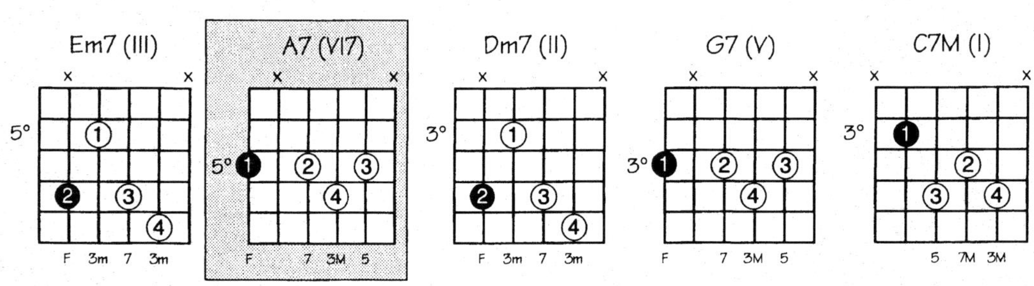

You may say that if we replace the Am7 with an A7, we are out of the D major key since A7 is not a part of this key!

Well not really, because the V(G7) and the I (C7M) are always good and well used together to make out the key. And to be truthful, the VI7 chord - which is known as the secondary dominant chord - intervenes only here to re-balance and give it power in the progression: this is to avoid the redundant three successive minor chords of the "perfect" anatole: III (Em7) - VI (Am7) - II (Dm7). Or we can say: by using the the VI7, it gives color to the anatole!

Besides, this VI7 opens up the very interesting possibility of harmonic substitutions that works with the tritone, which will give birth to the anatoles derived from the so-called "turnarounds".

But this is another story that we will be discussing later. Right now, just be happy with what you know in order to "let you turn" (play/record) the "perfect" anatole and the "altered" anatole.

THE CHRISTOPHE PROGRESSION

In the swing of jazz, you will also see another tonal harmonic progression, although this does not happen as much as with the major anatole.

We are talking about the progression known as "Christophe" and the measure where this is shown, in the harmony of "Jo's Remake". We will take the time to show you some lines of it here.

In the jargon of French speaking Jazzmen and through the analogy with the anatole, this progression is called "Christophe", that is named after the harmony of the "Christopher Columbus" song, where it is used. The "Christophe" has two main forms:

1 - The "I - I7 - IV – IVm" progression. For instance, if we use the key of G major:

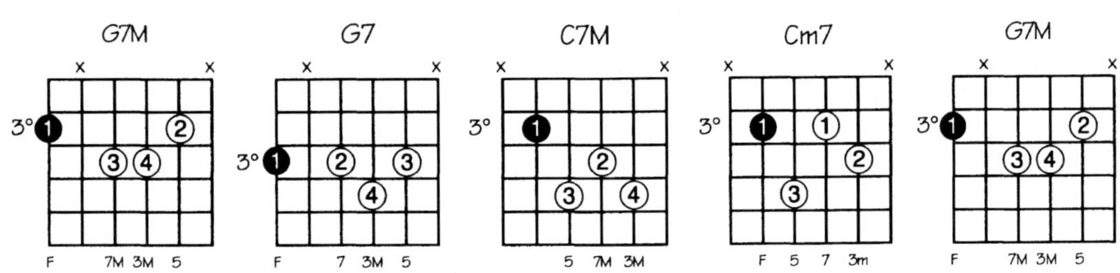

2 - The "I - I7 - IV - IV#dim7" progression. For instance, if we use the key of G (as in "Jo's Remake"):

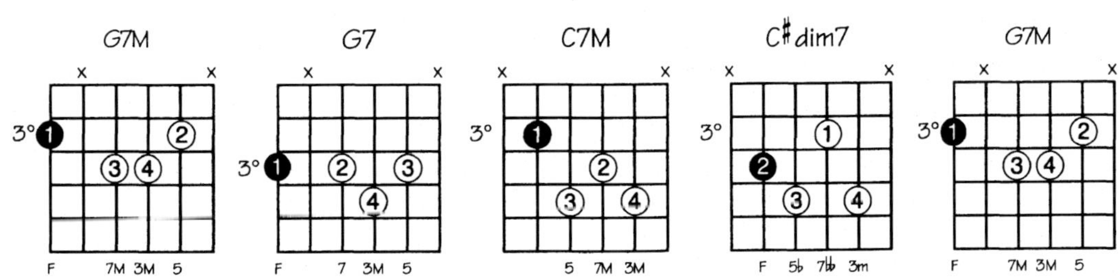

With these two forms, look at how "Christophe" makes use of the "I7", the secondary dominant chord, that is used to bring in the IV, by using the principle, as mentioned on page 4, chapter 6.

PART B2

Now let's look at the leads and diagrams for the rest of "Jo's Remake".

Jo's Remake (measure 17) explanations of melody

Measure 17 (as well as measures 64 – 65, see chapter 10) illustrates a discourse by Manouche, that is very often used: the use of natural harmonics. These sound perfectly well here because the general key of "Joe's Remake" is done in the key of G major. This is simply because the natural harmonics on the guitar produces a D6 chord (if you use standard chords), at the seventh fret (= the V degree of G major), and a G6 chord at the 5th fret (= the I degree of G major).

Does this mean that the general key of this song could have been chosen on purpose for the natural harmonics with the solo in mind? You be the judge.

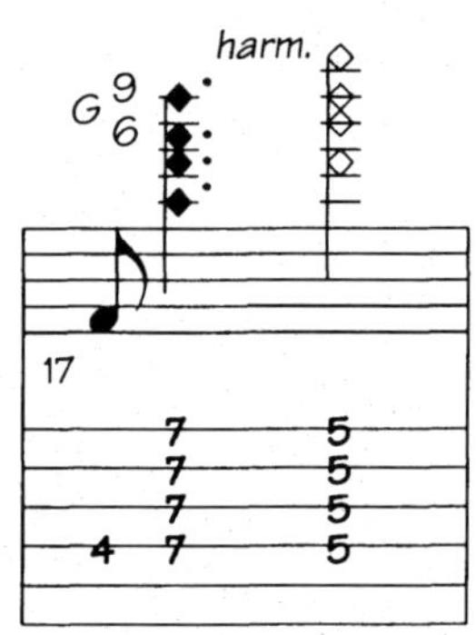

Jo's Remake (measure 23) melody and diagram #4

Here is a very important diagram that you should use often. It has a seventh dominant (V7 type) chord, to be played with the diagram of the minor chord (that is colored with a major second), which is located one half tone higher.

In measure 23 we use the B7 chord, which you can play the Cmin9 over. This is done to enhance the colored notes, which is very interesting when we use the B7: the augmented ninth (#9), the minor ninth (b9) and the augmented fifth (#5).

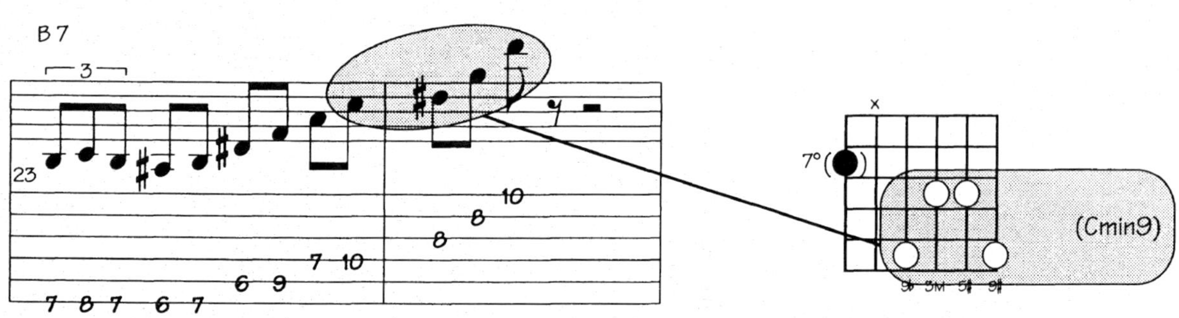

This B7 gives us the idea to think of an F7 (tritone substitution), as the chord that you can use before its II degree... and that is nothing other than the C Minor.

Jo's Remake (measures 25 and 28) explanations of the melody

The "Christophe" progression survives here, and you can see how it is treated melodically: by musically transposed motives that develops with the harmonies.

In addition to this, the two groups of ascending chromatic notes (tensions) puts together a "mirror" effect that makes it temporarely complicated. However, its aesthetic value must not be ignored.

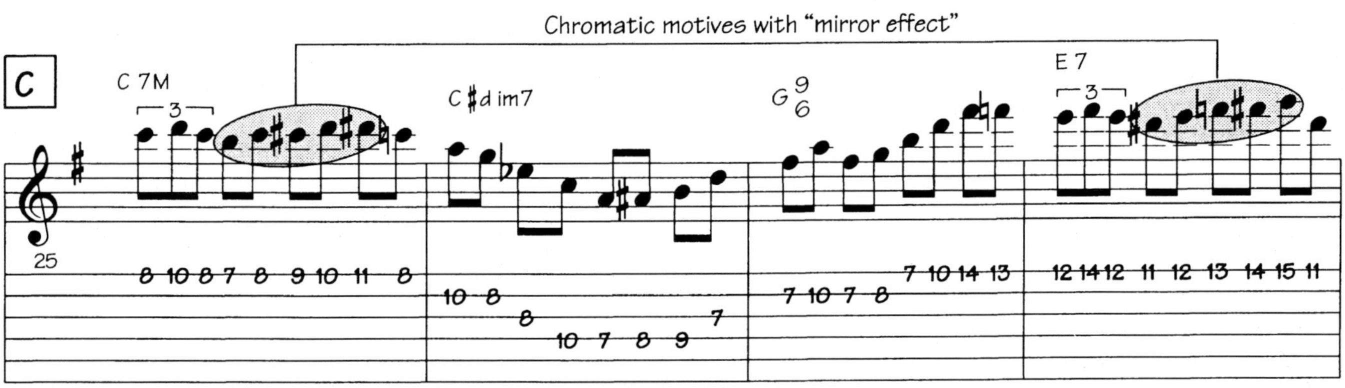

Jo's Remake (measures 29 - 32) lead and diagram #5

The first chorus is completed with a long lead that is based on the diagram and designated (★) notes of the C6 chord. This is in spite of the presence of D7 (take a look at exercise 19 in chapter 6), the tonic (G6) chord, that is strictly maintained, and done here for two reasons:

-The end of the diagram has the conclusion, where it is the perfect way to push the fundamental chord,

-The repetition of the lead here allows a certain harmonic "fantasy" (tension), much more than what we have explained... by adding a second chorus!

Pay attention when listening to the CD: at this point your listening is overpowered by the lead, which we hardly realize while listening and going through the first chorus to the second chorus!

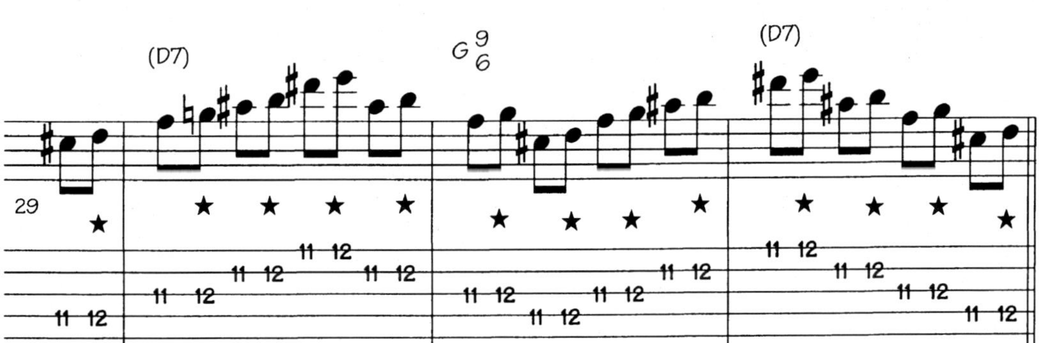

PART C

The continuation and finish of the first chorus of "Jo's Remake".

#35

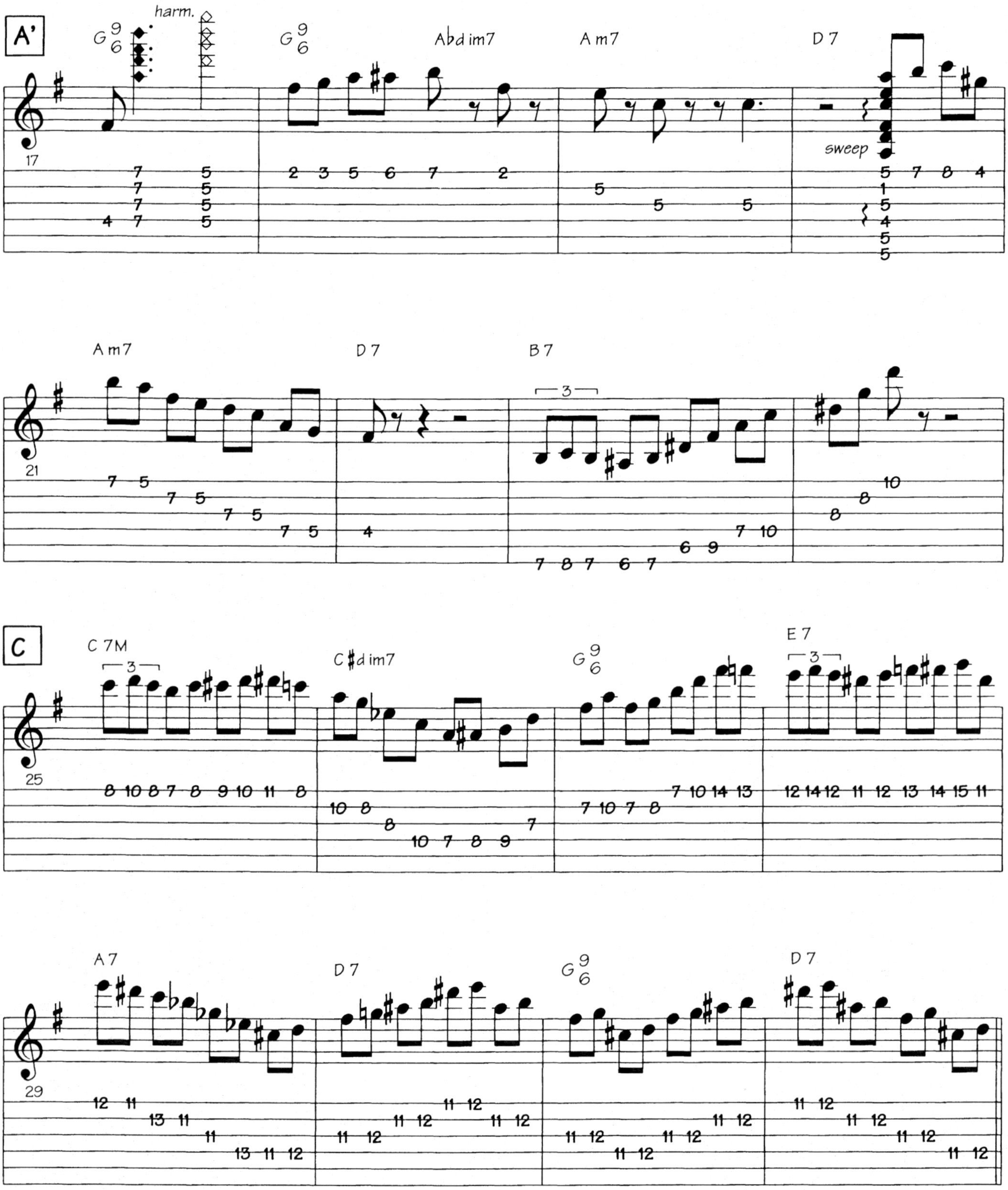

PART A

These exercises use the "designated notes" principle (compare with exercise 19, chapter 6), so that you will know how to change some selected notes of a given melody, while using various methods. This will enable you to form sentences with the vocabulary so that you can improvise with it.

Exercise 31 and 32 - designated notes of the G major chord

Here is a first cell, with some restricted notes, that uses the major scale and major chord, where the designated notes are the fifth and the root note. Of course, the inversion of this diagram with this cell on the opposite strings gives us another possibility, if we use it like that. (Exercise 32).

Play the notes in increasing numerical order.

Designated notes of G major (Exercise 31).

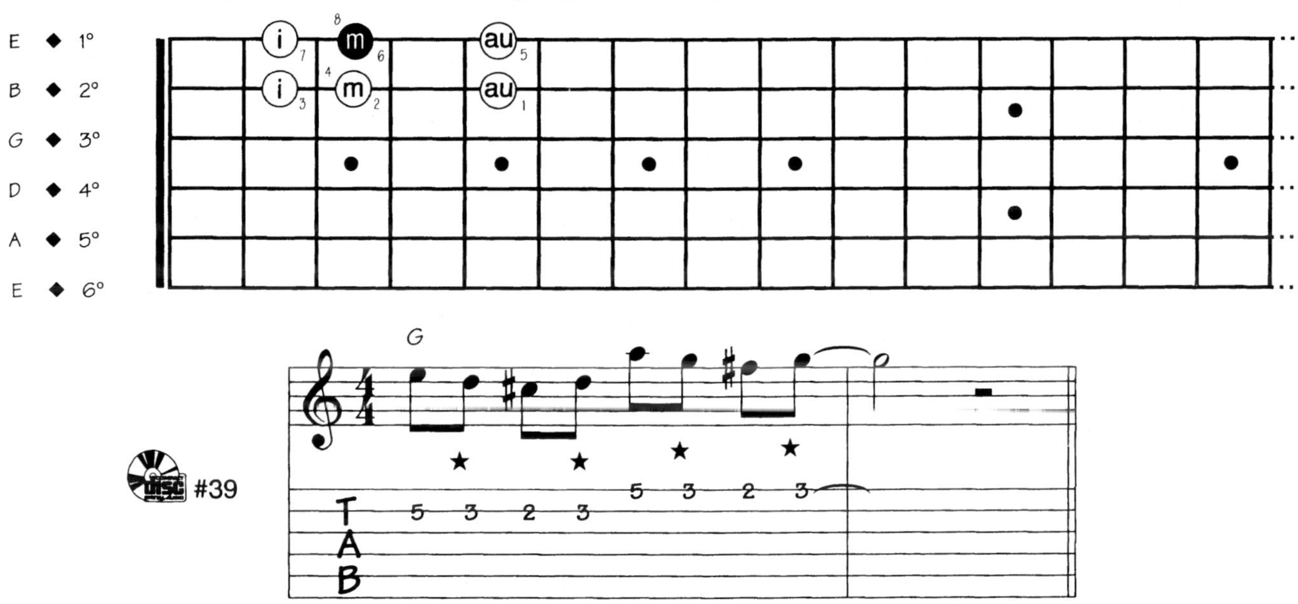

Designated notes of G major (Exercise 32).

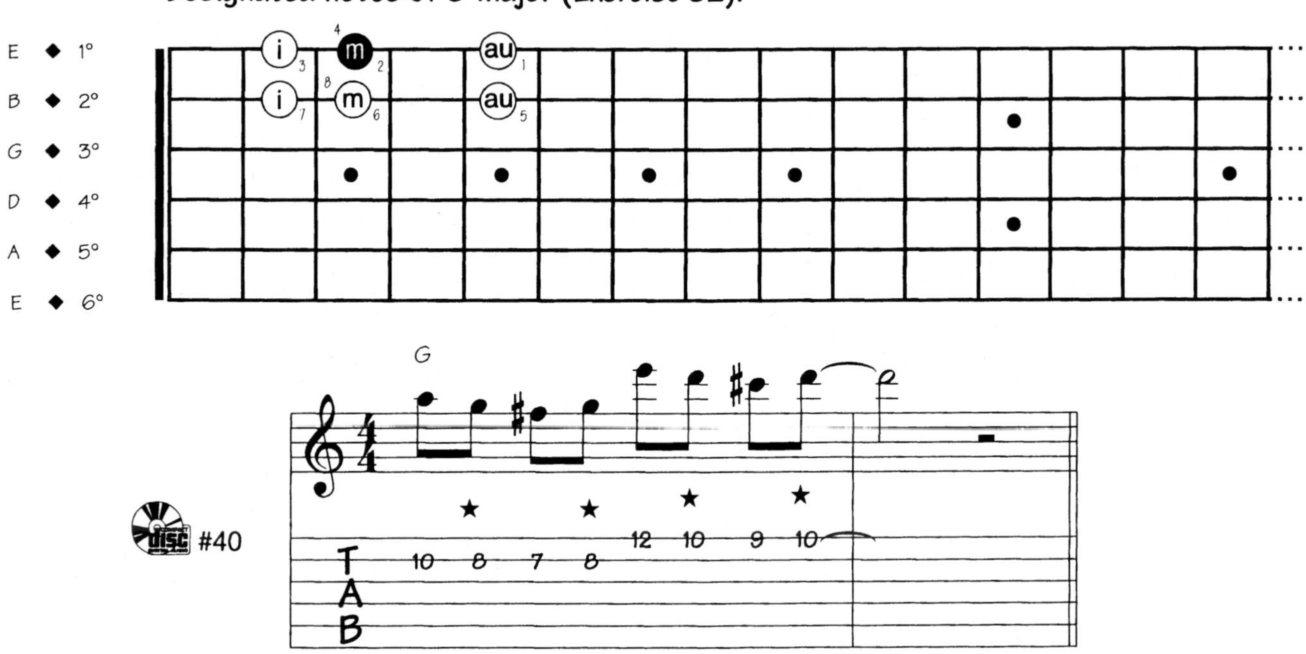

Chapter 10 / page 2

Exercise 33 and 34 - designated notes of the A minor chord

With the chords of the key of A minor, the principle of the designated notes is similar to those used with the major chords (which uses the major fundamental chords - the type I degree - or the dominant - the V7 type). Nevertheless, some light planning is needed to give the lead a realistic minor character.

Thus, in the case of a melodic cell, where the designated notes are the root note and the fifth of the minor chord, you will notice that this last note (the E note of this next exercise) is always preceded by chromatic steps. On the other hand, for a major or minor chord, the approach of the root note remains the same, it is always chromatic (the G# note, here afterwards).

Play the following notes in increasing numerical order.

Designated A minor notes (Exercise 33).

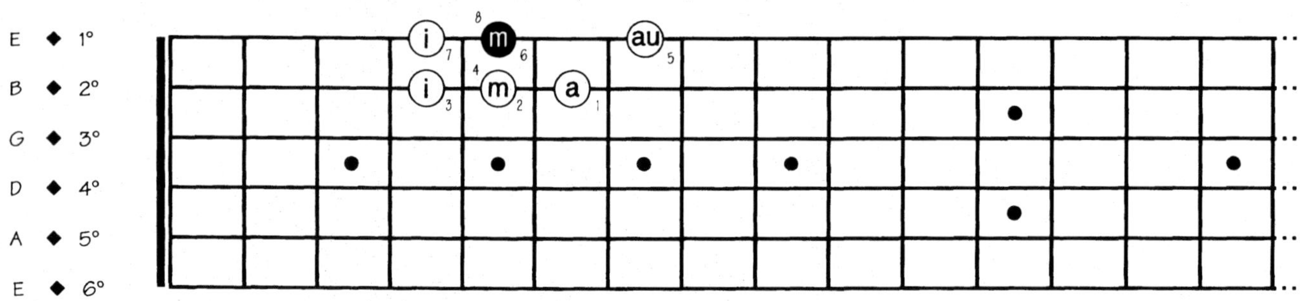

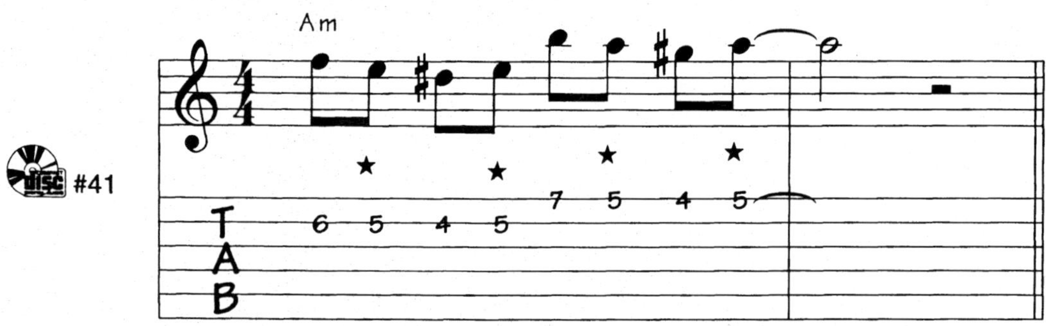

Designated notes of A minor (Exercise 34).

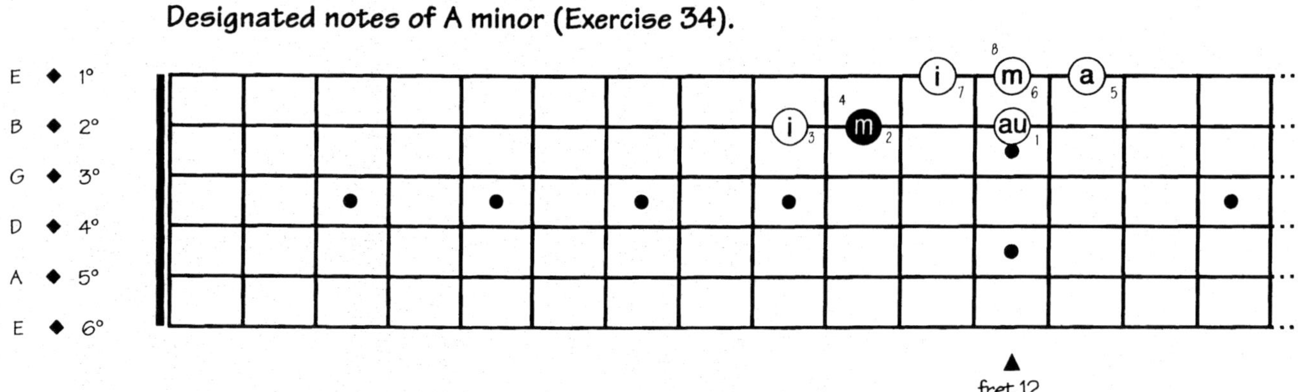

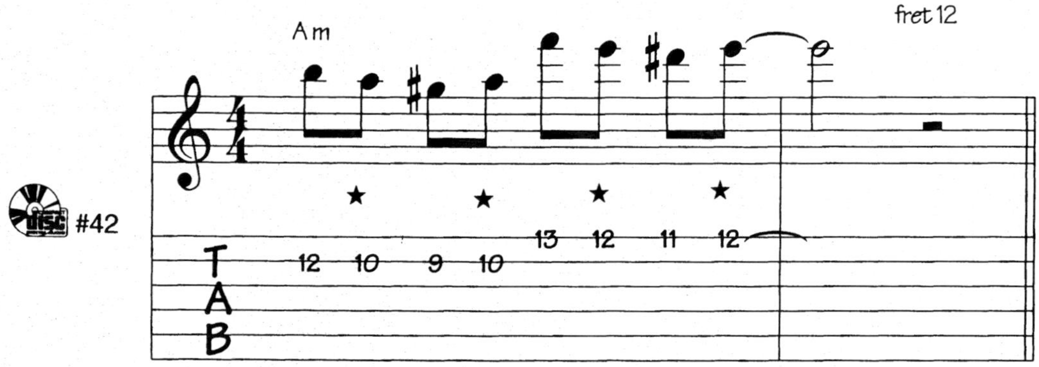

We will finish the exercises in this chapter with the study of some "VOICINGS".

The same goes for the leads. The study of voicings is an indispensable work in the entire matrix of the jazz guitar language. By knowing this it will let you, at times, produce more subtle and convincing rhythms. Besides, in the area of improvising the melody, you will develop your capacities in a very significant way, which enables you "to hear" the right choices of notes, that you need for a harmonic basis.

Technically speaking, a "voicing" is a constructed chord functioning with a group of other chords, that may be of the same type.

Of course, the group of chords in question rely mostly on standard harmonic progressions. The chord progressions that we often see. For example, with the anatole. We suggest that you force yourself to develop a real harmonic vocabulary by using the voicings, which we will study at the end of this chapter.

Now we are going to open fire with the major "II - V - I " progression.

The same goes for the progressions that follow. Use a metronome when you work on your progressions, using a 4/4 beat, marking each beat "drive" and by "putting these together": practice it over and over until each of the chords sound right.

Exercise 35 - voicings with II-V-I in G major (1).

The basic chords here are using the major II - V - I cadence (descending fifths: Am – D7 – G) which are boosted with a simple coloration.

But above all, notice the chromatic descending progress of the highest note (sharp) of every chord: it is with this process that it relies on the present voicings (we "make the chords sing!").

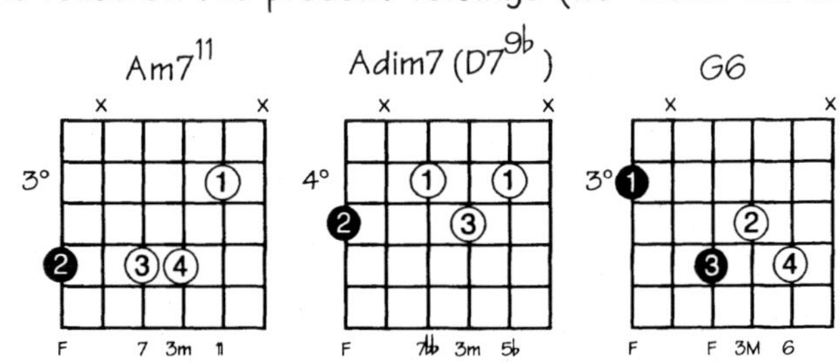

Exercise 36 - voicings with II-V-I in G major (2).

Here is another chromatic passage with the II - V - I in G, but ascending this time with the use of the dim7 chord, meaning the V7(D7) chord - a substitution that you are already familiar with, isn't it?

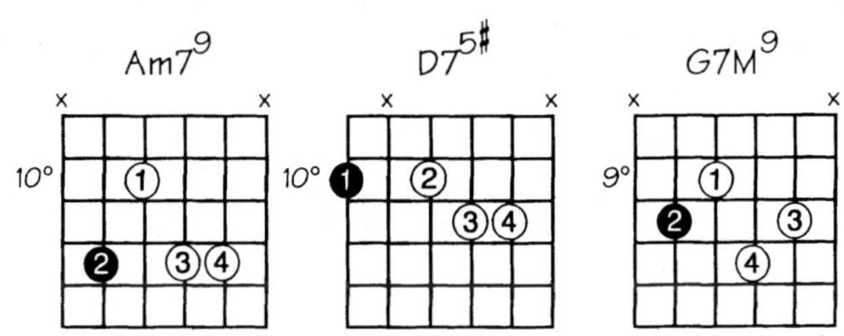

PART B1

We are now going to analyze the harmonic structure of "Jo's Remake" after we have studied the diagrams and the chords (chapter 8):

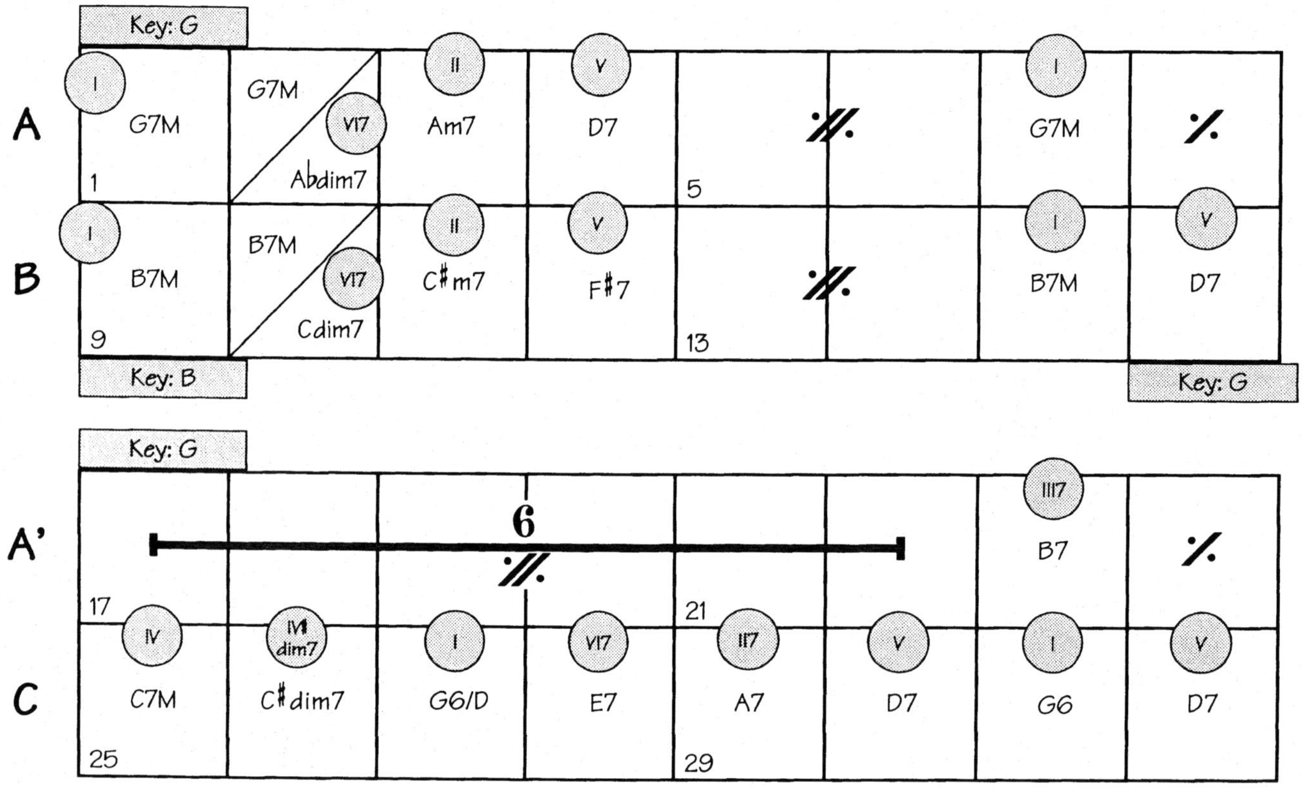

MEASURES 1-8: the key of G major, where the Abdim7 is a camouflaged E7, that is used to bring the Am7, with the V7 (E7) → Im principle, a provisional Am.

MEASURES 9 - 15: the same procedure will be done as was shown in section A. But it will be done with the B major key, at measure 16, where a D7 is a V in the key of G, and where it is used to re-introduce the A' section.

MEASURES 23 - 24: we use the key of G, a B7. This is a III7, a "secondary dominant" chord, which is used to introduce the C7M with the understanding that the C7M could be an Em7 (a diatonic substitution: the C7M and Em7 share common notes). Indeed, it is potentially the V chord which brings Em, always based on the principle that V (B7) → = temporarily the Im (Em). But, what a surprise, the resolution doesn't work with Em, but it will with this C7M substitution.

MEASURES 24 - 26: here we have the "Christophe" progression showing up in the key of G, with its IV#dim7 it is not necessary to look for a relation with a certain V7 (D7), which goes back through the fundamental chord, the G6. Surely, the presence of this IV#7 is not all that bad, but for right now, the explanation on how to make the progression is too long to explain, but we will discuss this later.

MEASURES 27 - 29: a cascade of dominant chords, which introduces one of the others (V of V of V). This results in the ultimate perfect V in the key G (D7). Also, be aware that the G6/D - E7 - A7 - D7 - G6 progression forms an anatole! We can easily qualify this here as "altered" in the measure where its III degrees and VI are "dominant" (it has much more color).

We will discuss voicings after we finish two more pages.

And since we are diving back into the diagram for "Jo's Remake" this gives us the opportunity to study voicings, by using the harmony of the theme. It is a fact that jazz - not only with Manouche jazz - is improvised music, including its rhythms.

In other words, it is like when you are asked to play an Am chord from the diagram. This doesn't mean that you have to hold yourself strictly to this chord. You can also play it by replacing a whole bunch of chords with the same types that belong to the same family (minor), which doesn't betray the global harmonic sense of the diagram.

"JO'S REMAKE" DIAGRAM - VOICINGS

A	G7M	G7M / Abdim7	Am7	D7	%%		G7M	%

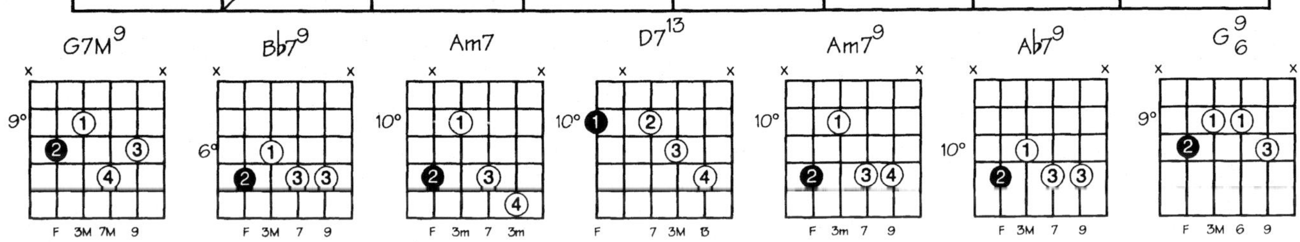

B	B7M	B7M / Cdim7	C#m7	F#7	%%		B7M	D7

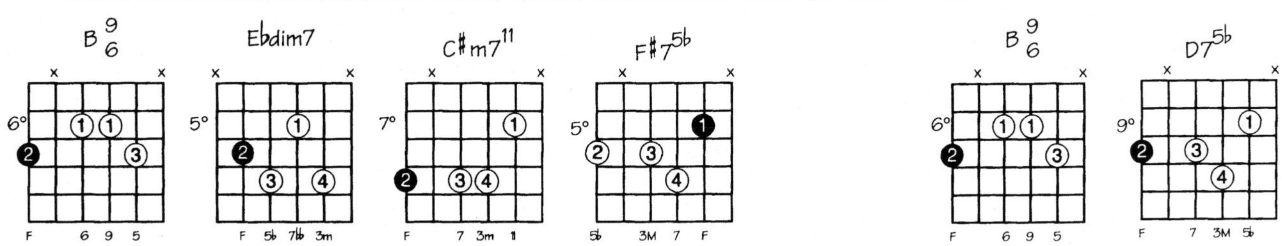

C	C7M	C#dim7	G6/D	E7	A7	D7	G6	D7

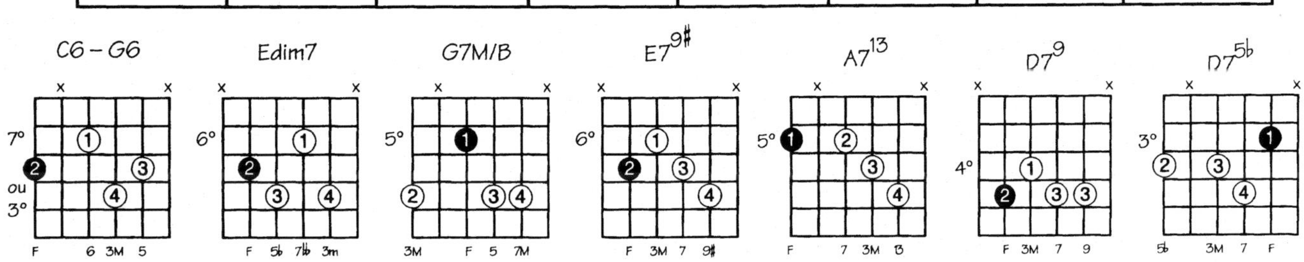

PART B2

We are now going to study the leads and diagrams of the second chorus of "Jo's Remake".

(measures 40 - 42) explaining the melody

Measures 40 and 42 demonstrate that it is possible to do a lot with very little, using a single note with some accents. Each uses the rhythmic approach of an improvised melody. The rhythmic element should never be neglected. Look where we place the accents: one note for every three, which gives it the effect of a triplet, although there aren't any in the phrase! Notice that this effect is reinforced by the attack of the pick: in groups of three (⊓ V ⊓).

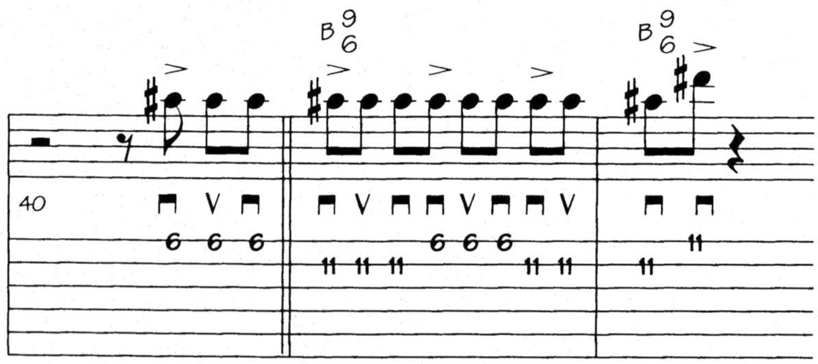

Jo's Remake (measures 45 - 47) explanation of the melody

These three measures show the dim7 arpeggio -- A#dim7 = F#7b9 -- combined with a series of ascending chromaticisms that aims for the resolution of the root note of the B7M chord (★ note).

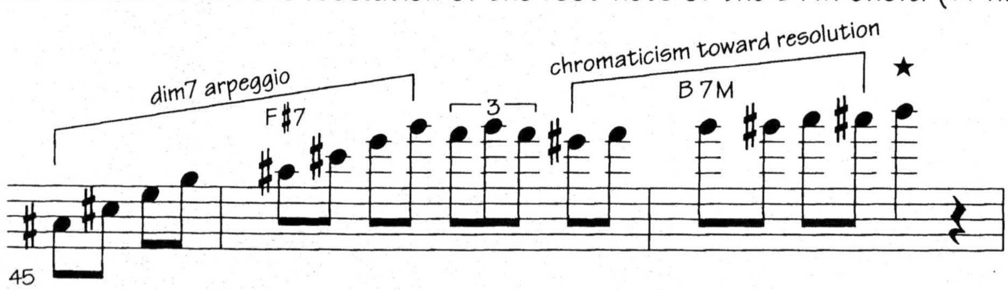

Jo's Remake (measures 49 - 50) lead and chord diagram #16

Designated notes (★) with the position of the G chord:

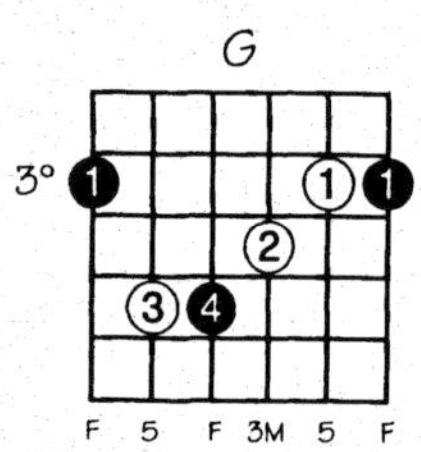

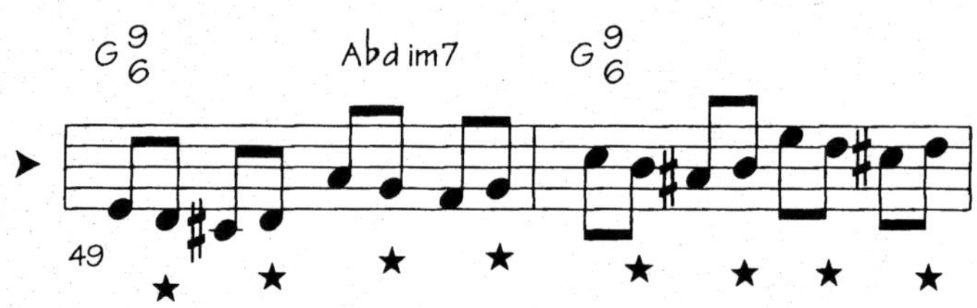

Jo's Remake (measures 63 - 64) lead and diagram #7

And the conclusion offers a chorus that uses the pentatonic scale, complete with natural harmonics on the same open strings. Look at the attack of the pick with the fretted notes, these are all down strokes.

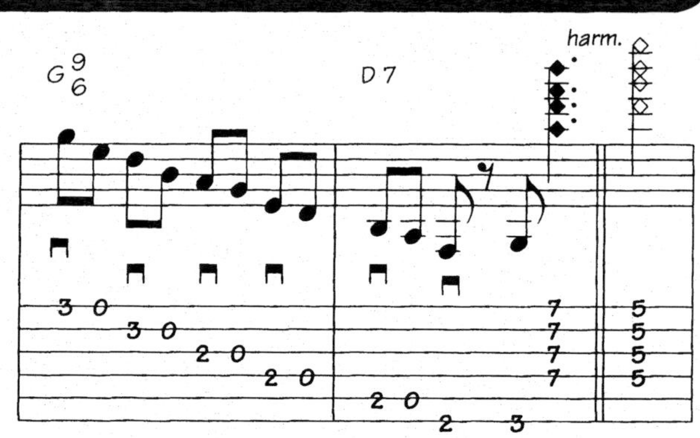

PART C

Here is the chorus of "Jo's Remake".

#35

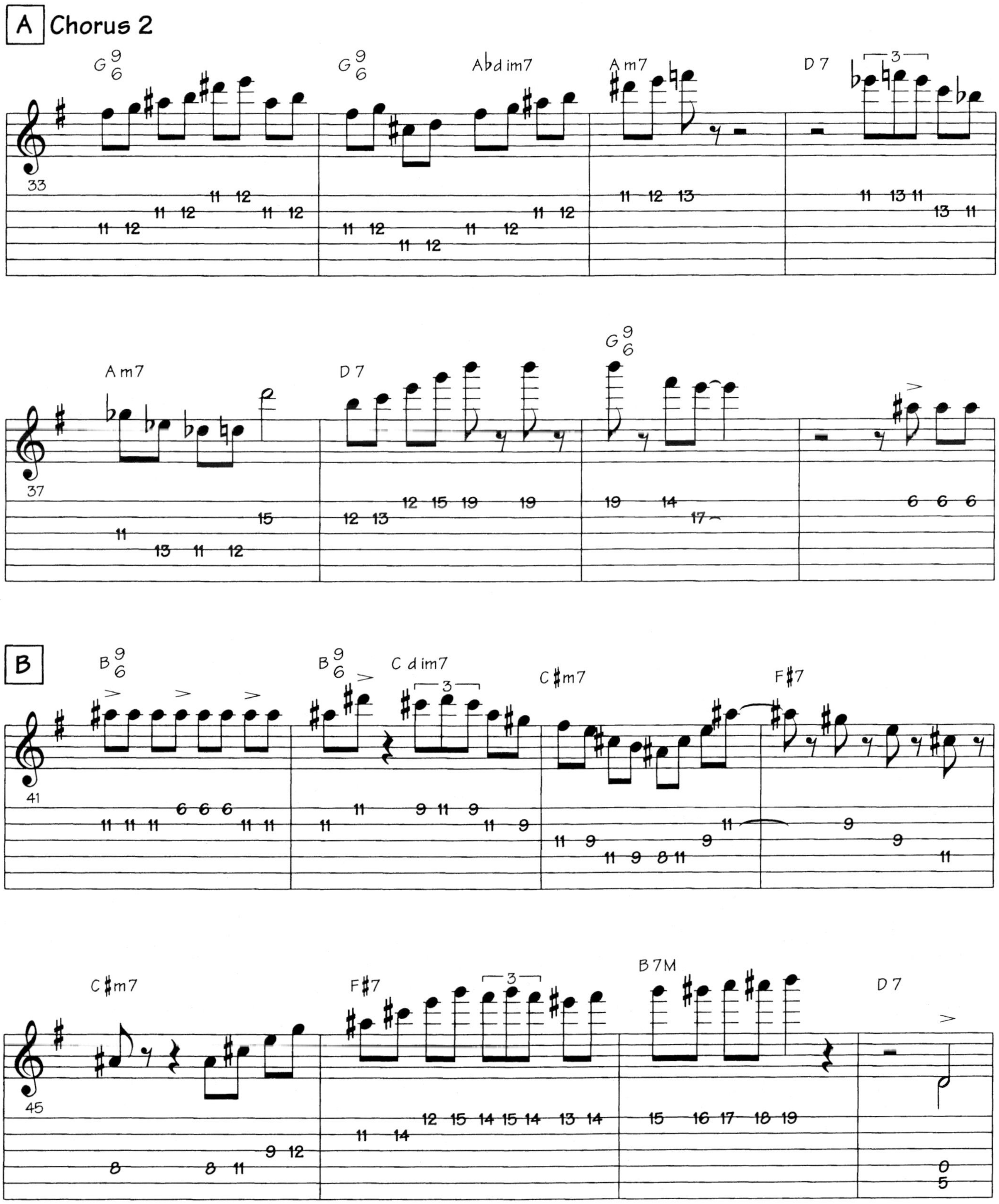

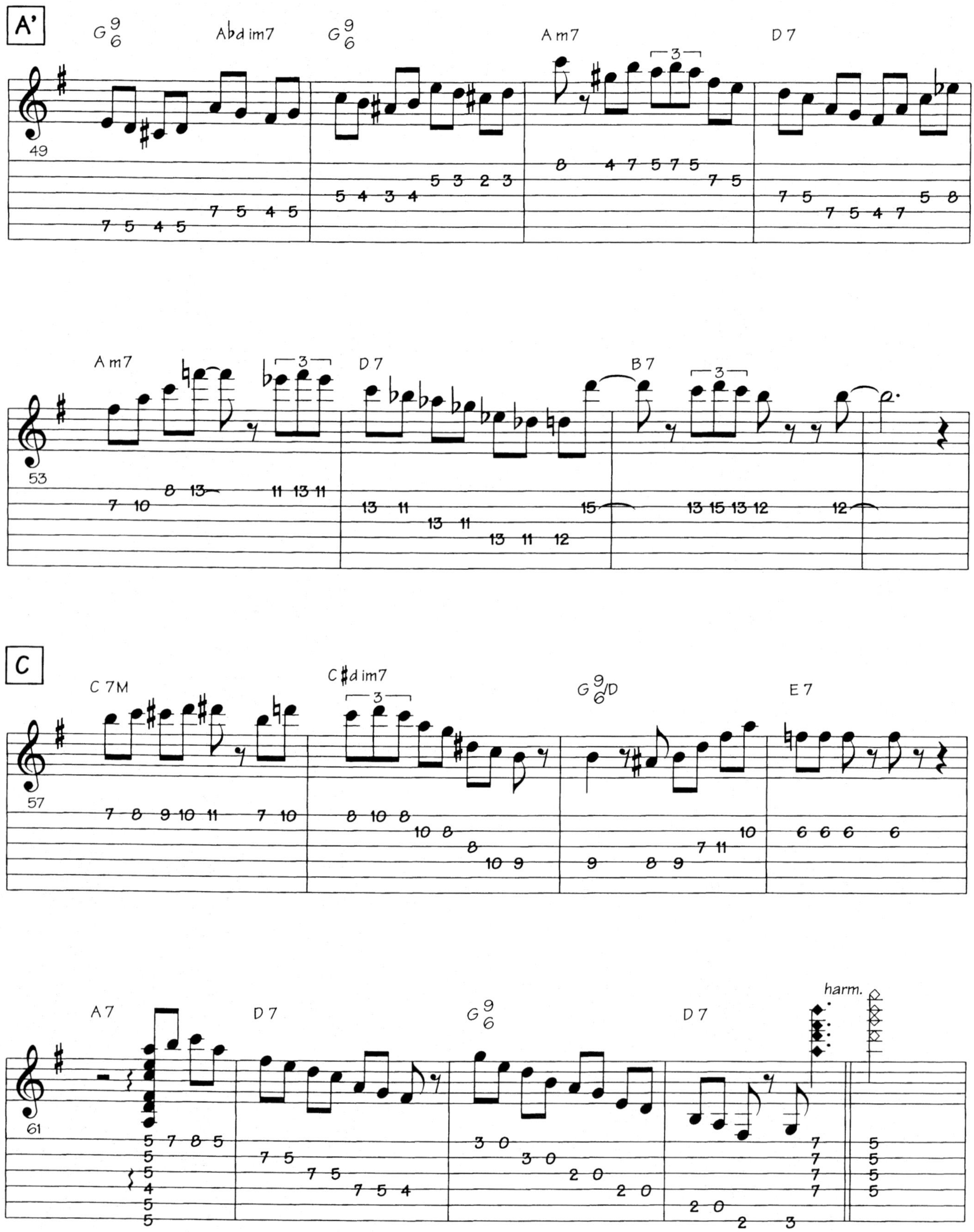
A'
G 9/6
Abdim7
G 9/6
Am7
D7
49
Am7
D7
B7
53
C
C 7M
C#dim7
G 9/6/D
E7
57
A7
D7
G 9/6
D7
harm.
61

PART A

Exercise 37 and 38 - designated notes with the G major chord

These first two cells rely on the major scale shown after the root note and goes as far as the fifth. As always, the notes conform to a procedure of permutations turning around the fifth and the root note of the chord (designated notes ★).

Notice how here the main index finger of the left hand (i) is used all throughout the lead of the whole diagram. This is also done with the descending phrase as well as with the ascending one.

Exercice 37 — #43

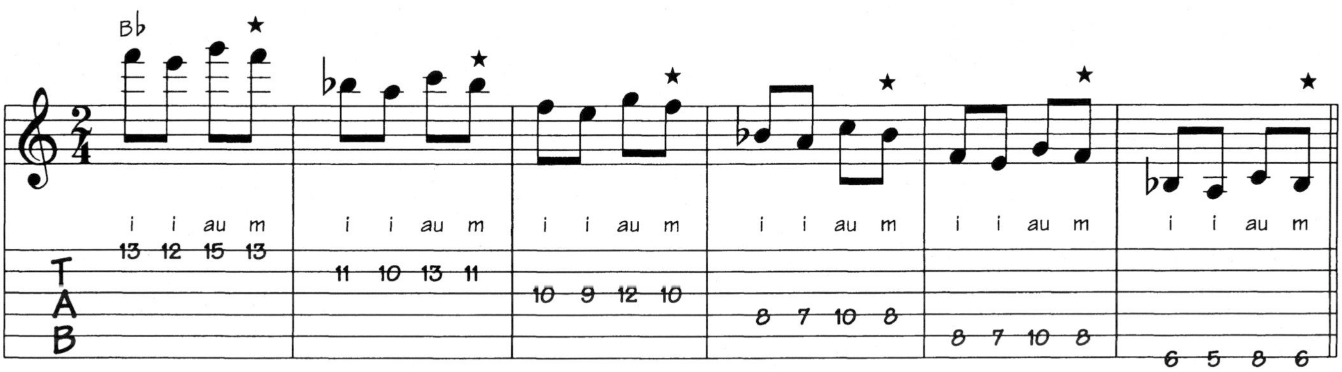

Exercice 38 — #44

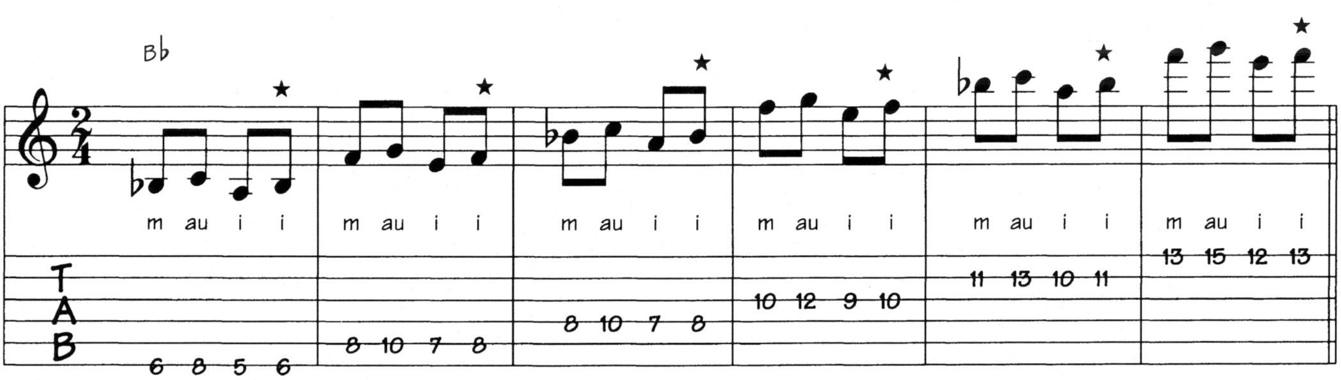

Designated notes with Bb major (Exercises 37 and 38 - diagram).

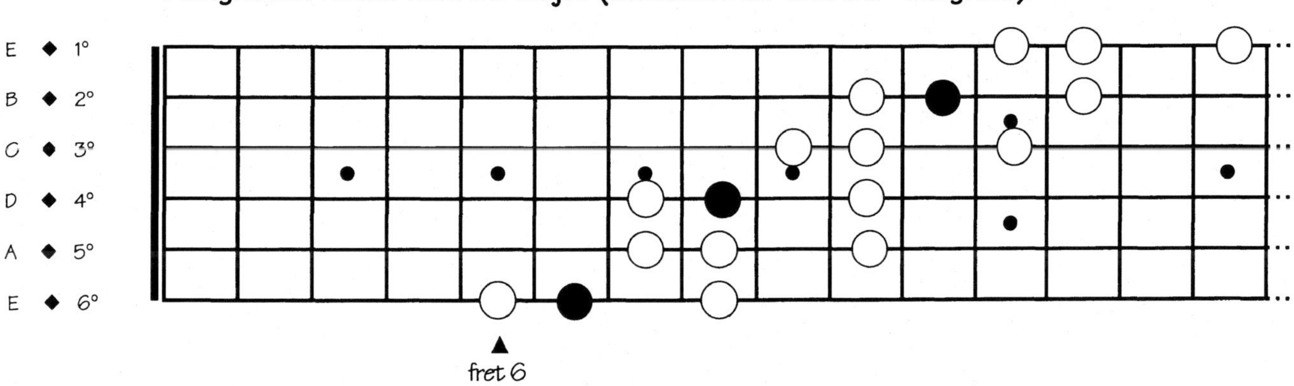

Exercise 39 and 40 - designated noes with the C minor chord

This, of course, will be based on the V degree of the central harmony in such a way as to form a mini V → IM - cadence with the minor harmonies, which determines the value of the phrase (tension → resolution).

The central harmony is Cm, and the arpeggio is the G (or substitutions), just as we have shown it below.

Designated notes / arpeggio with Cm (Exercise 39).

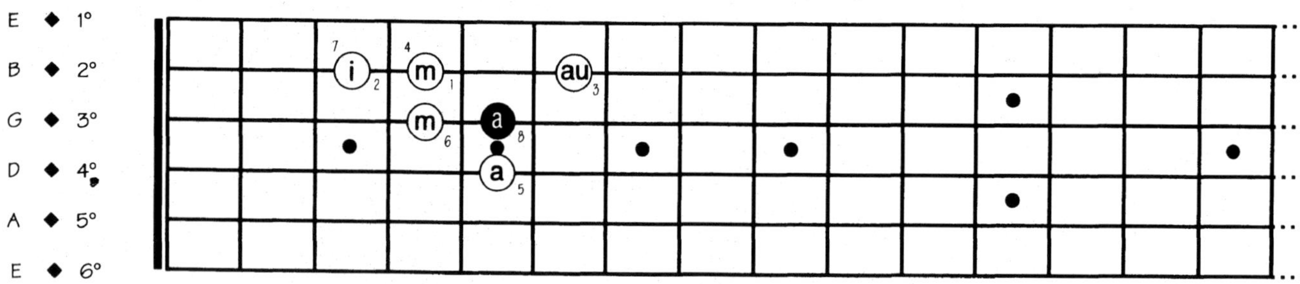

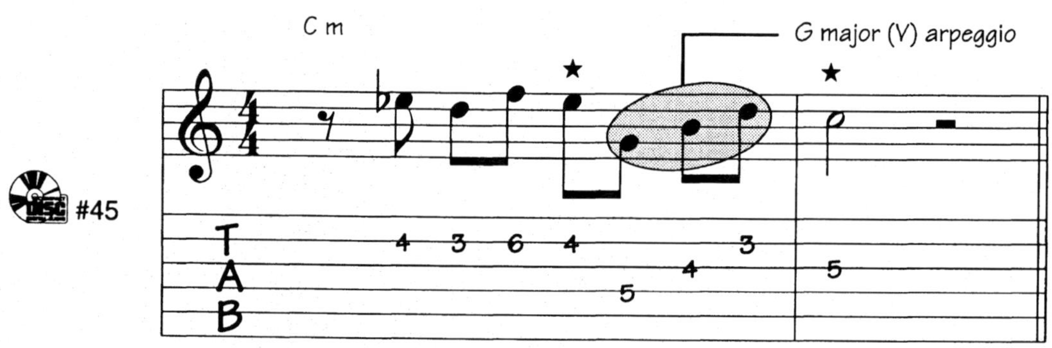

Designated notes / arpeggio with Cm (Exercise 40).

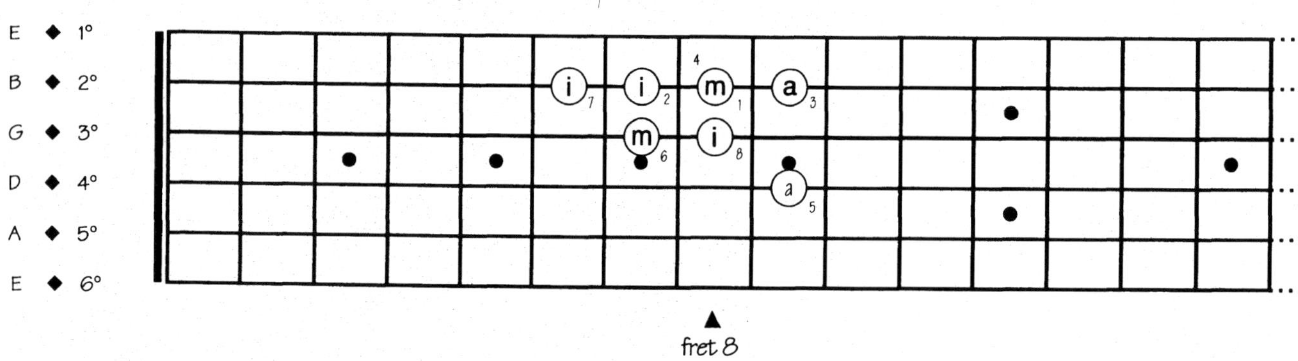

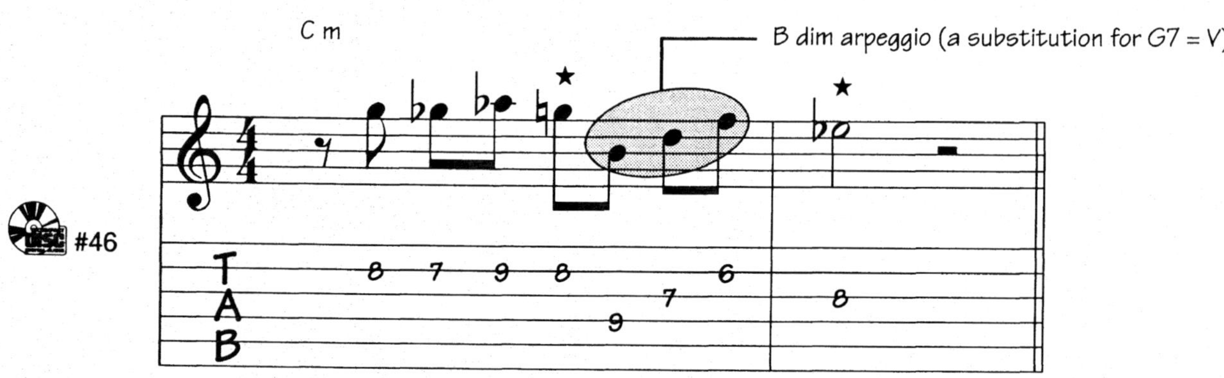

Exercise 41 and 42 - major "broken" scales

It is possible to work out long leads with the principle of the permutations of the notes. Moreover, these leads will be much longer when they rely on a large group of notes, such as relying on a scale.
The two following exercises illustrate this type of lead that you can use with the notes of a major scale.

Fingerboard diagram of a major scale - C major - reaching over (Exercise 41).

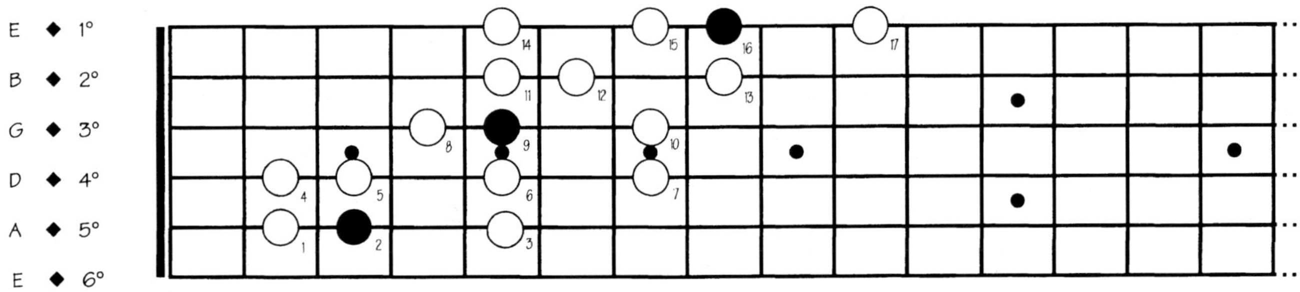

#47

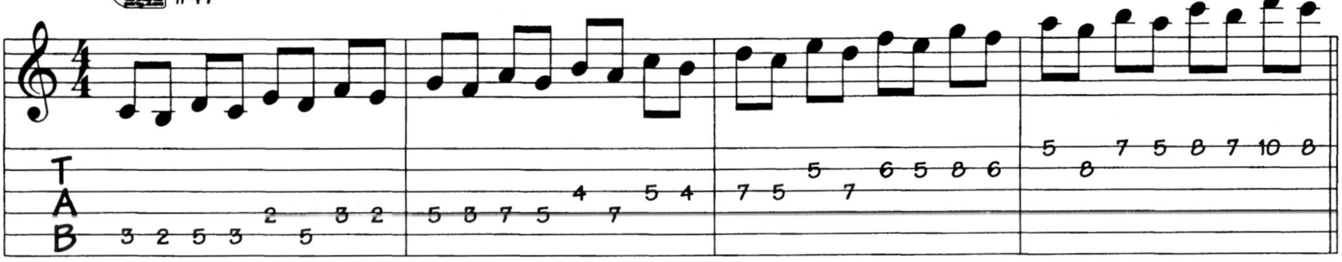

Diagram of a major scale - G major - in position (Exercise 42).

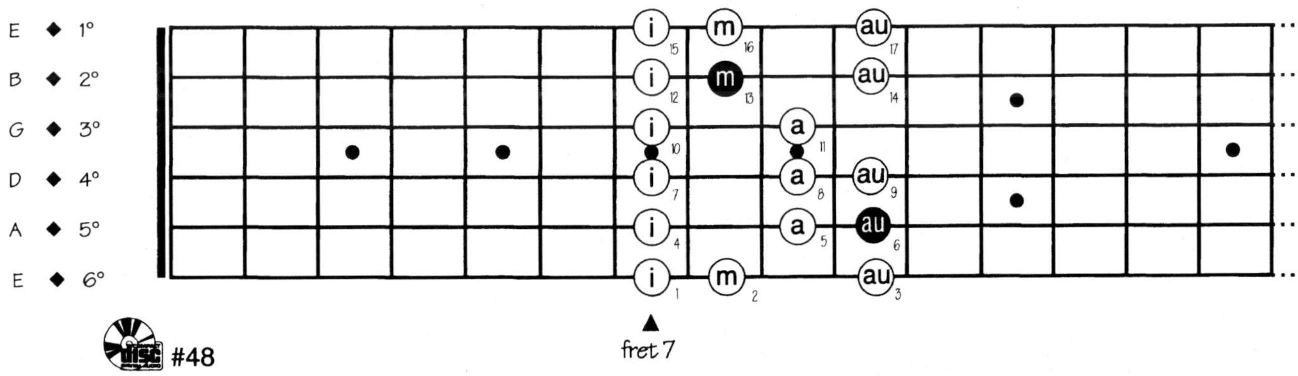

#48

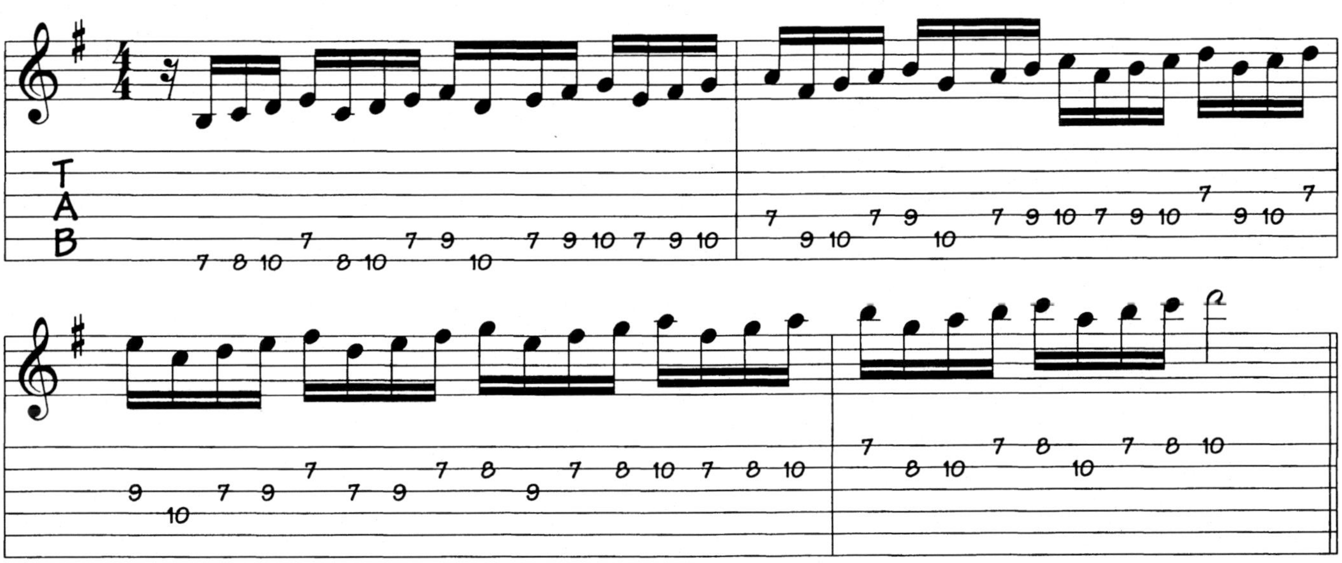

PART B1

In this last part, the theme of "Jo's Remake" offers an arrangement, which transposes the melody to a different key than the ones used at the beginning of the piece.

Here is the diagram of this final part.

It is basically the initial diagram, where the relationship between the chords stays the same (compare with chapter 8, page 4). Only the centers of the root notes are transposed - from G major to Bb major. The analysis of the harmonic structure is identical with those that we have looked at in chapter 10.

Jo's Remake

(final show)

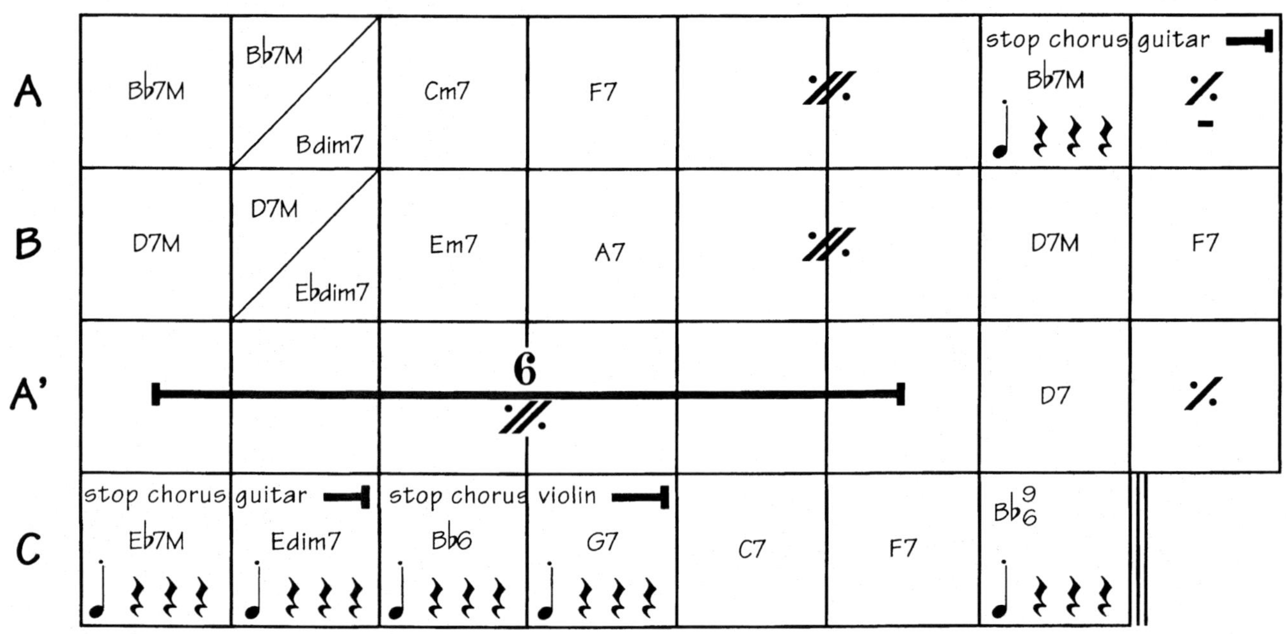

In this final diagram notice who makes the "stop chorus", according to the dedicated jargon.

As we have told you during chapter 1, the stop-chorus plays the role of a melodic springboard for a soloist and must be part of various and numerous processes, aiming at highlighting the total melody.

In this present notation, the first beats of the measures that concern us are marked with (♩), leaving the rest of the space open, where the soloist plays a mini chorus.

This procedure can be repeated, as it is shown here, or by being recycled in a much larger time frame. More often than not a stop is used. Here the chorus intervenes with the last two measures of the harmonic structure, at the time of its initial exposure of the theme, and, where its role is always the same: advance the discourse of the melody, whether it is improvised or not.

We complete this final diagram with some possibilities of chord positions:

Sections A and A'

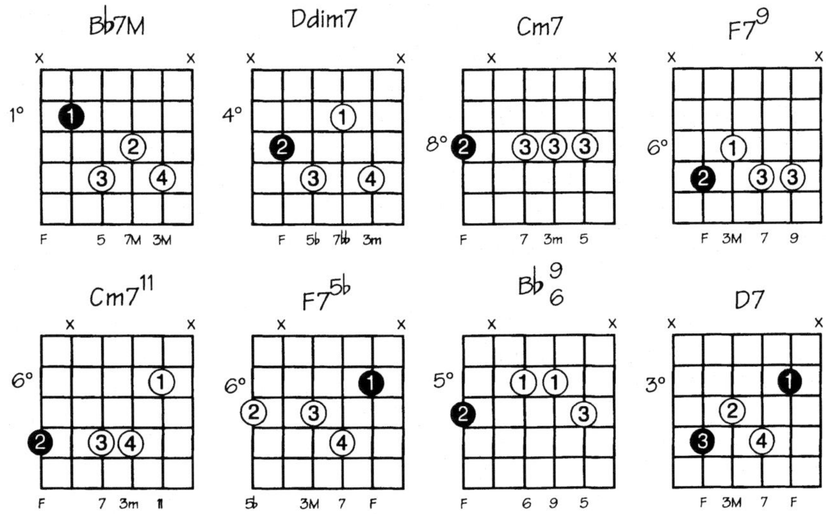

Section B

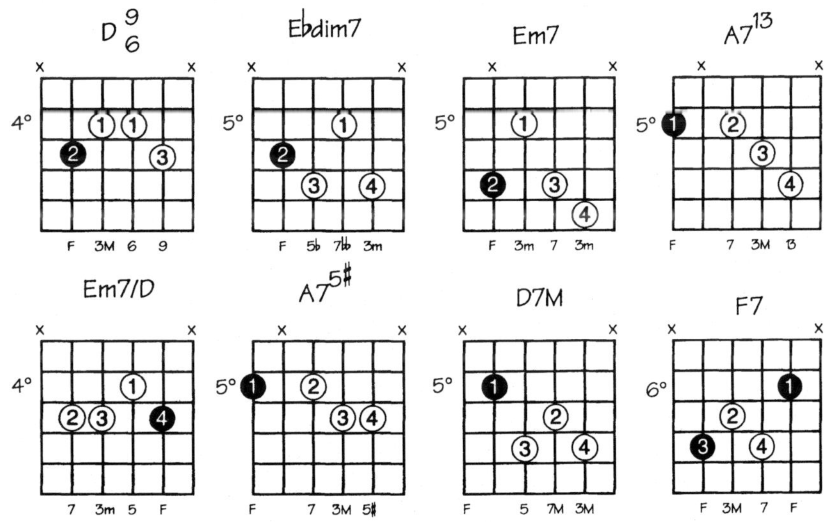

Section C

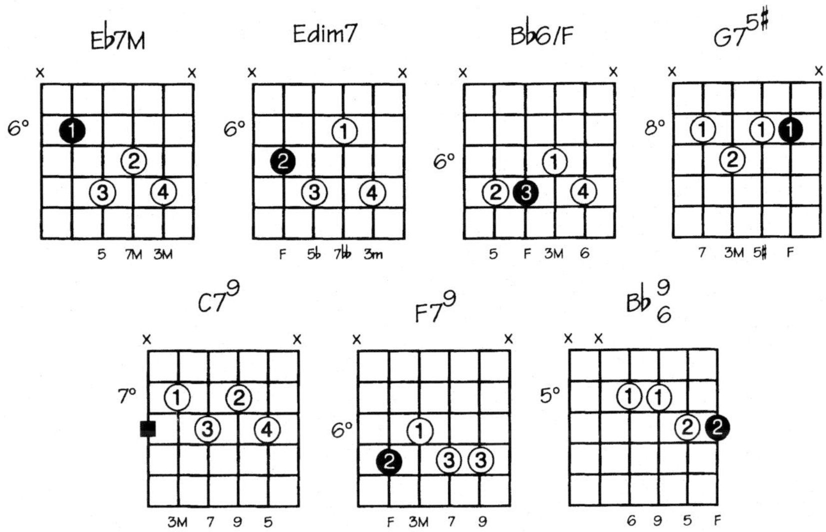

PART B2

We will now look at the diagrams and lead of the final theme of "Jo's Remake".

Jo's Remake (measures 6 - 9) lead and diagram #1

Measures 6 and 9 in particular represent the speed and virtuosity of the Manouche playing style.

This is well evidenced by the use of the chromatic scale with open strings (compare with exercise 14, chapter 4), which is significant, but this diagram continues with a single finger overreaching/sliding on a single string!

The purpose of this overreaching is to reach the root note of the D6/9 chord, stacked up for the first time. This must be done with great precision. When this is played incorrectly, it will lose much of its virtuosity effect.

In addition, the rhythmic flow is unusual enough: it uses a quintole of eighths, that means, five notes lasting as long as two quarter notes. Although it is simply a question of metrics: aim at the D note of the first beat of the resolvent measure and fill in the space of this previous note!

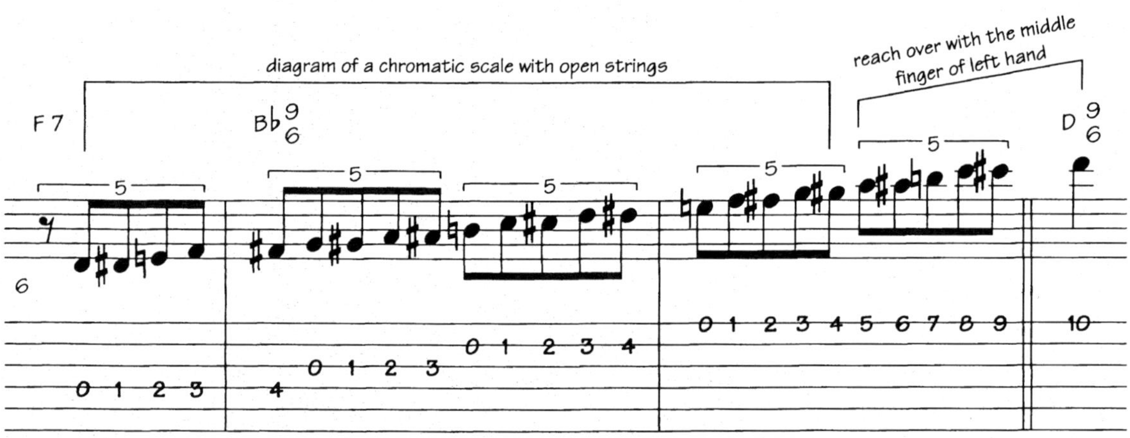

Jo's Remake (measures 25 - 26) lead and diagram #2

Finally, the last stop - the chorus relies on the diagram of the Eb6 chord, although it shows the notes of the major pentatonic scale of the same key.

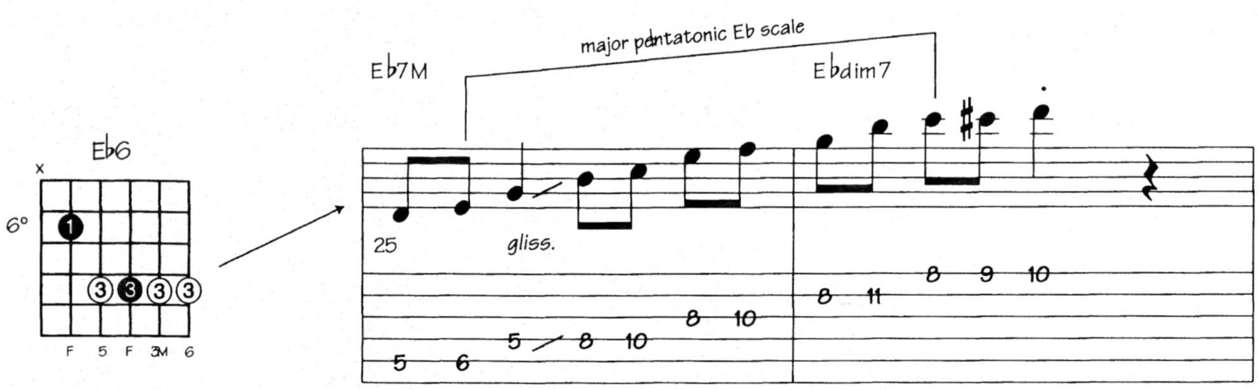

PART C

The final theme, including the improvised phrases, of "Jo's Remake".

Force yourself to really copy the string bends (measures 1, 5, 17, and 21); they are important for the style.

#49

A Final theme

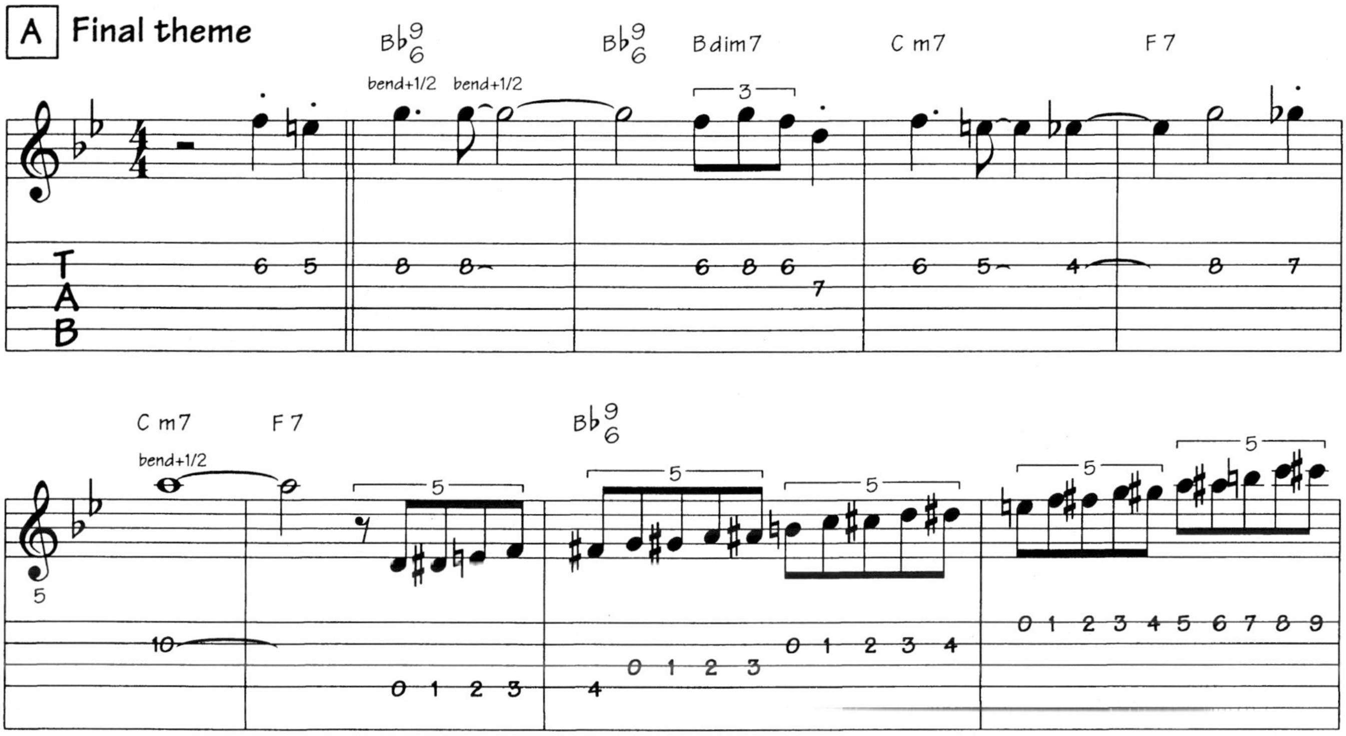

B

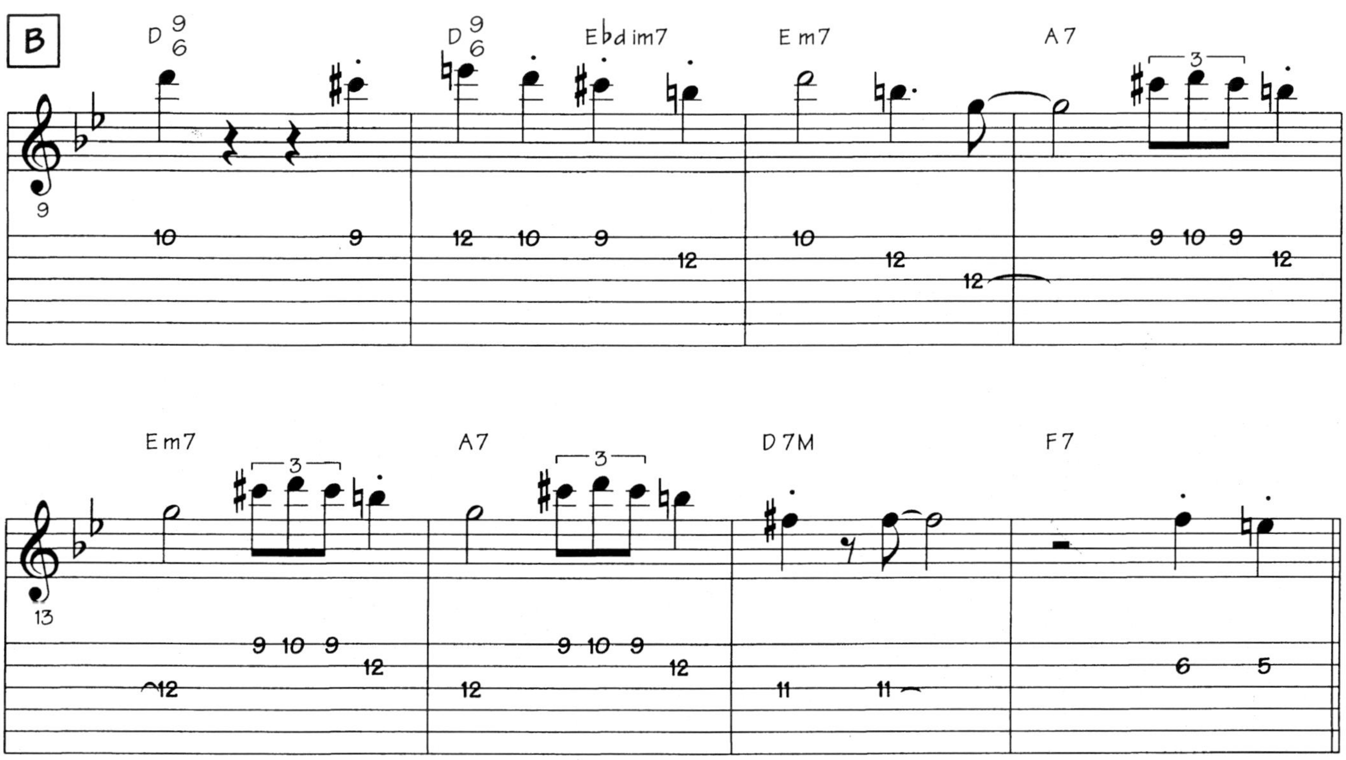

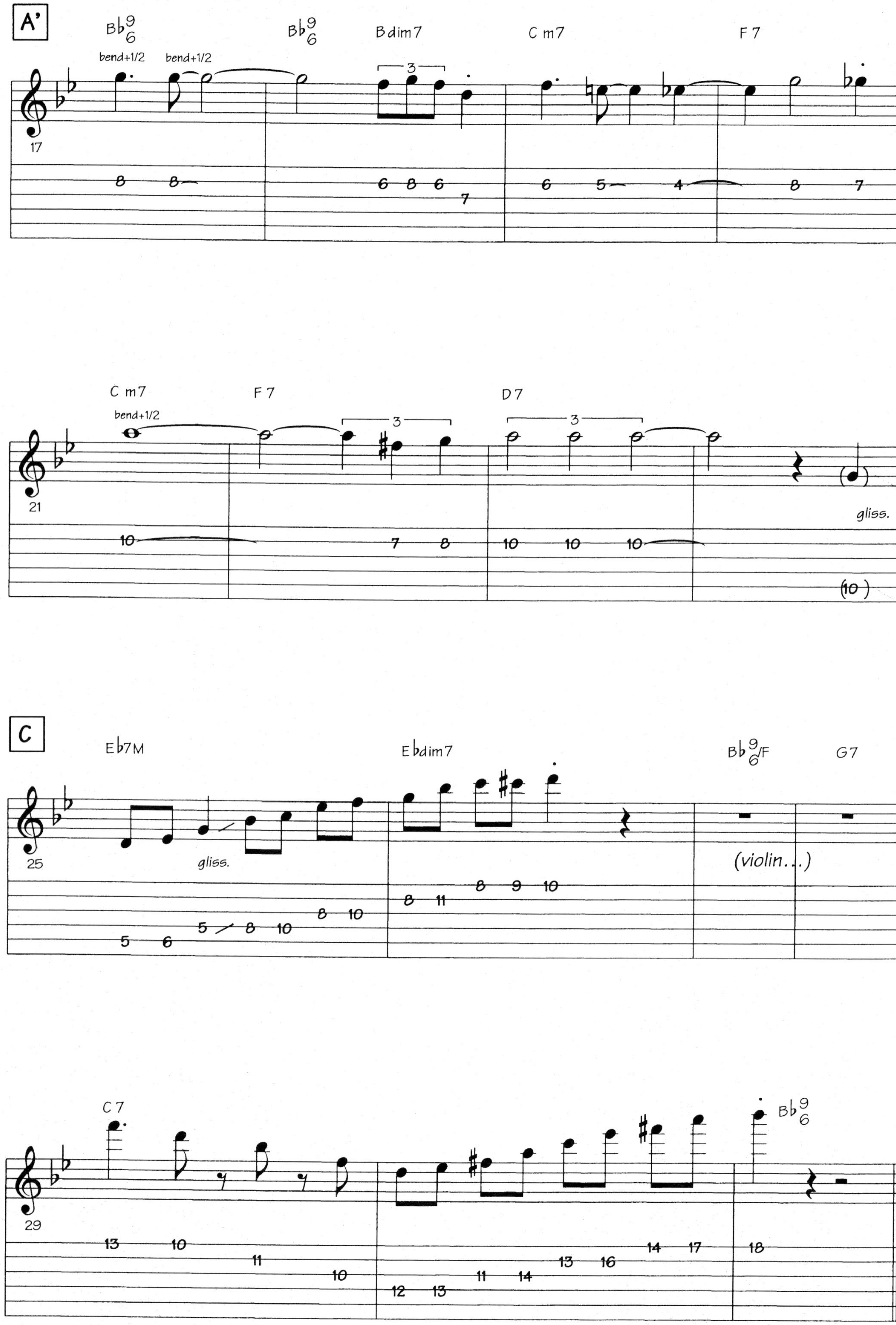
A'
Bb9/6
Bb9/6
Bdim7
C m7
F 7
bend+1/2
bend+1/2
C m7
F 7
D7
bend+1/2
gliss.
C
Eb7M
Ebdim7
Bb9/6/F
G7
gliss.
(violin...)
C 7
Bb9/6

PART A

We will use some quintuplets with chromatic eighths (see chapter 11). Here are two little exercises based on the tension → resolution principle, in the minor key.

Exercise 43 - a resolvent phrase with the Am chord

Do you remember the diagram of the harmonic minor scale (chapter 2)? Good, than this simple phrase ought to sound familiar to you. Play the notes in ascending numerical order.

Descending resolvent phrase with Am (the harmonic minor scale in the key of A).

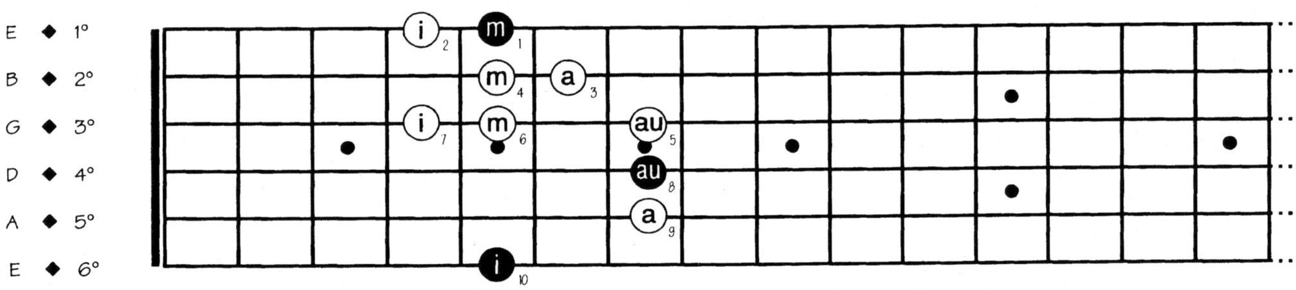

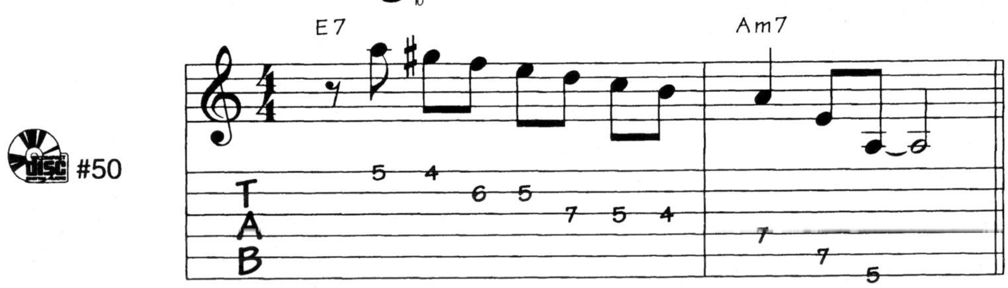

Exercise 44 - a phrase with the Am chord

It has the color of it, the number of notes (7), the way it is used in the context... and yet not! It is not a harmonic minor scale, but it is a near melodic ladder (scale) in the minor "Neopolitan*" mode. In this mode, the fifth (the E note) is almost done chromatically, because is uses two half tones in succession. This is something that you will not find in the minor harmonic scale. Play the notes in numerical ascending order, then play the phrase.

Minor Neopolitan mode, key of A.

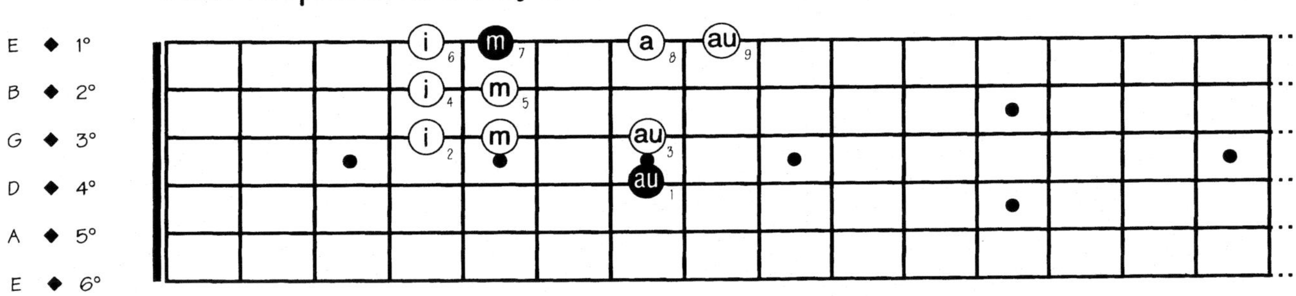

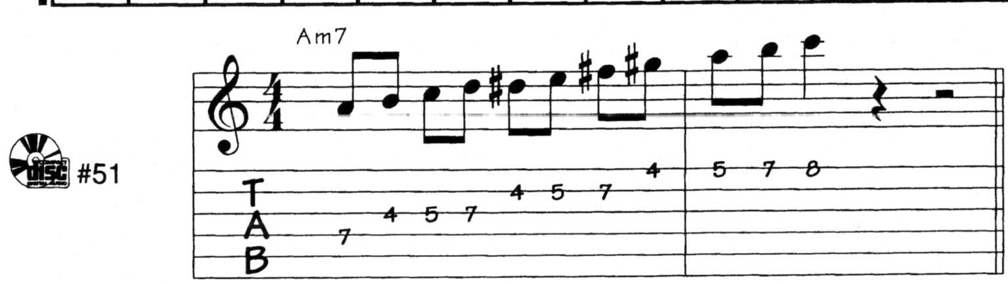

*Editor's note – the scale refered to as "Neopolitan" on this page is actually the melodic minor scale with a b5.

▪ PART B

As part of these first twelve chapters, we will give you a waltz in its entirety: The "Valse a Patrimonio", taken from the Romane Ombre CD.

Here is the diagram of that waltz:

Valse à Patrimonio

(Waltz of Patrimonio)

Its structure = 48 measures ABC – its entire structure = 128 measures ABACCABA

$\frac{3}{4}$ ♩= 200

A	Dm	Dm/C	$E7^{5b}$	%	Ddim7	C#dim7	Bb7	A7
	Dm	Dm/C	$E7^{5b}$	%	Ddim7	Gm6/A	Dm	%
B	D7	%	Gm	%	4 // (repeat of the previous 4 measures)			
	E7	%	Am	%	E7	%	$Em7^{5b}$	A7
C	D	F#7	Bm	D7	G	Ddim7	D	A7
	D	F#7	$G7^{5b}$	G	E7	A7	D	Gm6/A

As is always the case with Manouche waltzes, the time frame is a little unusual for jazz. Here, since we have three squared sections of six measures each, the progression of these sections does not follow the "standard" principle, such as the "AABA" principle.

This explains the fact that there is no solo with these harmonies, and this – "romantic stream" is uniquely composed with three counter melodies in a specified order, as is shown here: ABACCABA.

Of course, the harmonic rhythm is lighthearted, because of the relative speed of the beat and its basic rhythm: three beats per measure.

For this lead of the waltz, here are some possibilities for voicings:

Section A :

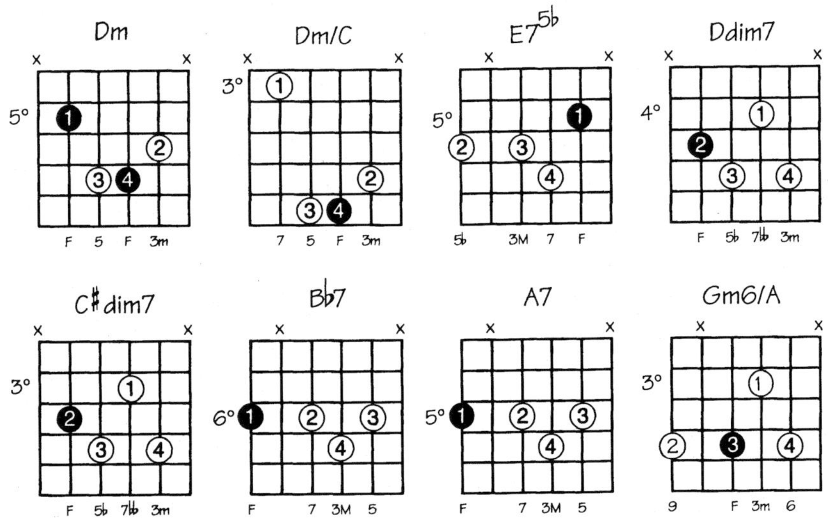

Section B :

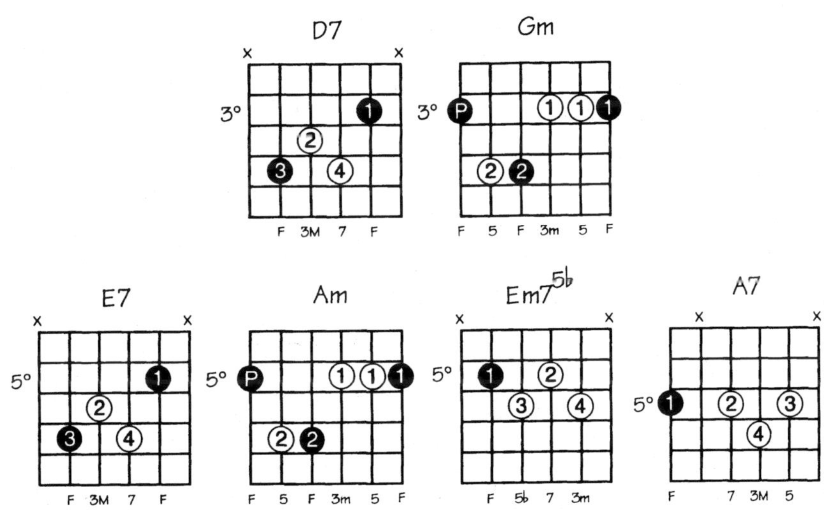

Section C :

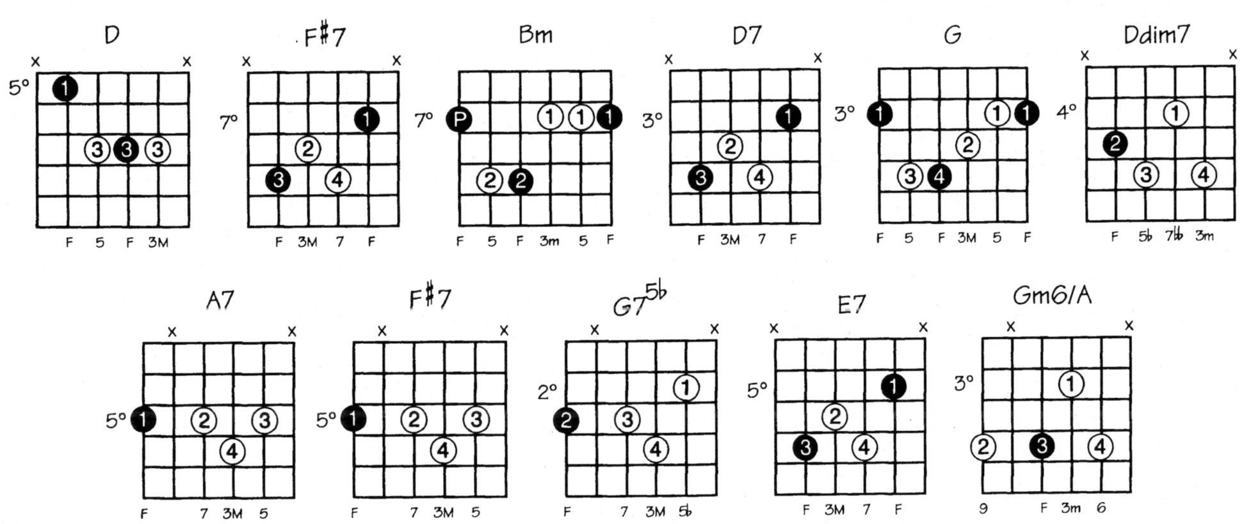

The analysis of this structure is as follows:

Key of: Dm

A							
I Dm 01	Dm/C	II7 E7^{5b}	⁒	II7 Ddim7 05	V C♯dim7	VI♭7 B♭7	V A7
Dm 09	Dm/C	E7^{5b}	⁒	Ddim7 13	V Gm6/A	I Dm	⁒

Key of: Gm

B							
V D7 17	⁒	I Gm	⁒	21 4 ⁒⁒			
VI7 E7 25	⁒	II Am	⁒	VI7 E7 29	⁒	II Em7^{5b}	V A7

Key of: Dm (measures 31–32)

Key of: D

C							
I D 33	III7 F♯7	VI Bm	I7 D7	IV G 37	I dim7 Ddim7	I D	V A7
D 41	F♯7	IV7 G7^{5b}	IV G	II7 E7 45	V A7	I D	V Gm6/A

Even if you do not intend to practice any of these improvisations, it wouldn't hurt to analyze them , and it may be of interest to you. Don't forget that the reason for this last analysis is to enable you to improvise, and to show the necessary components that you need to compose a good solo.

Three keys clear themselves here, where the ties occur: D minor (central pitch), G minor and D major. In other words, these 48 measures rely on a well-known major/minor (or visa - versa) "mirror" principle, combined with those modulations of pitches from its immediate cousins. Relatively, with the pitch of D minor, the G minor has an effective very close pitch: with the D minor being the I degree. The G minor chord could also be considered as a IV degree, if it didn't have the presence of the D7 (measure 17)!

• **Section A** - it is in reality formed with three fundamental chords, which affirm, with all its differences, the sentiment of the D minor tone. Of course, these three chords are the II, the V and the I.

– **MEASURE 3 - 4**: the E7 is the II7 chord (the secondary dominant chord).

– **MEASURE 5**: the Ddim7 is a camouflaged II7 - Ddim7 = E7b9.

– **MEASURE 6**: The C#dim7 is a camouflaged V - C#dim7=A7b9.

– **MEASURE 7**: The Bb7 is a camouflaged II7 (E7). In reality, here we have to use the famous tritone substitution (compare with chapter 6, page 4).

– **MEASURE 8**: Of course, we tackle the V chord, realistically called (A7), in a way to reintroduce the I (Dm) chord in the first measure of the second line.

– **MEASURE 14**: The Gm6/A (G minor six, A bass) is a camouflaged V chord, even if it really doesn't have the characteristics (without the C# note in the chord, which would be the major third of A7). But, where it occurs right before the I (Dm) chord, the Gm6/A cannot have any other purpose than to be a V (A7). Notice that in the passage this Gm6/A chord is typically done in the way of the manouche style, with its color as well as with its indication.

With this second line of section A, you should also look at the reduction of the harmonic flow, which we have already seen, that says, "Attention, this section ends and it is going to have a change in pitch".

• **SECTION B** - We are not surprised to find this in the first line: the V → progressions.

– **MEASURE 25**: The E7 is a VI7 that brings the II (Am) in its role, by using the dominant principle → provisional key. And in measure 29, the E7 is a "suspension" towards the A7 in measure 32.

– **MEASURES 31 - 32**: We have a II - V that drives back toward the D minor tone (section A), and a II - V which could also have been developed toward the tone of D major, indifferently!

• **SECTION C** - This section intensifies a little.

– **MEASURE 34**: The D major pitch is given by the fundamental chord in measure 33, the F#7 is a III7, which is used to introduce the VI (Bm) chord "the relative minor" of D.

– **MEASURE 36**: The D7 (I7) is the first chord of a progression that we have already seen, and we know it as the "Christophe" progression.

– **MEASURE 37**: The G is the IV of this "Christophe".

– **MEASURE 38**: By carefully looking at the four notes which make up the Ddim7 chord, you'll see that Dmin7 is another way to express the dimIV# (the G#dim7), that conventionally waits for its place in the "Christophe". Indeed, the G#dim7 has the G# (Ab) - B - D - F notes. These notes are exactly the same as those of the Ddim7 chord.

– The second line of the section C is similar to the first, an excepted flow of the harmony. The G7b5 chord anticipates the G chord which is advanced by one measure, in such a way that it frees the last four measures of the section, to use in it the conclusive and unavoidable II – V - I.

– **MEASURE 48**: Notice the appearance of Gm6/A. This means: "Attention, we are leaving the D major tone and return to the D minor."

PART C

Here is the melody for "Valse a Patrimonio", it doesn't have any difficult leads, but don't forget to study and practice it (especially the lyricism of the phrase with it's many triplets). Make sure you practice using the correct pickup measures into each section. Use it together with the complete structure, which will be 128 measures ABACCABA. Listen to the CD, if you need to.

#52

Valse à Patrimonio

music by ROMANE

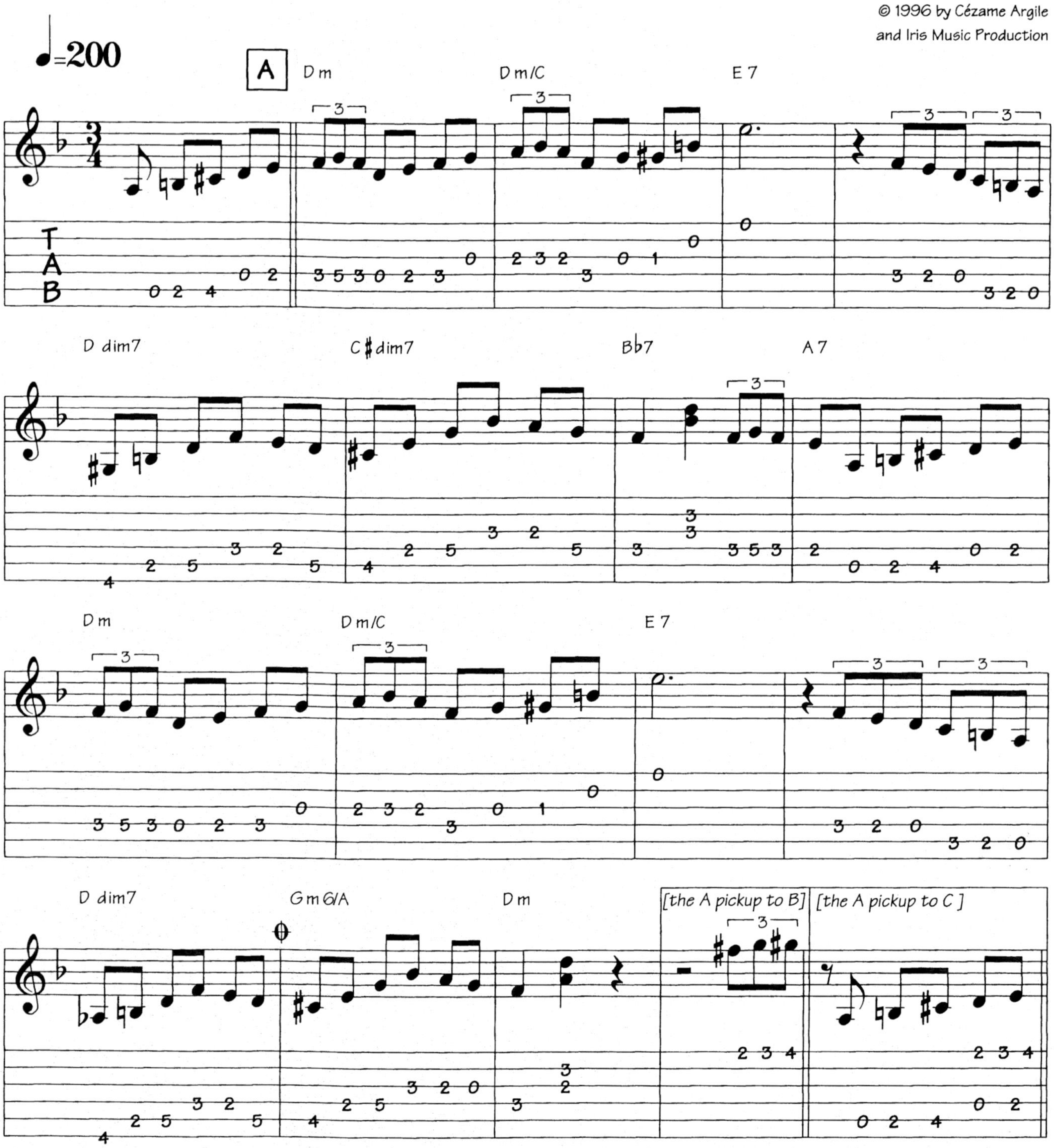

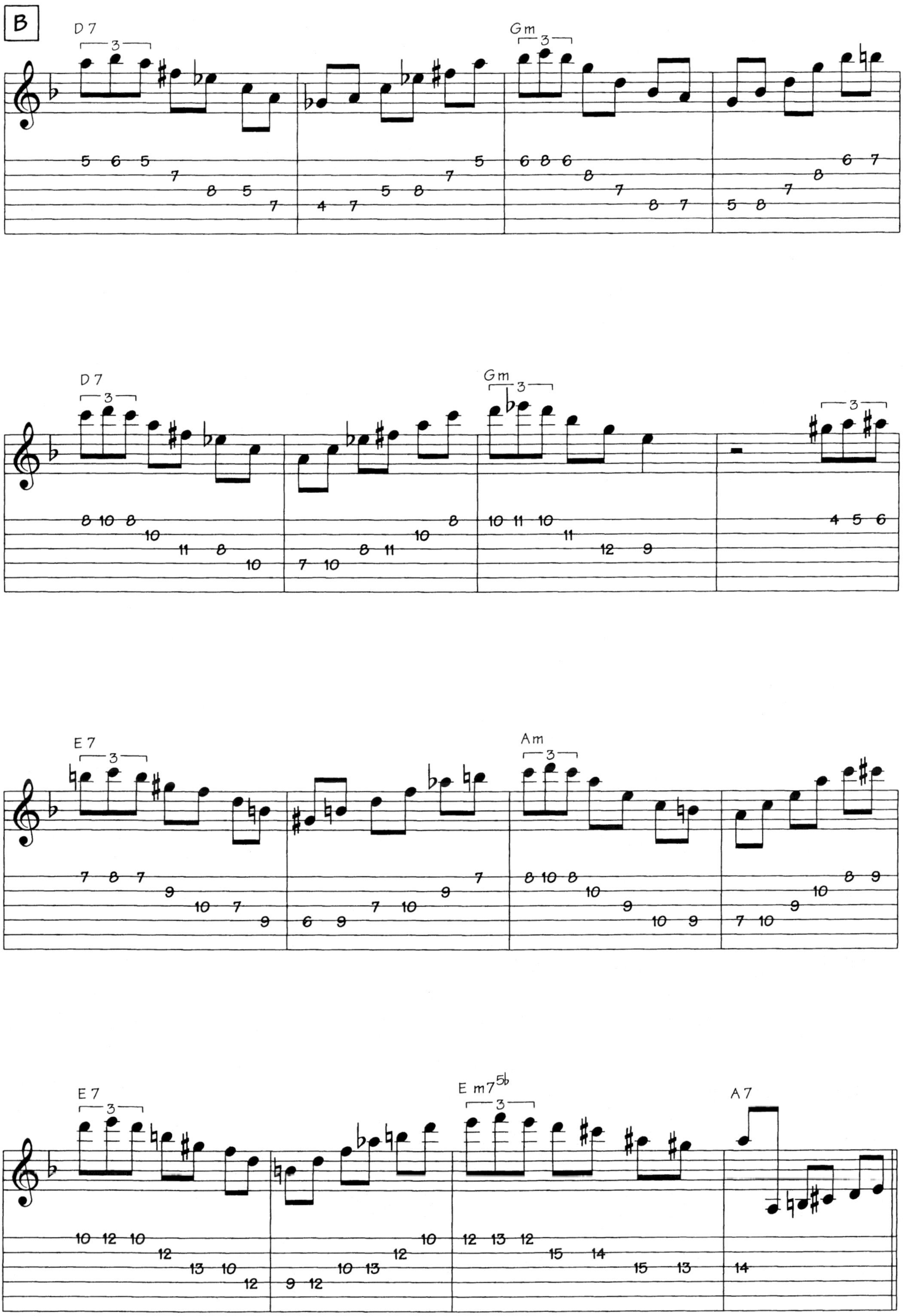
B
D7
Gm
D7
Gm
E7
Am
E7
E m7 5b
A7

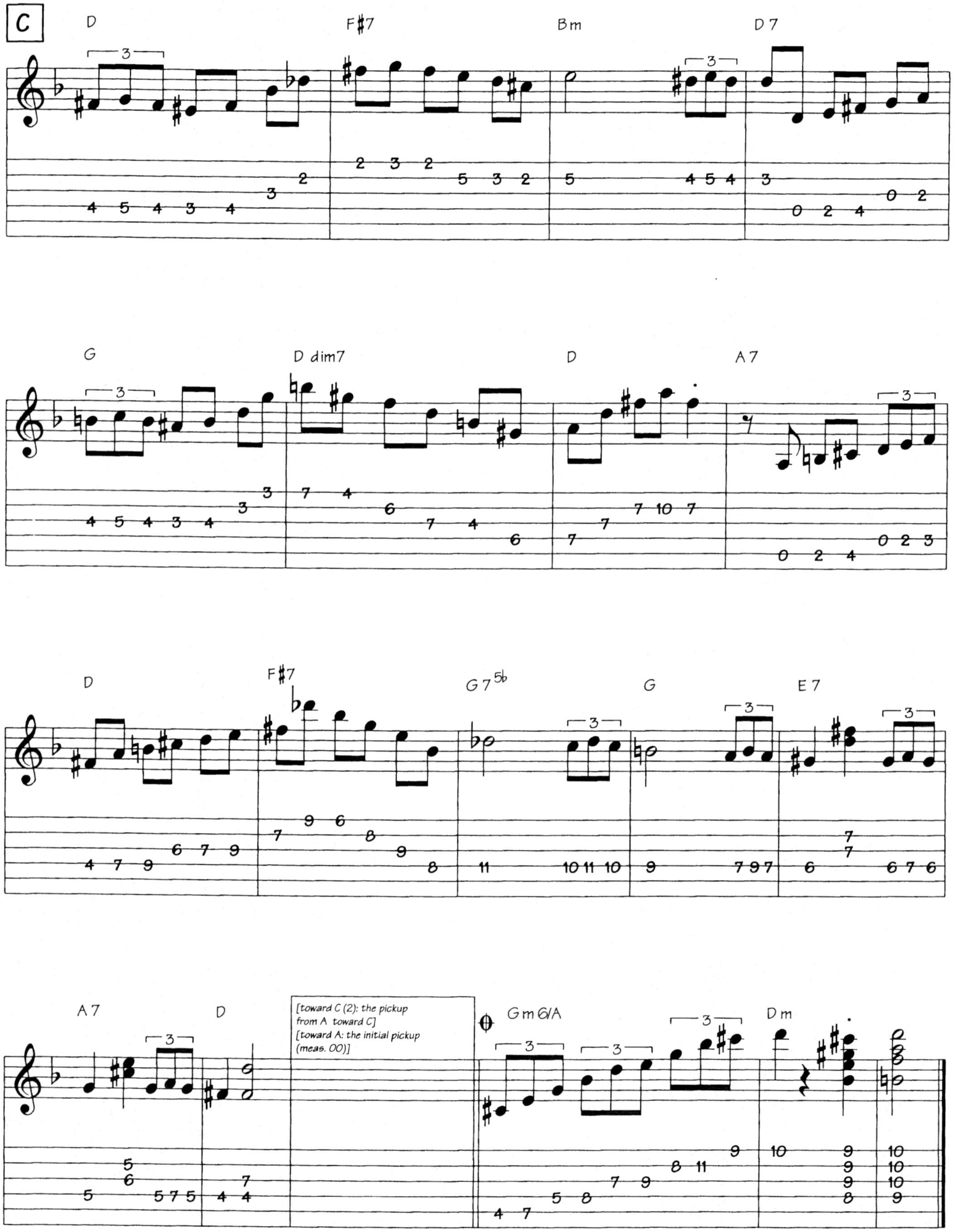
C
D
F#7
Bm
D7
G
D dim7
D
A7
D
F#7
G7 5b
G
E7
A7
D
[toward C (2): the pickup from A toward C]
[toward A: the initial pickup (meas. 00)]
Gm6/A
Dm

PART A

Exercise 45 - resolvent phrase in the key of C major

We start this thirteenth chapter with some very simple exercises.

The first illustrates the major scale and the dominant → root note principle, with two types of melodic resolution: that first measure is chromatic (the D# note, which changes to E and does not fit in with the C scale): the second measure is diatonic (the B note which changes into a D, becoming a part of the C major scale). Other than the fact that the resolution notes (E and B) take place on the strong beats, notice that in the passage of the chromatic resolution has a "Blues" color in the measure where, the entire chord (C), the augmented ninth (9# - here the D# note) is tradtionally considered a "Blue note".

#53

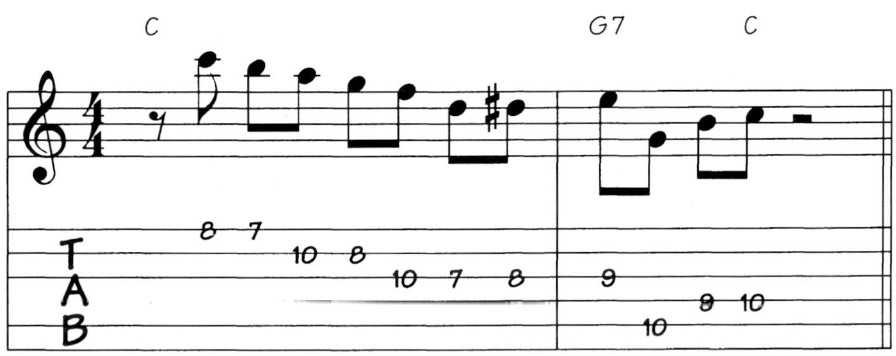

Exercise 46 - resolvent phrase with II-V in the key of D major

Always in D major, here is an illustration of what can be done by combining a scale (C major) with the resolvant chromatics (circled).

The first chromaticism resolves with the fifth of the Dm7 chord.
The second is triple: the point of resolution ("designated" note of each type) is the B note in the second measure, the note that corresponds with the major third of the G7 chord.
The third owing to the fact that this note Eb will not correspond with each characteristic note of the C7M final chord... and would, therefore, not form a resolution!
Finally, draw attention to the aesthetic order. Observe the starting point and the finishing point of this phrase: an ambitus of two octaves, very exact.

#54

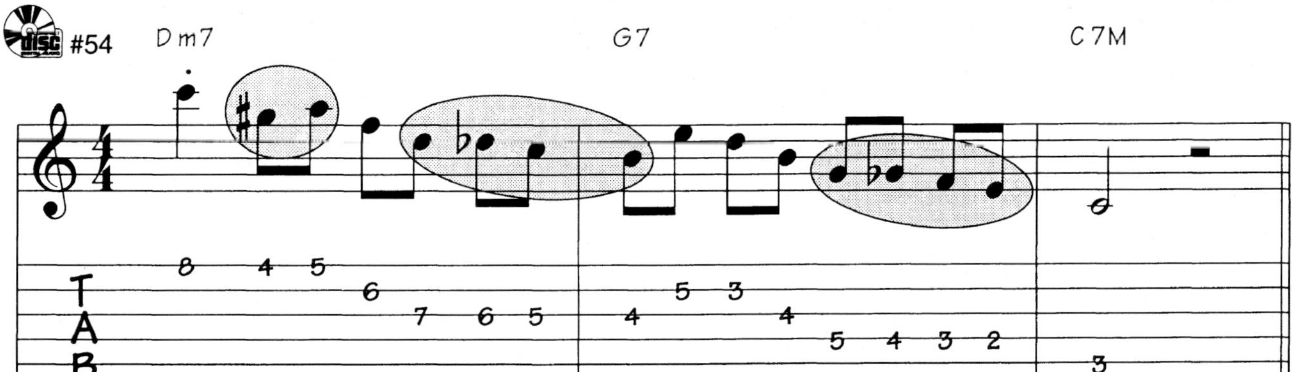

Exercise 47 - phrase in the key of A minor

Here is a third phrase, which is typical for the melodic conception of Manouche, based on the harmonic minor scale.

The starting point and finishing point are identical.

This time, no chromaticisms, but only two directions of the lead, which divides the measure in two equal symetric parts: an ascending arpeggio (of Am), and a descending arpeggio (of Dm).

The first arpeggio is based on the basic minor chord diagram (Am).

And the second arpeggio is the "dim7" arpeggio of G#dim7.

But by the attempt of constructing that G#dim7 with a Dm chord, is this the harmony that we are looking at?

If you have learned your lessons well, you can easily answer the question!

Yes, we will briefly repeat this property:

"The entire 'dim7' chord can be put in relation with a "7b9" type chord, where the root note is located a major third lower ."

In other words, the G#dim7 can be placed in relation with the E7b9 which is nothing other than the V degree of the key of A minor (look at the harmonization of the harmonic minor scale, chapter 2).

And now we understand why this procedure is typically like the Manouche's, which consists of avoiding the Dm chord (harmony of the moment) at the cost of the "dim7" arpeggio, which shows the E7 chord, to produce a melodic cadence V7 → Im (E7 → Am).

This phrase also represents the way Manouche applies the harmony in the melody, if the real harmonic structure is that of the one shown between parenthesis, as it is shown below, then that is how the rhythmic section should be played, to absolutely sound like Manouche, this is good and well the Dm.

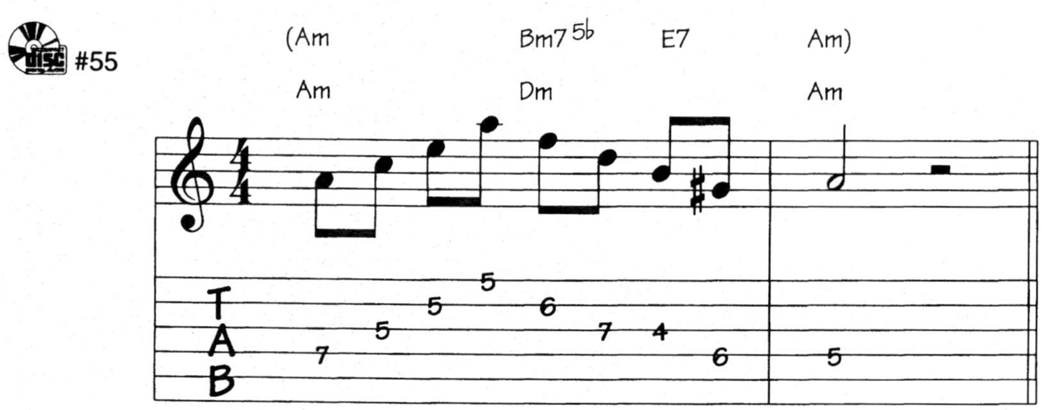

PART B1

We are going to study a new Manouche theme, by using the "Monticello" theme from the Romane Ombre CD.

Here is the harmonic diagram of this piece:

Monticello

The structure = Bolero, 40 measures ABA. ♩= 110

A	E7M	%	D7	%	E7M	%	G♯m7	C♯7
	F♯m7	%	D7	%	E7M	F7	E7M	B7 / E7
B	Am7	%	E7M	%	Am7	%	F♯m7	B7
A	E7M	%	D7	%	E7M	%	G♯m7	C♯7
	F♯m7	%	D7	%	E7M	F7	𝄌 E7M	B7
			𝄌 vamp ad lib.	‖: E7M	E7M / F7 :‖			

As indicated, "Monticello" is a bolero. The bolero is a musical form freely used in Manouche jazz. Without a doubt it is inspired by the piece "Bolero" by Ravel. Django Reinhardt had composed many themes in this form, like the strange "Bolero de Django"(1937) and "Troublant Bolero" (1953).

As a general rule, the speed at which the bolero should be played is relatively slow and the harmonic stream (frequency with which the chords occur), as well as the harmonic density (the name of the chords that makes up the harmonic structure) is modern. You also should be able to play the chord progression of "Monticello" by following its diagram without any difficulty since it is not necessary to correctly play it as the characteristic bolero rhythm, which we will study a little later in this chapter.

Otherwise observe that the structure of this theme deviates somewhat from the so-called "standard" ones. The A sections of this piece have a total of 16 measures.

Now we are going to show you how to play the chords of "Monticello".

Of course, you will observe that most of the chords, like the ones shown below, are slightly modified (these chords are enriched/colored), from the chords shown in the basic diagram on the previous page. This is owed to the fact that, and we will say it one more time, jazz is improvised music, where the "variations", as the harmony, melody or rhythm, are a part of the playing, that also represents the main part in jazz.

Intro (look at the recording of the CD) - the chords are played with the "lead" guitars.

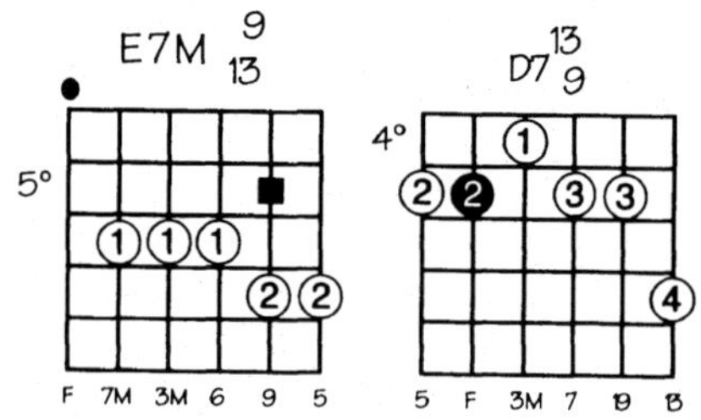

Intro - the chords are played with the rhythm guitars.

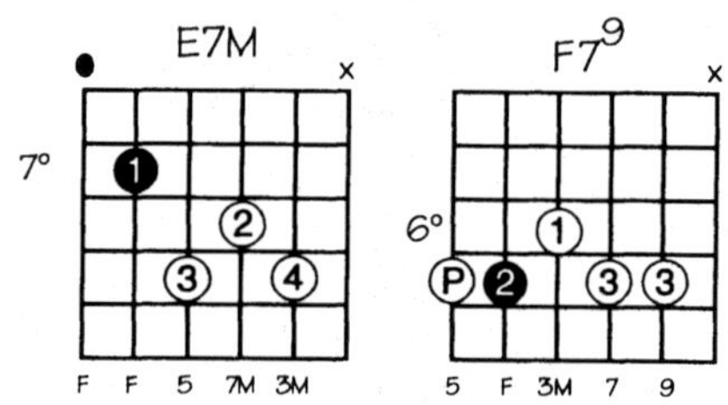

Section A:

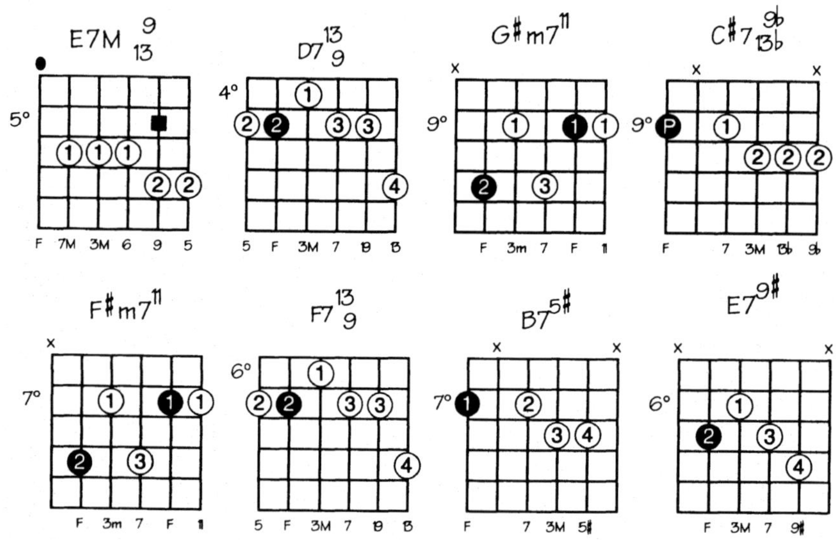

Section B:

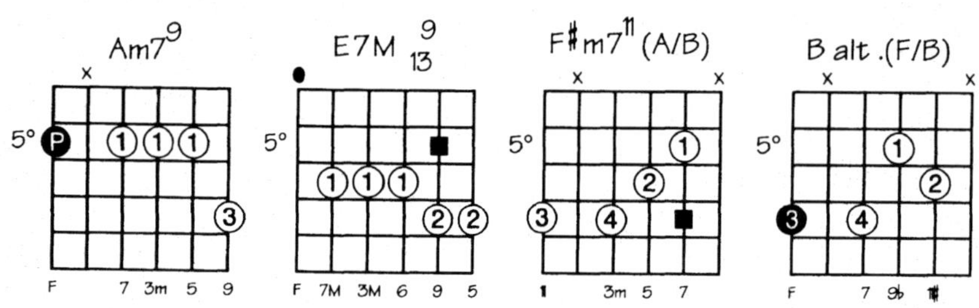

Coda:

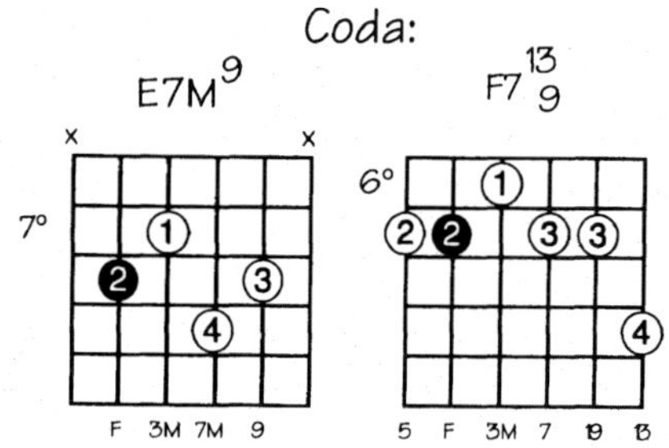

▪ PART B2

Now we are going to complete the rhythm lesson of "Monticello", by looking at the way the chords must be played with the bolero rhythm.

The chords used in "Monticello", as it is written, are in the pure rhythmic form:

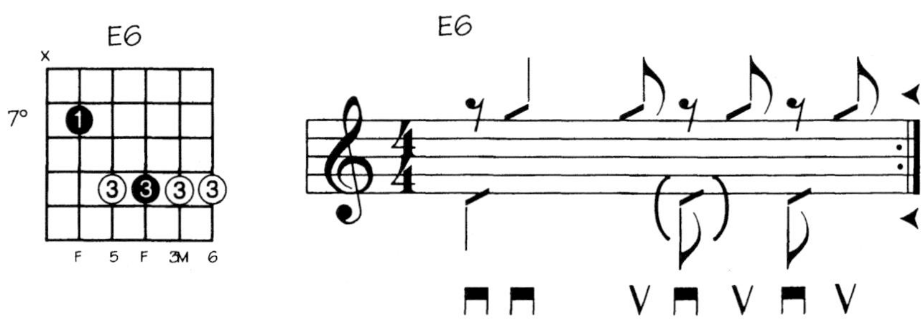

high notes of the chord

bass notes of the chord

Observe that all the high notes are played syncopated (not on the strong beats of the measure), with the exception of the first attack (quarter note), they are all done with up strokes of the pick.

On the other hand, the basses fall systematically on the strong beats, done with downstrokes of the pick. With respect to the third beat of the measure, the attack is shown between parenthesis, because this bass must be hardly heard, it 's only a suggestion. (In this case, it is often refered to as a "phanthom note.")

Train yourself to play this rhythm by practicing this measure non-stop.

Of course, there are many other variations of the bolero rhythm. Here is an example, as it is played by Django Reinhardt, the master, in "Troublant Bolero".

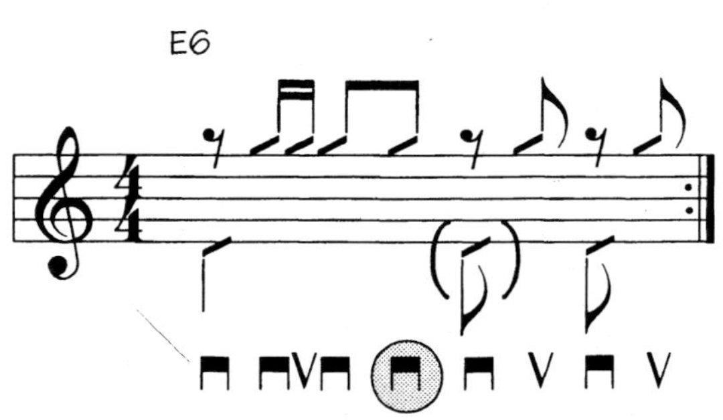

You could use this variation to accompany "Monticello", but pay careful attention to the way the pick is used. The difference is shown in the highlighted circle.

When listening to the CD, at the end of section A, just before coming to section B, notice that the rhythm section changes from the bolero rhythm. There are a series of quarter note triplets. Do the same with the accompaniment.

PART C

We suggest that you learn the melody of this theme before practicing the guitar solos with the harmonies of "Monticello" (chapter 14, 15 and 16).

#56

Monticello

music by ROMANE

♩=110

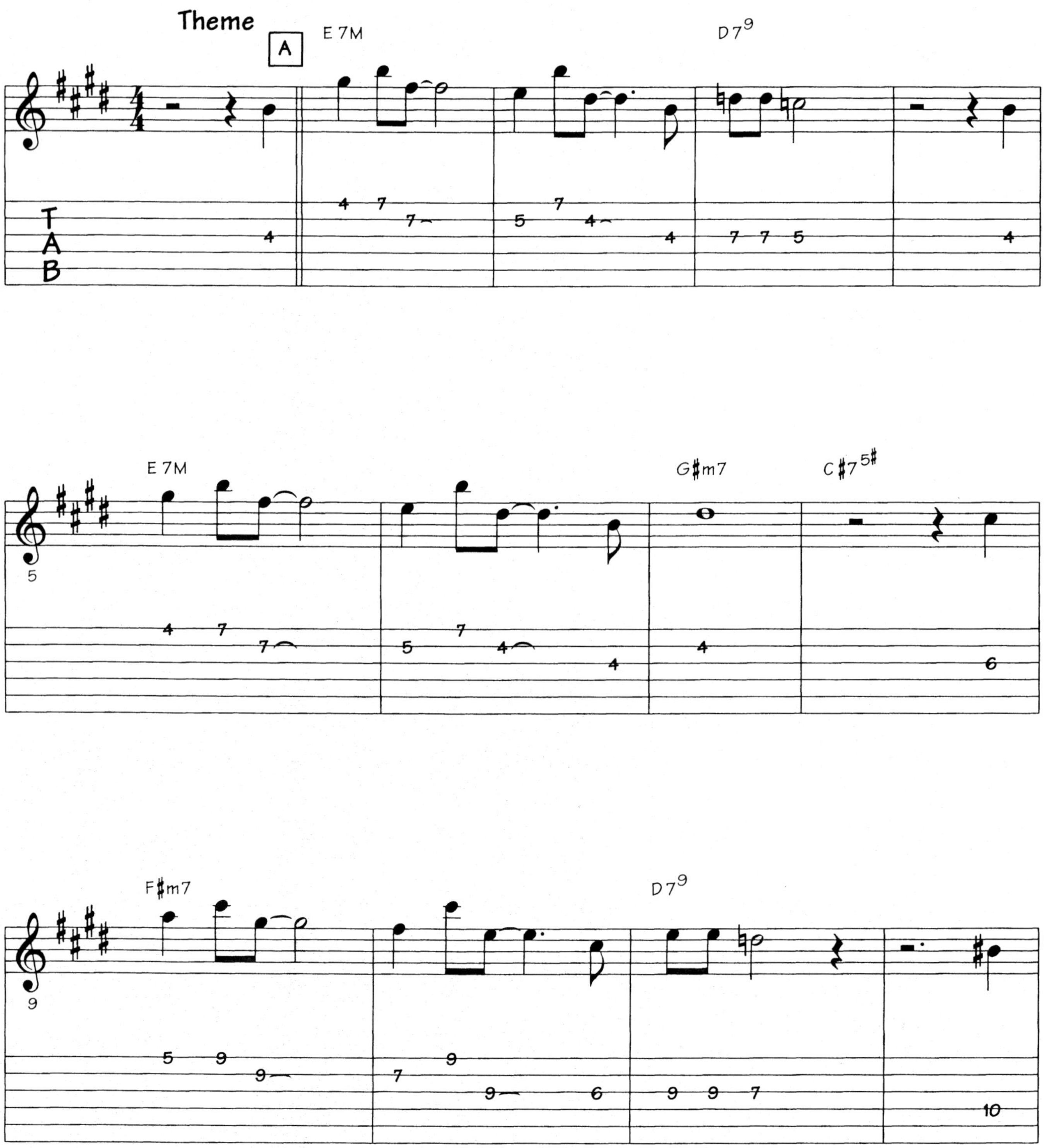

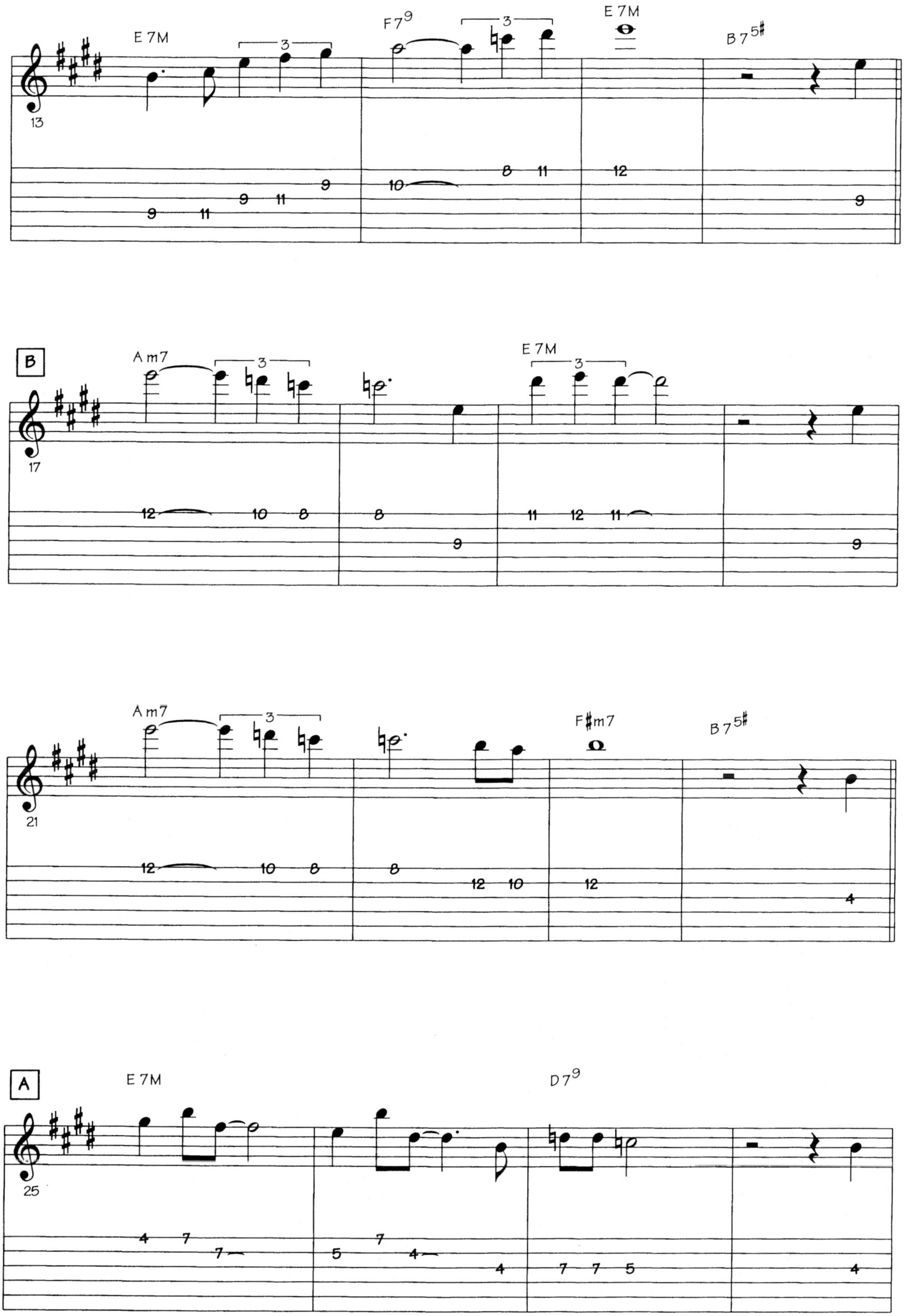
E 7M
F7 9
E 7M
B 7 5♯
13
B
Am7
E 7M
17
Am7
F♯m7
B 7 5♯
21
A
E 7M
D7 9
25

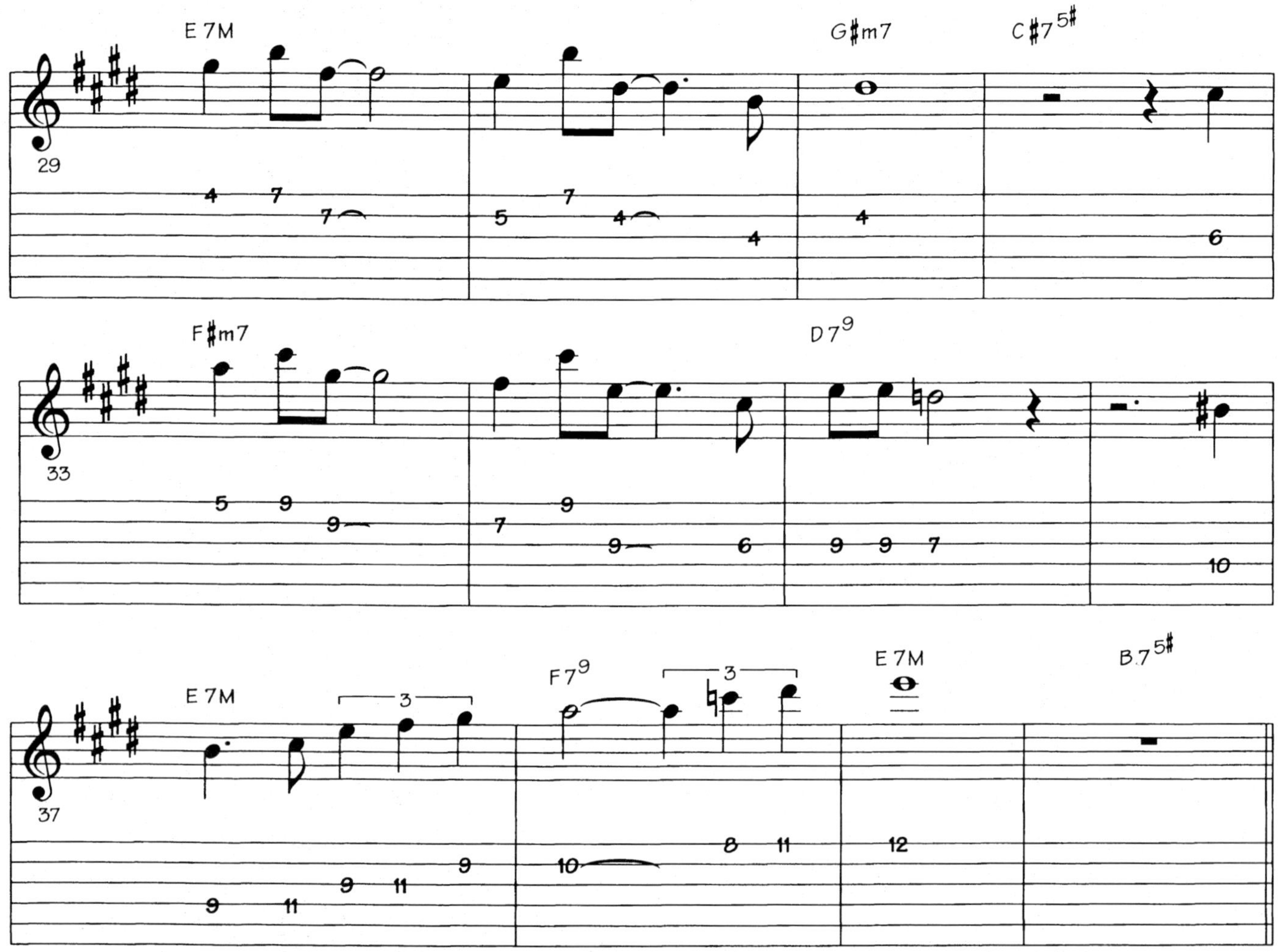

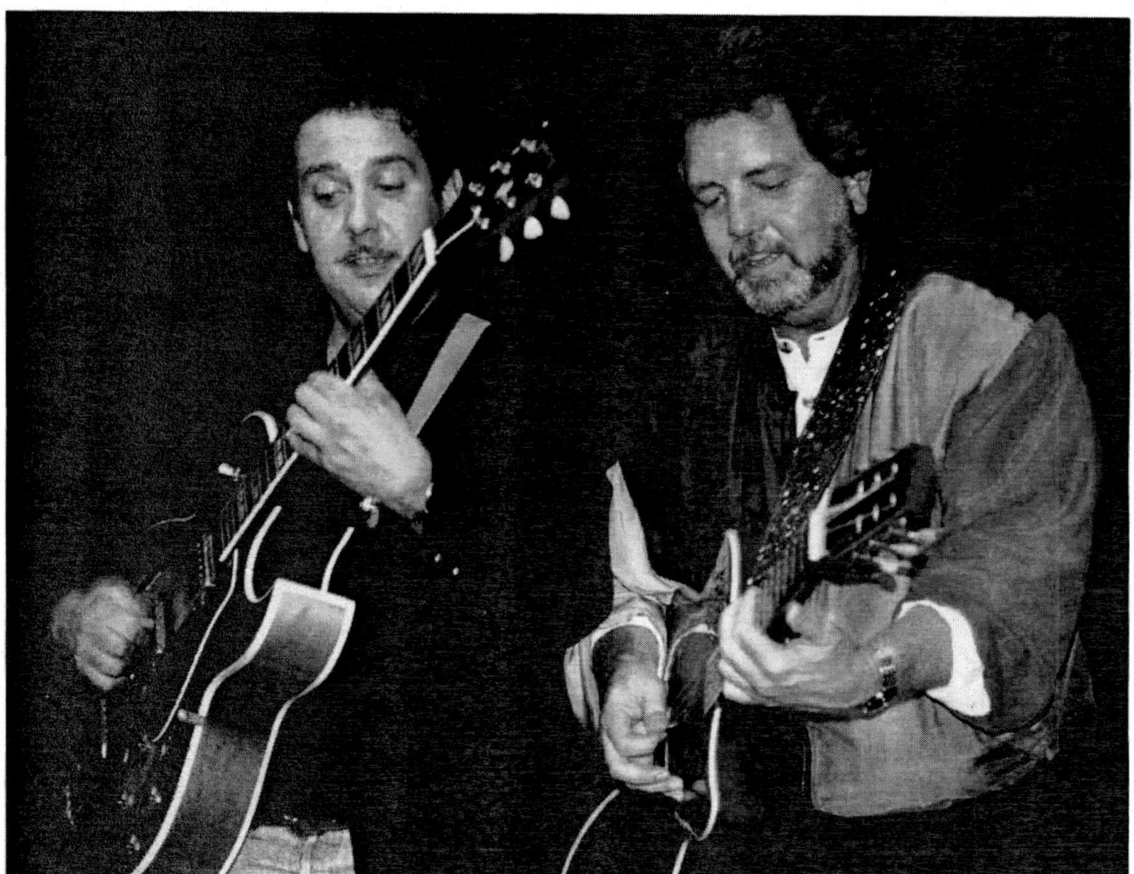

Romane, and Thom Bresh

PART A

Exercise 48 - The diminished scale

By having gone through some previous exercises, we've already seen the diminished scale. And certainly, at this stage of the journey, you are already familiar with its global sound, through its main 'ambassador' the "dim7" arpeggio.

But, in theory, we haven't spoken of this very common eighth note structure any more, which has among its structures the "A.L.T. (A Limited Transposition)" property (compare it with chapter 07, page 1).

As with the melodic concept, the diminished scale has come up rarely in music, unlike the "dim7" arpeggio/chord.

Whatever the case may be, this is a melodic scale that holds an extremely important place in music. To get the most out of it, we recommand that it is absolutely necessary to sing the melody in a way that comes natural to you, and in a major scale. With this goal in mind, the following simple observation will make a lot of things easier for you:

Diminished scale considered to start from the F# note:

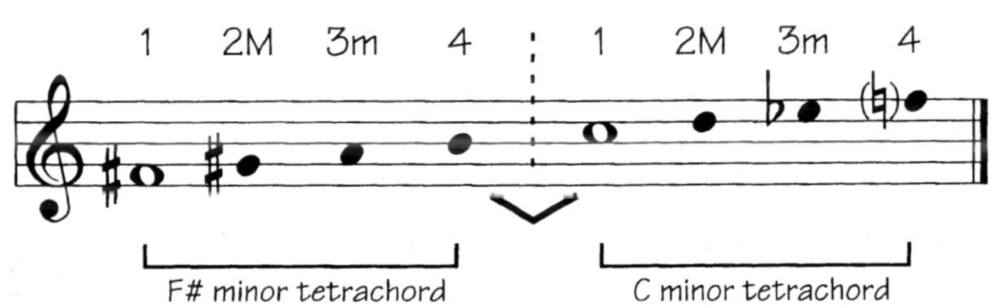

To make it easier for you to listen to it, we can imagine this scale indeed is being formed with two "tetra strings" (group of four notes joined together) opposite at a distance of the minor second (1/2 tone), or as two minor tetrachords where the root notes are at a distance of one tritone (As below, between the F# and C, we counted three tones).

As for its structure, it shares the octave symmetrically, that is, four intervals with minor thirds...

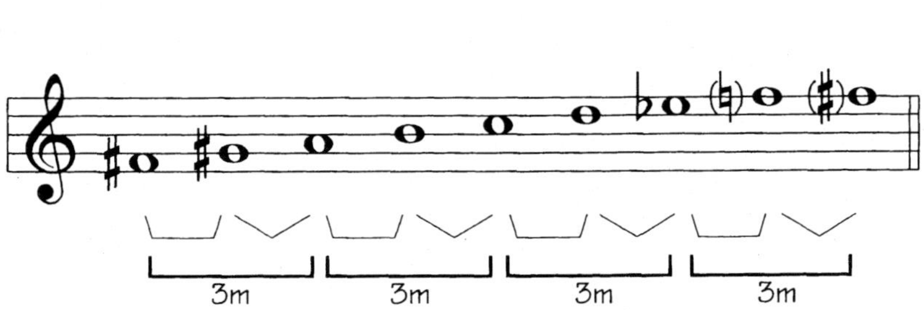

And in accordance with this regular succession of intervals it is easy to see that a given diminished scale can define three other diminished scales, at a distance of minor thirds apart. In other words, the diminished F#, the diminished A, the diminished C and the diminished Eb scales will all accept the same notes - of the "A.L.T." property, given by the diminished scale.

By comparison, to close this little tour of the theoretical horizon, notice that these interval successions (regularly alternated with whole and half tones) don't show us how to make that type of melodic scales (and not eight scales, stemming from the eight notes of the scale):

1 -- The "diminished" scale, which starts with the tone,
2 -- And its little sister, the "half-diminished" scale, which starts with the half tone.

On the guitar, take a D7 chord and play the half-diminished D scale, using regular up and down strokes of the pick.

#57

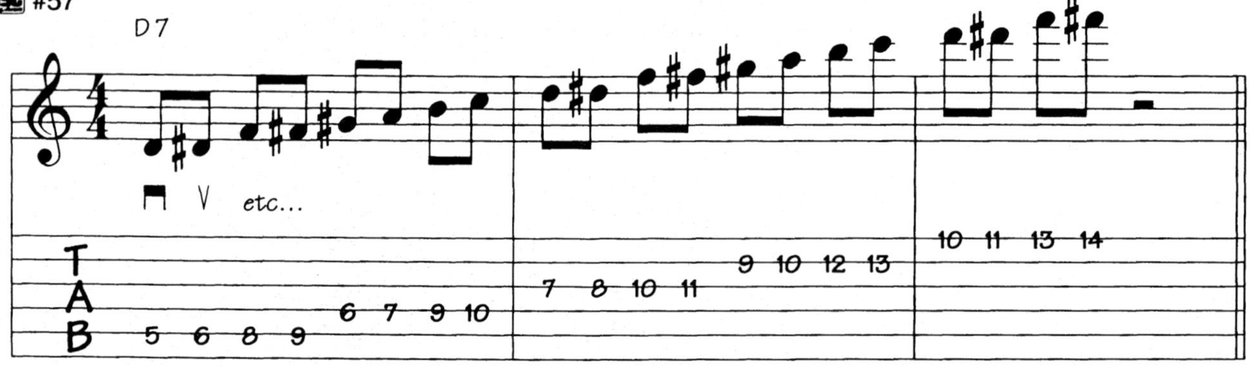

Exercise 49 - diminished scale with a G major cadence

Rhythmically, we have already met this kind of phrase (Exercise 23 and 25). But melody wise, we start here with a "7M" arpegio, while the harmony is dominant (D7); thereby establishing an improvisation, an important concept of the bi-scale, which we will come back to very soon and in more detail.

Observe that the resolution (with the G7M chord) of this phrase is done with the D note, which can be the fifth of G7M of the root note of D7.

#58

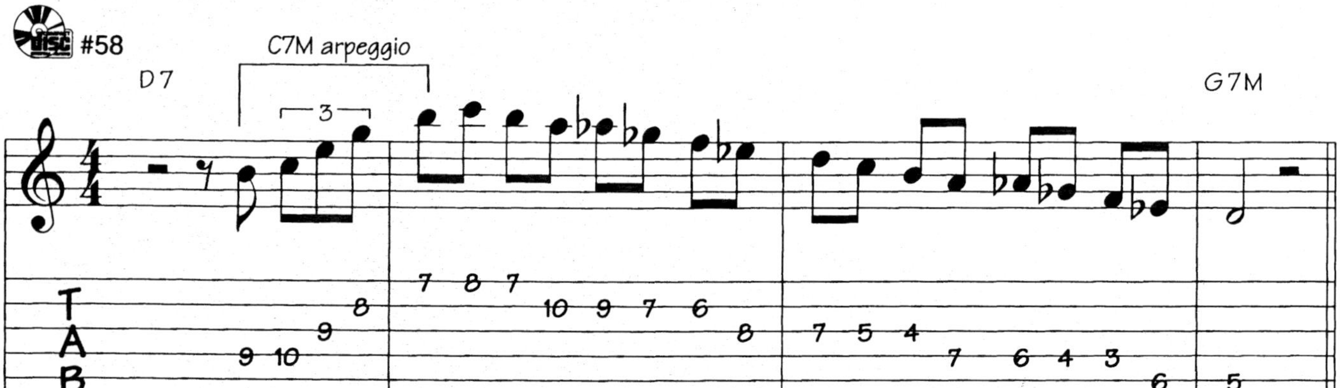

■ PART B1

Continue this study while using the diagram and the chords (chapter 13); we are now going to analyze the harmonic structure of "Monticello".

Monticello

Key: E

A

(I) E7M 01	%	(VII♭7) D7	%	(I) E7M 05	%	(III) G♯m7	(VI7) C♯7
(II) F♯m7 09	%	(VII♭7) D7	%	(I) E7M 13	(II♭7) F7	(I) E7M	(V) B7 / (I7) E7

B

(IVm) Am7 17	%	(I) E7M	%	(IVm) Am7 21	%	(II) F♯m7	(V) B7

A

(I) E7M 25	%	(VII♭7) D7	%	(I) E7M 29	%	(III) G♯m7	(VI7) C♯7
(II) F♯m7 33	%	(VII♭7) D7	%	(I) E7M 37	(II♭7) F7	(I) E7M	(V) B7

Although this diagram uses a single unique key, E major, at a first glance some of these sequences appear to be seemingly disconnected. It illustrates, some of these harmonic subtleties which jazz loves to juggle. Subtleties that are made while relying on logically solid principles.

MEASURES 3, 11, 27, and 35: the first of these subtleties is the presence of D7.

First of all, if we strictly consider the things from the key of E major, we would be tempted to define D7 as a chord that does not belong in E major -- this is the measure where no D7 occurs ,for certain, in the degrees of the E major scale, harmonized with thirds (compare it with the table on page 6, chapter 8). That is why it is analyzed as a "VIIb7".

And yet, we are sure that what we hear will agree with the notes, this chord sounds convincing, it does not give the impression of being thrown into this place at random, between the two root note chords.

Why does this D7 chord sound good here? There are two reasons. The first is located in the metric time frame. Besides, it is always possible, when the harmonic stream is sufficiently aired (which is the case here: a chord that lasts two measures only), to link chords together which apparently have no ties between them - a process that is allowed with modern jazz (it started in 1958) and is worked out with a lot with interesting harmonic structures.

Whatever the case may be, the second reason, which relies on the principle of substitutions, is by far the most important one, because it is the most satisfactory one that fits the perfect theoretical plan. In reality, the D7 is here a camouflaged chord of the II degree. Because D7(9,13) = F#7,5b(11): The E, F#, B and C notes respectively the 9, 3M, 13, and 7 with D7 correspond with the F#m7 in the 7, F, 11 and 5b. Note in the passage that a II chord can all be colored with a 5b and 11.

And that expresses the II degree that implies... the V degree, during B7: following the rule of : "the II precedes the V" (chapter 6, page4)... a V that inescapably re-introduces the chord with the root note, E7M, by virtue of the dominant ➞ root note principle.

To sum it up, we simply have to make a major II - V - I here, in which the II is camouflaged (a D7 for F#m), and the V evades, as is implied. To convince you of this, play section A and use the chords which are here (purely theoretical) - used with the real accompaniment, don't play the B7#5.

E7M	%	F#m7 5b (D7)	B7 5#	E7M

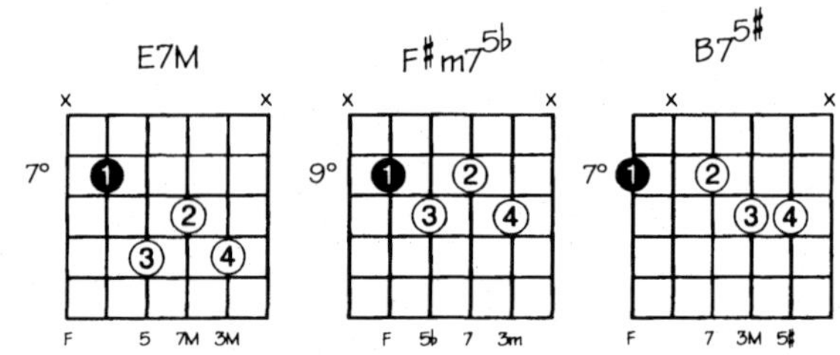

MEASURES 7 to 9: The chord we are aiming for is F#m7, the II in measure 9, which is introduced by its II - V, where it necessarily slides into a VI7, which is a secondary dominant chord.

MEASURE 14: This illustrates a basic tritone substitution: where the F7 replaces the B7, which will be the real chord of the V degree in the key of E major. Moreover, the one here was a long time coming, in order to appear in measure 16... but to introduce a I7 chord, which we directly carry out with the dominant (E7) ➞ root note principle (Am) of the first chord of section B.

MEASURES 17 and 21: This Am7 could appear unusual in the key of E major. Besides that, among the seven degrees of the last one, we do not find any Am chord. Evenso, we are going to continue to analyze this harmonic structure in the E major key. We do this for a one simple reason: the last chord of section A (E7), the first chord (Am7) and the second chord (E7M) of section B sketches a "Christophe" progression (compare this with chapter 9, page 5), where the IV#dim7 is evaded in such a way as to conserve the regular harmonic flow (using one chord during two measures). To see this, play section B by using the chords which are here like it is done with the real rhythm, do not play the A#dim7 chord.

E7 5b	Am7 (17)	A#dim7	E7M	E7 5b	Am7 (21)	%	F#m7	B7

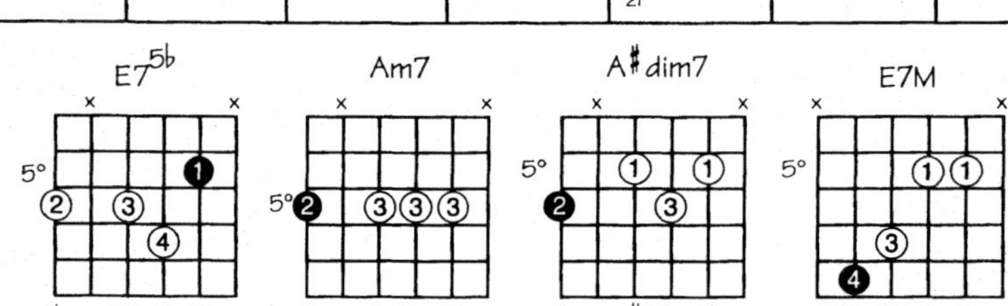

PART B2

Let's look at the leads, diagrams and procedures of Manouche which are in the beginning of the chorus of "Monticello". We saw the theme in chapter 13.

Monticello (measures 3 - 4) procedure #1

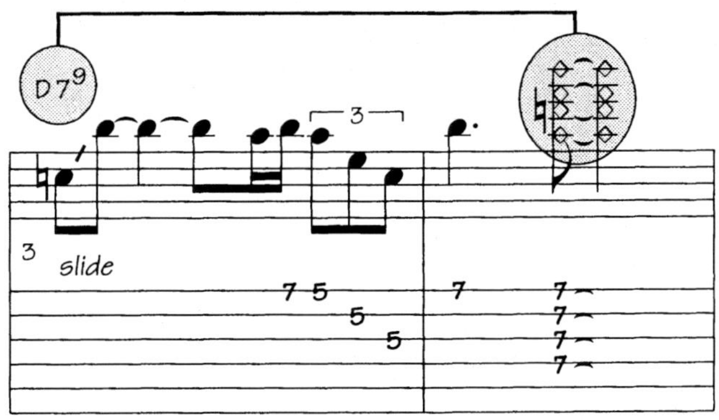

You have probably noticed that the Manouche solos freely use natural harmonics. However, except for the fact that these increase the value of the phrases, while giving them an interlying depth, the harmonics can also hold a function of their own. We have talked about this from the harmony point of view. Thus, in the case of the meausures above, the natural harmonics at the seventh fret are perfectly suitable for the D7 chord, introducing a more welcome coloration.

The A, D, F# and B harmonics are respectively the fifth, fundamental, major third and major thirteenth of the D7 chord, this is known as a global D7(13) chord. Take notice that this works here, and is all done in the area of the applicable harmony. A little later on, when we have no more secrets about chord substitutions (particulary tritones), you will realize that this procedure will give you interesting perspectives of the harmonic colorations while you are improvising.

Monticello (measure 8) lead #1

Measure 8 illustrates, in a quasi - academic fashion (1), the use of the harmonic minor scale (F# harmonic minor -- encircled notes), in relation to the harmony. In the Manouche playing style, this scale, although in minor, is used more often to construct phrases relying on the dominant chord - here the C#7(#5) - rather than using phrases based on a minor chord. This is owed to the fact that, harmonized in thirds, the harmonic minor scale develops a seventh dominant type chord which is very convincing within the context of the tonal minor with its V degree.
In a following chapter, we'll discuss this in detail.

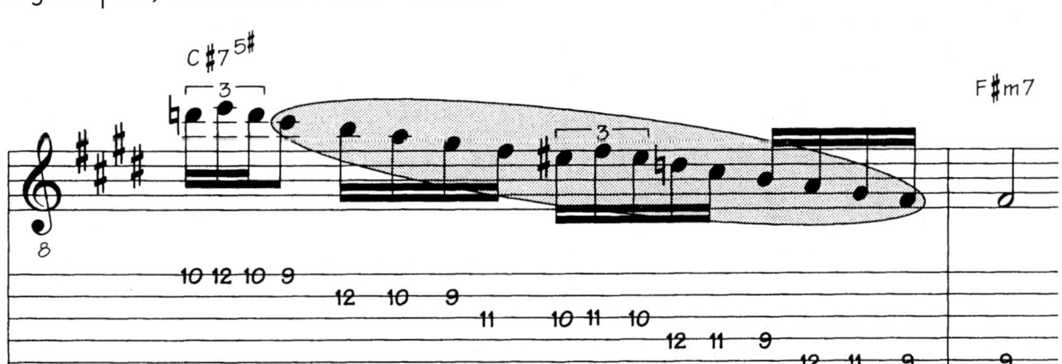

Chapter 14 / page 6

Monticello (measures 10 - 11) lead #1 and #3

Here we encounter a phrase that relies on the juxtaposition of two minor triads linked by the space of a minor third. It is interesting to know, that the harmony doesn't evolve around this space in the second part of the phrase (measure 11: Am triad with D7). The melody notes are not strictly constructed with the harmony that we are looking at. It is difference in the first part of the phrase (F#m triad with F#m7). In fact, this is commonly used procedure that relies on the following important rule:

"Each seventh dominant chord (Type V7) can be preceded by, or mixed with, a minor chord of which the fundamental is located one perfect fifth higher"

In other terms, D7 can here be preceded by, or mixed with, Am - the whole constituting a harmonic "II – V" (Am - D7) progression.

Thus remember this: "with a V7 chord, you can always improvise by thinking IIm".

And at this moment, as far as the concept of improvisation is concerned, the application of this principle lets you clear up your mind by simply thinking "juxtaposed minor triads with a minor third gap".

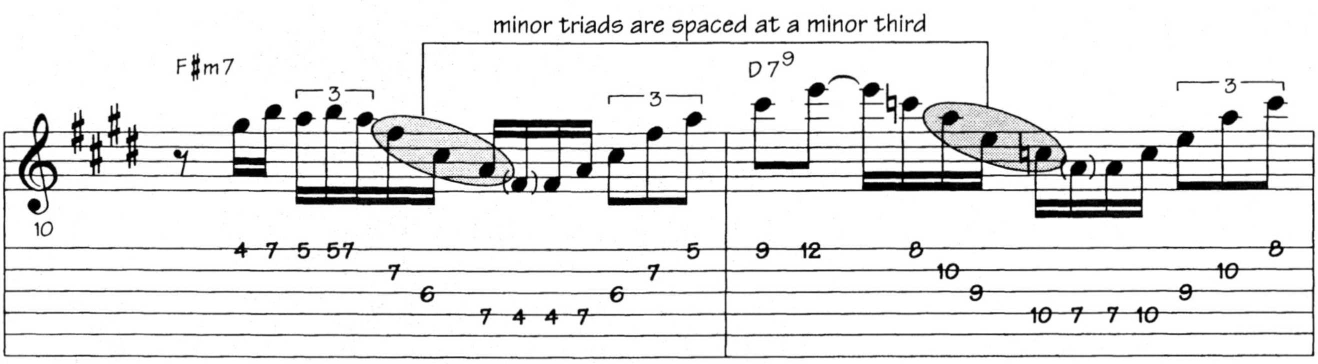

Monticello (measures 14 - 15) lead #4

Finally, with the last measures of section A, we find a phrase that relies, at times, on the major pentatonic scale of E (notes E, F #, B, and C#) and on the E6 chord diagram, shown in the middle of large skipping intervals.

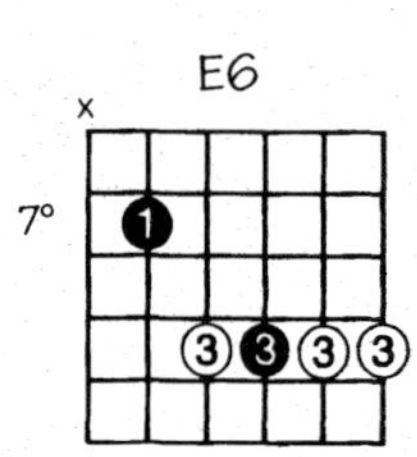

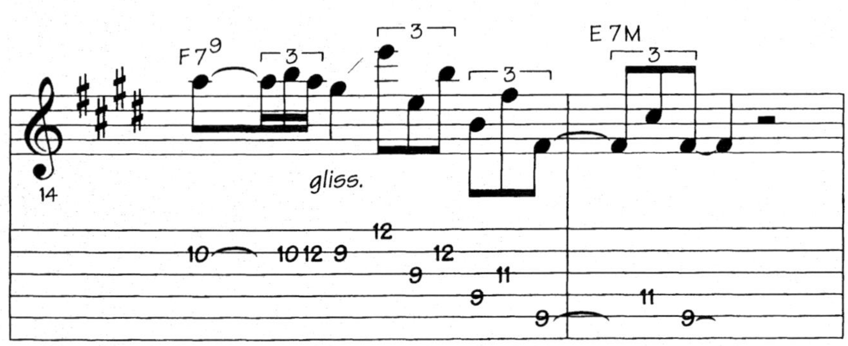

PART C

Here are the first six measures (section A) of the guitar chorus of "Monticello".

With regard to the many slides and where they are used, we recommand that you listen carefully to the CD to find out where exactly these are located.

Take your time to work with this chorus because syncopations and sixteenth note triplets are in abundance here.

#56

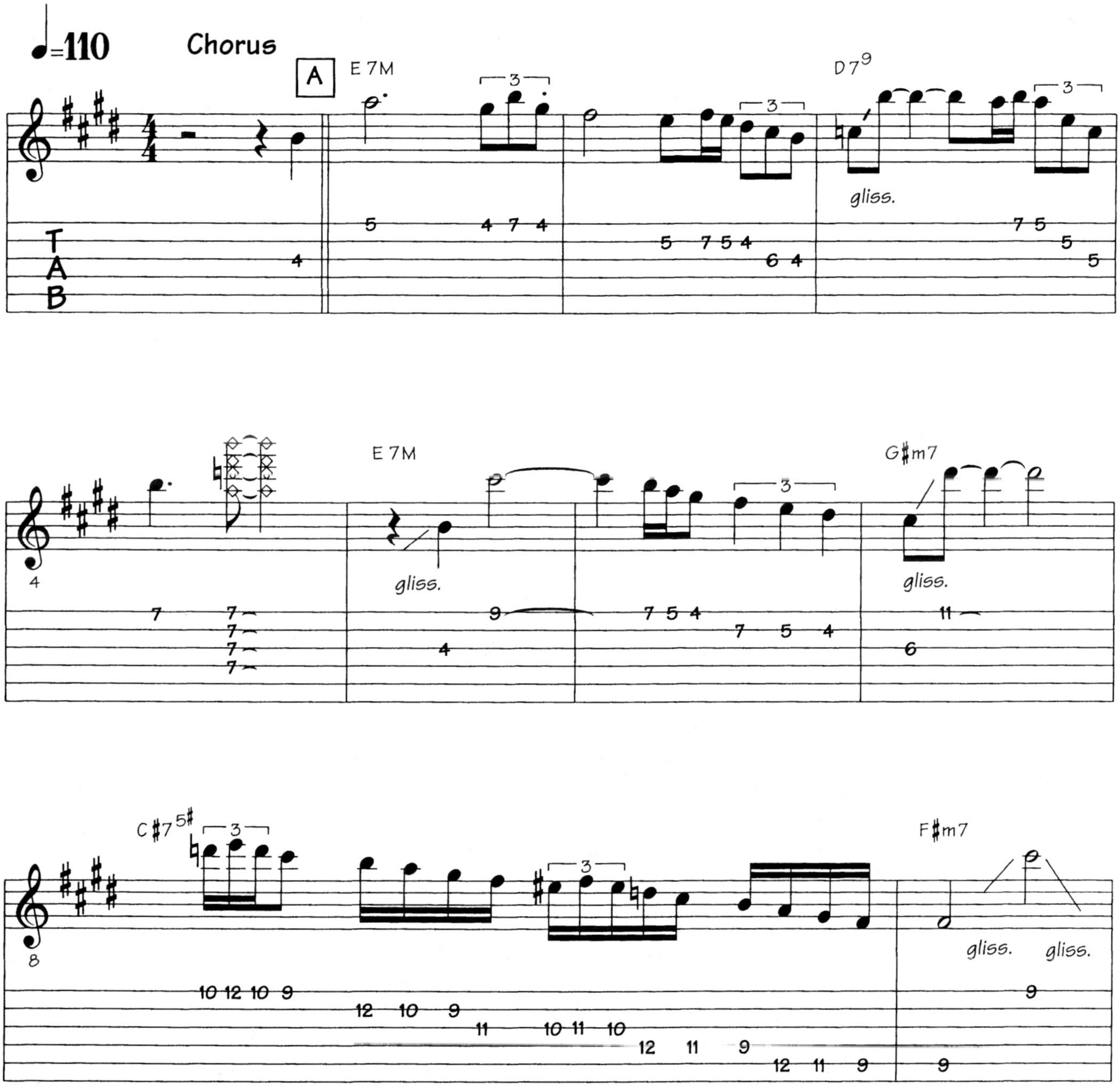

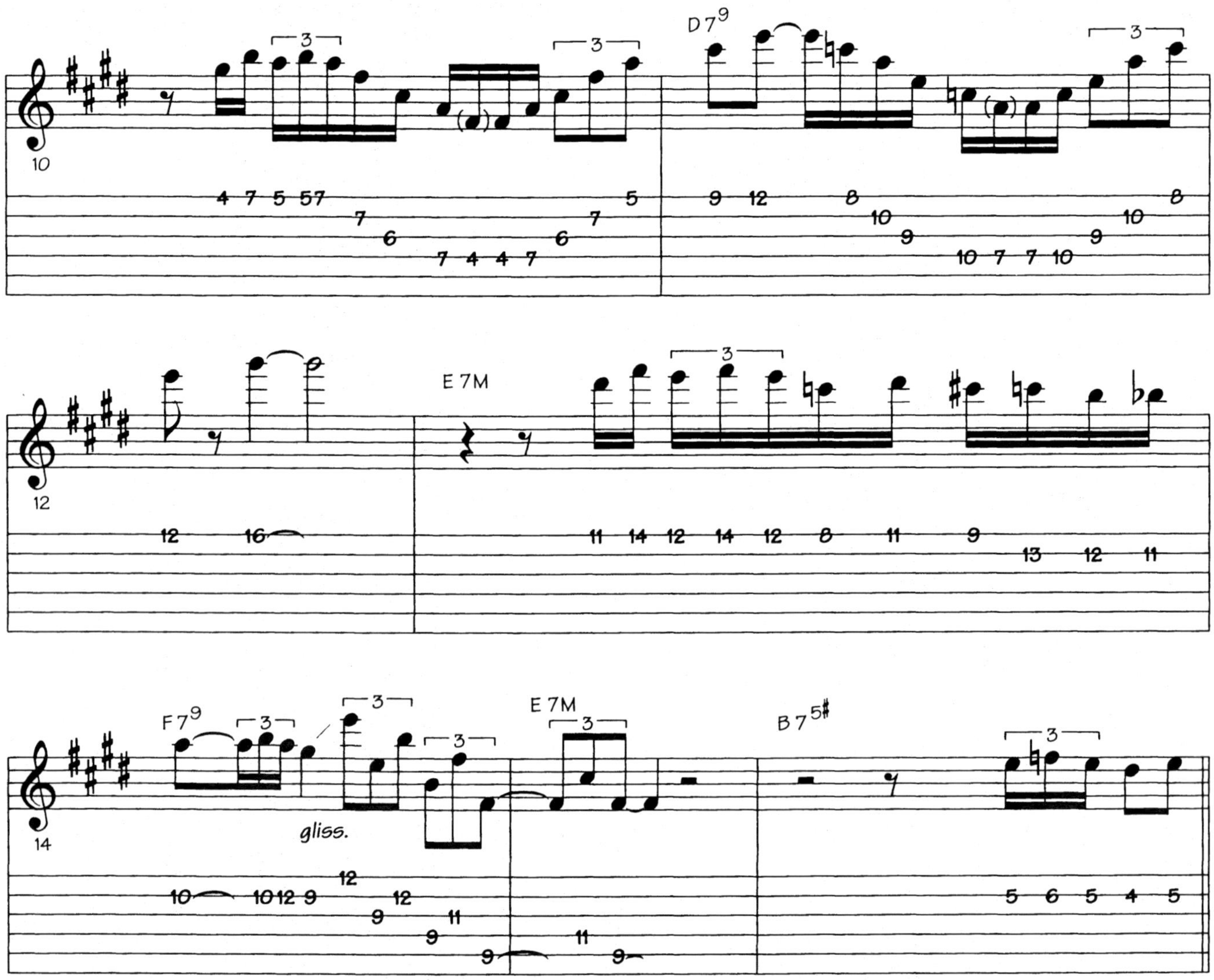

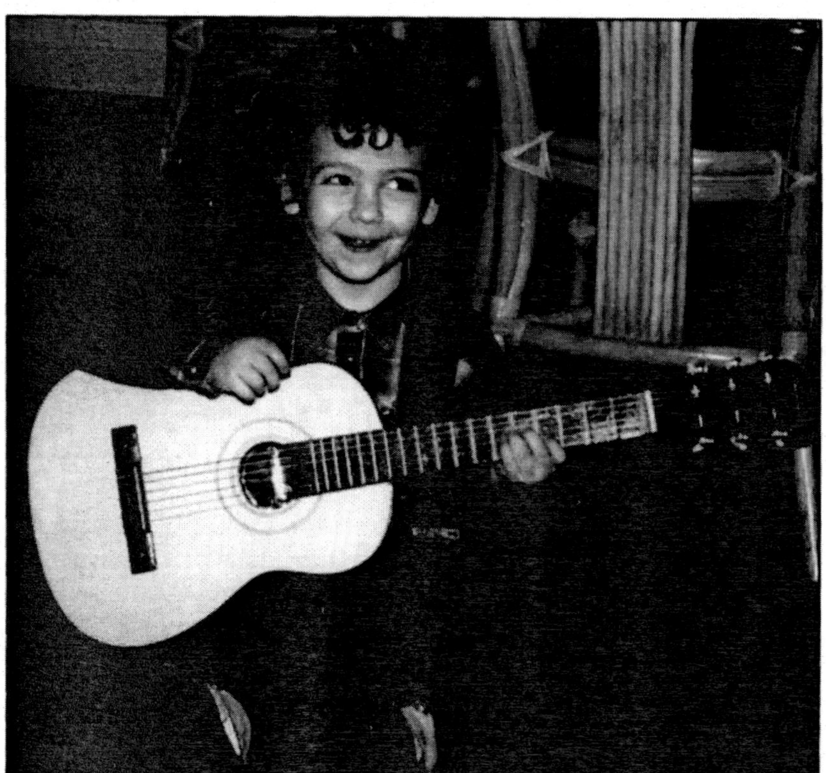

Pierre "Alix" Leguidcoq

PART A

Exercise 50 - melodic structure with the diminished scale

This exercise develops a melodic structure that is done with four combined intervals of the major second; all of these form the diagram with ascending steps. We should not refrain from joining it together with the diminished scale (or the dim7 arpeggio). As for the rest, this structure works in sections of eight notes that effectively makes it a complete diminished scale.

#59

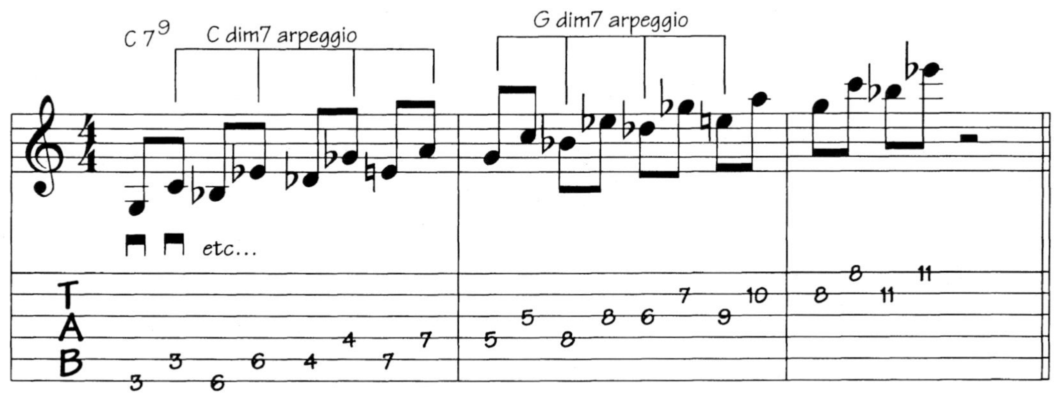

Notice that the start of the phrase is done with the fifth of the C7(9) chord, this chord is considered an Em7(b5) because we use this phrase to go, not toward the F major (by considering C7 as a V7), but toward the D major: by way of the II - V "Em7(b5) - A7 - D7M". In fact, the present harmonic structure is identical with that of the first measures of "Monticello", a preceding dominant chord, with a tone that is one step lower.

We can thus show you the following principle:

"The entire dominant chord can be used to introduce a major chord, where its fundamental is located one tone higher"

For example, as in the celebrated standard, "Night and Day", and done like the jazzmen and Manouche would play it:

|| B♭7(9) | % | C7M | % || instead of the "official feature: || Dm7(5♭) | G7(5♯) | C7M | % ||

This often provokes the indignety of certain jazzmen who, leaning on their pretenses of their theoretical knowledge and their immense culture, and who state in their destructive ways that Bb7(9) is wrong within this context. No, it is not wrong. In one part it sounds perfecty fine here, as well as in the other one, because Bb7(9) is just simply a different way to show Dm7(b5), which is a diatonic substitution - you should not forget this.

Conclusion: your musical ear and a sense of harmony doesn't necessarily require you to have a lot of knowledge. Certain musicians know how to play perfectly well by instinct and know how it must be played at that moment when it should be played, without ever having learned theory. Django was one of those musicians.

Exercise 51 - melodic layout/harmonic with cadences in fifths

Here is an exercise where it is only necessary to know two chord positions to play the lead with all its extensions. Besides playing arpeggios (as written), you could also play these strumming the chords (two chords per measure):

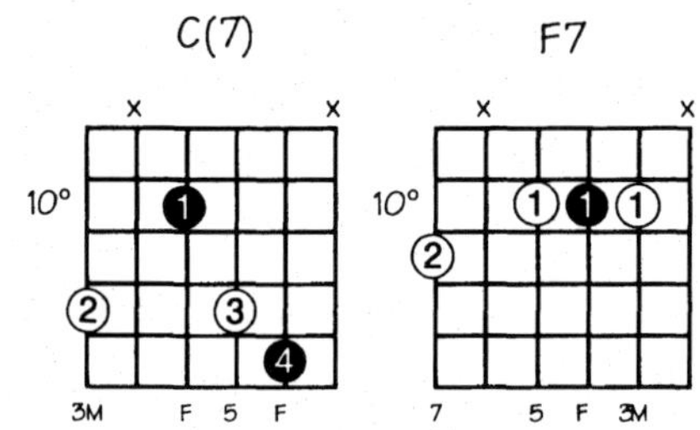

identical positions,(but transposed)
for all the other chords of the structure

#60

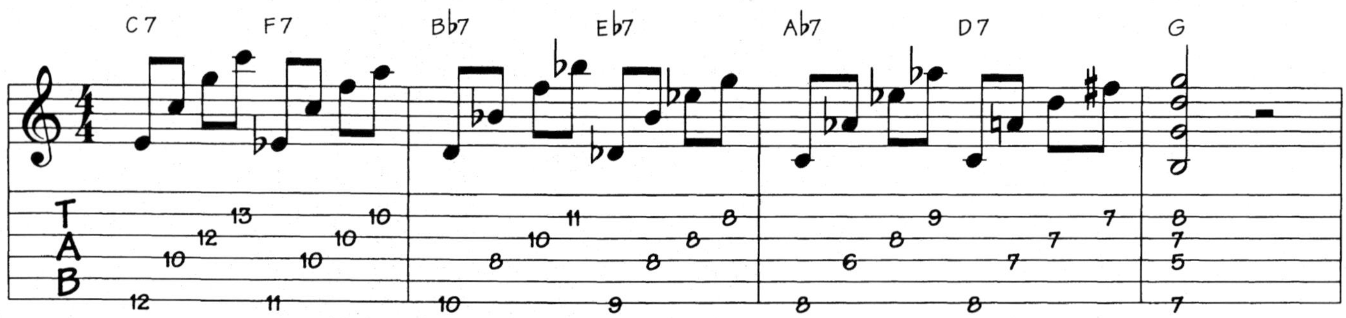

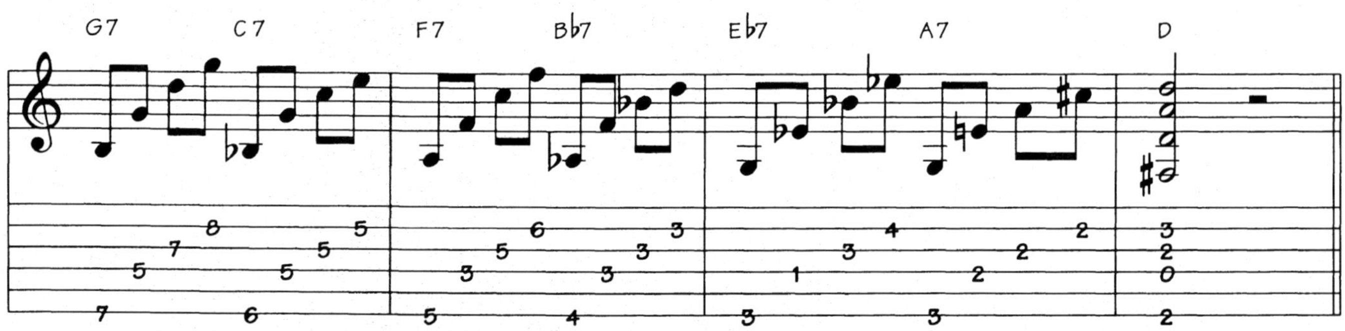

Exercise 52 - syncopated melodic structure with D7

The lead follows descending chromatics, which targets the root note and the fifth of the chord where it applies. The choice of the root note/fifth is not by chance (dominant → rootnote principle) and helps to form the rhythmic syncopation of this structure.

You can play this syncopated by simply playing each quarter note with a heavy beat.

#61

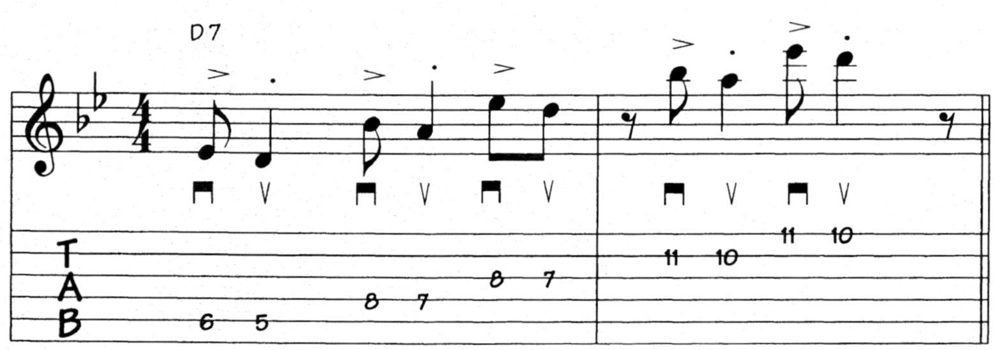

PART B1

THE TRITONE SUBSTITUTION

Well, here we are! Since we first talked about it, the moment has finally arrived to examine in detail, the theory and example, of the famous "tritone substitution" (T.S.).

First here are some preliminary details: the T.S., as it is called, is a harmonic concept all properly done in jazz (and actual assimilated music), one type of shortcut which, in a large measure, makes it easy to think globally within the proper jazz lingo - melodies, chords (improvised or not) - a shortcut that permits the creator marvelous choices with little to go by. In the Glossary a close definition has been given. Now here is the fundamental rule of the T.S.:

"All dominant seven chords (Type V7) can be replaced with a dominant seven chord (V7) of which the root note is seperated by three tones."

For instance, a B7 chord can be replaced with an F7 chord - and visa versa - the B (B7) and F (F7) are at a distance of three tones (or diminished fifth/augmented augmented fourth). You will notice that to reach the B note from the F note you count three tones up as well as downwards: in other words, the B notes divides the octave very precisely into two equal parts with three tones (from the low F to the high F). Or we can also say that the F note is exactly in the center of the octave that goes from the low B to the high B. And, of course, this works with all the "tritone" intervals that you can form with various notes of the music (G/Db, D/Ab, etc.).

Why can we replace the B7 with a F7, or F7 with a B7? Is this simply in accordance with this symetrical division of the octave?

No, there is a much more important reason for this. Examining the notes that make up the two chords, you will find:

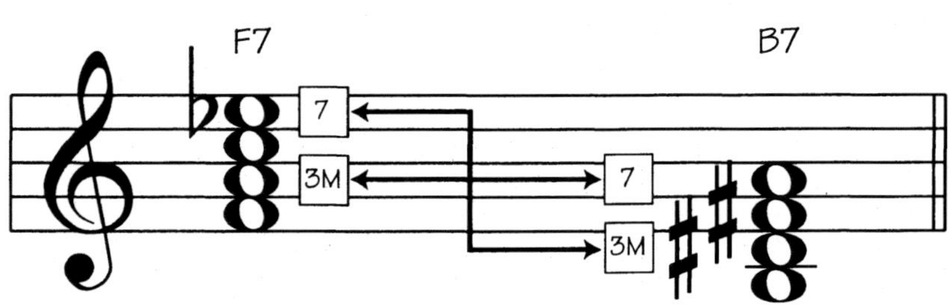

The characteristic notes of the first chord (the 3M and 7 = a dominant chord) are also the characteristic notes of the second, simply inversed, chord. These connections make the two chords interchangeable, and the T.S. relies on an extremely solid harmonic principle.

In passing, observe how the characteristic notes, 3M and 7, of any dominant seventh chord always form an interval of three tones: for F7, tritone A/Eb: for B7, tritone D#/A; in certain contexts, we even consider that this tritone is enough by itself to establish a dominant chord.

Now, what are the practical uses of the T.S.?

As you may have already noticed it in the preceding chapters, the T.S. shows up frequently in the harmony structure, in the analysis of the diagrams, the rhythm, and the coloration of the chords, within the structure of the melody: that is, improvisation phrases based on the tritone procedure, and the coloration of certain scales (whole tone, diminished).

To sum it up: the T.S. commonly governs the big lines of the musical composition in the measure where it is combined with other important concepts, such as the dominant principle → root note, the (major or minor) II - V - I progressions or the anatole, the diatonic substitutions, the rule of the II degree preceding the V degree, etc.

For instance, where we have a major II - V – I, where it is often the practice such as here:

|| Dm7 | G7 | C7M | ⁒ || → || Dm7 | D♭7 | C7M | ⁒ ||

tritone substitution: tritone between G and Db.

These can be translated into concrete terms with the following voicings (with basic chords or enriched ones):

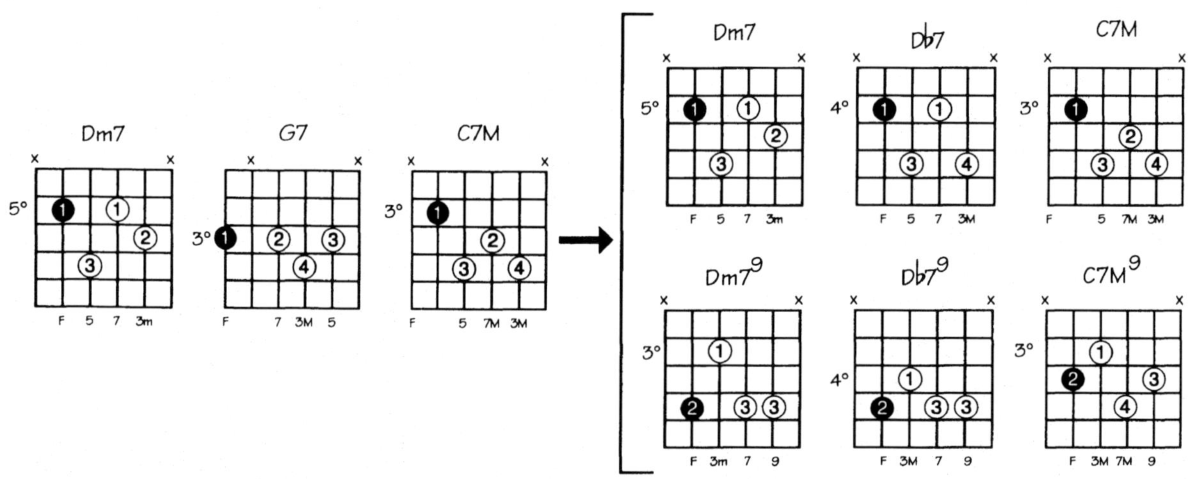

Of course, the T.S. can be applied where ever a dominant (V7) chord occurs. For instance, as with the II - V - I minor or the altered turnaround (= a turnaround with the VI7 degree, "dominanted"):

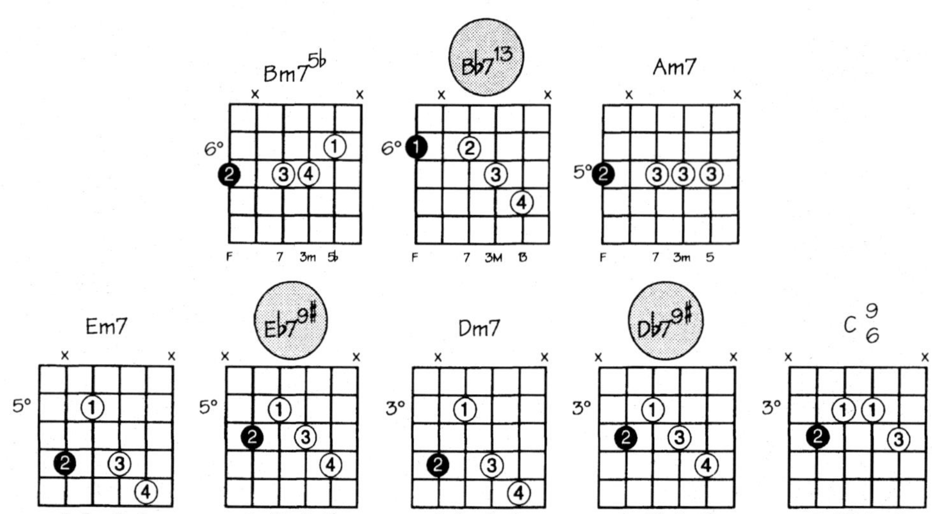

This can be used most places to construct improvised phrases. In chapter 16 (part 1) we will study the T.S.

PART B2

Let's go through and study the leads and diagrams that are used in section B of the "Monticello" chorus.

Monticello (measure 19) lead #5

Measure 19 shows an arpeggio of four notes based on the "7M" diagram, colored with a major thirteenth (13M, being the 7M + 6M - ★ notes).

The group of this phrase defines the E7M(13) harmony, an enriched harmony that conveniently uses the fundamental chords (I degree).

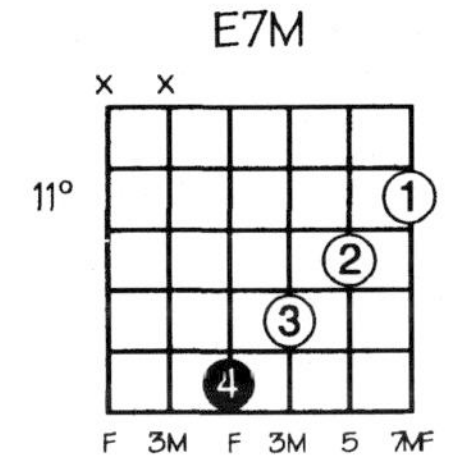

E7M arpeggio

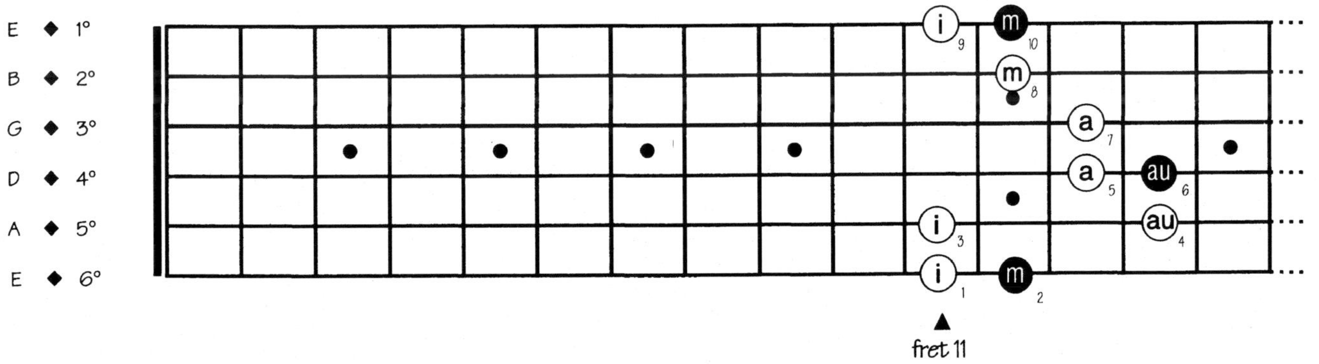

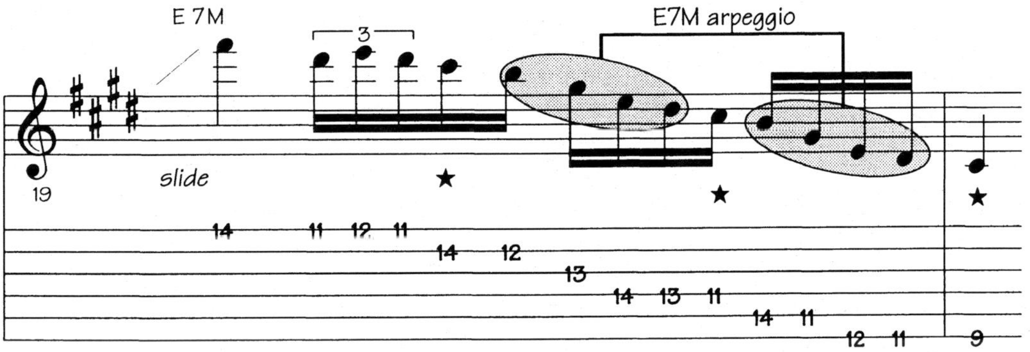

Chapter 15 / page 6

Monticello (measure 23) lead #6

This phrase, in sixteenth note triplets, relies on the following procedures: - the procedure, which uses the inversion rule that we have seen in chapter 14 (page 6).
This inversion rule is:

"All minor chords (II) can be followed by, or be mixed with, a dominant seventh chord (V7), or where its root note is one perfect fifth lower."

In the present case, the F#m7 chord (II) is therefore treated as a B7 (V7), not directly, but through our good friend the dim 7. This is the reason that it appeared at the beginning of the lead, the D#dim7 arpeggio, where the D#, F#, A and C notes respectively are the major third, the fifth, seventh and minor ninth of the B7 chord. The notes are perfectly adapted for this last reason.

--The phrase then links with the C minor arpeggio. A C minor with F#m7?

Yes. Do you remember the lead that we encountered in the chorus of "Jo's Remake" (Chapter 9, page 6), where the notes of Cm are played with the B7 chord? It is the same thing here, where we treat the F#m7 (harmony of the measure) as a B7, which conforms to the above stated rule.

Also notice the existing tritone relationship between Cm and F#. In reality, this part of the lead relies on the tritone substitution: B7 (for F#m7) / F7 (for Cm); between B and F, as well as between C and F#, all of these are three tones apart.

- Next, the phrase goes back down again, following the Cm chord diagram, by using all the melody recourses possible with that diagram. And finally, the phrase takes off towards the higher notes of the guitar, using once more the dim7 arpeggio. In the Adim7 arpeggio, the A, C, D# and F# are respectively the seventh, minor ninth, major third and fifth of the B7 chord, which finally surfaces in measure 24.

Again, notice the efficiency of the dim7 arpeggio to evolve toward the high register.

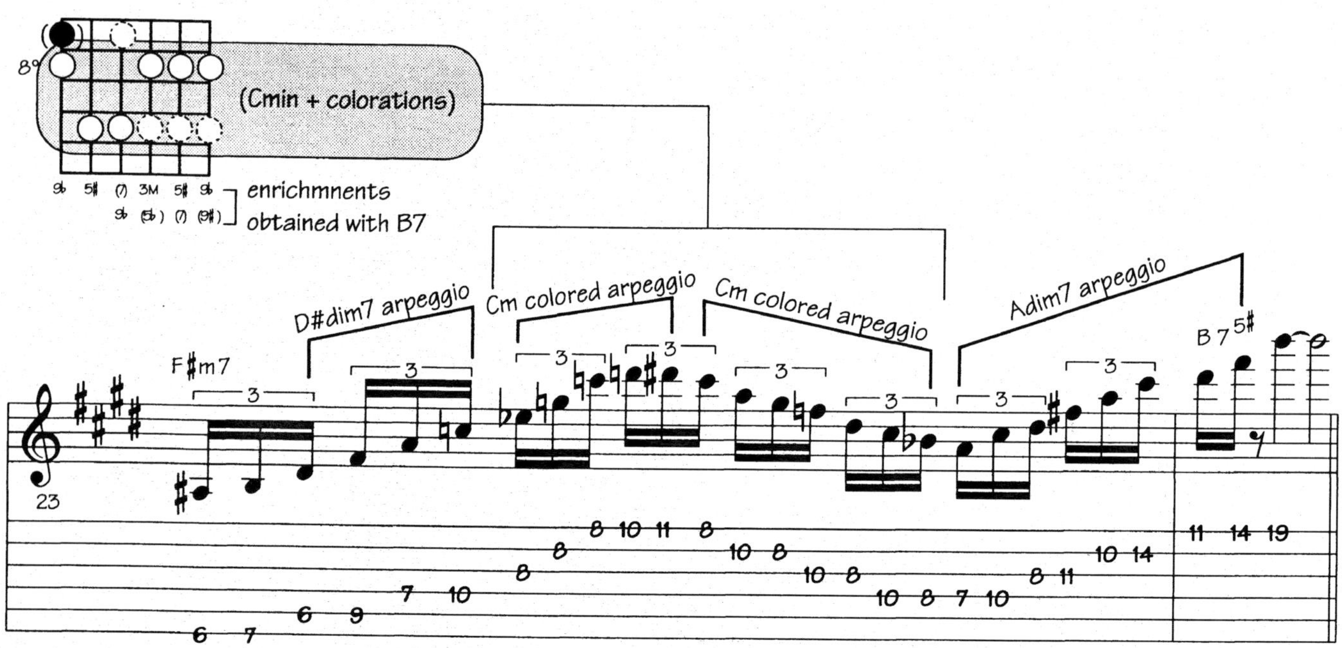

To sum it up, this excerpt is nothing more than a succession of four juxtaposed diagrams: the dim7 arpeggio + the minor ascending arpeggio + the minor descending arpeggio + the dim7 arpeggio.

PART C

Here is the continuation of the "Monticello" chorus, Section B.

In measure 17, the rhythm notation may seem strange to you. This is because the improvised phrase here has an eighth note triplet on two separate beats, that are syncopated and framed by two sixteenth note triplets.

By following the example of other phrases that we will see later in the chorus (chapter 16), it has to do with a free flowing fickle effect of the melody, a little like the image of automobile traffic during peak hours, an effect which fits perfectly in place with a slow beat (for a ballad) such as the one in "Monticello."

Listen to the CD to get the best feel for these phrases.

#56

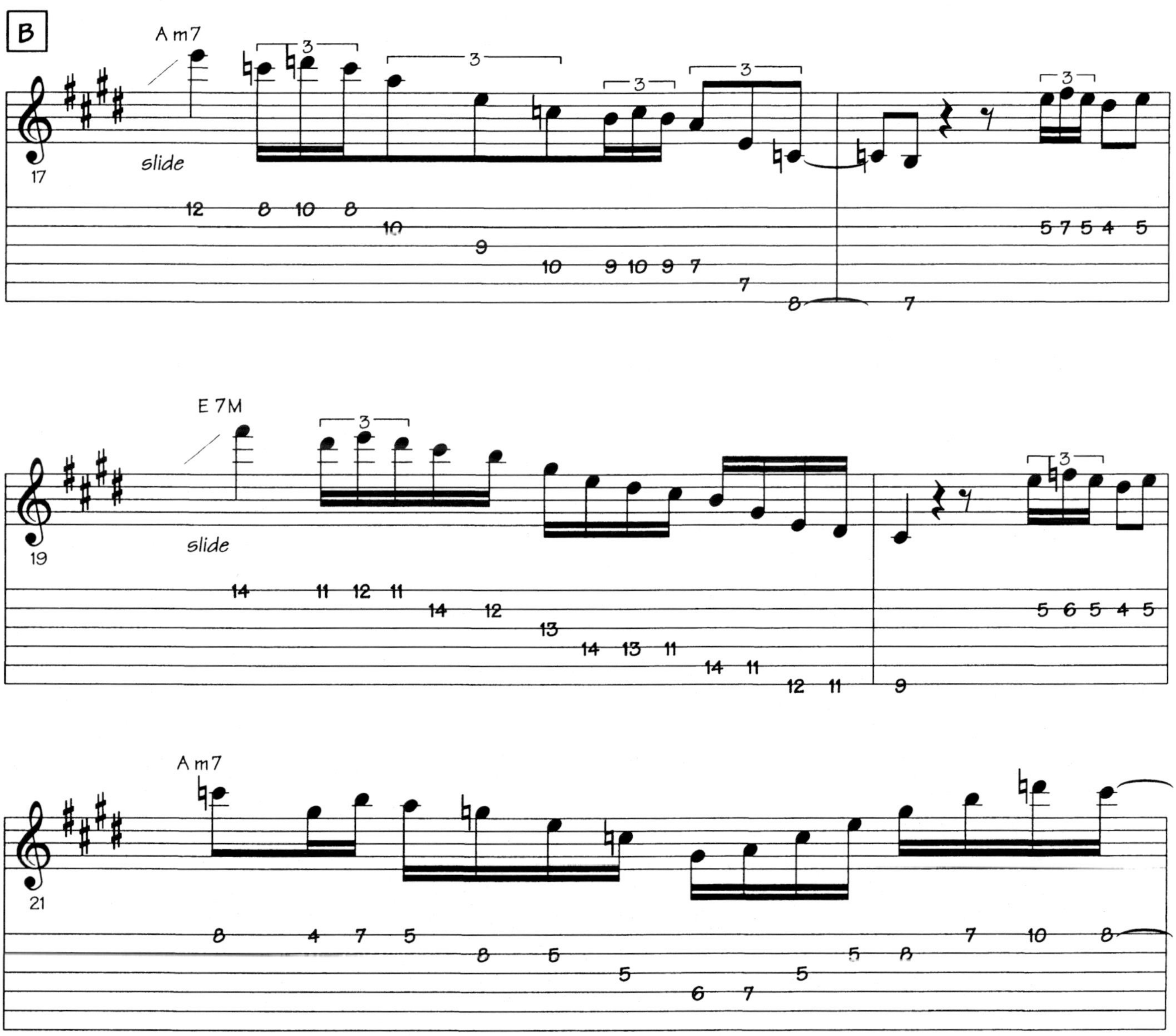

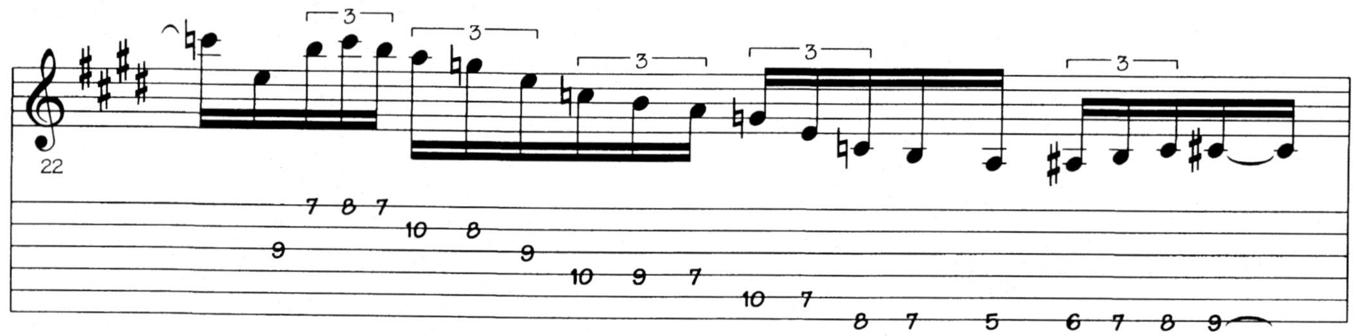

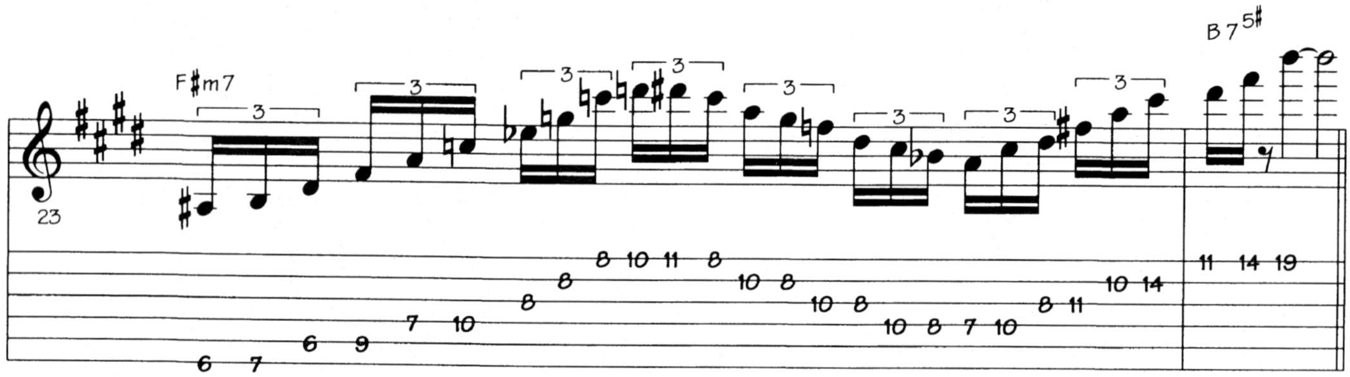

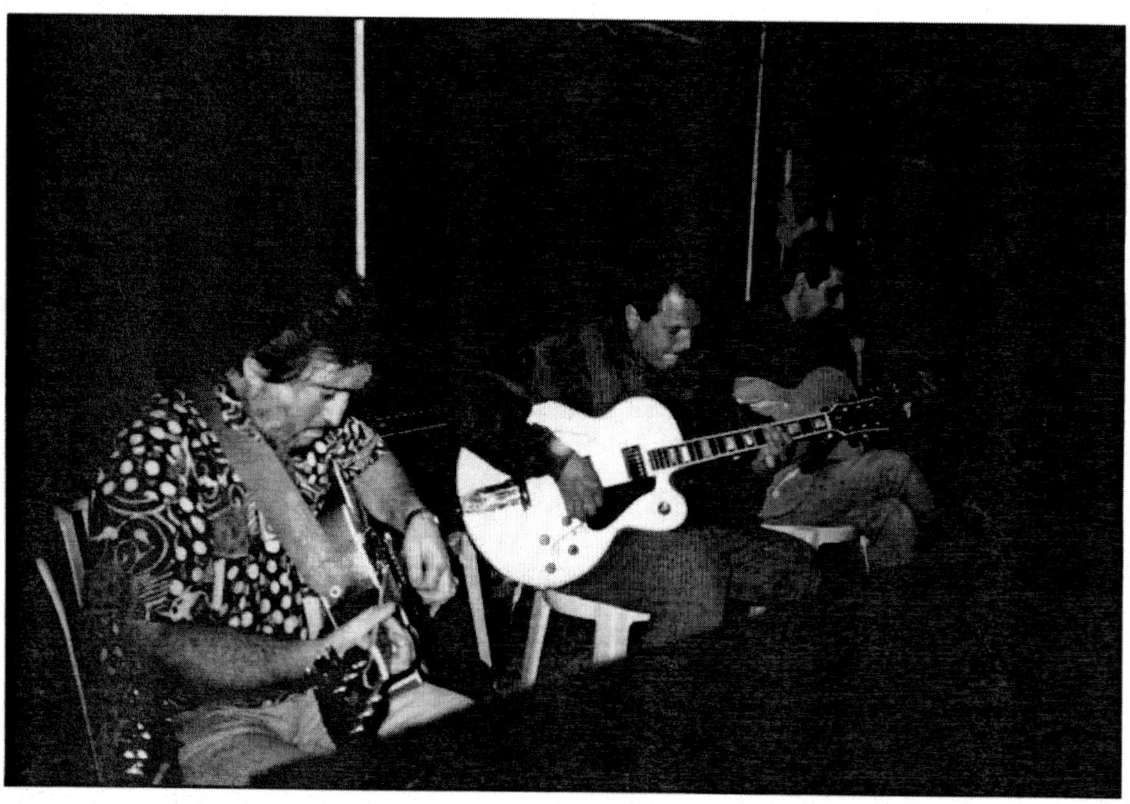

Patrick Saussois, Stochelo Rosenberg, Romane

PART A

Exercise 53 and 54 - Tritone phrases resolvent with the C chord

With the subject of the tritone substitution, and in the area of the dominant → root note principle, we have two very interesing phrases that combine the G and Db major arpeggios. Two tritone phrases, of course, since the G and D notes are three tones apart from each other.

The first phrase uses exclusively major triads:

#62

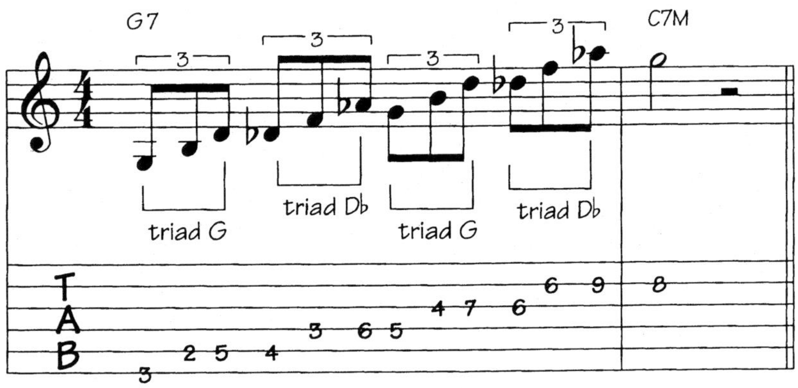

Here, the combination of the G and Db triads is for effect, for the enrichment of the harmony that we have here (G7), with the "11#" (Db notes) harmonic colorations and "9b" (Ab notes), which gives it a codified harmonic sound with the global G7(9b,11#) chord.

The second phrase uses major triads raised by a major second (2M):

#63

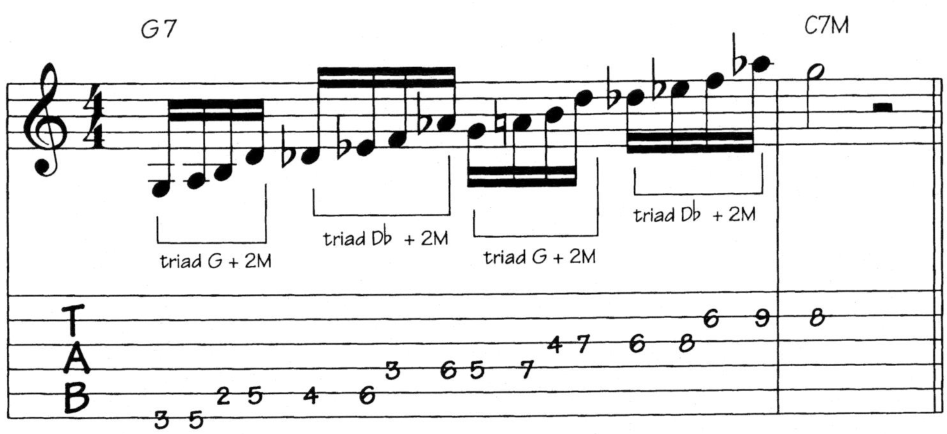

This time, the addition of the 2M (Eb notes) in the Db major triad determines the global G7(b9,11#,b13) harmony.

Finally, while being on the subject of resolving with the fifth of the C chords (G note) in each case, you will notice the triplets, with double eighths (a necessity to keep the time).

Exercise 55 - Tritone phrase resolved with the G chord

When using the T.S. principle, we can have another resolvent phrase, where the dominant seventh of the harmony is tritonely treated: the Ab major triad with the D7 chord (the Ab/D interval = three tones).

The resulting sound is that of the D7(b9,#11), as before.

#64

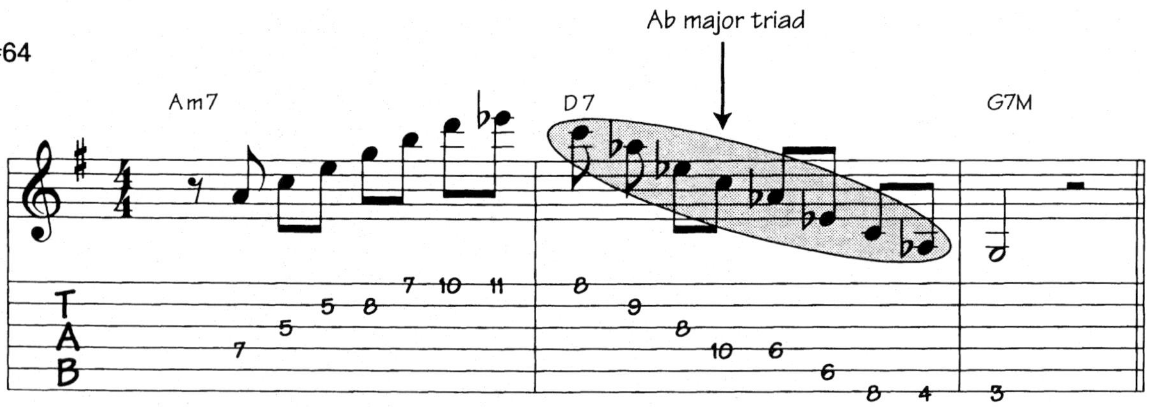

Exercise 56 - Resolvent tritone phrase with a turnaround in G

Taken from the direct source of the American jazz jargon, "turn around" is a general term which is used to make up various harmonic progressions that are based on the 'altered 'anatole, that is to say, on the anatole of which its "V" degree is "dominatized" (VI7). Editor's note: anatole = turnaround.

The present turnaround is called a "Be-Bop turnaround", for the simple reason that American jazzmen of the Be-Bop period (in the 1940's) are the ones that developed it.

Here is a melody based on the Be-Bop turnaround in the key of G major, which makes use of the major triad raised with a major second. The T.S.s are encircled.

#65

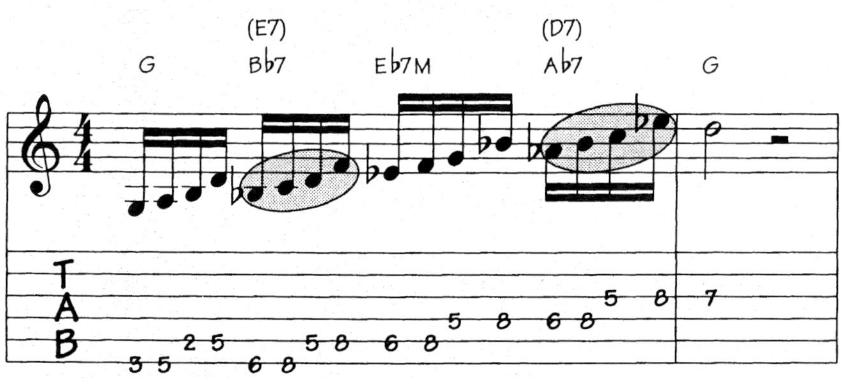

PART B1

THE TRITONE SUBSTITUTION (continued)

By going through the exercises presented in this chapter, you may begin to recognize, that when you use a T.S. to enrich the initial chord, for example, replacing the G7 with Db7, it returns as a G7(b9,#11).

But what happens if we decide to color a substitution chord – being substituted by, for example, a Db7(9) for the initial G7 chord?

It will always be around a T.S., of course, with the differ-nce that this operation should have an effect of coloring the intial chord in some other way:

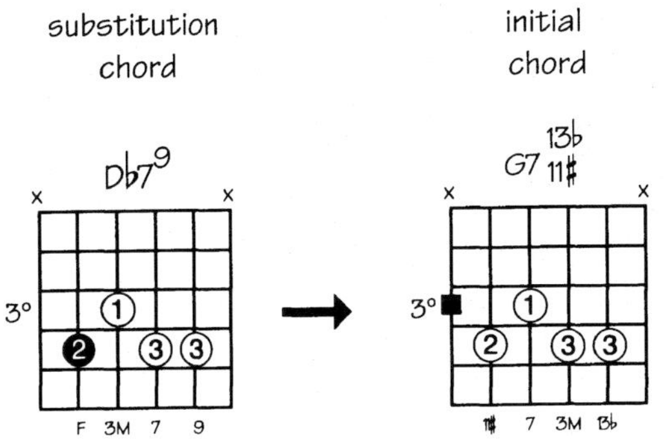

Here the initial G7 chord sees its root note and its perfect fifth removed at the cost of the two interesting harmonic colorations: "#11" (Db note, root note of Db7) and "13" (Eb note, the ninth of Db7).

Notice in the passage that the presence of the root note and the perfect fifth is not required to characterize a chord. On the other hand, with the third and seventh must be present.

And if we color the initial chord, we will get another case again, all being tritone substitutions. For example, we heighten the initial G7 with a thirteenth major (13M).

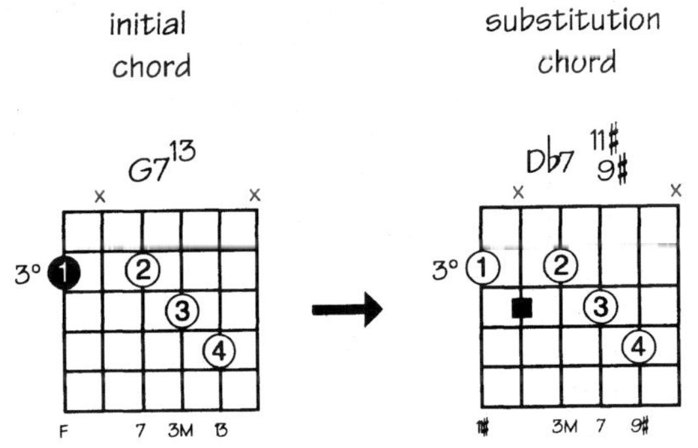

Then the Db7 sees itself being enriched by "#11" (the G note of G7) and the "#9" (the E note of G7), its fundamental and its perfect fifth that is being suppressed at the expense of these colorations.

Now, there are certain cases that deserve to be shown, in particular the cases that show the same harmonic symbols that are spaced three tones apart.

Without a doubt, you are already familiar with the dim7 chord, which we can analyze as a "7(b9)" chord (chapter 2 /page 4):

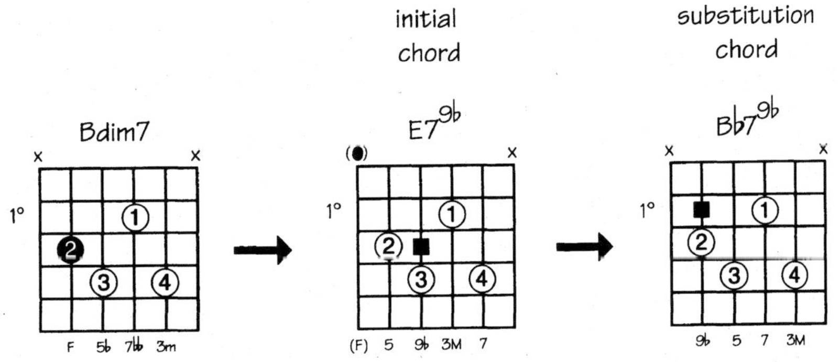

Another particular case, that of the 7(b5) chord that in addition of the 3M and 7, F and 5b, corresponds precisely by itself.

As in the case with the 7(b9) chord, the guitar positions are evidently indentical, which is convenient.

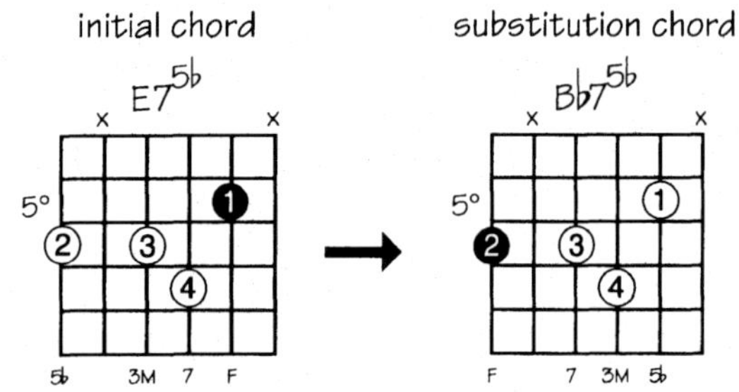

The third and last particular case (more or less in the category of the chords with four distinct sounds -- being the most manageable and mostly used) offers a strange harmonic sound which has only been entered lately in the harmonic vocabulary of jazz. It has to do with the 7(#9,13) chord:

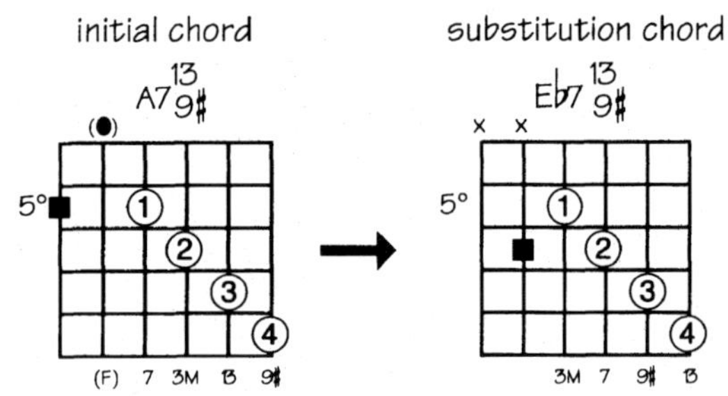

This being the case, it is not rare to encounter the extrapolations, when it is executed around the T.S., in such a way that it creates harmonic progression voicings with a resolvent vocation.

Here is one of those voicings, used the most in jazz:

It relies on a succession of tones and half tones (diminished scale) produced by the highest note of each of the chords, which are all dominant chords, with the exception of the last one, which resolves into the (I degree).

Besides, this voicing gives its all when it is produced over a low "pedal", which will always be expressed as the dominant (V7) of the chosen key.

In other words, if you resolve in A (major or minor), the pedal must be an E (the fundamental of the V degree, of the degree "with the dominant"), as shown in the example below:

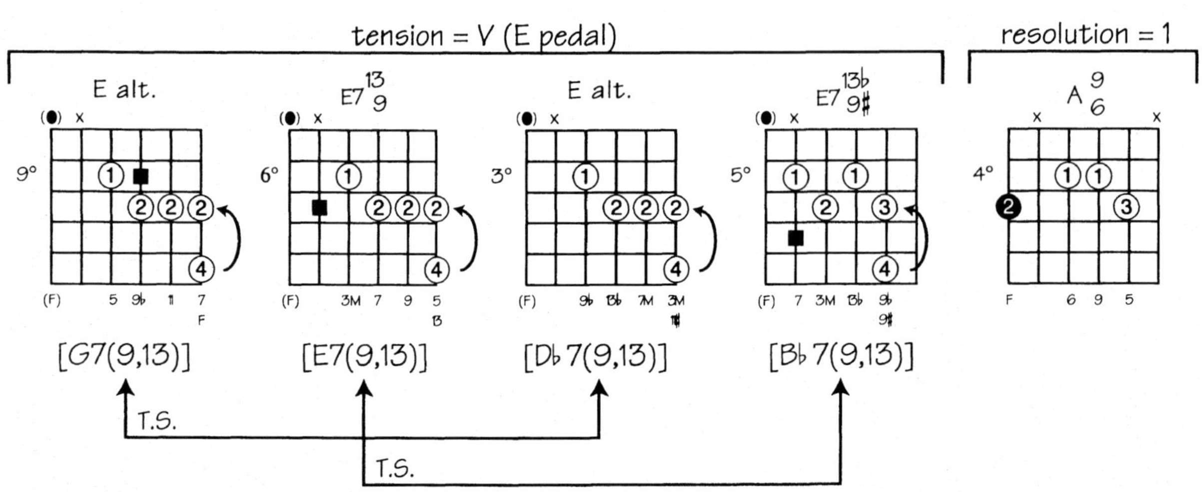

PART B2

We will now examine the leads from the last part of the chorus of "Monticello".

Monticello (measures 27 - 28) explaining the melody (#1 b is procedure)

The use of natural harmonics at the seventh fret colors the harmony with a certain depth. The procedure here is exactly the same as in measures 3 – 4 at the beginning of the chorus (chapter 14, page 5). We are concerned with the precise technique of these harmonics: these are done with the little finger of the left hand.

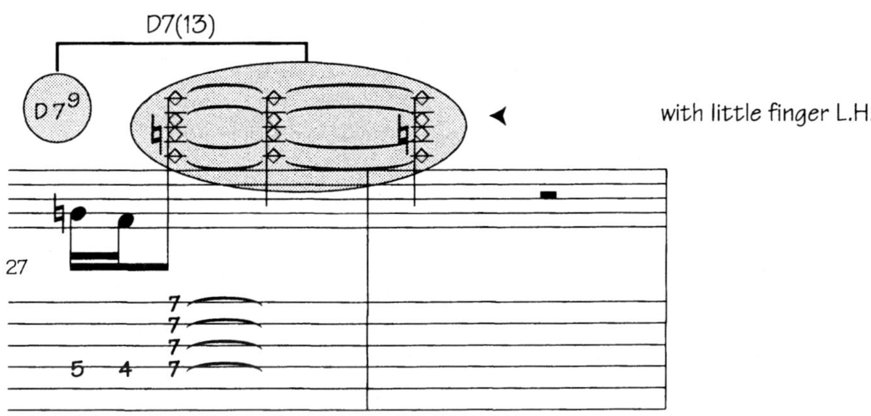

Monticello (measures 29 - 30) lead #7

In the "7M" chord diagram, that we previously studied (in chapter 15, page5), we have a vocabulary phrase that is often used with jazz improvisors. By building a body with the "7M" arpeggio as a basis, this phrase is built with a rhythm cell of three elements (note + silence + note), it is syncopated, and can be repeated in sequence as many times as desired. This procedure is used to create an unusual and interesting "syntax" effect that grasps the audiences attention:

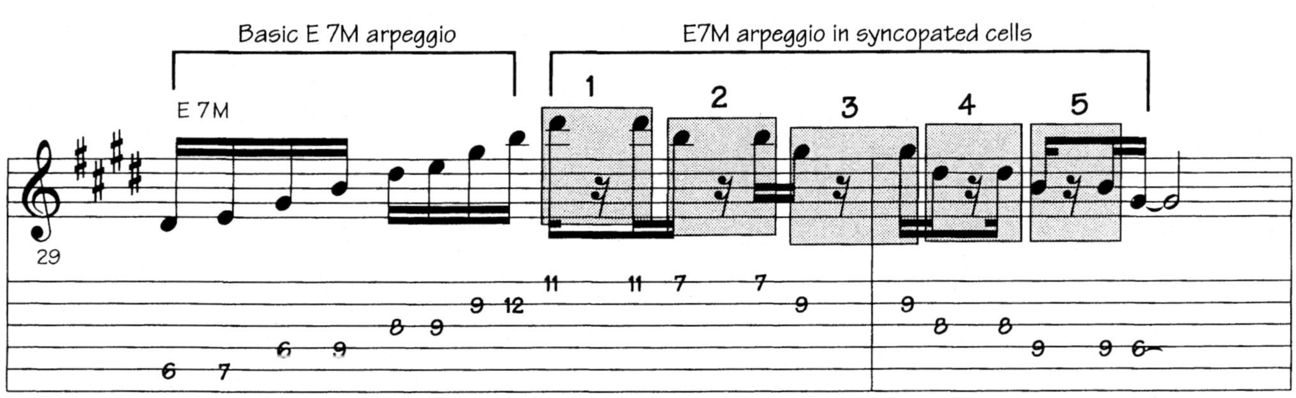

This demonstrates all the creative possibilities of the rhythm for a structured, improvised melody - an aspect that should never be neglected!

Monticello (measures 35 - 36) lead #7 and #8

Here is a "sweeping" lead that perfectly represents the Be-Bop style, a lead that at this point leaves the common vocabulary of all the jazzmen of today, who would have been sorry to discriminate against the Manouche!

It's very simple, and based on the perfect minor chord diagram:

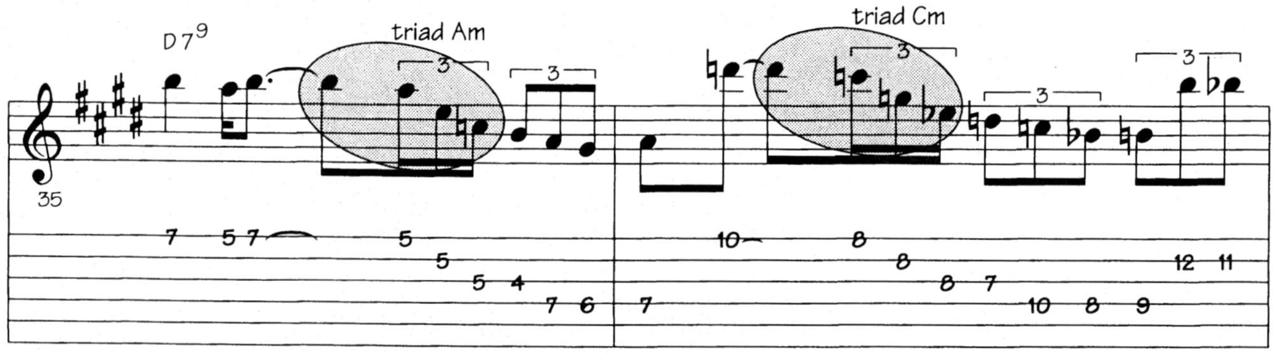

We see that the first of these sweeps calls for the principle mentioned on page 6, chapter 14, that is to "think / play" in terms of the II degree with a V type chord (Am triad of the D7 chord.)

As for the second sweep, it only centers moderately around the harmony that we are looking at now (the G note is ambiguous with D7), it's no less convincing for the good and simple reason that it brings the answer to the question that should have been asked with the first sweep, the "mirror" effect.

Besides, the linkage of minor triads separated with minor thirds (Am → Cm = 1 tone and a half), is a statement that barely touches the surface the dim7 chords.

So it isn't rare to hear, that with various improvisors, these sweeps continue from minor third to minor third (sweep Am → sweep Cm → sweep Ebm → sweep Gbm), to form a longer phrase which is convincing with the given harmony (D7). Try it...

Monticello (measures 39 - 40) lead #9

Finally, following the example of measures 14 - 15 (chapter 14, page 6), the chorus is completed with the E6 chord diagram in combination with the pentatonic E major scale (★ notes) to complete it. The ending should be thought of as diatonically descendent (diatonic = a succession of tones and half tones, forming the major scale in the majority of cases):

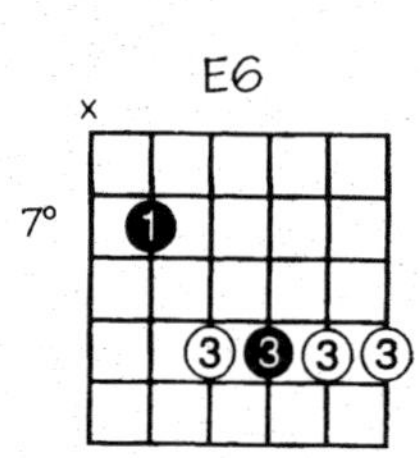

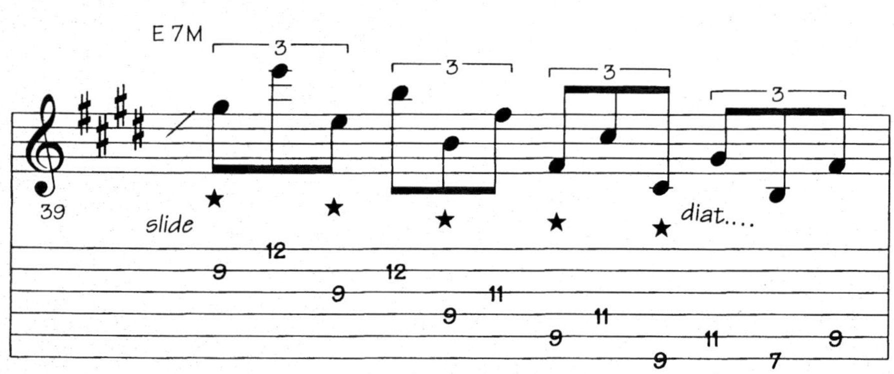

PART C

Here are the last six measures of the "Monticello" chorus. We have numerous ascending slides that increases the value of the melodic speech. Don't neglect these.

#56

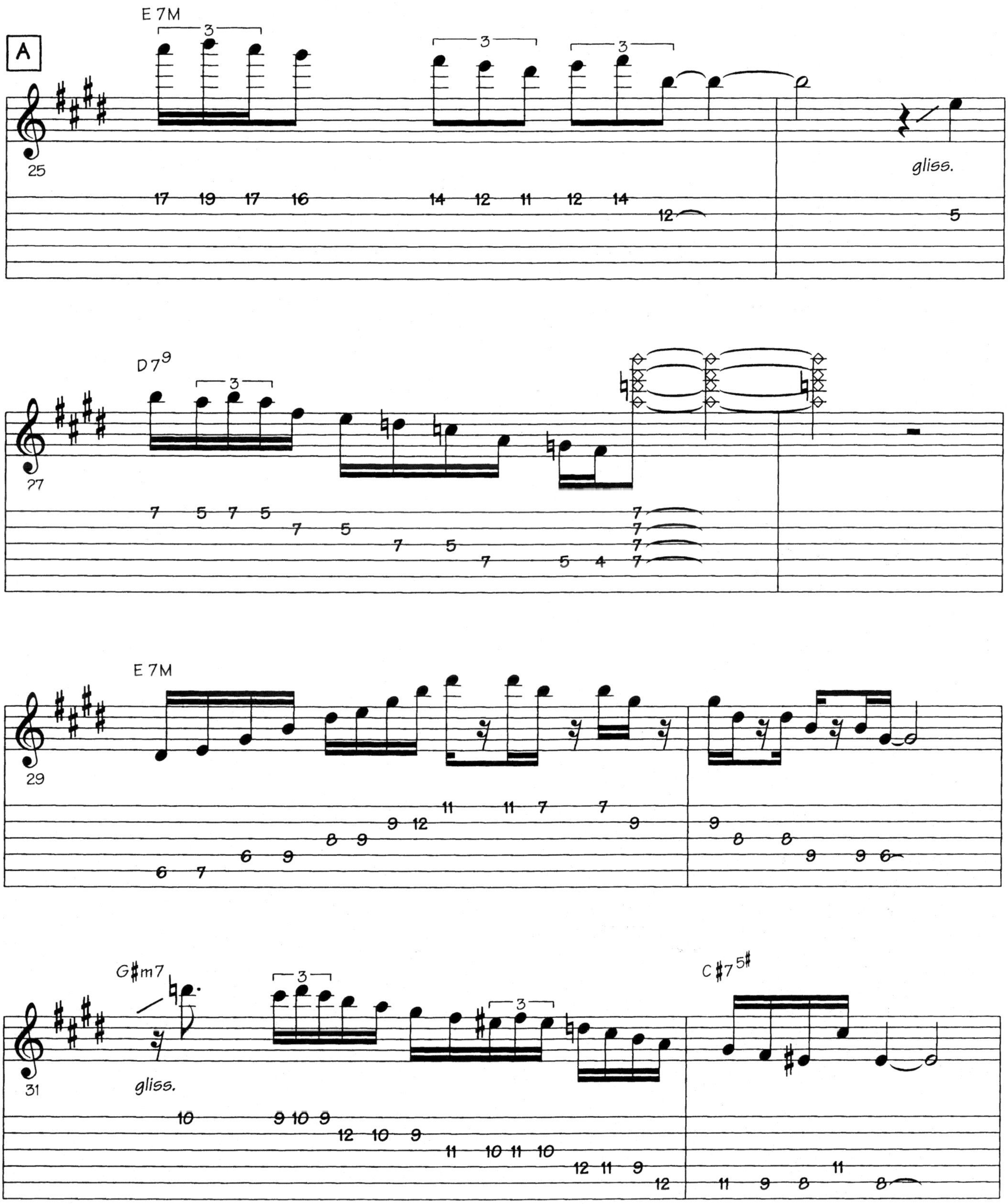

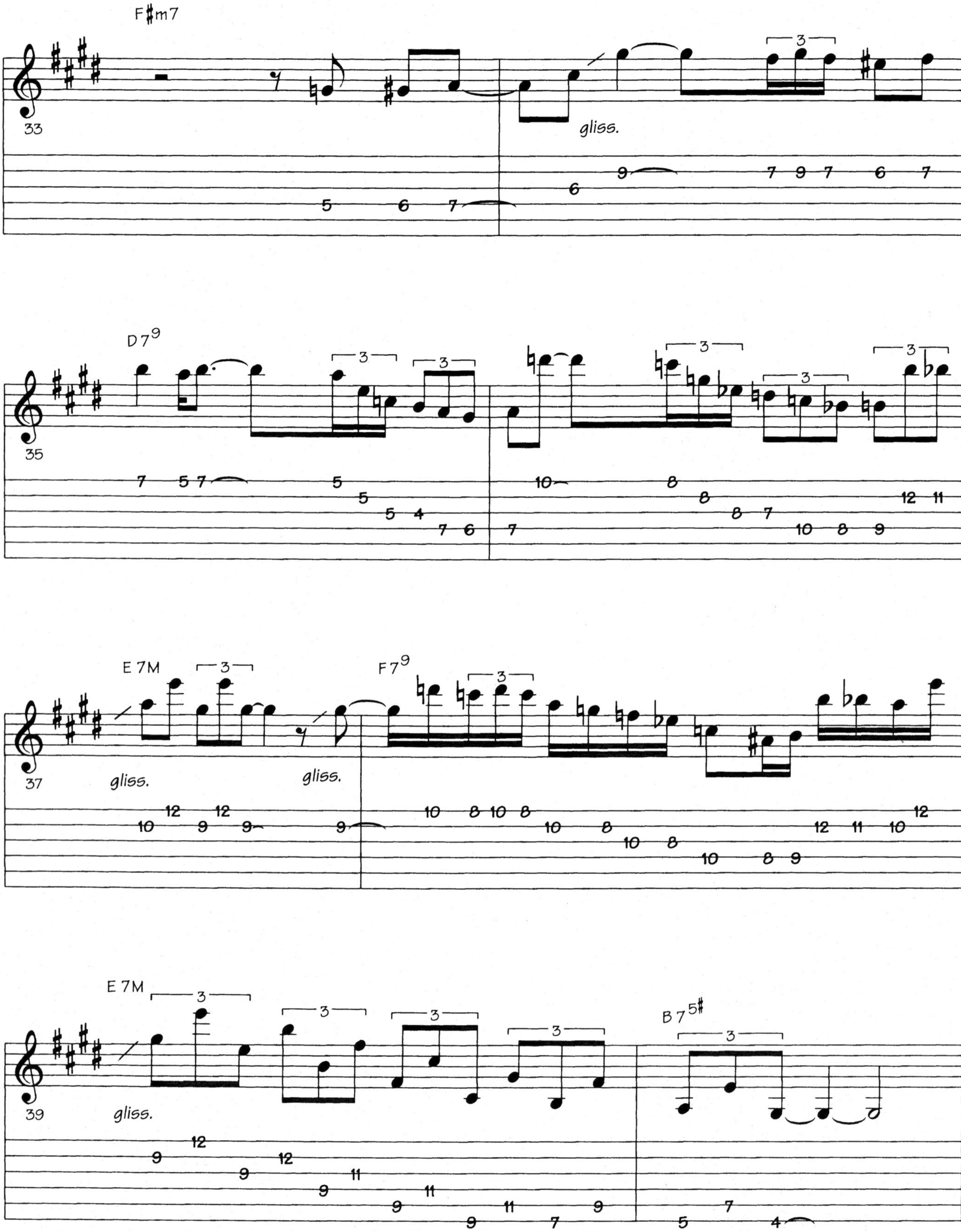
F♯m7
gliss.
D7 9
E 7M
gliss.
gliss.
F7 9
E 7M
gliss.
B 7 5♯

PART A

Exercise 57 - bi-tonal phrase with major triads of D7 (1)

In exercises 53 and 54 (in chapter 16) we had the experience of using these interesting phrases that could be constructed in combination with perfect major chords. And, with the illustration of the tritone substitution principle, these previous exercises combined major triads that are three tones apart.

Now we are going to see how it is possible to work out phrases that are as seductive in combination with the major triads that are one tone apart.

This generates, with the harmony (as below, D7), interesting colorations. It has the incompairable advantage to formulate, with a succession of notes, an unsurpassed optimal quality of the music, that is to say, the music quality of the 'perfect' major chord:

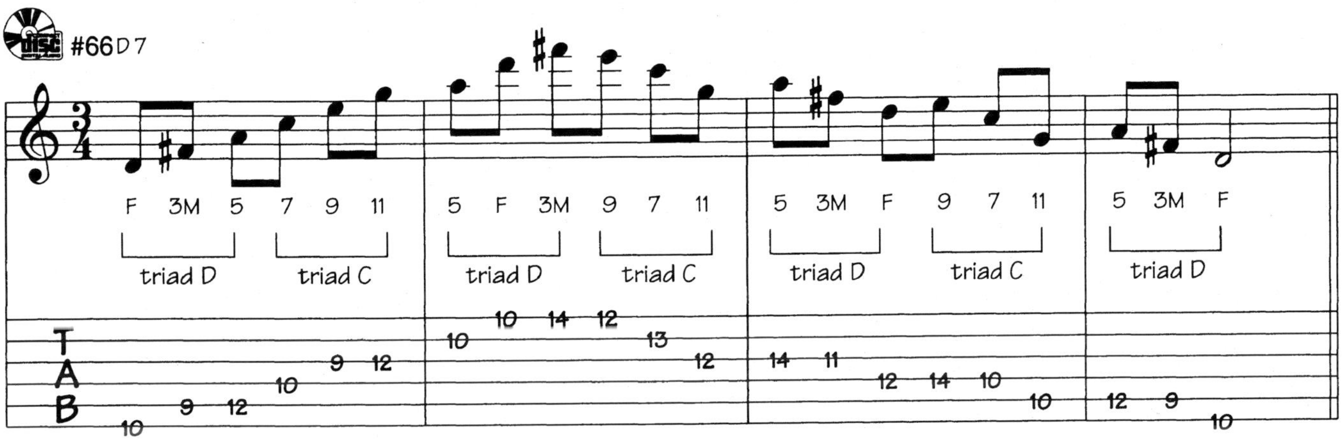

To visualize the fingerboard use the following diagrams. Play the notes in an increasing numerical order:

Bi-tonality with D7, ascending phase.

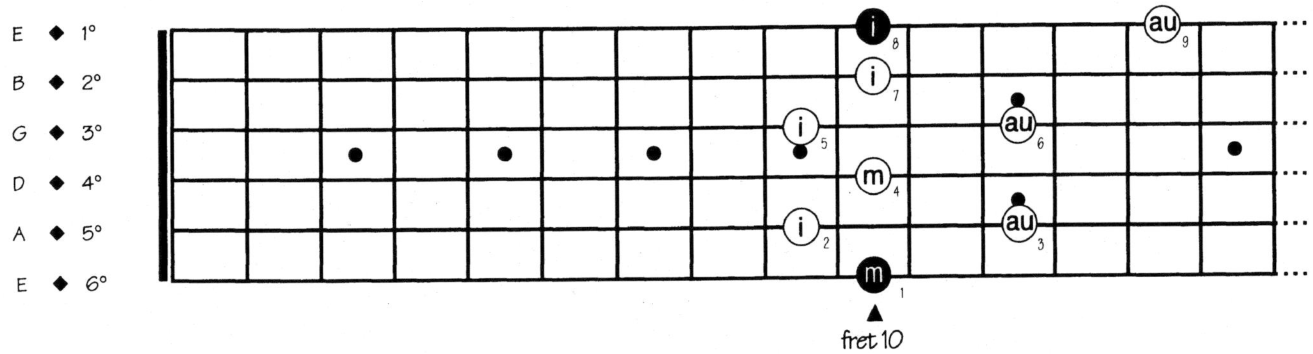

Bi-tonality with D7, descending phase.

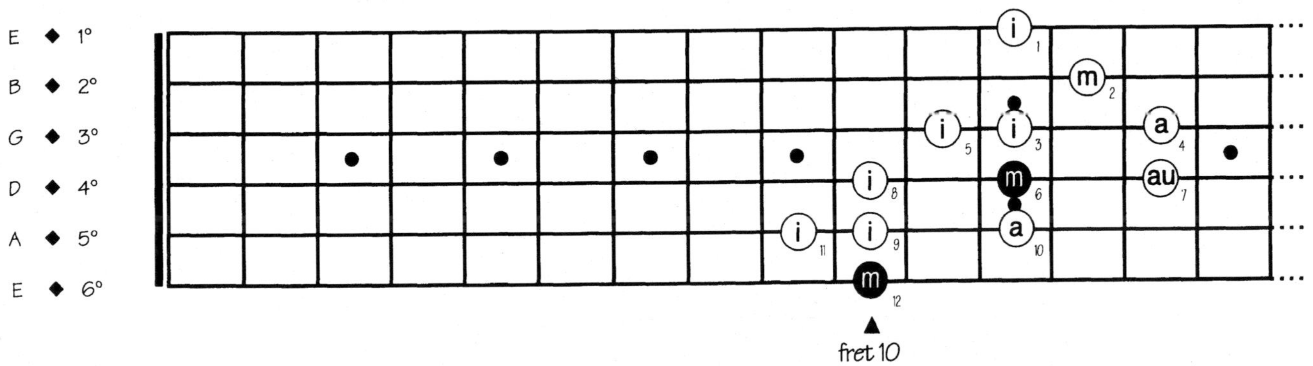

Exercise 58 - bi-tonal diagrams with major triads (C and D)

In view of working out phrases with bi-tonal improvisations that are compared with those of exercise 57, it is indispensible to adequately visualize the fingerboard of the guitar and the diagrams of the major triads (chord positions).

For this reason we give you the major triads of C and D major, which are the diagrams that will be of help to you.

Start by connecting these diagrams together in the form of chords (simultaneous notes).

Afterwards do the same by making arpeggios of the notes. Of course, develop the low register toward the high register, and reverse it.

To repeat it again, learn to combine those two diagrams of one group of chords with the other into one diagram (high to medium high, and visa versa).

#67

Major triads of C and D, alternately linked together - higher strings.

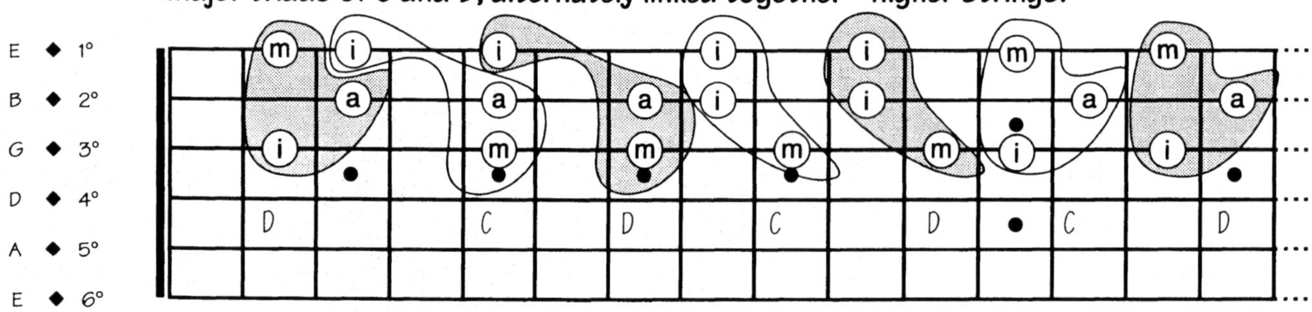

Major triads of C and D, alternately linked together - medium high strings.

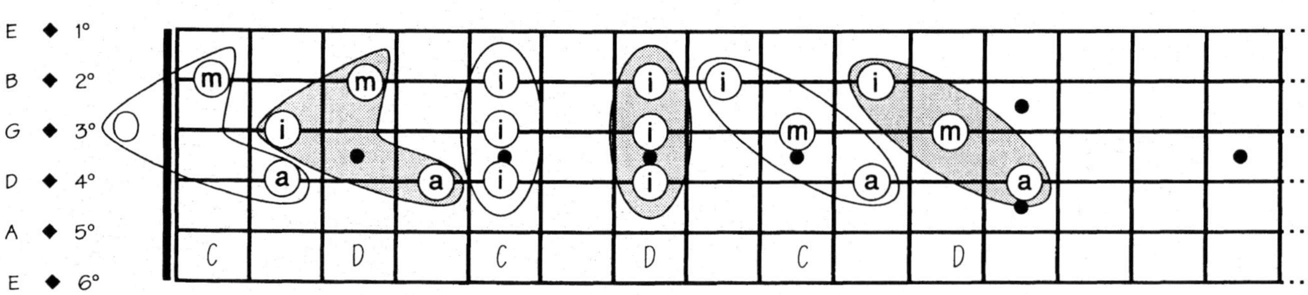

PART B1

The new Manouche theme that we are going to use is called "Destinee", and you can hear it on the Romane Quintet CD.

Here is the harmonic block diagram of this theme:

Destinée

structure = 48 measures AABBAA

♩= 240

A	Am	%	Gm	%	$B\flat7^{5\flat}$	%	Am	E7
A'	6 // (6 measures)						Am	%
B	Dm	%	Fm	%	Am 9/6	Am 9/6 / Cm 9/6	Am 9/6	%
B'	4 // (4 measures)				$E7^{9\flat}$	%	%	%
A	Am	%	Gm	%	$B\flat7^{5\flat}$	%	Am	E7
A'	6 // (6 measures)				⊕		Am	%
				⊕ FIN	$B\flat7^{5\flat}$	%	Am	

For its recognizeable swing groove and particular harmonic structure, "Destinee" is written more in the exact style of Manouche.

Its structure is a little closer to a standard structure: 48 measures using two A and B sections.

In the absence of a specified time signature, it is of course in 4/4 time – thus the harmonic flow is relatively light. In regards to the speed it is played at, it is "up" tempo, although it can be played much faster.

Now let's look at the rhythm chords for "Destinee".

Attention: if you look at the melody you will see that the chord positions are slightly unusual. This is because the solo guitarist must tune the sixth string one tone lower (drop D tuning). Later on you will discover the reason for this non-conventional way to play the chords.

Section A (solo guitarist - chording in low D):

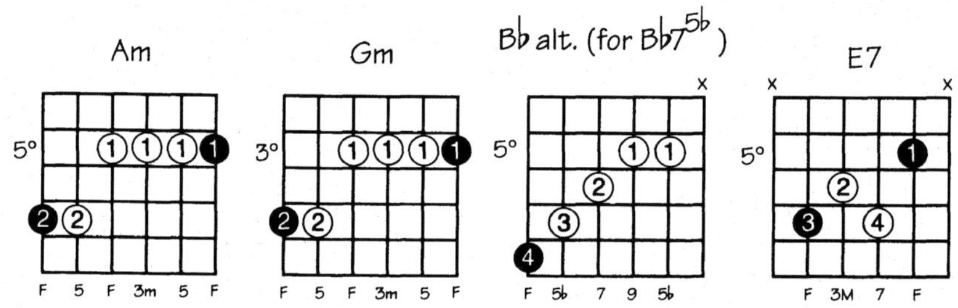

Section A (guitar accompaniment – standard tuning):

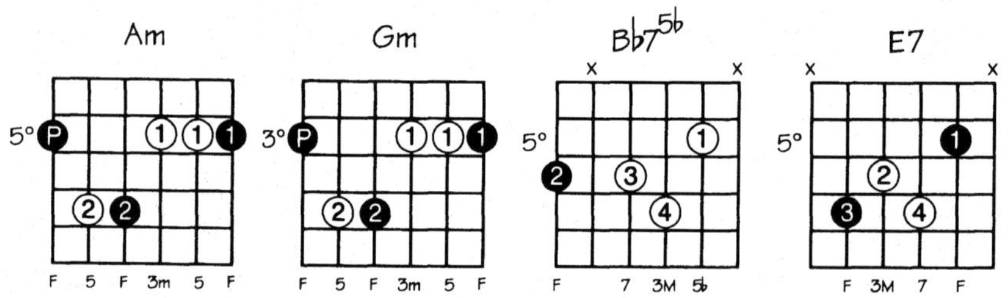

Section B (solo guitarist):

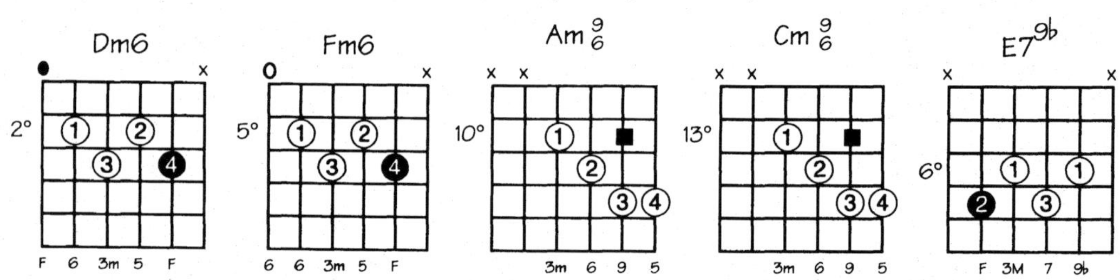

Section B (rhythm guitars):

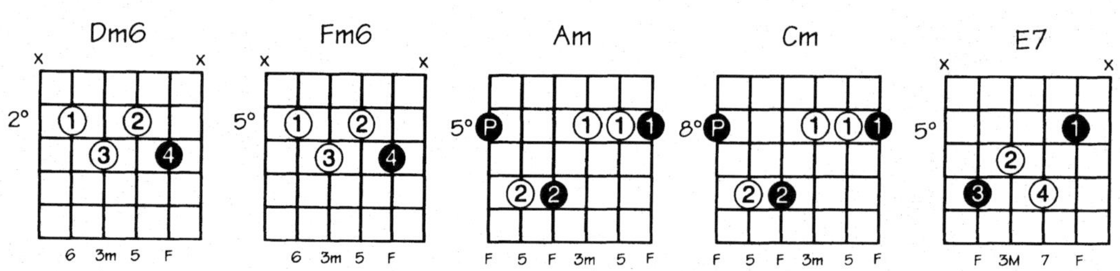

Coda- end (rhythm guitars):

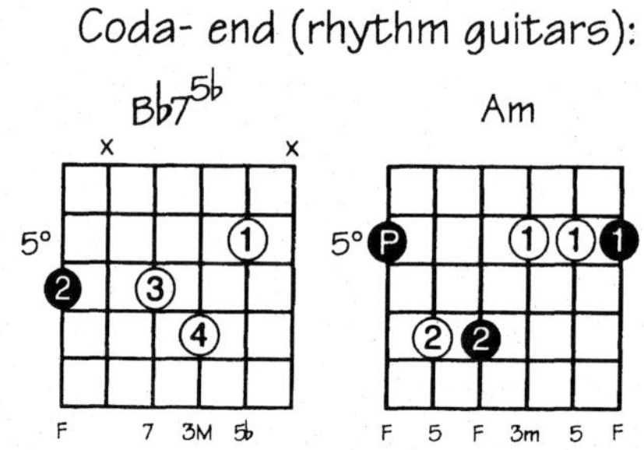

PART B2

Let's examine the melody of "Destinee."

Destinee - general explanation of the melody

As previously mentioned, the guitarist has to play chords with the 6th string tuned to the lower D.

This is not, of course, a fantasy of Manouche, but it is simply because the composer plays the melody in a lower register, out of the usual range of the instrument.

You can see a lower D in the phrases of the B section (measures 17 - 20 and 25 – 28.) In the melody of this theme the depth of this note and those that are connect with it becomes stronger; this will establish a little mysterious ambiance, bound with the idea of "Destinee" (fate/destiny). It's up to you to decide.

Whatever it may be, pay careful attention to the fingering tablature used to play the notes on the 6th string.

Destinee - lead #1 and #2

The key phrases of the melody have to be interpreted with the placements of the accents, the articulations and the precise attacks of the pick in such a way that you can establish a suitable "groove".

Here are the two key phrases for section A:

(1)

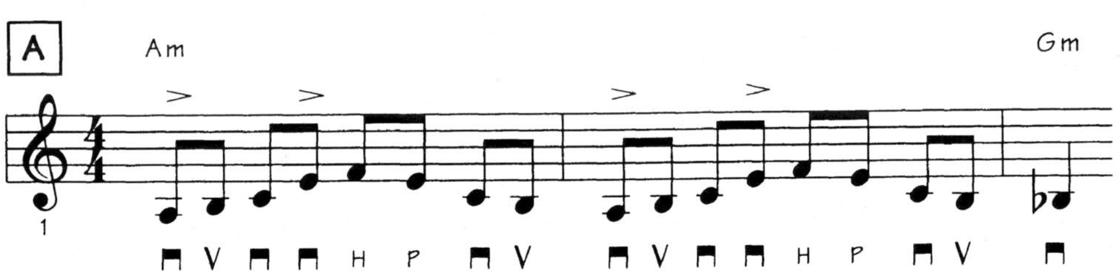

(2)

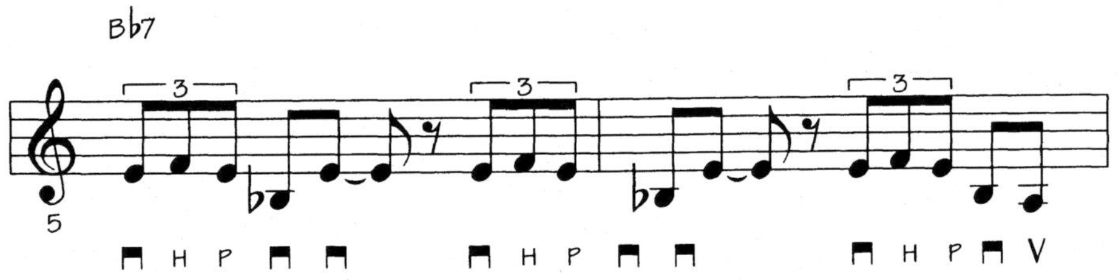

Notice the placement of the accents (>) on the lower and higher notes, which is a good way to mark the ambitus of the melody (here a perfect fifth). Notice also that the hammer/pull (HP) is always done after a down stroke of the pick.

The "ambitus" = a distance, counted in intervals, between the highest and lowest note of a given melody (or part).

Destinee - lead #3

In regard with the key of the phrase of the B sections, where the famous lower D and notes on the 6th string (circled) are, here are some techniques that must be employed:

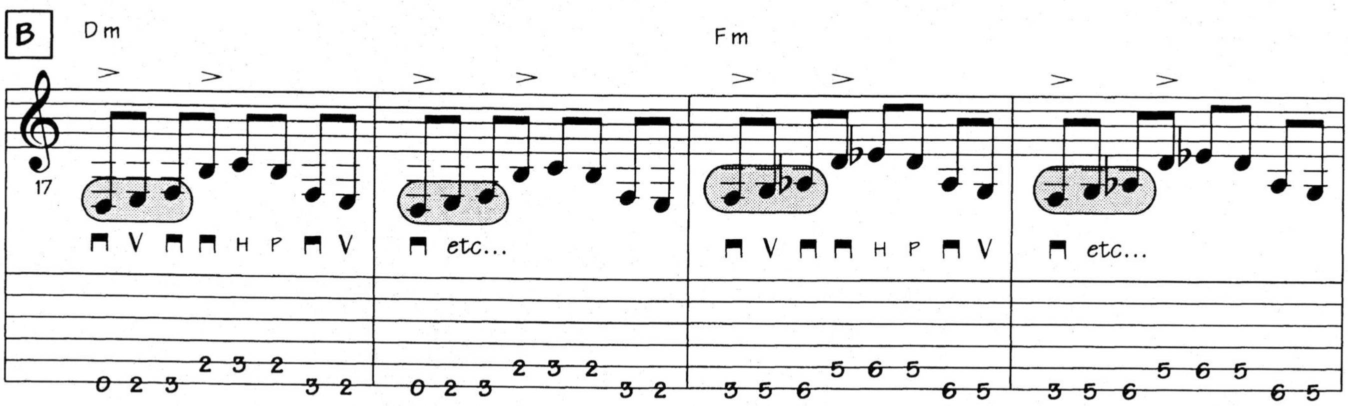

Of course, since it is almost an identical phrase in phrase (1) of the A sections, except for the center root note, the accents are placed at identical places: on the notes which limits the ambitus. The same observation goes with regard to the way the pick is used, as well as for the hammer-ons/pull-offs.

Destinee (measures 21 - 23) procedure #1

Measures 21 to 23 show a procedure that is often used in the way the Manouche play: the "rolling – slide" in chords.

Technically this rolling/slide is called a "tremolo" (shown with the ≢ symbol). It can be used with simple notes, and in this case, with chords.

We have already seen this procedure in "Swing For Ninine" (chapter 3, page 4). It's the same procedure, and uses the same chords, therefore, it is done with a pedal over the (lower A note), by striking very fast sixteenth note triplets with the pick held perpendicular to the strings in the manner to get a maximum volume. (1 - don't cheat by attacking the string with the edge of the pick! 2 - this is the right opportunity to make the wrist of your right hand smooth.)

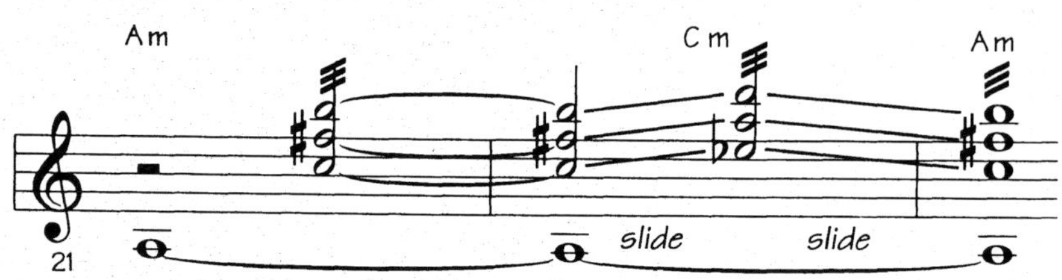

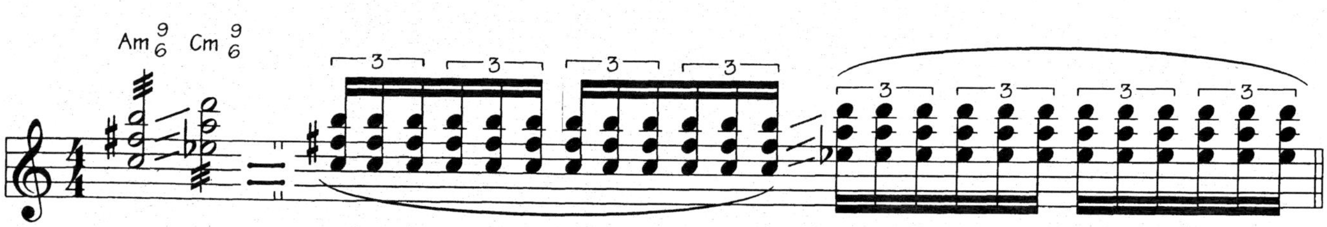

PART C

Here is the theme of "Destinee." You can find the recording of it on the Romane Quintet CD. As you can hear, the harmonics in measures 7 and 8 are enriched with an effect that is done by twisting the neck: put your left hand at the tip of your guitar neck and pull laterally (not very hard!) right after you have produced these harmonics.

#68

Destinée

♩=240

music by ROMANE

Theme = 48 measures AABBAA

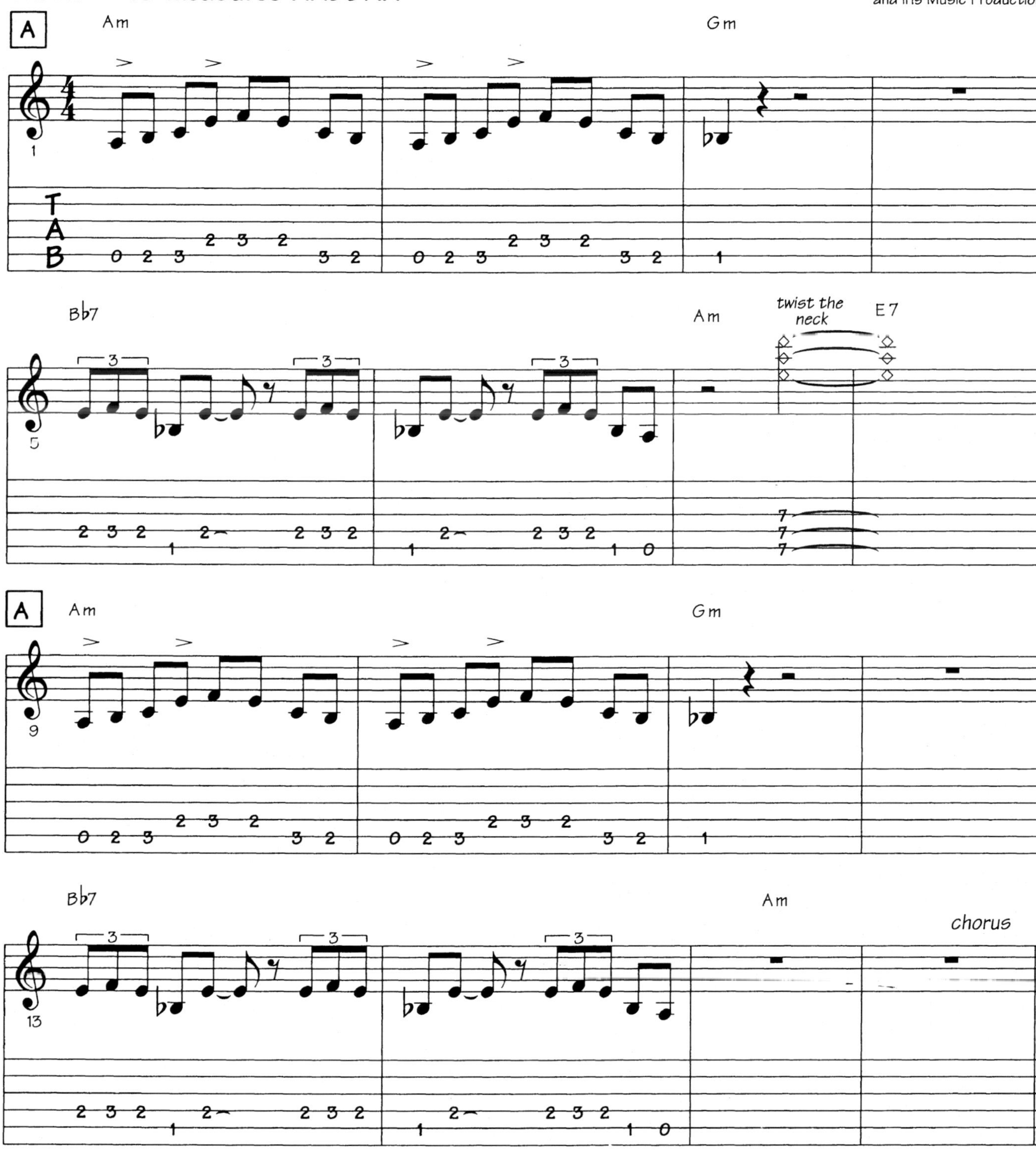

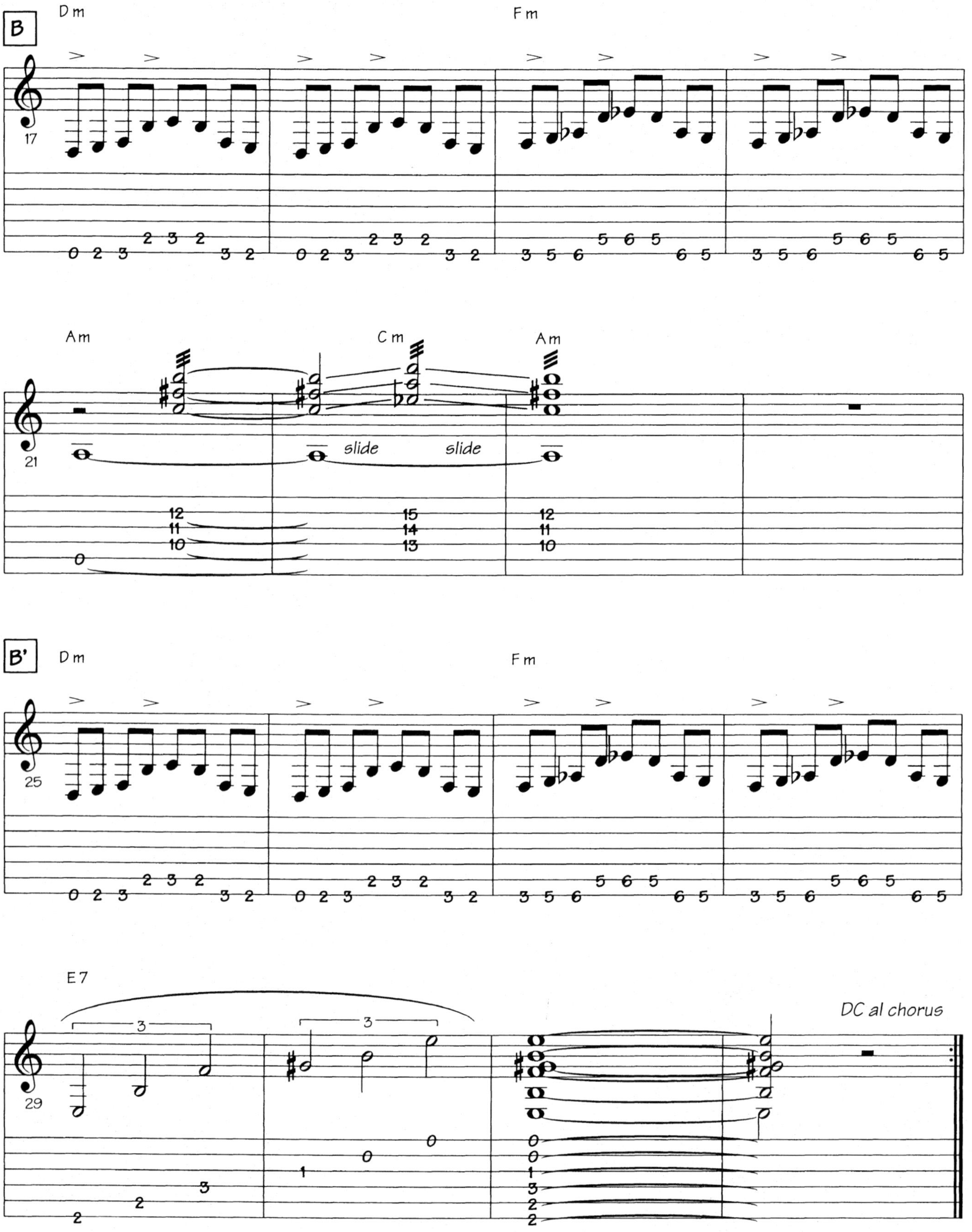
B
Dm
Fm
Am
Cm
Am
slide
slide
B'
Dm
Fm
E7
DC al chorus

PART A

Exercise 59 - lead of a D major cadence

This lead, as far as improvisation is concerned, is a part of the current vocabulary of jazzmen. It shows a new way to play a sweep with the pick. It will definitely produce its small effect, when it is played with a good "legato", together with an impeccable articulation and a fast beat.

Be careful how you use the pick.

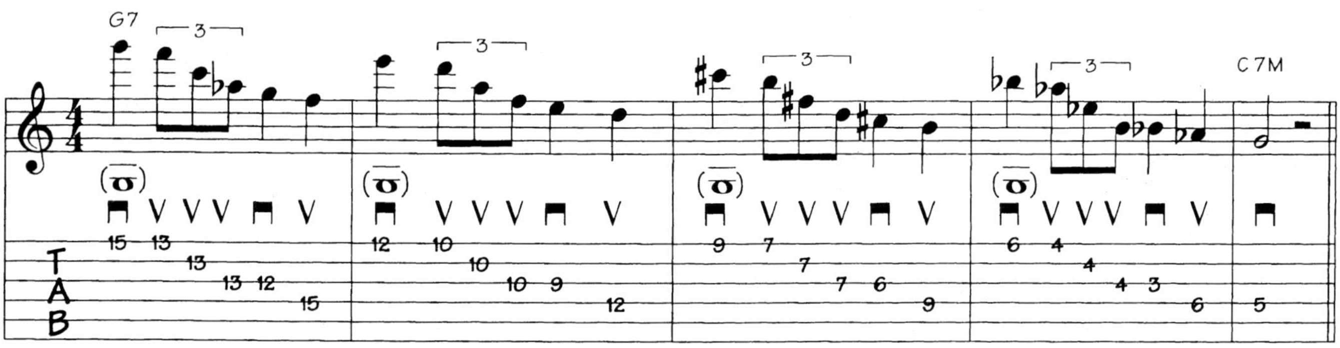

In the harmony, you will notice that this music works with the idea of the dim7 arpeggio: from one measure to the next, it is excactly the same diagram which uses gaps of third minors... tritone and tritone substitutions, of course!

Here you find the T.S. between the notes of measures 1-3 and 2-4, these notes can be regrouped with the same diagrams and the following harmonic symbols:

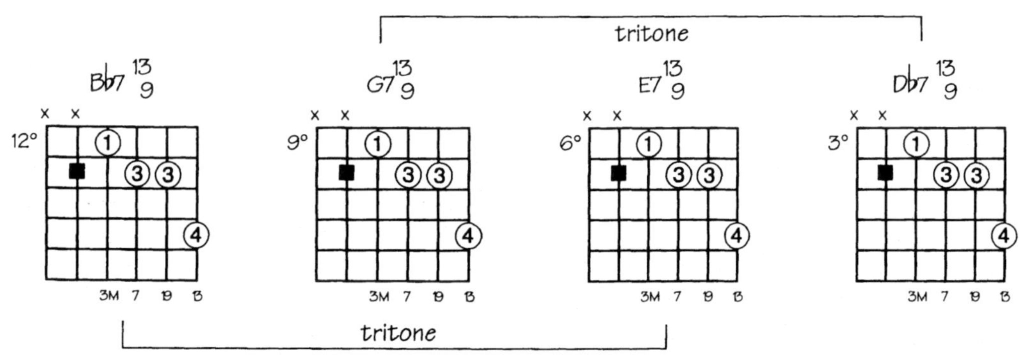

The resolution is done wth the CM7, this phrase tackles the fundamental chord with the V degree tritone: the Db7 in the place of G7.

Finally, you cannot play the lower G note (shown in parenthesis) - which is unfortunate - because you don't have a third hand! You have to face the fact that to show it well, all the phrases rely on the idea that the G7 will work with the C7M, despite the fact that the chords change. Ask one of your friends to play this lower pedal shown under the phrase (or make a good recording of it). You will understand this much better, when you listen to how this harmonic structure is created.

▪ PART B1

In the previous chapters you may have noticed that, under certain circumstances, the dominant seventh chords are marked with an "alt." type symbol (for example E alt., B alt., etc.).

Well, we are now going to have the pleasure of letting you in on the mystery without waiting any longer.

You must understand that a dominant seventh chord of the "alt." type is a chord that refers to a melodic scale, which is called an "altered" scale.

THE ALTERED SCALE

This altered scale gets its source from a melodic structure of seven notes. This is new for us, it is called the "melodic minor scale." Clearly, this altered scale is one of seven modes that can be created as a melodic minor scale. While we are on the subject, understand that we only keep the name of those modes that we are interested in.

The simplest way to state that this is a melodic minor scale, is that it has the D note as its middle root note (the name of the notes). The seventh of these modes generates the so-called "altered" scale.

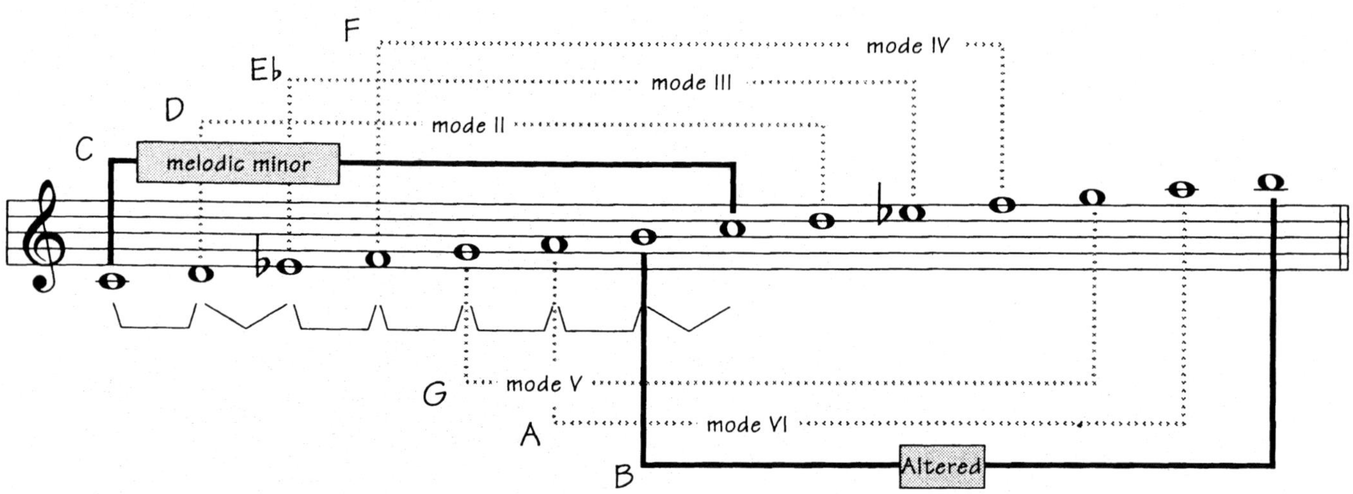

One observation stands out by itself: the melodic minor scale, which is composed of 5 tones and 2 half tones, has a strong similarity with the major scale, we could therefore be satisfied to basically define it as a major scale, of which the III degree would be lowered with a half tone (as shown below, C major scale with an Eb). You are shown this similarity specifically for what it is worth; it will namely enable you to use it as a mnemonic memory aid to study the altered scale. We are going to see how the minor melodic scale is put together. It differs greatly than the major scale, particularly from the point of view of the harmonies that it develops, and the use of these harmonies.

On the other hand, notice that any alterations of the notes, generated with the melodic minor scale, are not shown in the key signature (compare this with the remark made about the subject of the harmonic minor scale in chapter 2, page 3). Only the major scale (or its relative minor) are allowed to determine a key signature.

As a consequence, in the case where the melody admits the Eb by way of a unique alteration, nothing will be deducted, especially from what would establish the key of the melodic minor C. In the case where a melody yields a unique alteration of the Eb note, such a deduction would pure nonsense.

We are more interested in the 7th mode of the melodic minor scale, the altered scale. To begin with, let's look at its structure.

Altered scale (altered B)

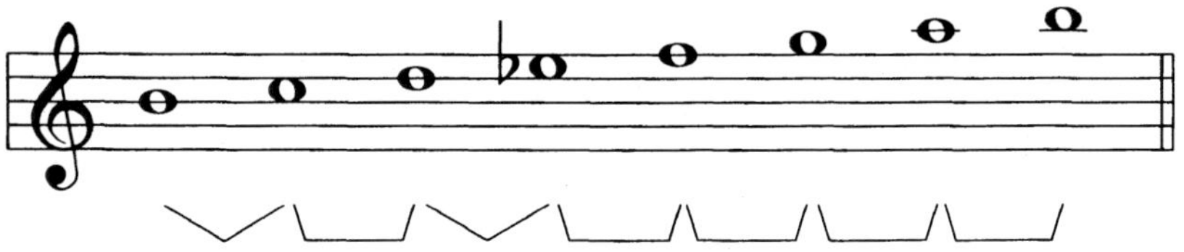

Can you hear the successions of the notes that you are already familiar with?

In the first four notes you will find a regular succession of half-tones and tones, in other words, the first half of the altered scale expresses itself precisely as the diminished scale (half- whole = 1/2t. • 1t. • 1/2 t. • 1t.), the scale that we have seen often and played, up to here (chapter 8). As for the second half of the scale, here is the evidence: it acts like part of a whole tone scale, which we also have already seen in chapter 7, pages 1 and 2.

To sum it up, the altered scale is a combination of two scales: a half-diminished scale (which starts with the half tone) and the whole tone scale.

The two scales are almost exclusively used with dominant seventh chords. We know this now from its harmonic structure. We can therefore better understand why certain dominant chords are shown as "alt.", when we make it stand out.

All of this doesn't explain however, what the term "alteration" is exactly based on.

We will start to harmonize the altered scale with superimposed thirds by developing this harmonization up to seven sounds, with the aid of all the notes of the scale, keeping this in mind:

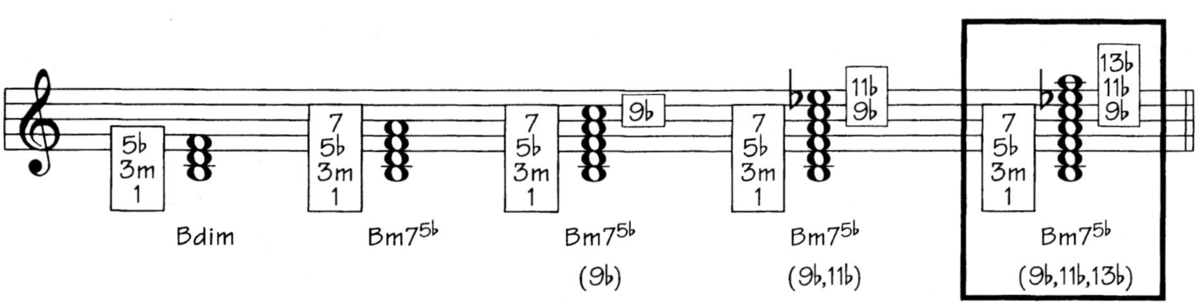

With the first (B dim) chord, a question arises: how could an altered scale have been used to improvise with a seventh dominant chord that has the same fundamental, but where none of its harmonization is developed?

Also, starting from the fourth chord, there is a much more astonishing question: the appearance of a major third with the coloration of a steadfastly minor chord! Because we cannot deny that the Eb (b11) note, or if you prefer the D#, can work as a major third together with the root note of the chord, the B note. As such, we get a chord with seven tones that contains both types of thirds.

Now the melodic minor scale is generating the altered scale, which is very different from our good, old friend, the major scale.

With keeping all this in mind the altered scale is one of the melodic scales among the more appreciated ones (and a most efficient one to boot). It's used to improvise with any of the dominant chords.

A popular use which relies on the "sleight of hands", the harmonic opposite, where the thorn like "b11" is transformed into a real major third, while the initial minor third becomes a (#9)coloration, which appears in the higher end of the chord. This gives birth to the "altered" chord which has all the attributes of a dominant seventh chord.

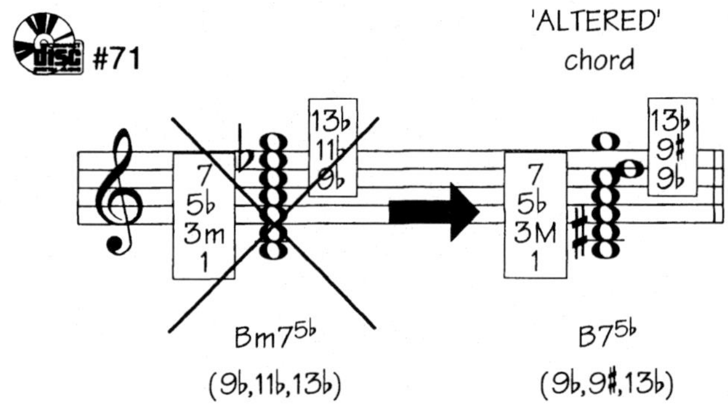

And the terminology "alt" is the result of the fact that the dominant chord, as it is defined, colors itself with the aid of the functions of the altered harmony: diminished 5th (b5), minor 9th (b9) augmented 9th (#9) and minor 13th (b13), the long awaited harmonic "non-altered" functions, which are the ninth and the thirteenth (9 and 13) - the perfect 5th was never considered to be a coloration.

Finally, we can conclude from this theoretic display the three following conclusions:

• Stemming from the minor melodic scale, the "alt." chord is a dominant seventh type chord of which the coloration is based on the altered harmonic functions: b5, #5, (or b13), b9 and #9. Consequentially, the designation "alt." would be used to globally mean that all dominant chords require all, or part of, these harmonic altered functions. For example:

C7(b9) or C7(#9) or C7(b9, b13) or C7(b5, #5) = **C alt.**

Moreover, the "alt." symbol could be used to mean that it is a dominant chord with a missing third, being the seventh, but which, by virtue of its harmonic context, the (II - V - I, turnaround, etc.), is known to be identified differently than as a seventh dominant chord. For example, with the II - V - I major, as shown on the other side:

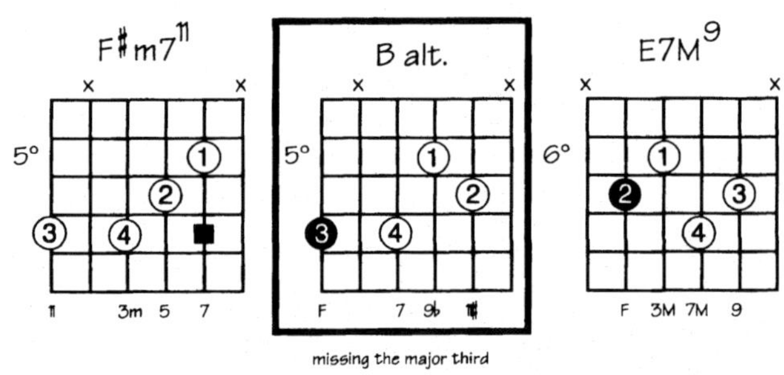

• The melodic minor scale, via its seventh mode, may be used to construct an improvised melody with all the dominant seventh chords, where its root note is located one half tone lower. For example, you could improvise by using the melodic Fm scale where we have an E7 chord (F → E = 1/2 tone apart), as is the case in the diagram of "Destinee."

And with this same diagram, you can directly plan how to improvise around the Fm chord, while the harmonic structure is in reality, centered around the Am key. This is a surprising relationship, which, at a first glance, was not too hard to determine.

• In the case where a chord has two types of thirds (M and m), the 3M must always prevail before the 3m, which then functions as an augmented ninth (#9).

PART B2

We are now going to study the diagrams and leads of the first guitar chorus of "Destinee".

Destinee (measure 1) procedure #1

This solo opens with fire by using two "bends + 1/2" (this means to bend the notes up a half tone). We benefit from this opportunity to simply see how the Manouche would play it. The note where the "bends + 1/2" applies to is always the one that is done first, and is never the resulting note after the bend. In other words, you must start a half tone below the desired higher pitch as indicated, and you can do this by bending the string up a half tone interval.

Destinee (measure 5) diagram #1

Measure 5 presents a worked out lead that has a new chord diagram. This results from tuning the sixth string of the guitar a tone lower than usual, to a low D. The sweeping diagram is similar to the one of Exercise 29 (chapter 9, page 3):

Sweep with Bb7 chord (non-standard chording).

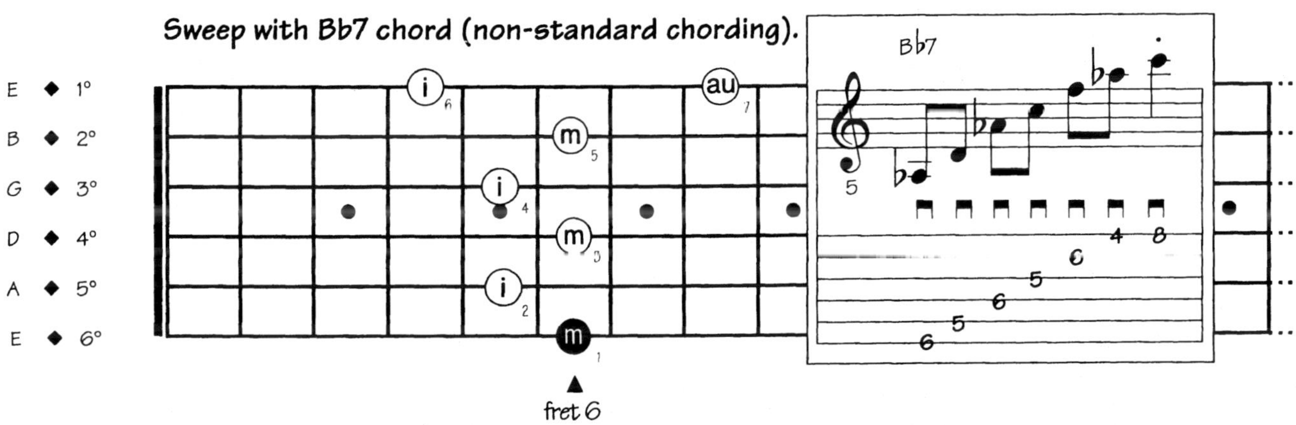

Destinee (measures 8 - 10) lead #1

With this phrase, which starts with a pickup at the end of measure 8, we find an illustration of the melodic minor scale. In this case it is the melodic Am (★ notes) where the diminished fifth is added in a way to halt the lead in its time frame, and to give it more value, with this (encircled) chromaticism, just as it is done in jazz.

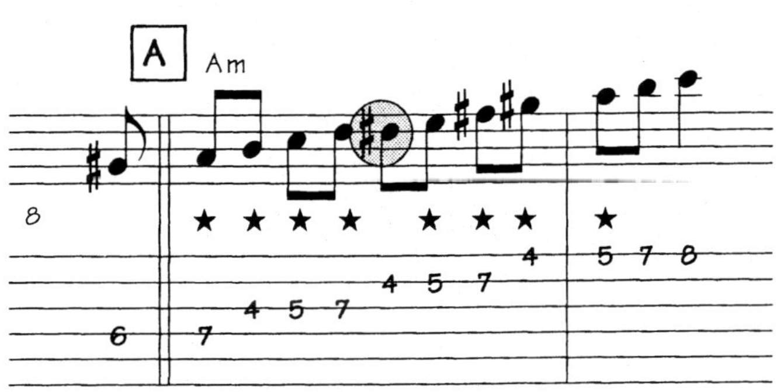

Destinee (measure 13) lead #2

Measure 13 introduces the T.S. (tritone substitution) since the phrase here is constructed with the augmented E (E+) triad and where the harmony now is Bb7: Bb7 to E.

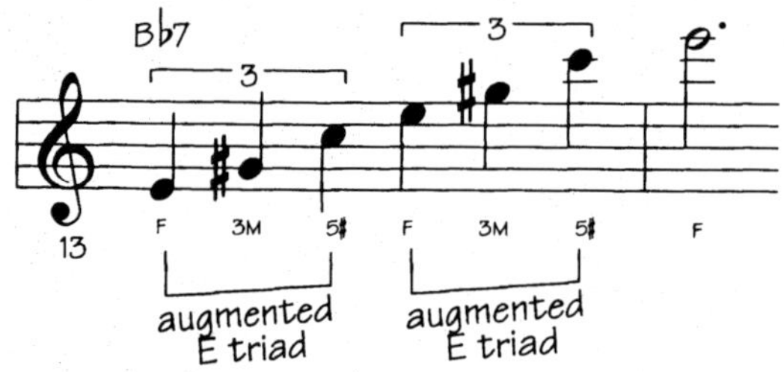

PS: the augmented triad, by following the example of the whole tone scale, is a chord with three tones. It has a root note (F), a major third (3M), and an augmented fifth (#5), which possesses the A.L.T. property (chapter 7, page 1).

Consequences:

• Each of the composing notes of an augmented triad defines an augmented triad, the E+ triad = G#+ = C+ (E, G# and C are the notes which compose E+).

• The augmented chord positions on the guitar are identically four frets apart (a 3M interval).

Example:

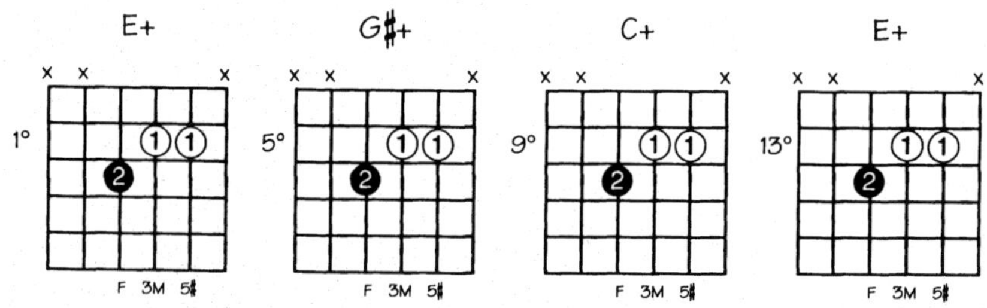

Destinee (measure 21) explanation of the harmony

Here, we have an interesting coloration, an Am7M(13), which gives us the opportunity to draw attention to substitutions. Look at these positions:

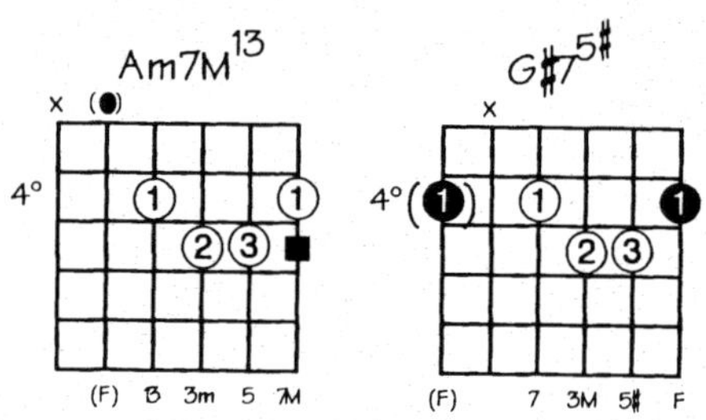

Here we have to make a substitution that is subject to the melodic minor scale. These two chords could be constructed with this minor harmonic scale. At a later time we will deal with this subject. Right now, know that only the choices of the bass (fundamental) makes these two chords different symbols, and a different name.

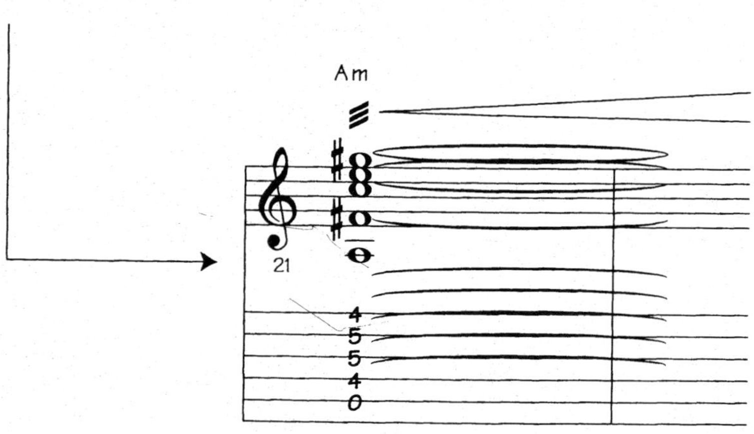

PART C

Here is the first chorus of “Destinee”.

Look how “with a stroke of the pen” the sixteenth notes are applied at the beginning of the long final phrase. This phrase is thus driven, ascending toward the sharp and then to descend again into some harmonic minor scale (the A harmonic minor). In other words, with the harmony being E7, we use the harmonic minor scale while planning to get it out of its fifth mode (E7 = V degree in the harmonic A minor scale).

#68

♩=240

Chorus 1 = 32 measures AAB

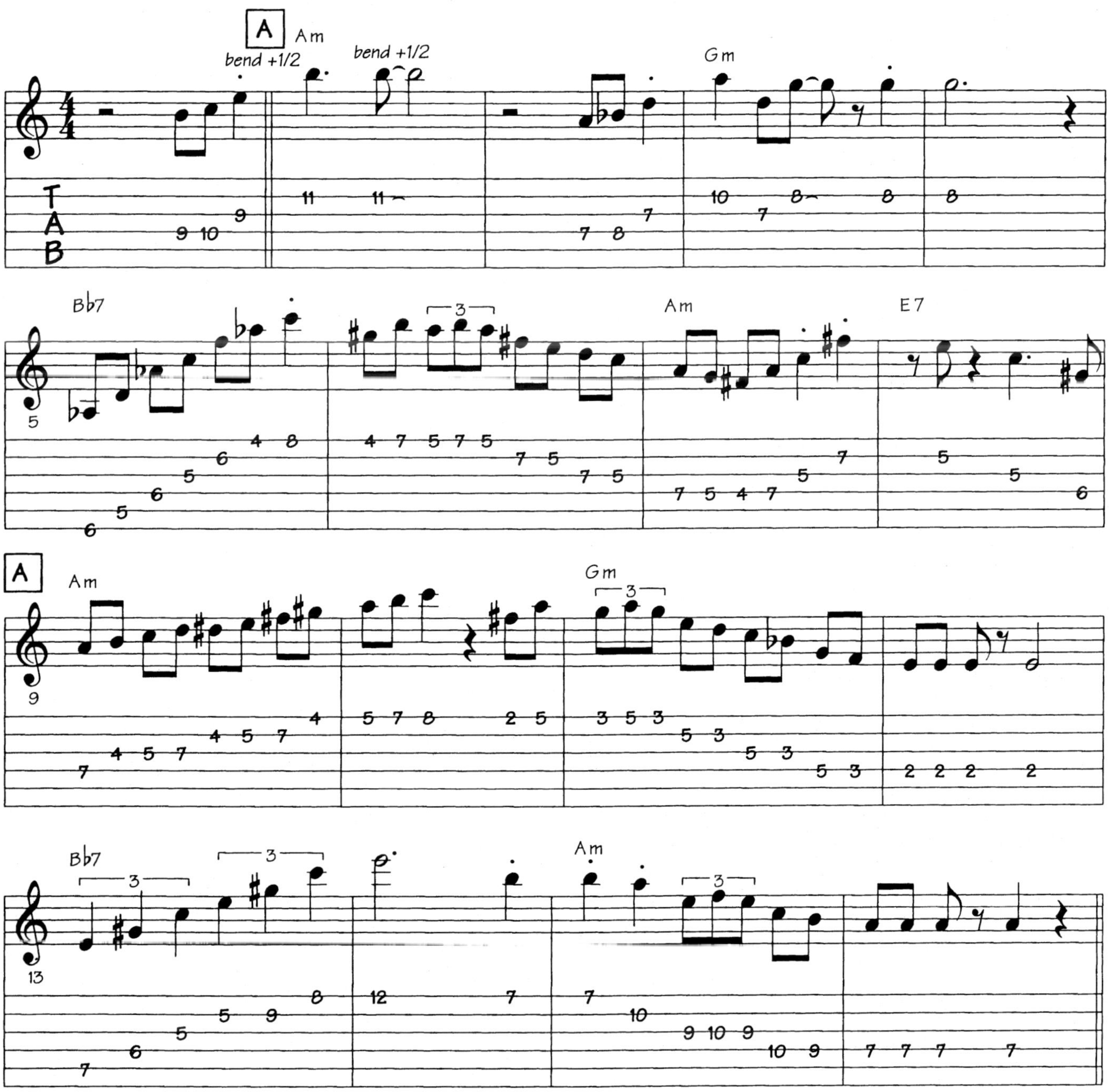

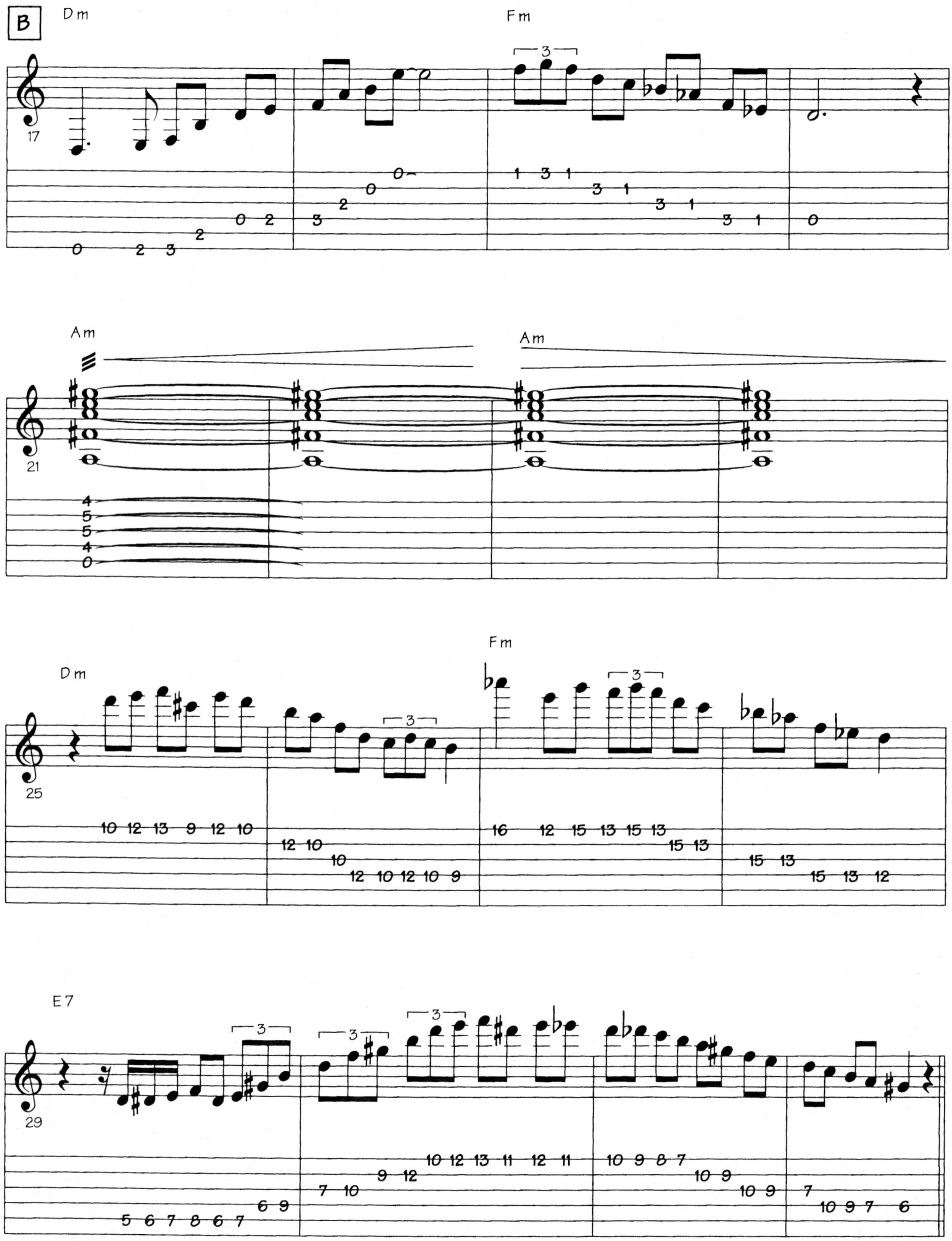
B
Dm
Fm
Am
Am
Dm
Fm
E7

PART A

Exercise 60 - melody by using the D major anatole (1)

During the next five exercises we are going to learn the techniques of improvising phrases. It is possible to exploit the tritone substitution with the major anatole (turnaround), which is often used for this purpose.

Examine this phrase here:

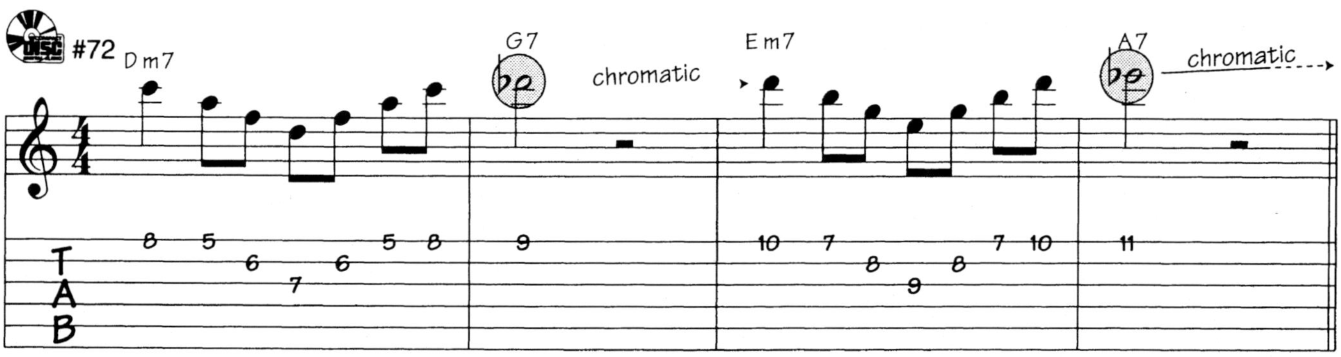

This phrase is built with ascending arpeggios and descending counter beats which correspond with the root note of the tritone chord.

As far as the G7 is concerned, it appears that the Db note, the root note of the Db7, is separated from the G7 by one tritone. We call it "devilish" in order to make it easy, while wondering why the tritone in the Middle Ages was qualified as a "diabolus in musica" (musical devil). If one would use it, he or she was found to be liable and excommunicated. Definitely, jazzmen could never have put down a single note, if they had lived during this period.

In reality, this note is often magical in the measure, it not only has its place within the desired harmony, it also lets you chromatically tie the first notes of the second sentence. The second sentence is exactly copied from the first, but with a gap of one tone higher (this is done very smoothly).

And with the group of harmonies of the anatole (turnaround), this magic note lets you create a homogeneuos melody and an increasing tension (a displacement going up), which gives it the simple idea of departing from a melodically structured discourse.

The fingerboard diagram and its corresponding chord positions are next. Play the notes in numerical ascending order:

1-- Dm Arpeggio (For the Em arpeggio: move two frets up).

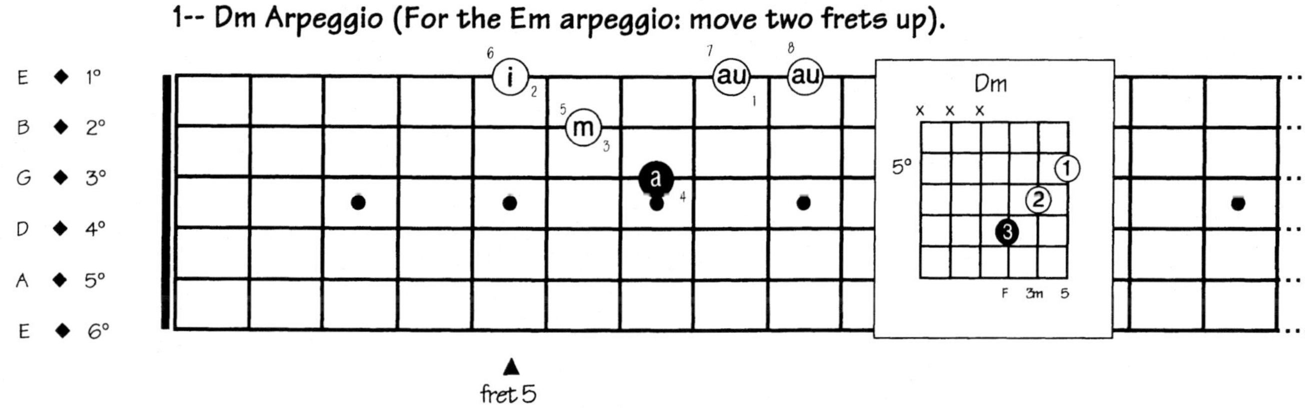

Exercise 61 - melody using the D major anatole #2

Since we have discovered this magic note, let's continue to use it.

We can continue to go higher by using the same procedure with the arpeggios.

The phrase will work like this:

#73

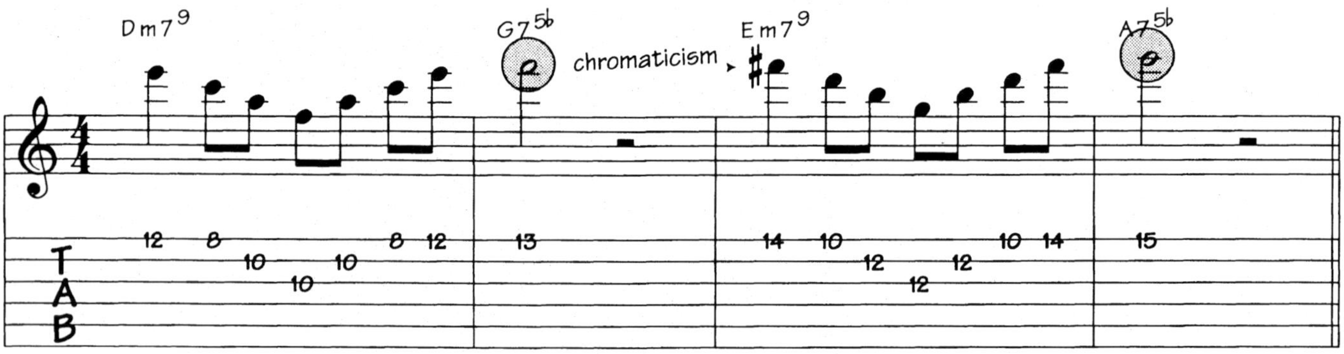

This time the arpeggios are majors, and you will see that these arpeggios are a diatonic relative of the ones in exercise 60: F for Dm, G for Em.

Of course, the chords are always the same, because we don't leave the C turnaround, and we turn these four measures together while the melody develops.

Here is the fingerboard diagram and their corresponding chord positions: play the notes in the ascending numerical order.

2 - F arpeggio (for the G arpeggio: move two frets up).

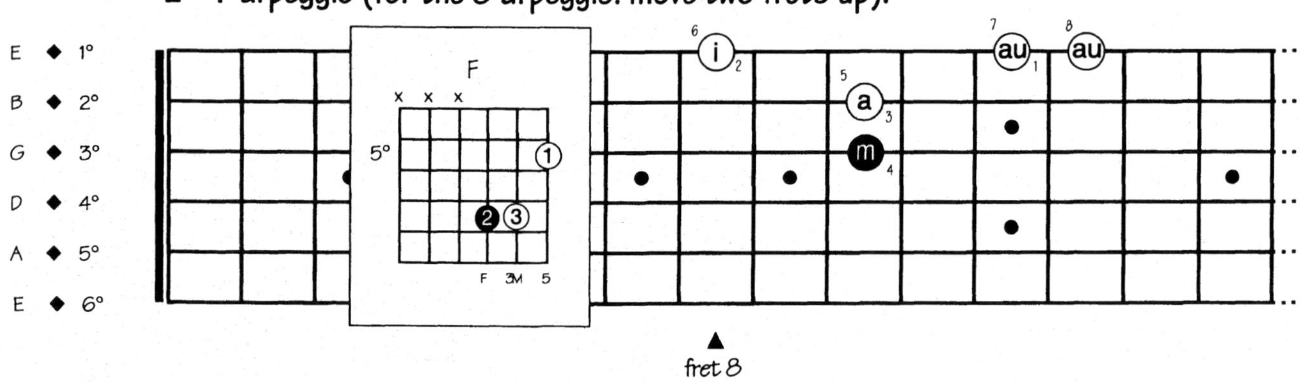

PART B1

Let's us analyze the lead of "Destinee":

Key: Am

A	(I) Am 1	%	(VIIm) Gm	%	(IIb7) $Bb7^{5b}$ 5	%	(I) Am	(V) E7
B	(IV) Dm(6) 17	%	(VIm) Fm(6)	%	(I) Am $^{9}_{6}$ 21	Am $^{9}_{6}$ / (IIIm) Cm $^{9}_{6}$	(I) Am $^{9}_{6}$	%
B'	25	4 //.			(V) $E7^{9b}$ 29	%	%	%

Although it contains many strange keys that are borrowed, the harmonies in "Destinee" are generally played in the key of Am.

In reality, this lead can be put in a narrow relationship with the entire first theme that we studied, although we have not analyzed it yet. We used it in "Swing For Ninine". This structure was:

Harmonic diagram of "Swing For Ninine".

Key: Am

A	(I) Am 1	%	(IIb6) Bb6	%	(V) E7 5	%	(I) Am	(V) E7
B	(IV) Dm 17	%	(I) Am	%	(IIb6) Bb6 21	%	(V) E7	%

In both cases the style of Manouche is still the same (a very recognized "groove"). It is not astonishing to see the strong likeness between these two harmonic diagrams and also the key.

It is for this reason that we now have the opportunity to give you a double comparative analysis. This has not been dealt with so far. There are certain technical forms within the structure of the harmony that we have to follow. These are the subtle uses of chord substitutions.

Analysis of "Swing for Ninine"

MEASURE 3: Bb6 is a tritone anticipation of the E7 chord (V) which happens in measure 5. Indeed, from E to Bb we count three tones. But pay attention: this anticipation is not a real T.S. because the chords, are within reason, all of the dominant seventh type. We could say that measures 3 and 4 are "covered by the shadow" of the T.S.

MEASURE 17: This is a transition with the IV degree of the key (very current for one section B).

MEASURE 19: This has the return of the tonic chord.

MEASURES 21 and 25: This shows an analysis identical with that of measures 3 to 6.

Analysis of "Destinee"

MEASURE 3: The Gm chord is a reduced VII degree of the key in question, because of the fact that the VII degree of a minor key is theoretically a dominant seventh. However, in reality, this Gm is a diatonic substitution for the B6 in the diagram of "Swing For Ninine" because:

To sum it up: via the Bb6, Gm revolves around the idea of E7, which of course is the V degree of the key. All that this is saying is that this illustrates the inevitable principle "dominant → key" one more time.

MEASURE 5: And here is the T.S. This IIb7 tritonelly expresses the E7, which, as a V degree of the key, is inescapably brought back to Am.

MEASURE 17: This is the same transition using the IV degree.

MEASURE 19: It is here that these two diagrams diverge. Indeed, from a strict theoretical point of view, the Fm6 is a VI degree reduced in the key in question, it is in reality a camouflaged V degree (E7) with a new sleight of hand that we are going to explain in detail.

First of all, notice the "6" coloration (major sixth) with the Dm and Fm chords. This is typically in the style of Manouche. This coloration once more gives birth to a four-note chord, which gives us an abundance of interesting substitutions.

Because,

First of all:
Dm6 = D-F-A-B [F-3m-5-6] = Bm7(5♭) [3m-5 -7-F],

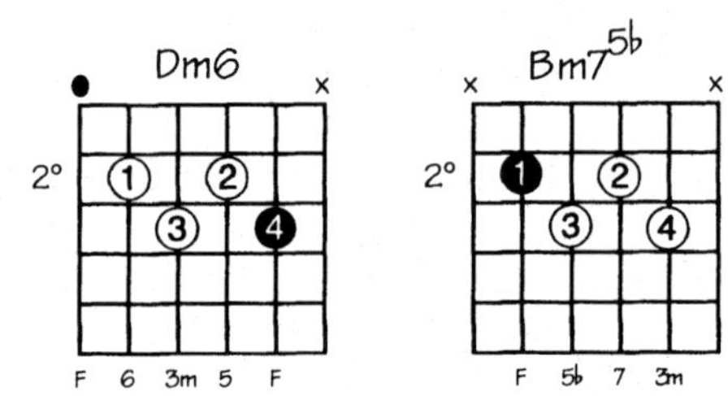

Secondly:
Fm6 = F-A♭-C-D [F-3m-5-6] = E7(9♭,13♭) [9♭-3M-13♭-7].

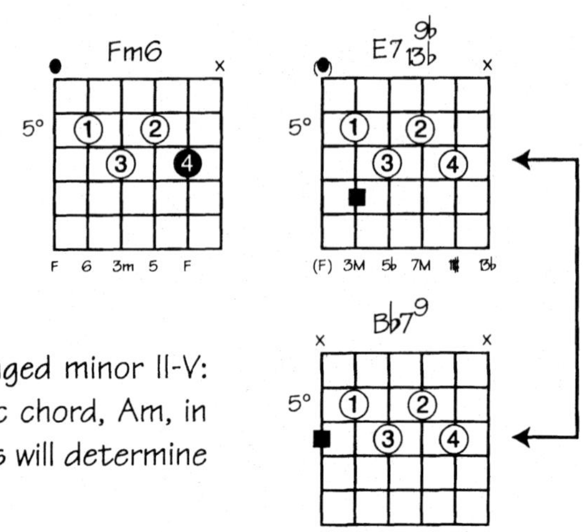

In other words, the Dm6 - Fm6 progression is a camouflaged minor II-V: Bm7(b5) - E7 progression which can only lead to the tonic chord, Am, in measure 21. We can also think of the Fm6 to be a Bb7. This will determine a T.S. with the other substitution, E7(b9/b13):

MEASURE 22: finally, the Cm6/9, is a reduced III chord in the key of A minor. It has no other ambition than to break the monotony that would be present if we let the Am6/9 last for four measures. This means, that the space of the minor third between the two chords should not be mentioned without the dim7 chord, this works everywhere when you want to link phrases and chords between them together.

▪ PART B2

We are now going to look into the second chorus of "Destinee" (CD Romane Quintet) which discusses the improvisation of the Manouche's leads.

Destinee (measures 33 - 36) lead #1

Here we have a speed/virtuosity effect, where the main difficulty arises where the two attacks are (⊓) in succession.

Pay careful attention on how to use the pick here, which combines accents on the 2nd and 4th beat. These are done identically in the two phrases.

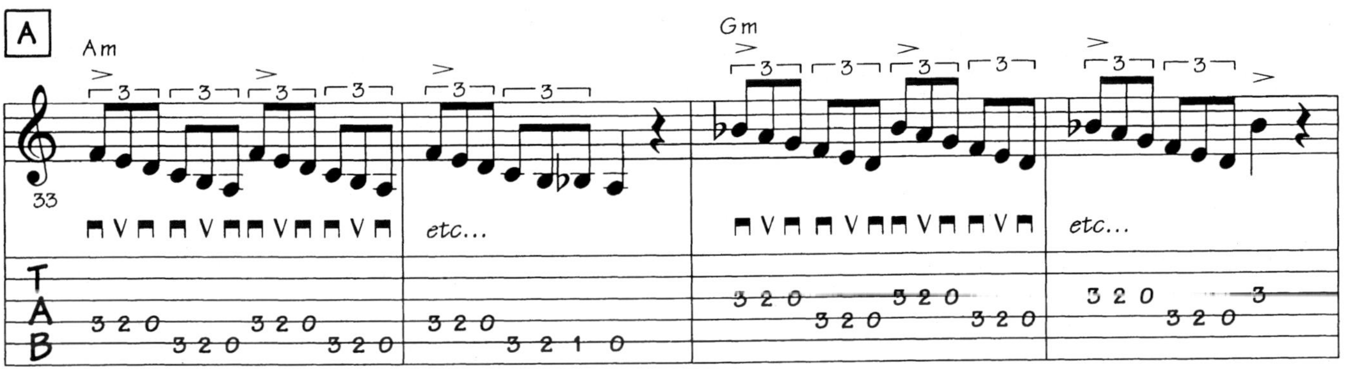

Destinee (measures 43 - 45) explaining the melody

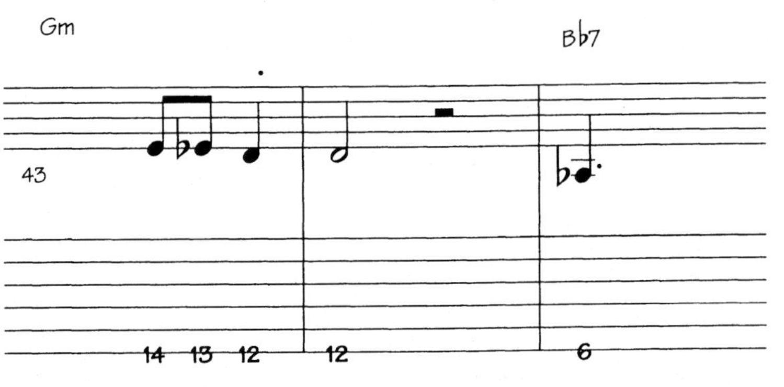

Attention: don't forget that in order to play the five notes above, your sixth string should be tuned to the lower D, which in this case is only used in the two "Destinee" choruses.

Destinee (measures 53 - 55) procedure #2

This little syncopated rhythmic phrase (encircled) gives us the occasion to speak about the technique involved with a particular characteristic aspect of jazz music: the style of "swing".

If we had to write the measures in question very strictly (for instance, with a classically trained musician in mind), the result would be as follows:

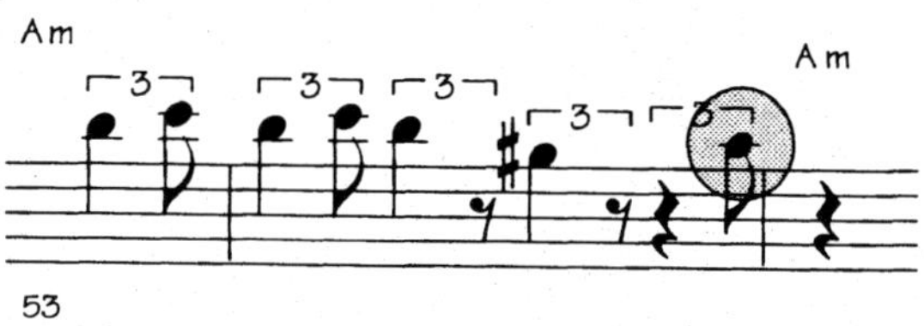

in the place of:

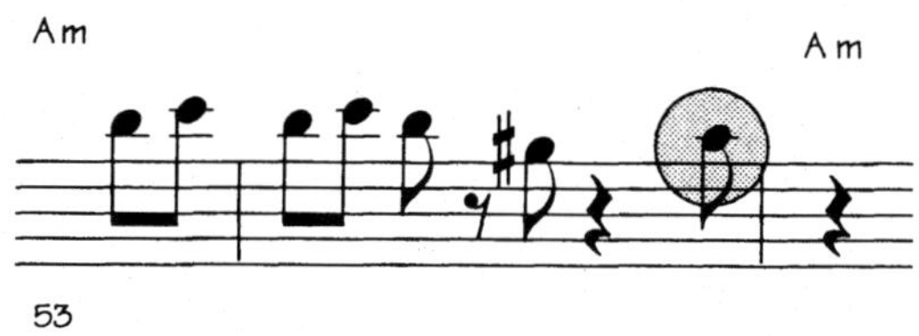

Finally, all pairs of eighths should be written as they are really interpreted, that's to say, redone in triplets where the first two eighths are tied (a quarter triplet). This rhythmic recast is done on the basis of what we call the "swing" phrase, which is used in jazz. This is very characteristic of swing.

But by writing it in triplets, you can imagine how much the music lines become loaded and difficult to read. The jazzmen also have, long ago, found a solution. It is done by writing the music in equal eighths, which must be played in unequal eighths, in triplets.

We simply call it the "swing feel" or (♫ = ♩♪) to indicate that the score of jazz ought to be interpreted as compound. Unfortunately, the entire problem remains because some performers are not in the habit of playing like this. It is then necessary to resort to strict writing and hope that all goes well; but the aptitude to make a melody "swing" is unfortunately a thing, that is in reality accomplished with playing by ear, experience and time.

Finally, the faster the speed, (more than 200 bpm), the more the eighths should be played straight, and visa versa.

Destinee (measures 61 - 62) lead #4

Finally, we see that the two chords end with a very architectural melodic phrase, which freely brings the famous "stop – chorus" closer, as we can see in the theme of "Swing For Ninine" (chapter 1, page 6). Here is a little variation of this "stop – chorus" using the same attacks with the pick, a much easier way of speeding up your playing!

Besides that, you have an illustration of creating a new phrase by getting away from an existing phrase. This is simply done with a rhythmic separation, a prior insignificant procedure that must never be neglected in the material you want to improvise.

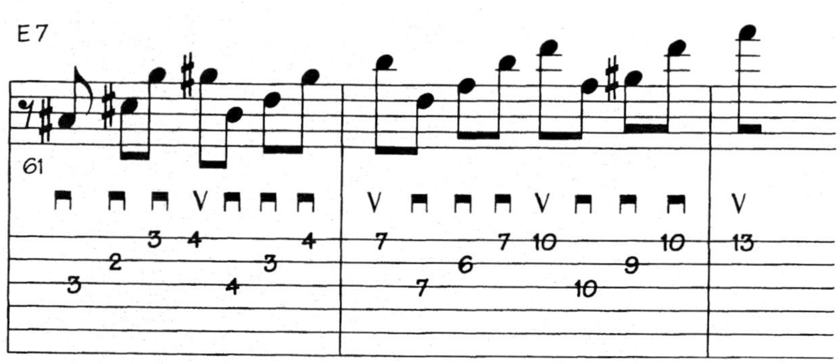

PART C

Continuing and the end of the chorus of "Destinee".

Be careful how you play the very high notes. Also take care of the notes where vibrato is used (measures 52 – 53), this gives more value to them and puts more "life" into it as a whole.

#68

Chorus 2 = 32 measures AABB'

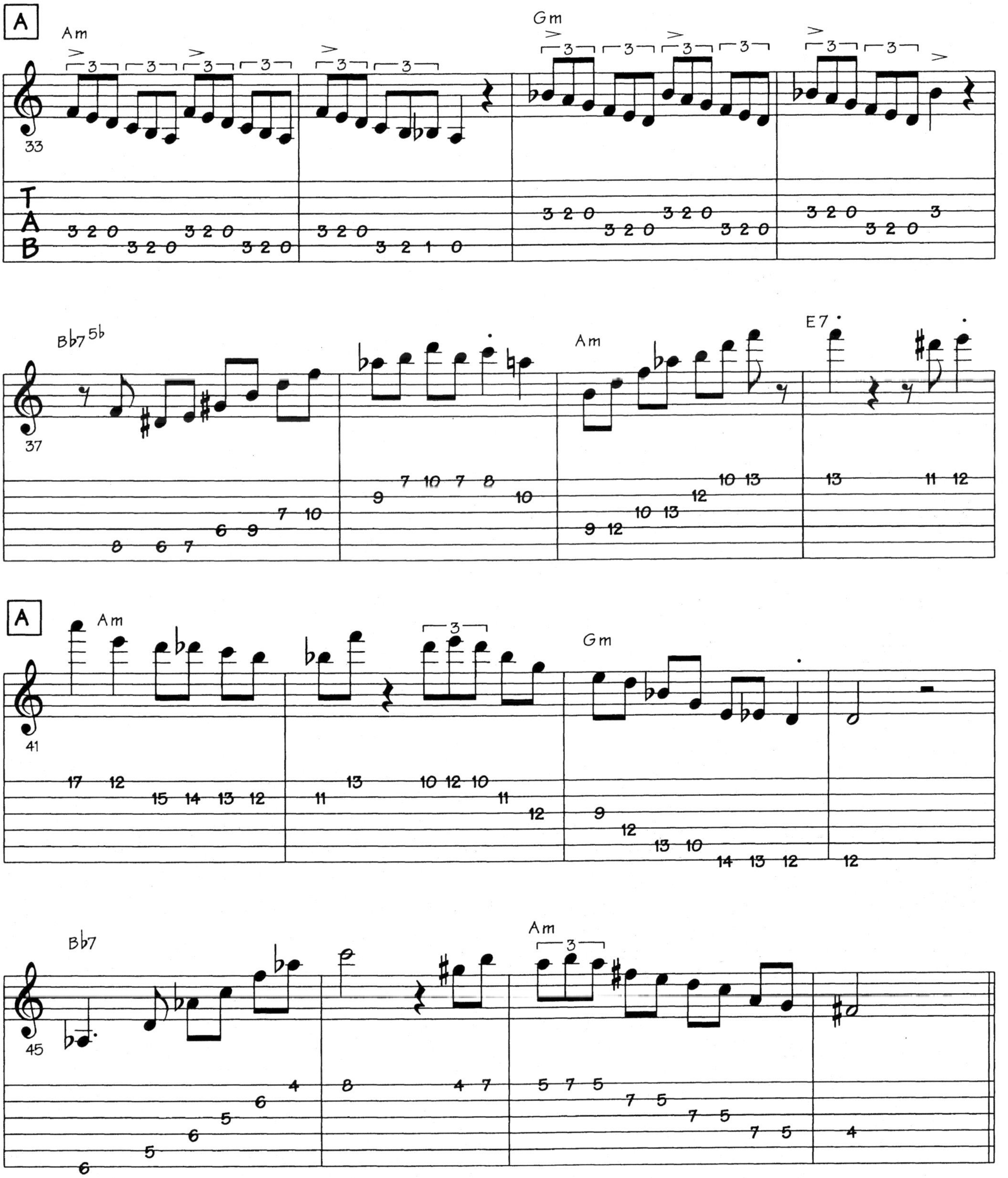

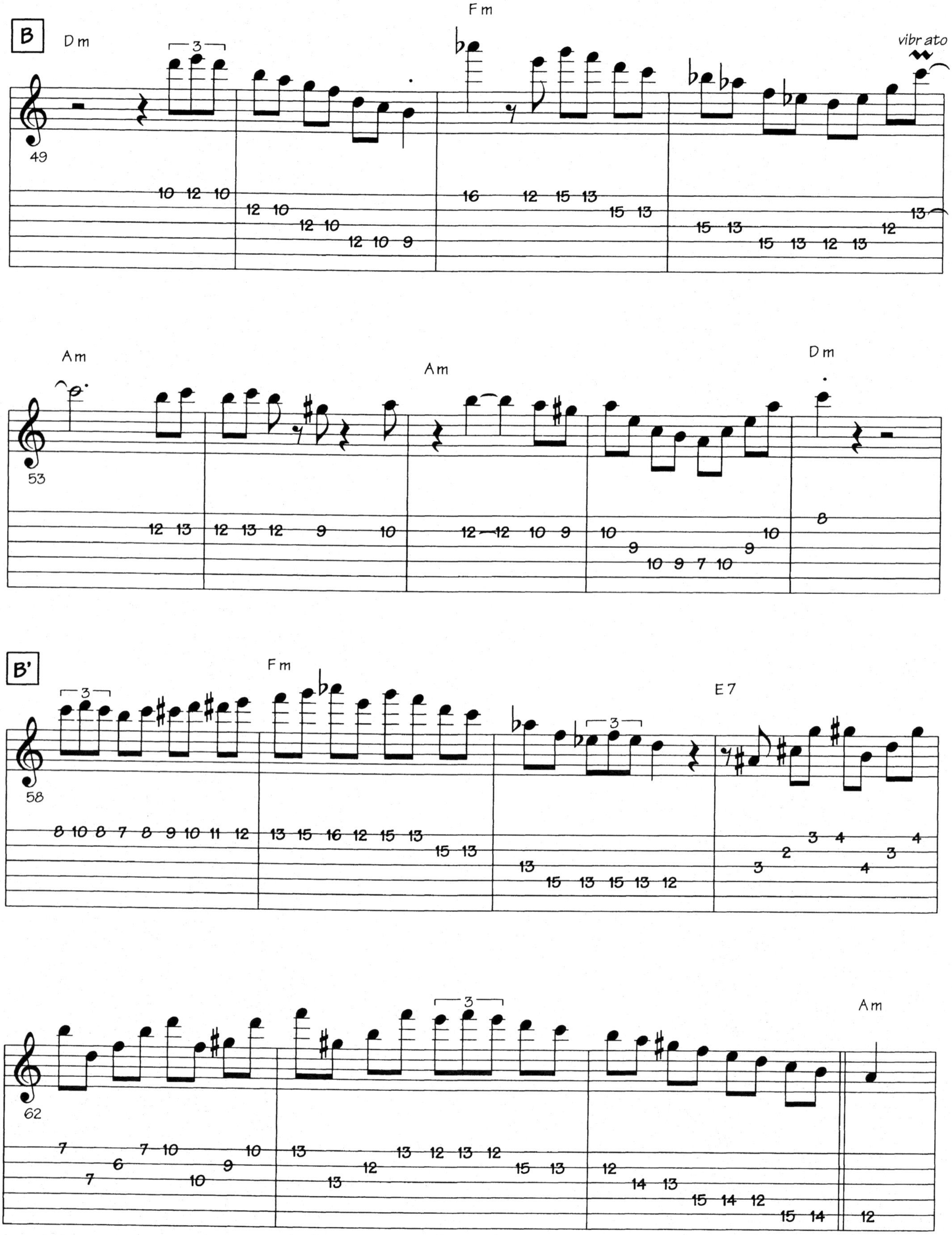
B
Dm
Fm
vibrato
Am
Am
Dm
B'
Fm
E7
Am

PART A

Exercise 62 - melody using the G major anatole (1)

We now continue the exploitation that started in chapter 19 of our "magic" tritone note, using the anatole (turnaround).

This time we are going to illustrate this with the key of G major by using the worked-out arpeggios on the medium high strings.

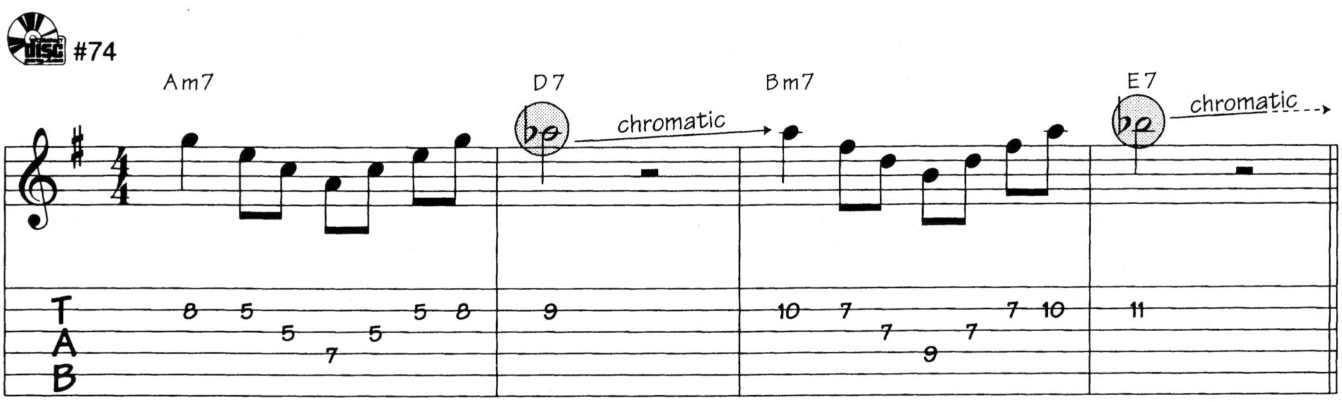

The fingerboard diagram with its corresponding chord positions, is shown below:

Play the notes in an increasing numerical order:

1- the Am arpeggio (for the Bm arpeggio, move up two frets).

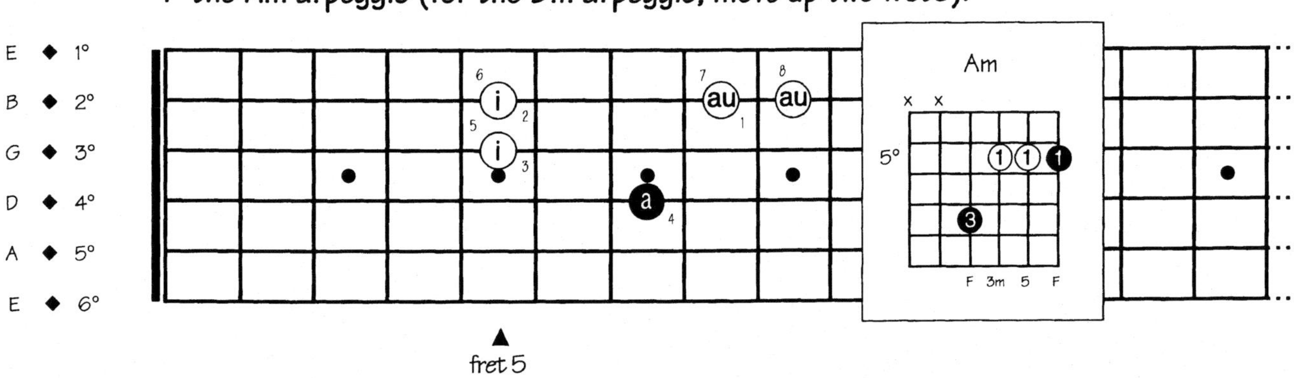

Exercise 63 - melody with the G major anatole (2)

We'll continue working with the arpeggios of the G anatole (turnaround), by using chromatic ties, which will give us the "magic" note:

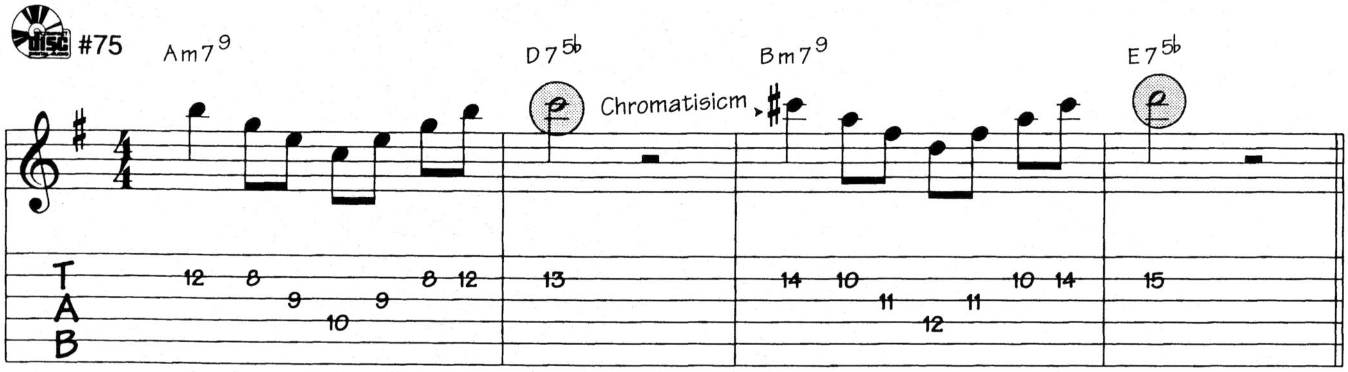

Notice here for the first time that the arpeggios are the diatonic relatives of the arpeggios in Exercise 62: C for Am, D for Bm (compare this with the exercises 60/61).

The fingerboard diagram with its corresponding chord positions is shown below:

Play the notes in ascending numerical order:

2 - C7M arpeggio (for the D7M arpeggio: move up two frets).

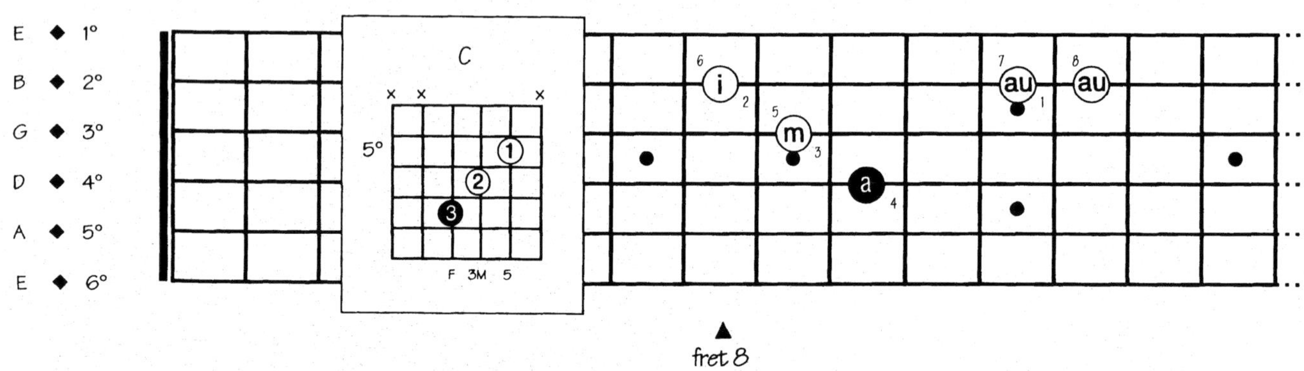

PART B1

Here is a new waltz to incorporate in your Manouche repertoire.

It is called "Dans Le Regard De Laura". You can hear it in two different versions on the Romane and on the Romane Quintet CDs.

The harmonic diagram is as follows:

Dans Le Regard De Laura

(Looking Like Laura)

3/4 ♩= 90

Global structure:
- 3x2 (intro)
- 32 AABB (theme)
- 2x2 (interlude)
- 3x16 AB (choruses)
- 2x2 (interlude
- 16 AB (final theme)
- 3x2 (coda fin)

x times

Intro. Interlude. Coda.	𝄆 Dm7M	$A7^{5\flat}$ 𝄇

A	Dm7M	Dm7	Gm7M	Gm7	$Bm7^{5\flat}$	$E7^{9\flat}$	$B\flat 7^{5\flat}$	A7
B	$D7M^{9}$	$A\flat 7^{5\flat}$	G7M	%	$E7^{11\sharp}_{9}$	%	A alt. (E♭/A)	% 𝄌

This piece has a peculiar structure because it uses an irregular split, where it systematically inserts a small recurring motive of two measures which is, this time, used as the introduction, the interlude and the coda.

The procedure of the "interlude" is often found in jazz. In most cases, it operates as a transition between different sections. Some interludes could reach up to eight measures. In France, we use the term "interlude", over the Atlantic it is called "vamp". This will seem rather mysterious for the non-initiated.

Finally, look how the metric structure is different between choruses (16 measures AB) and the initial illustration of the theme (32 measures AABB), which is a somewhat unusual procedure with jazz.

Chapter 20 / page 4

Let's see which chords we can play to accompany this waltz, except for those of the recurring motive in the two measures, which we will deal with later:

Section A:

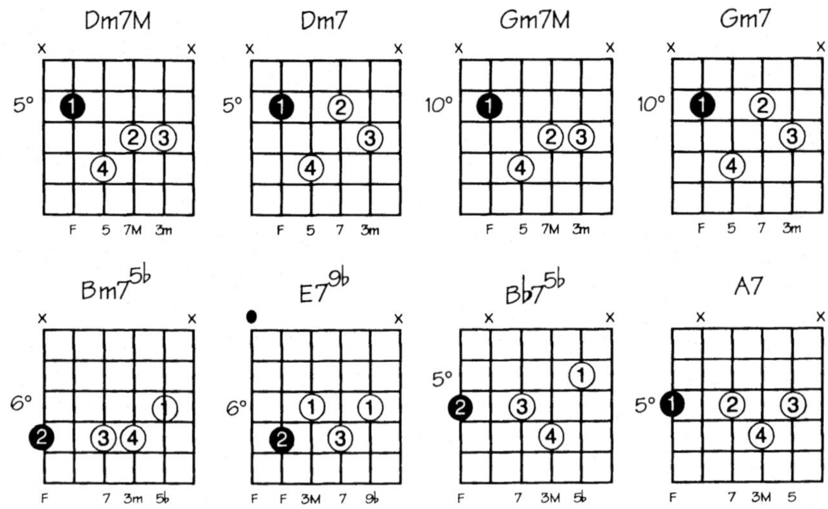

Section B:

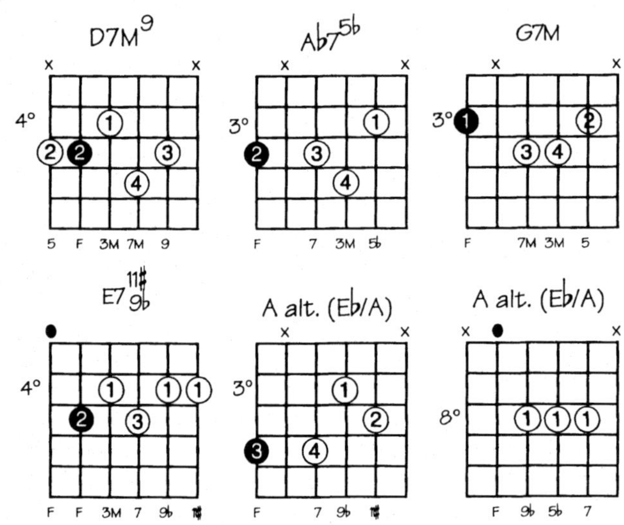

(option)

While listening to the CD, you should be aware that the interpretation of the accompaniment (in the theme) is not exactly the same from one section to the other. Section A is played "staccato", while section B is played "legato" (If you need to, look up the definitions of these terms in the glossary).

In general, when accompanying this piece keep an open mind, think of an earlier age in time, where it would be played on a hand-crank organ.

PART B2

At the end of this chapter, we will give you the theme and section A of the first chorus of "Dans Le Regard De Laura". We should, however, raise some points that must be considered in this music.

Dans Le Regard De Laura (theme) recurring motive

As we said before, this piece uses a little recurring motive in various places: in the intro, the interlude and the coda - two measures are repeated various times in the way it is written.

This recurring motive consists of two chords with four tones each that are strictly played in staccato. To make it easy to understand this, separate each note (a point over it means "picked" notes). To do it as in the introduction, you have to play this recurring motive as follows:

#76

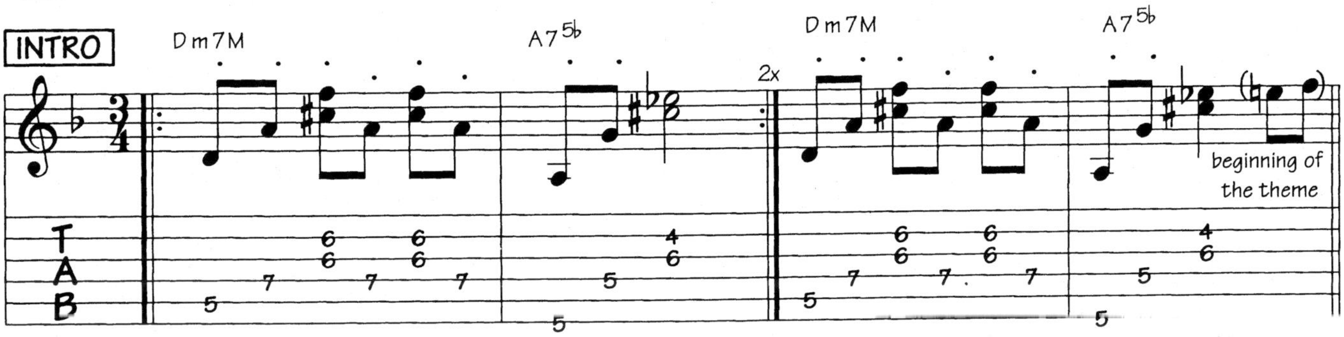

Dans Le Regard De Laura (theme) analysis of the melody

In music, the procedures for composing are extremely diversified. The list is too long to address in the present setting. This is a melodic "question-and-answer" procedure dealing with the harmony, in relation to the harmony.

The theme that we are using, is clearly one designed to show this procedure, by developing the melody with the logical thought of continuation, of which the conclusion is always a part of:

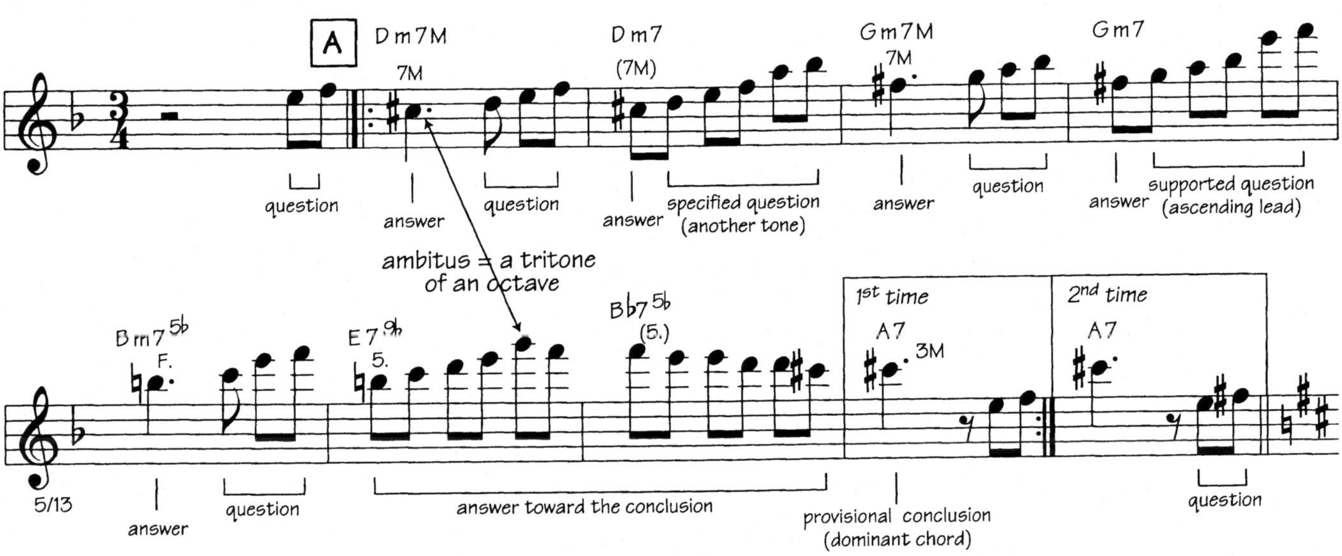

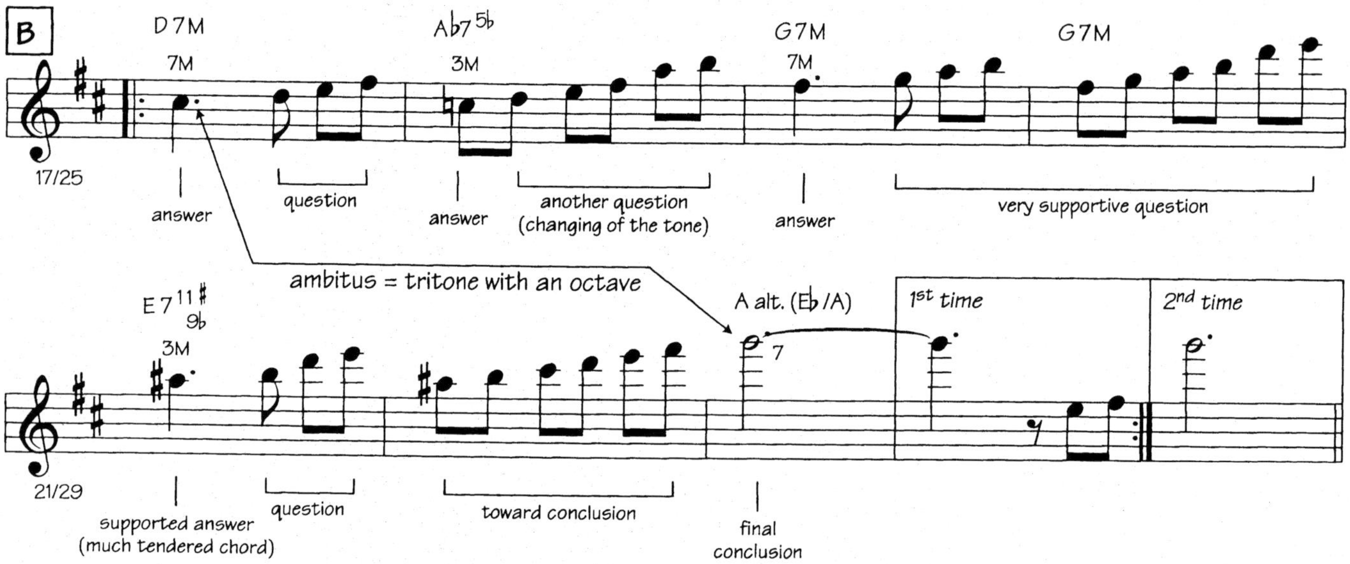

With aesthetics in mind, look at the detailed mechanics here, which are part of the development of the short melody of this waltz.

Notice how the "answers" are nearly always basic notes of the harmony (R, 3, 5 or 7). The result keeps an open mind that must proceed with an answer. Besides that, the melody will gain in value as far as the entire delivery goes. This happens only if you carefully increase the value of these notes with a vibrato effect (⁓) "answers" and "conclusion".

Notice the tritone ambitus of this melody, it gives you a global idea of tension and mystery (using a minor tone to begin with). This is not, however, incompatible with a certain tranquility, using a major tone next, but with very closed chords - namely the passing of the minor tone to a major tone with the same root note (here the D). It is the remaining process of a very up to date process involving a musical composition.

Dans Le Regard De Laura (chorus 1) explaining the melody

This first part of the chorus shows a very important aspect for improvisation: the timing of the phrases. Even more so, when it has to do with a slow tempo like we see here. It is the principle of specified notes combined with the intervening chromaticisms as marked. It also explains the impression of "elasticity" that takes itself away from this chorus, by using enough unusual rhythmic cells, although they are logically structured in jazz.

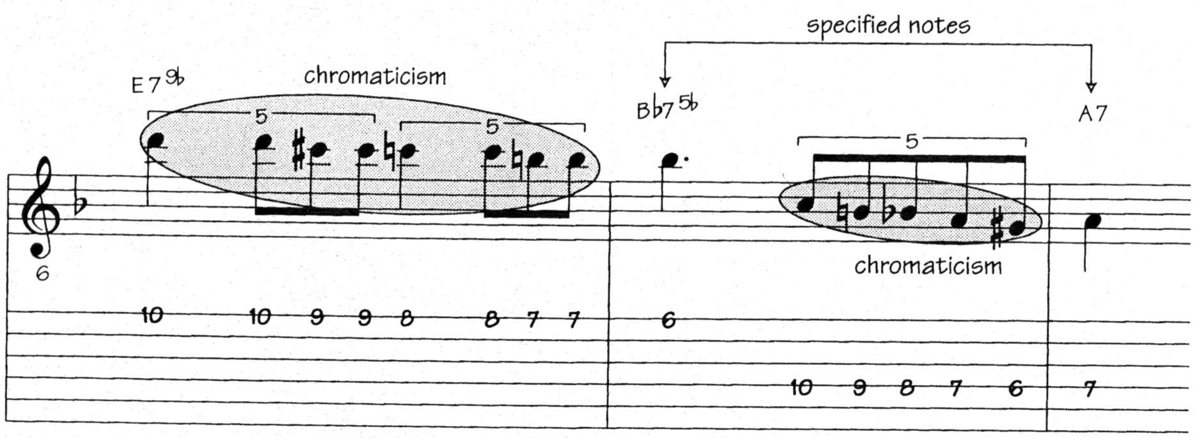

PART C

Here is the theme of "Dans Le Regard De Laura". Use the vibrato with all the answer notes, as soon as you can, particularly those with a long duration.

#76

Dans Le Regard De Laura

music by ROMANE

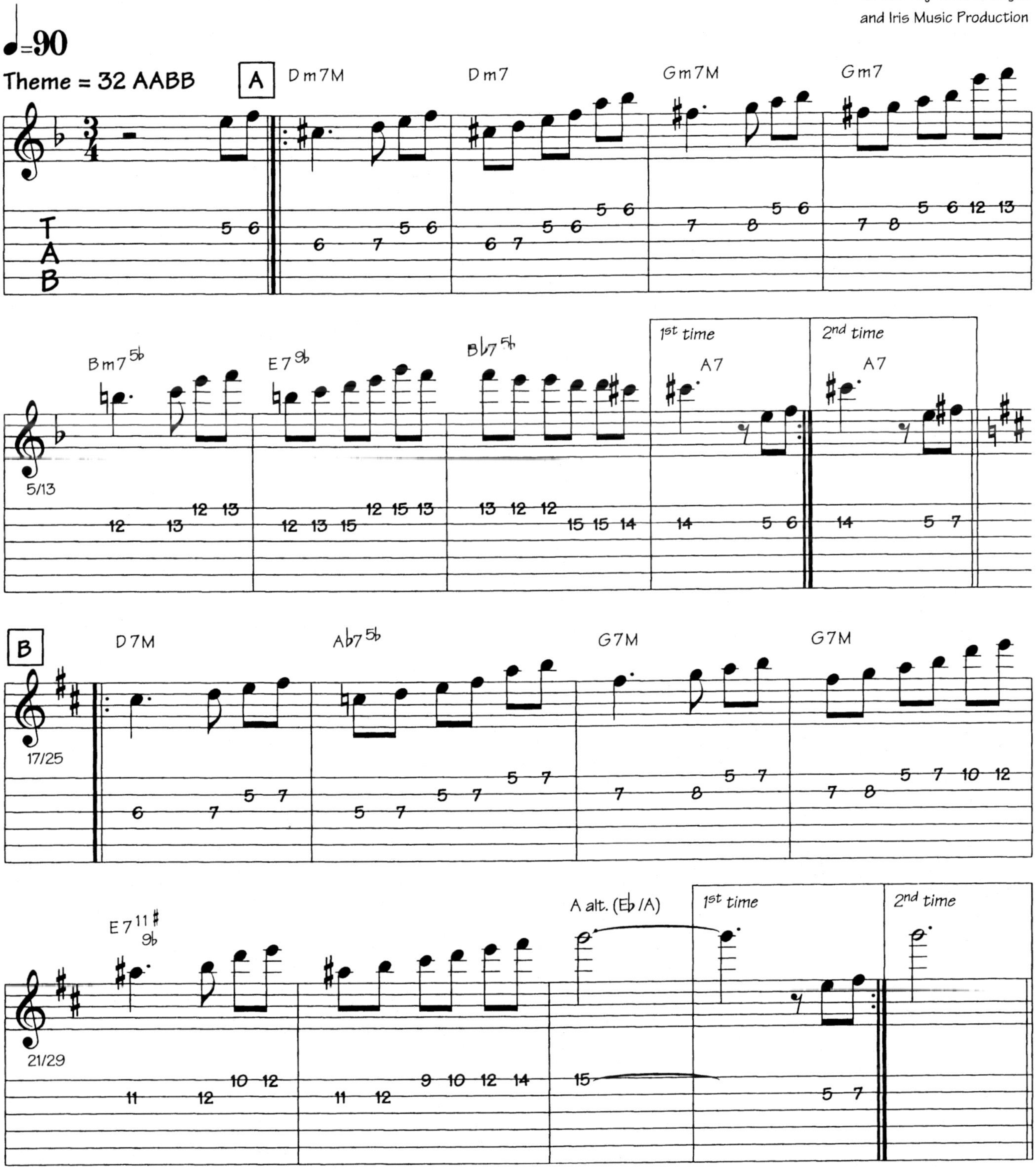

Chapter 20 / page 8

After the interlude of 4 measures we continue with the first theme shown, we join it with the first chorus of 16 measures.

If you aren't absolutely sure of yourself, listen carefully to the CD for where to place the quintuplets in measures 6 and 7.

This guitar chorus is taken from the CD version of Romane Quintet.

Chorus 1 = 16 AB

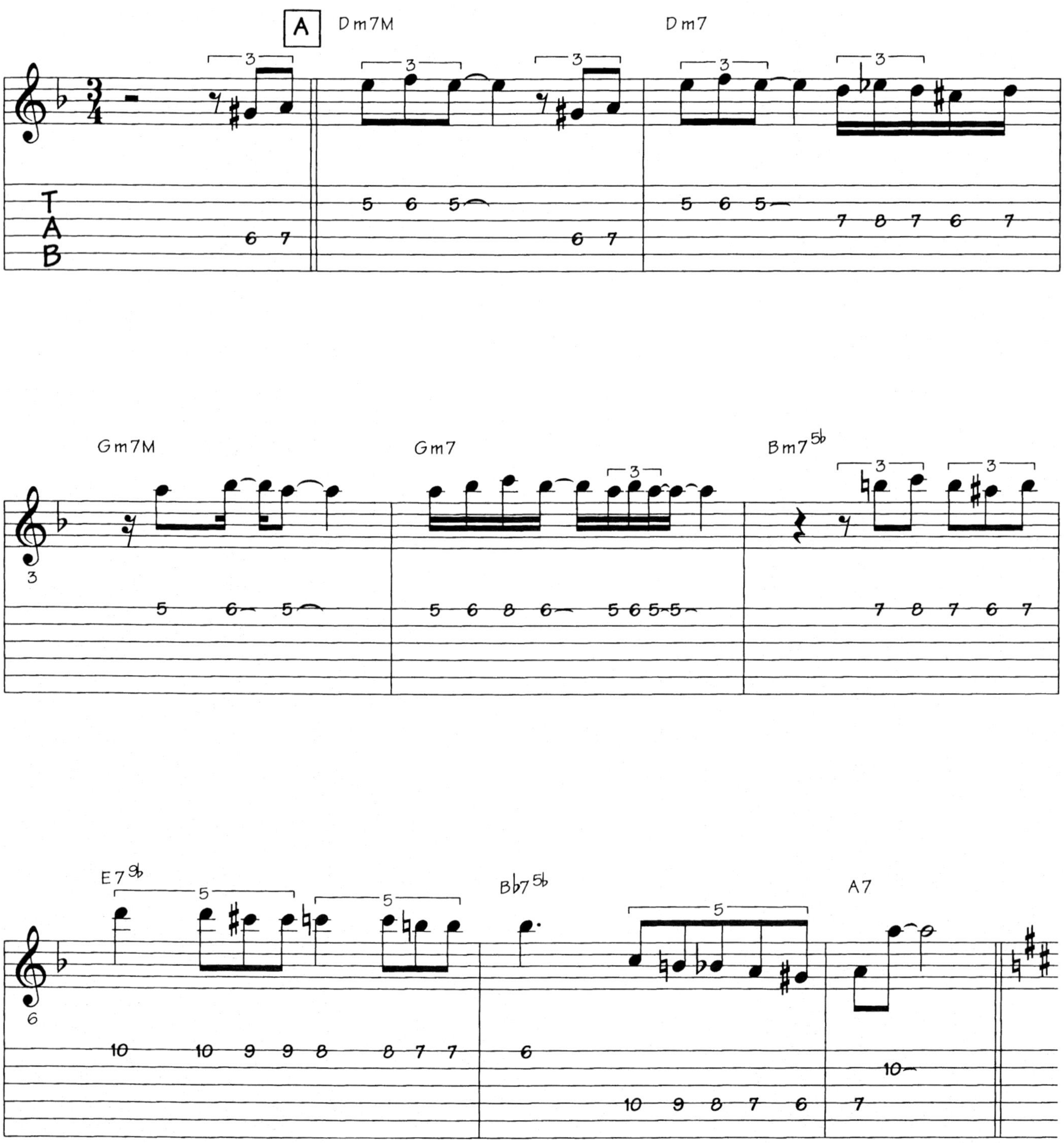

PART A

Exercise 64 - melody harmonized with the G major anatole

Here is the result of the four preceding exercises (chapter 19 and 20) with the anatole/turnaround and the "magic" note as a connection between the phrases.

If you have another guitar player avaiable, you can play this melody together, so that you can harmonize with it in thirds. This sounds powerful and great with two guitars. If not, you can record one of the other parts and play it back, so that you can play the harmonization at the same time.

This harmonization is in the key of G major, with the chords of the anatole/turnaround, thus:

#77

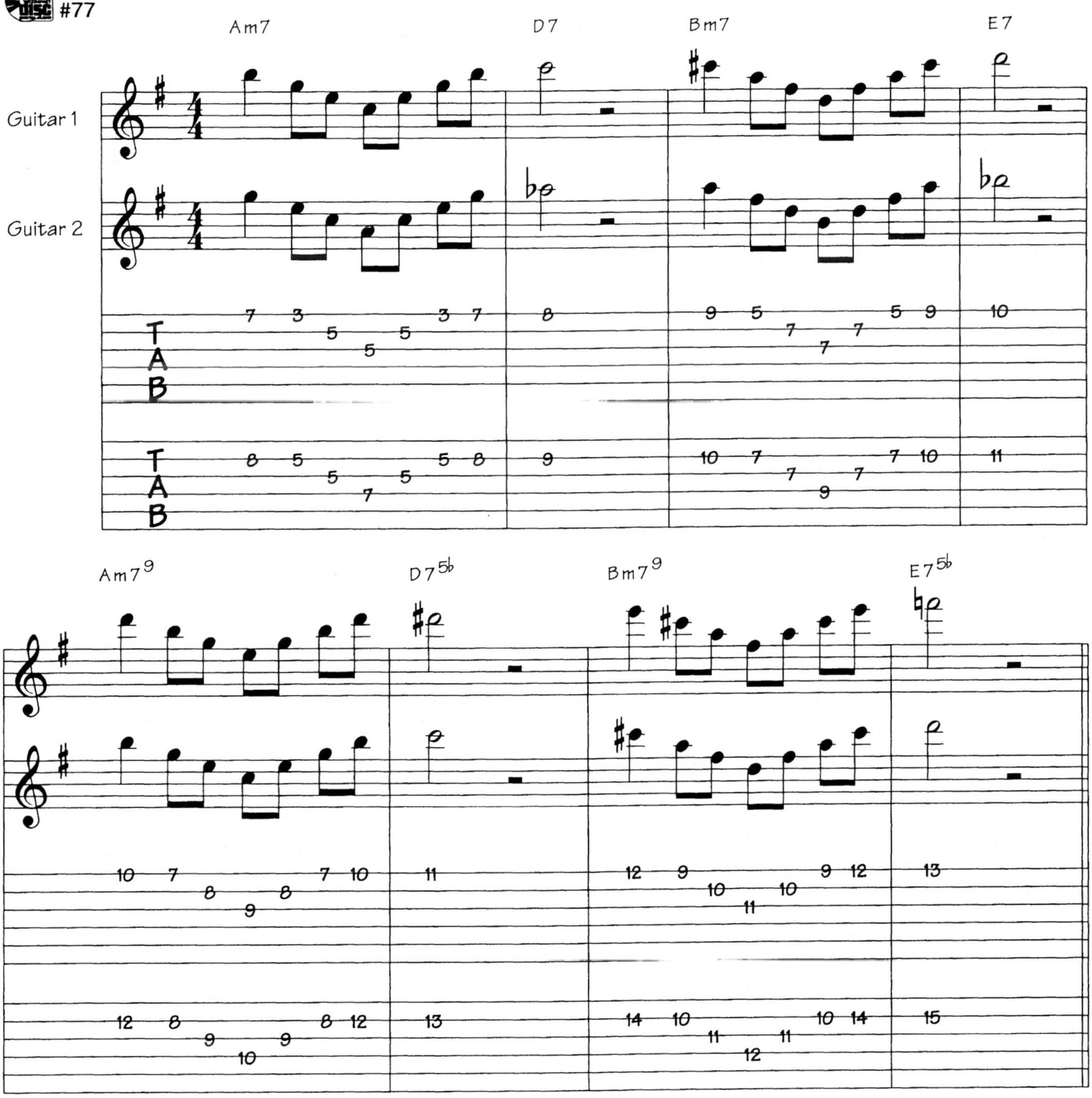

Exercise 65 - a progression with dominant altered chords

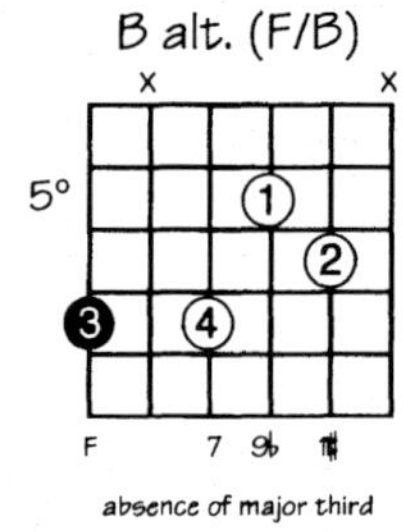

Do you remember the B alt. (F/B) chord?
As seen before, this chord is missing a third. But these chords still belong to the dominant class with its particular coloration, as well as in the harmony that is always used to form an "altered" type chord (compare this with the last measures in the bridge of "Dans Le Regard De Laura").

During our study of the scale and the altered chords (chapter 18), we have seen this chord and specified it with an "alt." symbol. This was done to define it as one of the dominant seventh chords, where either its major third or its minor seventh is missing, and here the "F/B" chord is in between (the F/B is a major triad - F - with the b5 at the bass - B).

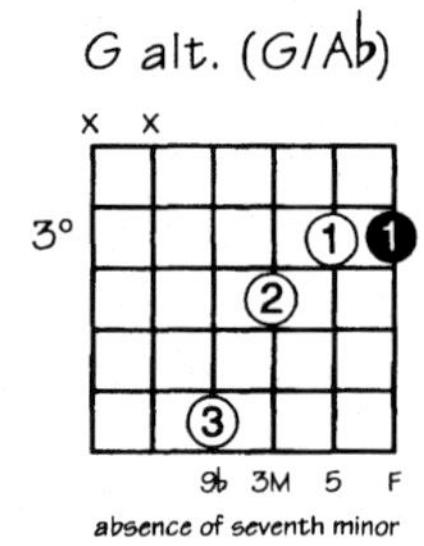

With this exercise, let's discover another chord of the same type, just as convincing and used as much: that forms a major triad with the one where we add a 9b at the bass. The resulting chord will lack a minor seventh and be classified, by virtue of the context where it is always used, as an "altered" type chord (V degree).

Let's put this chord in a harmonic context: it is a tension (V = G7) driven by a resolution (I = C7M).

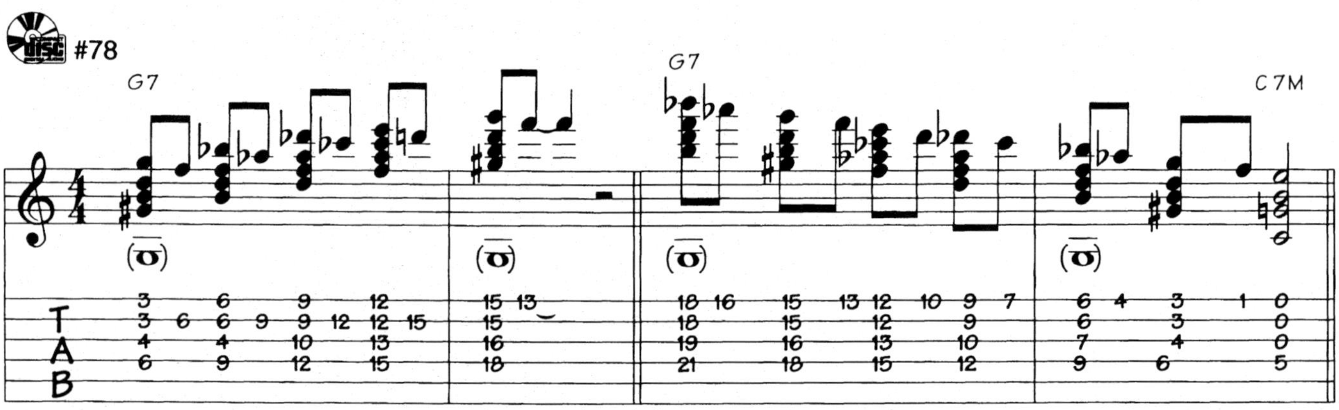

We will look at this once more, the chord is systematically linked together and spaced with minor thirds, which of course gives us a "dim7" arpeggio and its procession of a tritone substitutions.

On the other hand, as in the case of exercise 59 (chapter 18), the lower G note appears here, clearly showing that the entire harmonic phrase relies on the idea that G7 goes with C7M, despite the fact that the chords change.

Finally, notice in the passage that this "G alt." can be put in relation with another altered chord (this one complete), that is nothing other than the V7 of the A minor key... the relative minor of the C7M. Thus we could have resolved this harmonic phrase perfectly with an Am chord.

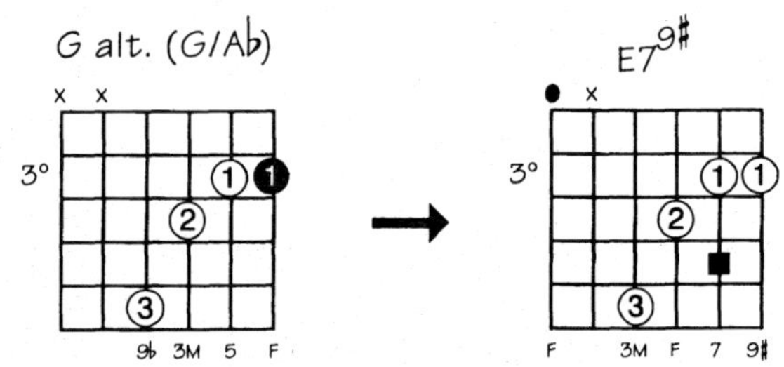

▪ PART B1

Let's continue analyzing the harmonies of "Le Regard De Laura".

Here is the new diagram.

A — Key: Dm

1				5			
I	I	IV	IV	IIm de II7	II7	ST de II7	V
Dm7M	Dm7	Gm7M	Gm7	Bm7^{5b}	E7^{9b}	Bb7^{5b}	A7

B — Key: D

9				13			
I	ST de I7	IV		II7		V	
D7M^{9}	Ab7^{5b}	G7M	%	E7$^{11\#}_{9}$	%	A alt. (Eb/A)	%

From one section to the other, the principle used appears as it is shown: having the same central root note - D, which follows the same trend, but modulating from the minor key to the major key.

The keys of the chords of the I, IV and V degree nearly meet in the same areas. The two sections are only different with the way they use the principles and substitutions. The details of which are given below:

MEASURES 1 – 2: chords with the root notes in the two frets. Two types of seventh (7 and 7M), these do not change the quality of the chord, which remains a fundamental chord.

MEASURES 3 – 4: using the IV degree, with the same colorations as the fundamental chord. Of course, like in measures 1 - 2, these colorations do not change any of the global function of the chord.

MEASURE 5: here we have the use of a strange chord in the key of D minor. Indeed, we find no Bm7(b5) among the seven degrees of the natural minor D scale (or, the F major scale that starts with its VI degree - see the table in chapter 8, page 6). In fact, having been given that measure 6 introduces an E7 chord, the Bm7(b5) chord functions as a transition of the II degree of this E7 according to the principle shown in chapter 14, page 6, which is:

"All the dominant seventh chords (V7) can be preceded by, or mixed with, a minor chord of which the root note is located one perfect fifth higher."

The Bm7(b5) is located a perfect fifth above the E7. This principle relies on the idea that to form a II-V progression, even if this progression doesn't resolve with a fundamental chord.

MEASURE 6: in the capacity of the II7, the E7 is the V7 of the real V of the D minor key, known to us as the A7 chord, which finishes the eight measures of section A.

MEASURE 7: the T.S. of E7, the Bb7(b5) chord, could also be considered as an E7(b5), as was discussed on page 4, chapter 16.

MEASURE 8: the A7, that entered into the scene with the unavoidable V of the key in question, will give us the opportunity to explain the following important principle:

"All major, minor or seventh dominant chords can provisionally be considered as a chord of the I degree, and can, as a result of that, be introduced with A II - V progression."

Thus, this A7 is effectively the result of the II - V in measure 5.

Now, with regard to measures 5 – 8, as well as to the global area of the D minor key, we can also consider the following things, as shown here:

The Bm7(b5) = VI... the E7 = II7... the A7 = V... a VI – II – V that forms a part of the harmonic progression with which you are certainly familiar with at this point, the anatole, but in the minor key this time.

MEASURE 9: here is a minor anatole, which resolves into major. To be honest, you must wonder why this has so much more authority than the D note, which never had this status. As a matter of fact, it will never have a particular preference for the major or the minor (here, the center static root note: D minor key, then the D major).

MEASURE 10: the T.S. of D7 (I7) makes a passage (by using descending chromatics) to the IV degree in measure 11. Notice here that by following the example of section A, the harmony still plays with alternating sevenths: D7M → D7. But in the case of the D7, there is a noticeable difference: a minor seventh combined with a major chord that is called a dominant (tension) chord, which freely calls for another chord (resolution). However, this was not the case with Dm7 in measure 2.

MEASURE 11: the "Resolution" of Ab7 with G7M, the IV degree of the D major key.

MEASURE 13: the E7(b9,#11) works exactly the same way as the E7 in measure 6: this is the V of the real V degree which takes place in measure 15. With this chord, we let the passage know that if one replaces the tonic E by a Bb (T.S.), we get:

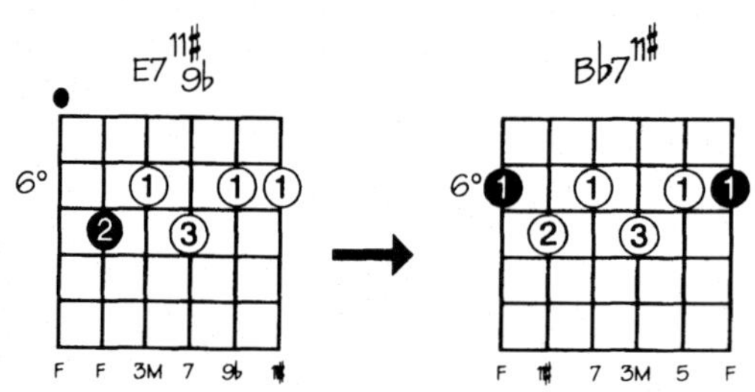

MEASURE 15: finally, the A7 introduces the V degree in the key of D major. This final chord is special because it misses the major third. It is for this reason that it is shown as "A alt.". But it performs no less than an authentic V. As we have been told, on the one hand it maintains a lower A (bass) in the key in question, and it is in the other part brought in by an II degree (E7) of this same key. Besides this, its altered quality, as well as its length (two entire measures) indicate the imminent return toward the D minor tone.

PART B2

Now we are going to study specific points of the first chorus of "Dans Le Regard De Laura."

Dans Le Regard De Laura (measures 9 - 10) lead #1

Measure 10 starts with a chromatic descent. Measure 10 shows a very academic illustration of the T.S: the use of the Ab major triad (encircled) that we saw with the same harmonic analysis as illustrated in the diagram, with the understanding that it is a D7. We count three tones from Ab to D.

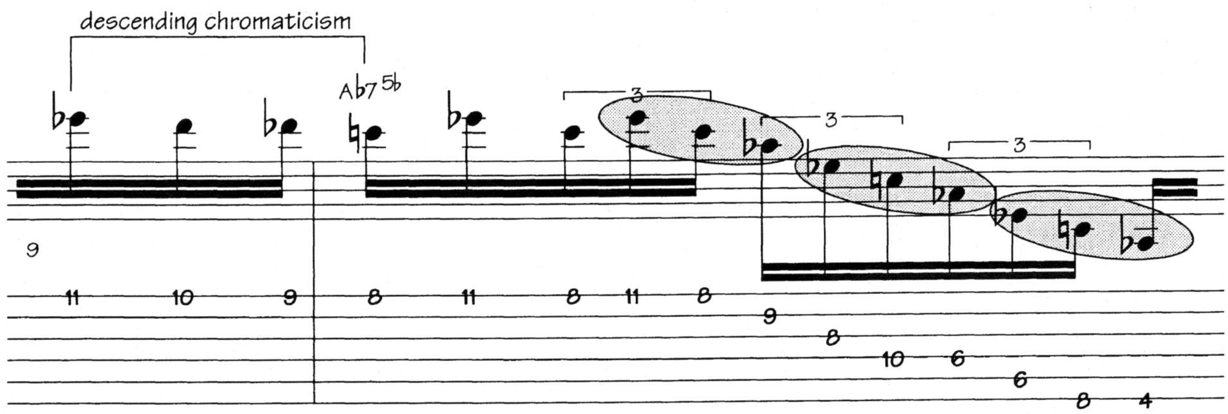

Dans Le Regard De Laura (measure 13) lead #2

The whole tone scale appears here in its primitive form. The current use of this scale is very appropriate with the harmony that we are now looking at.

Indeed, after we examine the harmonic functions, which have cleared themselves of the six notes, it becomes apparent that they form the whole tone scale. We will consider that it starts with the E root note. It seems that this corresponds exactly with an E7(9,#11) chord:

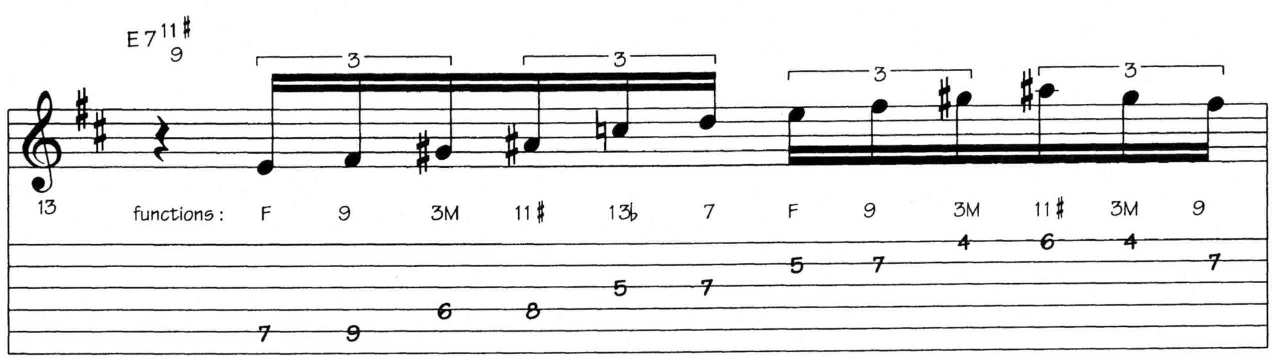

Dans Le Regard De Laura (measure 14) lead #3

The development of the whole tone scale with a structured melody forms a cell of four notes that evidently progresses... by tones! The fingerboard diagram is very easy to remember, and leads you in the direction that you want it to go:

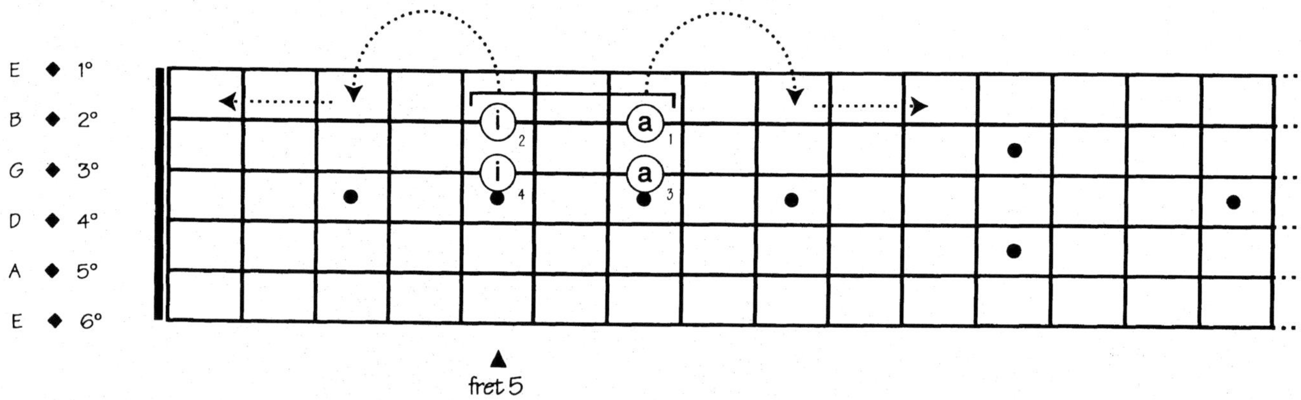

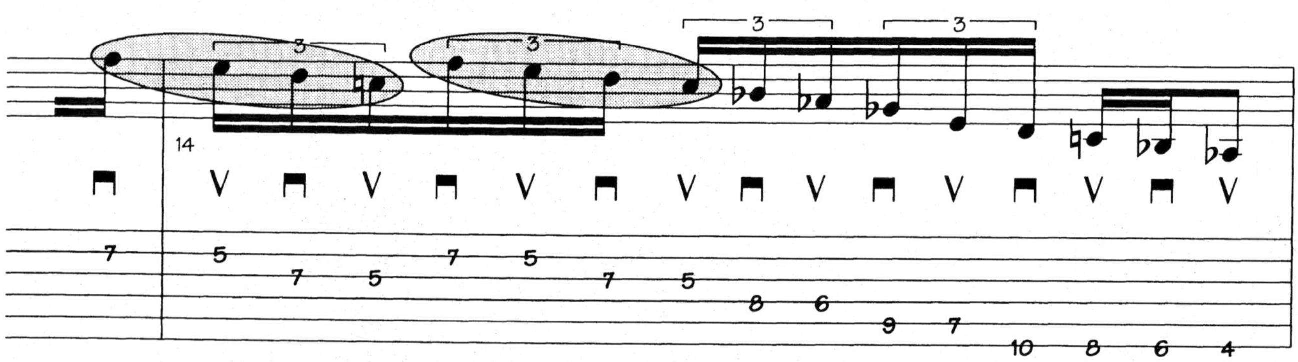

Notice how all the notes are regularly played with up and down strokes of the pick, when you use this whole tone scale.

Dans Le Regard De Laura (measure 15) lead #4

In short, measure 15 shows a tritone arpeggio: the combination of two major triads where the root notes are located three tones apart from each other (A and Eb). This of course corresponds perfectly with the harmony that we are looking at now. It is a major Eb triad supported by an A in the bass.

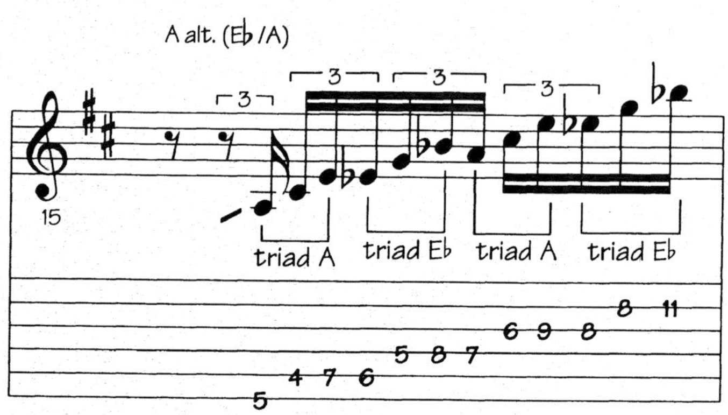

PART C

Continuing the first chorus of "Dans Le Regard De Laura".

Watch out for the slides that decorate this solo.

You should listen for the quintuplets in the last measure. Listen to the CD, because you must recognize how jazz is improvised, especially in the case of the note for note summaries. Nothing could be more efficient, and pay off better than to let your listening work for you!

#76

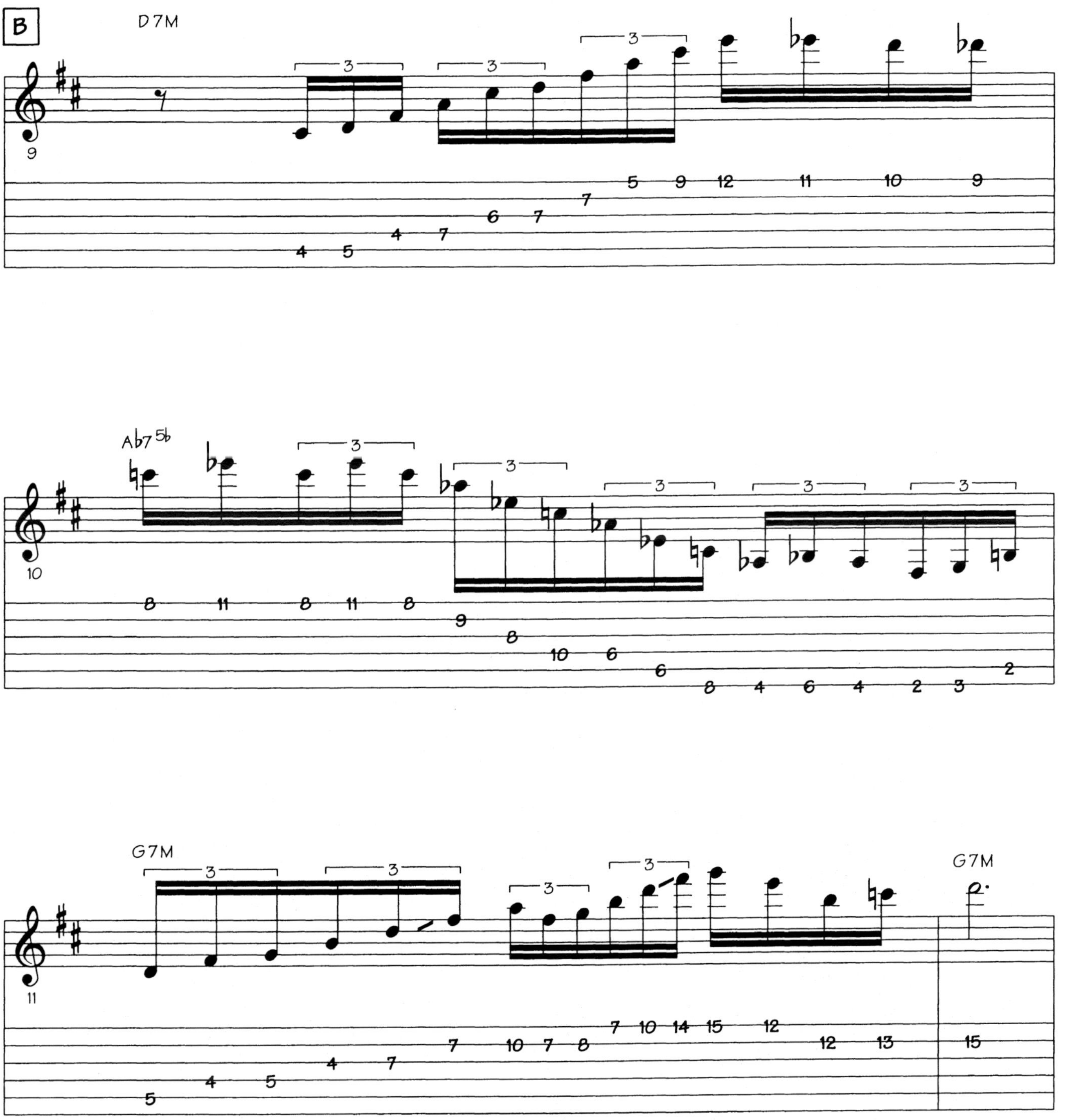

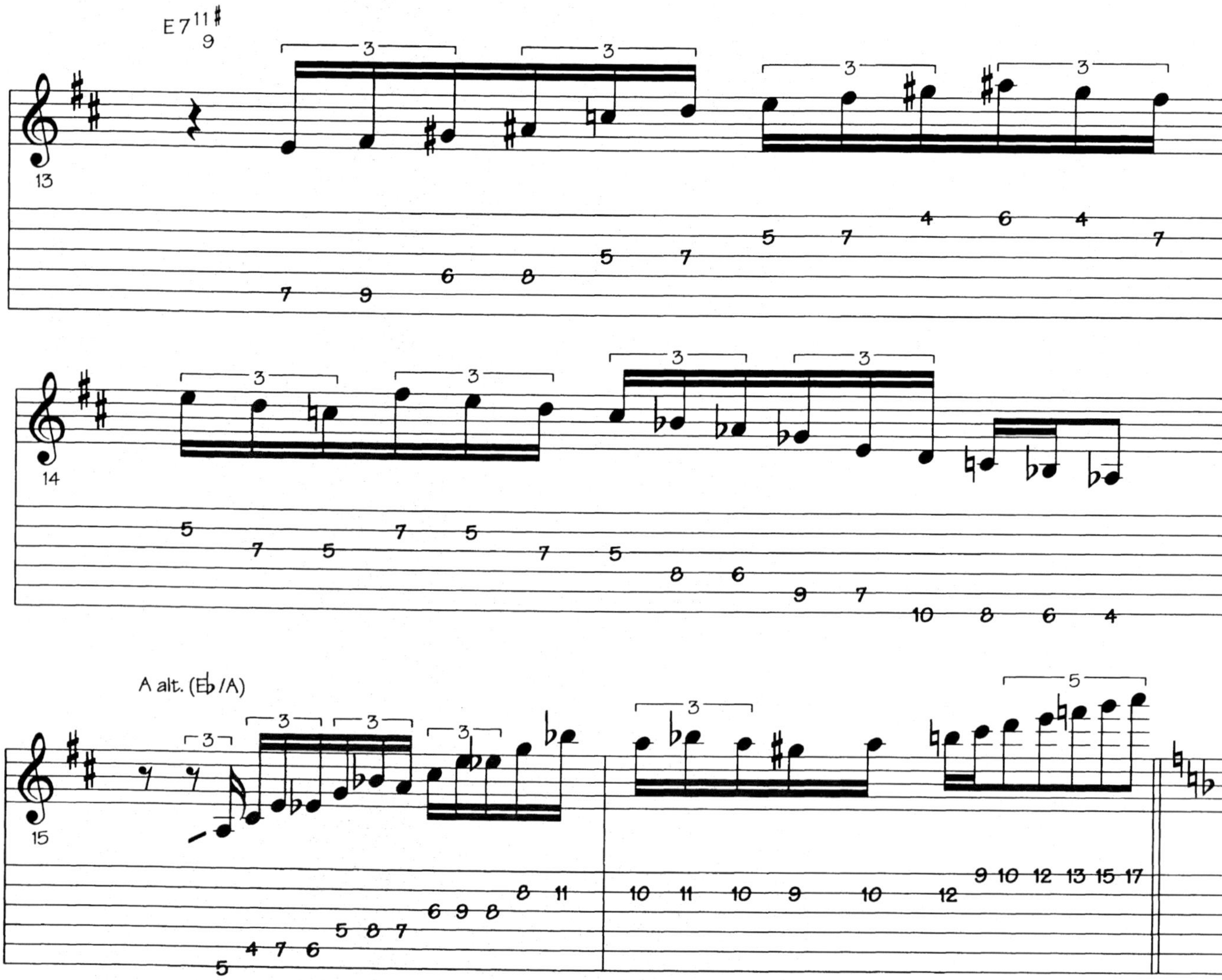

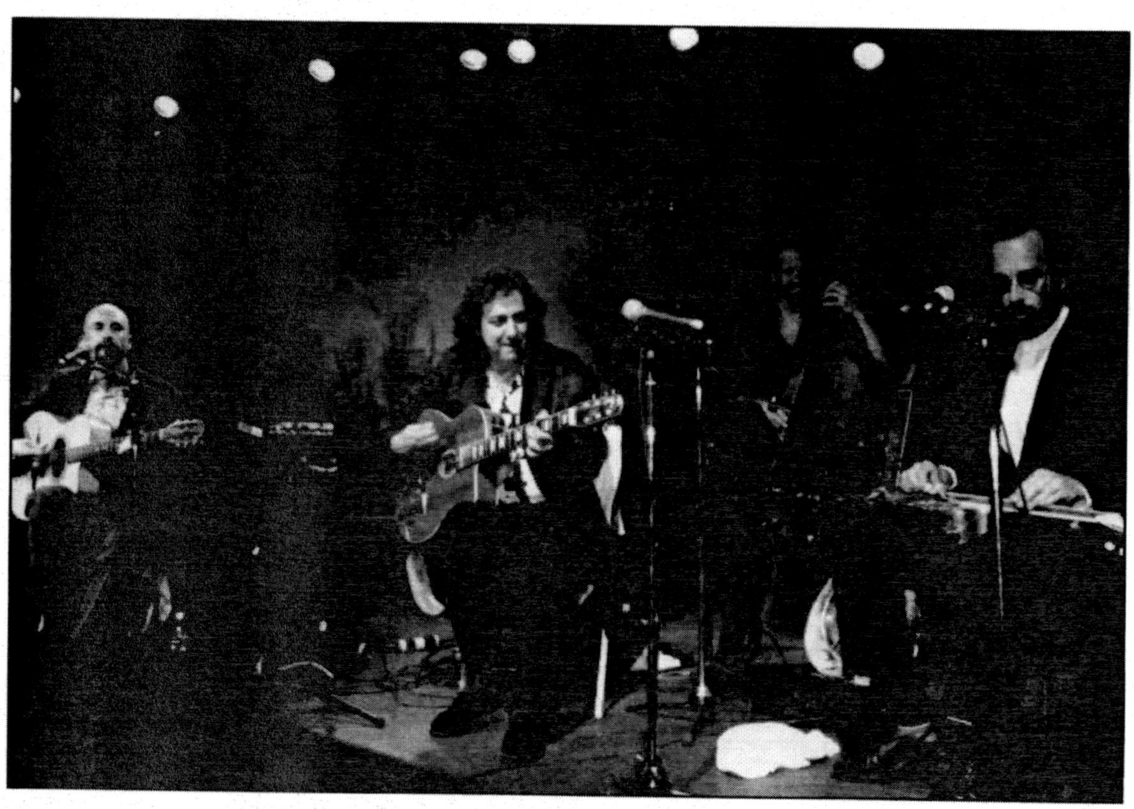

Philippe "Doudou" Cuillerier, Romane, Doug, Bob Brozman

PART A

With the exercises in this chapter you must make an effort of loosening up your finger joints by playing the chords that are next, which are very typical in the Manouche playing style in the rhythm section.

Exercise 66 - Manouche voicings with the anatole (1)

To start with, here are the positions which the Manouche freely use with the progression of the harmonic anatole, it is labeled this way because it is the "Manouche anatole".

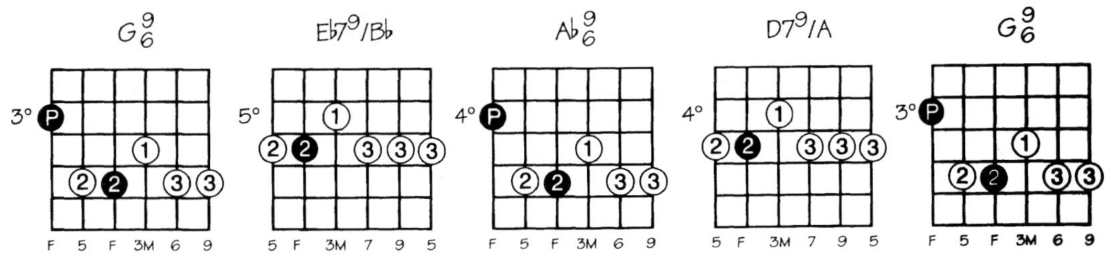

Watch out when going through the chords without forewarning the other musicians around you, especially the bassist. The modifications are done here with the anatole that is commonly used (in G major it will form: G - E7 - Am - D7 - G).

Exercise 67 - Manouche voicings with the major II - V - 1

Let's continue with the II - V - I in the making, where we still use half-barred chords and with the selected anti-academic position of the thumb:

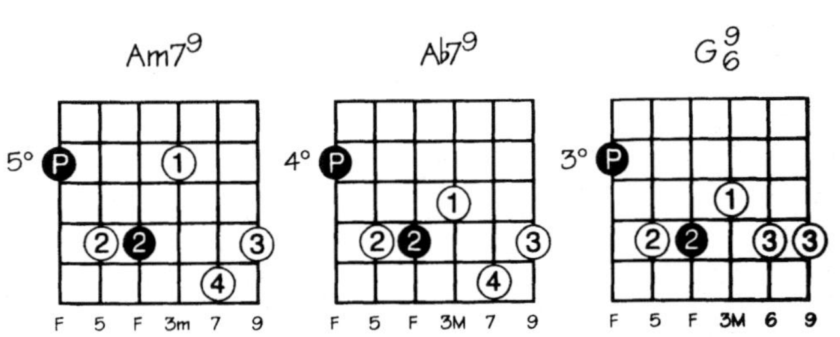

Exercise 68 - Manouche voicings with the anatole (2)

Here is a long developed voicing that is always in the key of G major, based on the usual anatole, which is:

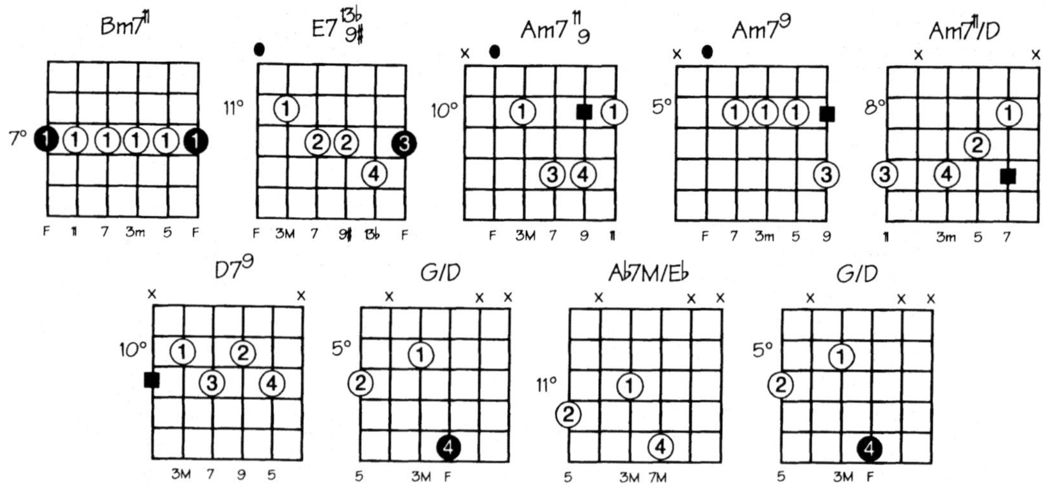

Notice that the last three chords of this voicing form a very convincing cadence to make a harmonic conclusion (end of the section, coda final, etc.). Otherwise, we can simply indicate the fifth chord as a C/D, being a C major triad, with a D in the bass. But it is preferable to write Am7(11)/D because, in the key of G major, this symbol clearly expresses that it has to do with the II degree (Am) going toward a V degree (D7).

Exercise 69 - Manouche style harmony, continued

Continuing with the harmony where, from one chord to the next, the higher voice is static while the bass descends chromatically. This makes this collection of "broken fingers" perfect! It is the procedure of the counter movement of voices, which governs the development of the voicing worthy of its name. Then again, the 'end' character of this chord progression should not escape you when listening to it using the CD!

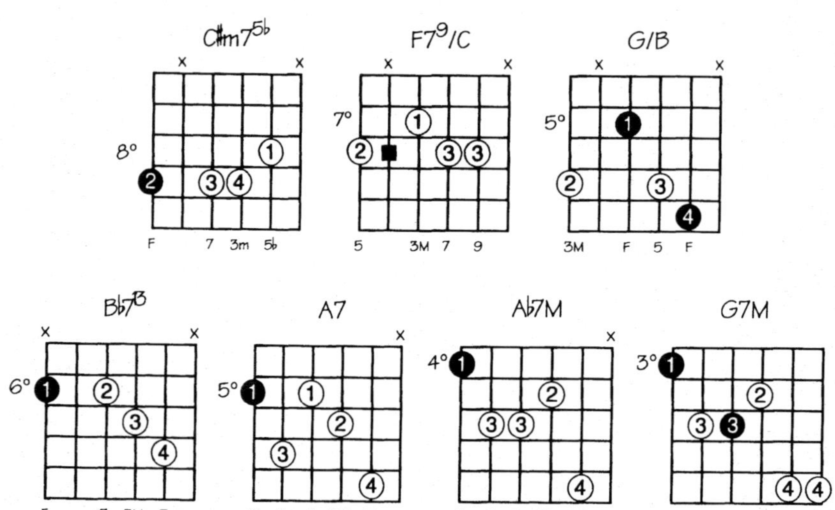

PART B1

In chapter 18 we studied the altered scale, stemming from the minor harmonic scale. We are now going to show you how to complete the harmonization of the melodic minor scale perfectly.

The structure and function of these note components are as follows: (using the melodic C minor):

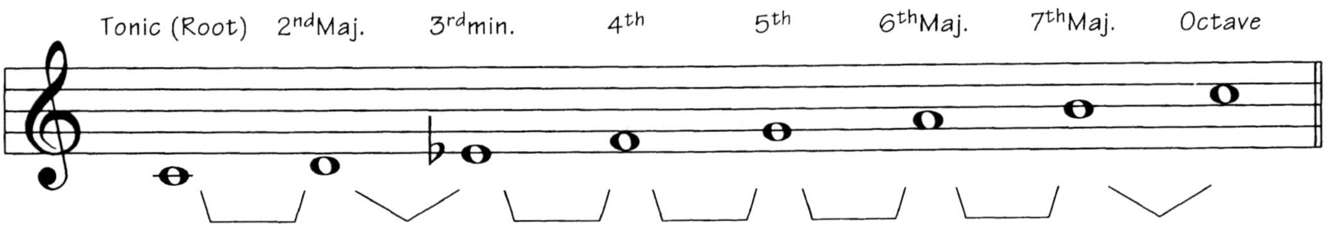

Remark: notice that the Eb, the only alteration present, is not put in the key signature. You should never put an alteration "b" or "#" in the key signature.

We immediately see what type of chords this scale produces, when we harmonize these by stacking three thirds (M or m) above each of the seven notes. This procedure gives us chords with four distinct pitches (tones):

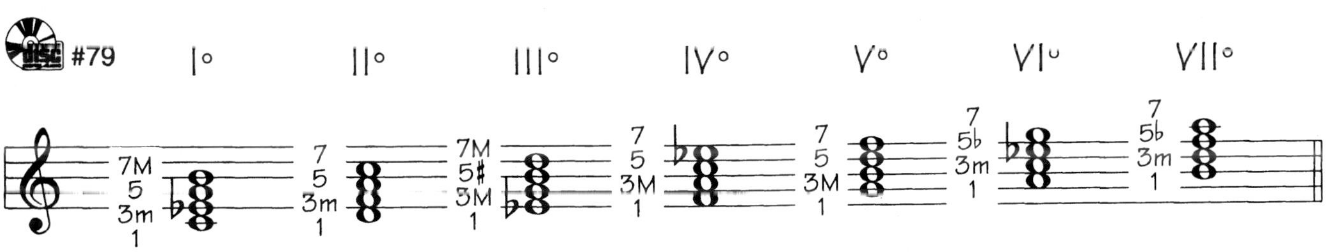

Harmonic symbol with 3 notes:	Cm	Dm	Eb +	F	G	Adim	Bdim
Harmonic symbol with 4 notes:	Cm7M	Dm7	Eb7M5#	F7	G7	Am7^5b	Bm7^5b

Of course, notice that this is a harmonization in theory only. Consider what has been shown in chapter 18, (page 4). In practice we always have the VII degree work as a dominant chord and not as a minor chord, like it is shown here.

You will notice from this, by following the example of the minor harmonic scale (chapter 2, page 3), that the harmonization of the minor harmonic scale presents a very important fact. Namely: it develops a seventh dominant chord 1 - 3M - 5 - 7: here G - B - D - F = G7, with its V degree.

Otherwise, the I and II degrees will develop into a minor chord (Cm and Dm).

Conclusion: the melodic minor scale is capable of forming, as is its minor harmonic cousin, a minor II - V - I cadence (here, the Dm -G7 -Cm) a topic of higher interest, however, we will come back to this later.

Right now we will finish our lesson on the minor harmonic scale, while thinking of another important fact that takes away its harmonization: the presence of a second dominant chord, with the IV degree.

We know that all dominant chords, whatever they are, are potentially a step to form a "dominant → root note" (V7 → I, M or m) cadence. We then know that this second dominant chord highlights the melodic minor scale with a very interesting modulating angle.

Indeed, with the F7 (IV degree of the melodic minor C scale) it is possible to head for the Bb major, within reason that is. There is a strange key among the melodic minor scale. The C minor melodic scale is a basis to improvise with, using a harmonic altered anatole progression (III -VI7 - II - V - I). This is all made possible since its first four chords are all descended from the harmonization of this scale.

degrees of Bb major (anatole):	III°	VI7°	II°	V°	I°	
	‖ Dm7	G7 |	Cm7	F7 |	Bb7M |	⁒ ‖
degrees of melodic minor C:	II°	V°	I°	IV°	—	

This can all be summed up with the following principle:

"All minor melodic scales can be used to improvise with an anatole progression, of which its center root note is placed one tone lower."

Otherwise, the IV degree of the melodic minor scale gives the maximum guarantees of tonal efficiency with the harmony. By successively harmonizing up to seven sounds, we develop the following functions:

#80

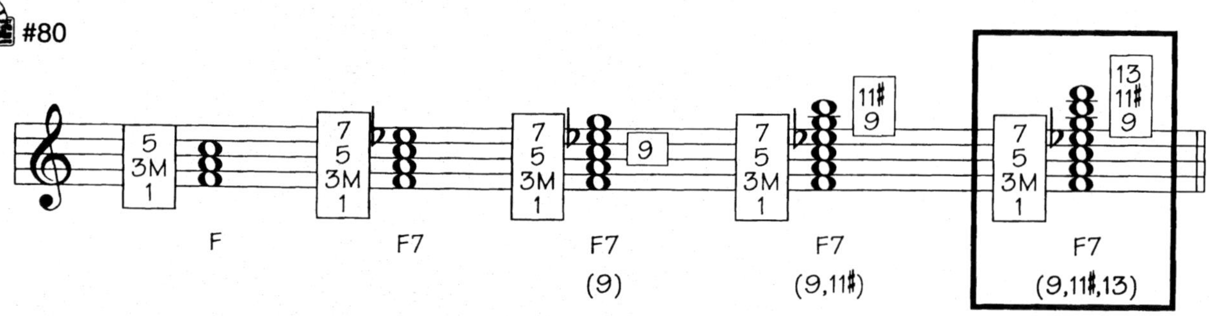

With these "9, #11, 13" colorations, this dominant chord, is in effect particularly adapted for the tonal subject. Here are some examples: 7(b5), "7(9, #11)", 7(#11,13) etc.

Thus, when we are about to improvise with an F7 chord, we'd rather use the melodic minor C scale, that is centered on the F note. We would rather do this than using Bb major (Bb7M = I degree if F7 = the V degree) that is centered on this same F note.

This is done for the reason that with the F7 the C melodic minor doesn't give any ambiguous notes within the tonal structure. On the other hand, the Bb does create ambiguous notes, namely the Bb note, the perfect fourth (or 11) for the F7. In principle, this note must only be used as a "passing note". It should have a short value away from the heavy beat, without any accentuation.

Whatever it may be, this is a case of personal taste... improvising should always remain a form of expression, without any of the theoretical hindrances.

PART B2

We are now going to study the leads in the style of Manouche that we find in the final chorus of "Dans Le Regard De Laura".

Dans Le Regard De Laura (measures 20 - 22) lead #5

This shows the flexibility of the melody when a note of the harmony is designated (The #11 in measure 22). This is an ascending chromaticism in three movements, shown with the cell of rhythmic repetitions, and moved in relation to the strong beats (the triplet in eighths is placed between the first and second beat in measure 21):

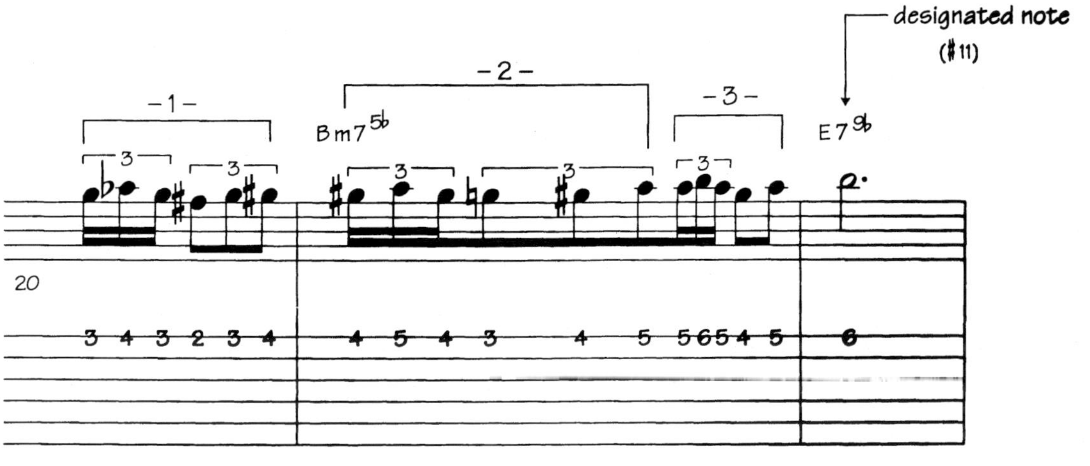

Dans Le Regard De Laura (measures 26 - 27) lead #6

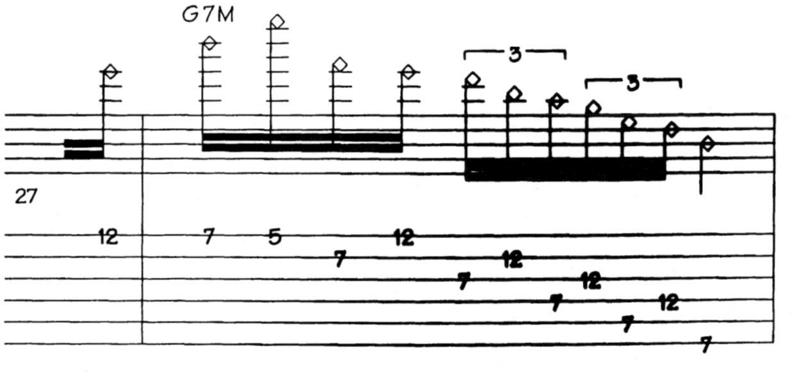

This use of natural harmonics is, without a doubt, a signature of the Manouche.

Besides the notations in the TAB, we have the fingerboard diagram (next page), so that you can play most of the notes of this lead.

Play the notes in the ascending numerical order.

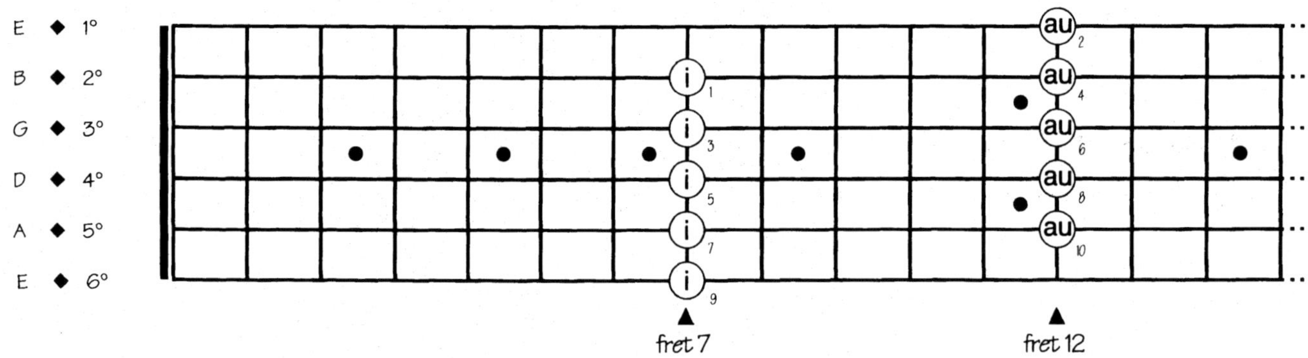

Since we speak of the harmonics that we always use with the harmonies in the G major key (or possibly those of E minor - the relative minor of G major), you can play the following variation shown here:

Play the notes in the ascending numerical order. (pay attention to the same harmonics that are used twice):

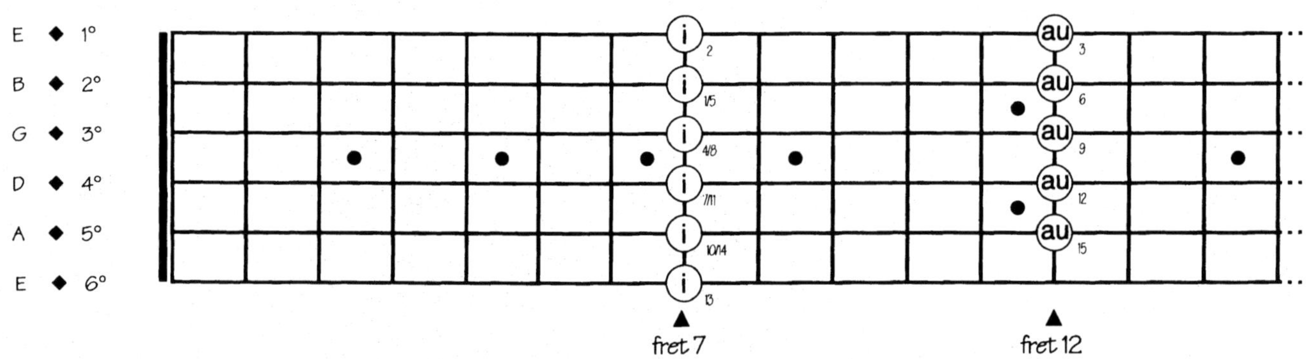

PART C

The continuation and end of the second chorus of “Dans Le Regard De Laura”.

Listen to the CD carefully to get the best subtleties, the “flexibility” of the delivery of the melody.

Also pay attention to the slowing down of the beat (rall...) in the final measure.

#76

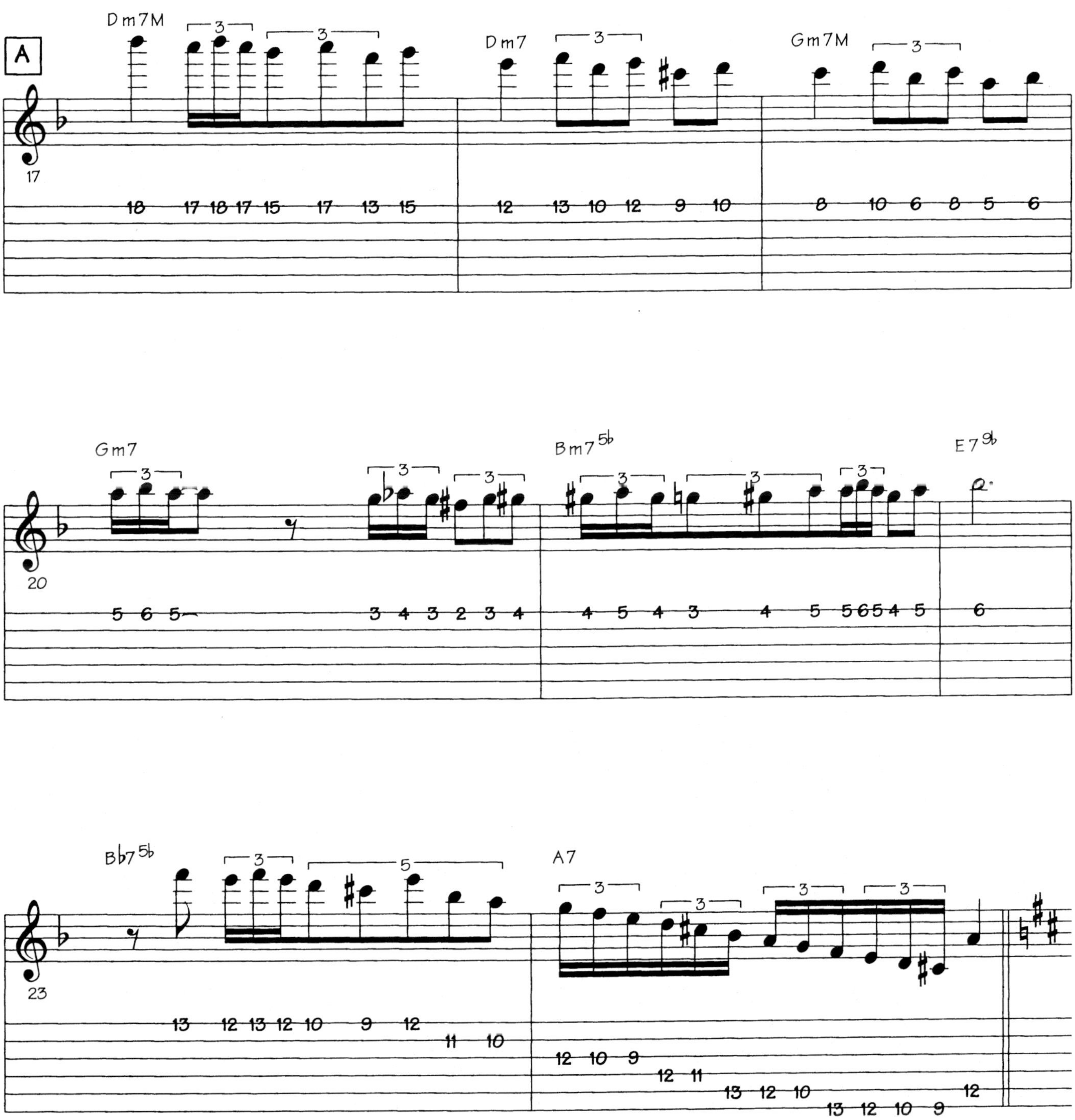

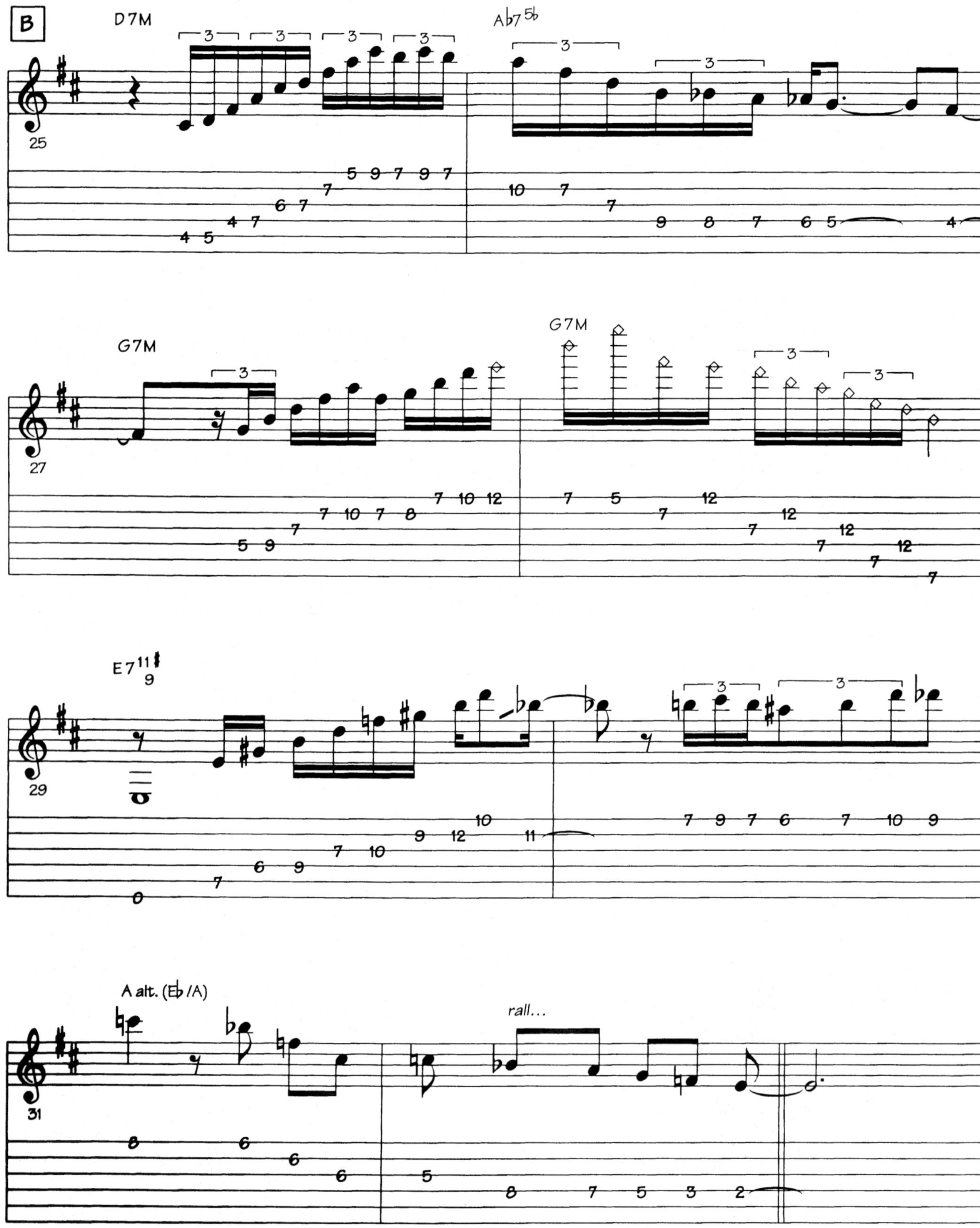
B
D7M
Ab7 5b
G7M
G7M
E7 11# 9
A alt. (Eb/A)
rall...

PART A

Exercise 70 - melody with skipping intervals (1)

By following the adventure of "Arc En Ciel" - we suggest that you study this chapter, as well as the next one, which comprises of the series of the exercises that we have here. These are "classical" in nature. The objective is that you practice with the skipping intervals while listening to it, and that you practice in such a way so that you develop the melody lines around the "revolving" notes.

In each case you have the freedom to choose how to attack the notes: with the pick (using any method) or by playing finger style, as the classical guitarists do.

Developed from the scale of major C, the first of these exercises is as follows:

#81

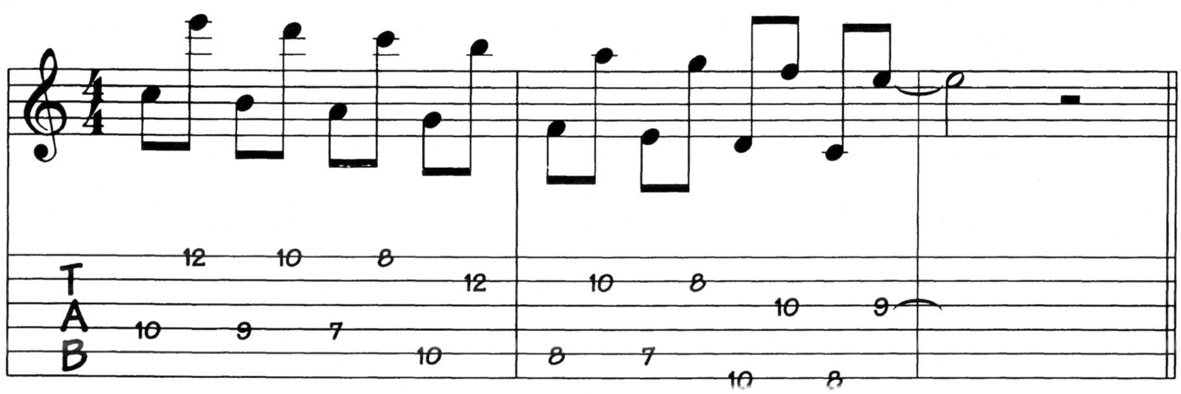

Exercise 71 - melody with skipping intervals (2)

Here is the second exercise with skipping intervals revolving around one note (encircled); relies on the A harmonic minor scale.

#82

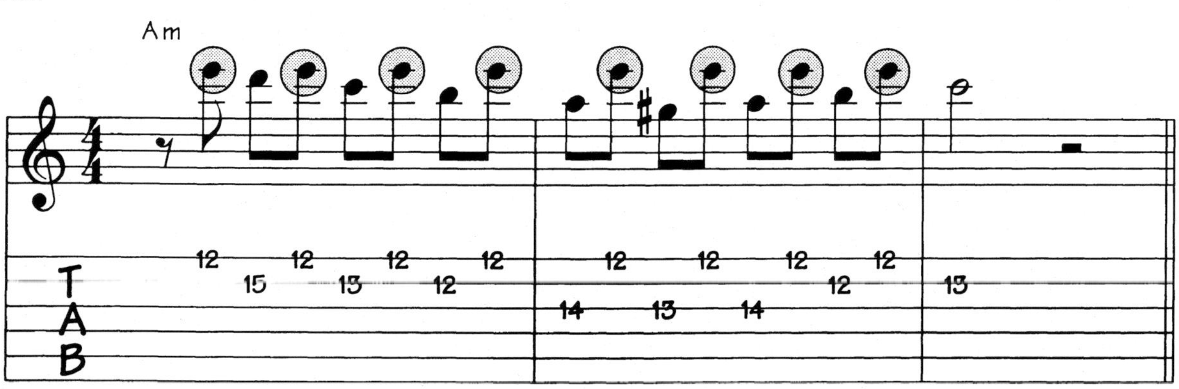

Exercise 72 - melody with skipping intervals (3)

Here is the third exercise, done in the harmonic minor A scale, but with a different harmonic development.

#83

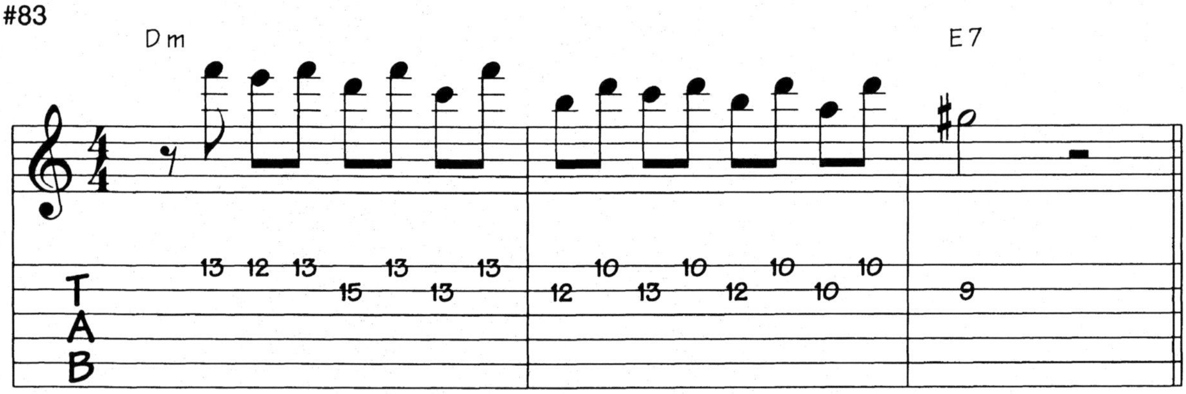

Exercise 73 - melody with skipping intervals (4)

Finally, this fourth exercise combines and summarizes the three preceding ones. It is done with the A harmonic minor scale.

#84

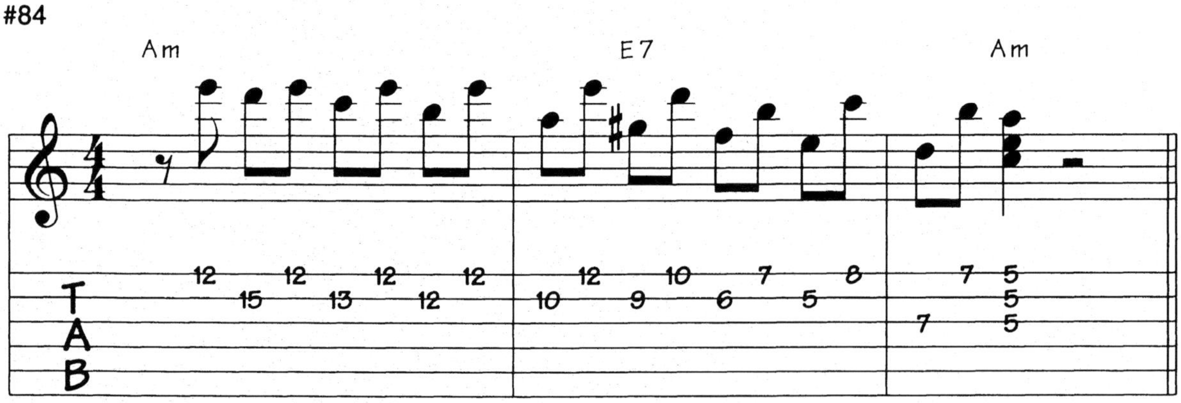

PART B1

THE SUBJECT OF RHYTHMIC STRUCTURES AND STYLES

As you will see, "Arc-En-Ciel" is written with a 2/4 time signature, a time that is not too common in jazz. However, that doesn't make this theme a military march (one!... two... one... two!).

To be truthful, the choice here of 2/4, is the fruit... of a conditioned reflex. This is a simple reflex of the jazz composer who is absolutely used to the traditional metric "standards". By taking the development of the melody into account, our 2/4 is exclusively aimed at a familiar structure: 32 measures.

You can use 4/4 time perfectly in the measure: we than have to count, not eight, but six sixteenth per measure. Then its metric time structure should not be 16 measures. On the other hand, the same result could have been obtained if we used another very current rhythmic structure, the 2/2 time or "barred C" (¢), or better yet, the 8/8 time (this is presently used more frequently).

How do we choose which rhythm is correct, the 2/4... 4/4... 2/2... 8/8, when the choice of the rhythm structure is eventually called for, in order to write a freshly hitched musical composition?

It is evident that we cannot discuss the subject here in detail.

The global musical composition implicates so much and there are so many different styles (Western, fusion types, etc.) It requires more than just a few pages to discus the topic from the bottom on up to its infinity. Nevertheless, we will limit it to jazz music only. This way it will be possible to bring out some practical observations, using those that play a considerable stylistic role.

– 60% of jazz compositions use the 4/4. What inspired us most is the simplicity of its elements, the evidence of its pulsation, its metric adequacy with regards to the melodies with its excellent 4/4 rhythmic structure in western music, as used by poets.

The 4/4 in jazz is used for slow tempos as well as for fast ones. These are used for the ragtime styles, swing, Manouche style, bebop, cool, hard-bob, modal, jazz rock and fusion – in other words, nearly in all the jazz styles.

– 25% uses 2/2. The difference depends on one hand what style is used, and on the other hand the speed of the piece, even if one can place the same number of notes precisely (quarter, eighths, triplets, sixteenths, etc) in 4/4 and 2/2 time.

Have you already tried to do the quarter notes of a samba with your feet? Annoying, isn't it? On the other hand, if you mark the whole notes, all goes like it would go in roulette, the pulsation of this samba feels naturally, obvious for the body as well as in spirit. It is simply a question of splitting up the rhythm in two, the 4/4 time (musical beat "with quarter notes") toward the 2/2 time (musical beat with "half notes").

The 2/2 time in jazz is used with all these so-called: "Afro Cuban" styles: Samba, Bossa – Nova, Calypso, Bolero, Rhumba, Mambo, Cha-Cha, etc.

During the 50s and the 60s, the jazz interest in this music was immense. Today, the Afro-Cuban influences give it a still more distinct feeling in jazz. It is even likely that all this 'binary" music, with its incredibly polyrhythmic richness, has had an influence in such a way that should not be neglected. These are the recent creations of new styles, called "Fusion", like the way Miles Davis does it. He was the main brain behind it during his best years.

10% use 3/4. With three beats, of course it's a waltz, the Manouche use it often in jazz. However, it equally appears in the other styles, notably swing, and in the form where it takes on a very interesting dimension, with a bewitching character.

Finally, the rest of the 5% is used in the so-called "composite" measures. In jazz, the best evidence of this is illustrated in the celebrated theme "Take Five", where the 5/4 rhythm is used, which is realistically split in 3/4 and 2/4. The recent styles (Fusion) have also used composite measures, because they get their inspiration from non-Western sources, where the 7/4, 9/8 and others, like the 13 1/2/ 4 are current.

To sum it up, you have to keep in mind that the choice of rhythmic structure in jazz is closely influenced by the kind of presumed musical composition. It occurs even more often, with all the various elements that makes up the melody, where the desired harmonic trends and accompaniment will determine the correct choice.

For example, an accompaniment with a "walking bass" will always lean to the 4/4 or 3/4 time.

A melody with a fast beat relies on a harmonic airy stream, where the rhythmic balance should be a determining factor of the composition, and will dictate that the 2/2 is used.

In conclusion, we'd like to show you how to put your compositions on paper, if you so desire to do so. You should first start with determining its style and metric time structure. Draw a big diagram divided into eight measures and put down the supporting chords of your melody while counting the beats per measure. By doing this, you will easily determine whether your composition will start with a pickup and where the possible difficulties with the rhythm of the melody are located (generally with syncopations). These sections are repeated in the structure, etc. In short, it gives you an indispensable shortcut to finish it perfectly, thanks to the diagram. And it is only then that you will take a pen and write the notes on the staff without any hesitation.

PART B2

We are now going to study 2/4 time in "Arc-En-Ciel".

This "piece" (as we call it in classical music) has two melodies, therefore, we can play it with two guitars.

In these pages, which include TAB, we will mark it precisely for you so that you can memorize the melody of the first voice (guitar 1): these are chord positions... with the expectation that this first voice is entirely based on our eternal procedure that uses DIAGRAMS.

The second voice is more linear, follow the corresponding TAB.

Arc-En-Ciel (measures 1 - 4) musical notation of voice #1

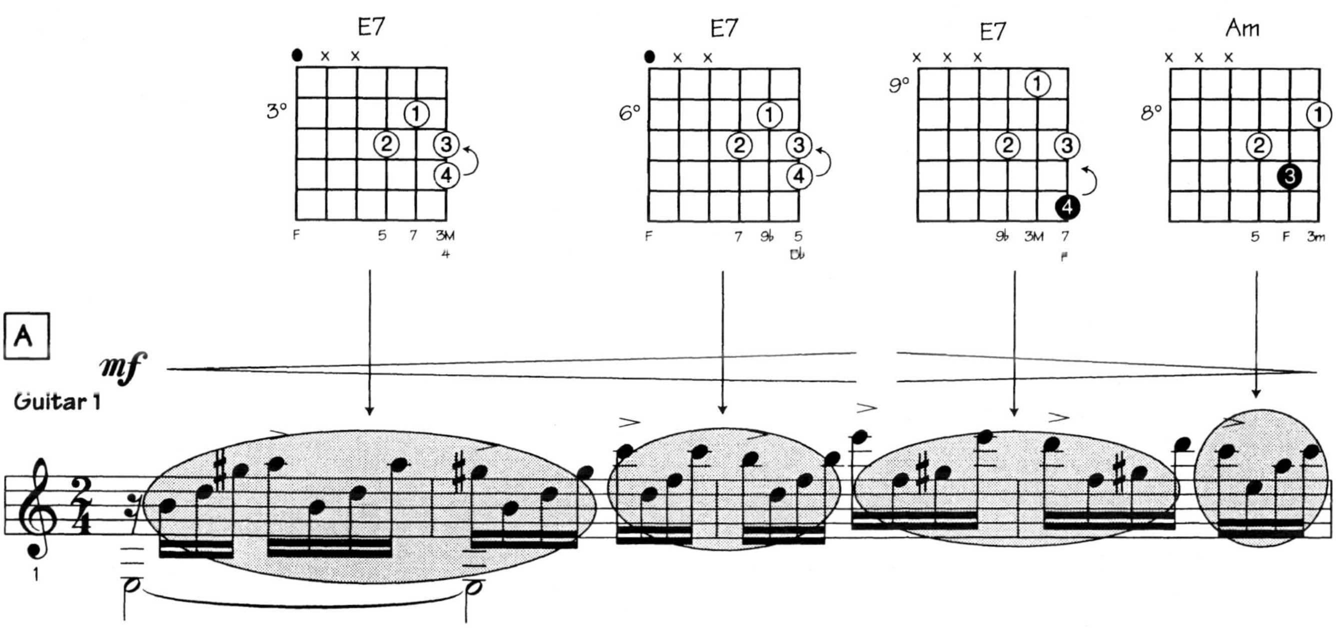

Look at these four measures: these rely on the dominant → root note principle in the key of A minor, by the way of an old known dim 7 arpeggio.

The E7 chord is indeed separated by three frets (minor third) according to the exact construction of the dim 7 arpeggio.

Arc-En-Ciel (measures 5 - 8) musical notation of voice #1

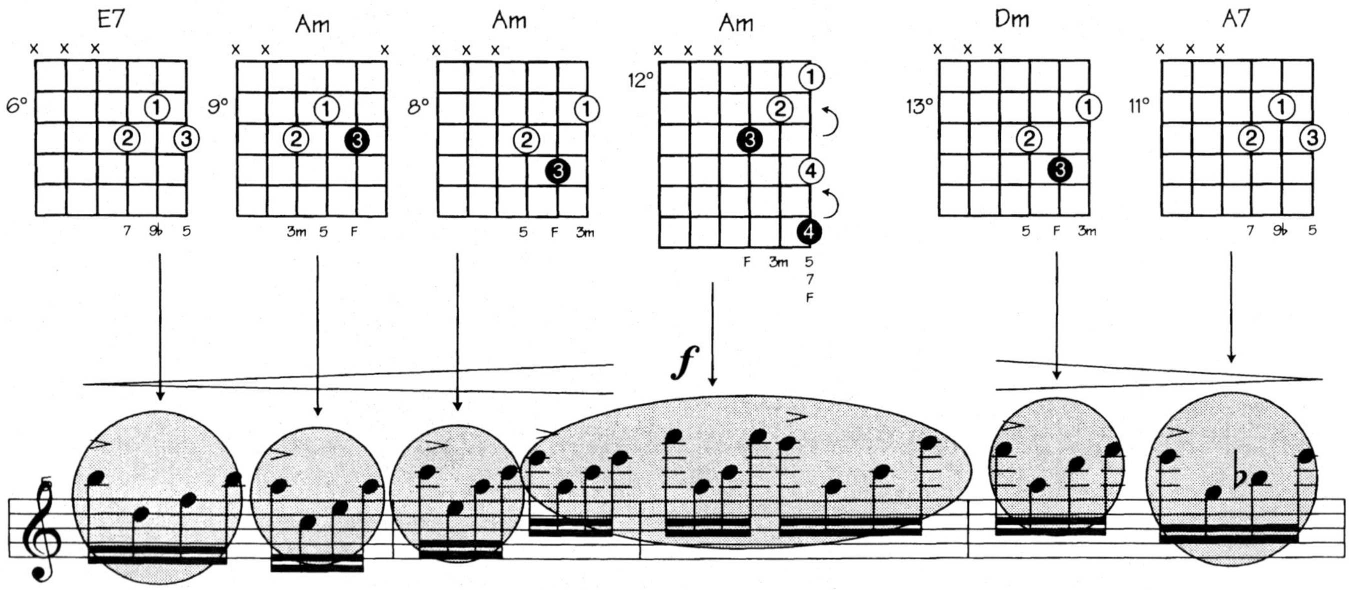

Note that in these measures the first and last chords are determined by the second voice. These lack the third, and it is difficult to indicate it at first glance.

Arc-En-Ciel (measures 9 - 12) musical notation of voice #1

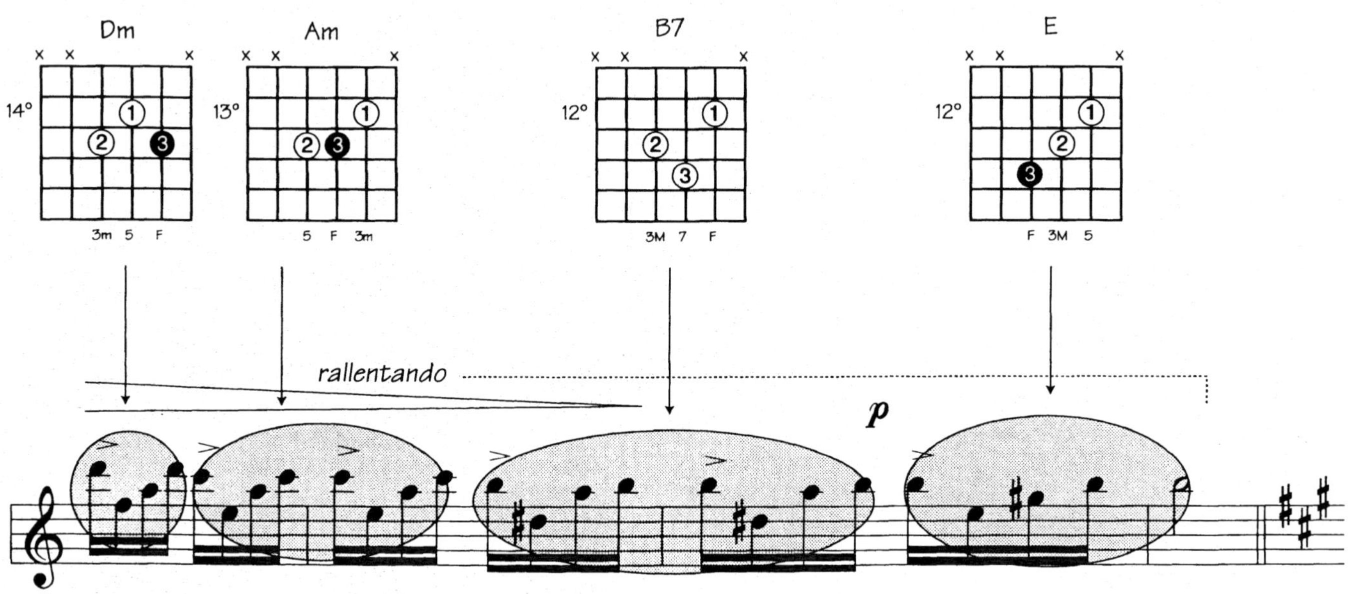

PART C

Here is the score of the "Arc-En-Ciel" theme that you can hear on the Romane CD, and it shows you how to play section A, which has 12 measures.

Arc-En-Ciel

#85

music by ROMANE

structure = 62 measures AABAAB

Allegro moderato ♩ = 104

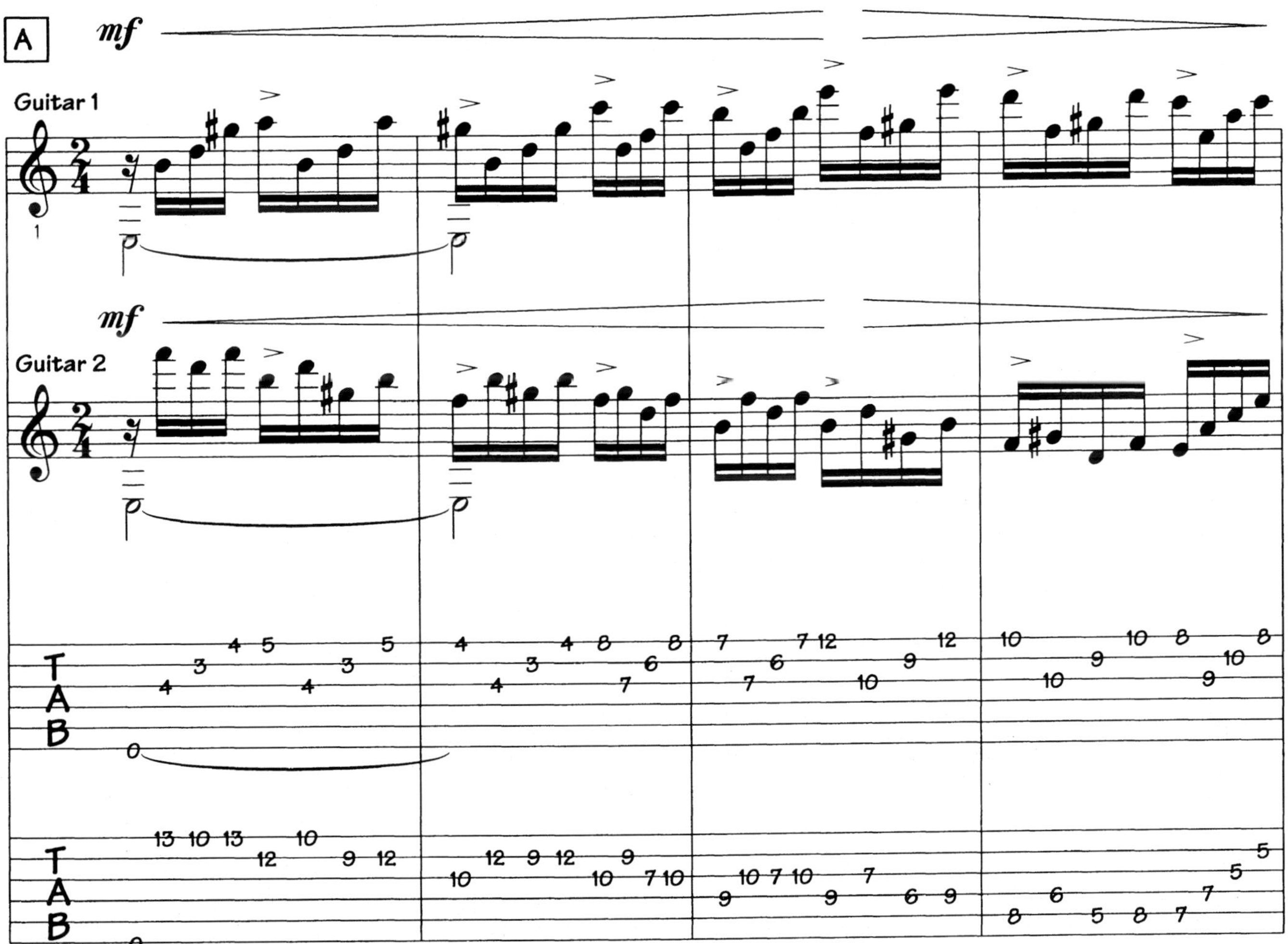

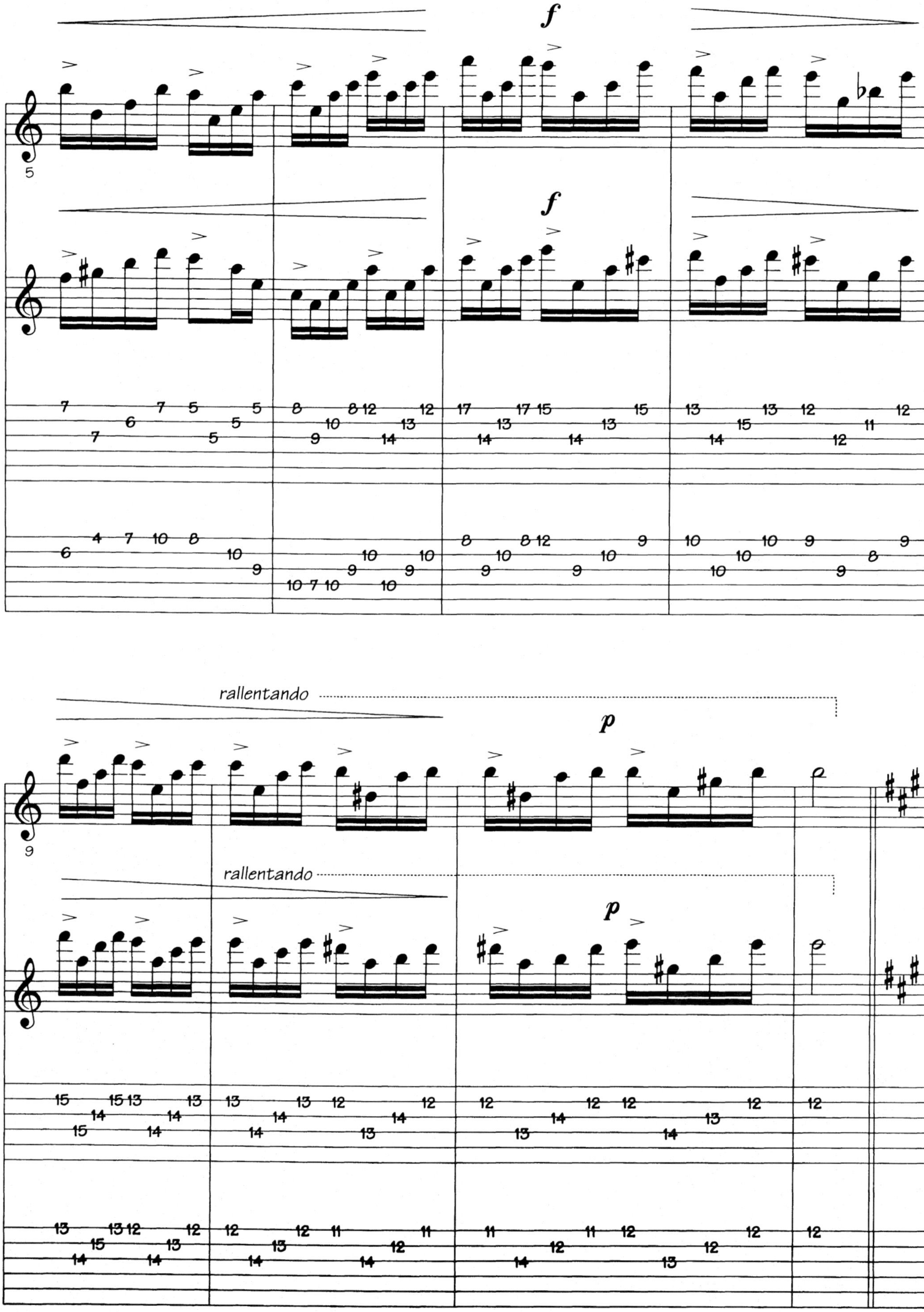
rallentando
rallentando

PART A

In the same vein as exercises in previous chapters, we have a musical arpeggio exercise that is inspired by J.S. Bach. Thus it is in a classical form, where even the ears of Django Reinhardt would not pay attention to it. It also seems to be strange for the those looking at it for the first time.

Exercise 74 - classical form arpeggios

Here we use one note per string. The right hand and the pick will do these classical arpeggios with one sweep. I give a thousand pardons, Mr. Bach, for this modern time jargon! It is because we have a lot of attacks with the pick going (▬).

For the first measure we will show you the indications of the fingers of the right hand:

I = index finger   m = middle finger   a = ring finger   au = little finger

For the rest, use the same pattern. Notice how the five notes for each finger form the simple major, minor or diminished chord positions:

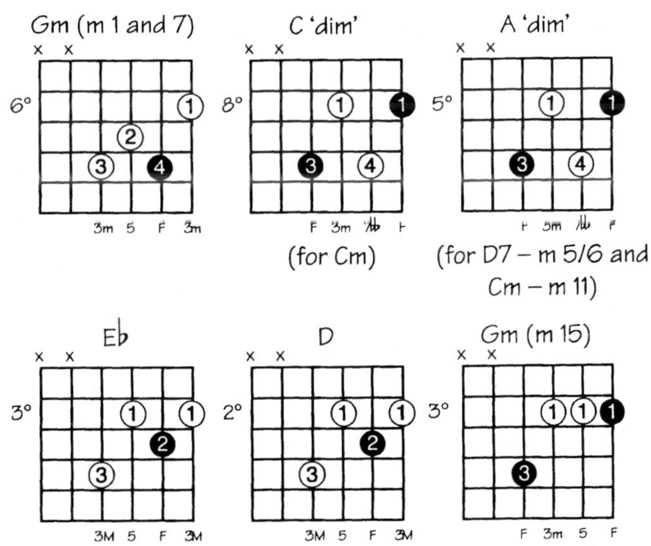

In measures 3 - 4 and 11 - 12, look at how the diminished arpeggio is used, the Cm is a disguised Am7(b5), which introduces the D7. This diminished arpeggio is completely used in a way to keep time with regular eighths. Nevertheless, it is used as a complete dim7 arpeggio: separated by three frets.

Once you have memorized this diagram, use its logical architecture to work out the phrases of the vocabulary to improvise. (You should never forget that the great classical works started as improvisations, before it was ever put in its final form on music paper).

For example, one way to do it is to take out the (silent) notes, add in sixteenth note triplets combined with trills, reorganize the timing between the notes (in pairs of unequal eighths, pointed eighths and double pointed ones), etc. In other words, show your imagination in your work. Be sure that if you do it this way, it is never done in vain.

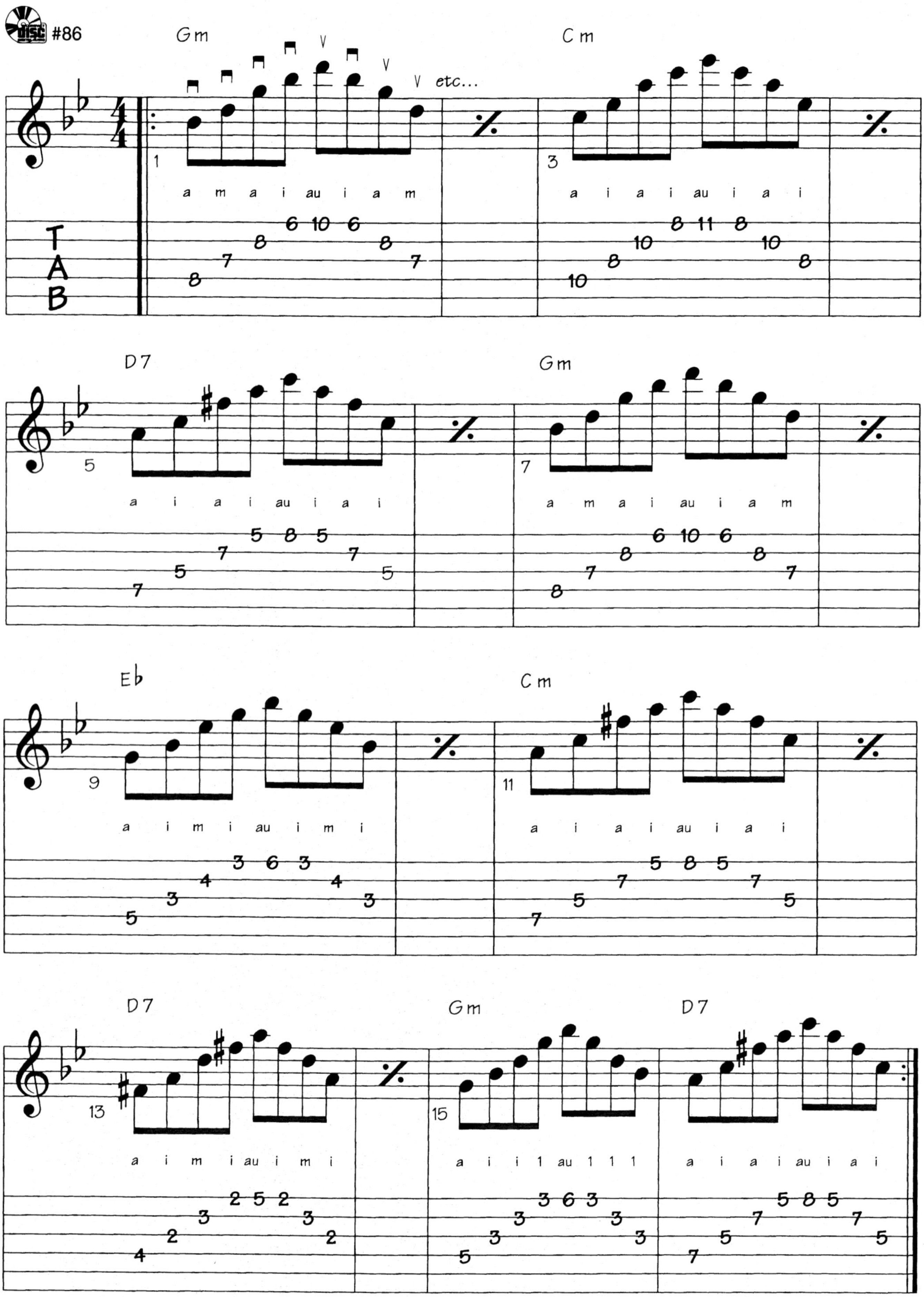
#86
Gm
Cm
etc...
a m a i au i a m
a i a i au i a i
T
A
B
D7
Gm
Eb
Cm
a i m i au i m i
D7
Gm
D7
a i i 1 au 1 1 1

PART B1

TERMS, SYMBOLS AND ABREVIATIONS

As you have already noticed, the score of "Arc-En-Ciel" has many symbols and indications that show you how to play dynamically. One word about the changes, it must enrich the music, this is an indispensable part of the music.

The current symbols that indicate these changes are as follows:

— ***p*** = abbreviation for "piano"(softly). The sound level should be low. You should have a picture in mind of the pedal which mutes the sound of an acoustic piano (which the term comes from).

— ***mf*** = abbreviation for "mezzo forte". The sound level should of moderately soft.

—***f*** = abbreviation for "forte". This indicates that the music should be played loudly.

The palette of dynamic changes also has the triple piano (***ppp*** or pianissimo: as soft as possible) and the triple forte (***fff*** or fortissimo: extremely loud), which go through a certain number of intermediaries.

This palette with graphical symbols matches those that are included in one of the many measures of the score, and which are used to metrically change the values of keeping time. The symbols that are most widely used are:

— The "crescendo"
This indicates that the sound should increase, from one measure to the other, until it is no longer used.

— The "decrescendo"
This of course is the opposite of the "crescendo".

There are many other types of changes and symbols that show you how to interpret music. Nevertheless, we have given you the ones that are essential for classical music and which are not much used with jazz (except when orchestrated). Improvised music is not written in the abstract. We hope that some of our readers willl go through many adequate theoretical works, and get deeper involved with this topic.

Now that we know this, we would like to say that, musicians play music to create. Or we can say it another way: it is the fundamental feeling of musical art.

It is only secondary that we use these terms, symbols and abbreviations. By saying this it might have the result of displeasing some sensitive orchestra musicians! The practice of interpretation cannot have but one school of values. In one word, it's only one way to show it, but not the only one.

THE HARMONIZATION WITH TWO VOICES

Here we will discuss the addition of a second voice to an existing melody. We can see an example of it in "Arc-En-Ciel".

When we compose and add a second voice, as we see in the many marvelous and numerous fugues bequeathed us by the great master of fugues, J.S.Bach, a major point should be mentioned:

When adding a second voice to the first, the second voice must absolutely make sense with the melody, and be musically correct. It is out of the question to write a second voice that does not belong there. The second voice should also be as convincing as the initial melody.

Therefore, the subject that we are going to discuss is that of classical counterpoint, which today is known as a "counter voice". Most often, these are separated with thirds and sixths in relation to the first voice. This first voice determines what makes up the second voice. But it is not necessary that this second voice has to be strictly parallel with its big sister. It is not even recommended.

As a general rule, the second voice also has to avoid repeating the notes at the same height. This is particularly the case in an area where the voices cross. When the crossing of the two voices are at the same point it is a so-called "unison"!

For you to create this form of music, if you feel like doing it, exercise and repeat the exact passages of "Arc-En-Ciel", where you will see:

— counter voicing with opposite movements: one voice descends while the other goes up (section A),

— counter voicing with parallel movements: often with separated thirds (Section B),

— unisons: two rising crossing voices.

Of course, what works in double counterpoint must also work in triple counterpoint. But it is obvious that in this case the challenge to do so is distinctly harder.

In the case that you use three voices in jazz or harmony, it gives the more reason not to do this because of its complexity. It becomes impossible to do so.

Whatever you will do, go and work on the counter voicings with the melodies that you compose (if you already haven't composed anything, start to do it without waiting any longer). You will get the hang of it with a little practice. Your ability to add voices while improvising will gradually improve. We guarantee it.

PART B2

As before, we are adding the TAB. Here are the diagrams which will help you memorize the melody of the first voice/guitar, relative to section B of "Arc-En-Ciel".

From a melodic view point, and to "return to Ceasar what belongs to Ceasar", we remember that the melody, done with arpeggios in this theme (in particular in section B), comes close to the "DOCTOR GRADUS AD PARNASSUM". This is one of the six fascinating pieces for piano by Claude Debussy in its celebrated "Children's Corner". In hindsight, all musicians can be a victim of the musical culture which was created during his childhood!

The other part of the harmonic structure of "Arc-En-Ciel" comes closer to "Dans le Regard De Laura", in the measure where the procedure that is used in the composition is the same: in section of A in the minor key (D minor), and a section of B in a major key with the same central (D major) root note.

Arc-En-Ciel (measures 13 - 15) voice diagrams #1

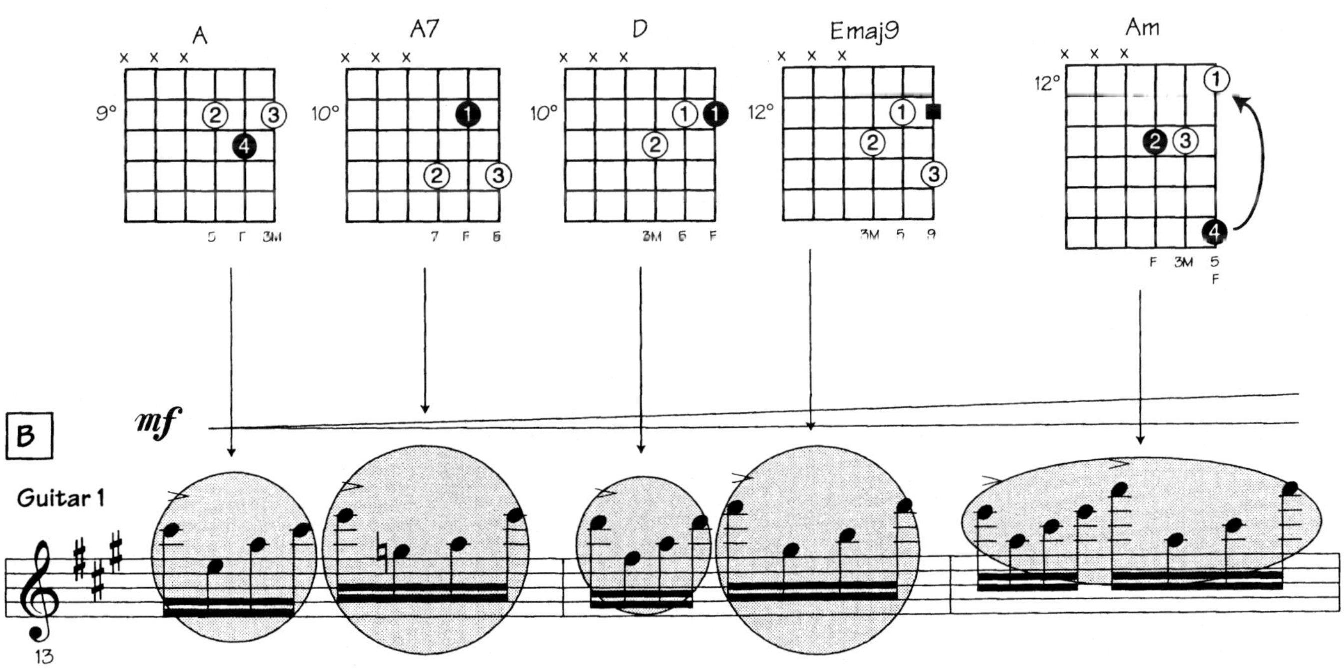

Arc-En-Ciel (measures 16 - 17) notation of voice #1

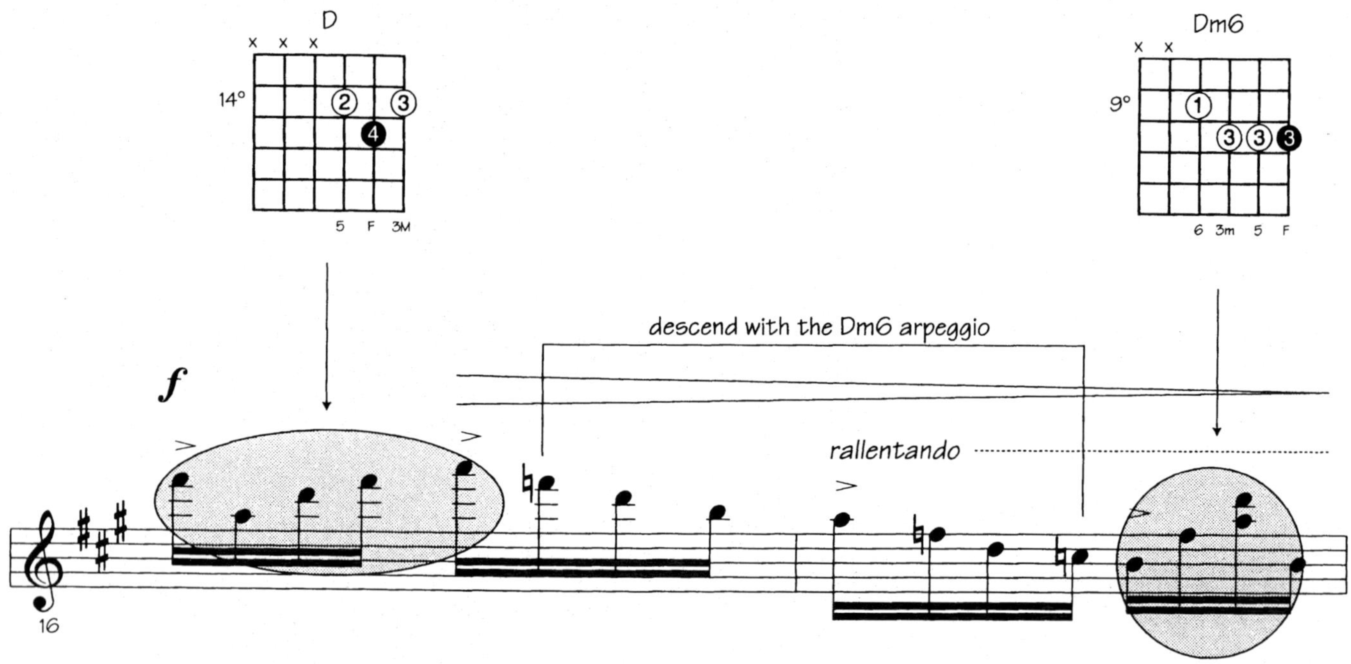

Arc-En-Ciel (measures 18 - 20) notation of voice #1

With the final dominant chord (E7), simply move all diagrams up three frets.

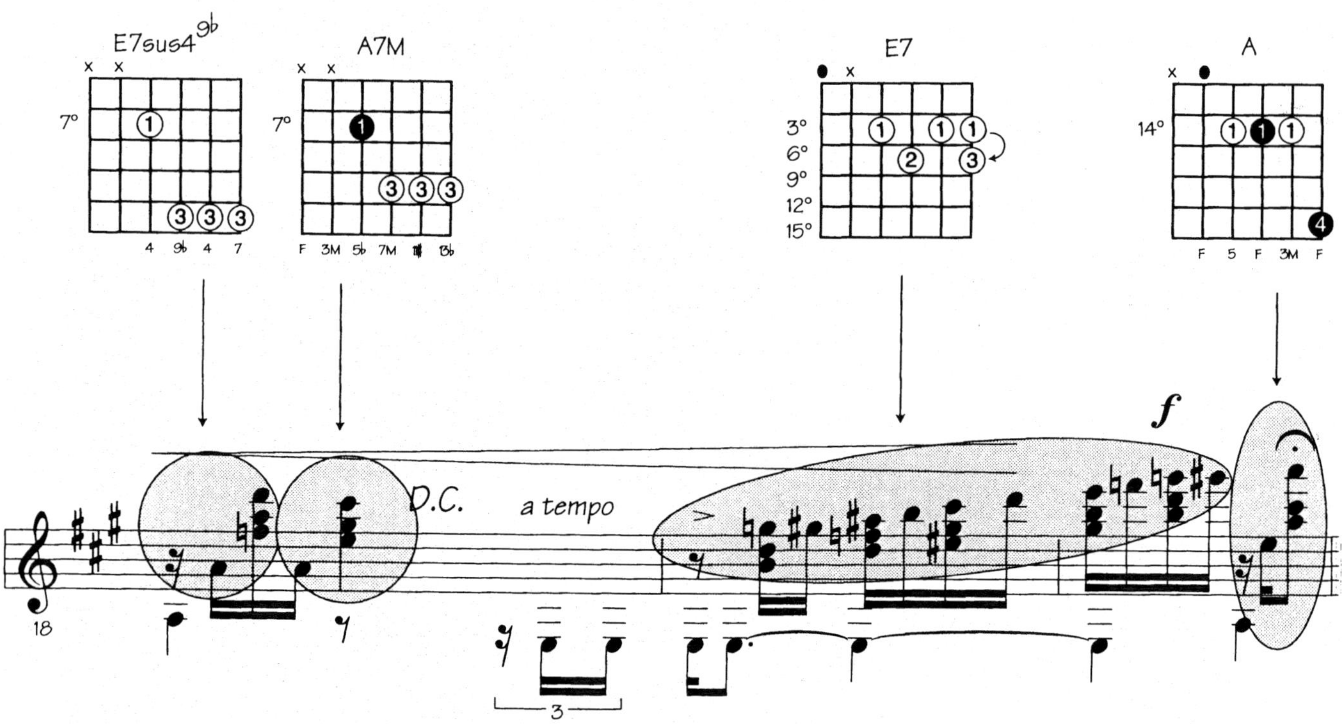

PART C

This closes this twenty-fourth chapter. We will now continue and finish the score for the two guitars of "Arc-En-Ciel", section B.

The piece has not been totally finished. The "keep time" symbol (a tempo) specifies that you have to return to the initial beat as used before (quarter note = 104). This symbol will undo the rallentendo, which shows up at the end of section A.

Of course, the same goes for measures 17 and 18.

Finally, if you are familiar with knowing the musical symbols, you will notice the 𝄐 this is a fermata, when placed above a chord (or note) it means that you should sustain the duration as long as the performer(s) likes it (or the conductor).

Now you have it all. Get going!

#85

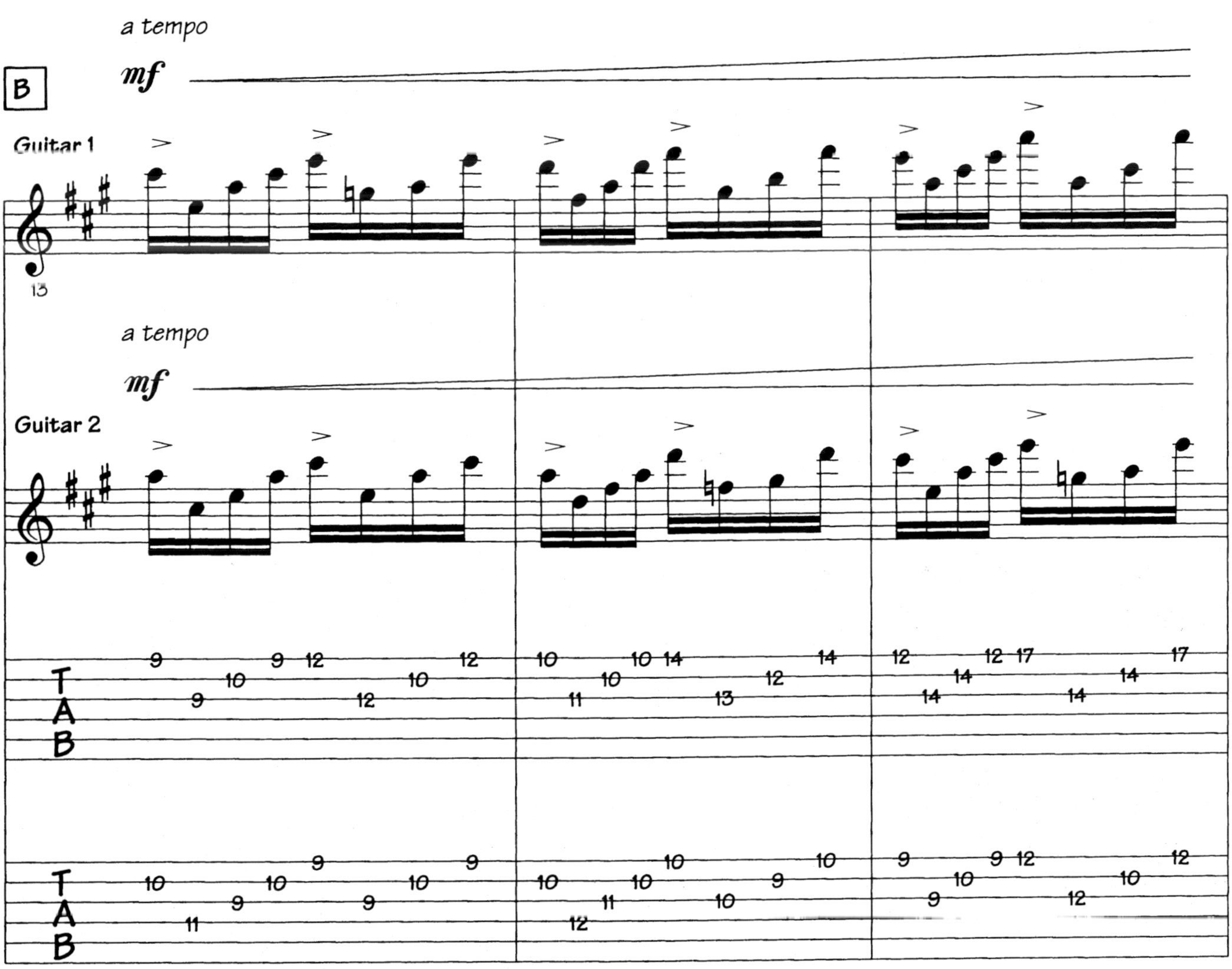

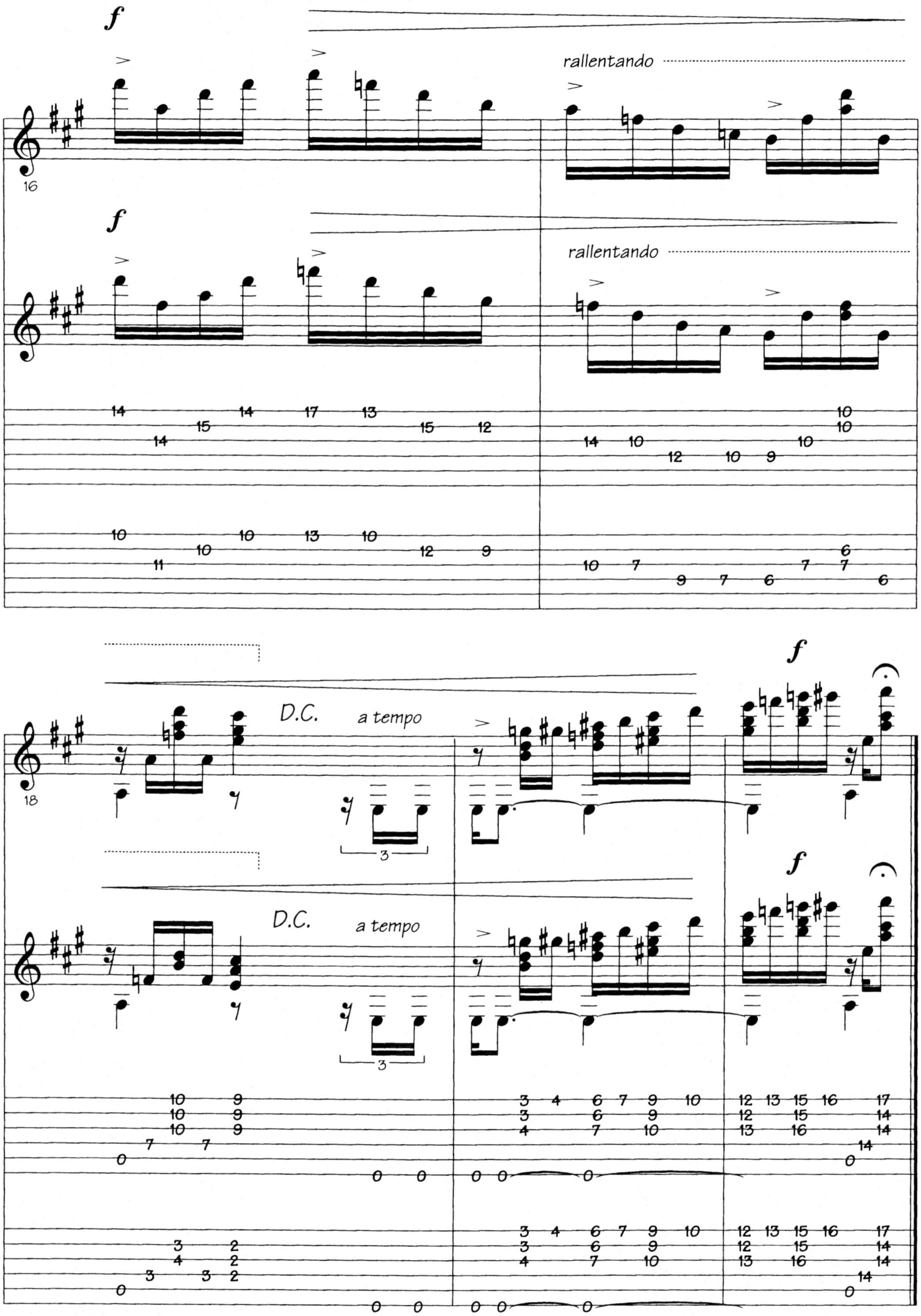
f
rallentando
16
f
rallentando
18
D.C.
a tempo
D.C.
a tempo
f
f

▪ PART A

In chapter 25 all the exercises that we are going to give you will be centered on the actual jazz theme and the study of their various aspects.

All other chapters that we are going to study at this point will be those of "Gypsy Fire" (available on the Romane Ombre CD). In the preliminary exercise, a spotlight lights up the introduction of this theme.

Exercise 75 - Intro to Gypsy Fire, using a whole tone scale

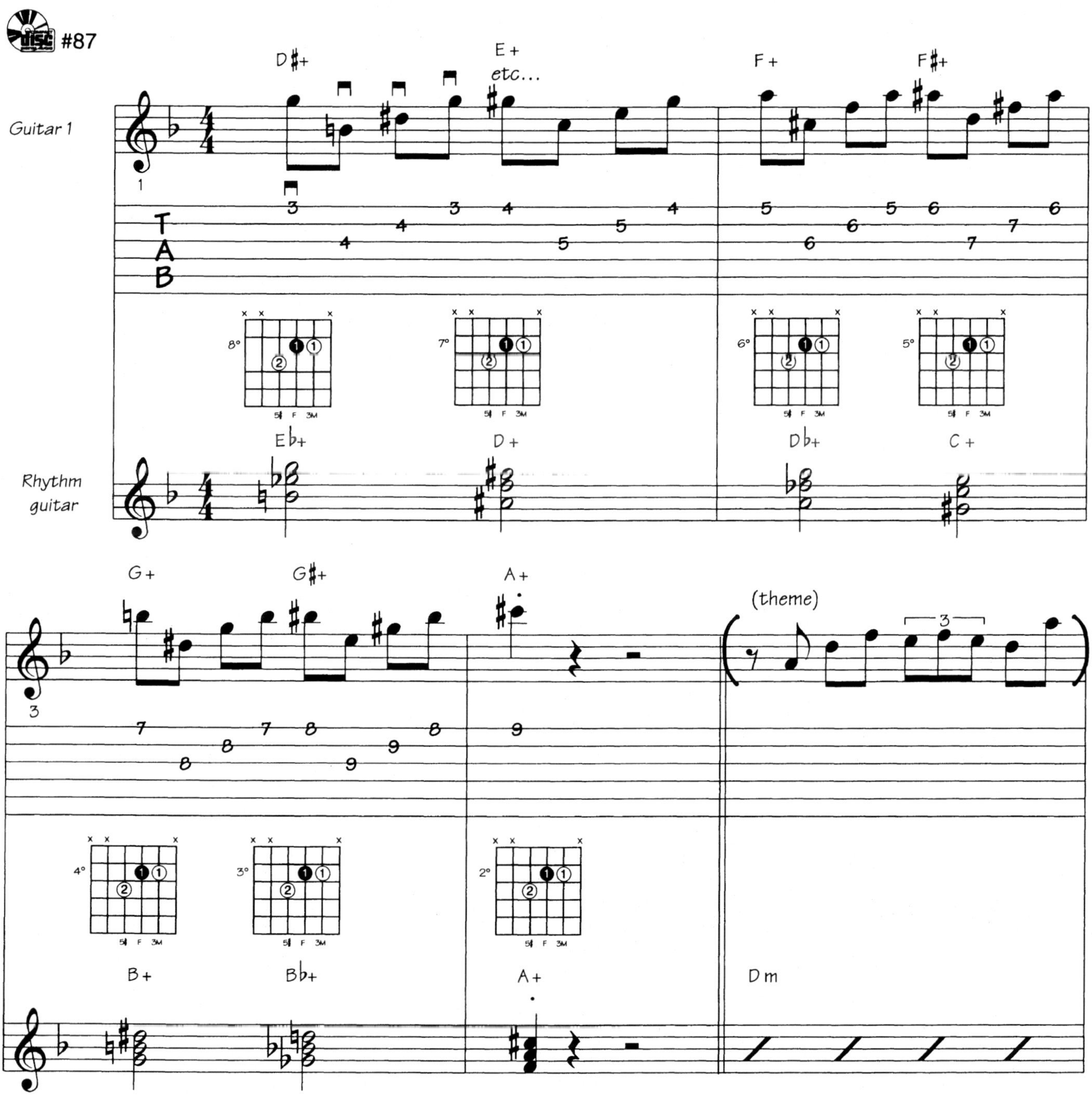

Chapter 25 / page 2

By listening to the disk you will without a doubt detect the four measures of this introduction, which relies on the whole tone scale (chapter 7).

An explanation here may be necessary. This is done exclusively by using the so-called "augmented" triad: a chord made up with three tones, a root note (F), a major third (3M), and an augmented fifth (#5). This group is shown with a "+" sign.

Indeed , the "+" chord is excellently represented by the whole tone scale in the measure where all its composed notes restrict the intervals of the major second, or its entire tones:

Whatever the case might be, we are more interested in these three measures because of the particular way the whole tone scale is used, that's to say:

- with the contrast of the melody/harmony, the arpeggios of guitar 1 and chords of the other guitars,
- with the movements of the counter melody: guitar 1 goes up, the other down.

We have already seen (chapter 24, page 4), that in the area of harmonization we must always look for the counter movements. And now we see, that the whole tone scale has a particular interesting harmony .

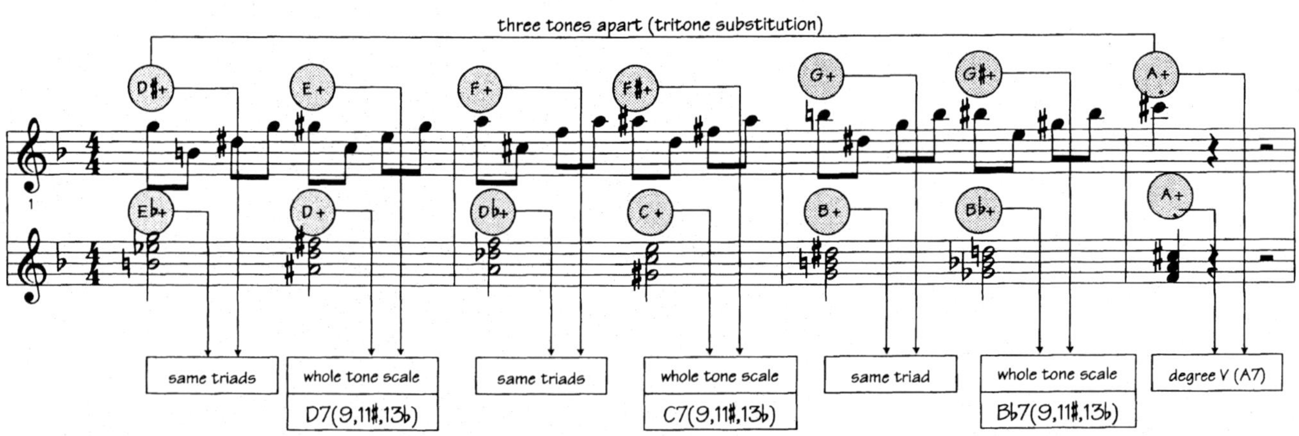

The object here is to prepare the first chord of the theme (Dm). We academically let it precede with V (A+) that will all start with a T.S. of this last (E+) chord. But here we have the "A.L.T." property of the whole tone scale (and also of the triad "+"). This is the combined succession and chromatics of these triads, created for the effect to express (a chord with two) the entire whole tone scale with these very convincing intermediate dominant chords. For example, the D+ goes to E+, that is the D7(9,#11,b13), which is the D whole tone scale (but also the E whole tone, etc.).

This shows you a very interesting principle:

All augmented triads could be used - on an improvisational basis - with a dominant chord of which the root note is, being identical, located one tone higer or lower.

For example, using the A+ triad (or the F+ = the same notes as A+) to improvise with a G7, you color this chord with "13" (or #5).

Finally, notice that the Bb7 (T.S. of E7) introduces the marvelous final: A+.
For the rest, all the chords of this intro are brought about by a chromatic resolution with a higher half - tone!

PART B1

We are still using the theme "Gypsy Fire", and will look at its structure which the harmony relies on. The basic diagram of this piece, typically in the style of Manouche, is very classical in nature.

Gypsy Fire

structure = 32 measures AABA

♩= 240

A	Dm	⁒	E7	⁒	Gm	A7	Dm	A7
A	6 ⁒⁒						Dm	⁒
B	E♭7⁹	⁒	G♭7⁹	⁒	A7⁹	⁒	A7⁵♯	A7⁵♭
A	Dm	⁒	E7	⁒	Gm	A7 ⊕	Dm	⁒
		⊕	A7 / A+	B+ / G♯+	D♯+ / G+ / F+	G+		

As for the rhythm chords, you can use the following:

Sections A :

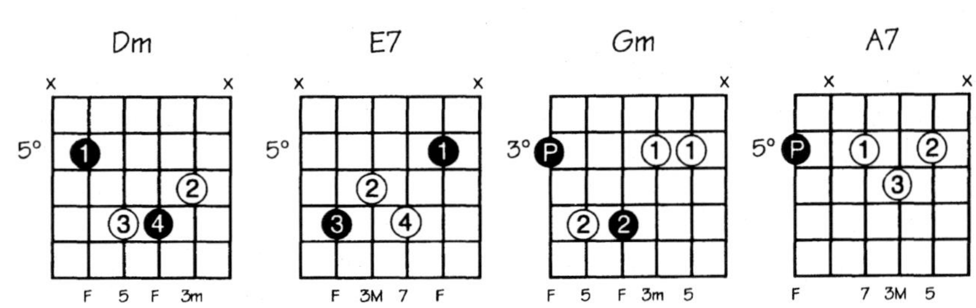

Section B :

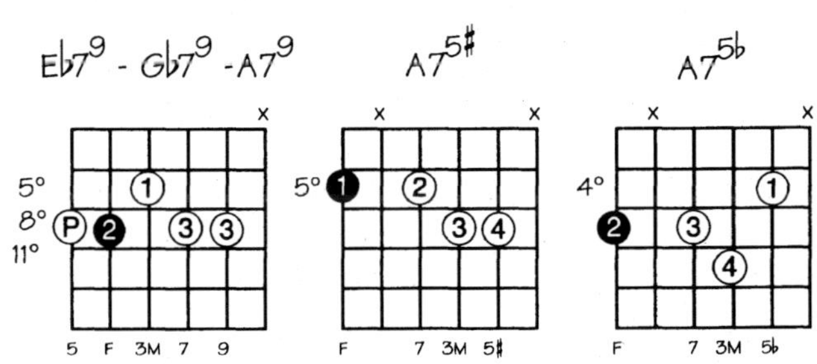

Coda :

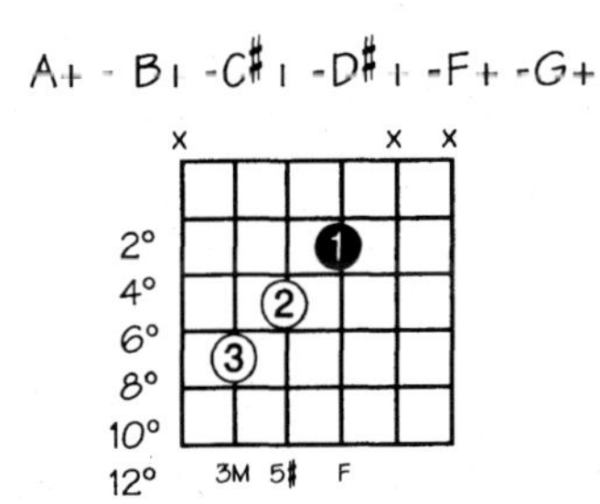

The analysis of the harmonies reveals some scattered eccentricities that show up in the 32 measures:

Key: Dm

A	Im Dm	%	II7 E7	%	IV Gm	V A7	Im Dm	V A7
A	6 //						Im Dm	%
B	IIb7 $Eb7^{9}$	%	IVb7 $Gb7^{9}$	%	V $A7^{9}$	%	V $A7^{5\#}$	V $A7^{5b}$
A	Im Dm	%	II7 E7	%	IV Gm	V A7	Im Dm	%

Here, the whole structure can be considered as having one single and same key: the D minor.

In the A sections, we have the principle degrees of the key: the I, IV, and V among which the II7 slides. This II7 is known as a "secondary dominant" chord, in the measure where the II degree of a minor key is normally a minor chord. The II is, therefore, "domineering" and, in general, is preceding directly the realistic II that, in the present case, doesn't happen. Measure 5 presents a IV (Gm), and not the expected IIm (Em). In reality, everything here is a simple affair of substitutions, used to spice up the harmonic structure. Indeed, the A section could have dressed up the traditional aspect very well, which is here:

A	Dm	%	E7	%	$Em7^{5b}$ (Gm6)	A7	Dm	A7

Thus, by simply coloring the Gm with a sixth (Gm6 = Em7(b5), the four last measures constitute a pure II - V - I minor, which gives us a very good and strong melody. Try it!

In section B, the V degree (A7) reigns as an almost absolute master:
– the four last measures are made up exclusively,
– the IIb7 (Eb7) is its T.S. (the E and A root notes are three tones separated from each other),
– only the IVb7 (Gb7) seems to want to throw trouble into this nice harmony...
But, we can ask ourselves the following questions:
What is the T.S. of the Gb7? The answer is: C7, and, in some way, did this C7 leave the (natural) D minor key? Absolutely: this is the VII degree, a VII degree that can, by strengthening the V, be used to take back the I degree (Dm, in measure 1 of the third A).

In the key of D minor, the C → Dm (VII → Im) is usually considered as a cadence, although this one is not as convincing here, nor as useful than the V → I progression.

Whatever the case is, the bridge relies on the idea of tension before it comes to a rest: that is the first chord of the third A section, and all these dominant chords (tied between them as substitutions) where it is perfectly used. This tension is equally favored with the separation of the Eb - Gb - A (by minor thirds) between the chords which overshadows the dim7 chord.

PART B2

The last pages of this chapter will use the "Gypsy Fire" score, where we are going to study its various "ingredients".

In a general way, the melody of this theme relies on a constant melody/rhythm, that you have certainly already become accustomed to with the material of the Manouche playing style: eighth note triplets.

And you will notice that the triplets are used in almost all the measures:

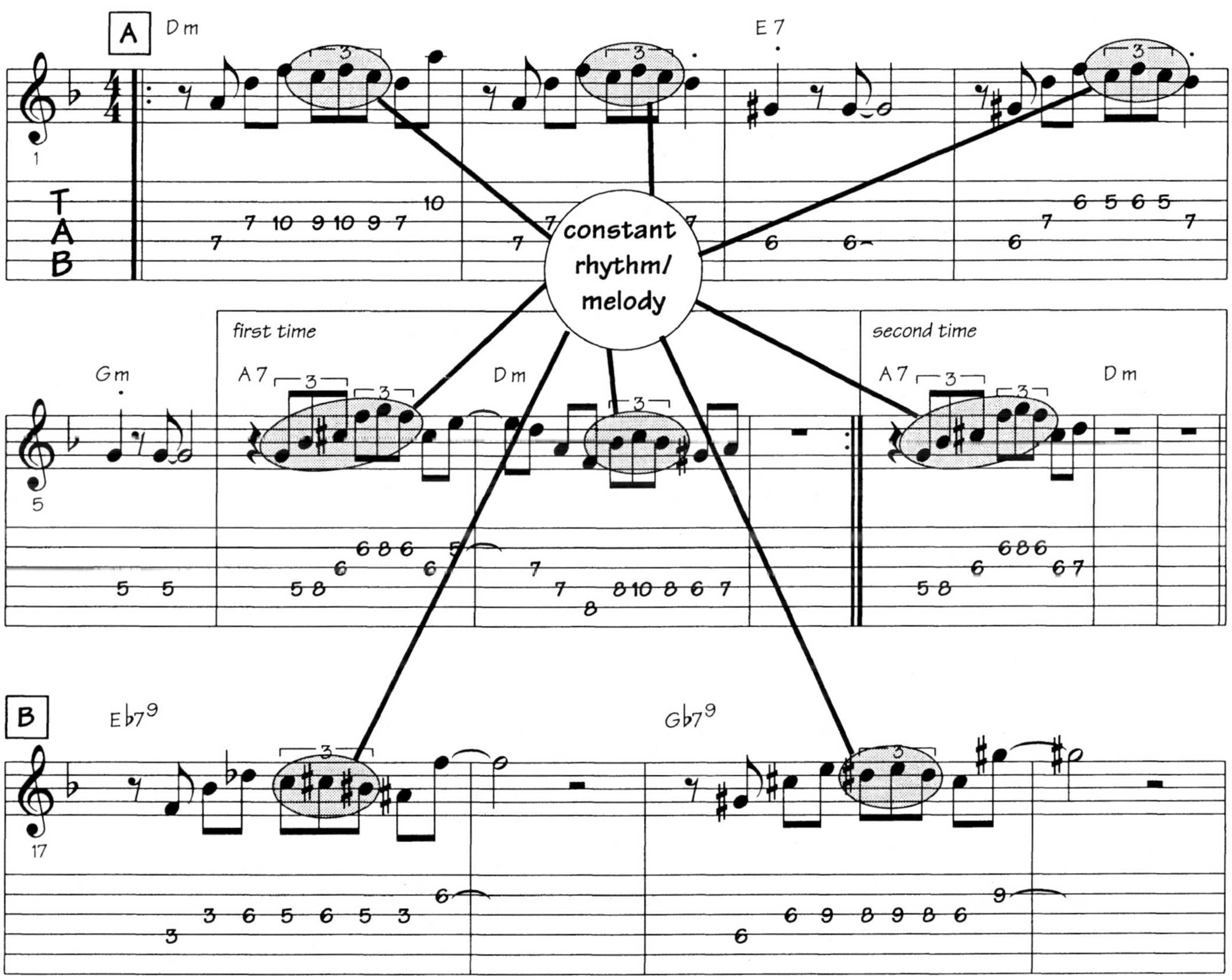

Surely, with the rhythmic layout, the triplets are a typical Manouche signature... this is a "Manouchery"! Thus the "Gypsy Fire" melody is formed and it takes on its form by means of this simple ingredient.

We give you a little precision technique: All triplets in this theme (and others too) are done by striking only the first note, the other two are played with a double tie, by using push and pull, known better as hammer-ons and pull-offs (H./P.)

So, when playing this melody, if you feel that it doesn't turn out as it should, you can listen to the CD and compare it. Make sure you pay attention when playing the H. /P. ties with triplets.

Gypsy Fire (measures 6, 14, and 30) sweeps with triplets

In the vein of exploitation, we also encounter successive triplets that use a sliding sweep, that should be discussed when we look at how to use the pick.

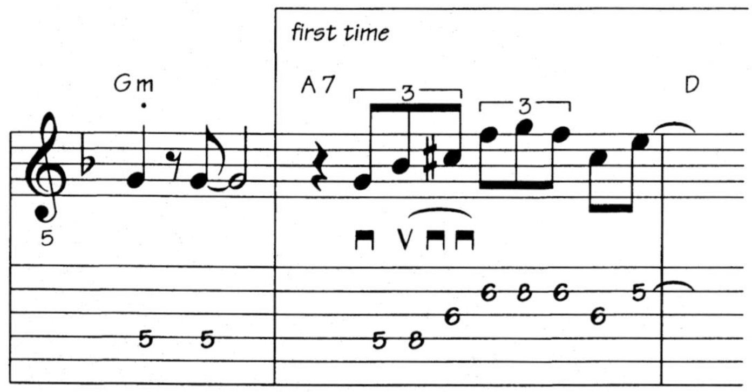

Gypsy Fire (measures 23 and 24) featured speed

In the two last measures of the bridge we will encounter a speed/virtuoso phrase, which will remind you of measures 7 and 8 of the "Swing For Ninine" theme (chapter 1, pages 6 and 7).
The two phrases are constructed exactly the same way, with the same placements of the accents (>), although it has certain rhythmic differences.
In reality, the rhythmic arrangement of the "Gypsy Fire" lead is the easier one. You can also use this arrangement with sixteenths notes if you play "Swing For Ninine", by having the same freedom (besides, this one is less complicated to read). However, it is different than the first, because the present lead relies on the seventh augmented fifth arpeggio, and less on the diminished arpeggio:

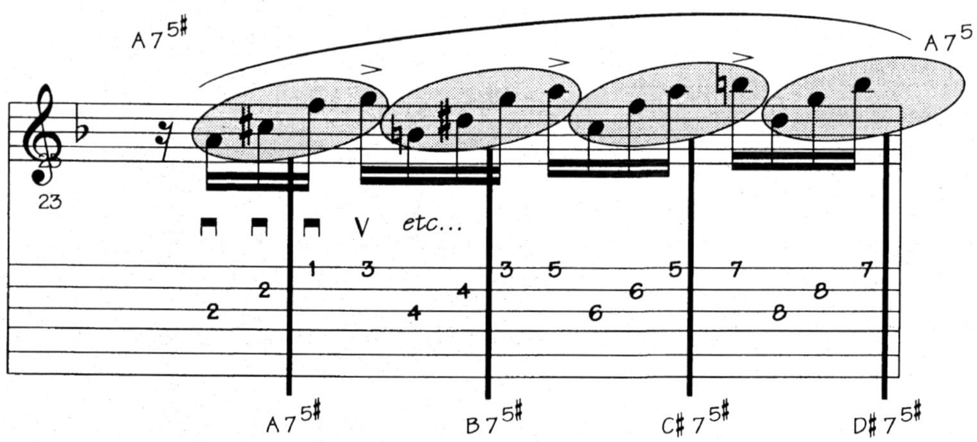

Notice that in the passage of this chord progression, with the 7(#5) chord, is done with whole tones, which gives it the advantage in measure 24 to let the harmony coincide with its tritone substitution: the A7(b5) with D#7(b5), because we effectively count three tones between the A and D# (or Eb) notes.

This lead is also discussed, simultaneously, in the harmonic climate of the introduction, and the final coda. Both are based on the whole tone scale and the harmonies that it develops: augmented triads and dominant seventh chords of which the fifths are altered.

PART C

And here is the melody of "Gypsy Fire". We worked hard to learn to respect the 32 measures, the AABA structure well, by looking at this score and by keeping count of the repeating measures (1st time, 2nd time).

#88

Gypsy Fire

music by ROMANE

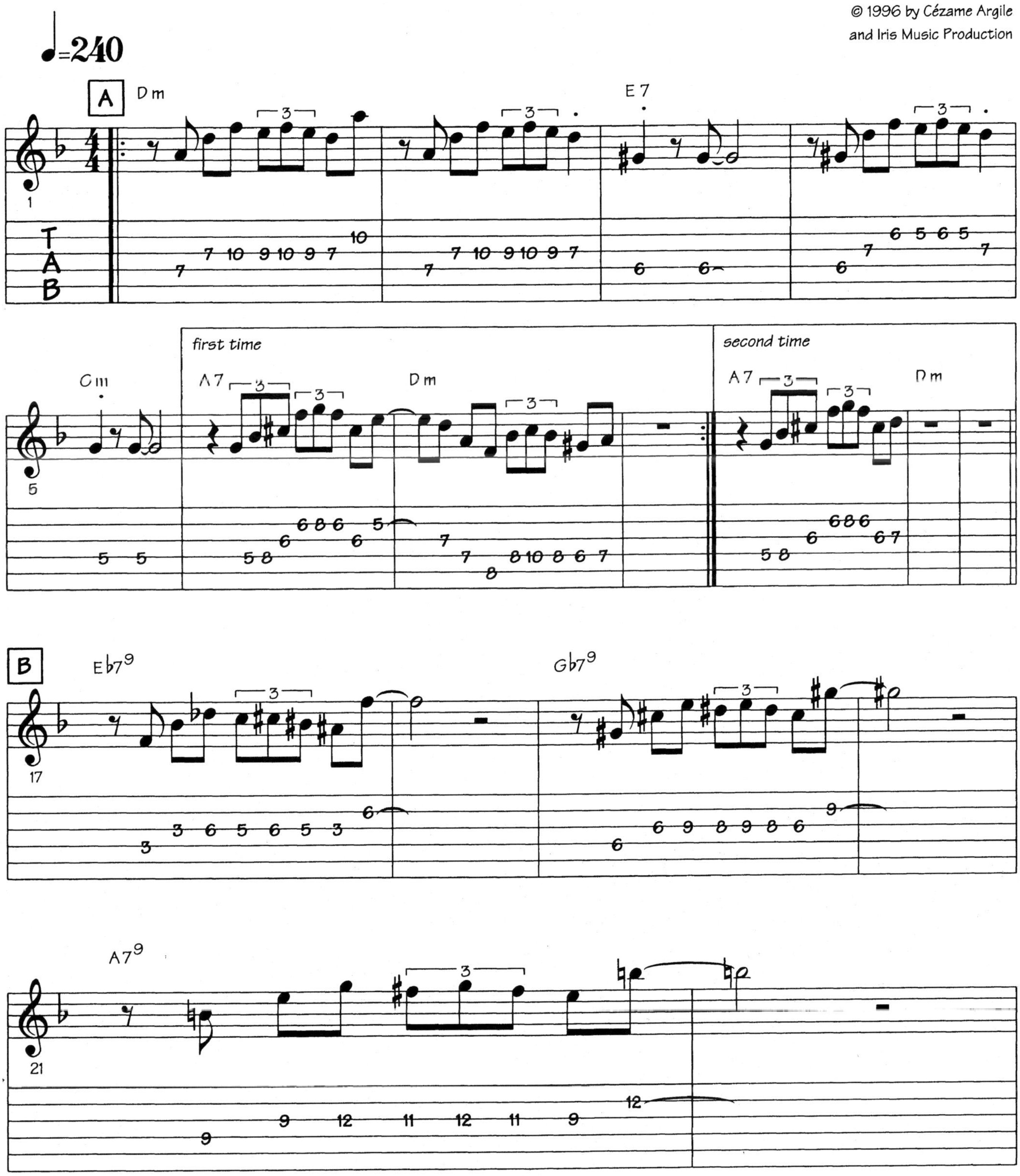

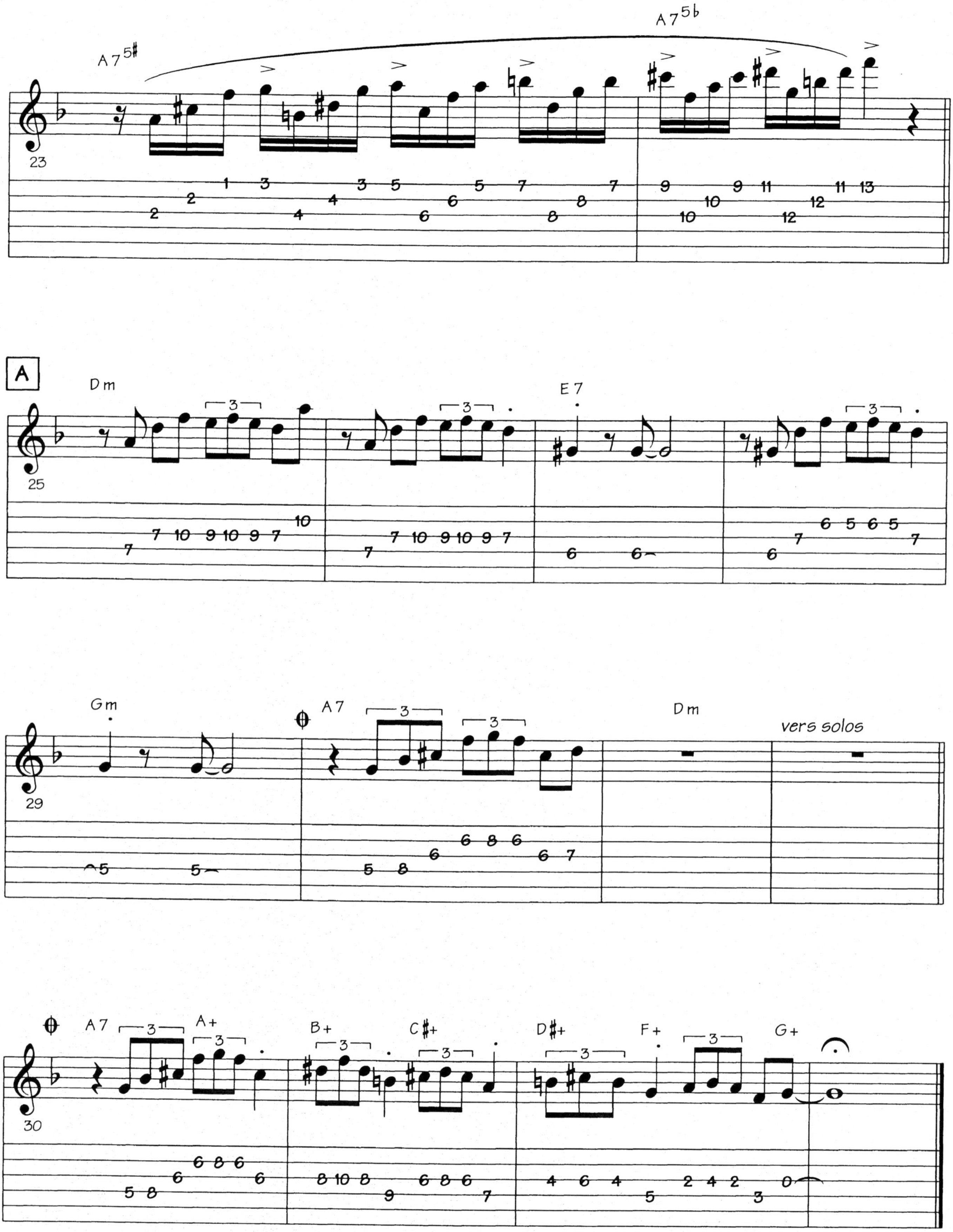
A7 5#
A7 5b
A
Dm
E7
Gm
A7
Dm
vers solos
A7
A+
B+
C#+
D#+
F+
G+

PART A

Exercise 76 - Valse a Django

Here is a new exercise that we will use until chapter 32. It's going to spread out over 128 measures. In reality, it is a lot more than an exercise since it is about one of the Manouche theme styles 'fetishes'. The "Valse a Django" is also known under the "Montagne Sainte - Genevieve" title. It is signed by Django Reinhardt, and this is a theme that all Manouche-like guitarists should have in their personal repertoire, with each ad-libbed slide that gives it their own personal stamp. It is also a condensed type which particularly represents the way Manouche plays the guitar: with major virtuoso minor and diminished arpeggios, triplets and trills, minor harmonic and chromatic scales, with a thrusting drop of a pin, glides, harmonics… in short, it's all there - or nearly all!

Valse à Django

(Django's waltz)

Basic harmonic diagram - the structure = 128 measures AA'AA'BB'AA' $\frac{3}{4}$ ♩= 190

A	Em	%	%	%	Em	%	Am	%
	B7	%	%	%	F#m7^{5b}	B7	Em	B7
A'	Em	%	%	%	E7	%	Am / E7	Am
	Am	%	Em	%	B7	%	Em / B7	Em
A	Em	%	%	%	Em	%	Am	%
	B7	%	%	%	F#m7^{5b}	B7	Em	B7
A'	Em	%	%	%	E7	%	Am / E7	Am
	Am	%	Em	%	B7	%	Em / B7	Em
B	D7	%	G	%	Am	D7	G	%
B'	D7	%	G	%	Am	D7	G	%
B	D7	%	G	%	Am	D7	G	%
B'	D7	%	G	%	Am	D7	G	B7
A	Em	%	%	%	Em	%	Am	%
	B7	%	%	%	F#m7^{5b}	B7	Em	B7
A'	Em	%	%	%	E7	%	Am / E7	Am
	Am	%	Em	%	B7	%	Em / B7	Em

Chapter 26 / page 2

We are now going to give you the harmonic diagram and chord positions of our version of the "Valse a Django" with regards to the chord positions of the basic diagram, shown on the previous page, by now in the book you will know how to determine these by yourself - and this will be an excellent exercise.

Re-harmonized diagram (arrangement by Romane)

A	Em	B7/F#	Em/G [a]	B7/F#	Em	Em/G [b]	B7/F#	B7
	Cdim7	Ebdim7	Gbdim7	$C7^{5b}$	B7	B/A	Em/G [a]	B7/F#
A'	Em	B7/F#	Em/G [a]	%	G#dim7	E7	Am E7	Am
	Am7	$D7^{9}$	G7M	C7M	$F\#m7^{5b}$	B7	Em B7	Em
A	Em	B7/F#	Em/G [a]	B7/F#	Em	Em/G [b]	B7/F#	B7
	Cdim7	Ebdim7	Gbdim7	$C7^{5b}$	B7	B/A	Em/G [a]	B7/F#
A'	Em	B7/F#	Em/G [a]	%	G#dim7	E7	Am E7	Am
	Am7	$D7^{9}$	G7M	C7M	$F\#m7^{5b}$	B7	Em B7	Em
B	Am7	$D7^{9}$	G7M	G#dim7	Am7	$D7^{9}$	F#7	G6
B'	Am7	$D7^{9}$	G7M	G#dim7	Am7	$D7^{9}$	G6 D7	G6
B	Am7	$D7^{9}$	G7M	G#dim7	Am7	$D7^{9}$	F#7	G6
B'	Am7	$D7^{9}$	G7M	G#dim7	Am7	$D7^{9}$	G6	B7/F#
A	Em	B7/F#	Em/G [a]	B7/F#	Em	Em/G [b]	B7/F#	B7
	Cdim7	Ebdim7	Gbdim7	$C7^{5b}$	B7	B/A	Em/G [a]	B7/F#
A'	Em	B7/F#	Em/G [a]	%	G#dim7	E7	Am E7	Am
	Am7	$D7^{9}$	G7M	C7M	$F\#m7^{5b}$	B7	Em B7	Em

Sections A and A'

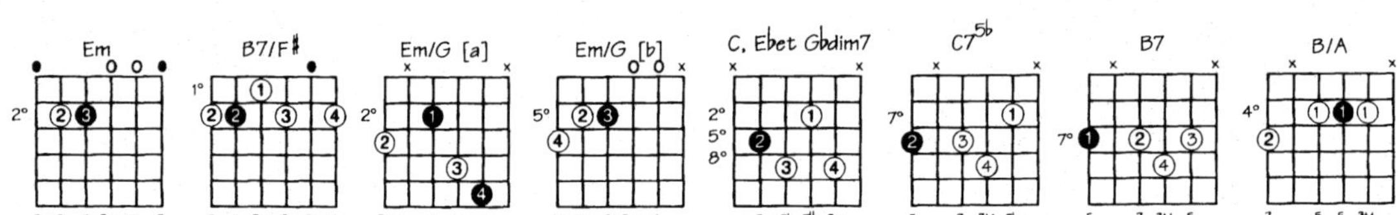

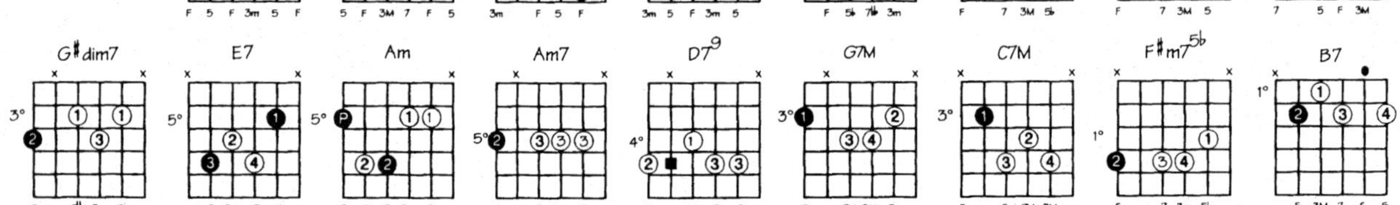

Sections B and B'

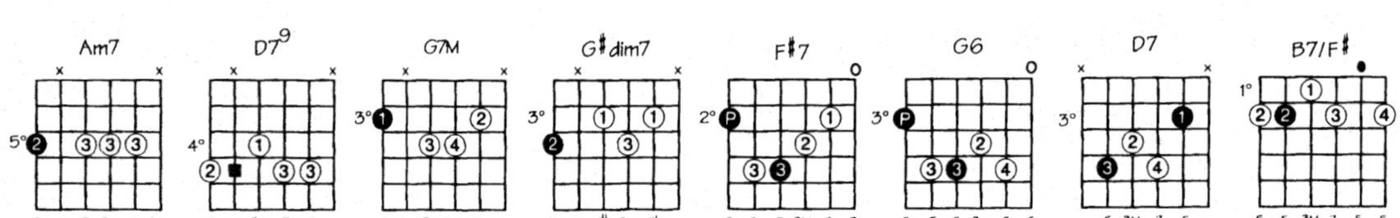

The superstructure of our waltz has been established. We are going to check out how the melody is structured, of course.

#89

Valse à Django

(Montagne Sainte-Geneviève)

(St. Genevieve mountain)

music by Django REINHARDT

Arrangement by Romane

128 AA'AA'BB'BB'AA'

♩=190

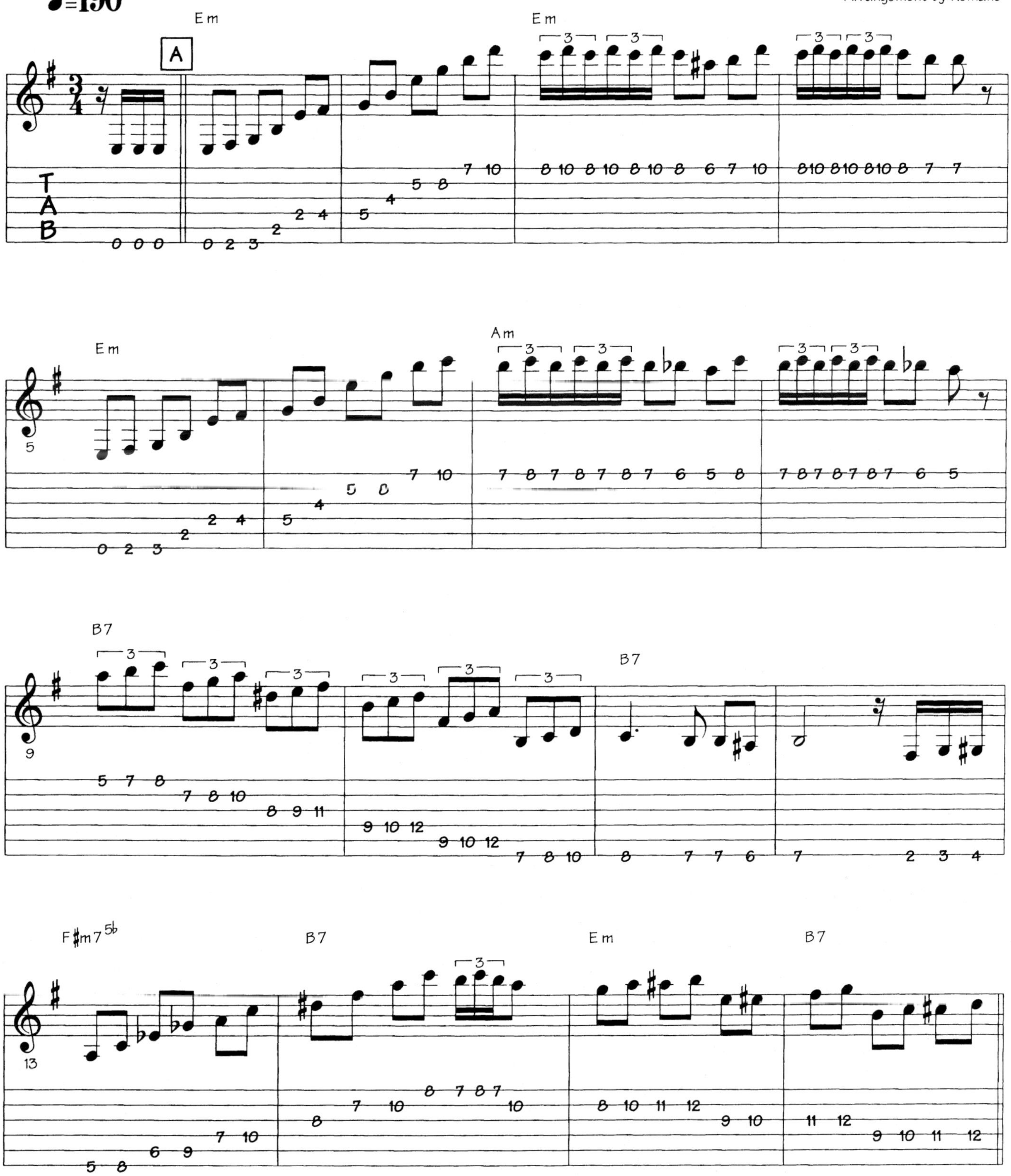

PART B

We continue with our lesson on "Gypsy Fire". This time, we'll deal with the chorus, which gives the particulars of the Manouche playing style that we already know, as well as new ones.

Gypsy Fire (measure 0) Pick up

As it is often done, this chorus starts before the first measure with a pickup. This pickup uses two ascending chromatic notes, where the second one is the "sensible" note (A), being the fifth of the harmony (Dm), in measure 1. And this sets up the key in the best possible way.

It is simple to start a chorus, but we must have some idea of how it works. Therefore, here is an idea that you can put in a little corner of your memory. For the rest, we have the same type of procedure at the end of measure 2, with the use of our well-known thrusting "stroke of the pen", with chromatic sixteenths.

Gypsy Fire (measure 11) inversed thrusting lead

Until now, all the driving "strokes of a pen" that we have seen were ascending. Measure 11 suggests one that descends, and it is as much driving as it is heightened by the use of an open chord where the harmony (E7) permits it:

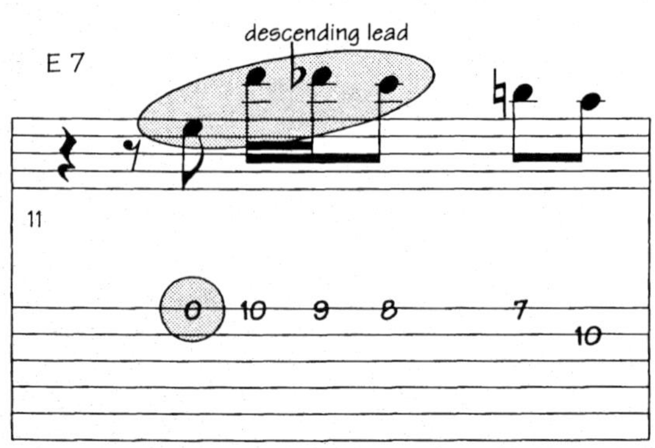

Gypsy Fire (measures 17 - 20) diagram of the phrase with the "II of the V"

This is not the first time we have seen this diagram. However, it has merit to point it out again, having its importance with the general subject of working out improvised melodies. In this case, the trick is to build the phrase around the m7 chord with a dominant chord, where the root note is placed one perfect fifth above it. Thus the phrase in measures 17 - 18, where the harmony is Eb7 (V momentarily), is worked out with the Bbm (I of V) position. The same procedure is also followed in measures 19 - 20, stopped with a space of a minor third:

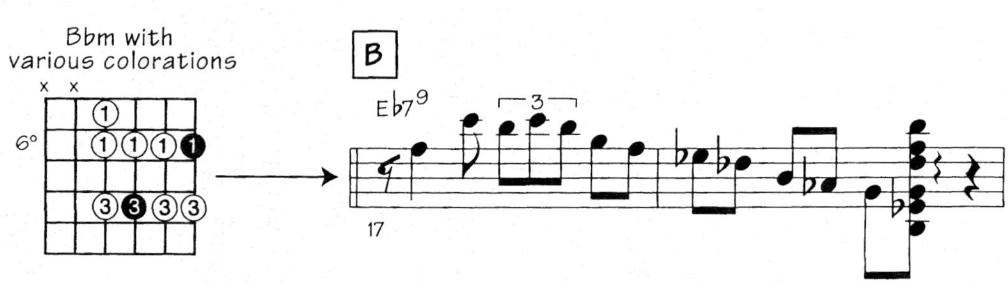

And this "II with V" diagram continues to be exploited in measure 22. The phrase ends with a series of metric chromaticisms that designate the A note, in measure 23:

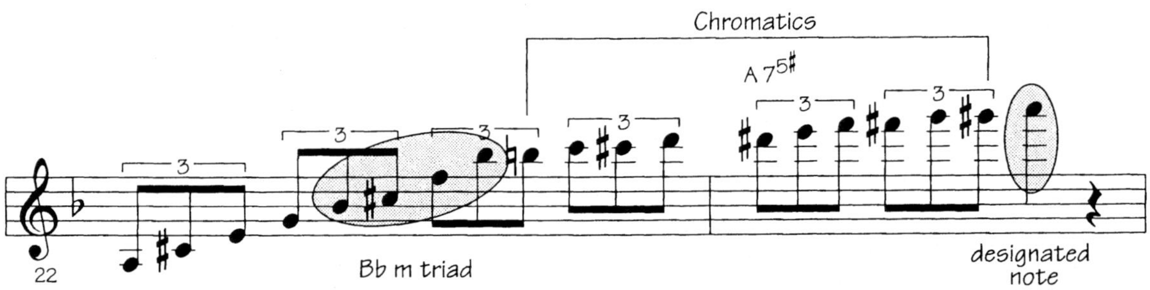

Gypsy Fire (measures 25 - 26) designated notes with Dm

Appreciate the continuity of ideas with these improvised phrases: the continuation after a designated note by using a chromatic lead, linked to another lead that uses the same principle as that of the designated notes:

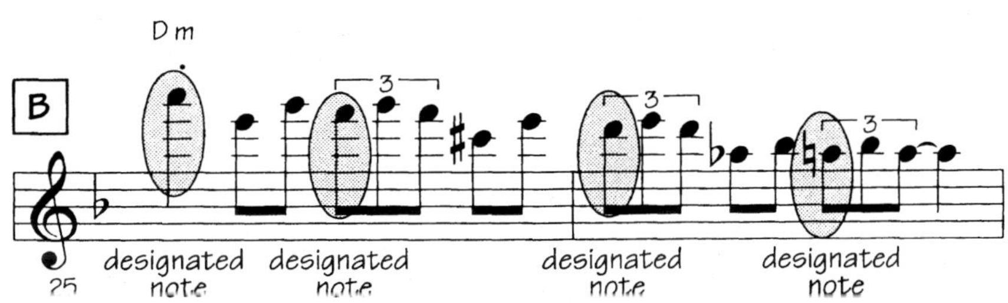

Gypsy Fire (measure 2) driving lead

Again, here is our driving "stroke of a pen", with sixteenth notes. As before, it is descending, and an invitation for an ascending phrase.

At a later time, we would love to insist upon the importance of this "stroke of a pen" procedure and the material of the Manouche playing style. It is a signature of the style: look at it carefully, and have a good memory if you really want to sound like a Manouche. Also look how the notes are used and are always disposed of with chromaticisms, either going ascending or descending, but never with diatonics (full and half tones) or another way.

Gypsy Fire (measure 32) conclusion with manouche color

Finally, the last measure of the chorus drives the nail on the head as far as "Manoucheries" are concerned, but with the pure structure of the harmony this time by using two typical colorations: the seventh and the major sixth with a minor chord.
And, since we are here, let's add some syncopations.

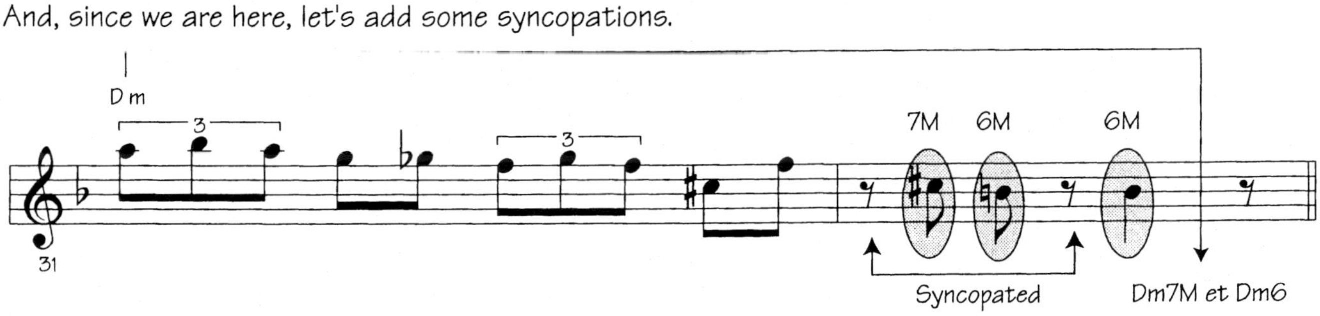

PART C

Here is the score with 32 measures of the "Gypsy Fire" chorus that you can hear on the Romanne Ombre CD.

Be careful while playing the high notes, because the beat is faster. In measure 18 (section B) you work hard to really learn how to do the sweep very fast (⌇) which is done with the Eb7(9) chord. It is of important in this chorus (and the others), to stay with the style that sounds very much like that of the Manouche. Finally, don't forget the slides in measures 17 and 19.

#88

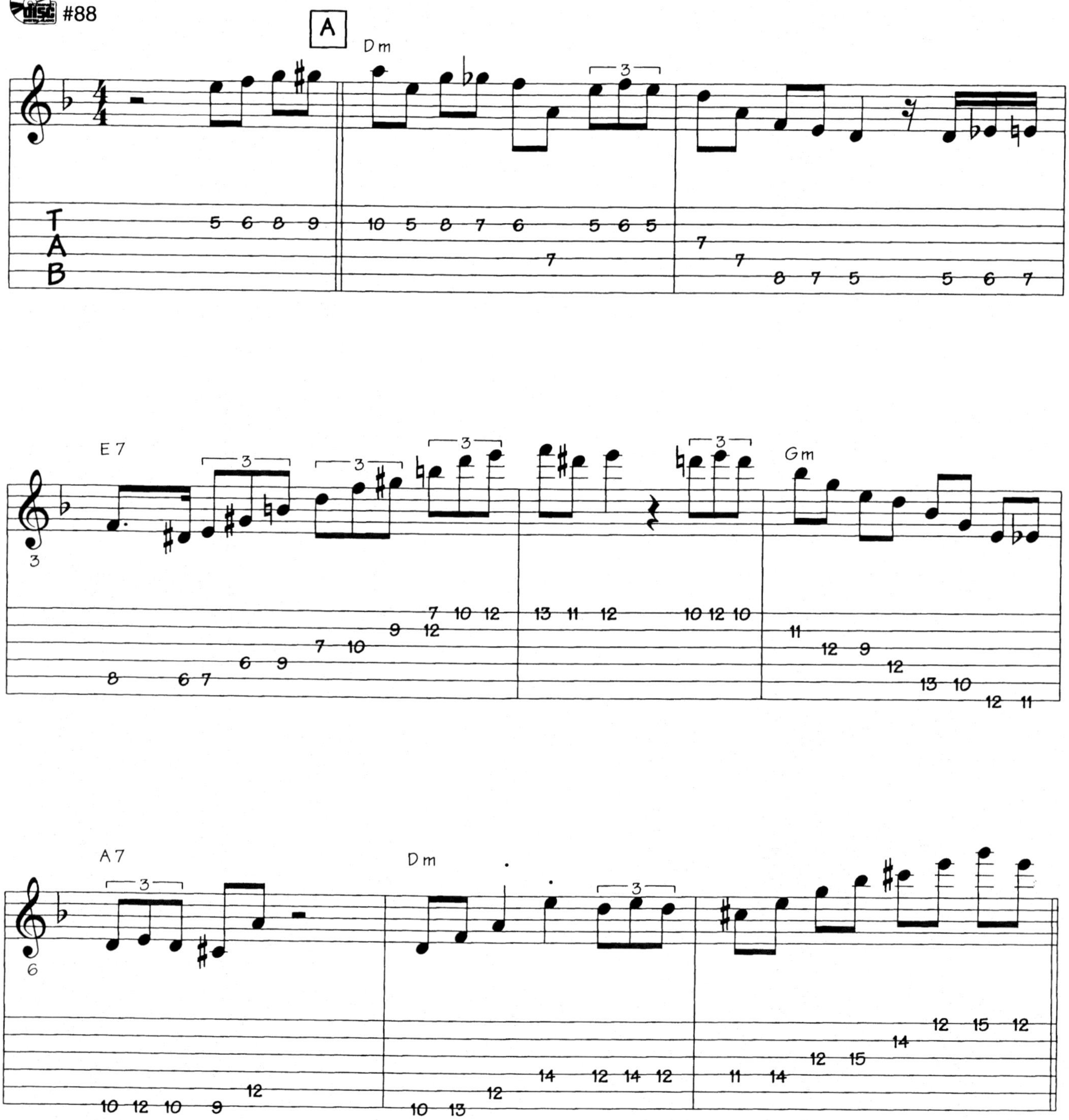

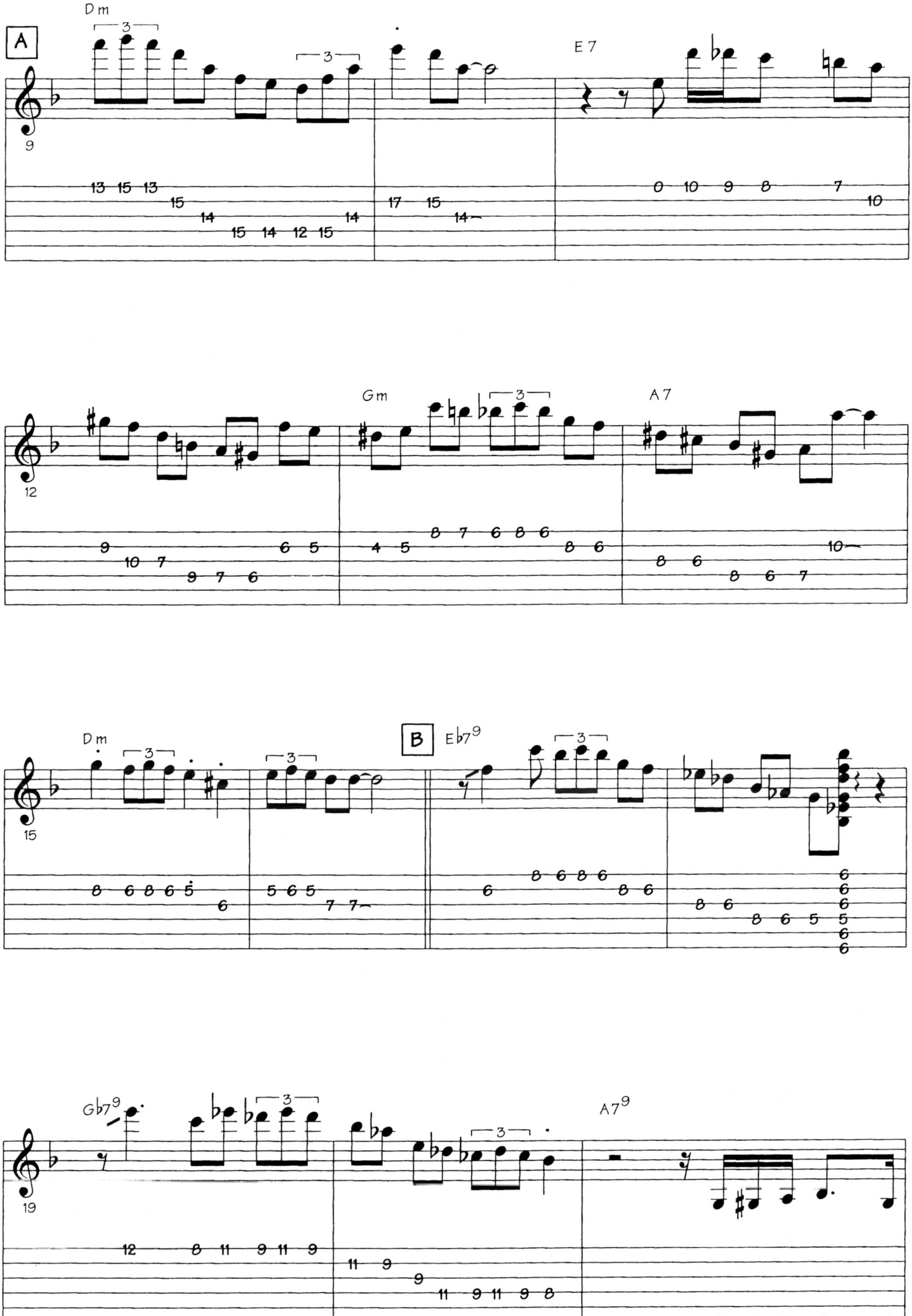
A
Dm
E7
Gm
A7
Dm
B
Eb7 9
Gb7 9
A7 9

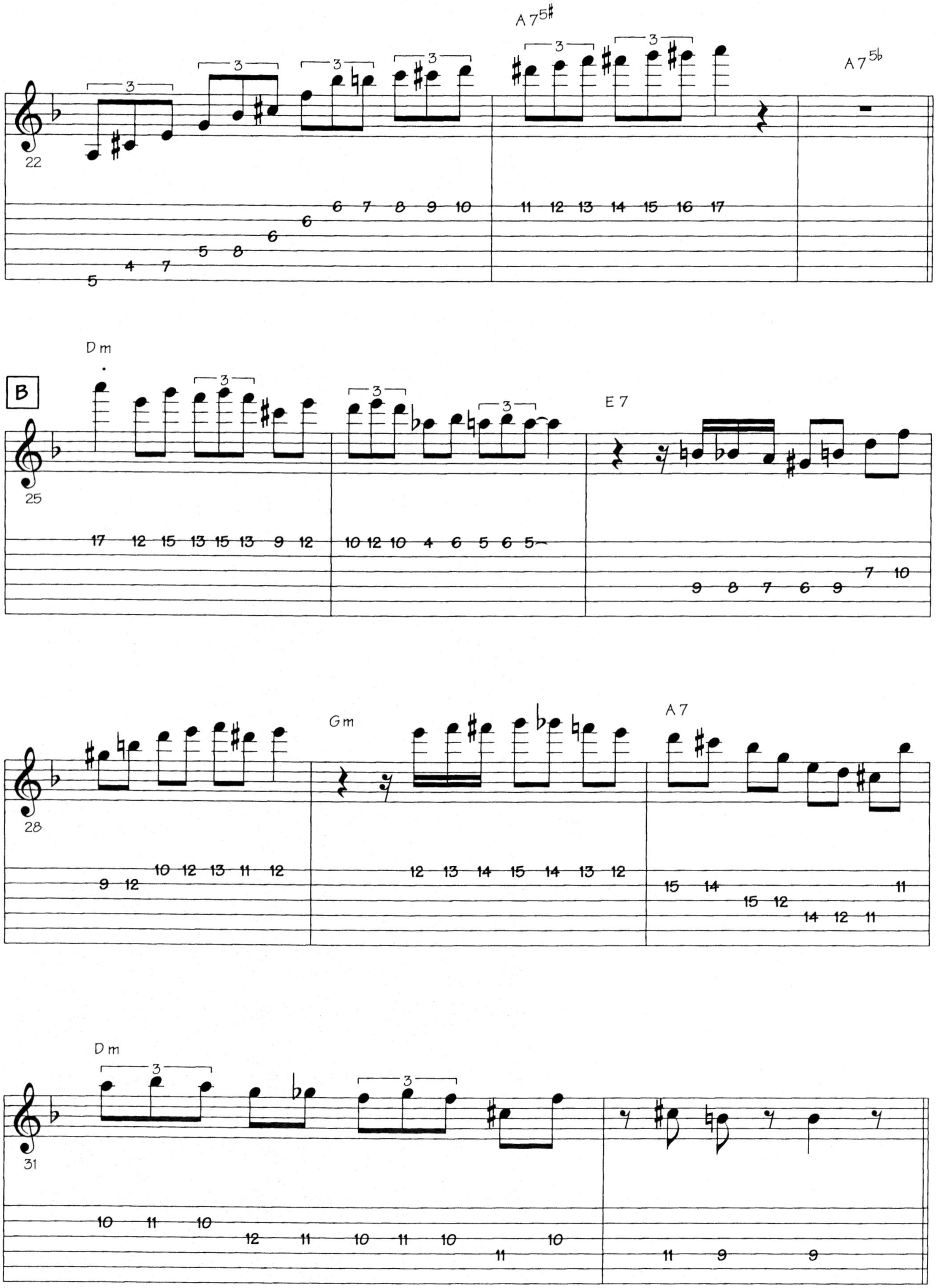
A7♯5
A7♭5
B
Dm
E7
Gm
A7
Dm

PART A

Exercise 76 - (continuation) Valse a Django

Continuation of our theme - exercise: the "Valse a Django". In this A' section of the melody, it uses trills all throughout (sixteenth note triplets, separated by one tone or a half tone), as in section A.
Be very careful when executing the trills because they are generally an important aesthetic element of the Manouche waltzes.

#89

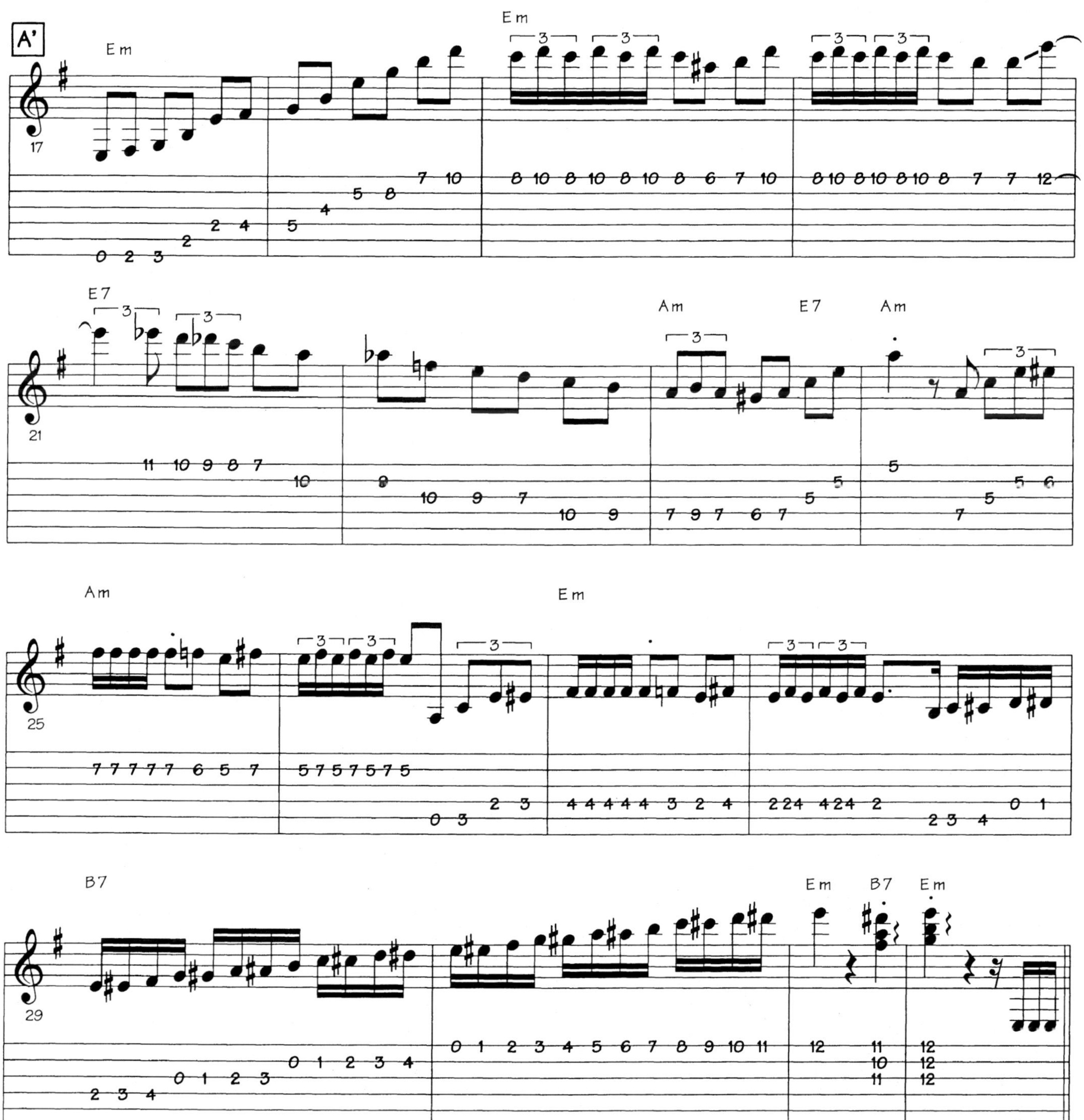

PART B

Taken from the Romane Ombre CD, we'll now study the theme "Manège". Here is a diagram that shows the structure of the harmony, theme, choruses, and the rhythm chords:

Manège

structure = 32 measures ABAB - diagram of the theme ♩= 250

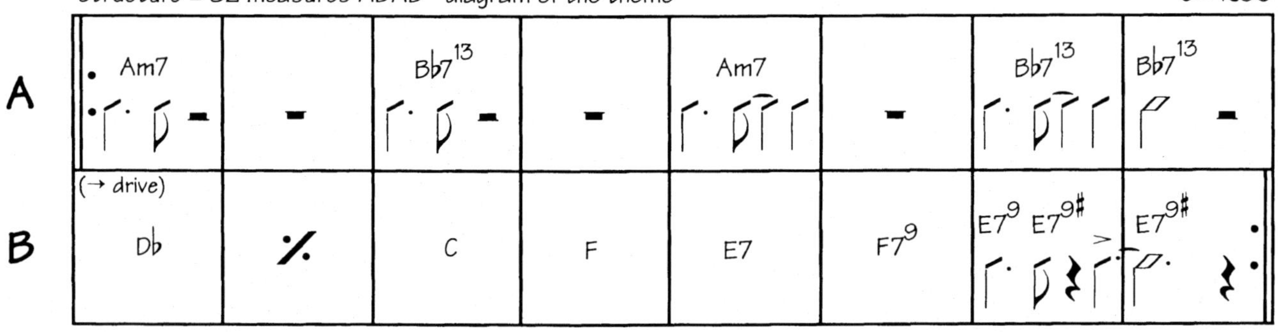

Diagram of the choruses

A	Am7 (1)	⁒	Bb7[13]	⁒	Am7 (5)	⁒	Bb7[13]	⁒
B	Db (9)	⁒	C	⁒	E7 (13)	F7[9]	E7	⁒

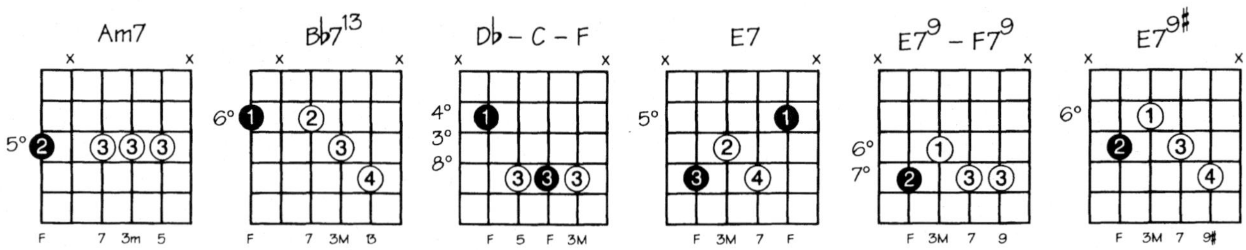

The analysis of this harmony structure is simple. The key is static: A minor. But, of course, each of the little subtleties will show up by itself.

Key: Am

A	(Im) Am7 (1)	⁒	(IIb7) Bb7[13]	⁒	(Im) Am7 (5)	⁒	(IIb7) Bb7[13]	⁒
B	(IVb) Db (9)	⁒	(III) C	⁒	(V) E7 (13)	(VIb7) F7[9]	(V) E7	⁒

MEASURES 1 - 8: alternate reiterated cadences, of the I to the IIb7 (T.S. of the V) and visa versa.

MEASURE 9: the bIV chord is nothing other than the T.S. of the chord which drives with III. In other words, the major C chord is introduced with a major chord that is located a perfect fifth higher (compare this with the main explanation in chapter 6, page 4) and is tritonally substituted with (G → Db = tritone).

MEASURES 13 - 16: this prepares the return of the Im (at the beginning of the diagram), through its V degree (E7),- interrupted by a VIb7, which is nothing other than the T.S. of the chord (provisional V: B7) which drives with E7, the realistic V degree. This is thus exactly the same principle as that of measures 9 to 13.

On page 6 of this chapter we find the the melody of "Manège". In the prelude of this last study, we want to get rid of some principles that governed over the development of this melody.

Manège - Explaining the theme

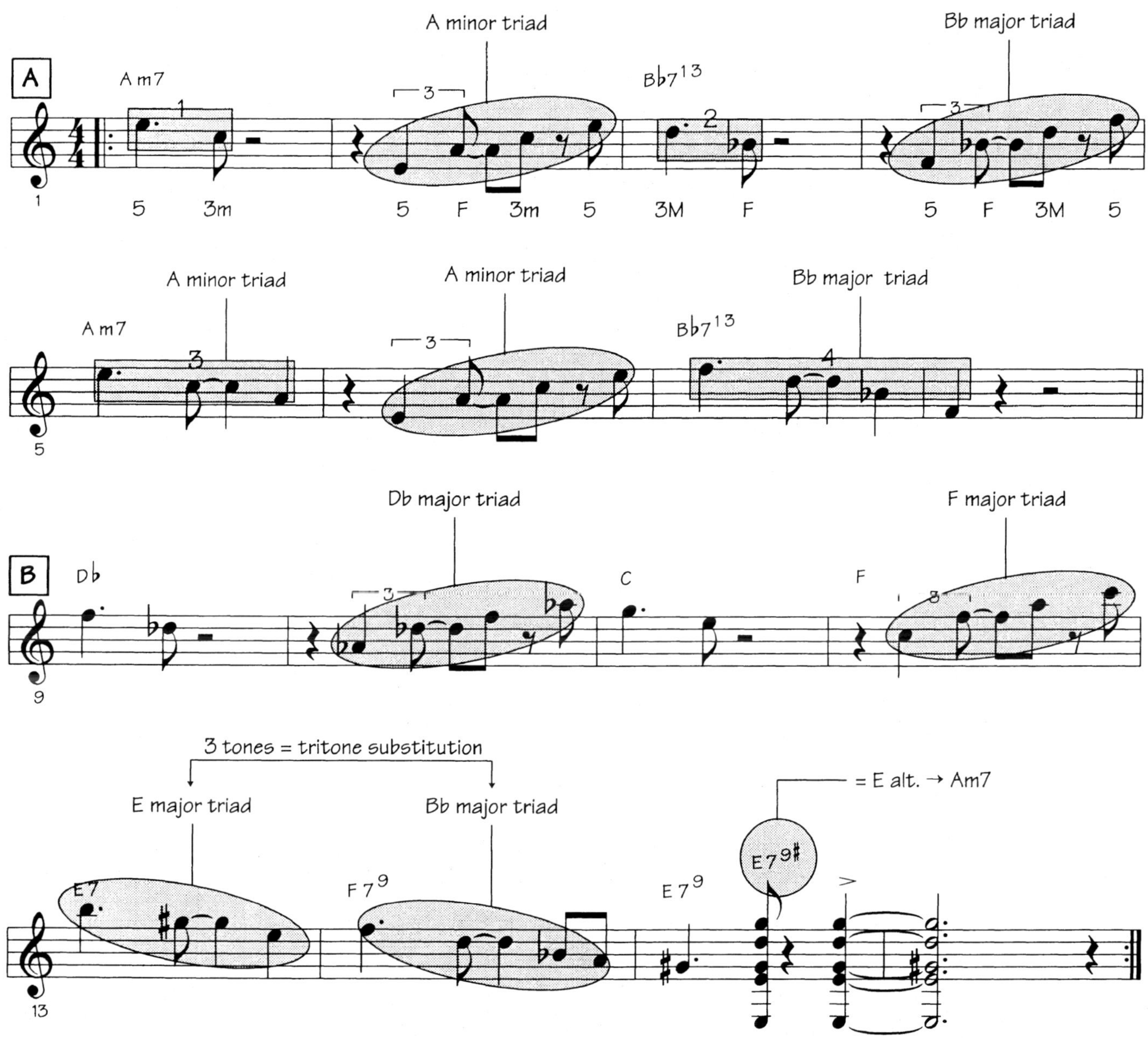

The driving force of this melody is the principle of the arpeggio, applied by going around and around with major and minor triads. These are excellent musical units relative to the harmony that we see here. This theme relies almost totally on this principle.

Observe also:

– the procedure of the melodic progression forms a "mirror" (encircled 1, 2, 3 and 4),

– the progression of measures 13 - 14, where the dominant of the (A minor key) is shown in two possible ways: as an E7 (V) and as a Bb7 (T.S. of E7). Globally the harmony of these last four measures is E7, in spite of the presence of F7 (measure 14), that is done for no other reason than to break up the monotony of the arranged rhythm.

– the use of the E7(#9) chord, an alt. type chord, which drives back in a very certain and convenient way, toward the I degree of the key (Am7, measure 1).

Chapter 27 / page 4

Let's finish "Manège" by studying two suggested guitar choruses.

Manège (chorus 1) Stop chorus

This solo opens fire with a particularly fierce stop - chorus that is embedded in the Manouche playing style: the chromatic scale. This one uses open chords. Note that the final (designated) note corresponds harmonically with the major ninth (9M) of the first chord in the diagram (Am7), the lead that starts with the root note of the E7 chord, the V of AM7.

Manège (chorus 1, measures 5 - 8) dead notes

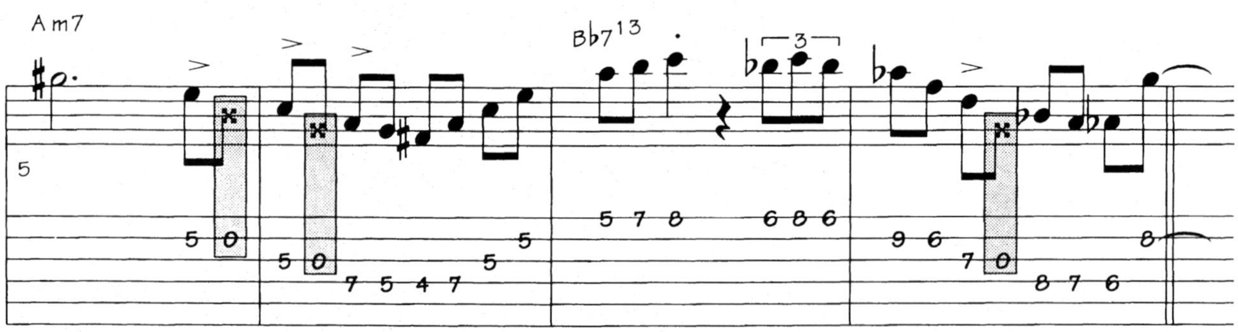

By using short attacks and dynamics, the "dead notes" are most often sounded with an undetermined pitch. We have already seen examples of this when we studied the preceding choruses ("Swing For Ninine", "Monticello"). Nevertheless, these illustrations present a new interest in the measure where it uses open strings, which takes place in the harmony that we are looking at: namely, the open B and G, respectively the 9M and 7 of Am7. At the same time notice the accents which precede each dead note. Listen to this passage on the CD.

Manège (chorus 1, measures 14 - 16) expecting melody phrase

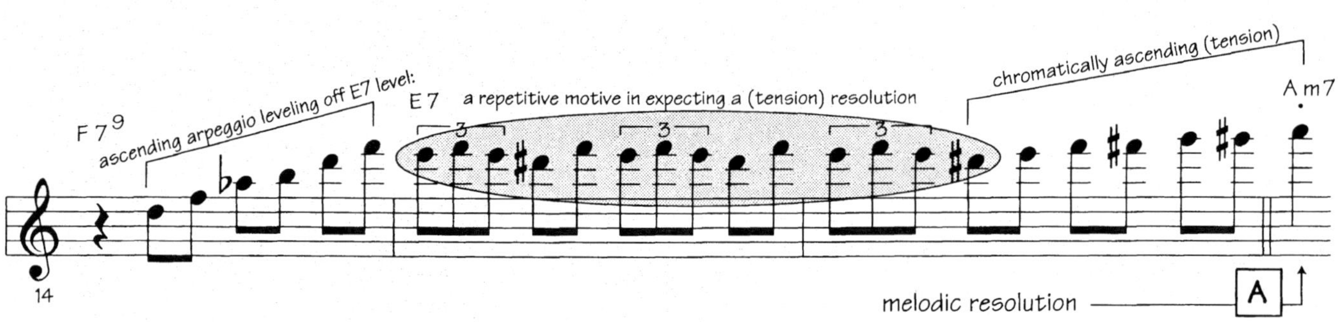

Measures 14 and 16 show an improvisational procedure that has an aesthetic important value.

Here we are looking at a very regular rhythmic phrase, which combines many elements (arpeggios, triplets and chromatics), whereby the objective is to mark and maintain tension whenever necessary, which results in the melodic resolution.
And, of course, this operation is done with the V chord (E7), which drives the Am7, the resolution chord.

Manège (chorus 2, measures 21 - 22) designated notes

In measures 21 and 22, we recover a procedure which we have already seen in the way a Manouche improvises: those designated notes (★) in relation to the harmony we are looking at now. Notice that these corresponding notes here are shown as triads of the Am7 chord.

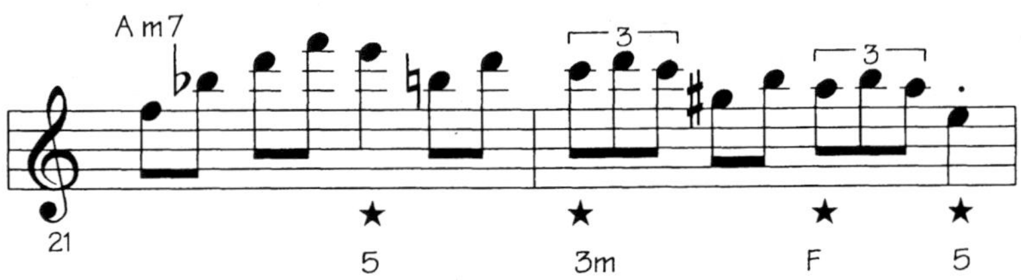

Manège (chorus 2, measures 25 - 26) Chromatic sweeps and II for V

Here we have a driving chord sweep, combined with a short ascending chromaticism (encircled). It starts decent with the notes based on the Abm chord that conforms with the principle that we seen many times over in the course of this chapter (Chapter 14):

All dominant seventh chords (V7) can be preceded by, or mixed with, a minor chord of which the root note is placed a perfect fifth higher.

Notice in this subject that the harmony, the (Db), is thought of as dominant, namely the Db7.

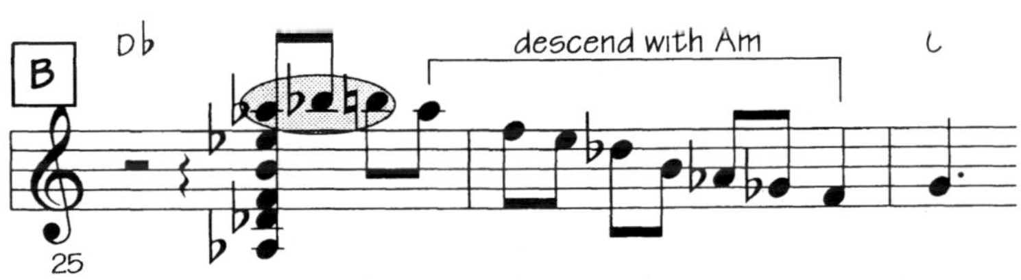

Manège (chorus 2, measures 29 - 32) minor harmonic scale

Finally, the second chorus is completed with a long and interesting illustration of the minor harmonic scale, in which triplets play a major role. Also look at this lead, made up with notes from the A minor harmonic scale. (This is easily recognizable by its G# note, which is isolated among the exclusive "natural" notes). This lead exploits the last V degree, a degree that itself exactly developed an E7 chord, as it must be done with the harmony here.

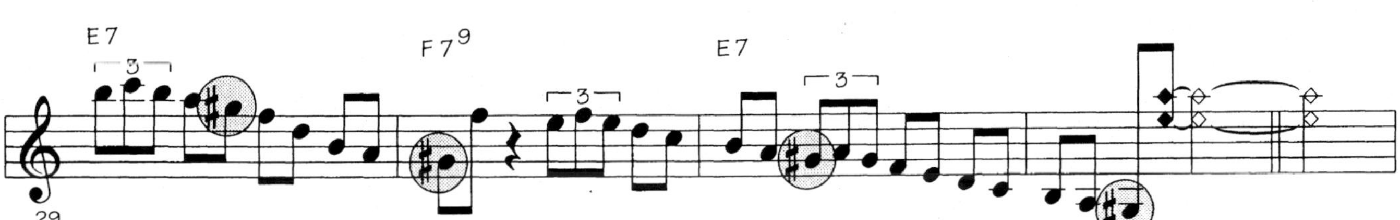

PART C

Here is the theme of "Manège".

It is important to keep the rhythm in time. Therefore, we have opted to write certain compound passages (paired measures) in a way to really underline the syncopated swing. But the other passages are written binary (paired measures), the interpretation should also be compound, of course.

#90

Manège

♫ = ♩♪ (triplet) ♩=250

music by ROMANE

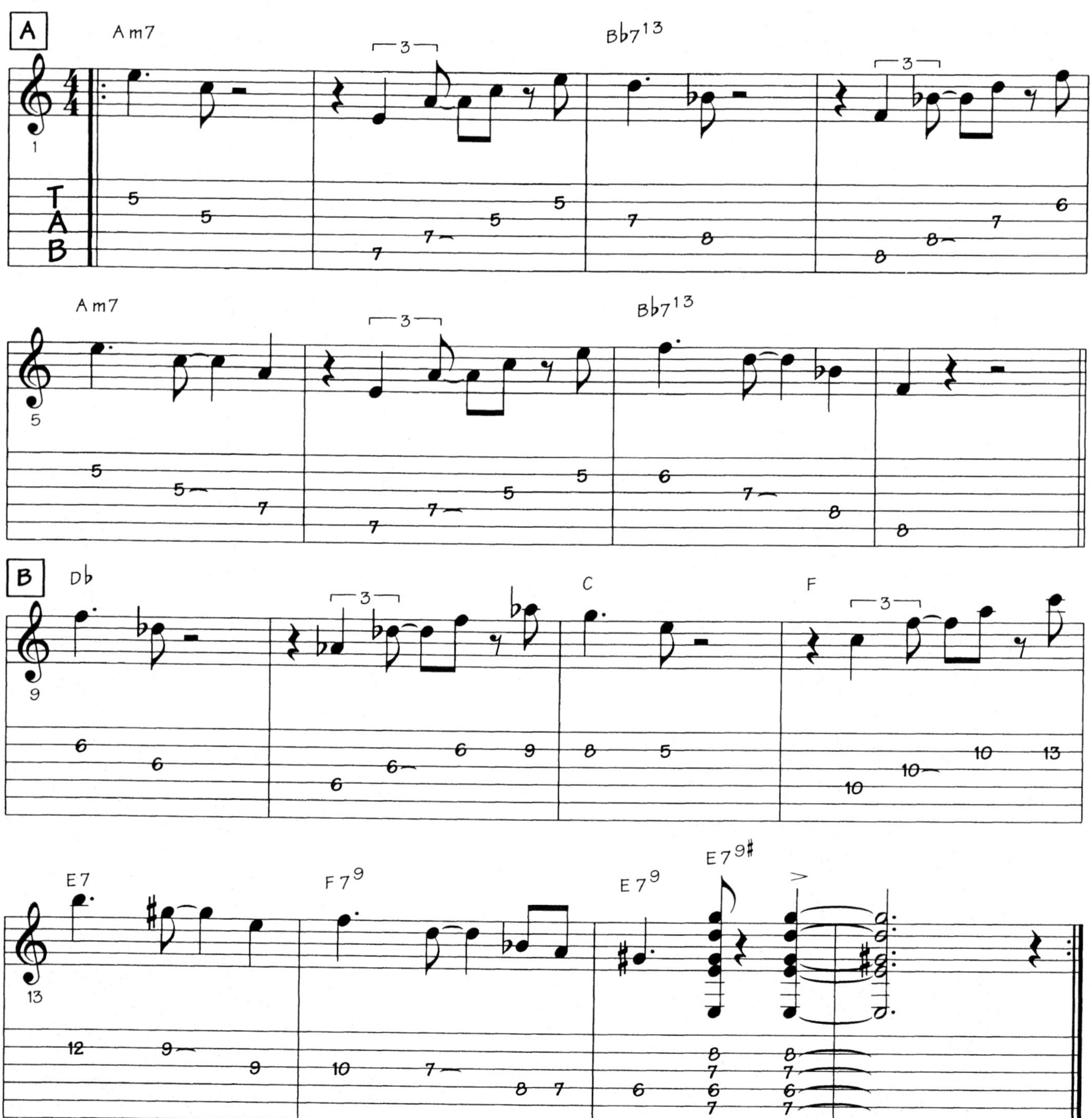

We are now going to continue with the violin and accordion choruses on the Romane Ombre CD, so that we can finish the two guitar choruses of "Manège".

With regard to the rhythm diagram of measure 19, don't panic. It is simply a triplet with quarter notes where the last two together are subdivided with eighth notes, and the five notes together last exactly as they should: two beats. Once more, listen to the CD in order to be really sure of the timing.

#91

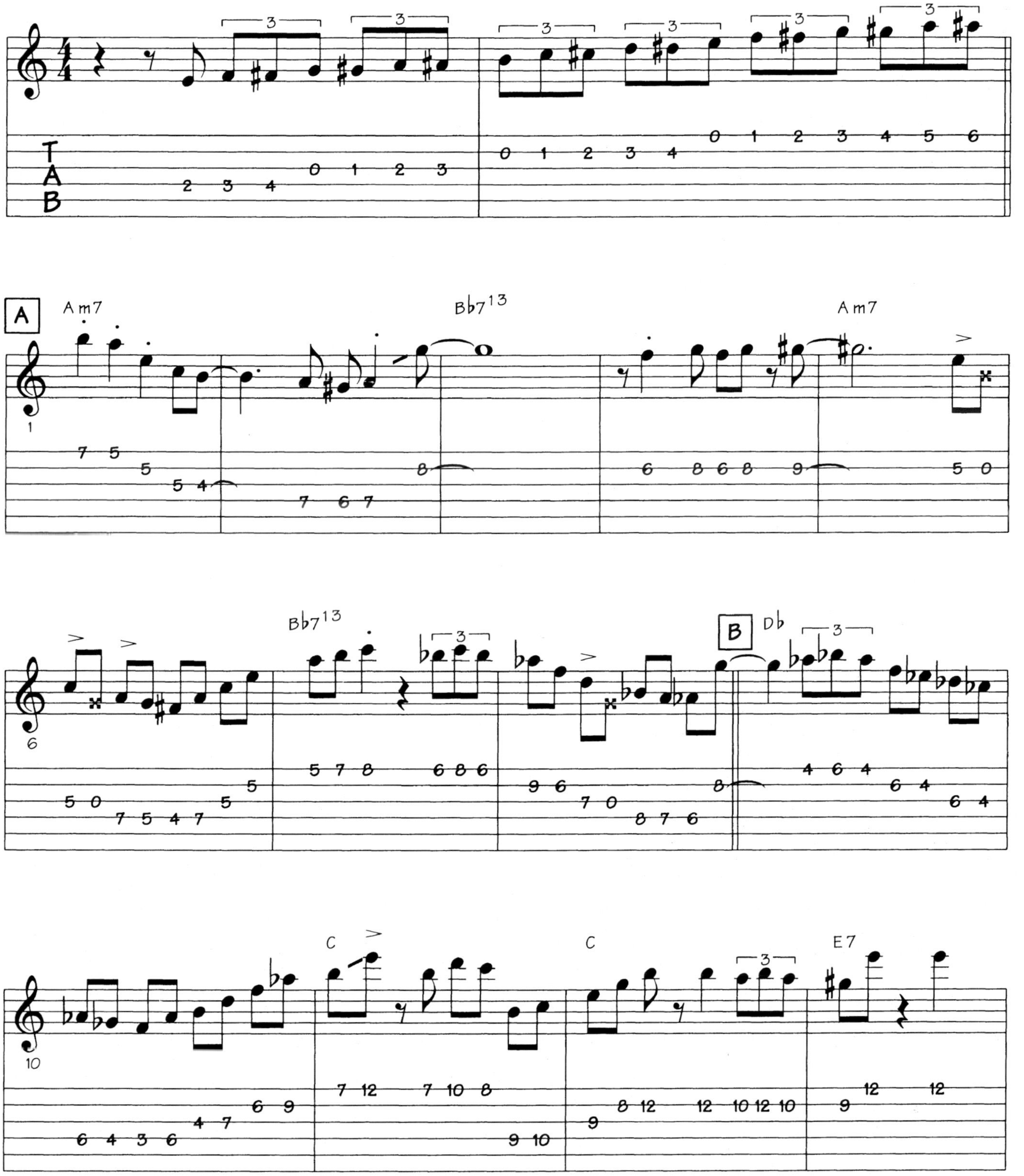

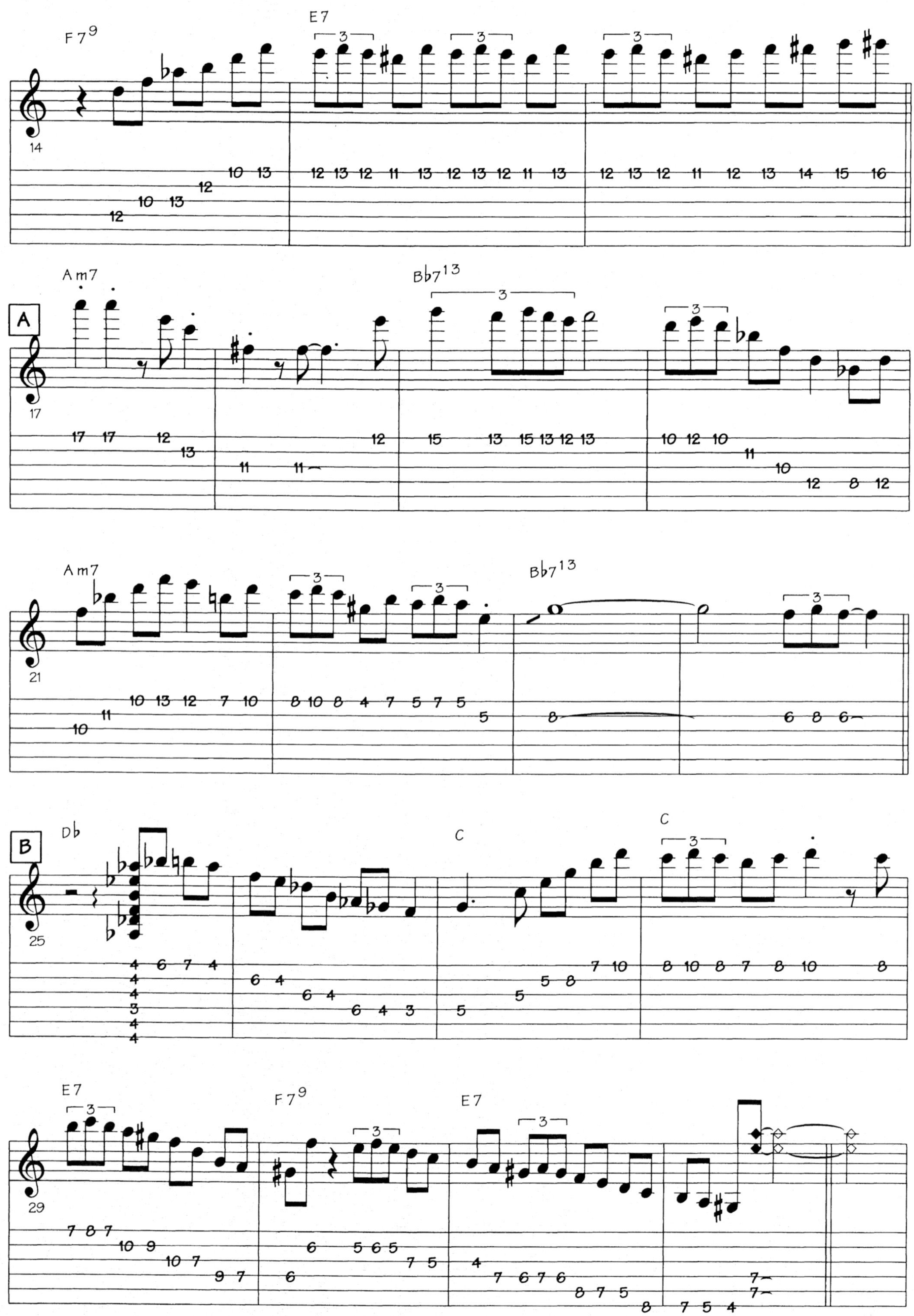
F7⁹
E7
Am7
A
Bb7¹³
Am7
Bb7¹³
Db
B
C
C
E7
F7⁹
E7

PART A

Exercise 77 - introduction of Ombre

Before playing the studies that follow, listen to the "Ombre" theme (Romane Ombre CD) and make an effort to play the chords keeping time as in the introduction.

As always, the subject is to introduce the chord of Gm (the beginning of the theme), and that we use the "dominant → root note" principle: the Gm is introduced by D7, which itself is brought by the Eb7 (A7).

Also notice how the contra-bass is inserted during the rests (question/answer principle).

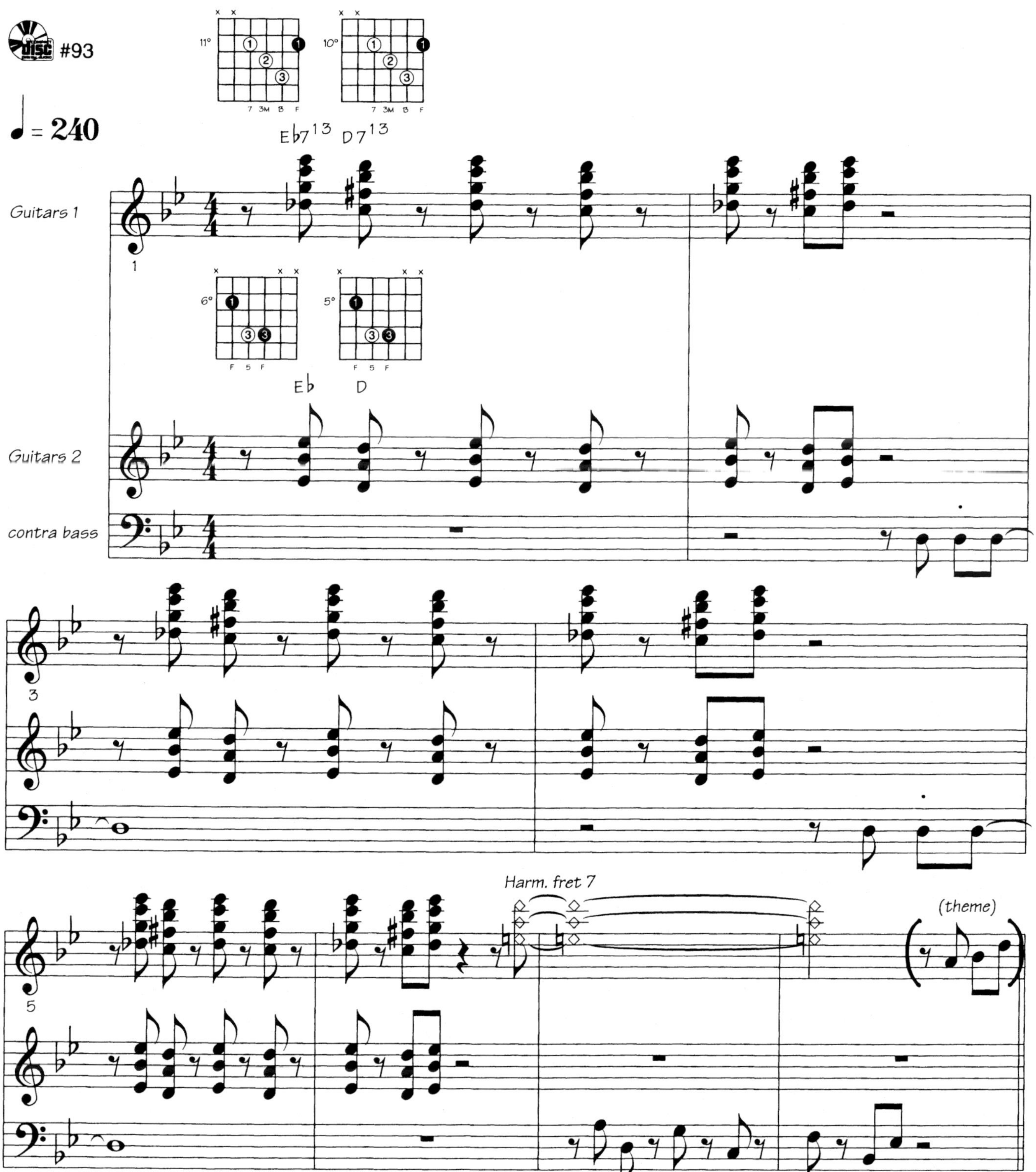

PART B1

After the introduction, here is the diagram of "Ombre".

Ombre

(shadow)

structure = 16 measures AB (3 times) - diagram of the theme — ♩= 240

A	Gm6	%	C7^{5b}	%	Gm6	%	Ab6	%
B	Cm7	F7^{9}	Bbm7	Eb7^{9}	Am7^{5b}	Ab7^{5b}	Gm6	–

Chorus diagram

A	Gm6	%	C7^{5b}	%	Gm6	%	Ab6	%
B	Cm7	F7^{9}	Bbm7	Eb7^{9}	Am7^{5b}	Ab7^{5b}	Gm6	D7

By following the example of "Manège", the structure of this theme revolves around 16 AB measures. The melody of this theme is repeated three times, each chorus follows exactly the 16 AB structure.

If you have any difficulty playing the syncopation in time with regard to measure 15, the best thing for you to do is to listen to the CD. And with a minimum of concentration, your listening can promptly solve this problem.

As with the rhythm chords of this peace, these register perfectly with the style of the Manouche in this piece.

Section A :

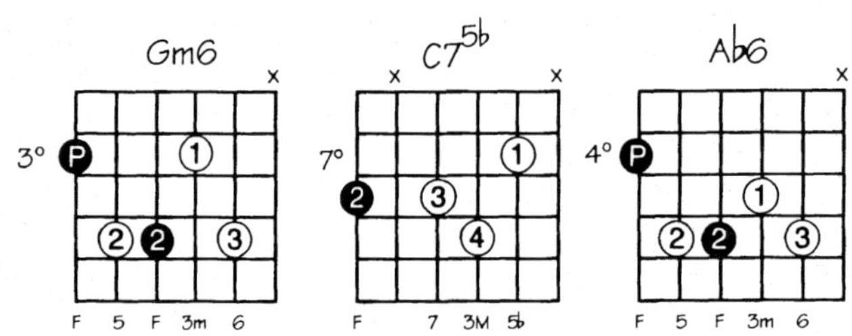

Section B :

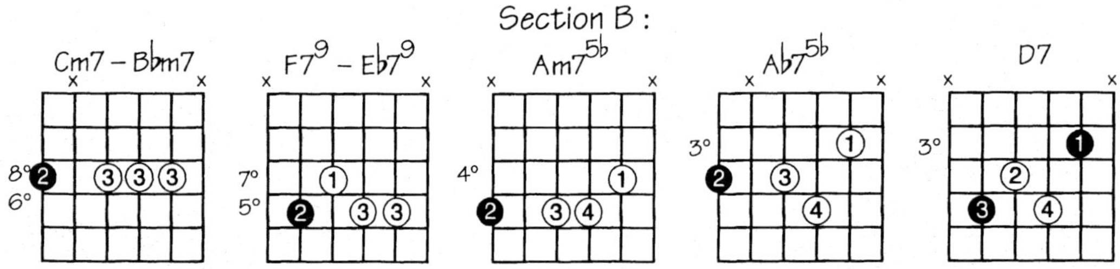

"Ombre" presents an individual enough harmonic structure, so that the analysis shows it is possible to sensibly depart the "beaten paths" of the harmonic composition without being disappointed with its result.

The "beaten paths" here are the various principles which maintain one key, and you are already familiar with its name. Or, at least what it has to do with section A. The structure in "Ombre" doesn't show any tonal evidence of the jazz standards that we generally like.

Here is what it turns out to be:

	Key: Gm						Key: Ab	
A	1 (Im) Gm6	%	(IV7) $C7^{5b}$	%	5 Gm6	%	(I) Ab6	%
B	9 (III) Cm7	(VI7) $F7^{9}$	(II) Bbm7	(V) $Eb7^{9}$	13 (II) $Am7^{5b}$	(IIb7) $Ab7^{5b}$	(Im) Gm6	(V) D7
					Key: Gm			

MEASURE 3: if the first two measures are to be analyzed other than by the tonality of G minor, the presence of IV7 seems to be questionable again in the measure where, with its IV degree, this G minor key doesn't develop a C7chord (but a C7m chord).

But then, are we really in G minor? Yes, this IV7 is widely used in jazz, and more precisely in the blues where, in a major key, the harmonic structure is done traditionally - it is even an essential characteristic of the harmonies with the blues - a IV7 chord.
And that gave us everything to enthusiastically qualify "Ombre" as a Manouche blues !

MEASURE 7: if the structure of "Ombre" is BLUESY by the presence of the IV7, it is like Manouche with its evolution of using a strange chord in the initial key. In effect, each Ab major chord does not exist in the key of G minor.
And the relationship between G minor and A major, has therefore two minor/major keys placed one half tone apart. This is a harmonic signature of Manouche: examine the new harmonic structure of "Swing For Ninine" (chapter 19, page 3), you will recognize this characteristic.

MEASURES 9 - 12: here we have the altered anatole in the key of Ab. However, in the measure where this anatole doesn't resolve (it's not an Ab in measure13) and where, in another part, we are in another section (B) of the structure, we prefer to consider this entire group of four chords as a continuation of the II - V progression with descending tones and without particular ties between them.

MEASURES 13 - 16: finally, the return of the initial G minor key in the middle of a minor cadence where the IIb7 chord is none other than a tritone substitution for D7 (from Ab to D we count three tones), it is the V of the Gm6 chord.

Now we are returning to study harmonic theory.

With this subject, here and in following chapters, we are going to devote some pages to give you certain information that will greatly benefit you with mastering the guitar chords.

Since the beginning of this book you have learned to play a certain number of chord positions, within various contexts and, we suppose, you always have been happy with their voicings.

But maybe you have asked yourself at this stage: how can we make such beautiful chords, because it sounds like it was done without any difficulty, all by itself or among the other chords (voicings), and how can I play it on the guitar?

Are there precise procedures to get these results? Or are these exclusively coming from "inspiration", from patiently accumulating it, by listening to it, or by spending hours while plunging your nose in dictionaries with 23,456 chord positions?!

With regard to the last hypothesis, we immediately insist that you don't worry about it (and you will be spared headaches!): in the matter of chords, chord dictionaries let you get the knowledge and the mastery that you want, with little effort.

The musical ear, the experience, and much more… the Manouche guitarist that knows something.
When you have inspiration, it compares with listening and having experience, but at a much higher level. This is when the technique really becomes second nature, and all the principles and theoretical procedures are understood and assimilated.

Yes, there are procedures that are simple enough and very efficient.

These procedures to master the chords are divided into three sections:
1) limit the choice of chords,
2) work rigorously with their reversals,
3) know their substitutions.

LIMITED USE OF CHORDS

You have, without a doubt, looked at the last pages of this book, at the jazz chords that mainly uses four tones. These are at times rich and manageable when the harmonic functions are respectively (R - 3 - 5 - 7 - 9, etc.), other than the fact that these chords are freely deprived of the root note and/or the fifth, at the cost of such and such particular colorations.

This being the case with our strict musical system of twelve equal half tones between them (a system called "tempered tuning"), you probably have never asked yourself, "How many distinct chords can you make with four notes?"

In other words, what is the exact number of combinations, by using four notes in our musical system, that we can define, when we "double it" without transposing?

The answer is 43: from the chord that will be formed, for example with "C - C# - D - D#" (that is extremely dissonant). We designate it under the generic terms as a "cluster" until we have the one that forms the "C – E – G – B" (C7M), while passing through "C – E – G – A" (C6), etc.

43 four-note chords… it's little and it's a lot.

Little, because the size of the number is totally human. This is lot and enormous, if you consider all the inversions and transpositions that you have to go through when you write a "hyper-mega" chord dictionary (but be calm, we never intended to do so)!

If we can only use three notes, we get 19 chords. On the other hand, with five notes it goes up to 66, and for six notes to 80!

Good, this is all done here for you, so that you can make the absolute necessary choices by knowing the chords… because it is out of the question to play and master the guitar with 43 distinctive chords, of course! From a pure musical point of view; this will even be a fundamental mistake.

If this is the case, do we have to restrict our choices with those types of chords in particular?

– It is known that the tempered system was institutionalized over the course of three centuries. This was done to encourage the rapid expansion of the TONAL CONCEPT (→ modulations, leisure displacements of the central key in the course of one single and same musical work - a radical concept different of the true modal procedure) which is a favorite with the westerners.

– It is known that the MAJOR SCALE is the melodic "stepladder" which lets you, by excellence and between all of those, create works with a tonal character. (95% of the western musical creations rely on the tonal principle. This is the case in jazz.)

You should know these tonal type chord that are generated by the major scale. You have already learned these special chords, the groups that used four tones. These special chords, are composed with thirds of the major scale, come in four types. These are summarized below:

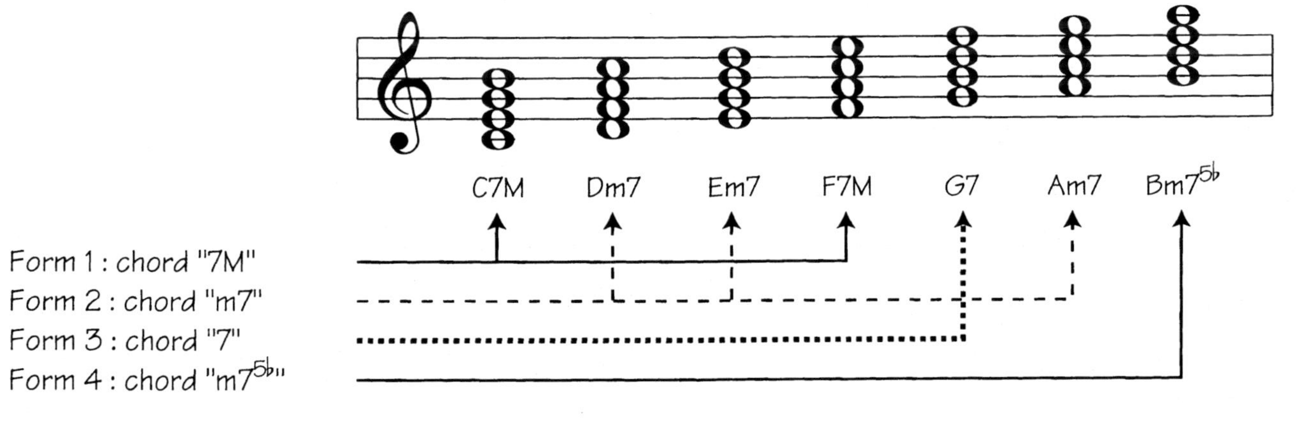

Thus for the time being, when you master these four types of chords, with all its possible angles, (the inversions in various registers, transpositions and substitutions), we guarantee that you will have the skill in most situations to use these when you need them. Then you can spend your time to become an expert at it, in particular, and with the preferred order, of these chords above, done with different harmonizations (notably, the superpositions with fourths) and scales that are close to the major scale, such as the harmonic minor scale or the melody.

We are now coming to the real technical part of the subject, and will discontinue with our chord choices:

THE CHORD INVERSIONS

When we have a chord with four sounds, and we want to determine the inversions of these, we have to do it in three successive stages, where the precise name of the chord (symbol) doesn't have any impact:

A) Determining the initial "close" position: this determines the arrangement in which the composing intervals are reduced to the minimum size. All the notes of chords must be joined there, by following the example of the terms of a scale.

For example, to leave the B - F - E - C group, we can choose the initial close position the relationship of E - F - B - C, which is composed of the minor second (E - F), an augmented fourth (F - B) and a minor second (B - C).

B) The inversions of the initial closed position: this is disposed of in turn with the sharp of each of the composed notes, without modifying the initial spaces of the intervals between these last ones. Thus, a chord with four tones will give us three inversions. This gives us a total of four chords.

C) To open: we are leaving each of the four closed positions, to modify the spaces of the intervals between the composing notes according to certain well defined processes.

In the category of the four-note chords, the theory offers us a large palette, which gives us over six related procedures. Thus, with the exception of the closed positions, all the chords, which are determined by these procedures, are the "open" chords (separate notes):

1 - "close" positions,	4 - "drop 2/3" positions
2 - "drop 2" positions,	5 - "drop 2/4" positions
3 - "drop 3" positions,	6 - "double drop 2/drop 3" positions

At the end we get 24 chords that are all perfectly distinct from each other, although these all use the same four notes. As far as the convenient and practical American term "(to) drop" is concerned, it means to lower. In this case, we have to lower some of the composed notes of a given chord to a lower octave, or possibly 2 octaves lower ("double drop 2").

Good, in order that you don't get discouraged, we immediately determine that the guitar doesn't have much to do with procedures 2 and 3, but rather with procedure 1, which is relatively isolated.

In order for us to know what the choices are, here are, guitaristicly speaking, the three known A B C chapters, that we will call it this time. We give you, at random, as an example, the four E - A - G - C notes.

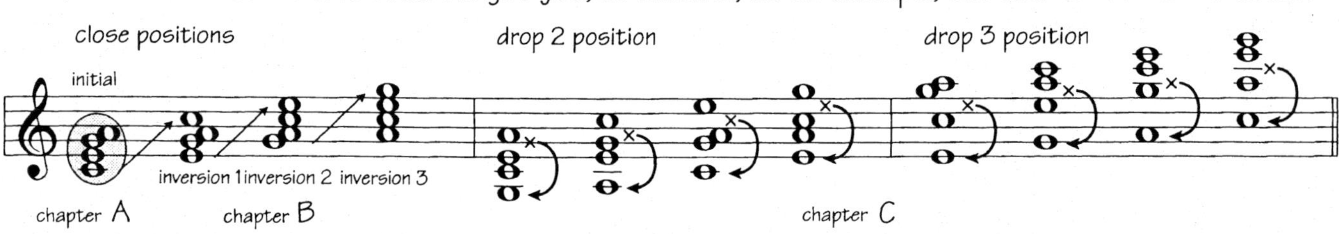

The four "drop 2" and "drop3" positions are thus obtained by taking the second and third notes of each of the four chords in a close position an octave lower, and expect that the highest note of a chord is always considered to be the first.

Now that we have shown you this, we will continue to study the inversions in the next chapter.

PART B2

For a warm up to study the "Ombre" melody, we would like to make certain remarks of a general order.

Ombre - Architecture (construction) of the melody

This melody (section A) uses a certain number of simple procedures:

– The pick up is repeated in the form of a question and answer. The height of the melodic punctuations.

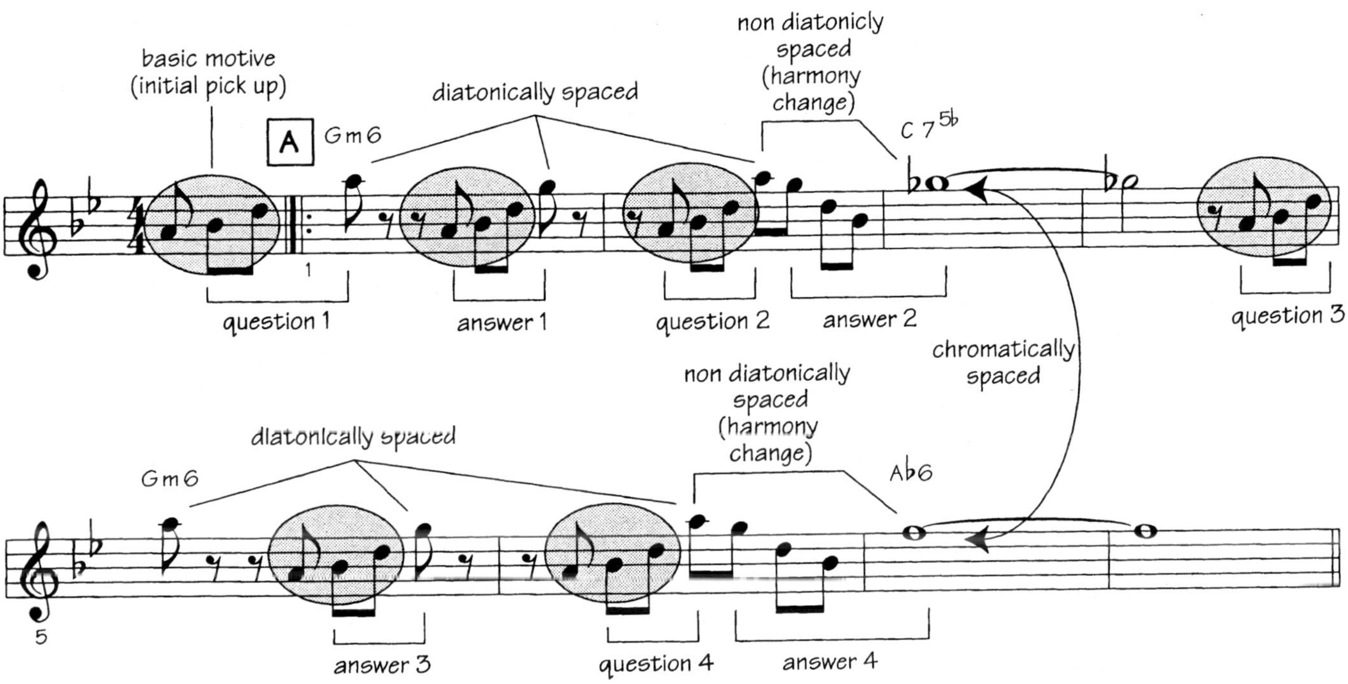

Notice the function of the harmony with the punctuation in measure 3: if the Gm chord lasted four measures, this Gb (or F#) would have a 7M. This will get us the following principle:

"The use of the 7M coloration with a minor chord, potentially a II degree, gives birth to the b5 coloration (or #11) with the chord that follows, potentially a V degree (IIm → V7 progression)."

In regard with the chromatic spacing that rules between the punctuation of measures 3 and 6, notice that the movement is going in the opposite direction from each other: the harmony goes up four tones (Gm → C7), while the melody descends a half tone (Gb → F).

In section B, the principle of the question and answer form continues, with rhythmic differences. But this time, the motive is not static; there is a diatonically descending movement:

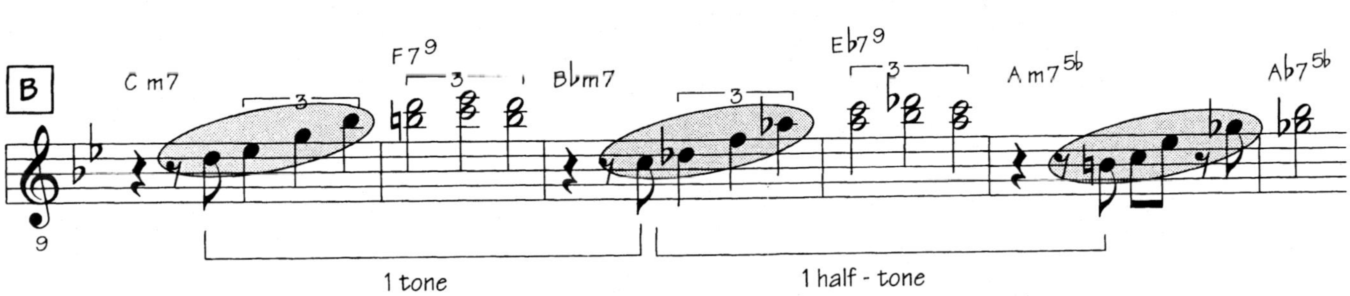

PART C

Here is the score of the "Ombre" theme.

On the CD, after the proper spoken introduction (page 1 of this chapter), notice that the melody is played, in the form that the intro is played twice, the first time with two guitars together, and in the lower range (one octave lower than the part below). Then, still together, the theme of 16 measures is played two additional times, in the octave as written.

#93

Ombre

(shadow)

♩=240

music by ROMANE

32 ABAB

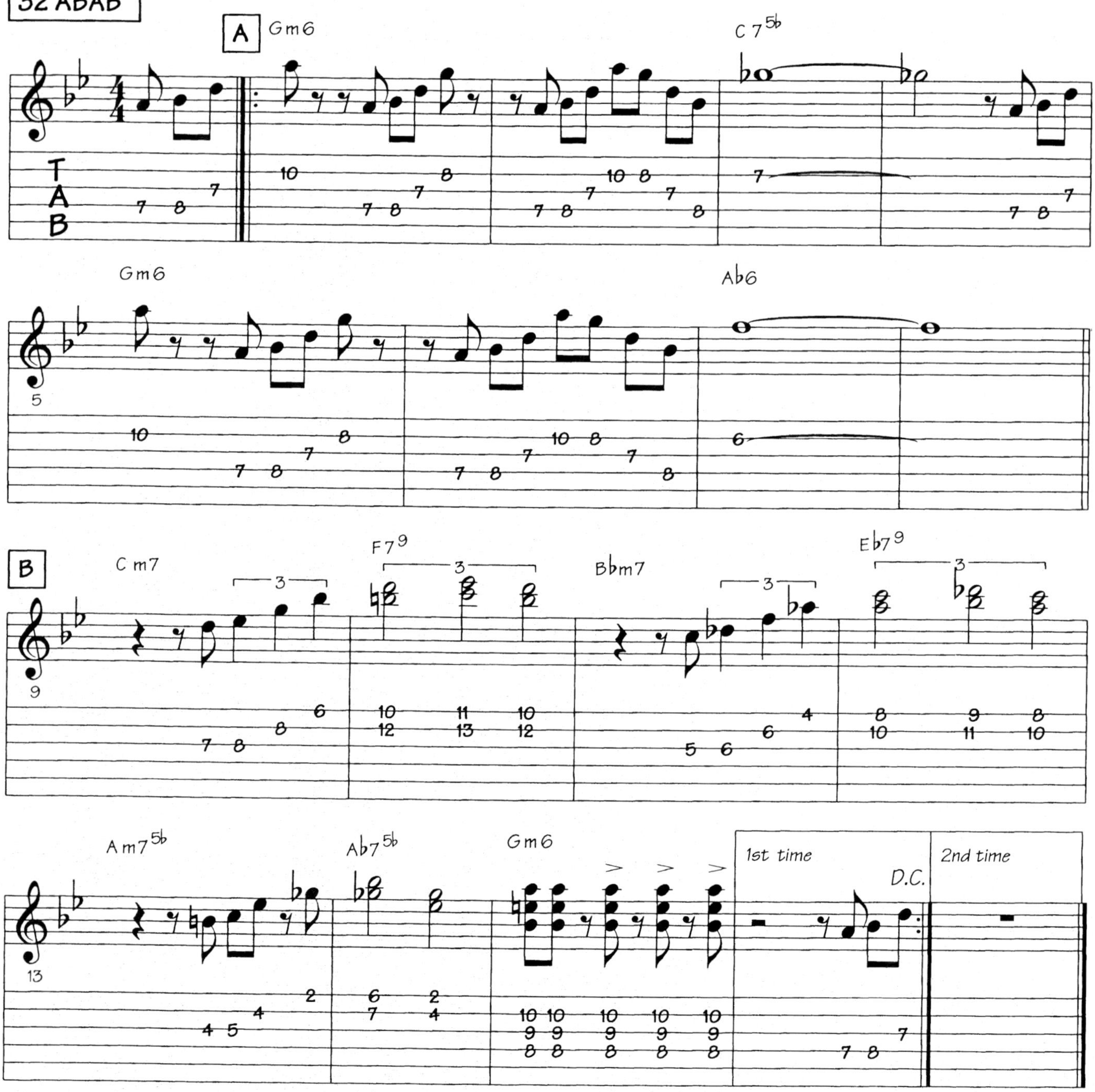

PART A

Exercise 76 (continuing) Valse a Django

We continue our waltz by doing an exercise. Study the second sections of A, A' and B. For your information, the second A and A' are identical at first (chapters 26 and 27) except that the measure of the pickup (encircled) is differently done so that a logical transition between the sections is certain. And to make it easy to study we prefer to give you a complete "go around", deprived of all the repeat symbols or return symbols.

#89

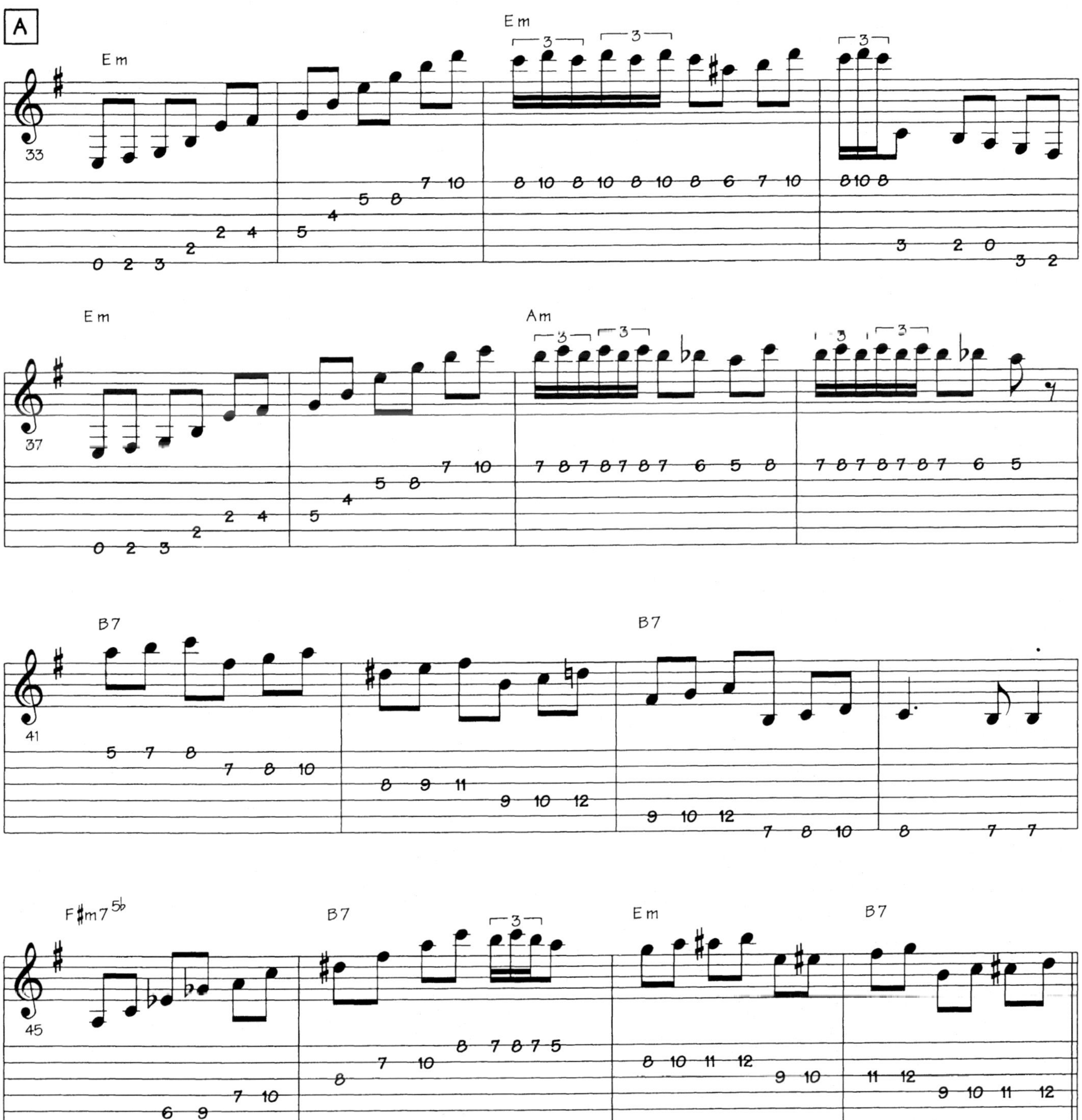

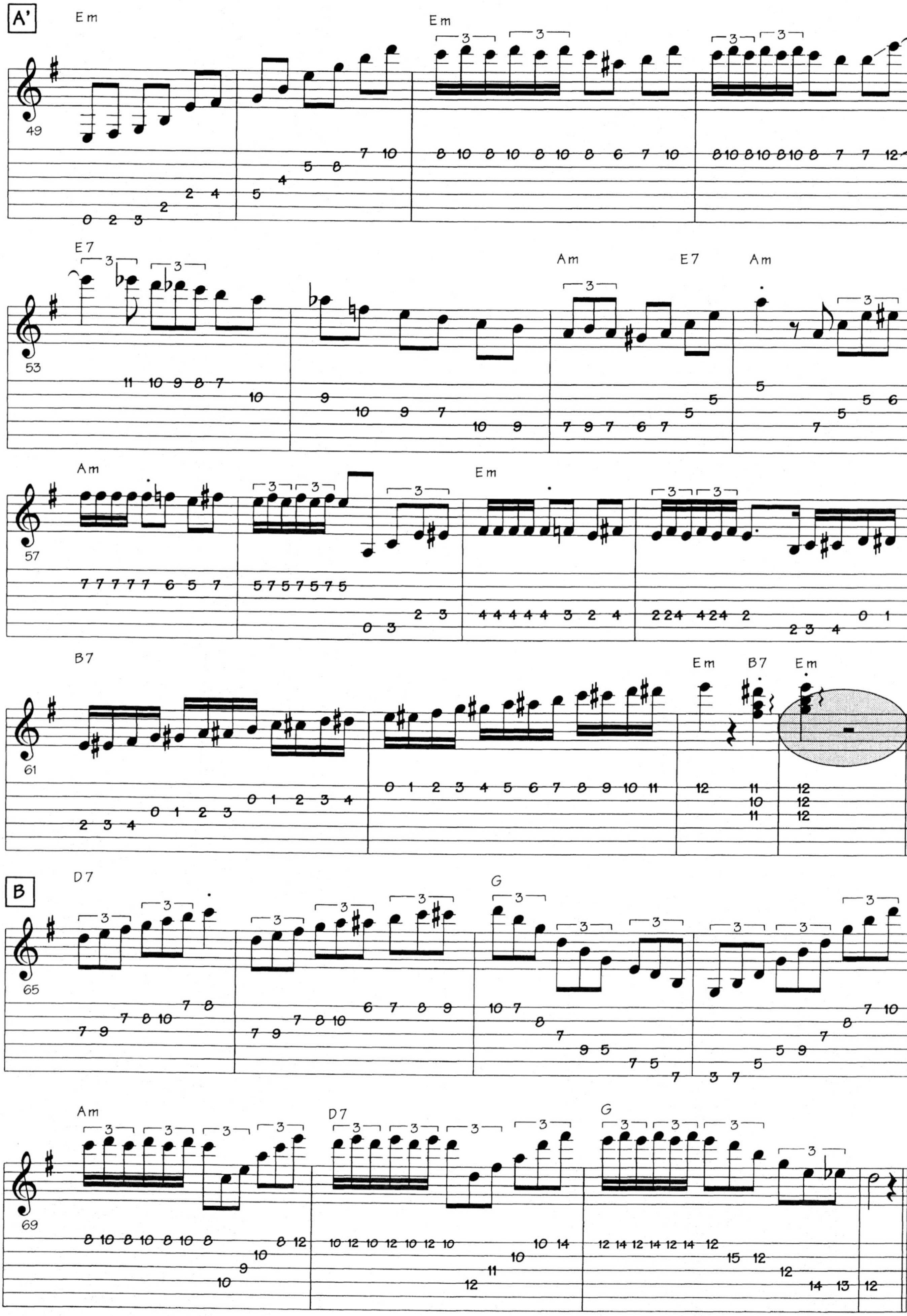
A'
Em
Em
E7
Am
E7
Am
Am
Em
B7
Em
B7
Em
B
D7
G
Am
D7
G

PART B1

THE CHORD INVERSIONS (continues)

In chapter 28 we were shown that the practice of chord reversals in jazz is limited and has four priority choices of chords with four tones. In the other part, we were shown those that have the theoretical procedures that let us determine these inversions.

Now we will continue to study the guitaristic inversions in detail with our most important chords, beginning with the M7 type.

— Study of the CM7 inversion:

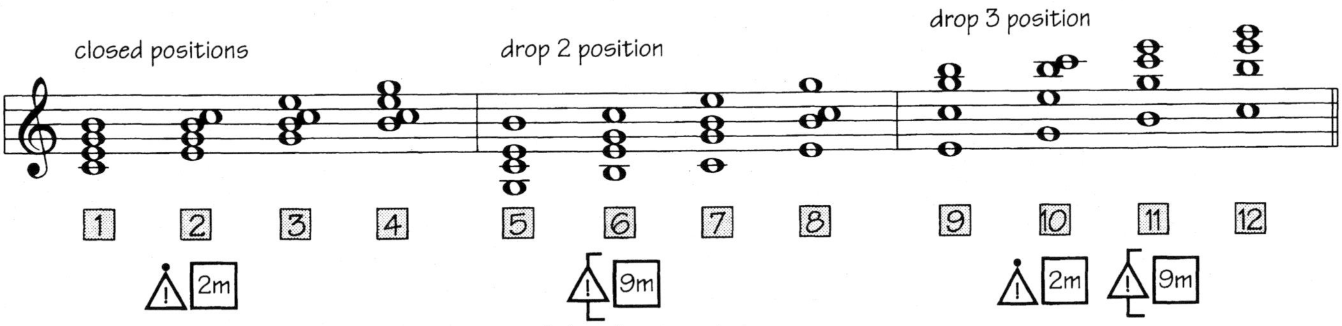

avoid this: the minor second interval between the two upper voices.

avoid this: the minor ninth interval between any two voices (here the low B -- high C).

Here are those chord positions that you can theoretically generate on the fingerboard, with all the registers together.
Technically, you should practice all the chord positions with a metronome, in order to combine them, and to make it convenient for you. You should do it in the best "legato" way, strive carefully to get a perfect sound while using all the merged notes.

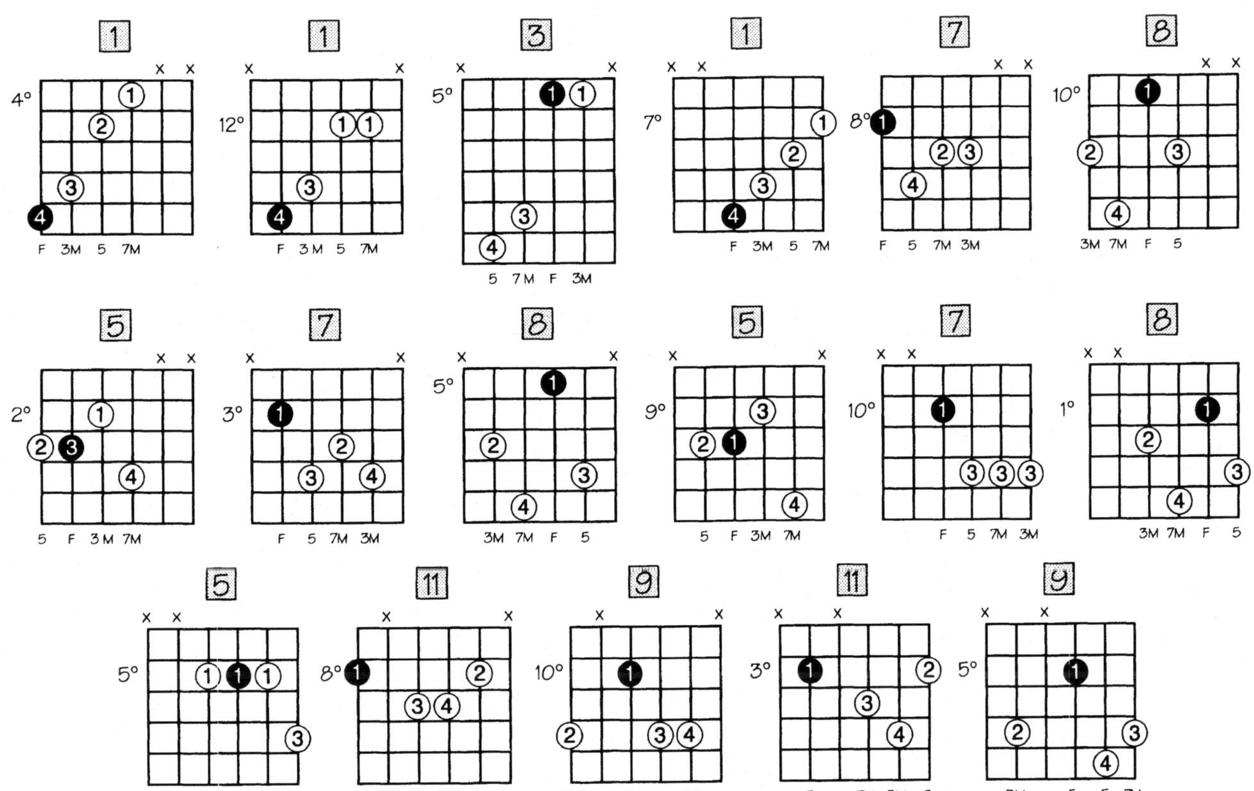

— **Study of the C7 inversion:**

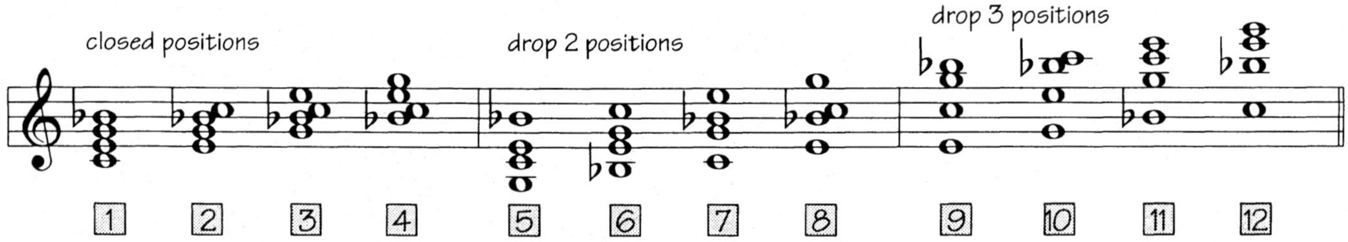

Here are some of these theoretical chords generated on the fingerboard, where all the registers are merged. You will see that C7 (and all its transpositions) doesn't have any inversions "to be avoided"; its four note components don't define any interval of a half tone (m2). As a consequence, the guitar has more C7 positions than those of CM7.

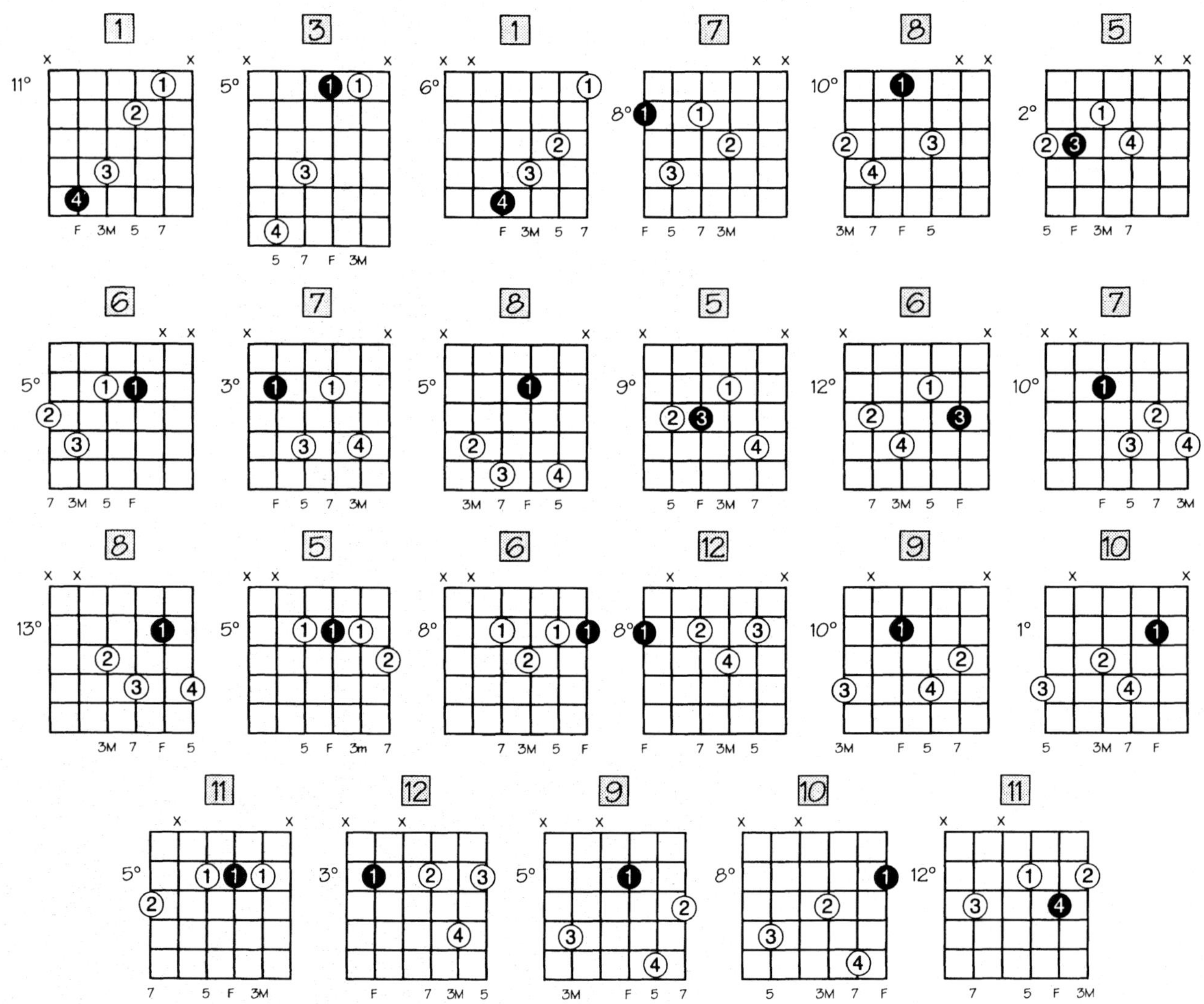

Here, certain chords are particularly pleasant to hear: number 4, 6 and 11, because the higher three notes of the chord form a major triad, which represents the perfect consonant harmony. Certainly, chord number four is a closed chord, which is practically impossible to play on a normal chorded guitar. On the other hand, number 11 has an excellent sound that is freely used. Otherwise, although these chords are theoretically correct, the number 5 inversion has little value, because we know that the interval that separates the two higher voices is a tritone. It doesn't fit in if it is used this way. All the more so since the chord isn't colored with any harmonic enrichment.

PART B2

We are now going back to "Ombre", of which we studied the diagram and theme in chapter 28.
On the Romane Ombre CD, the first (studio) version of this piece has two guitar choruses, split into two groups of 16 measures each. To finish this 29th chapter, we suggest that you study these two choruses.

First we have some observations about this subject.

Ombre (chorus 1, measures 0 - 4) minor harmonic colorations with mirror effect

The first measures of this chorus use the principle of the "mirror" effect, which we have already seen many times. With the harmonies that we have here, the symmetry relies on a note with a very precise coloration, that of the M7 with Gm, which develops toward b5 with C7:

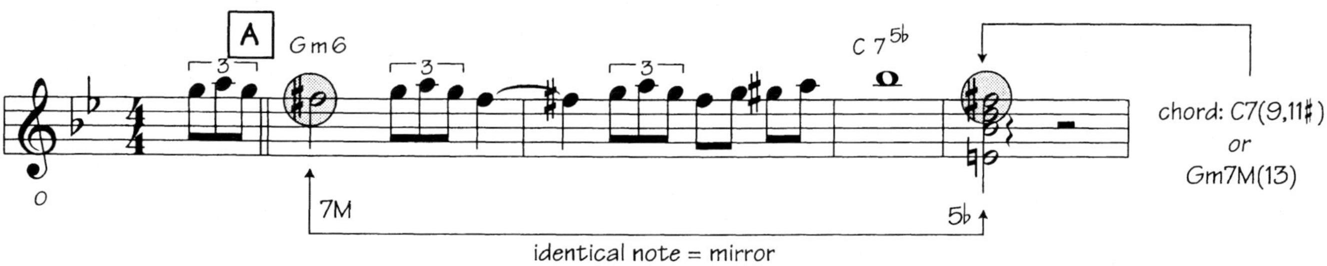

In its improvised melodic form, we recover the re -affirmation of the possible corresponding harmonies between a II chord (Gm) and the V (C7), using the principle as shown in chapter 28 (page 7).

Ombre (chorus 1, measures 14 - 16) virtuosity

This chorus finishes with a dim7 arpeggio and the diverse possible colorations with the chord diagram of Ebm (altered D scale):

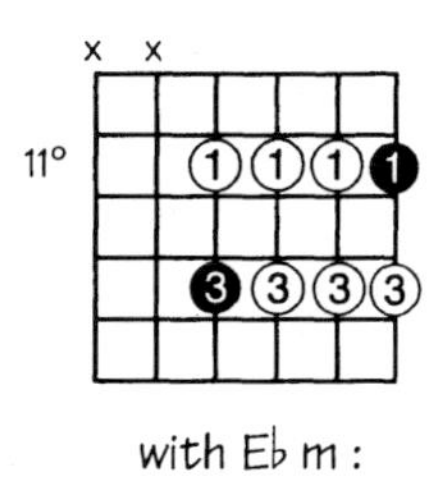

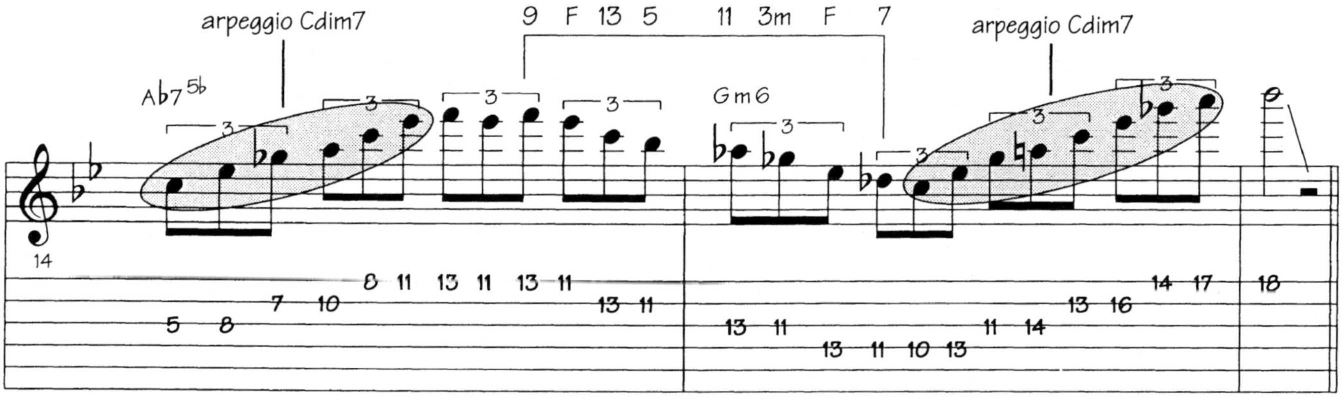

Notice the TAB: the virtuoso effect is made easy with the almost regular use of two notes per string.

Watch the following sections in the second chorus of "Ombre":

Ombre (chorus 2, measures 1 - 4) harmonic colorations with mirror effect

When an idea is good, you should not hesitate to re-use it. That is why the first measures of the second chorus has the same mirror effect as chorus 1, however, with a small change in the octave and with a light metric displacement:

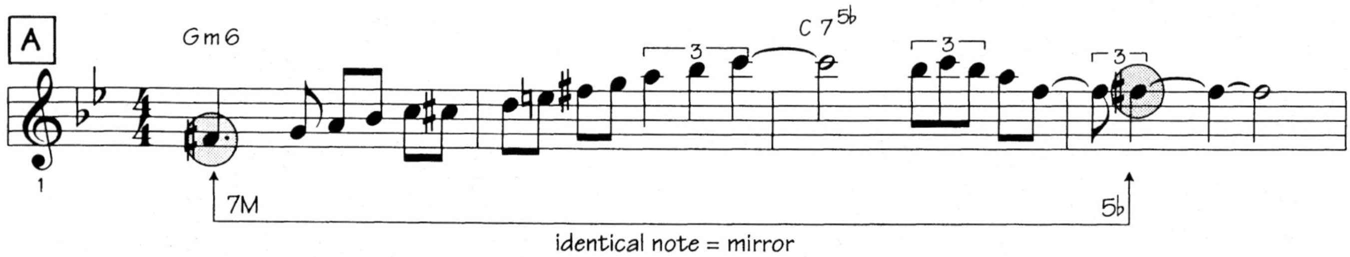

Ombre (chorus 2, measures 5 - 6) dynamic dead notes

We often have had the occasion to observe the Manouche playing style, and notice that they freely use open chords. Here, played in the form of "dead notes" (X), the open B and G chords are used to make an improvised dynamic phrase, by making its action easy going. Of course, these dead notes have a light sound intensity and their tone is hardly audible, although we have a lot of these in the rhythm.

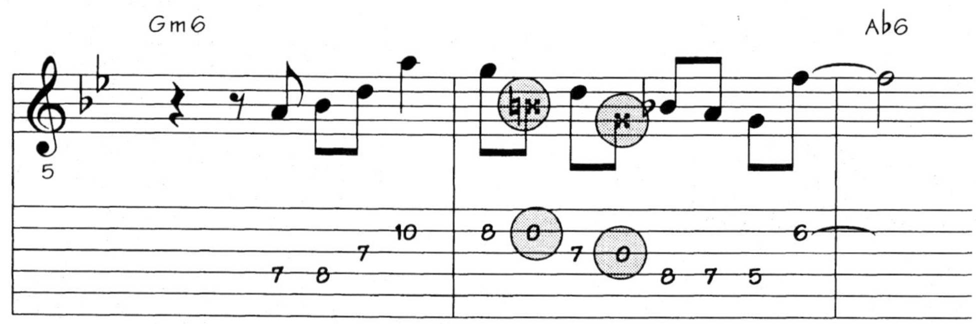

Ombre (chorus 2, measures 13 - 16) diminished scale

With the second chorus we finish with a brilliant illustration of the diminished scale (D diminished) which is used to leave the "M13" harmonic coloration of the Ab7 chord - or still yet, the harmonic coloration of the "#9" of the D7 chord. The D7 is a tritone substitution for Ab7 and a realistic V degree which drives a Gm (I degree) chord.
Also notice the progress on the TAB; four notes per string.

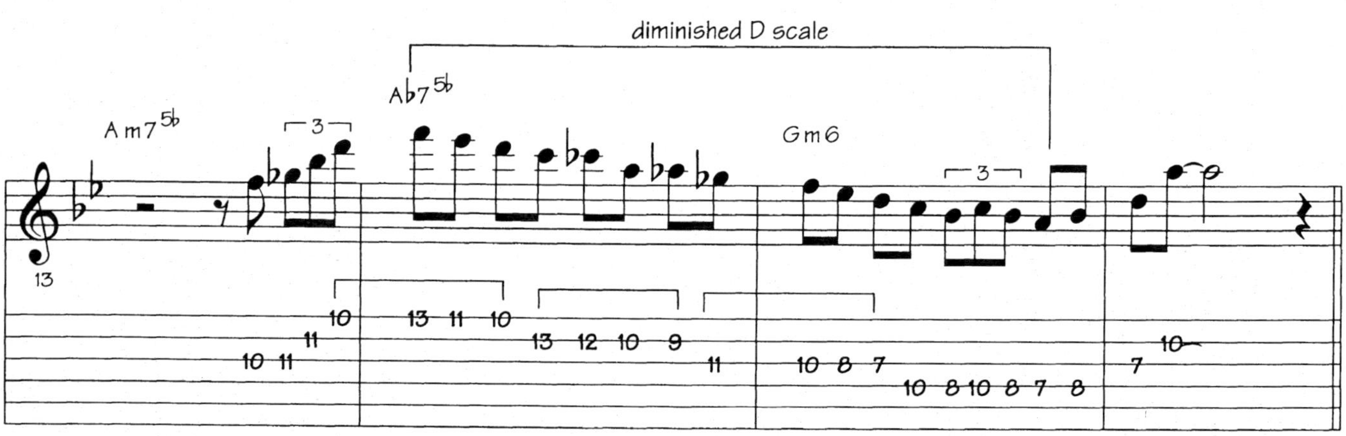

PART C

Here is the score of the first chorus of "Ombre" (studio version); watch out for the slides in measures 9 and 16.

You could eventually connect this #1 chorus together with #2 chorus (next page), although, on the CD these two choruses will be played separately by a violin and accordion.

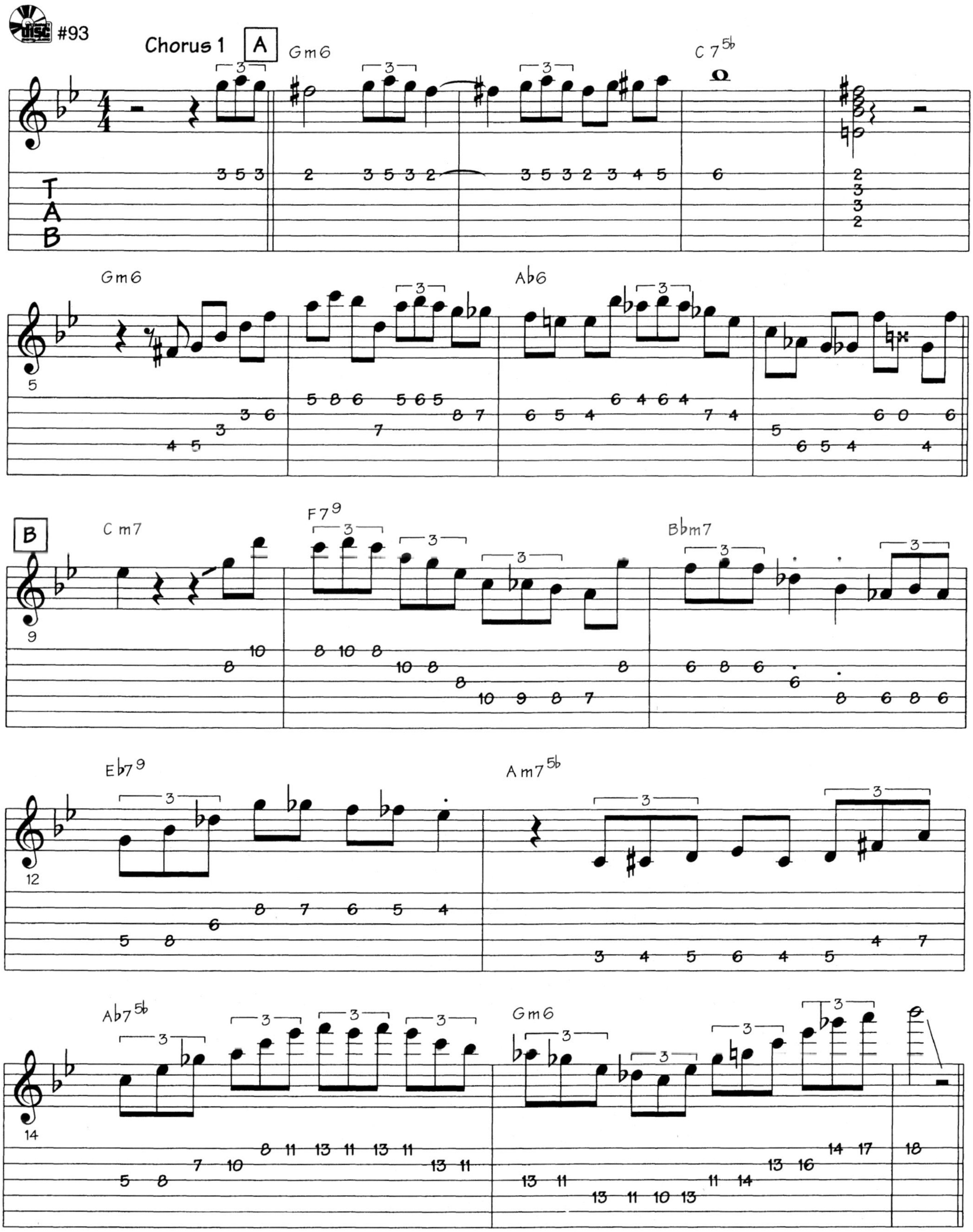

Chapter 29 / page 8

Here is the second guitar chorus of "Ombre".

#94

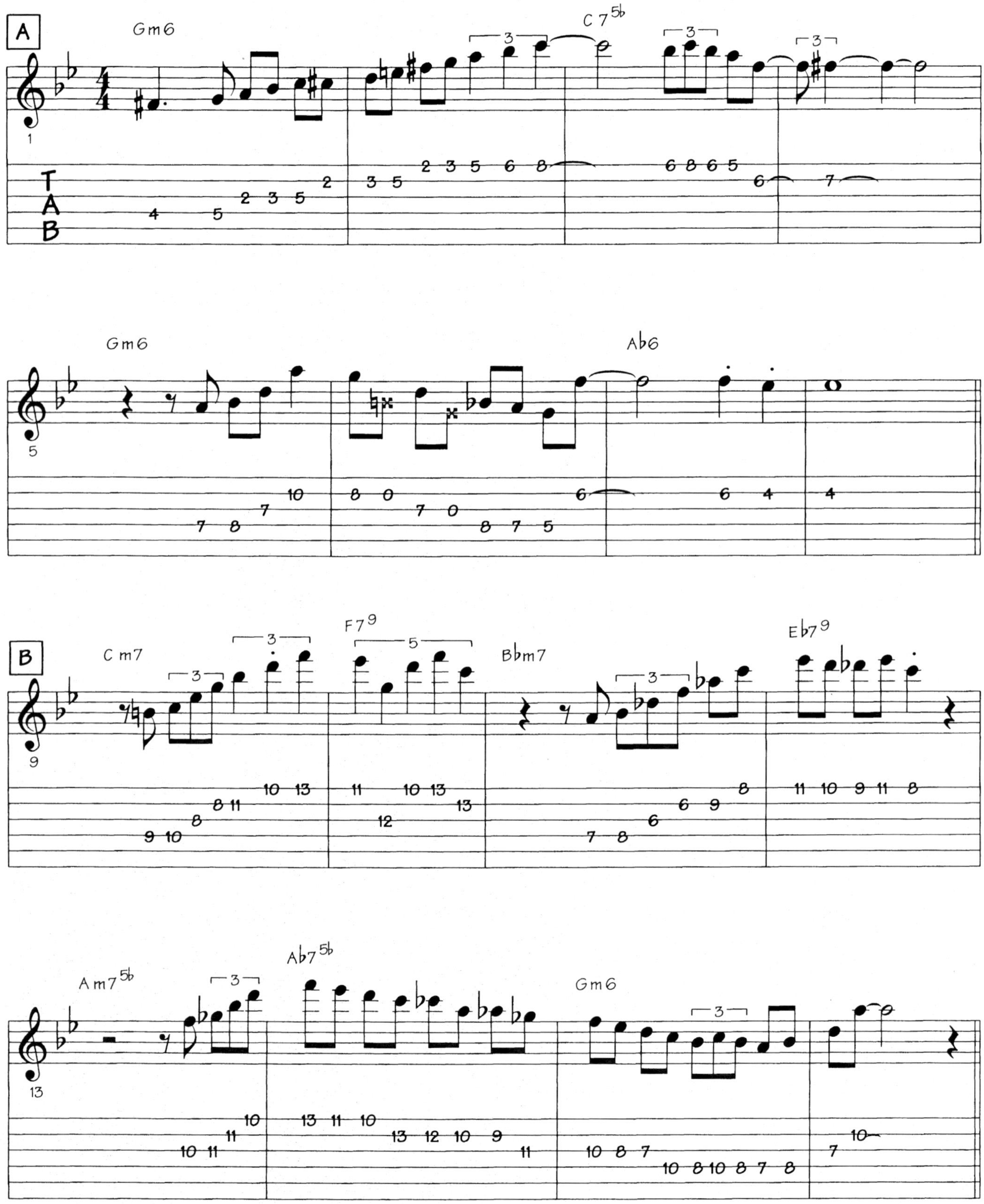

PART A

Exercise 76 (continues) Valse a Django

We are continuing with the previous chapters. Study section B' of the "Valse a Django". The continuation of the second B' section is found in chapter 31.

#89

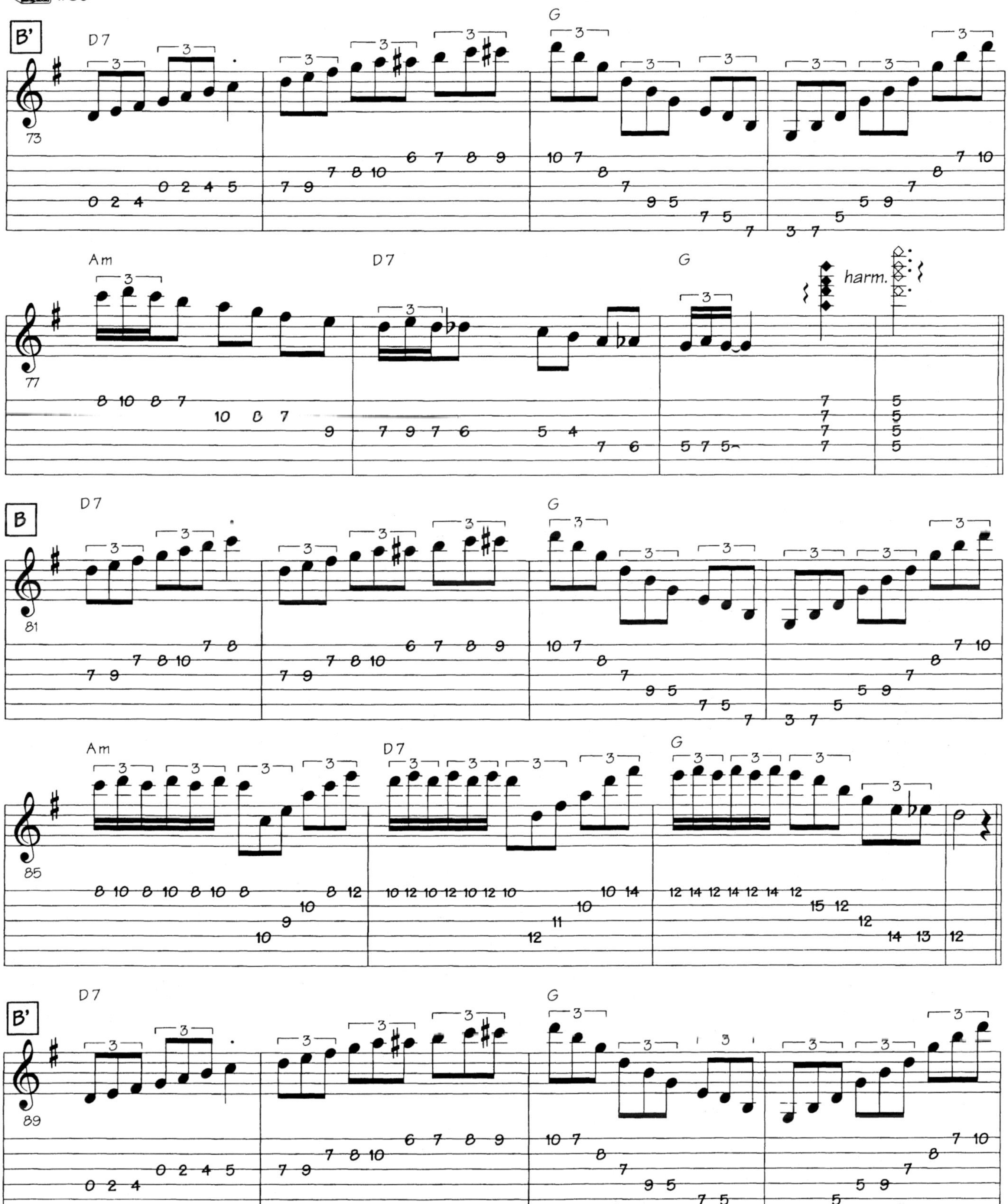

PART B1

THE CHORD INVERSIONS (continued)

– Study of the Cm7 inversion:

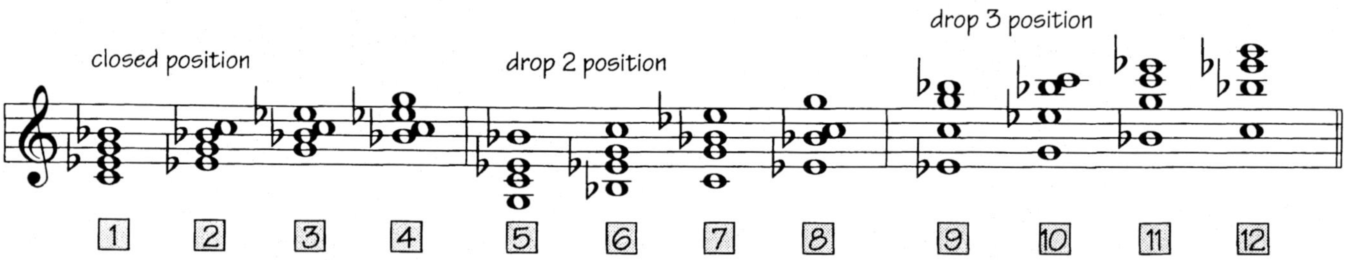

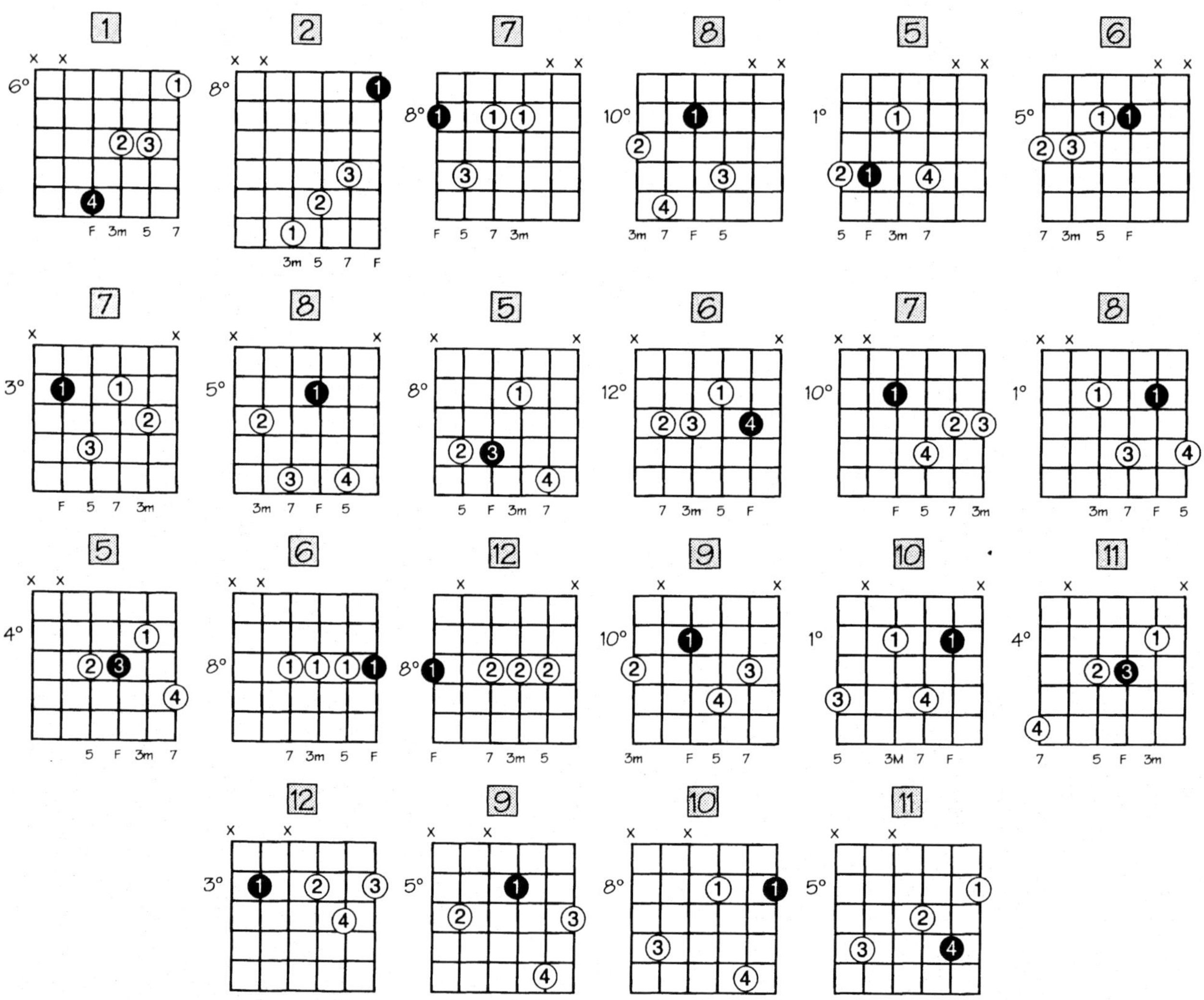

– **Study of the Cm7(b5) inversion:**

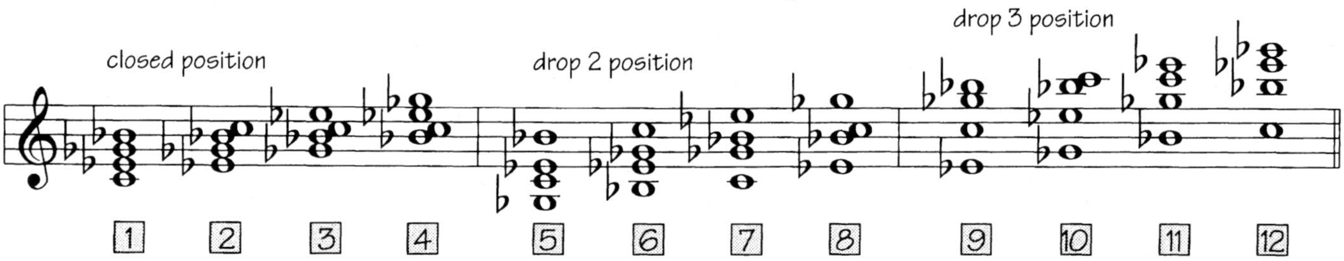

We don't encounter any chords that should be avoided in the measure where the notes make up the Cm7(b5), which does not define any minor second (m2) intervals. In addition, by examining these theoretical chords, here are those positions that we will get on the fingerboard:

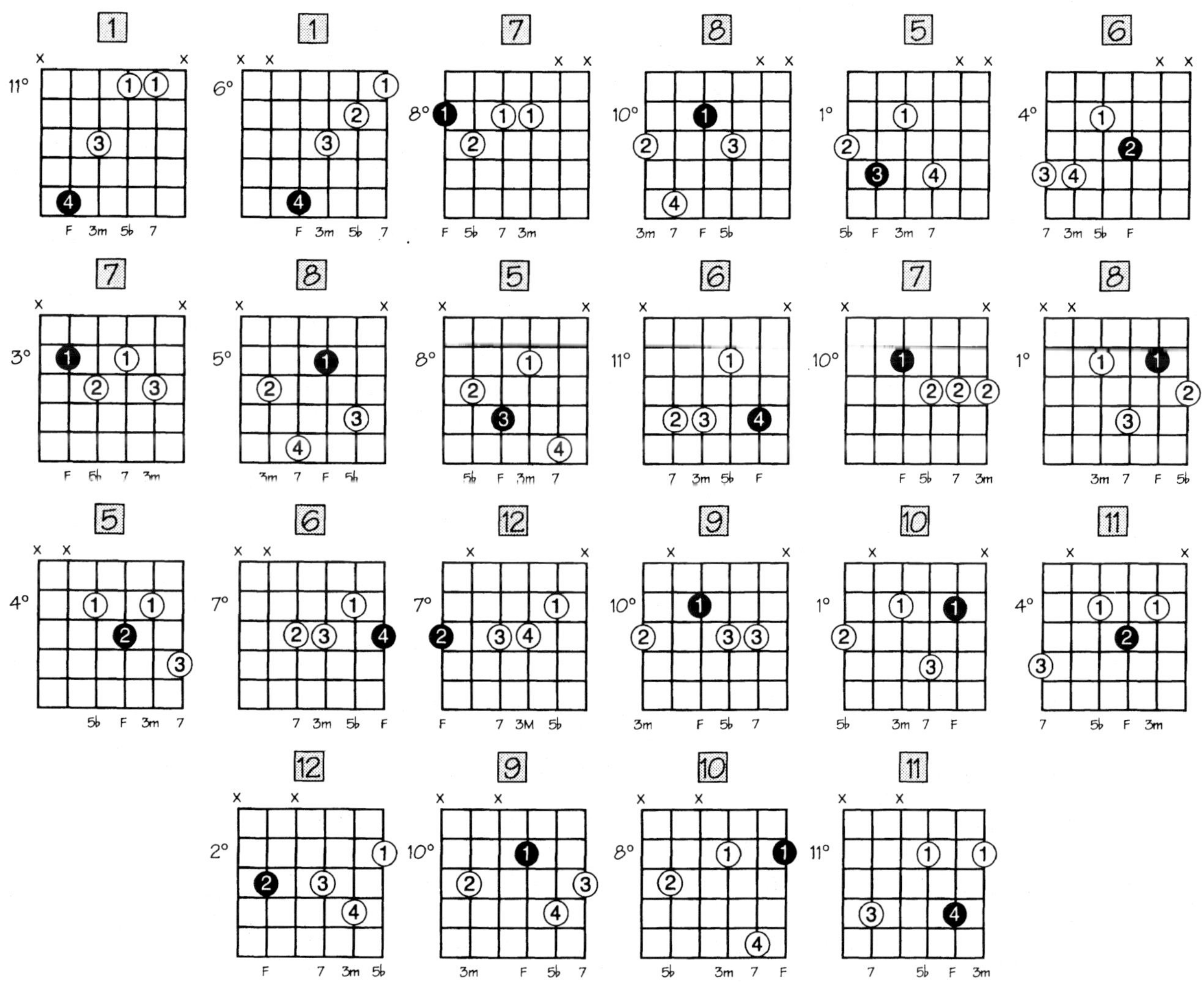

There are a little over 80 positions to mainly work with, for reasons that we will explain later.
Among these chords you will be able to favor those where the root note is in the bass, as well as those that give a particular balanced sound or the ones that you find harmonious.
If you memorize them all, with the idea in mind to work out and use these voicings, it will be easier to develop your musical talent, because it will be a great help to you.

To develop your talent more, we'll give you the third and last part of methods to master chords: the complete knowledge of substitutions in relation to those chords from which you can make your choice.

THE KNOWLEDGE OF SUBSTITUTIONS

At this point of the journey you are familiar with chord substitutions, and have already and painstakingly practiced these with interest. While we are on the subject, we are going to do some general review that will go together with these "novelties", by studying in detail the substitutions, which generate our four types of tonal chords.

The CM7, Cm7(b5) chord substitutions:

– The four notes which make up the CM7 chord can be analyzed on the basis of another root note which is the A note, because:

C - E - G - B = F - M3 - 5 - M7 = m3 - 5 - 7 - 9, therefore,
CM7 = Am7(9) without a root note, this is a diatonic substitution: I degree → VI substitution.

– The four notes that make up the C7 chord can be analyzed on the basis of another root note which is the Gb note (or F#), because:

C - E - G - Bb = F - M3 - 5 - 7 = #11 - 7 - m9 - M3, therefore,
C7 = G7 (b9, #11) without a root note nor a fifth, this is a tritone substitution: II → V degree.

– The four notes which make up the Cm7 chord can be analyzed on the basis of three other root notes, which are the Eb, Ab and F, because:

C - Eb - G - Bb = R - m3 - 5 - 7 = 6 - R - M3 –5 = M3 - 5 - M7 - 9 = 5 - 7 - 9 – 4, therefore:
Cm7 = Eb6, this is a diatonic substitution: VI degrees → I degree,
Cm7 = Ab7M(9) without a root note, this is a diatonic substitution: III degree → I degree,
Cm7 = F7sus4(9) without a root note, this is a composite substitution.
Of course, these equivalencies are well known: Cm7 = Eb6 = Ab7M(9) = FM7sus4(9).

– Finally, the four notes which make up the Cm7(b5) chord can be analyzed on the basis of four other root notes which are the Eb, Ab, D and F notes, because:

C - Eb - Gb - Bb = R - m3 - b5 - 7 = 6 - R - m3 - 5 = M3 - 5 - 7 - 9 = 7 - m9 - M3 - m13 = 5 - 7 - m9 – 4, therefore,
Cm7(b5) = Ebm6, this is a composite substitution,
Cm7(b5) = Ab7(9) without a root note, this is a diatonic substitution: VII degree → V degree,
Cm7 (5b) = D7 (9b,13b) without a final nor a 5th, this is a composite substitution...
(a tritone, like the previous one)
Cm7(b5) = F7sus4(b9) without a root note, this is a composite substitution.
Of course, Cm7(b5) = Ebm6 = Ab7(9) = D7(b9, b13) = F7sus4(b9).

You can see the diatonic and tritone substitutions under a slight differently angle, which allows you to better understand the practical mechanics and implications of substitutions in general.

As with the "novelties", these substitutions are simply added to practice improvising with the D7sus4(b9) chord, by knowing that the scale of this chord is related to it: it is simply enough for you to think around the F7(9) - or still yet, the alt. B (B7(b9, b13)).

Now, our knowledge of substitutions related to the four tonal chords gives another implication, which is also very interesting. This is a precious short cut as you will see.

For example, when you want to work with and memorize all the Cm7 positions, you should be working on and memorizing all the corresponding positions. Of course, you also have to know the substitutions of this chord: the Eb6, AbM7(9) and F7sus4(9).

You will have at your disposal, by knowing only four chords and their positions of the Cm7, thirteen combinations of numerous symbols among the more efficient ones. And then we know that, on the fingerboard of the guitar, the transitions can be done by simply moving the chords on the fingerboard without changing any finger settings. We will leave it up to you to count the number of chords that you rapidly can use.

Certainly, the difficulty is in the mental interconnection that is necessary for doing each substitution. There is technically less to do, because the work is enormously simplified. In addition, the more you practice the chords and voicings, all these interconnections becomes automatic. For the rest, we illustrate this in the last chapter, and an application which will not let you be indifferent when you hear it.

Now that everything is finally clear, we will finish the group of the theoretical inversions of any guitar chord that has four tones. We are now going to choose the particular colored ones, in such a way that you will get an optimal understanding during the various chapters while we continue with this subject.

The harmonic G7(9, 13) symbol in theory tells us that this is a chord with six distinct tones, before we reduce it to any four. This requires the necessary practice:

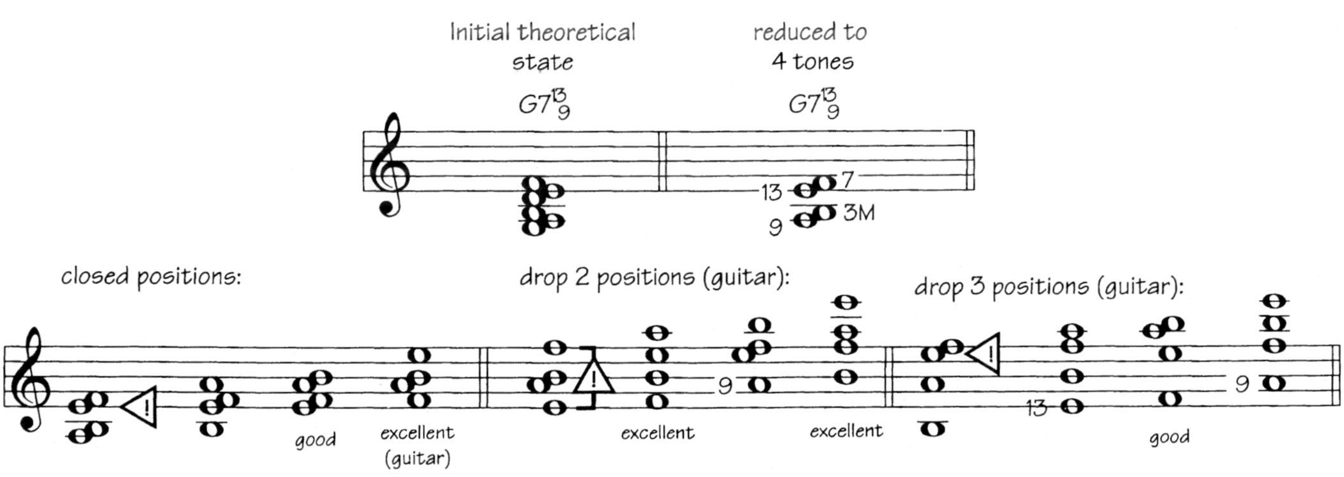

It is easy to see that with these 12 possibilities that we have with this dominant seventh chord, less then half of those are really of an interest to us, because of the second and ninth minor, but also for the fact that the colorations do not always happen there, where the chord will sound very convincing: in this case here it is the lower 9 or 13, that's to say, below the M3 and 7, the notes which characterize the chord. Nevertheless, the inversions, which remain valuable, can all be used. In order for us to understand this with regards to the substitutions in this figure, you should know:

G7(9,13) = D♭7(9♯,13♭) = F7M(5♭) = Dm6/9.

PART B2

We have taken from the Romane Ombre CD the "Chasses Croises" theme, which we will study in the next three chapters, this should satisfy those guitarists who have been waiting to get their hands on this (these) arrangement(s) and orchestration(s). These are the disciplines that are of a great musical interest to us.

"Chasses Croises" is a minor blues theme, a musical form which deviates somewhat from the Manouche characteristics. However, this will still give you an excellent opportunity to express yourself in a different way. This proves all together that the music form is everything.

This piece is arranged in the form of a "combo" or small group. It is written for four guitars and a string-bass. (The accordion and violin parts on this CD can be played by guitars 2 and 3). This theme relies on a motive/riff principle (which is a favorite with the blues). The arrangement is inspired by the "big bands", and by the guitarist that plays it! It is easy to see that the title of this piece, "CHASSES CROISES" (Mixed Up), is not at all by chance, when we compare all the parts, that are different from each other.

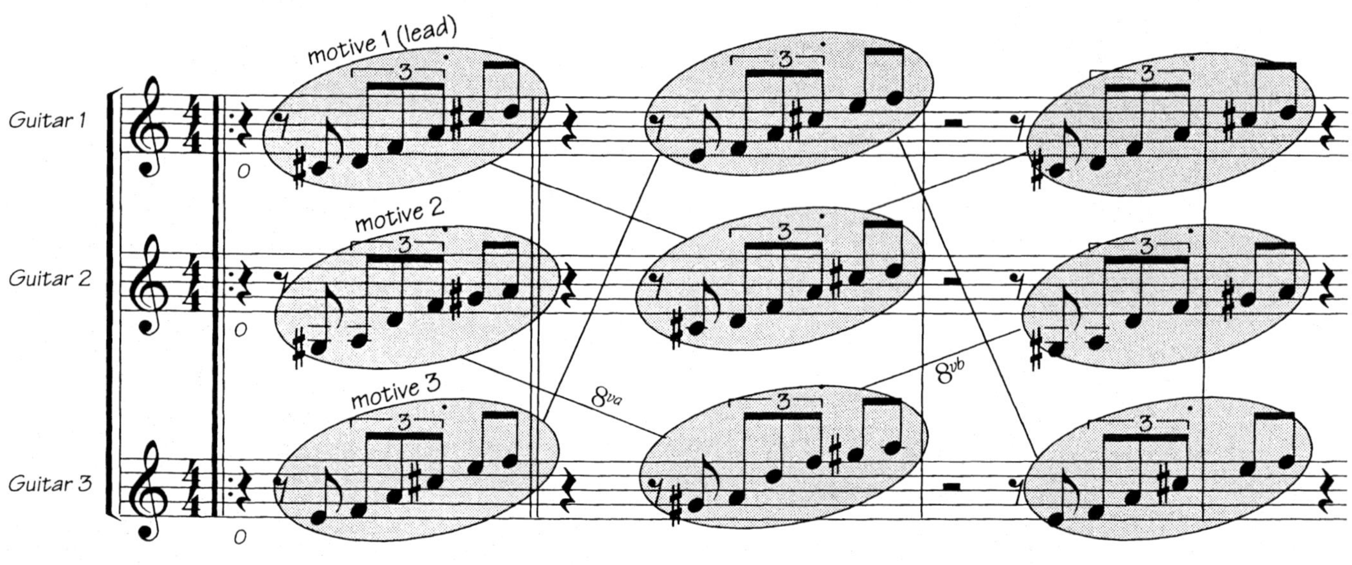

So the three voices cross their respective motives while their intervals of thirds express the requisite harmonies.

In the partial score above, notice that the F note doesn't work as a M3 (of which the D note will be the root note) but as a #9, which is what we call in the jazz and blues a "blue note", this is in the measure where D7 (and not Dm7) is the harmony which supports the melody.

In the dialogue with the rhythm which is systematically intervened by rests, the riffs are played until measure 8, where a pedal is given for guitars 3 and 4 and the string bass in beats 2 and 4. Guitars 1 and 2 produce a series of superimposed chords (polychords) constructed with the V degree of the key which is inescapably driven to the stop-chorus of guitar 1.

Since you are not very familiar with these syncopated forms, the exposure to this theme might cause you some small problems, at least in the beginning. Listen to the CD first while carefully following the score, then play the guitar parts, with a sleight of hand, using the music as shown above.
In addition, if this isn't enough, we recommend that you take a little cue from Count Basie's big band, by opening up your ears. We can not repeat it enough, listening is the musician's best friend!

PART C

Now we give you the scores of "Chasses Croises" for guitars 1 and 2. If you'd like to get a look at how to keep time with this theme, and its various elements put together, look at the "score" (orchestra partition) shown on pages 6, 7 and 8 of Chapter 31.

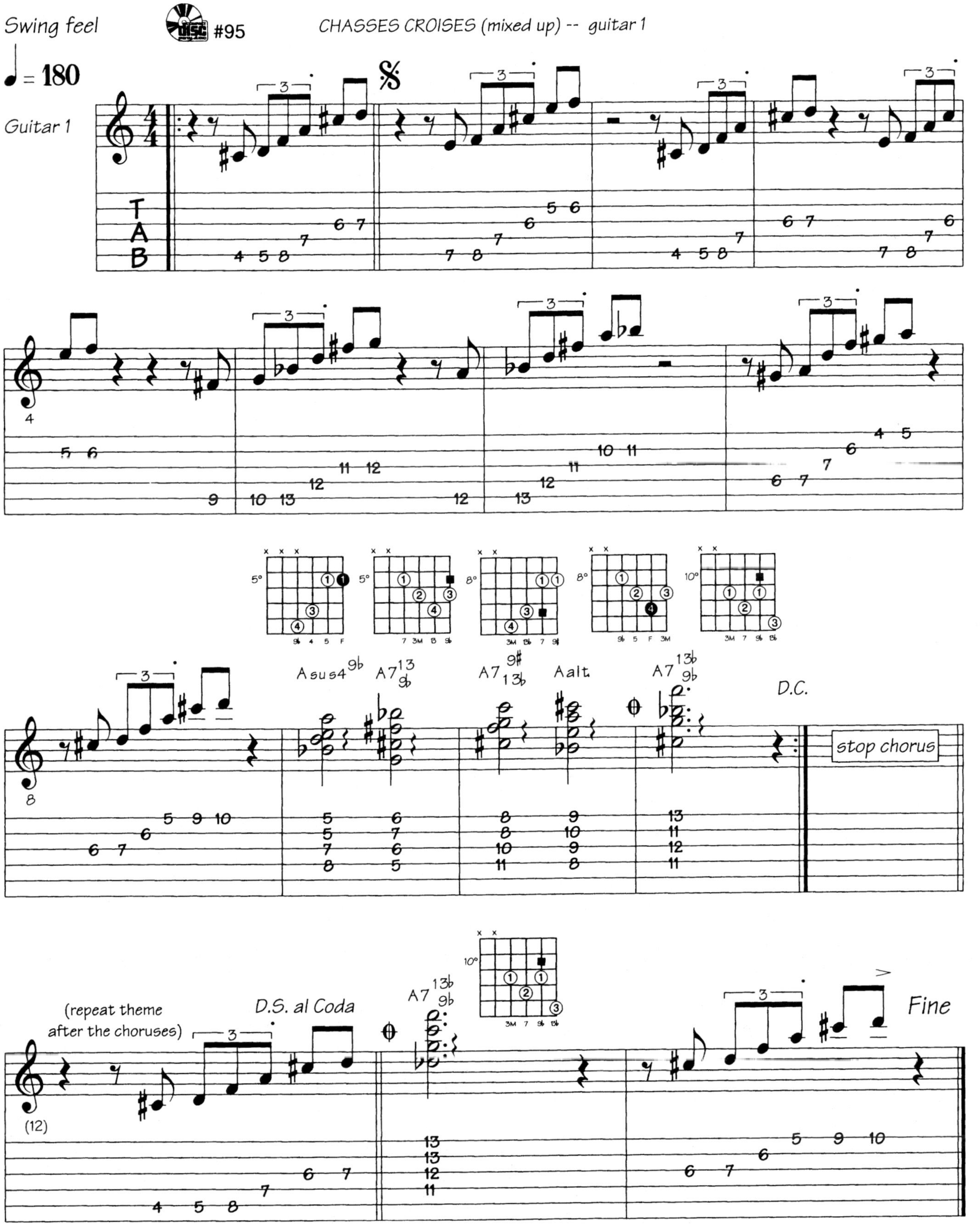

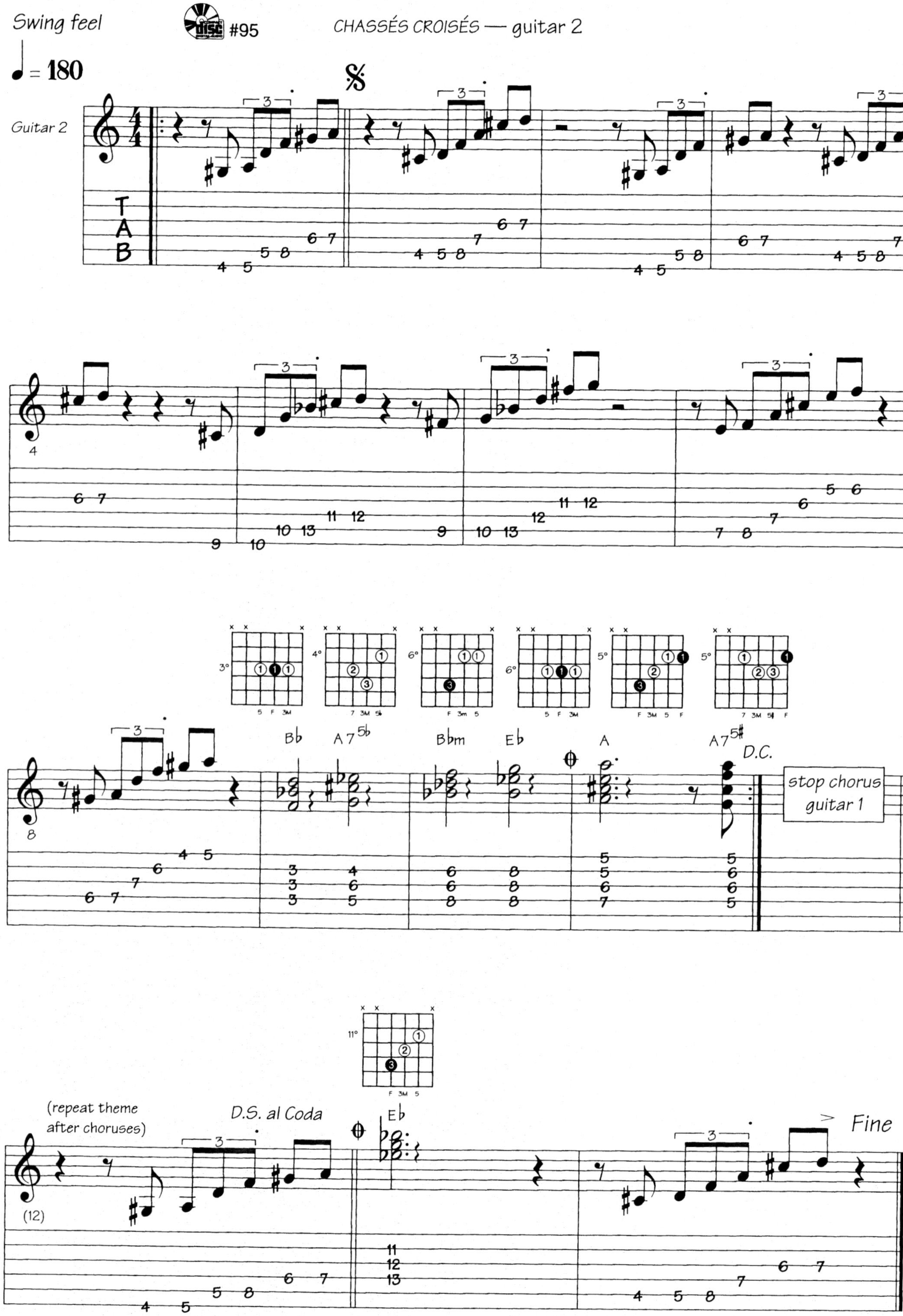
Swing feel
#95
CHASSÉS CROISÉS — guitar 2
♩ = 180
Guitar 2
B♭
A7⁵♭
B♭m
E♭
A
A7⁵♯
D.C.
stop chorus guitar 1
(repeat theme after choruses)
D.S. al Coda
E♭
Fine

PART A

Exercise 76 (continues) Valse a Django

This is the last part of the second B' section (notice the differences of the pickup which equals a return to section A) and the progression with the final repeat of the A sections.

#89

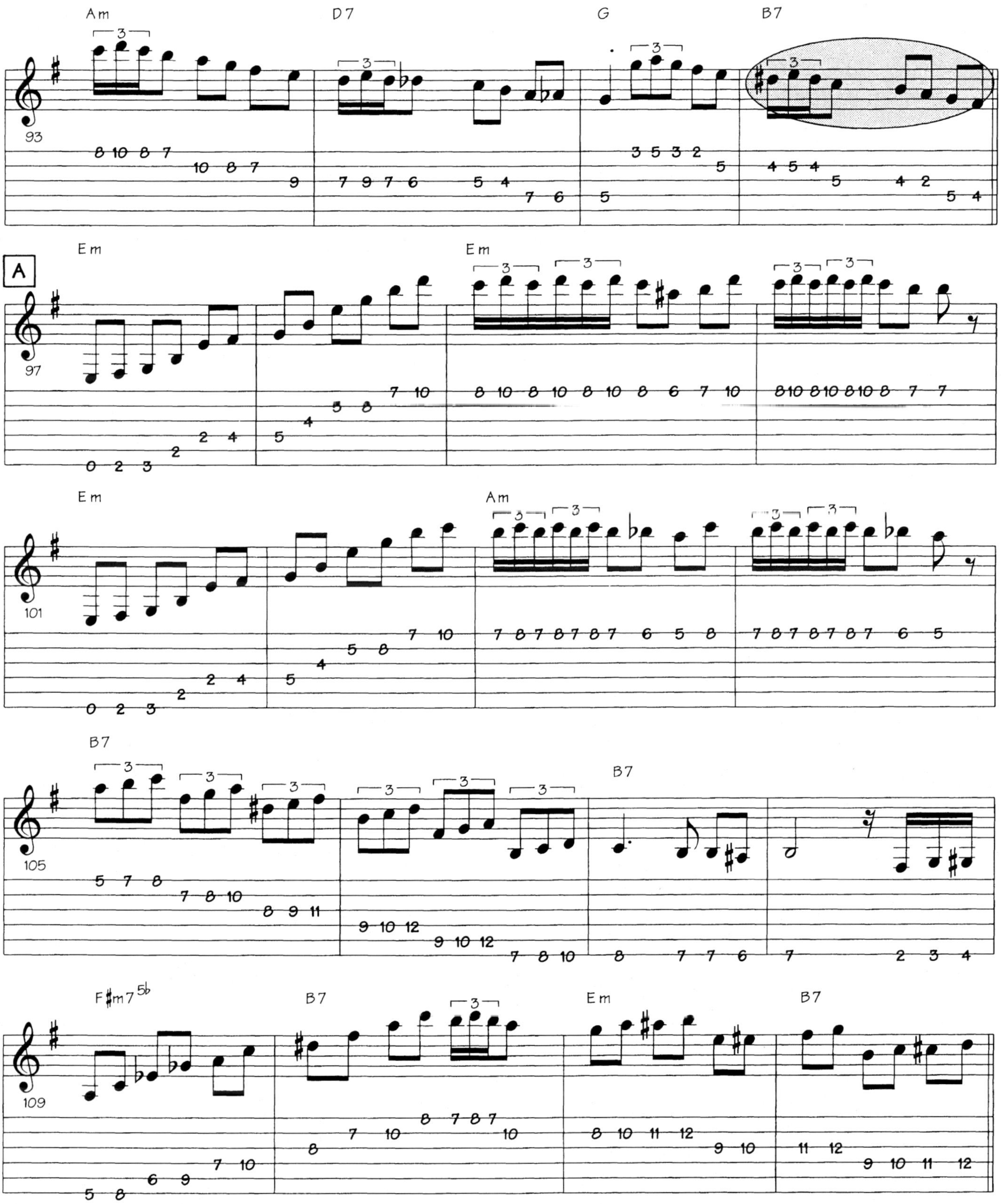

PART B

Now we continue with "Chasses Croises": the score, which regroups all the instruments. This will give you a general view of the ensemble, and also the individual scores of guitars 3 and 4.

Before coming to these last ones, we still have one more thing to say about guitar 2. At the time of repeating the theme (the end of the piece), watch for the chord at the coda, which is different than those initially shown (measure 1).

Otherwise, all the mixed scores came from the division of this piece. With the score on the CD, this division is as follows:
– Measure 0: pickup (riff),
– Mesures 1 - 8: melody themes (riffs),
– Measures 9 - 11: superimposed chords + (rhythmic pedal),
– Measure 12: same as measure 0 (→ renewal of the indicated second part, or from the D.C. symbol, which means to resume from the beginning),... or the stop chorus (→ the end of the second part),
– 2 guitar choruses of 24 measures with the blues diagram in D minor (see score),
– 2 accordion choruses,
– 2 violin choruses,
– 2 string bass choruses, which finishes in measure 23, at the expense of the pickup, with the final repeat of the theme. In the score, this is a delicate passage that concerns the two measures close to the D.S. al coda symbol: starting from the (𝄋) sign over again (from measure 1, not measure 0) to the Coda (+) (10 measures total).
– Coda: 2 measures, of which the riffs this time are written in unison.

Now we go back to the theme.
The role of guitar 3 is versatile: shown (measures 0-8) along side guitars 1 and 2; giving a more supportive rhythm together with the string bass and guitar 4. Where shown, notice that guitar 3 starts up over the two others, but ends below, just before the accordion superimposes:

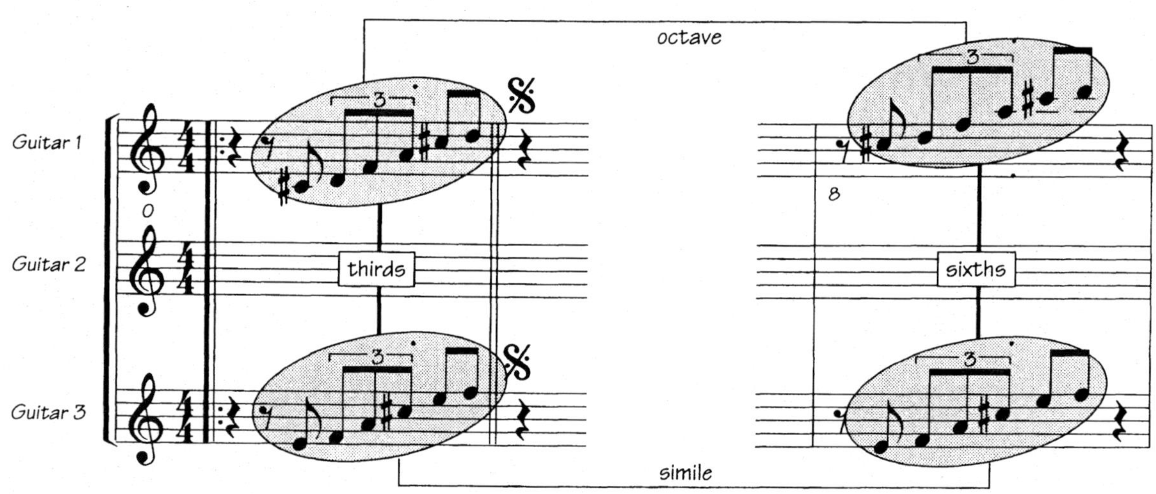

Here, we give guitar 1 more importance which is the main voice/lead, with a "higher crescendo". This is the conclusion, which is done in a way to be expressed with the last tension of the theme, a little before the final overlapping tension that is produced with the superimposed chords.

As for guitar 4, it is exclusively used for rhythm. Except in the choruses or where it will be satisfying to "pump", this guitar part is exclusively set up for syncopated harmonic punctuation or for counter beats.

Look at measures 0-8, all the chords are spaced out and out of the strong beats.
To set all this up, the secret is to stop at the riffs, by looking at all the chords systematically that happen one half beat after the last note of each riff. You can eventually, mentally, add a note with these riffs (encircled), and patch your chord up with an eighth, which immediately follows this addition:

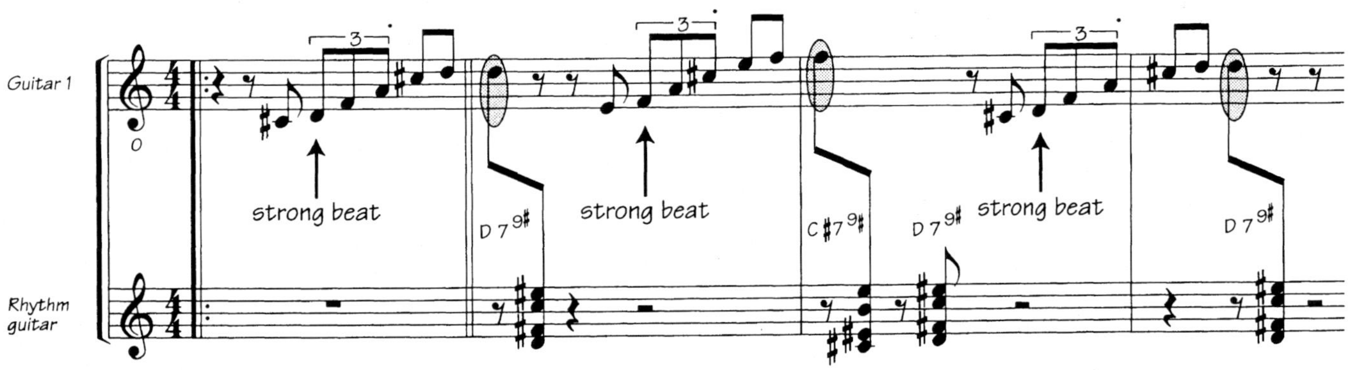

The riffs should be set up well for the other members of the orchestra. The secret is to look that all the triplets that systematically occur on a strong beat. Knowing this, the set up of the riffs is much easier.

Keep a steady beat , and in the measure where the riffs and rhythm interact, these eight measures of "Chasses Croises" will stop being long and become amusing!

In measures 9 - 11, accenting the off beat is distinctly classical and much easier. Certain parts, that overlap (chords/pedals) are not syncopated. You need a good mental knowledge of the strong beats in the measure: first and third for guitars 1 and 2, second and fourth for guitars 3 and 4 and the string bass.

With a little help, you can hear these and the string bass part on the CD. Listen to the last one and follow the score of this instrument (look at the score) and pay attention, especially with measure 11, the end of the chorus and coda.

Finally, a word about the chords used in the syncopated punctuations (measures 1 to 8).
All are of the same 7(#9) type, which is very blues like (#9 is a blue note) and more often linked to chromatic movements where it is plainly a tritone substitution.

Look at measure 4:

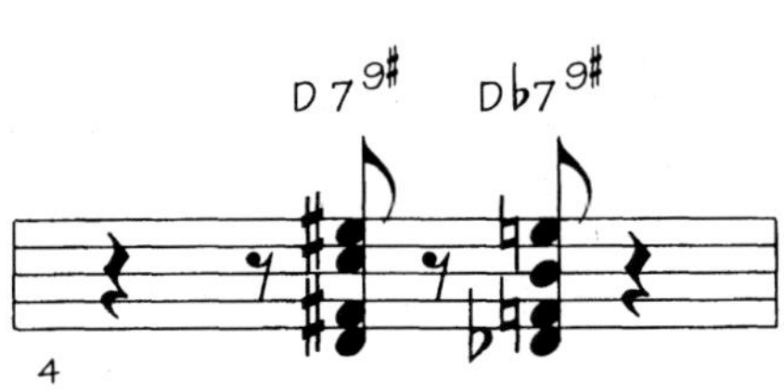

Following the D7(#9), Db7(#9) plays the role of the IV7 degree that occurs in all the real harmonic blues features, precisely at this place (measure 5, to help with the syncopated moves).

This IV7 is G7 in accordance of the tritone substitution:

Db7(#9) = G7(#11, 13), without a root note of fifth.

PART C

Continuing the scores of "Chasses Croises", this time for guitars 3 and 4.

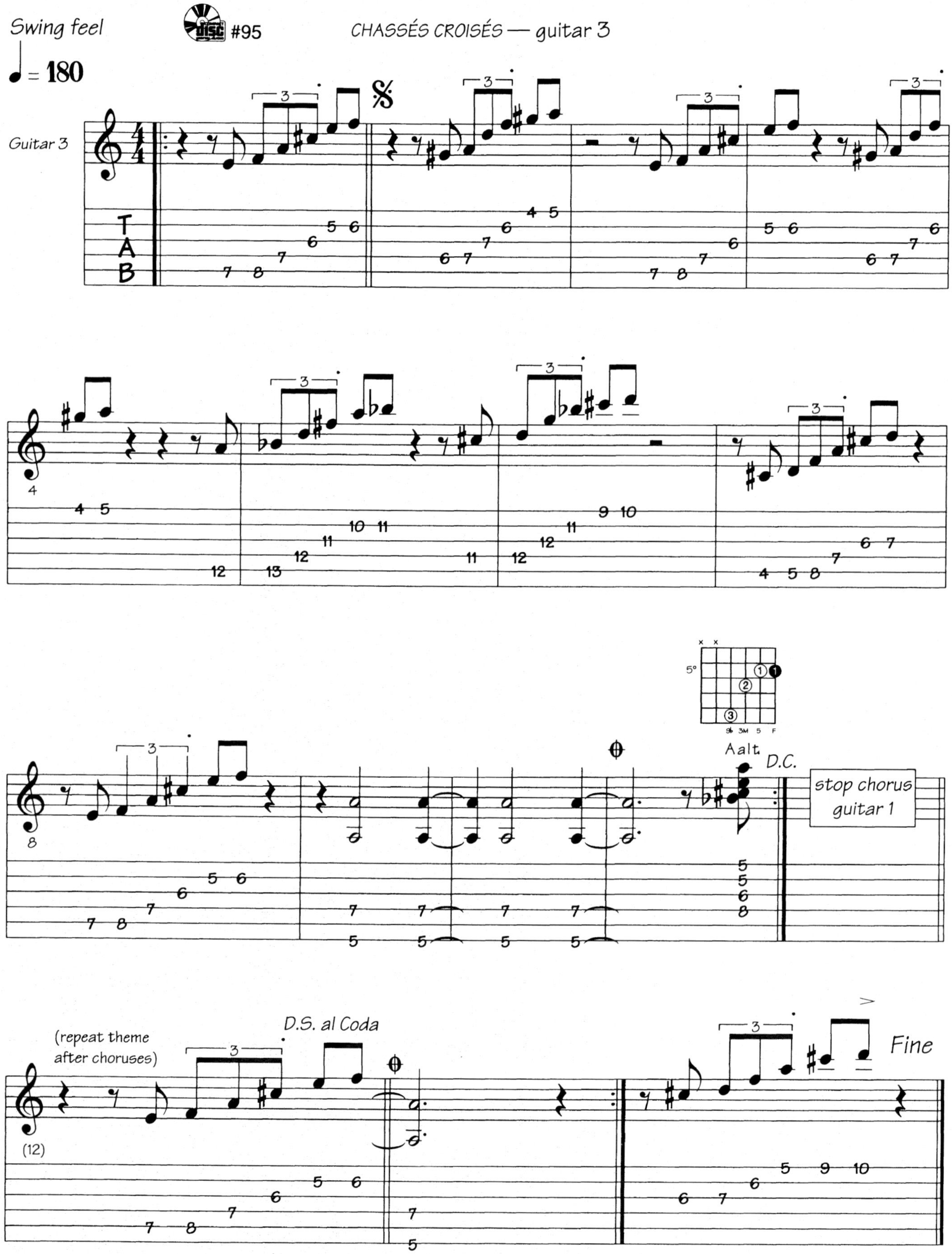

CHASSÉS CROISÉS — guitar 4 (rhythm)

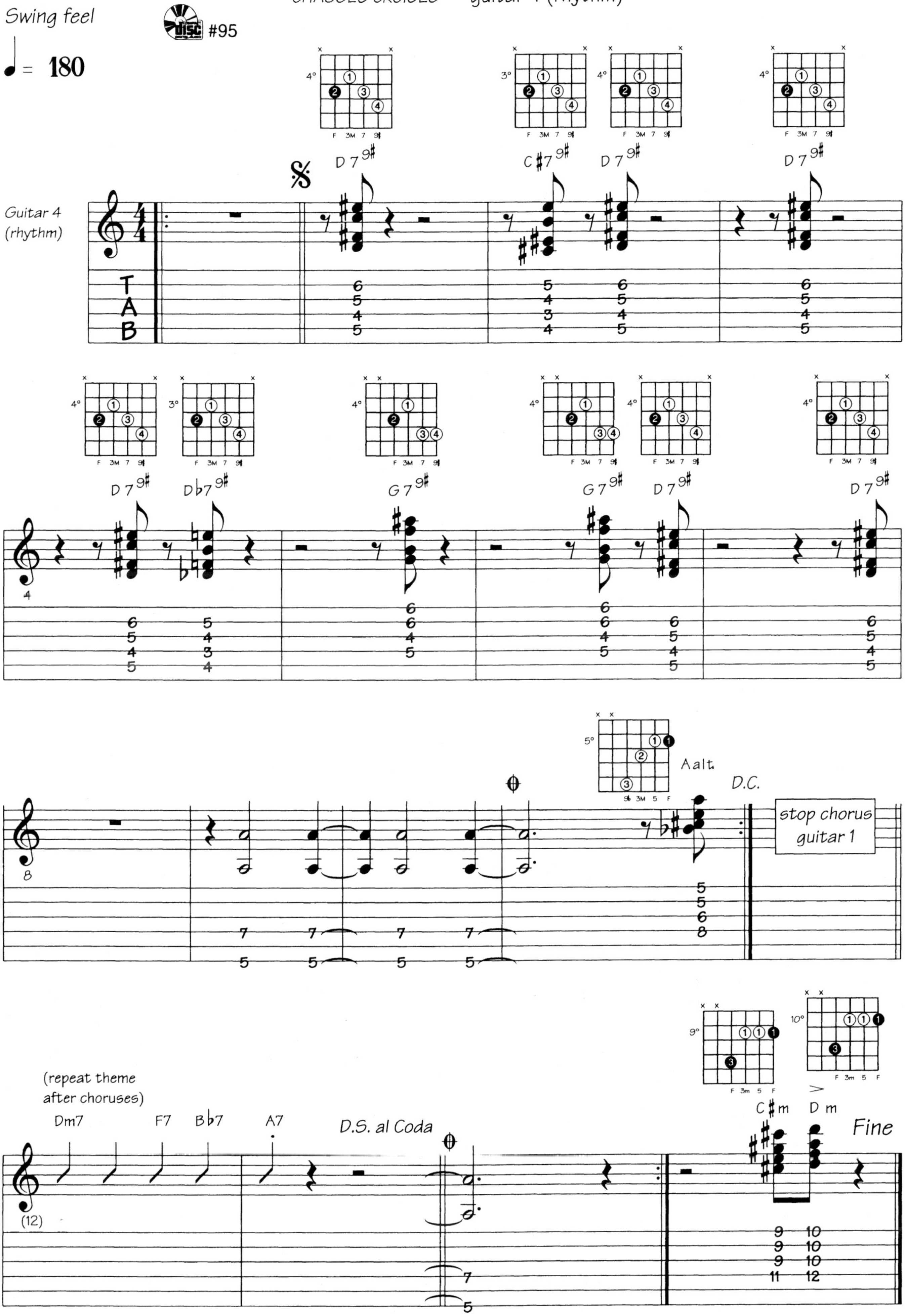

As promised, here is the "Chasses Croises" score, thanks to those who arranged it.

#95

Chassés Croisés

(mixed up)

music by Derek SÉBASTIAN

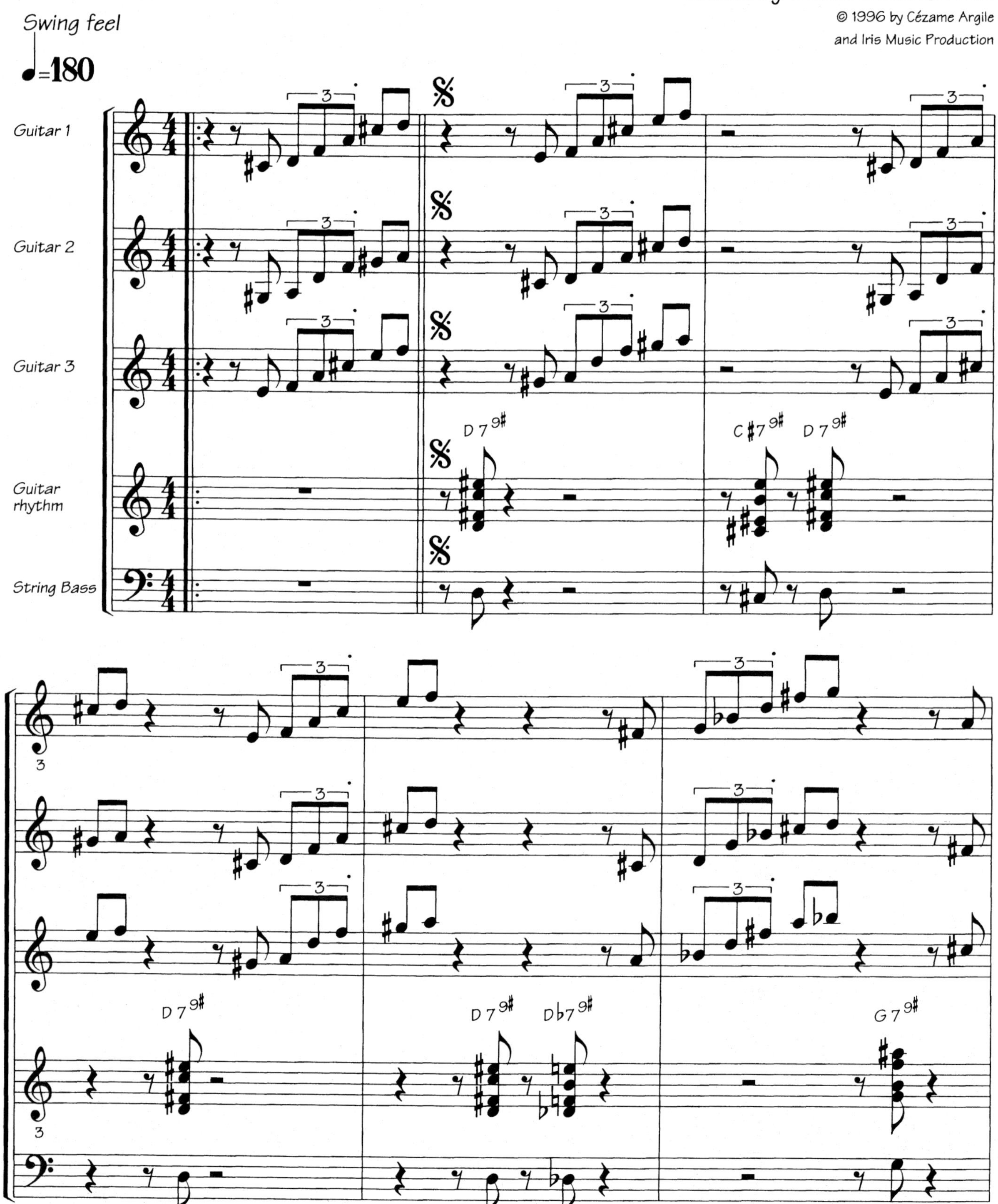

CHASSÉS CROISÉS — score / page 2

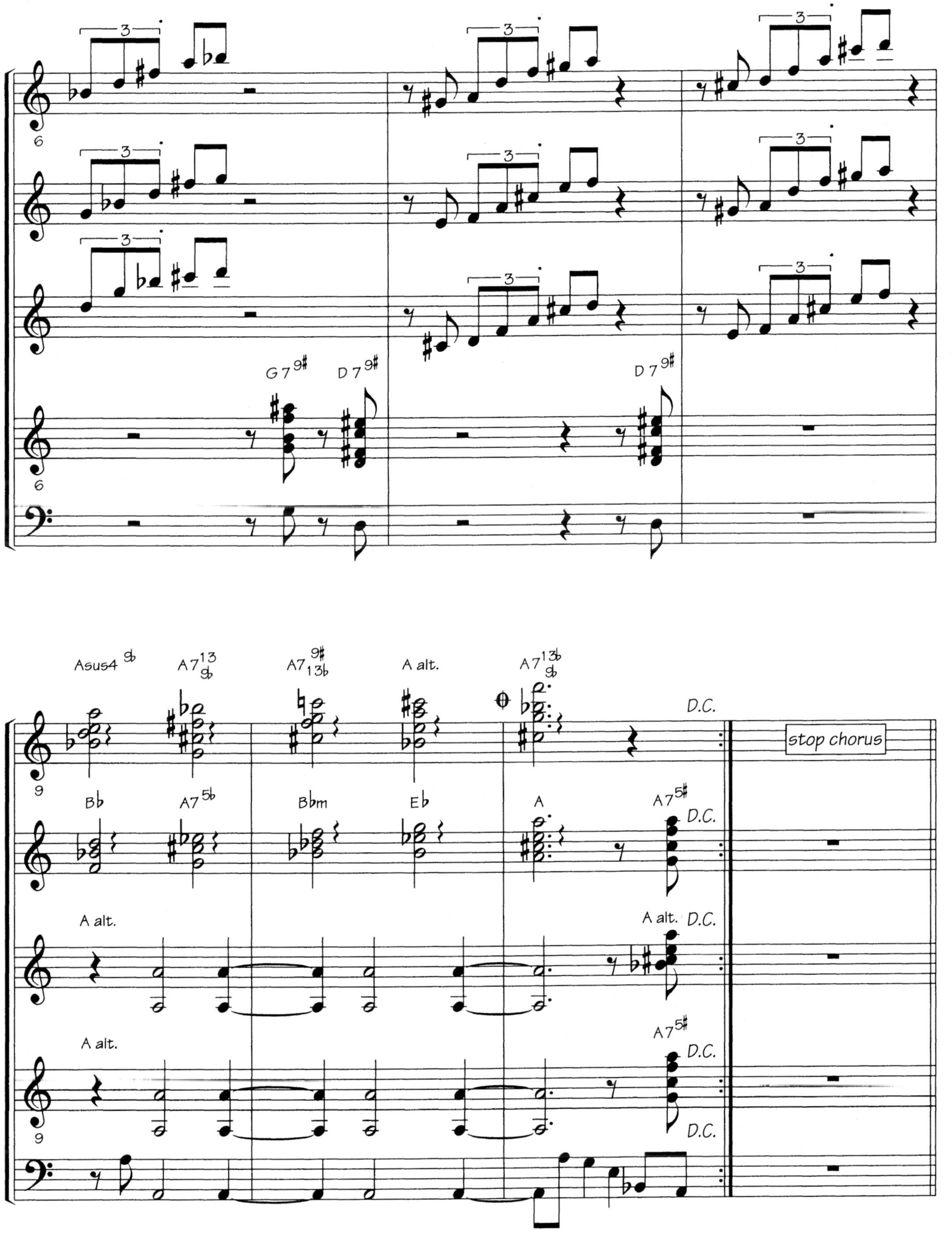

CHASSÉS CROISÉS — score / page 3

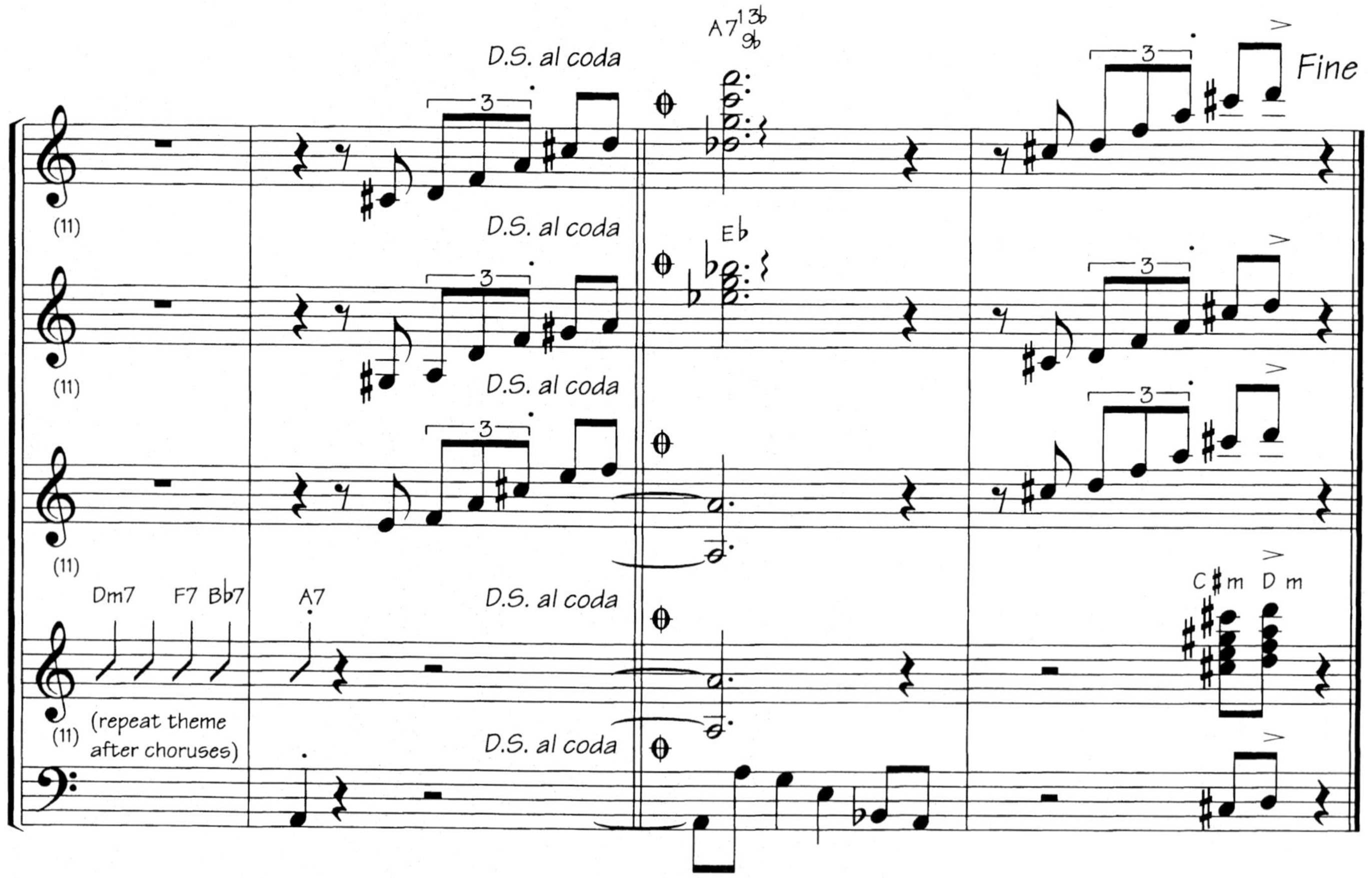

Harmonic diagram for the choruses —

Dm7	Em7$^{5\flat}$ / A alt.	Dm7	Am7$^{5\flat}$ / D alt.
Gm7	Bb7^{13} / Eb7^{9}	Dm7	C7$^{5\flat}$ / F7^{9}
Bb7^{13}	Eb7^{9}	Dm7 / F7^{9}	Bb7^{13} / Eb7^{9}

PART A

Exercise 76 (continued and ending) Valse a Django

In addition, here we come to terms with our study of the theme from "Valse a Django". All together this piece forms a metric structure of 128 measures AA'AA'BB'BB'AA'.

Notice the slides in measure 116, (which we saw in measures 19 and 52), also notice the accent placed on the last chord.

#89

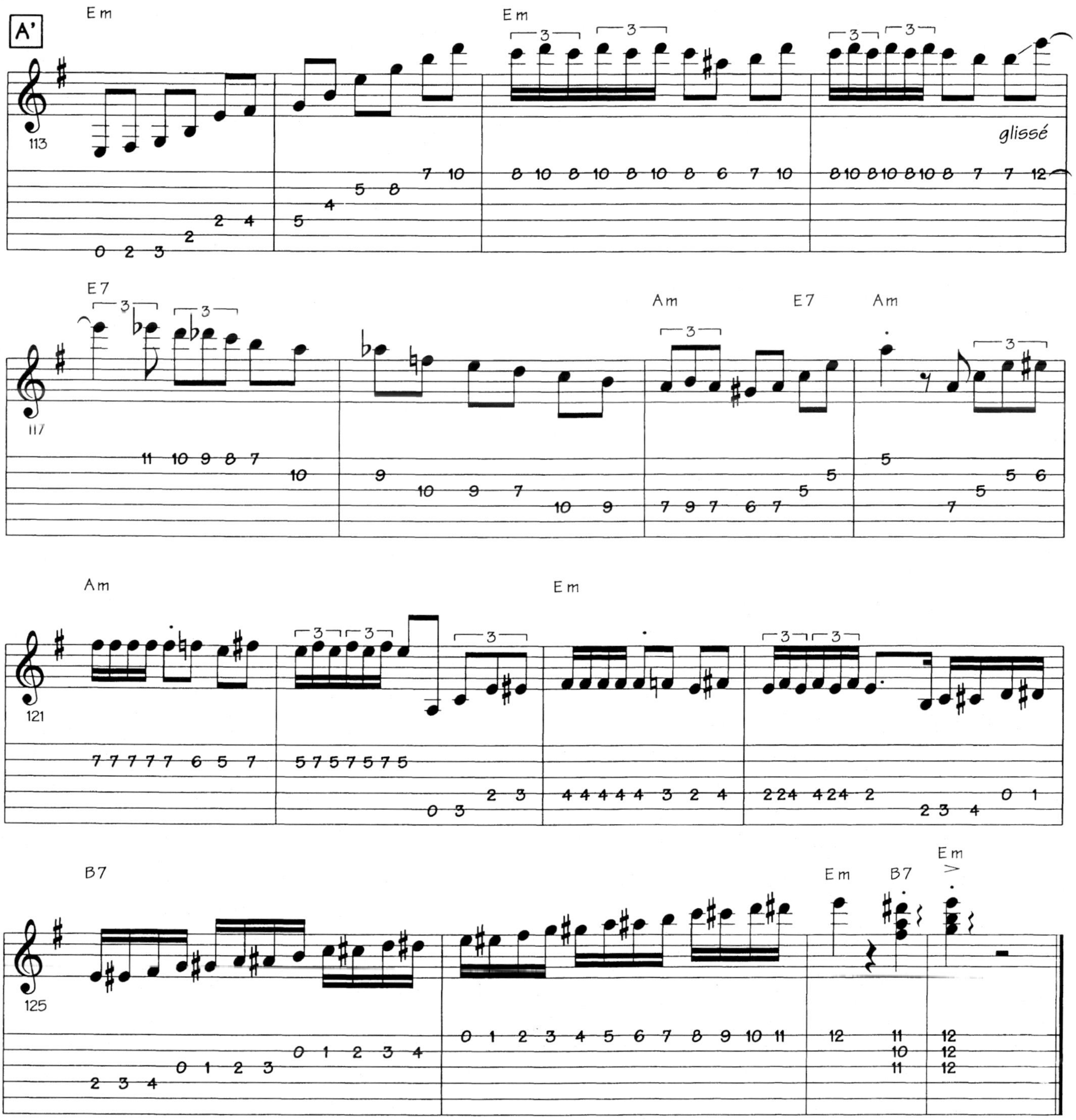

▪ PART B1

We are going back to "Chasses Croises" (chapter 31), to study the various harmonic aspects and rhythm, starting with the accompaniment diagram of the choruses.

On the CD you can hear two types of guitar accompaniment. One is the traditional "drive" with its regular notation in four times: the other (choruses, accordion and violin) offers a more modern signature, where syncopated punctuation plays an important role. This is particularly the subject that we want to develop here.
Nevertheless, we will look at some chords and positions which create this chorus diagram.

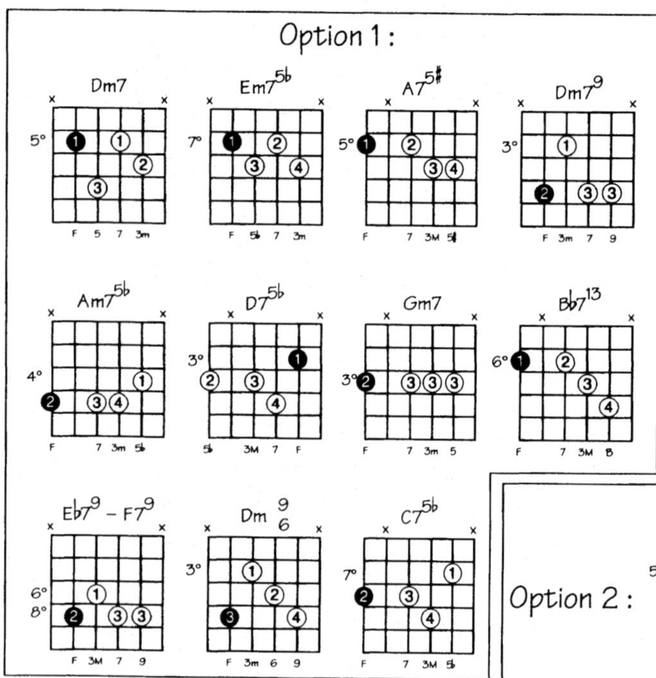

Dm7	Em7 5b / A alt.	Dm7	Am7 5b / D alt.
Gm7	Bb7 13 / Eb7 9	Dm7	C7 5b / F7 9
Bb7 13	Eb7 9	Dm7 / F7 9	Bb7 13 / Eb7 9

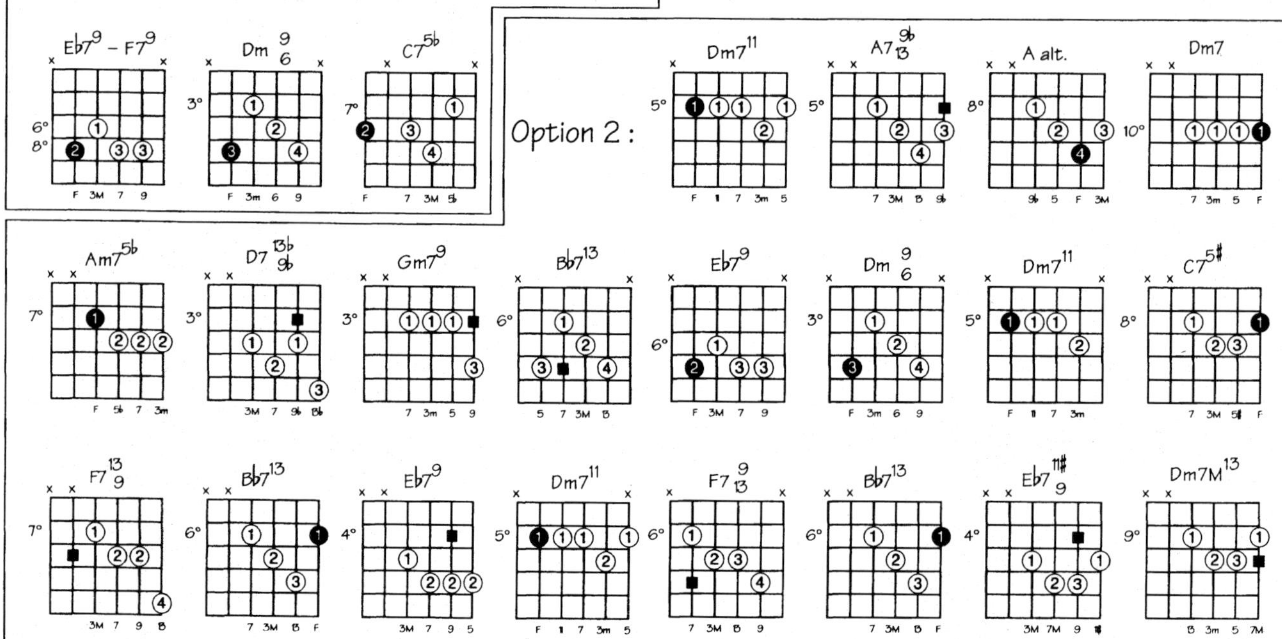

The two options here are concerned with the accompaniment of the choruses. The first one is more dedicated to the "drive" style accompaniment.
On the other hand, the chords of the second option present a little stronger bass root note and grouped together forms the voicings, which will lend particularly well to the syncopated punctuation.
This kind of accompaniment could be done in many ways. Although, it relies on the principle of short, diversified rhythm sections, in the line of harmonics, sections where this syncopation is abundantly used.

By means of the chords in option 2, we can develop a syncopated, punctuated accompaniment for "Chasses Croises" that could look like this:

#95

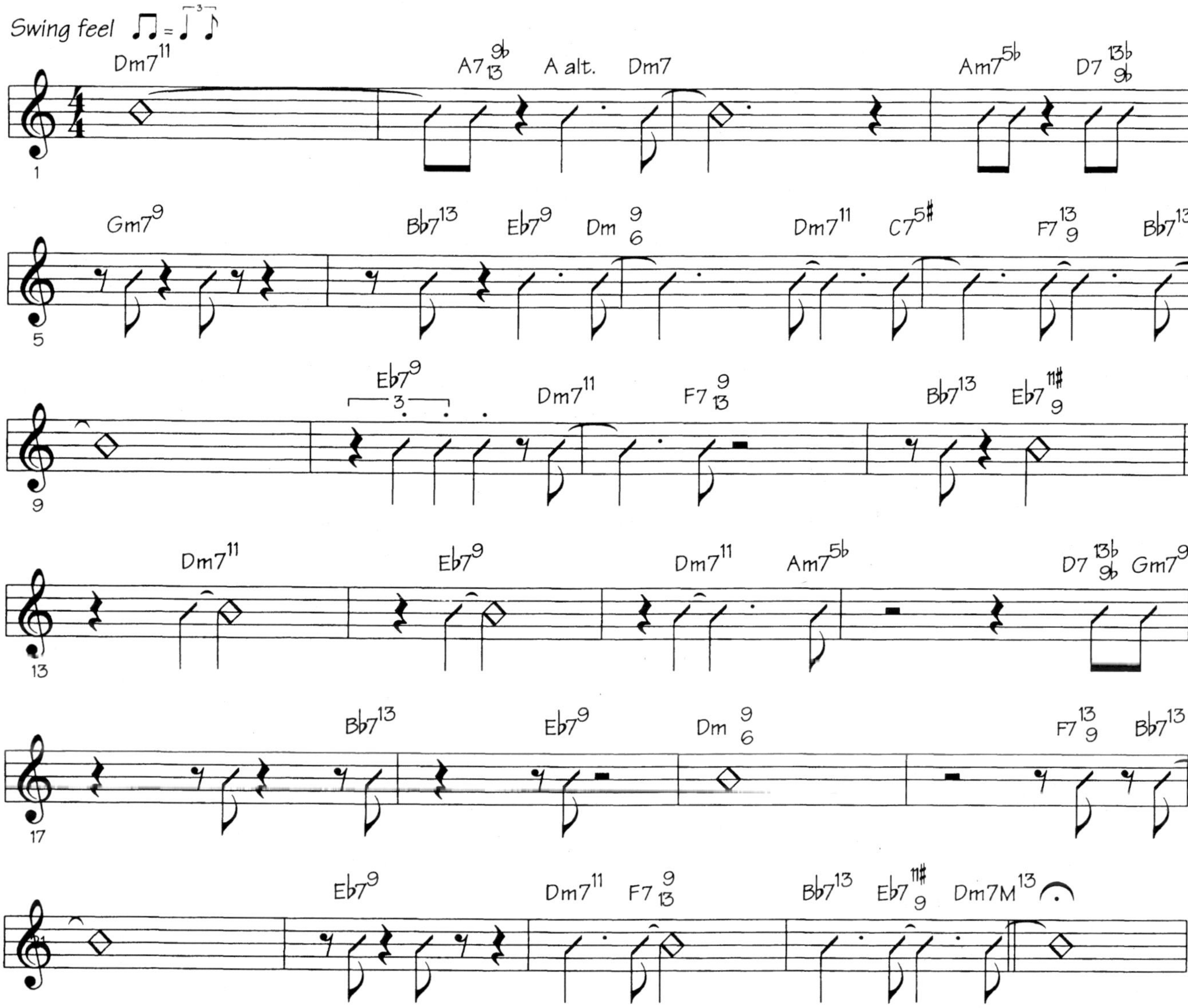

Given that this has to do with accompaniment, the notation here is simplified purely to indicate the rhythm. With this type of score, the rhythm/chords/voicing association should be coherent but nevertheless, discreet and subtle. In other words, you must not lose sight that this accompaniment is exclusively intended to support a soloist.

In reality, the accompaniment offered here is a little to tight to assure an optimal way to support a soloist: by doing this, you should never risk to "cut the notes away from under his fingers". Always listen carefully to how the soloist plays. Its how you listen to him (or eventually to the other members of the orchestra) that creates the harmony of the moment. Always be ready to properly punctuate. If needed, don't be afraid to remain silent, your punctuation could be done with one single chord, expressed with nothing more than an eighth improvised at the right moment. A full stop doesn't need to be made to produce some tones... and it is much more relaxing than to make the rhythm "drive"!

We merely offer this tightly titled accompaniment as an illustration, so that you can get new ideas from it, which you can exploit and which will benefit you.

Now what remains to be analyzed is the lead of "Chasses Croises".

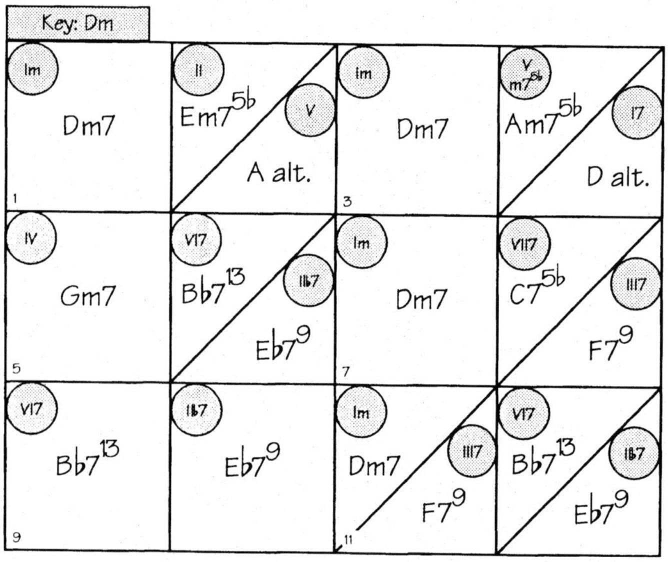

Whether it will be major or minor, all the blues have certain characteristics, which let them be identified as such. In the metric make up, a blues usually counts 12 measures. But this is not enough. In measures 1 , 7 and 11, it uses the I degree chord. Furthermore, measure 5 uses the IV chord.

If these conditions are united, you will play a realistic blues. If not, it more often becomes a blue's imitation, like those in the style of "hard-bop" of the 1950s-'60s, done in great abundance.

Therefore, "Chasses Croises" is a blues since it has all the mentioned characteristics in the minor key. In a moment, we will look a little how these harmonies work:

MEASURES 1 - 3: the I chord, shown at the beginning, is being reintroduced in measure 3 because of its II - V (Em7(b5) - A alt.). Look in the passage at how the V is an "alt." chord (and not simply a dominant A7). Within the minor tonal context, the "alt." quality, is always welcome for the V degree.

MEASURES 4 - 5: very simply, the IV is used via its II - V (Am7(b5) - D alt.) In addition, this is the only reason to look at Vm7(b5) and the I7, chords, which are all strangers in the D minor key. For the rest, this last one stays since the IV degree (Gm) presents itself.

MEASURES 6 - 7: and here are the tritone substitutions. Bb7 is the T.S. of E7 and serves in accordance with the shown principle in chapter 6, page 4. Eb7 is none other than the T.S. of A7, the V degree in the D minor key. In measure 7 we return to the I degree.

MEASURES 8 - 10: with the measure 6 model but, this time, with the fighting fifths, C7 and F7 serve to introduce the Bb7, which itself brings the Eb7, the chords of which we have already respectively detailed in how it works.

MEASURES 11 - 12: before leaving the diagram, the last placement of the I degree, the Dm, to leave of the one that developed the traditional "turnaround", ending (compare Chapter 9, page 5)... of that its function is to "turn around" from the D minor climate, before it returns in measure 1, at the time of the new chorus.

At last, here is some very useful information regarding other colorations that you can apply with other chords of this feature, information you can use to color the chords which make up the feature of other works.

- The minor chords can be colored with the exact fourth (4) or eleventh (11). The major ninth (9) works also, but is less convincing with a type m7(b5) chords. b9, b13 and 13 colorings: in a tonal context, are absolutely excluded.
- The dominant substituted tritone (Bb7 and Eb7) value only the ninth (9) and/or the thirteenth (13) majors. Eventually, the augmented eleventh (#11).
- The dominant chords link together the fifth with all types of coloration: b9, 9, #9, #11, b13 or 13. But in any case (within the tonal context) the right eleventh (11).

PART B2

To close our chapters dedicated to "Chasses Croises", we are going to use these last pages to study the two guitar choruses that are on the CD.
First, let's explain a few points.

Chasses Croises (chorus 1) general explanations

With the conceptual plan, the first chorus makes use of three repeats to build the melodic phrases. This motive is very typical in jazz while improvising the melody. Being made up of (compound) eighths, placed immediately after a triplet:

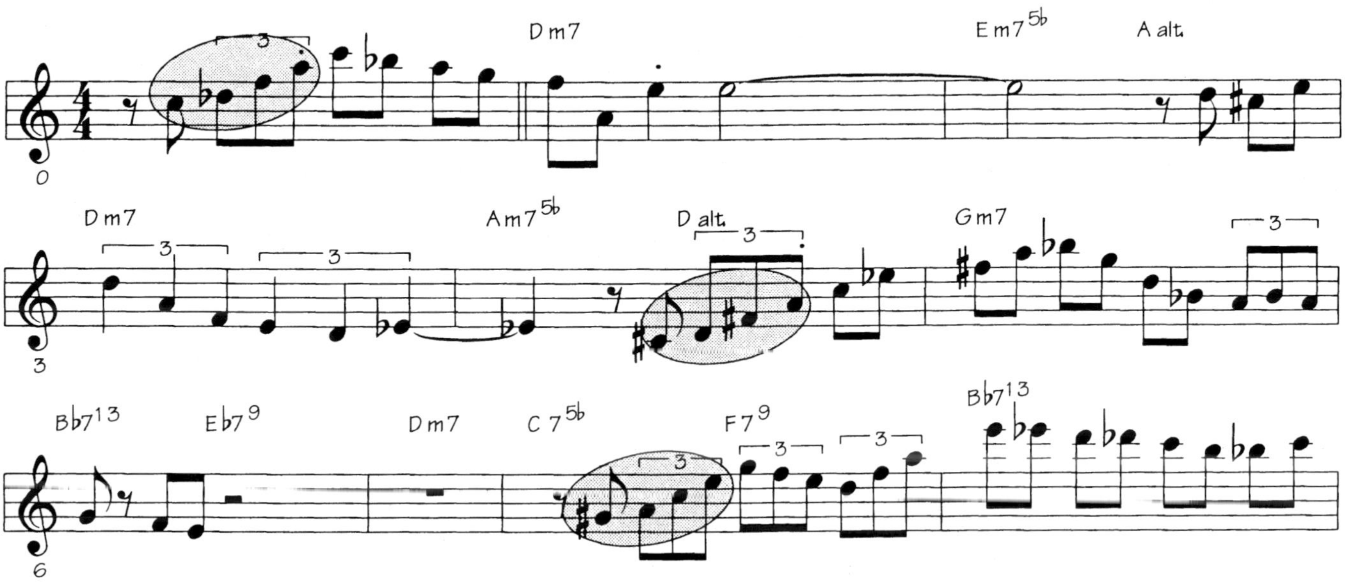

It is proceeded with logical aesthetic rhythm, so you will not miss anything, of course, benefiting thereby by improvising the right way.

Chasses Croises (chorus) stop chorus

Now then, the first chorus starts with a stop chorus, seen at the end of the theme based on the tritone of the harmony of the moment: A7.

Indeed, this stop chorus is thought of as an Eb7 chord (from A to Eb and an inversion, we count three tones), which produces the following colorations (in relation to Eb7):

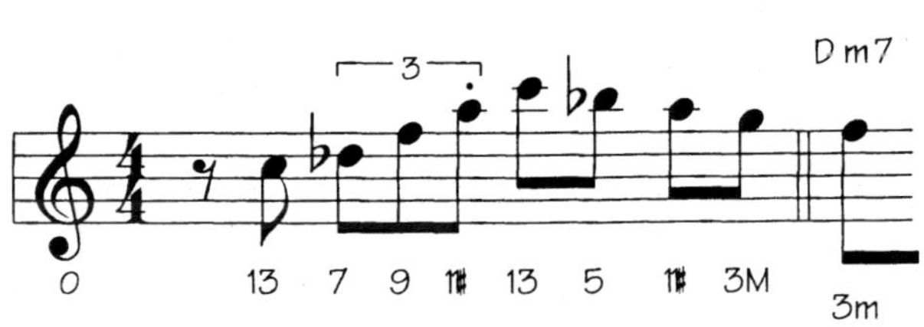

Chasses Croises (chorus 1, measure 12) Be-bop sweep

In measure 12 we find a lead characteristic of Be-bop. This is not the first time that we have encountered this type of rhythmic motive where sweep picking plays a part. The whole secret of a good execution is in the left/right hand coordination and the inherent legato.
Listen well to the CD.

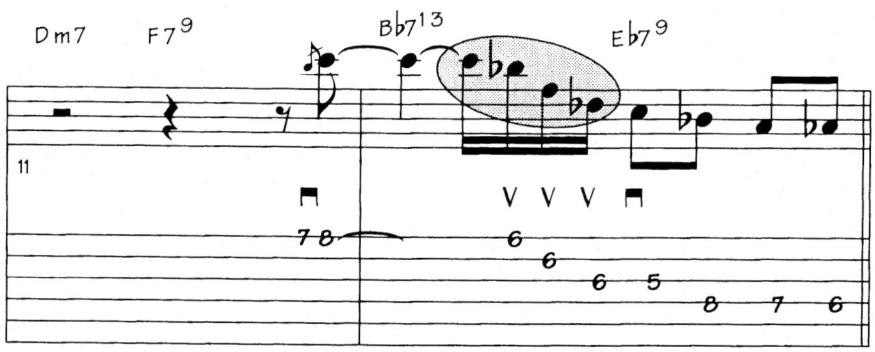

Chasses Croises (chorus 2, measures 18 - 19) Delayed mirror effect

Measures 18 - 19 of the second chorus illustrates the logic of thinking of the melodic speech in the measure where this lead is the mirror (with a long delay) of the first strong comparable lead, this occurs in measures 8 - 9 of the first chorus:

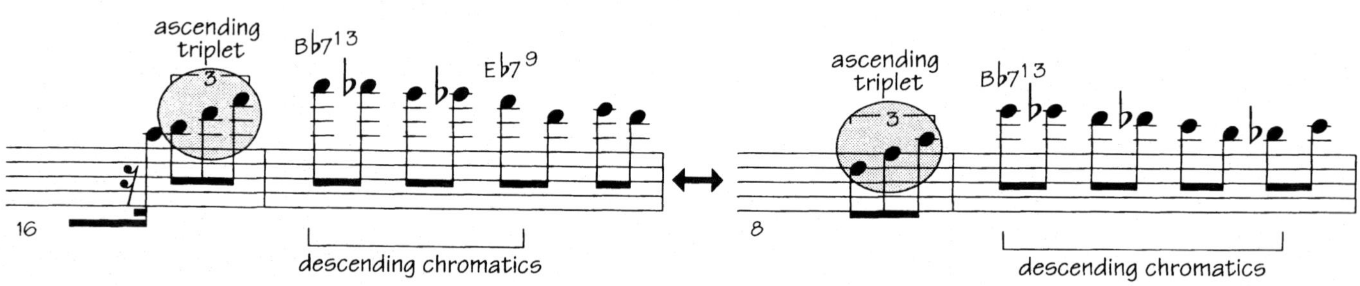

Chasses Croises (chorus 2, measures 23 - 24) strange notes

To finish this second chorus with the minor blues subject, there are some notes with strange sounds that appear in the harmony (final turnaround) that want to come back.

Whatever it may be, these strange notes are not "blue notes", but you need these if you are playing the Manouche style. These harmonic colorations are gladly used in the style, in a minor context: M7 and M6.

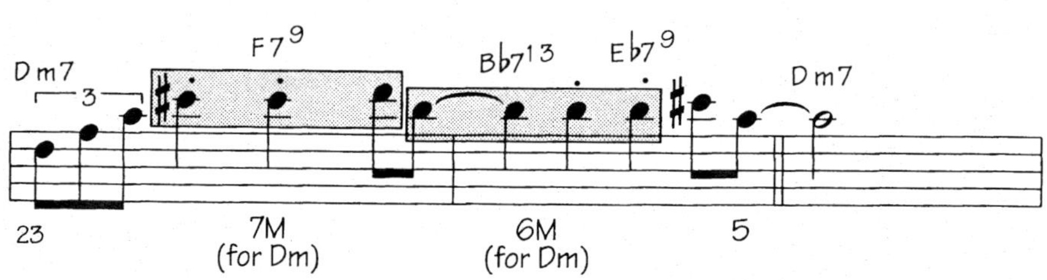

PART C

Here are the two elevated choruses for guitars of "Chasses Croises".

With regard to the quarter notes in measure 17, this is not so magical as it seems: it is simply placing five quarter notes in the space of three beats. Listen to the CD to locate this passage.

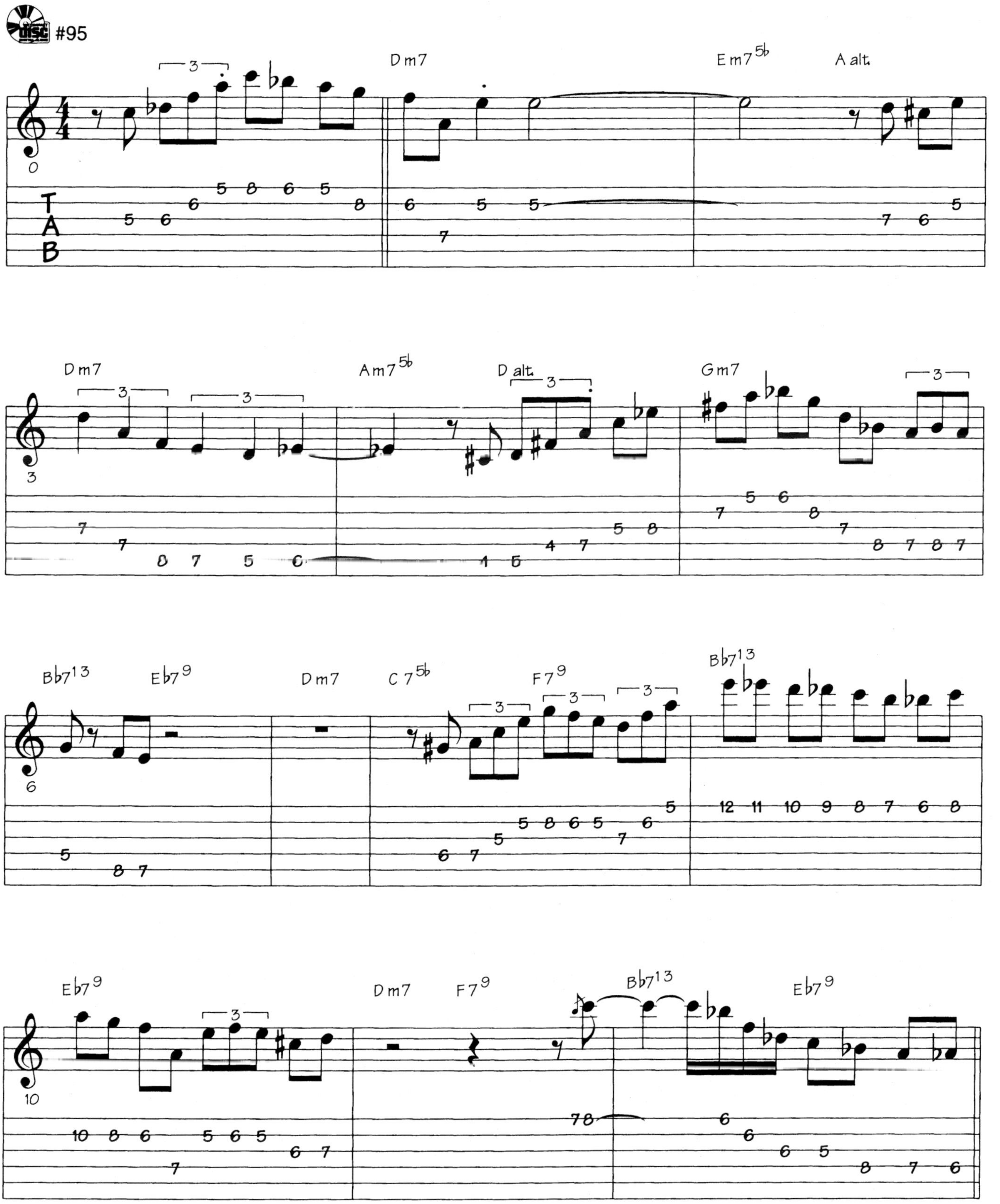

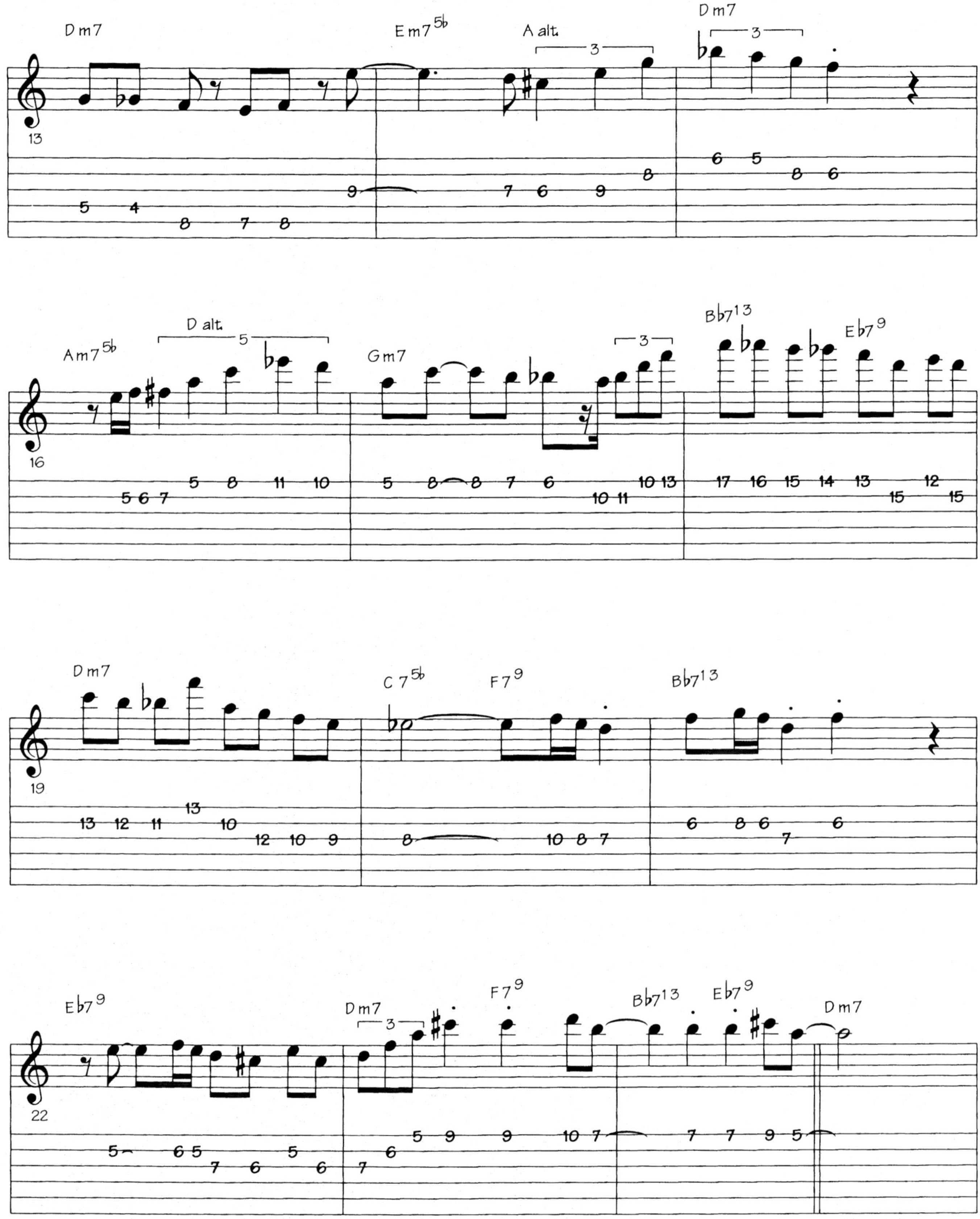
Dm7 Em7 5b A alt. Dm7
Am7 5b D alt. Gm7 Bb7 13 Eb7 9
Dm7 C7 5b F7 9 Bb7 13
Eb7 9 Dm7 F7 9 Bb7 13 Eb7 9 Dm7

PARTS A & B

In chapter 33, we begin with the last lead in our journey. With this fact, we are going to modify our usual focus by abandoning our preliminary exercises to benefit from the detailed study of the jazz theme which will use in the remaining chapters in the book. And since this theme is the last that we will study, we are going to spoil you!

It is titled "My Foolish Heart" and for once it is not written by Romane nor Derek Sebastian, but Victor Young, who has done a number of marvelous melodies which became Hollywood standards in jazz, for instance, "Stella by Starlight" (stemming from the very amusing film Doctor Jerry and Mr. Love). In short, "My Foolish Heart" has 32 measures ABAC done with a very slow beat, it is a ballad. We will use an arrangement for two guitars, plus a string bass, and, eventually, drums.

This theme has already been recorded by a number of jazzmen (if possible, listen particularly to the pianist Bill Evans - Live at Village Vanguard, 1961, or John Mc Laughlin - Electric Guitarist, 1978). This arrangement is a totally unedited, made up version, not recorded as of this day, so you will be the first to see it.

In its original written version, the melody of My Foolish Heart is as follows:

My Foolish Heart (Victor Young / Ned Washington)

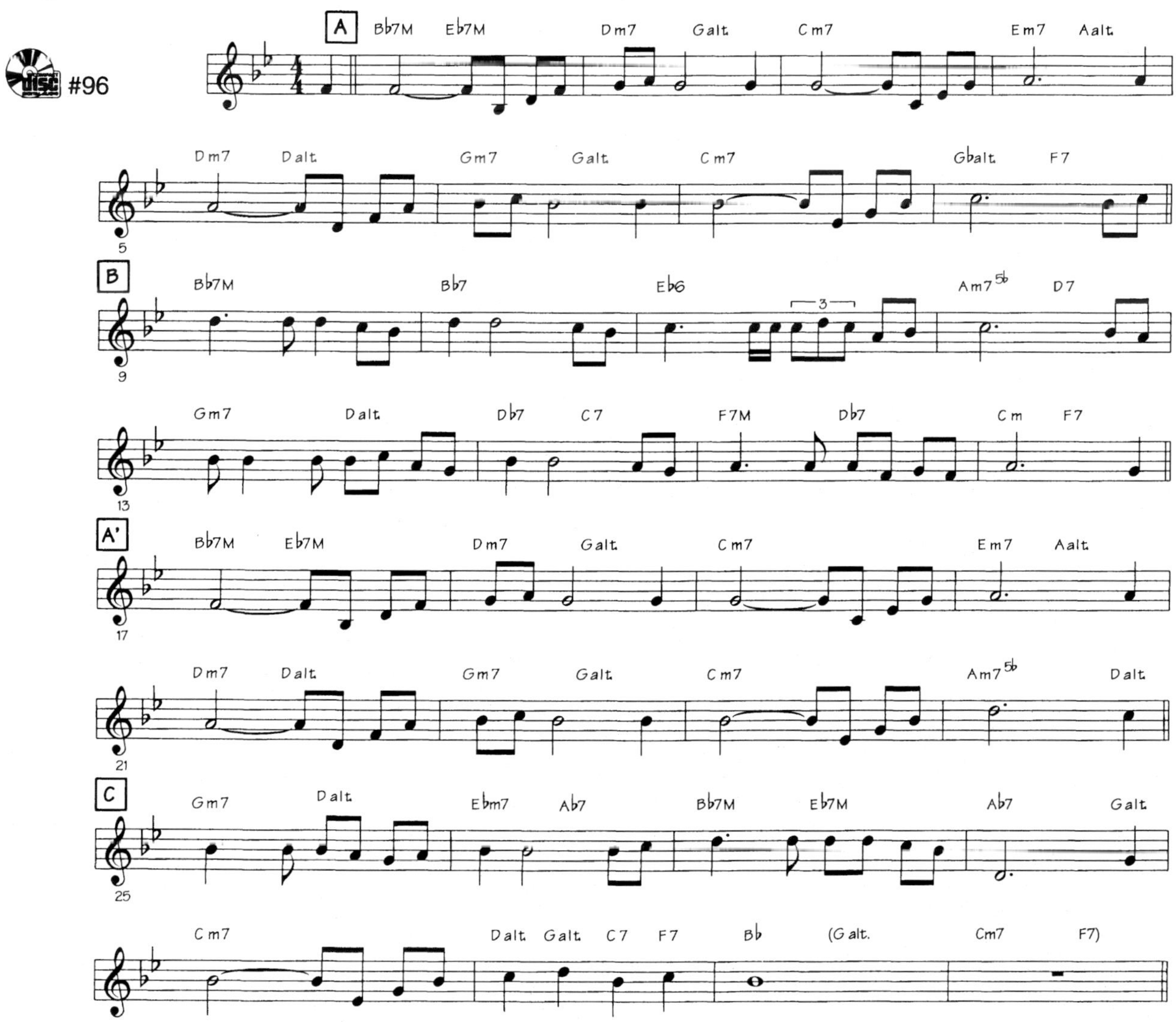

This melody gives us the following diagram of the theme:

The diagram is split up for the theme — ♩= 60

A	Bb7M / Eb7M	Dm7 / G alt.	Cm7	Em7 / A alt.	Dm7 / D alt.	Gm7 / G alt.	Cm7	Gb7 / F7
B	Bb7M	Bb7	Eb6	Am7^{5b} / D alt.	Gm7 / D alt.	Db7 / C7	F7M / Db7	Cm7 / F7
A'	7 %							Am7^{5b} / D alt.
C	Gm7 / D alt.	Ebm7 / Ab7	Bb7M / Eb7M	Ab7 / G alt.	Cm7	D alt. / G alt. / F7 / C7	Bb7M / G alt.	Cm7 / F7

It has a large harmonic density, therefore, it is all the more metrically split up for this presentation with 32 measures. But don't panic, this is a slow piece. It is so slow, that even in the choruses, it could be split in a relative way, giving value to the dynamics instead of giving a 64 measures diagram, it is more airy and easier to read. Use it as a reference mark to accompany the choruses (see chapter 35, page7).

Whatever it may be, the theme is shown in 32 measures ABAC, and here are some basic options (that you will find less and less in the pages to come) for the chord positions. By following the example of "Chasses Croises", you could make use of syncopated punctuations:

Sections A and A':

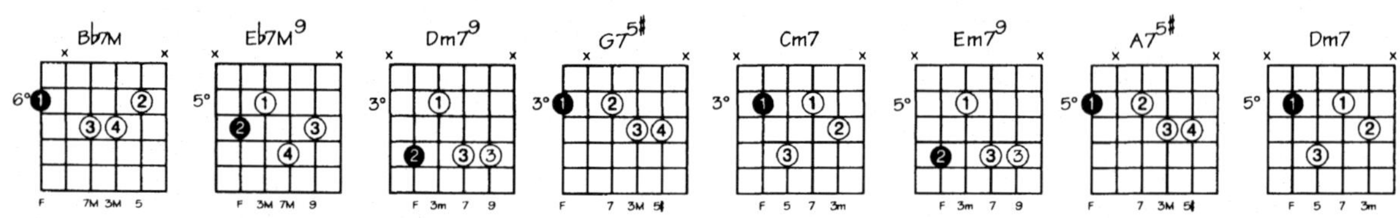

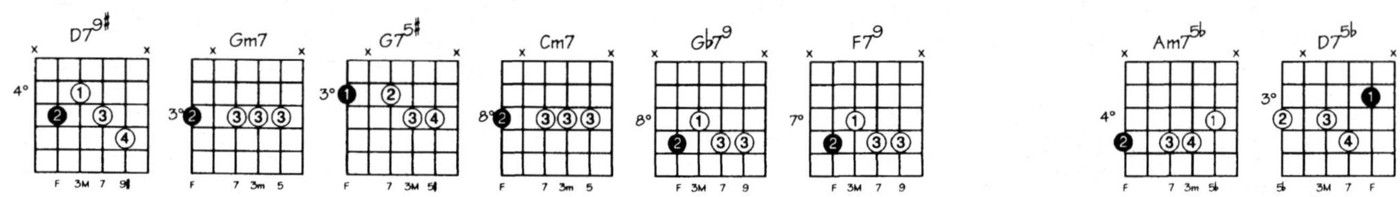

Section B:

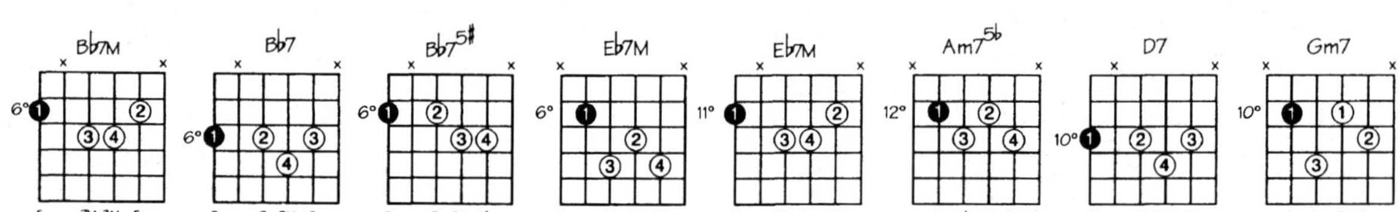

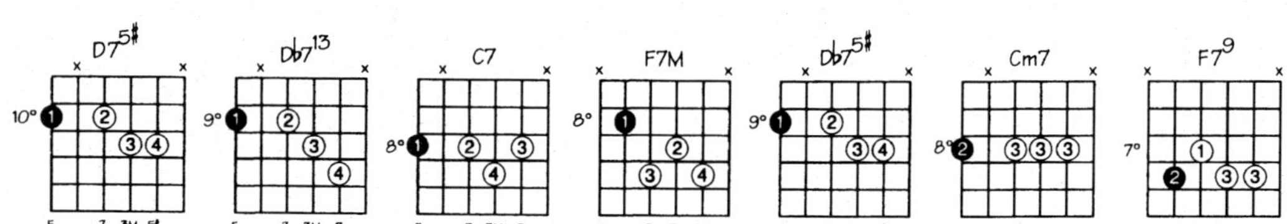

Section C :

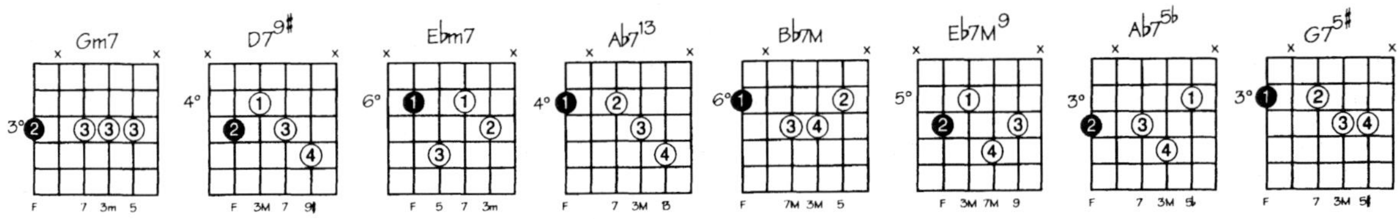

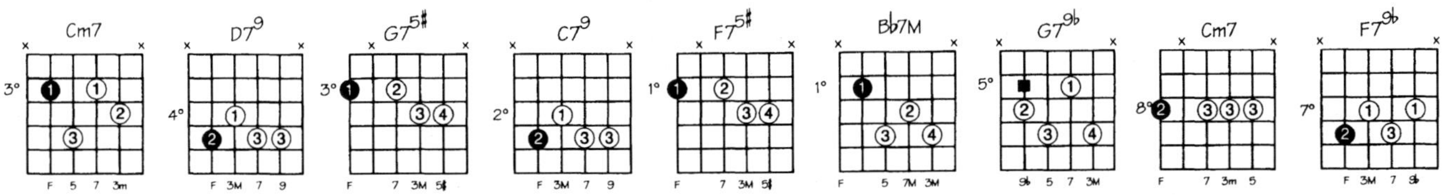

Let's go through the harmonic analysis of "My Foolish Heart", via the diagram in 64 measures.

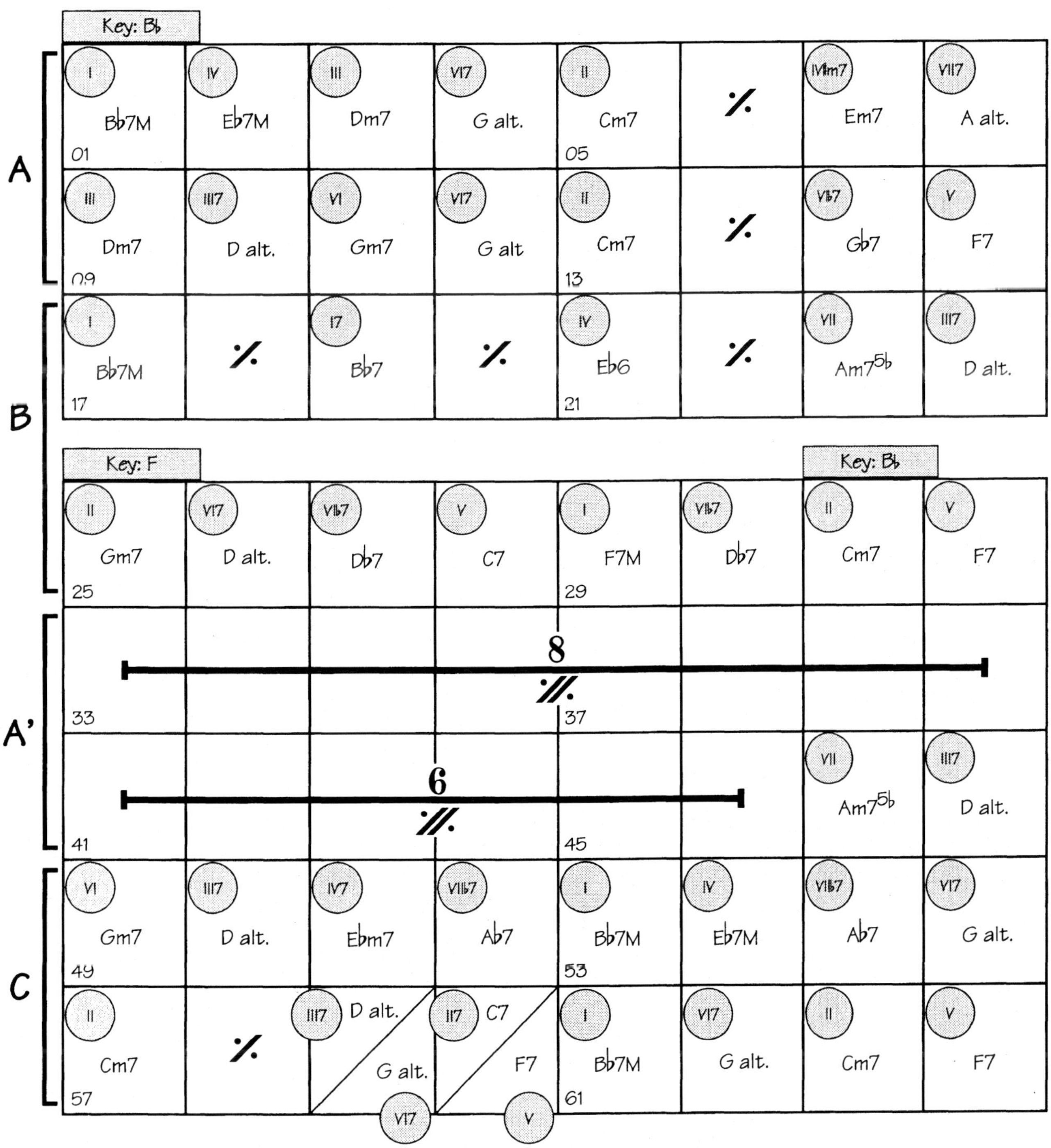

This lead cannot pretend to take away the "the academics of the circle of fifths". "My Foolish Heart" is reinforced with chords that are arranged going down the circle of fifths. And these are not the first six measures that contradict this fact.

MEASURES 1 - 6: the I chord is being placed at the entrance, summing up descending fifth degrees of the Bb major key done through IV, III, VI and II. Missing from this first salvo is the VII chord (which should have been inserted between IV and III). Of course, the VI is used to introduce the II, in accordance with the customary "dominant (G7) → root note (Cm7)" principle.

MEASURES 7 - 8: the key of Bb is going strong until we hit the #IVm7 in measure 7. Does this change our key? No, not only does this Em7 sound superbly well, but it is the ideal springboard to introduce the VII, which is dominant, it even reintroduces our original key in measure 9.

MEASURES 9 - 14: Now we are back on track with Bb major, because the III is a diatonic substitution of I. Of course, the III7 and VI7 respectively serve to bring the VI and II degrees in a more convenient way (dominant principle → key).

MEASURES 15 - 16: now we are at the end of the section, which ends with the V chord. In measure 15 we see a VIb7 (Gb7) which is none other than the T.S. of II7(C7), and the V (of V) equally could have been made a forerunner, in accordance with the dominant principle → key (C7 → F7).

MEASURES 17 - 24: half of a diminished harmonic rhythm, we enter a calm zone: with the I7 we created a small grain of tension, the better to introduce the IV with in two measures. Then, a provisional II -V in person as Am7(b5) - D alt. which introducse the relative minor key Gm? Yes and no.

MEASURES 25 - 30: Yes, we stay in Bb major. No, four measures later, there is a FM7 which would not know how to be taken for a V, being given that it is a (M7). Consequently, the Gm7 serves as a transition to modulate in the key of F major. And between this Gm7 and FM7, a cascade of dominant chords continually appears until the real V (C7).

MEASURES 47 - 48: classic cadence of fifths being driven with the VI (Gm7) of the key.

MEASURES 49 - 53: do you remember the harmonic feature in "Monticello"? We had the progression of D7 → E7M. The same procedure is used in measures 52 - 53: the I is brought by the VIb7, knowing that the VIb7(9) is equivalent to IIm7(b5). There is only a small difference, the reinforcement of Ab7 in the middle of Ebm7. And under a certain point of view, this cadence Ebm7 → Ab7 (= provisionally "II - V") can for an instant let us think that we could have gone to the key of Db major. But no, since the choice is possible, we opt for homogeneity and stay with Bb major while putting BbM7 in measure 53, then EbM7 in measure 54. For the rest, the melody is very explicit in this topic (the D note = #m of BbM7).

MEASURES 55 - 56: we have dominant chords which mutually call themselves out to bring the II.

MEASURES 57 - 64: after a rest with the II, things continue. At the end of the section is a pushed I degree with evidence at the end of the lead. And for that, there are no thirty-six solutions: pick up! A dominated, integrated pick up with compression of the harmonic rhythm (measures 59 - 60). And we then can pose like a flowery chord of the final key and quit using the pickup for a second time to launch a second chorus (measures 63 - 64).
And there you are. This is our last harmony analysis, and we hope that you will get some fruitful lessons out of it, like all the preceding ones.

And now, we come quickly to the subject: our arrangement for two guitars.

Of course, it has to do with the melody, which we have to harmonize and use the aid of some "chosen" chords. These are not mistakes in the harmony in this arrangement, but our ears maybe are not yet ready to receive the density of the harmony with "polytones" which are offered here. If this is the case, be confident and have patience. Open your ears and all will be clear at the point mentioned.

With the rhythm diagram, this arrangement should not be particularly difficult, this is not the part of the string-bass, you are a guitarist, and that doesn't mean here that it is only a complimentary title.

With regards to the interpretation of the "groove", it is a little more delicate. Generally, the slow beats demand concentration and suppleness. If you are not accustomed to it, don't burn thru the chapters and start rigorously playing in tempo. Then, bit by bit, you will be freed from the technical contingencies relative to all these new chords and their rich sound, and you will start to feel the throbbing as the "groove" searches you out to be reborn.

In the upcoming chapter we will give you a part of the score (chapter 35, pages 5 - 6) with separate guitar parts. These are the last ones you should work on. There is no tablature. In reality, tablature is a written form hardly used by jazz guitarists, who for a long time prefer notation and diagrams.

You can play these chords two ways:
– with your fingers, using them together in a single stroke, like a pianist does.
– with a pick, using very fast arpeggios with the notes. More guitaristicly: an arpeggio with a heavy thumb stroke, like Wes Montgommery. This is a matter of personal taste and you are the only judge on which one you will choose.

From a general point of view, these two guitar parts are worth it. Guitar 2 is slightly easier being given that it plays the role of a second voice, or is made defective with wrong melodic reference marks.
We start using guitar 1 which exposes the theme and suggests, from here to there, pure melodic interventions. Besides, this guitar 1 can stand alone sufficiently by itself, in case you decide to play "My Foolish Heart" as a guitar solo, without accompaniment, as was magnificently done by Joe Pass.

Finally, we hope that you will have your friends who play guitar and enjoy sharing your studies help with this duo of the arrangement of "My Foolish Heart". If not, get support from your tape recorder which will give you the opportunity to know both parts, a double task which will enrich your musical ears.

The presentations have been made, we are going to go over the study of these guitar parts, and give details of some of the numerous polytonalities which makes them up. We hope that this gives you an optimal understanding of the harmonization procedures of the guitar, and gives you the possibility to arrange some type of other jazz theme of your choice.

To harmonize with the guitar, the fundamental leading line is, of course, the melody, which combines itself with the preceding harmonies, and is as important. Also the material and an ear has to get its word in, that is likewise enormously important, as well as knowing the theory.
With this last aspect, we encounter a certain quantity of chords in "My Foolish Heart", which are simply indicated as "alt.", a terminology that, if we ignore its significance, we seriously risk compromising the harmonization.
Compromising the harmonization? No, you have studied this book from the beginning, this way of indicating it is not completely mysterious.
You will find the choice of colorations totally natural that we have used for the chord in measure 2, divided between the two guitars:

• My Foolish Heart, guitar 1/a

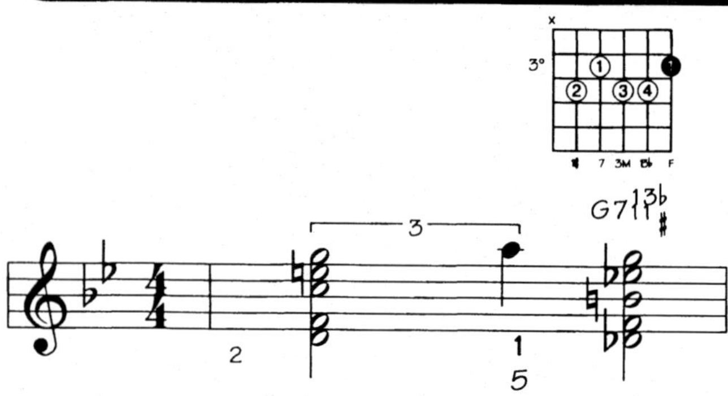

Besides, the indispensable M3 and 7, which characterize the chord, this guitar part calls the colorations #11 and b13 or, if you prefer, b5 and #5 (Db and Eb notes) which are the colorations of the "alt." type, responding to the globally required symbols: G alt.

• My Foolish Heart, guitar 2/a

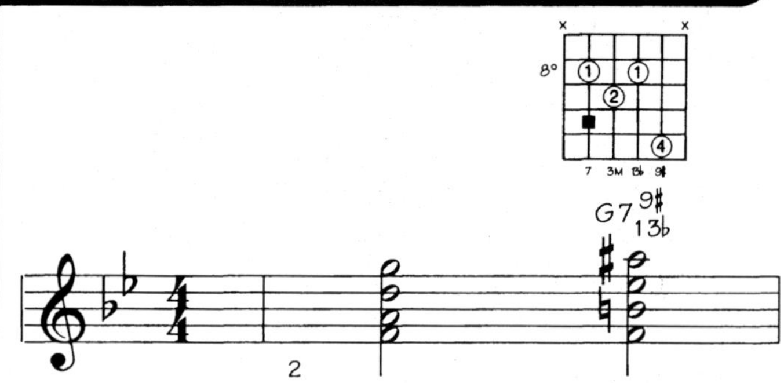

The second guitar plays a G alt. chord and is opting for the b13 and #9 colorations. It is also perfectly correct to look at the basic symbol when asked.

And at the beginning stake we get a polytonal chord ("polychord") G7(#9, #11, b13), very rich in sound and set up with six distinctive notes, or with three doubling up together (M3, 7 and b13), producing a "chorus" effect (natural, not electronically) which is inherent with this type of superimposing sounds.
Try this polychord many times. The A section of "My Foolish Heart" gives you a second one as dense, with rising triplets of measure 5:

• My Foolish Heart, guitar 1/a

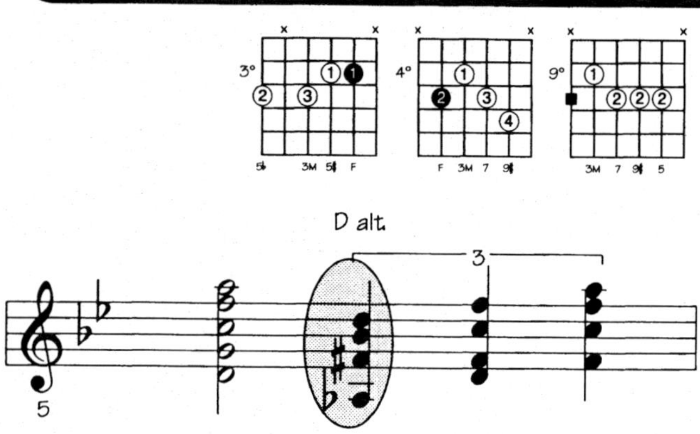

The same colorations as before the b9, #11 and b13, - but differently done between the guitars, and with another root note. Notice also the #11 (or b5) in the bass.

• My Foolish Heart, guitar 2/a

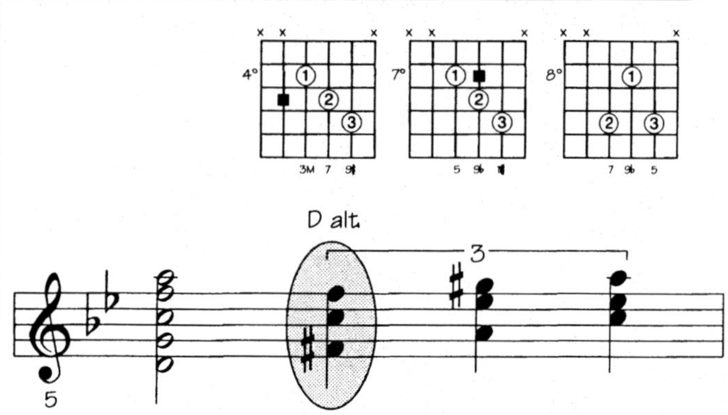

The second guitar is satisfied with a so-called M3-7-#9 triad and it gains by linking it with gaps of m3. The advantage: easy fingering, but also having respect for the demanded harmony, together with guitar 1.

PART C

Here are the guitar parts of "My Foolish Heart" which concerns section A. The continuance and the ending of the arrangement are given in chapters 34 and 35.
A word of explanation about the fingering shown for the isolated notes (guitar 1): the higher numbers tell you which string to use (ex: **3** → G string), the lower numbers tells you which fret is used on the neck as in tablature, but without the six lines.

MY FOOLISH HEART — guitar 1 / a

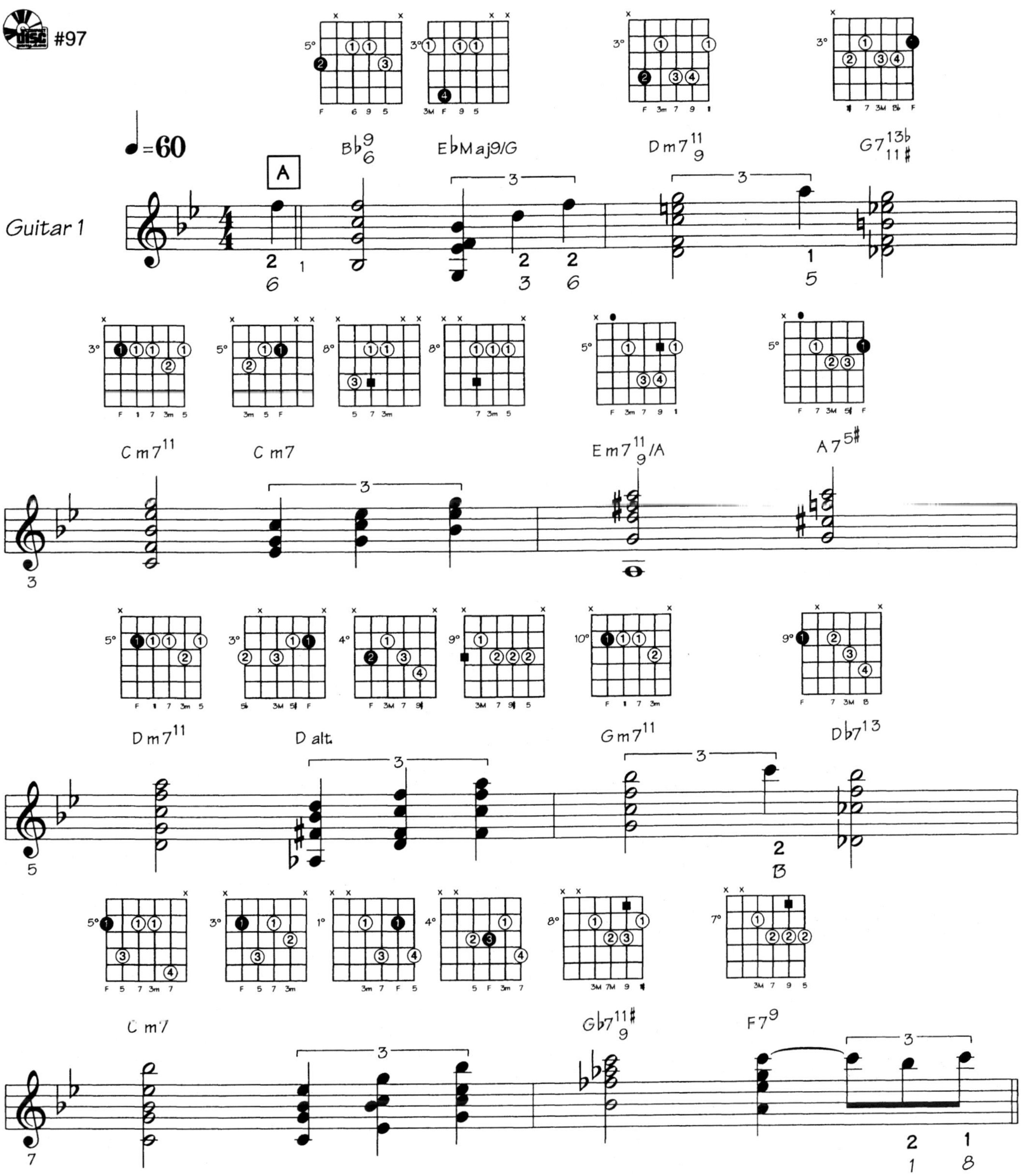

MY FOOLISH HEART — guitar 2 / a

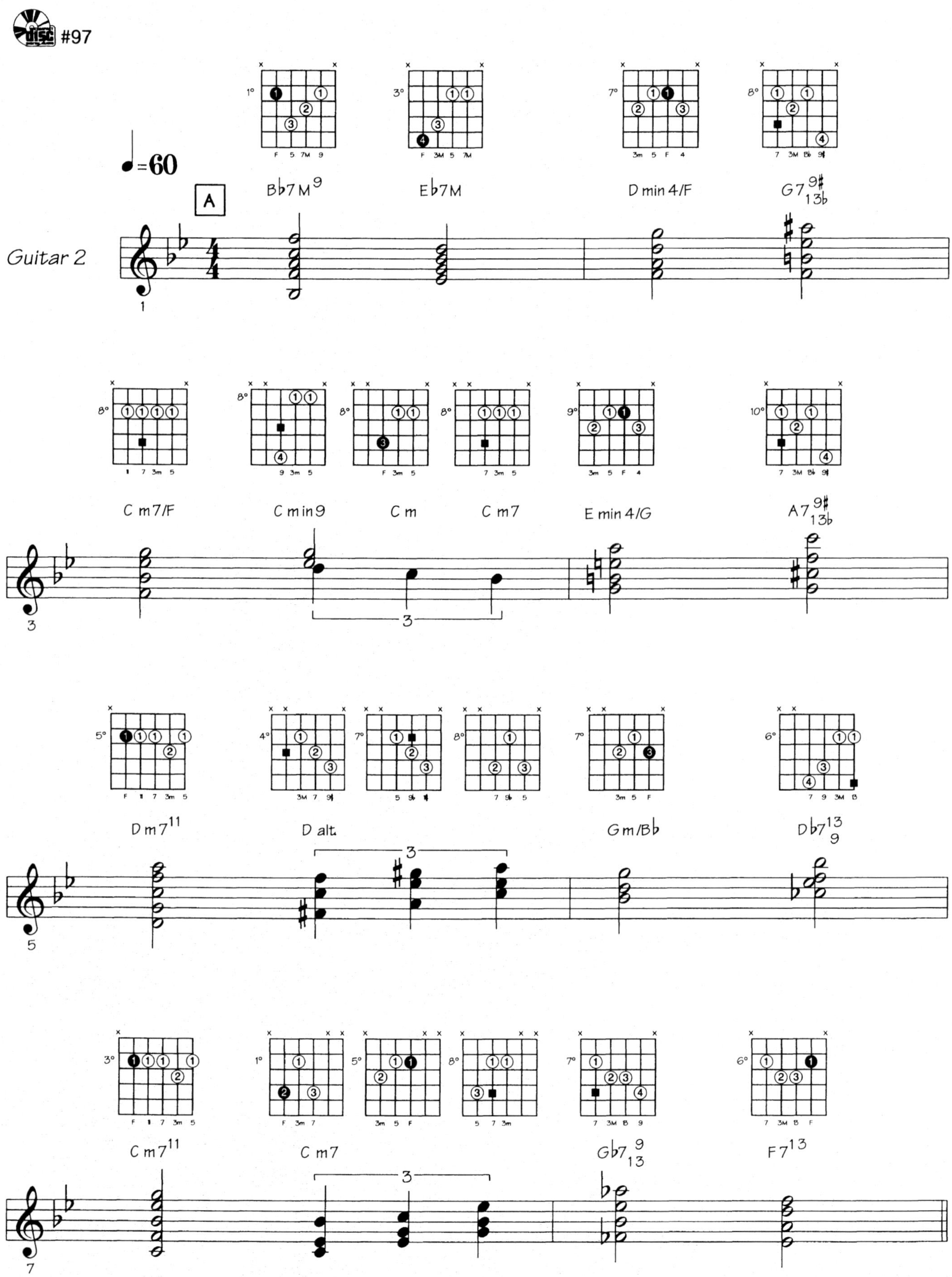

PARTS A & B

Let's pursue our study of the guitar parts in "My Foolish Heart".

In this case it is going to be about the B and A' sections, where we still see the "alt." type polychords, as in measure 10: E7(#9, #11, b13). This E alt. is particularly efficient here because it is reinforced with a low root note, the lowest note on the guitar. When the harmony permits it, don't hesitate to use these lower root notes (equally called "pedals" when held) that are on the open strings.

In the area of harmonizing melodies (among others), we would like to review some important points concerning the way to create chords (from a minimum of four distinct notes):

A) With all major, minor or dominant chords:
Notes based on R - 3 - 5 -7 can indifferently be left with the voices, knowing that one M3 or m3 is placed under a D of the first octave (D1) = one tone lower then the low E on the guitar) will have a great tendency to produce a confused sound, which is hurting the ears by being disconcerned with the character of the chord that makes this third "cavernous". This restriction does not concern the guitar. But, there could be a day when you have to write for another instrument.

B) Wtih all open major chords ('drops'):
• The 9 and 13 colorations (or 6) must by placed in the higher voices, preferably above the M3 and /or the M7. Of course, this remains really for the combinations (9 with 13, or 6/9 being 6 without 7M). Certainly, to consider a "C/D" (C triad, D in the bass), where the D note is 9, the chord sounds excellent and is often used, but this is in fact an Am7(11).
• The #11 (= b5) coloration could eventually be represented with the low chord (voice 4).
• The #9 and 11 (= 4) coloration are unusable in a tonal context, being ambiguous in tone.
As for the 9 and b13 (= #5), which are very modern colorations for the major family, we would thus have:

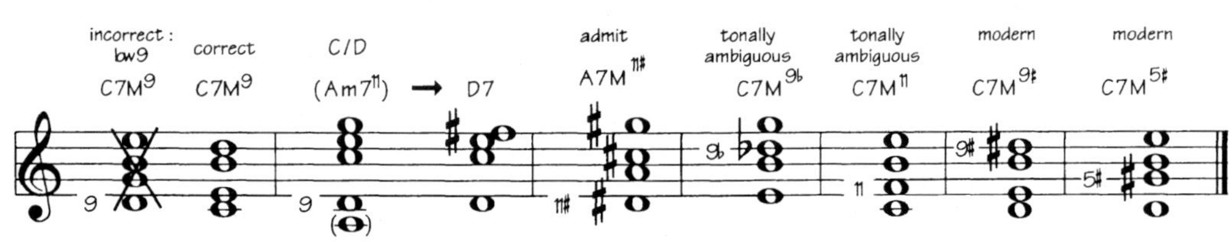

C) With all open minor chords:
• The 11 coloration could be placed indifferently within the voice. It produces the same excellent sound when it represents voice 4 (see above) Am7(11) → Dm7.
• Otherwise, the 4 coloration is freely used in place of the m3. For example, D7sus4 in the place of Dm7.
• The 9 coloration should be placed in the higher voice, never in voice 4, and preferably above the m3 and/or the 7(M or m). Of course, this really remains with the combinations (9 with 11, 6 with 9 being 6 in the absence of 7... for example, Cm6/9).

To summarize the valuable sounds or confusion with an illustration and minor family, we will have:

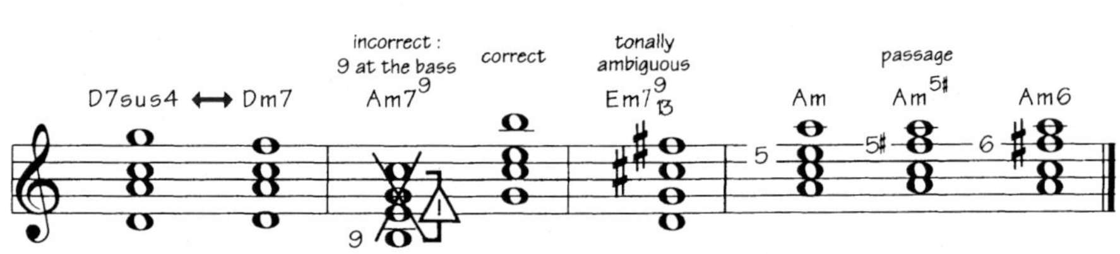

D) With all open dominant chords:

• The 9, #9, b3 (=#5) and 13 colorations must be placed in the higher voices, preferably above the M3 and/or the 7. This remains with numerous possible combinations (except 9 with b9, 9 with #9 and b13 with 13).

• On the other hand, the b9 and #11 (= b5) colorations could be placed differently with the voices, including in voice 4, as we already have seen so many times ("My Foolish Heart", guitar 1, measure 2, second chord: 11 on the bottom). There is one restriction, the case of the b9 with 11 combination, the colorations will be in the higher voices.

• The 11 (= 4 in the presence of M3 and the 7) coloration is unusable within the tonal context, being tonally ambiguous, this will not necessarily say that this type of chord is inaudible (look at the lines below this paragraph). On the other hand, the 4 can be "suspended" at the M3. Or if you prefer, the 4 can momentarily replace the M3. As in the case of G7sus4 that precedes G7.

To summarize with an illustration of the valid or confused sounds, it is the dominant family, we thus have:

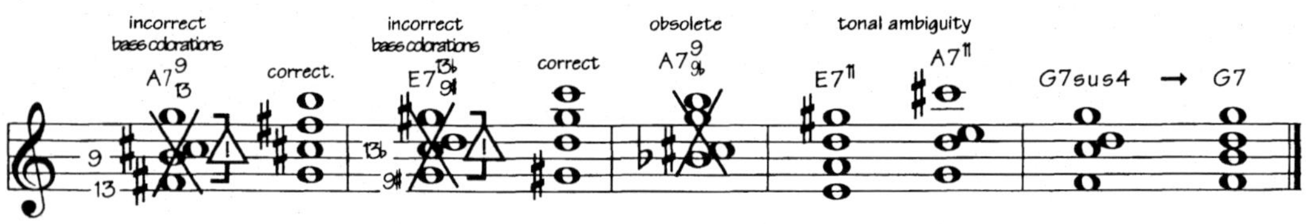

E) The closed positions:

Whatever the family is, the chords in close positions don't have any restrictions, except those that are concerned with the known tonal ambiguities, as quoted.

F) The inversions:

Finally, a small recall (Chapter 29), don't neglect to take the precautions on the subject of reversals:

• to avoid the m2 (1/2 tone) interval between the two higher voices of the chord, on a guitar it isn't a problem.

• avoid the m9 (1/2 tone + octave) between any two voices. With this m9 interval, there are some exceptions, which can be illustrated with two chords:

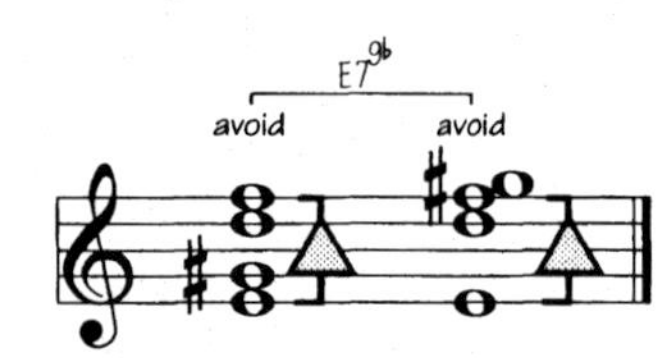

With all this information, we return to our arrangement of "My Foolish Heart", section B.

With our very dense E alt. chord (measure 10, second chord) we have reached a spot where the harmonic tension is loosened with the EbM7 chord brought by chromatic movement: E7 (T.S. of Bb7) → EbM7. And with Eb7 this major chord, between two lower notes in the harmony (5th and 6th), we meet a movement of a passage, which momentarily produces a modern and interesting harmony: M7(#5), compare it with the upper paragraph B:

• My Foolish Heart, guitar 1/b

• My Foolish Heart, guitar 2/b

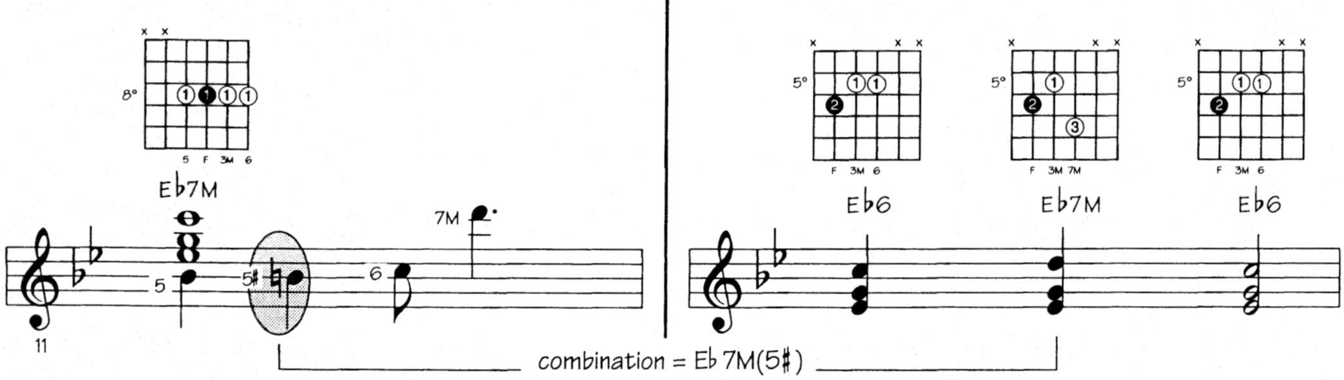

In measure 11, the EbM7(#5) is blocked in, also examine the other harmonic colors combining the basic M7 and 6 notes to make the EbM7(13) chord, M7 and 6 become 13, left between the two guitars. Also in measure 11, except the string bass, observe how to loosen the harmonic tension (created in measure 10): by using a regular rhythmic line, called a "walking bass":

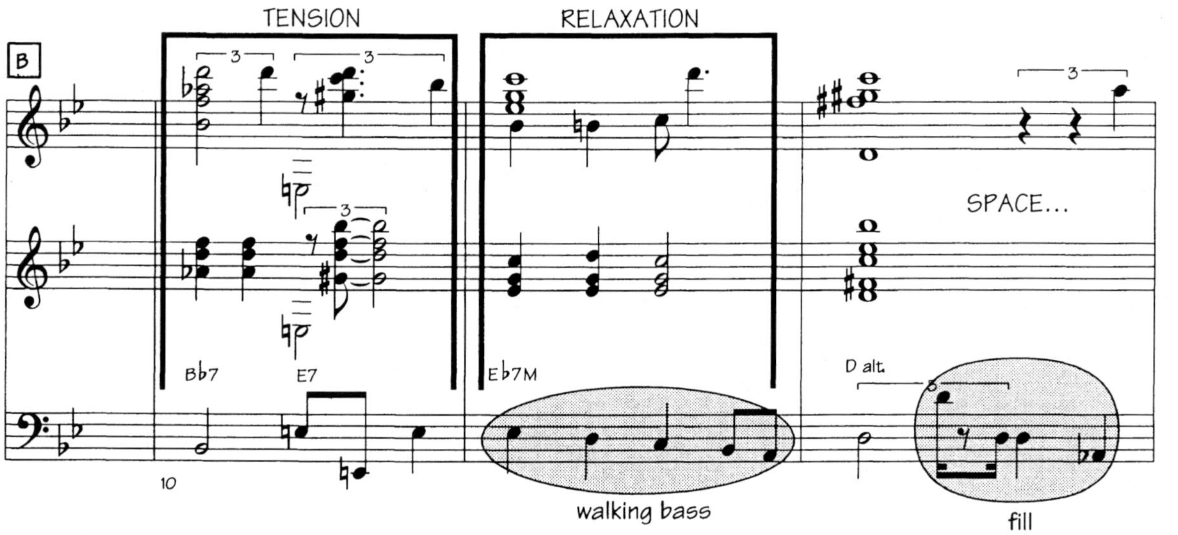

Otherwise, you will notice in the score (chapter 35, pages 5 and 6) that, from a rhythmic point of view, the little dense passages can be tactfully handled in various ways by the exploited guitars, on the other hand, the string bass which profits by "furnishing" the space while doing this. The jazzmen call these "fills". This is the case in measure 12. This being so, this procedure must not become systematic at the risk of loosing all its charm, by imagining a forest deprived of all its light.

In measure 13, we raise two observations:

– in the guitar 2 part, we have an illustration of this current substitution, which consists of replacing a minor chord with a sus4 chord. Compare this with paragraph C above: which uses theG7sus4 in place of Gm7. A substitution which is played by guitar 1 at the same place, producing a global harmonic Gm7(11)sound:

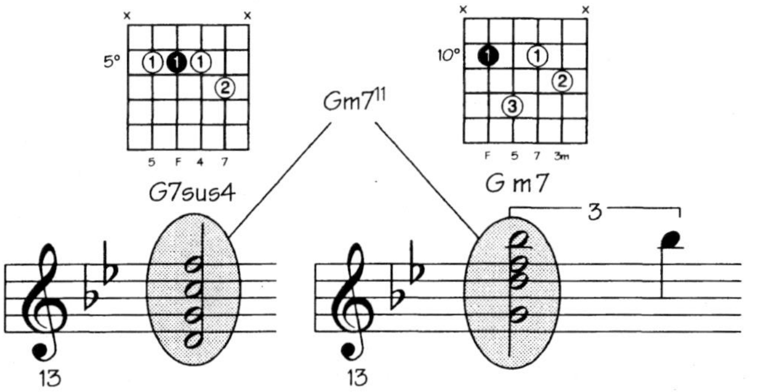

– in the guitar 1 part, the second portion of the measure mentions an "alt." type harmony where all of the melody is not harmonized. Certainly, the case produces other areas of arrangements, but here, the absence of harmonizing is desirable in the measure where it slides among these isolated notes as a tonal ambiguous coloration with a dominant chord: the 11 dominant chord: the 11 (= a perfect quarter), a coloration which must be treated as a passing note:

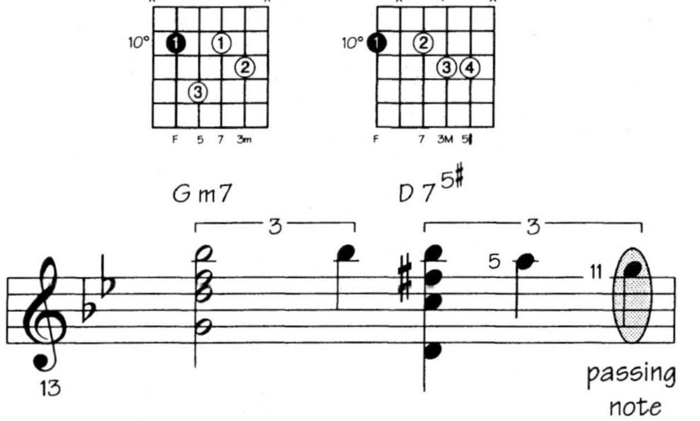

Now, if harmonizing this G note was an absolute necessity, it is not on the basis of the harmonic symbol (D alt.), it would be convenient to do so (tonal ambiguity), but on the basis of the immediate preceding harmony, knowingly the Gm7. The way to formulate it is to use a tonal type V - Im progression, that's to say, and once more: dominant (D alt.) → tonic (Gm). See opposite side:

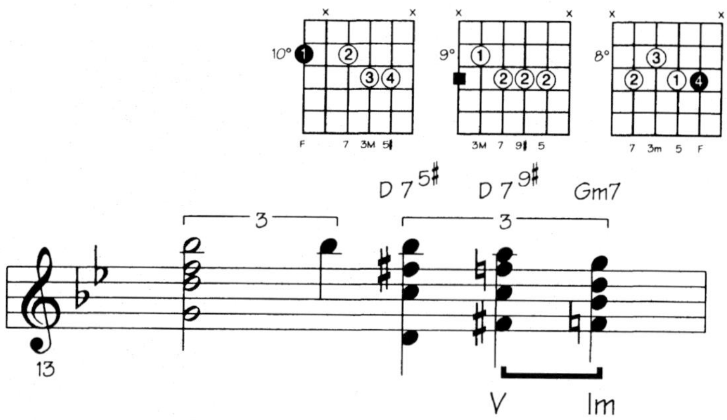

The third section, A', is the same as section A, except for the two last measures. By the way of section A, you will see that measure 8 also presents an ambiguous tonal coloration with the harmony: the second triplet is the 11 (Bb note) in relation to the supporting chord (F7). And of course, this coloration is treated the same way as in the case of measure 13: a passing note, all the more where the rhythmic values are short (triplets).

The second part of measures 7 and 23 (sections A and A') illustrates a direct application of the theory that we approached in chapters 28, 29 and 30, concerning chord inversions. And in this fragment of the arrangement you will recognize some of the Cm7 inversions which you have already studied (chords blocked in). This is done with guitar 1 and guitar 2, and guitar 2 offers a variation of it with three notes only, however, it is done without missing any of the indispensable notes that characterize the harmony:

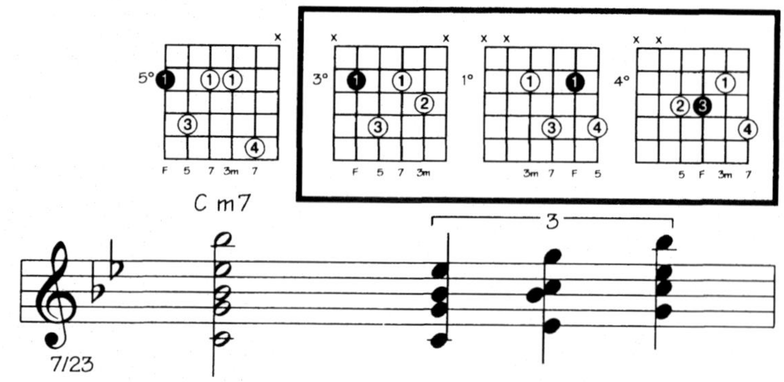

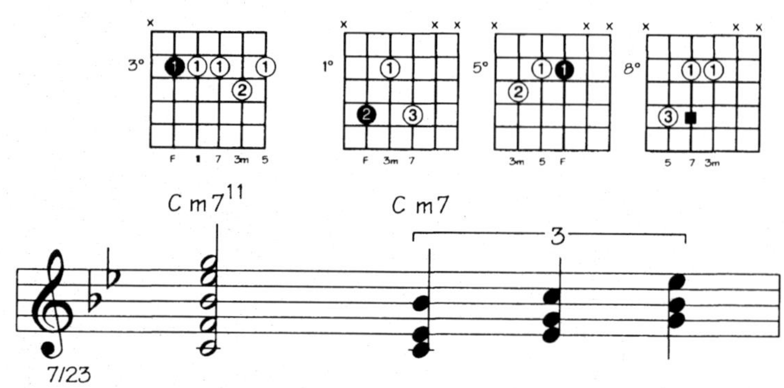

Finally, in measure 24, section A', the first chord has an interesting coloration which is the basic Am7(b5) chord, where the result, between both parts, is Am7(b5, 11):

• My Foolish Heart, guitar 1/c

• My Foolish Heart, guitar 2/c

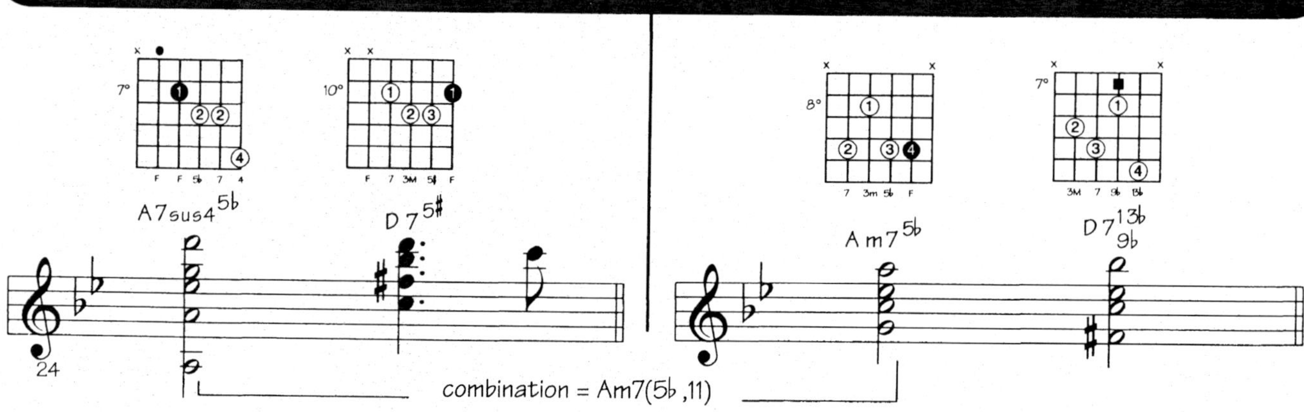

PART C

The four pages included in this chapter give us the continuation of the guitar parts (sections B and A') which we began to study in chapter 33.

#97 MY FOOLISH HEART — guitar 1 / b

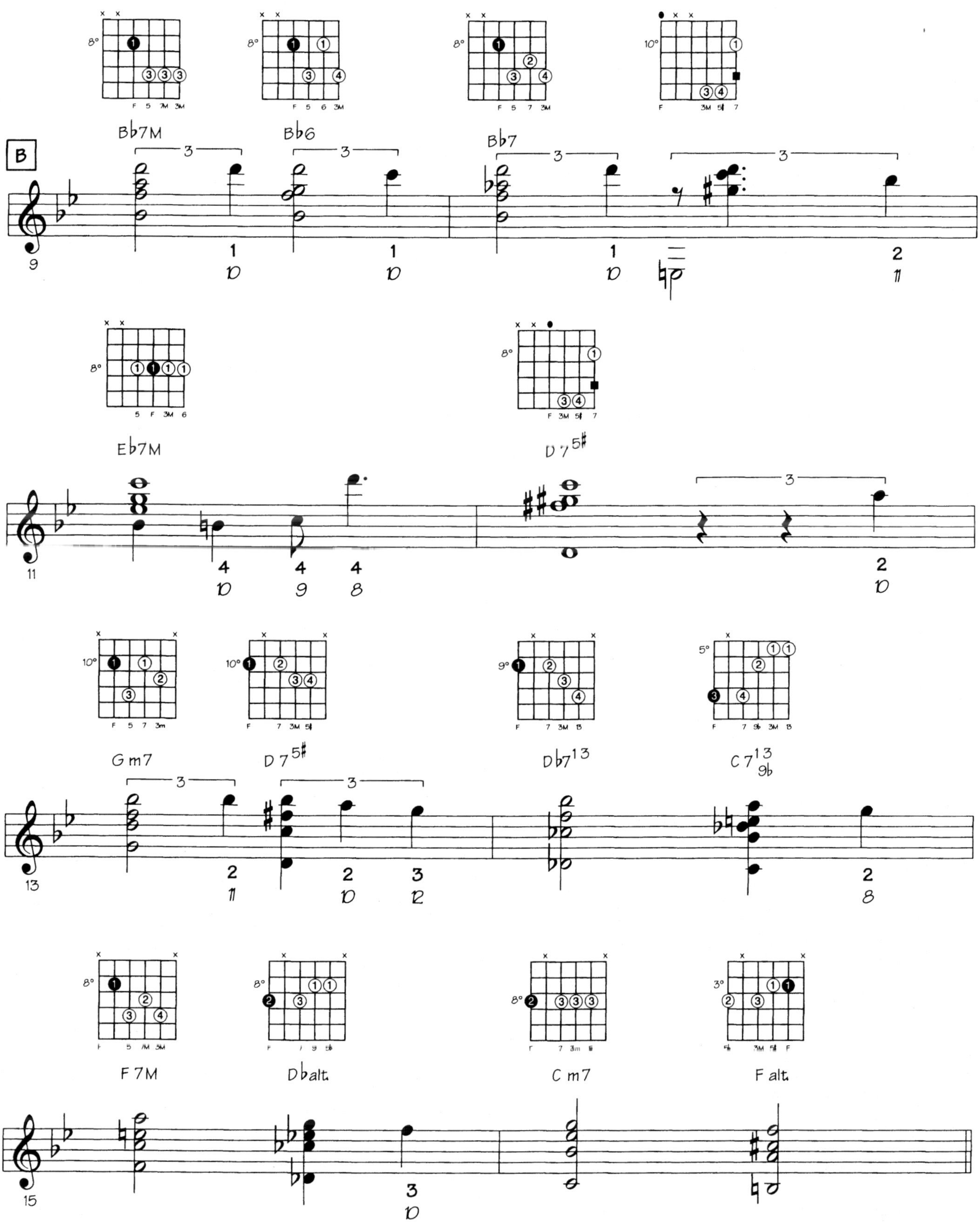

#97

MY FOOLISH HEART — guitar 1 / c

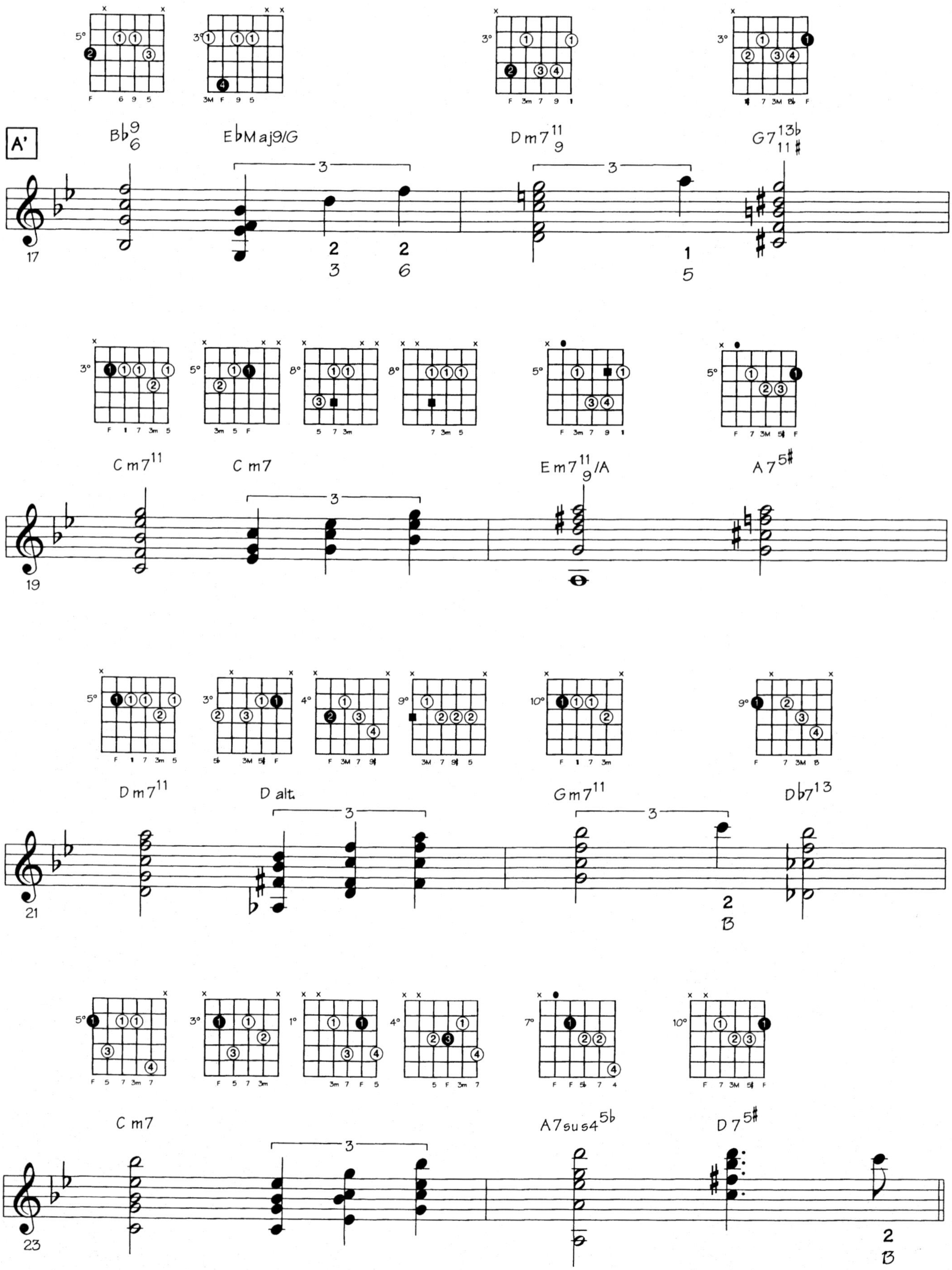

#97

MY FOOLISH HEART — guitar 2 / b

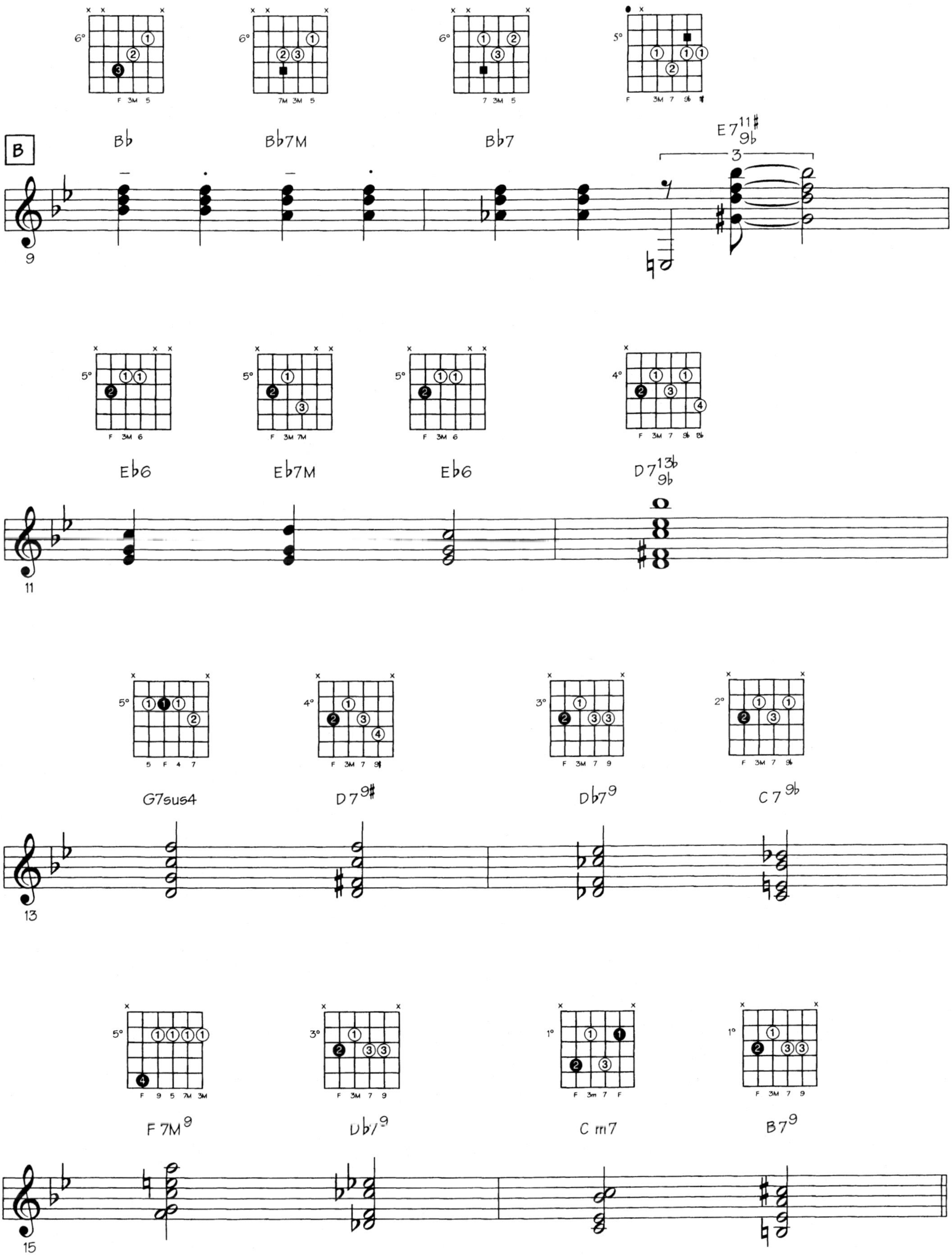

#97

MY FOOLISH HEART — guitar 2 / c

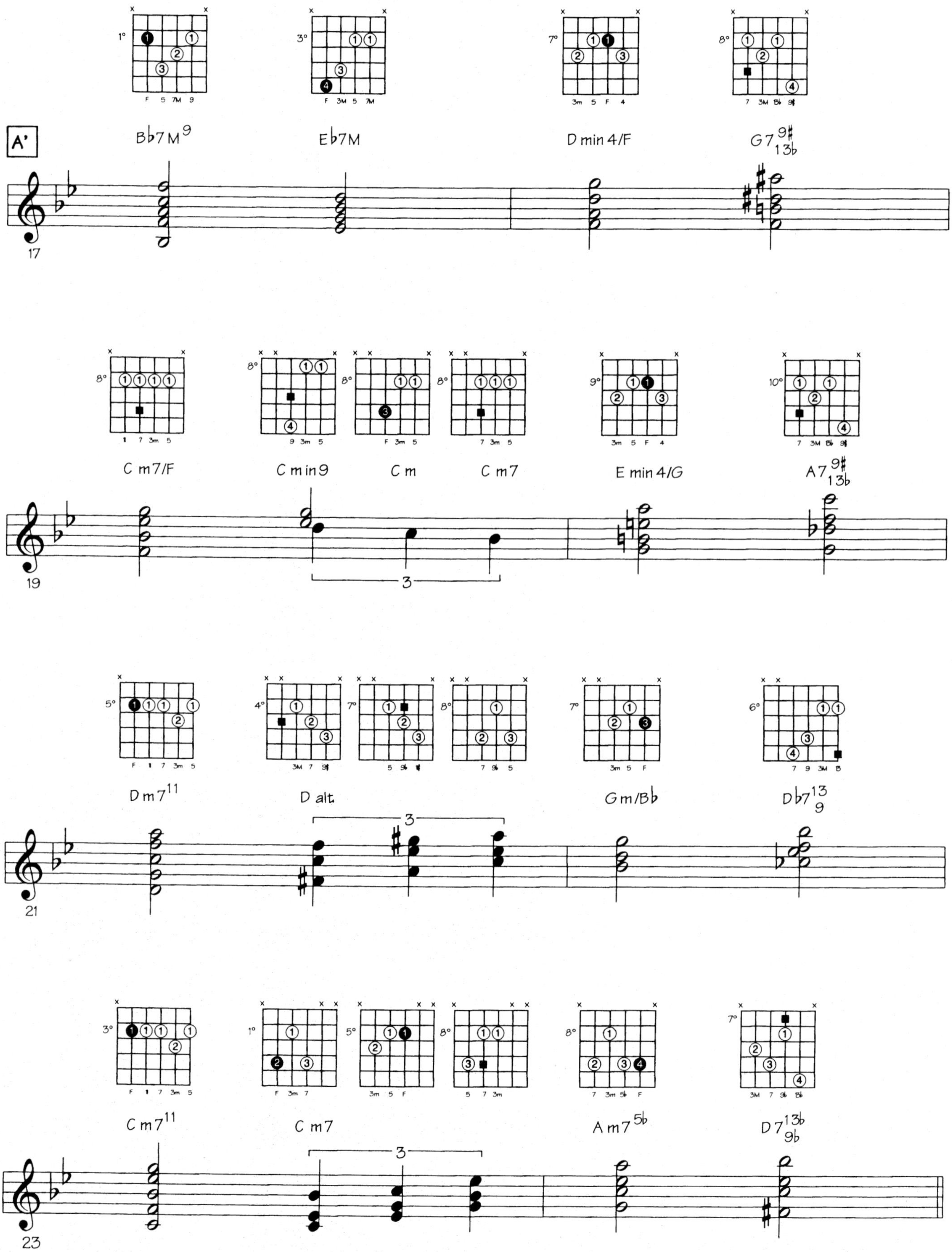

▪ PARTS A & B

In chapter 35, we will finish the guitar 1 part, section C, of "My Foolish Heart".

In measure 25 guitar 1 presents the 11 coloration with a dominant chord. This ambiguous coloration must be treated as a passing note, by following the example of measure 13 (this is exactly the same case of the harmonic illustration for the remainder):

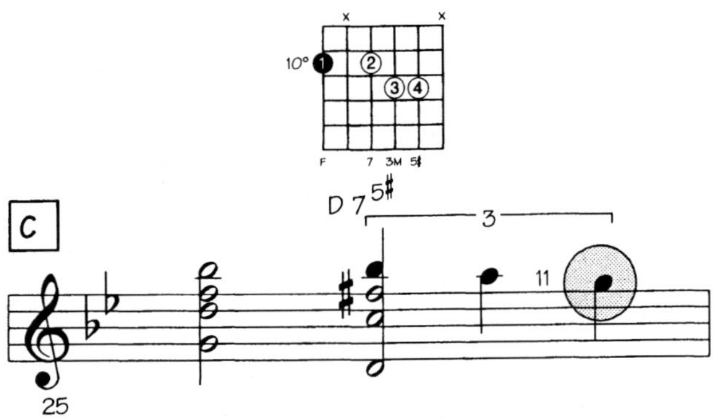

In measure 27, notice the second chord played with guitar 2: it is made up of R - 9 - 5 - M7 and, although it is being deprived of the M3, adds up to be EbM7(9) altogether. Indeed, it can be recognized otherwise, considering the harmonic context in which it is placed: which is the key of Bb major that develops an EbM7 chord with its IV degree. However, you can eventually add the M3 that misses this EbM7(9), the guitar position which makes it easy:

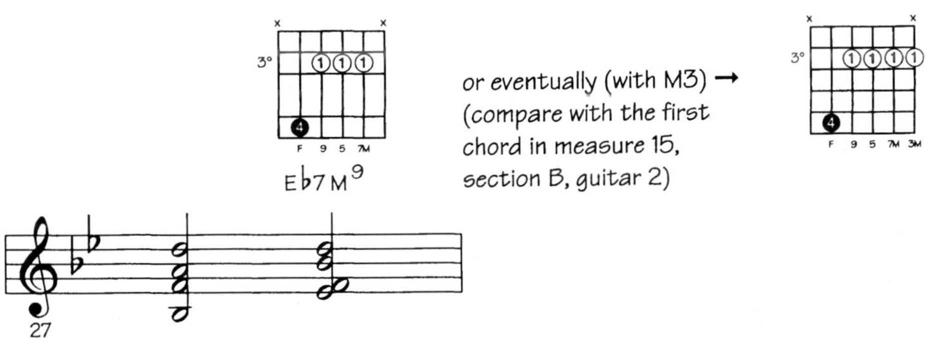

In measure 29, guitar 2, is an analog procedure for the first chord, which is made up of m3 - 5 - R – 4, and indicated by Cmin4, which is given if it doesn't have the 7. But it will not be less than this Cmin4, joining those who play guitar 1, which determines the global harmony of Cm7(11). This "m7" sound is otherwise solidly affirmed in the second part of the measure, where we recover our continuation of the inversions of Cm7, by following the example of measures 7 and 23.

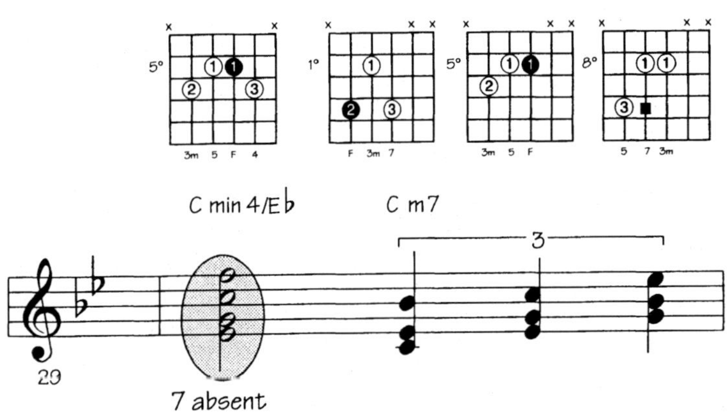

In measure 30 we have slightly modified the melody line in a way to increase the richness of the four dominant chords arranged in descending fifths (or ascending fourths):

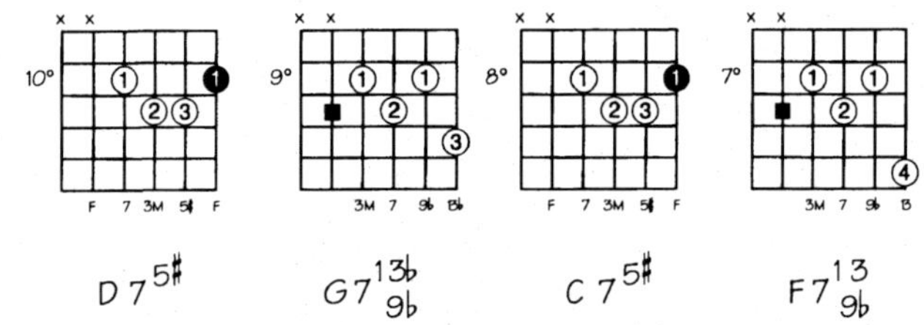

initial line:

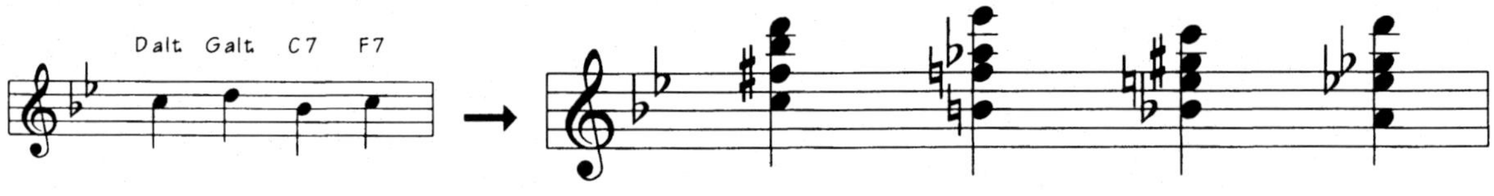

This modification gives us the opportunity to see how guitar music is written one octave higher than it really sounds. In other words, the C notes contained in the two measures above sound exactly with the same pitch, but the measure on the left is written for the guitar, while the one on the right is written for a "concert" (piano part).

Otherwise, notice that the chords of guitar 1 proceed symmetrically with the harmonic colorations: (#9) → (b9, b13) → (#9) → b9, 13). The last chord - F7 - nevertheless, receives a (major) 13 in the measure where it is the V degree of the key. This 13 is indeed the D note, a natural component of the Bb major scale.

Measure 30, is in the key of Bb, its pickup, its ultimate V degree, however, the Bb chord (root note) doesn't appear in measure 31. What are we supposed to do there? It gets worse, the second guitar uses a totally foreign chord, the BM7, and persists afterwards with B6/9. Is this arrangement suddenly derailing?

Not at all! The goal here is to get a harmonic "caesarean", to create a surprise, interest and drive guitar 1 in a better way with a stop –chorus. This "caesarian" is similarly reinforced by the dynamic intervention of the string bass, which starts to double up the relative beat without, losing view, of the initial Bb major key: look at the instance where it uses the F note, which is none other than the dominant before inescapably taking back this key. And finally, it developed here, an always welcome coloration, although modern, for a chord of the major family: the #11, via BM7/F, where the F note is #11.

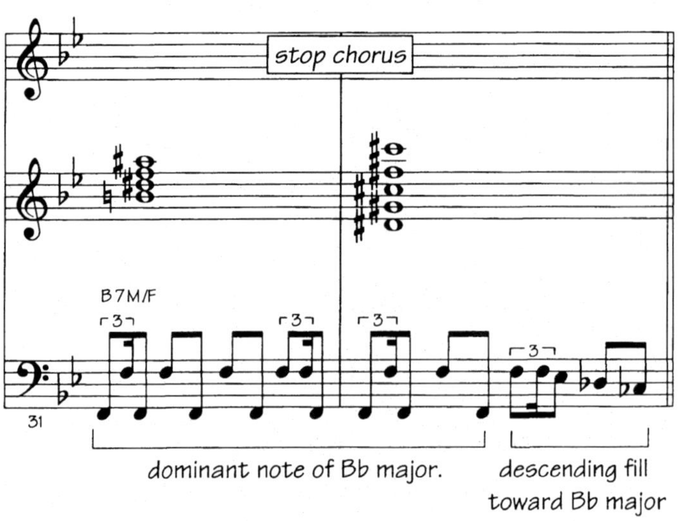

Finally at the repeat in the theme after the choruses, there is a coda that should start with measure 31, at the place of the stop-chorus, which spreads over five measures.

Our explanations with this arrangement finish here. On page 8 of this chapter, you will find a suggestion given to you in the global form to play the complete "My Foolish Heart", and we hope that this festival of harmonics with jazz will fascinate you.

PARTS C

Here is the continuance and the end, including the coda, and guitar parts of "My Foolish Heart".

#97 #98

MY FOOLISH HEART — guitar 1 / d

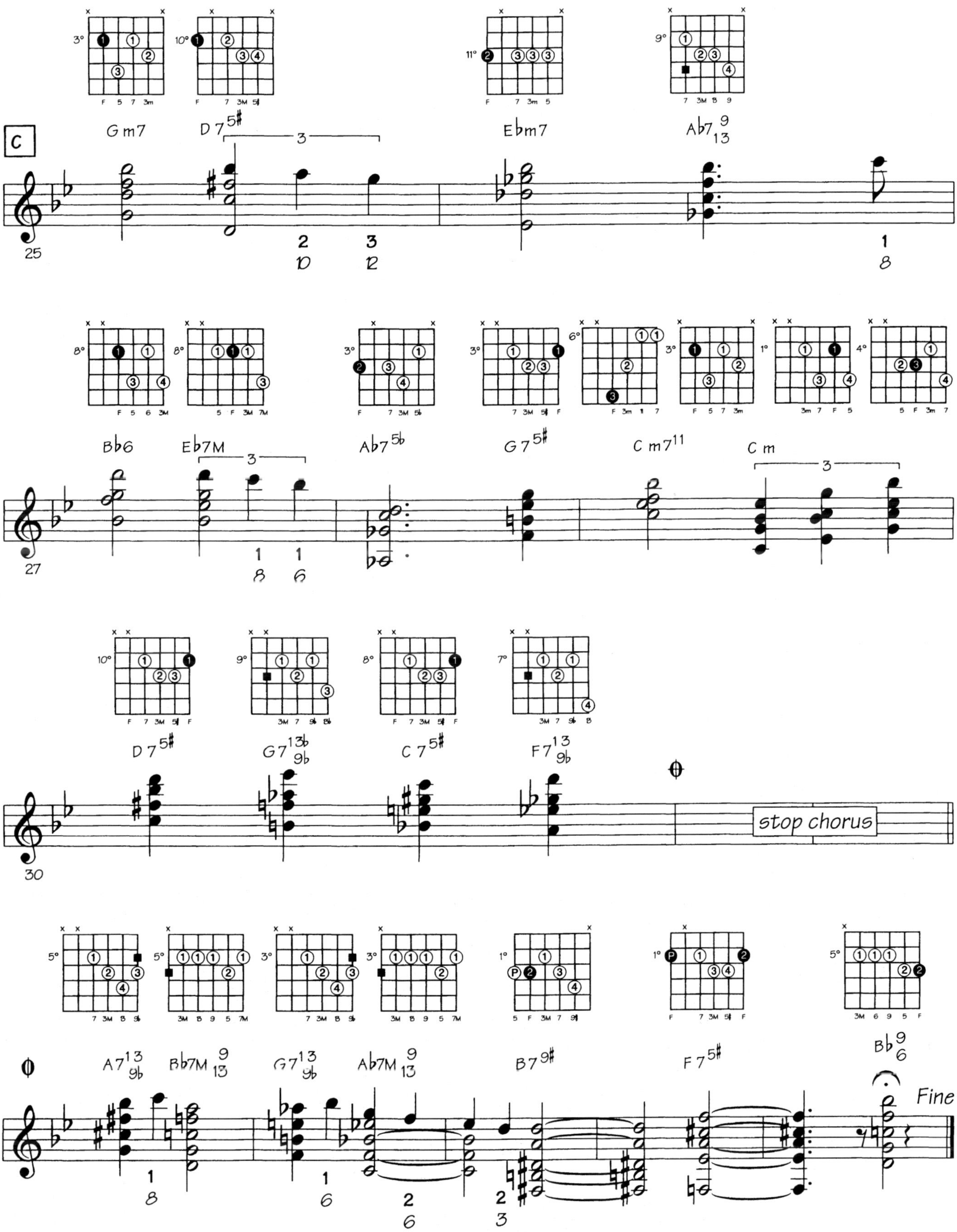

MY FOOLISH HEART — guitar 2 / d

#97 #98

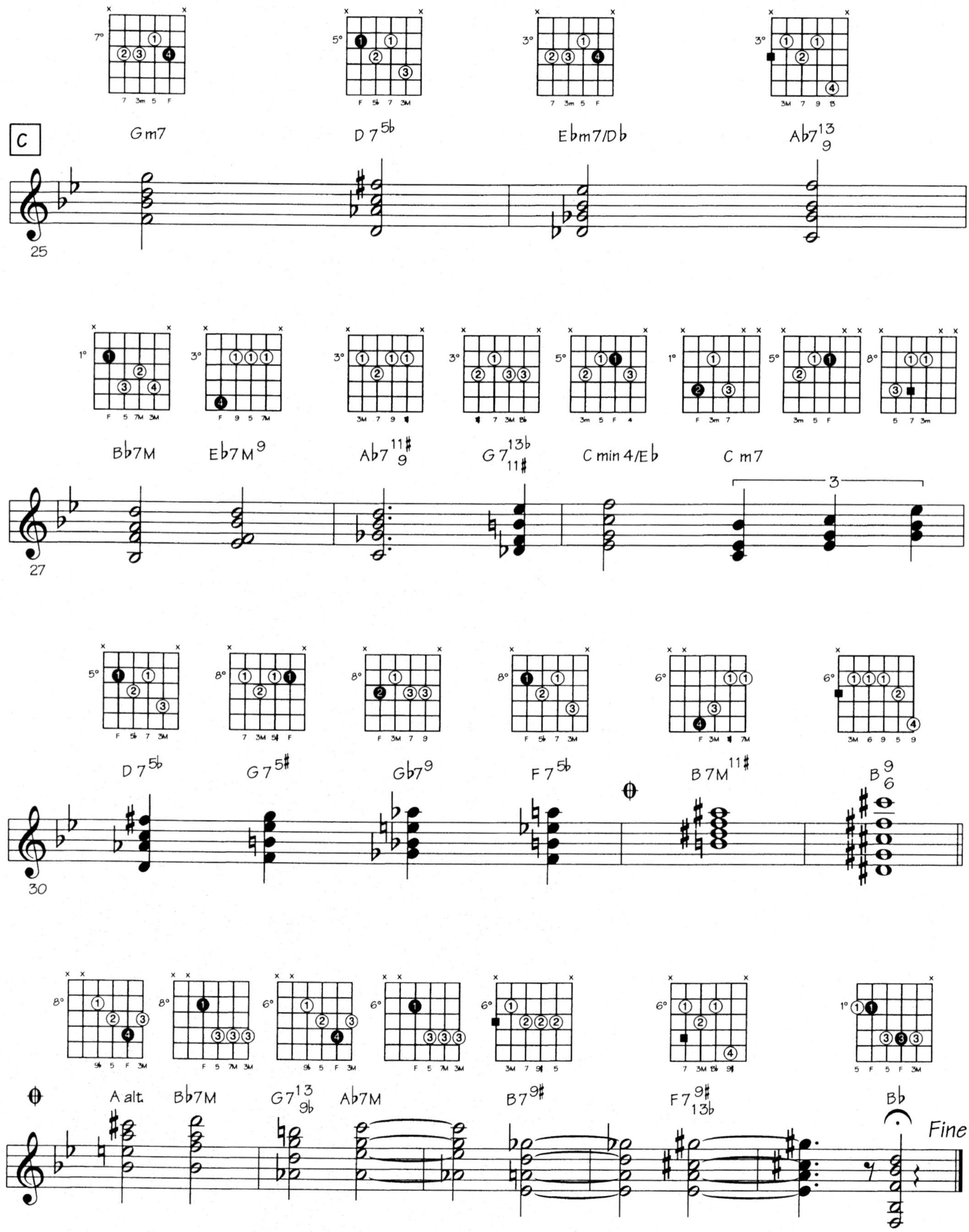

Here is the complete score of "My Foolish Heart". And with regards to the structure of 32 measures ABA'C, watch of the first and second returns.

#97 #98

My Foolish Heart (Victor Young / Ned Washington)

structure : 32 ABA'C

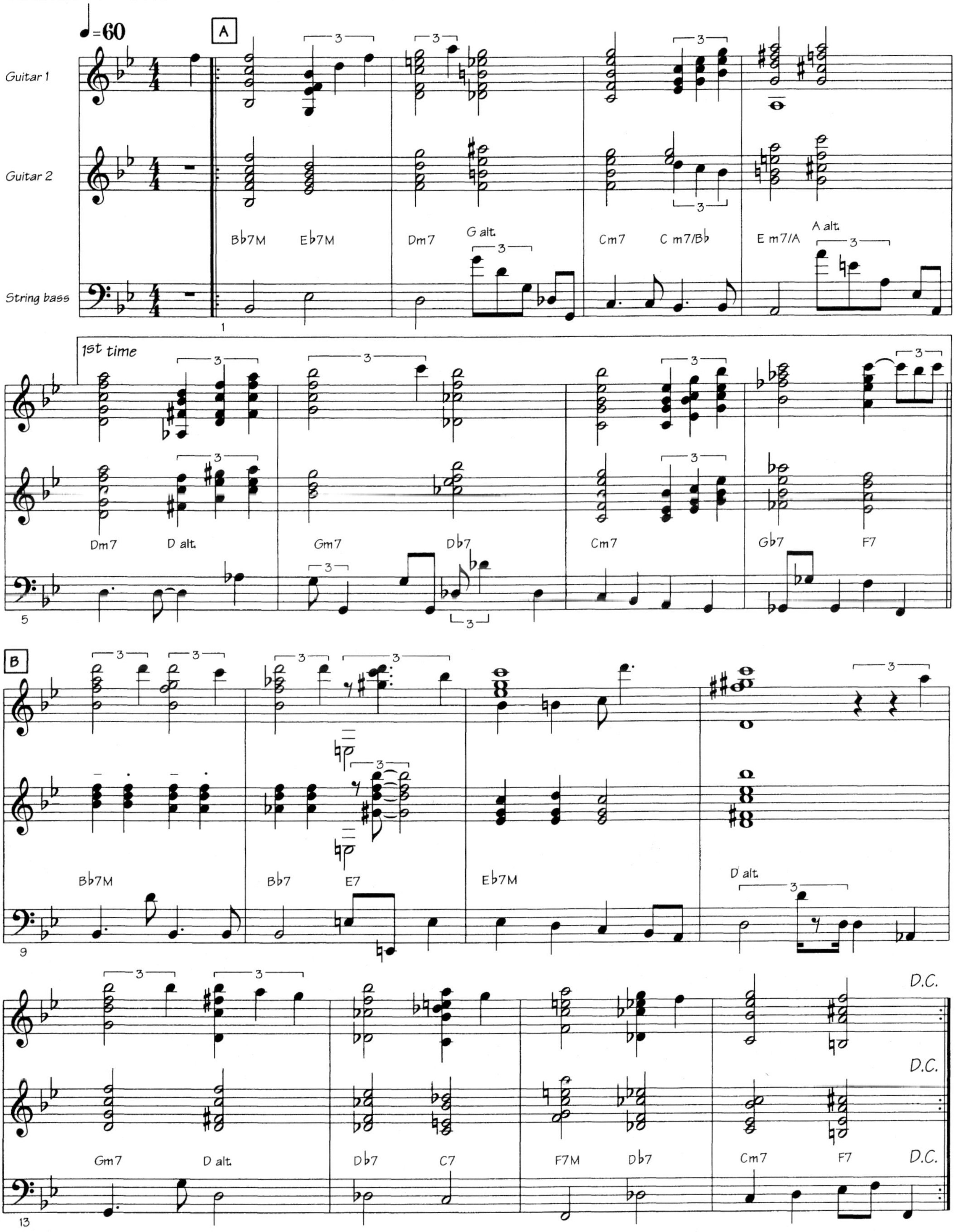

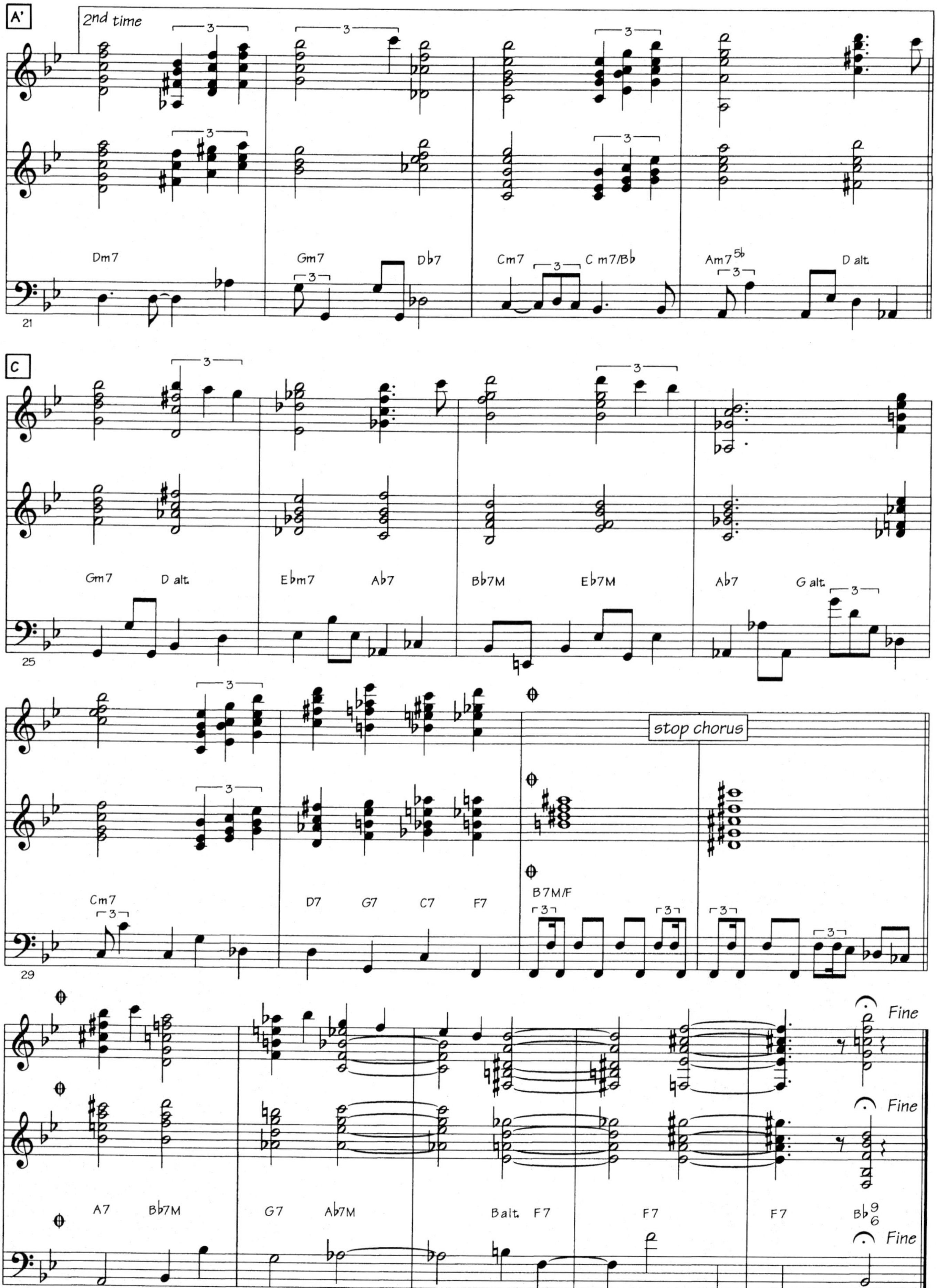
A'
2nd time
Dm7
Gm7
Db7
Cm7
C m7/Bb
Am7 5b
D alt.
21
C
Gm7
D alt.
Ebm7
Ab7
Bb7M
Eb7M
Ab7
G alt.
25
Cm7
D7
G7
C7
F7
B7M/F
stop chorus
29
A7
Bb7M
G7
Ab7M
B alt.
F7
F7
F7
Bb 9 6
Fine
Fine
Fine

Finally, we regroup the two versions of the harmonic feature. Do you remember the 64 measure diagram that relieves much of your thinking during the choruses, as well as for improvising the melody and for the accompaniment, when these are done here at double speed?

My Foolish Heart

Double diagram (→ accompaniment of the theme) — ♩= 60

A	Bb7M / Eb7M	Dm7 / G alt.	Cm7	Em7 / A alt.	Dm7 / D alt.	Gm7 / G alt.	Cm7	Gb7 / F7
B	Bb7M	Bb7	Eb6	Am7^{5b} / D alt.	Gm7 / D alt.	Db7 / C7	F7M / Db7	Cm7 / F7
A'	7 %							Am7^{5b} / D alt.
C	Gm7 / D alt.	Ebm7 / Ab7	Bb7M / Eb7M	Ab7 / G alt.	Cm7	D alt. / G alt. / C7 / F7	Bb7M / G alt.	Cm7 / F7

Double block diagram (→ accompaniment of the choruses) — 𝅗𝅥= 60

A	01 Bb7M	Eb7M	Dm7	G alt.	05 Cm7	%	Em7	A alt.
	09 Dm7	D alt.	Gm7	G alt	13 Cm7	%	Gb7	F7
B	17 Bb7M	%	Bb7	%	21 Eb6	%	Am7^{5b}	D alt.
	25 Gm7	D alt.	Db7	C7	29 F7M	Db7	Cm7	F7
A'	33 8 %				37			
	41 6 %				45		Am7^{5b}	D alt.
C	49 Gm7	D alt.	Ebm7	Ab7	53 Bb7M	Eb7M	Ab7	G alt.
	57 Cm7	%	D alt. / G alt.	C7 / F7	61 Bb7M	G alt.	Cm7	F7

Of two diagrams shown, the one with 32 measures is used to show the make up of the theme, by knowing that the counting should be done in "quarter" notes. The other diagram is enlarged to 64 measures, being intended for those choruses, as it is traditionally and commonly done for ballads, with a very slow beat, the rhythmic stream is doubled, in relative time. This procedure is very dynamic for the general "groove" of the piece, in the part of the choruses. It seems to give the impression that the harmonies suddenly last two times longer. But in reality, it's not so:

The diagram of 64 measures lasts exactly as long (time wise) as the diagram with 32 measures. Technically, as you can see by looking at the last two measure of the string-bass part, the quarter notes in the initial count (normal tempo, theme) are considered as eighths in the larger diagram (choruses, double tempo).

To finish up, here are some suggestions given in a form to develop in its entirety the melody of "My Foolish Heart":

– exposure of the theme with 30 measures ABA'C,
– two measures of stop chorus for guitar 1 (measures 31 - 32, section C),
– chorus for guitar 1 with 64 measures (larger diagram) ABA'C,
– chorus for guitar 2 with 64 measures ABA'C.
  - GT1 → measures 1 – 4 (section A),
  - GT2 → measures 5 – 8 (section A),
  - GT1 → measures 9 – 12 (section A),
  - GT2 → measures 13 – 16 (section A),
  - GT1 → measures 17 – 20 (section B),
  - GT2 → measures 21 – 24 (section B),
  - GT1 → mesures 25 - 28 (section B),
  - GT2 → measures 29 -32 (section B - pay

– attention to measures 31 - 32, the tempo must start at single speed = back to the initial tempo).

THE ARRIVAL

Well now, some more pages, and we have come to the end of our voyage, which you should have wanted 8 to 18 months ago.

Chapter 36, has a comprehensive test, which covers all the information that has been given to you. It also gives you the opportunity to test your knowledge that you have acquired. Good luck, you will find all the correct answers at the end of the book.

There you have it. We expect that this adventure in the Manouche style jazz guitar has given you the best of the various aspects, which let you discover new musical areas and let you progress with your art, and that it has motivated you personally as a musician.

Thank you for your attention you have given us with the music!

Romane Derek Sébastian

COMPREHENSIVE TEST OF KNOWLEDGE

This test has 50 questions. Each question is worth 8 points. The entire test is worth 400 points. The multiple choice (MC) questions only have one right answer. There is only one right answer for each question.

If you can get at least 280 point you are doing very well and are on your way. Be sure to concentrate.

THEORY AND GENERAL KNOWLEDGE

Question 1 worth 8 points

A pickup never lasts more than 1 measure.

❑ true ❑ false

Question 2 worth 8 points

The "𝄎" symbol is a variation of the "𝄍" symbol, and is used the same way.

❑ true ❑ false

Question 3 worth 8 points

The notes that form the order of flats in the key signature are separated with intervals of:

❑ an octave ❑ ascending fifths ❑ ascending fourth

Question 4 worth 8 points

A natural minor scale is a major scale that starts from its fifth note.

❑ true ❑ false

Questions 5 worth 8 points

An ambitus is:

❑ the ability to coordinate the two hands while practicing the guitar.

❑ the ambiguity between two notes of the same pitch but with distinct names.

❑ The total distance in intervals between the lowest and highest note of a melody, or part of a melody.

Question 6 worth 8 points

The melodic "A.L.T" (A Limited Transposition) scale with the following intervals 2M - 2m - 2M - 2m - 2M - 2m - 2M - 2m is called:

❑ diminished scale ❑ an augmented scale ❑ a whole tone scale ❑ a half-diminished scale.

Question 7 worth 2x4 points

a) The chord that has the following notes, from low to high: G - E - B - D is in the position of:

❑ closed ❑ drop 2 ❑ drop 3

b) The chord that has the following notes, from low to high: F - A - C - E is in the position of:

❑ closed ❑ drop 2 ❑ drop 3

Question 8 worth 8 points

A chord with any 4 distinct notes composed with intervals of perfect fourths belongs exclusively to the category of inversions:

❏ closed ❏ drop 2

❏ drop 3 ❏ drop 2/4

Question 9 worth 2x4 points

a) As long as we are looking at the melodic concept, at what period in the music history did the diminshed (and/or half-diminished) scale first appear?

b) During what decade of the XXth century did "hard-bebop" first appear in jazz?

HARMONY

Question 10 worth 2x4 points

a) A "7/9" chord has a root note - M9 - M3 - 7.

❏ true ❏ false

b) A "7M13" chord has a Root note - M3 - 5 - M13 - 7.

❏ true ❏ false

Question 11 worth 8 points

The harmonic "C alt." symbol is the same as the global "C7(b9, 13)".

❏ true ❏ false

Question 12 worth 8 points

The harmonic "E+7" symbol is the same as the "EmM7".

❏ true ❏ false

Question 13 worth 2x4 points

Are these harmonic symbols likely coherent?

a) CM7(b9, #9) ❏ yes ❏ no

b) C7sus4(9) ❏ yes ❏ no

Question 14 worth 2x4 points

a) The "B7" chord is the V degree of which major key?

b) The "Cm7" chord is the III degree of which major key?

Question 15 worth 2x4 points

a) The "A7M" chord has the diatonic "F#m7" chord as a substitute.

❏ true ❏ false

b) The "Em7(b5)" chord has the diatonic "Bb7" chord as a substitute.

❏ true ❏ false

Question 16 worth 2x4 points

a) What is the tritone substituition of the "Bb7" chord?

b) What is the tritone substitution of the "Cb7" chord?

Question 17 worth 8 points

What are the II - V - I chords in the key of Bb major?

Question 18 worth 8 points

What are the II -V -I chords in the key of D minor?

Question 19 worth 8 points

The [Am7 -Ab7 -GM7 -CM7 - F#m7(b5) - B alt.] ⁒ harmonic progression is in the key of:

❑ A minor ❑ F# minor ❑ C major ❑ G major

Question 20 worth 8 points

In the [Bbm7 - A7 - G#m7(b5) - C#alt. - F#m7] ⁒ harmonic progression, the A7 chord responds to:

❑ the dominant (A7) → tonic principle ❑ the tritone substitution principle

❑ the diatonic progression principle ❑ any of these three principles

Question 21 worth 8 points

All the dominant chords can be used to introduce a major chord with its root note located one tone higher.

❑ true ❑ false

Question 22 worth 8 points

To introduce the "Gm7" chord in a harmonic structure, it is possible to use the following chord:

❑ A7 ❑ B7 ❑ D7 ❑ E7

Question 23 worth 8 points

To introduce the "Am7" chord in a harmonic structure, it is possible to use the following chord:

❑ C7 ❑ Eb7 ❑ Bb7 ❑ B7

Question 24 worth 4x2 points

Which chords make up the harmonic "anatole/turnaround" progression of the following keys:

a) G major ?

b) Bb major ?

c) D major ?

d) Eb major ?

Question 25 worth 8 points

The "D alt." symbol is the same as the "D7(b9, 11)" symbol.

❑ true ❑ false

Question 26 worth 8 points

Show, in the initial closed order, the notes that make up the "GM7(#11, 13)" chord:

Question 27 worth 8 points

The "AbM7(9, #11)" symbol determines a chord with the following character:

❐ tonal ❐ poly tonal

❐ A tonal ❐ tonally ambiguous

Question 28 worth 8 points

a) The harmonic equivalence of "Ebdim7 = F7(b9)" without a root note is:

❐ accurate ❐ not accurate

b) The harmonic equivalence A7(#9, 13) without a root note or without a fifth = Eb7(#9, 13) without a root note or without a fifth is:

❐ accurate ❐ not accurate

Question 29 worth 2x4 points

a) Which chord is designated as the IV degree of the minor melodic F scale?

b) Which chord is designated as the V degree of the minor harmonic G scale?

Question 30 worth 8 points

Harmonized in four voices, the whole tone scale exclusively generates dominant seventh chords.

❐ true ❐ false

Question 31 worth 2x4 points

a) The harmonic equivalency of "Cm6 = Ab7(9)" without a root note is:

❐ accurate ❐ not accurate

b) the harmonic equivalency of "G7(#9)" without fifth "= Db7(#11, 13)"" without a root note or fifth is:

❐ accurate ❐ not accurate

Question 32 worth 8 points

Of the following two types of harmonic progressions, which is called a "be-bop turnaround"?

❐ || DM7 - F7 | Em7 - A7 || ❐ || AM7 - C7 | FM7 - Bb7 ||

Question 33 worth 2x4 points

Do the following group of notes specify a "christophe" harmonic progression?

a) || EbM7 - Eb7 - AbM7 – Ab7 - EbM7 | ./. || ❐ yes ❐ no

b) || AM7 - A7 - DM7 - Ebdim7 - AM7 | ./. || ❐ yes ❐ no

IMPROVISATION

Question 34 worth 8 points

To improvise with the "G7 chord", it is possible to use the "Bdim7" arpeggio.

❐ correct ❐ incorrect

Question 35 worth 8 points

Is it possible with the "Eb7" chord to base its improvisation on the "Am7" chord?

❐ correct ❐ incorrect

Question 36 worth 8 points

To improvise with the "F7" chord, you could use the F major arpeggio combined with the C# major.

❒ correct ❒ incorrect

Question 37 worth 8 points

The whole "dim7" chord can be put in a relationship with a "7(b9)" type of which the root note is located one minor third lower.

❒ true ❒ false

WRITING

Question 38 worth 4x2 points

With the correct key signature, write one octave of the following scales:

E major

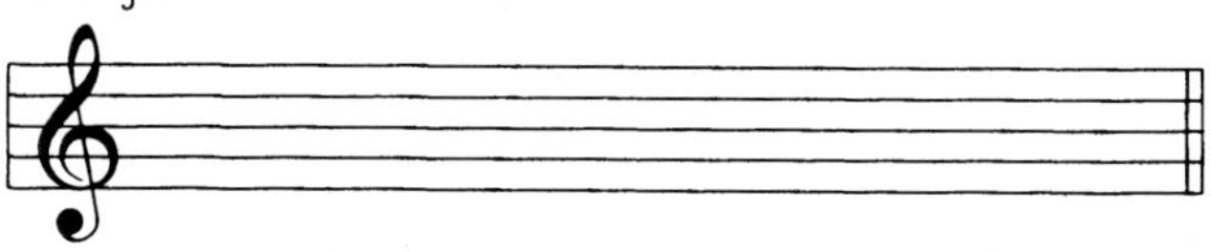

Ab major

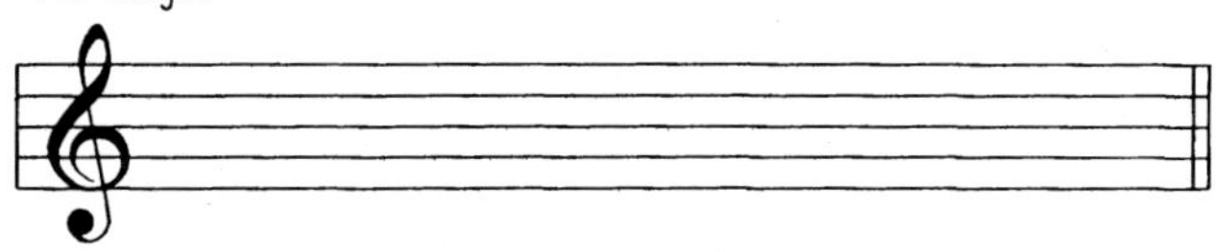

F# major

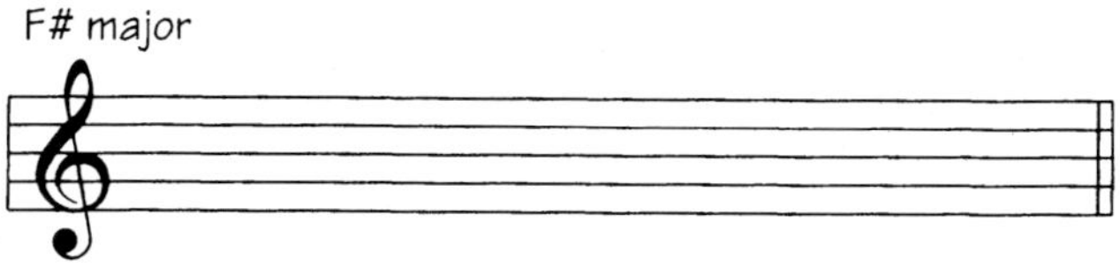

Gb major

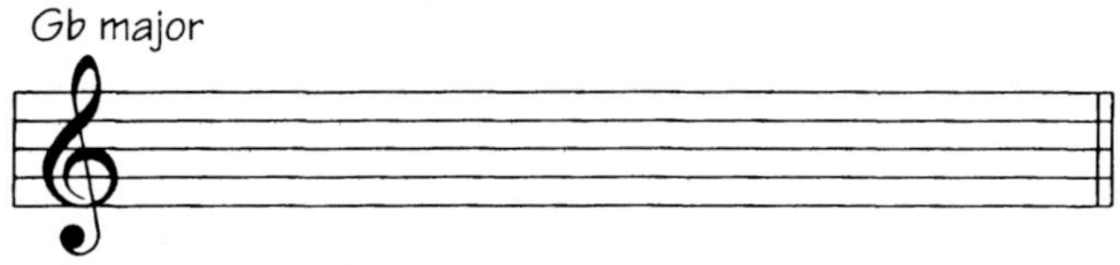

Question 39 worth 4x2 points

With the correct key signature, write one octave of the following scales:

natural minor D

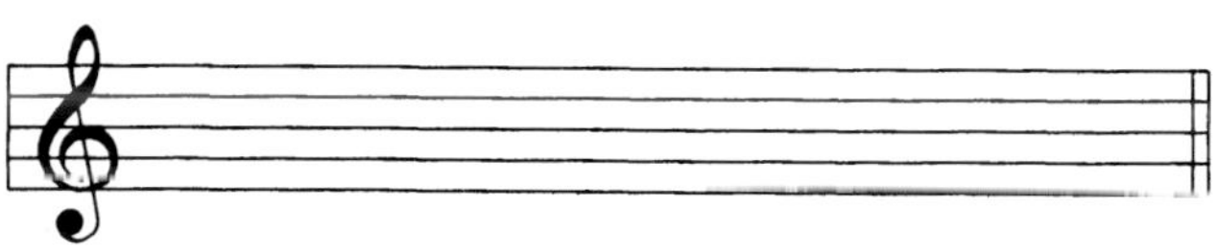

natural minor Eb

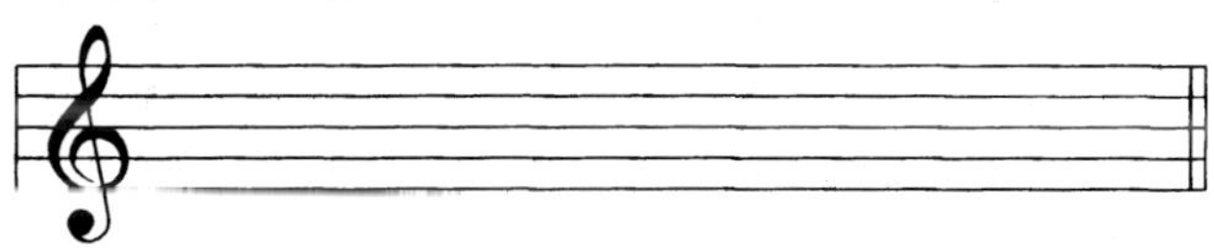

natural minor F#

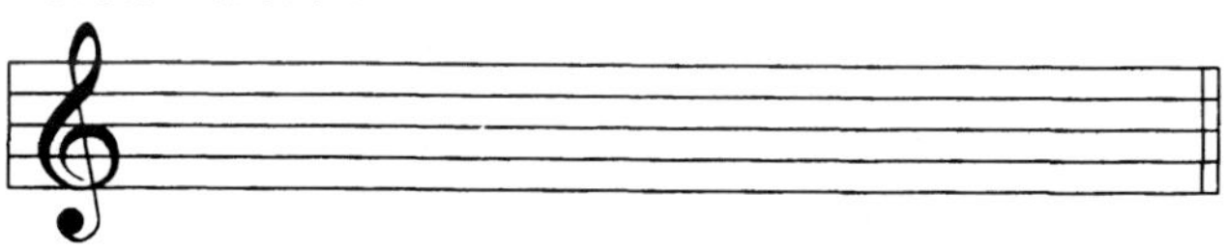

natural minor B

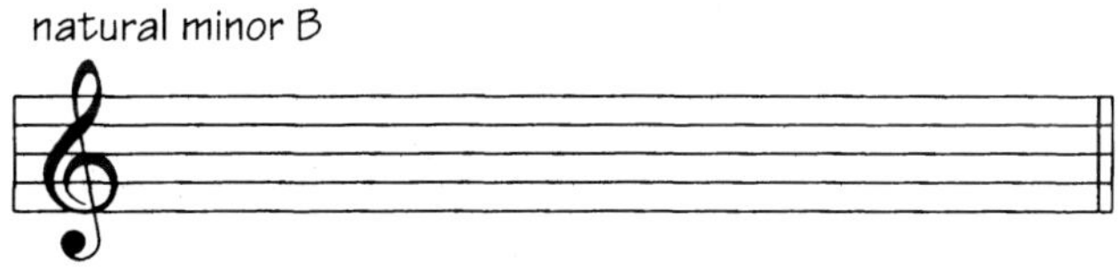

Question 40 worth 4x2 points

Write one octave of the following scales:

harmonic minor D

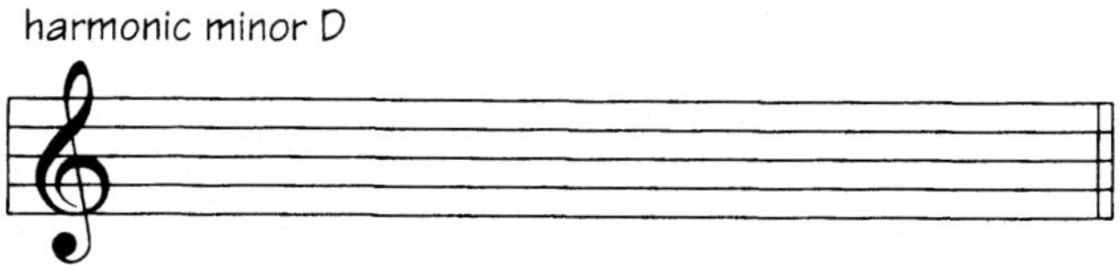

harmonic minor G

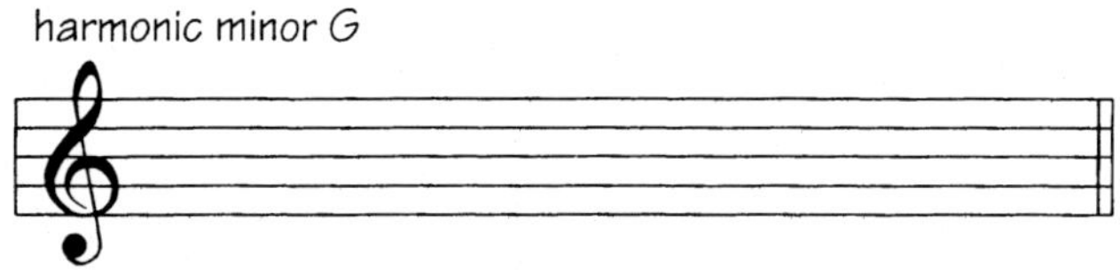

harmonic minor F#

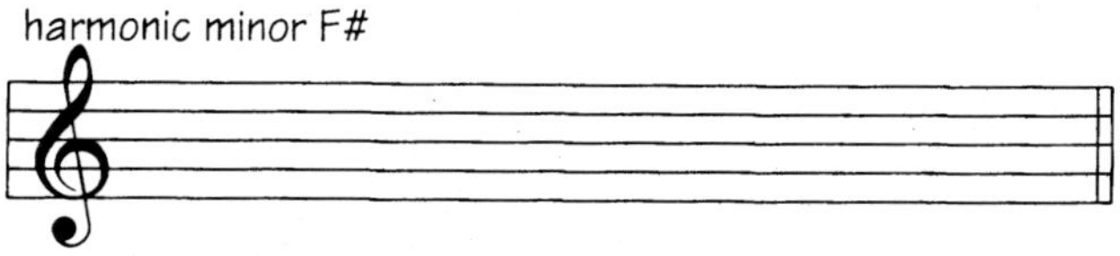

harmonic minor E

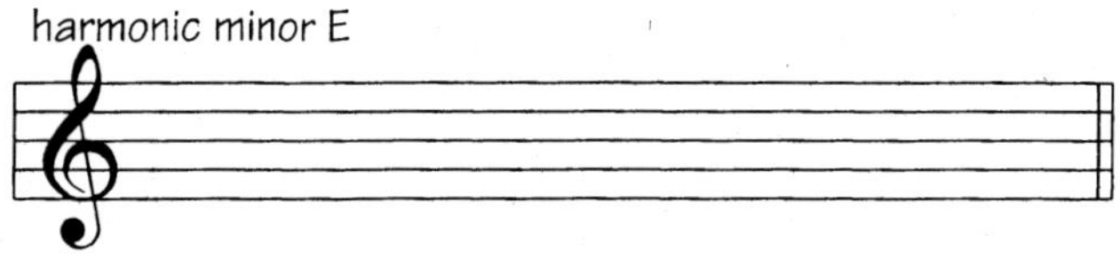

Question 41 worth 4x2 points

Write one octave of the following scales:

melodic minor Bb

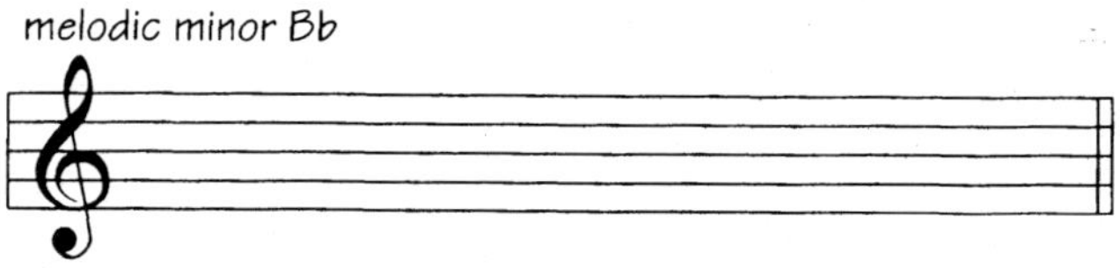

melodic minor G

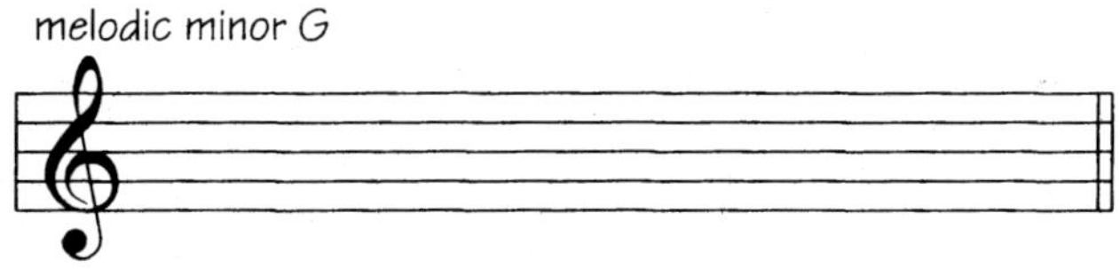

Question 41 continued

D# altered

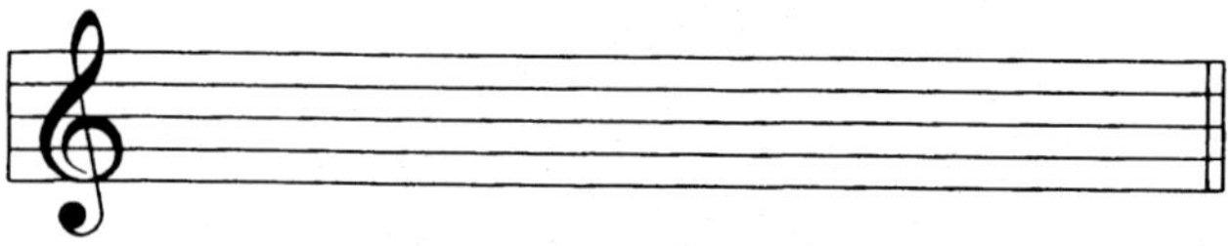

E altered

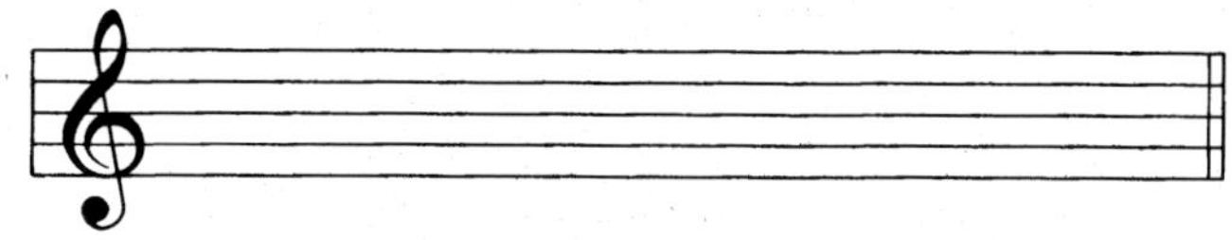

Question 42

worth 4x2 points

Write one octave of the following scales:

Whole tone F

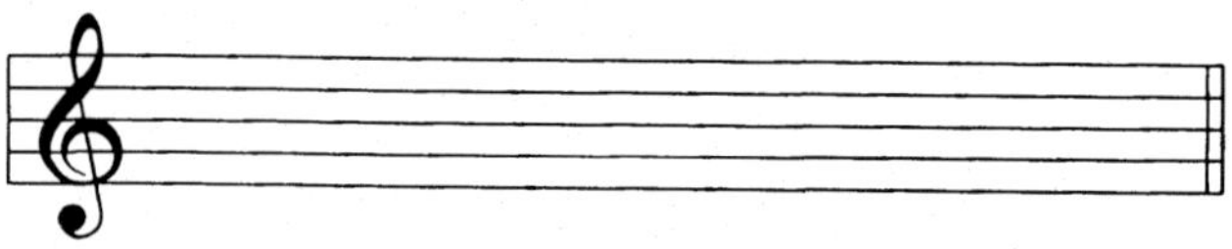

whole tone Bb

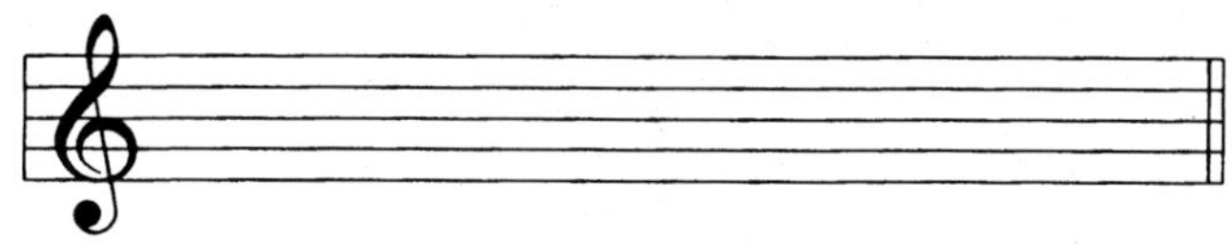

A diminished

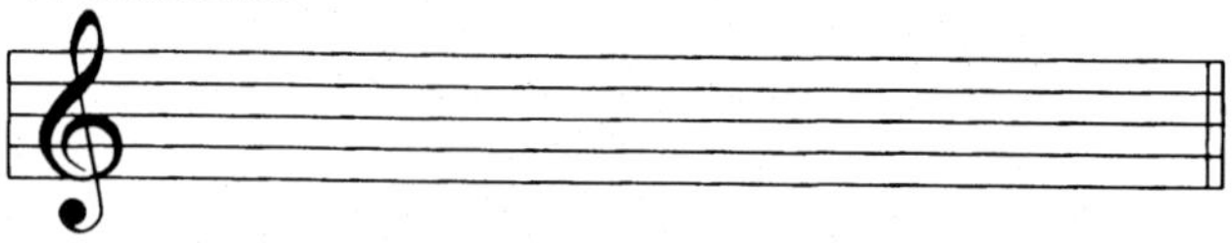

D half – diminished

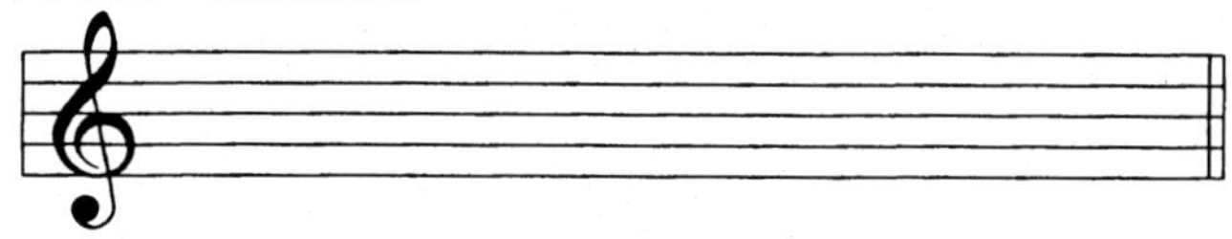

Question 43

worth 8 points

These four measures are composed by a pianist. On the blank staff, transcribe it for the guitar.

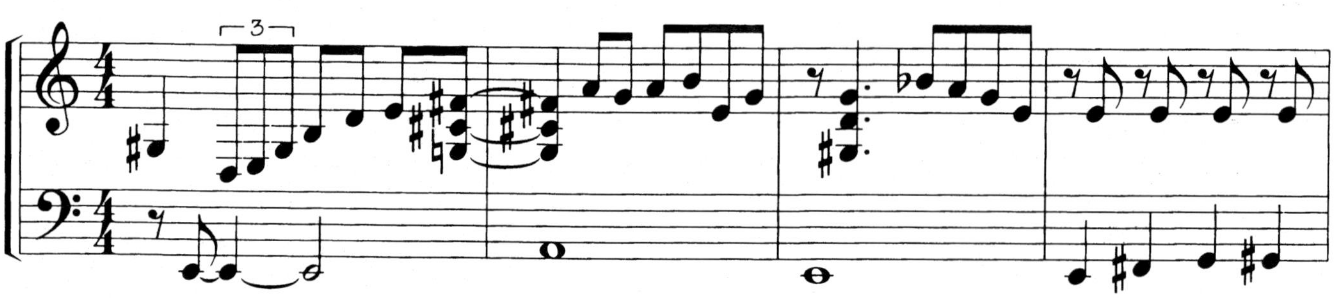

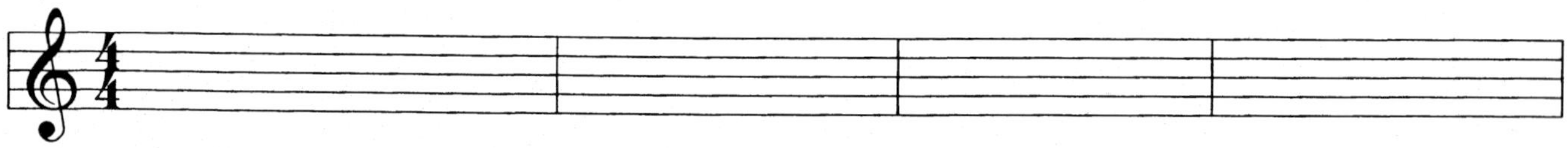

Question 44

worth 8 points

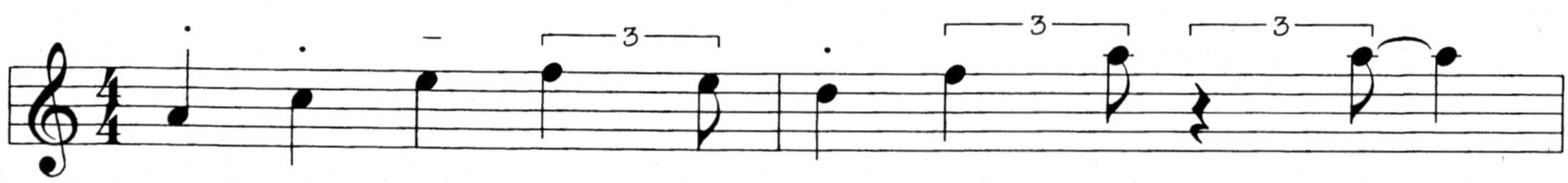

Rewrite the little fragment of the melody above, in the way that a jazzman is accustomed to read it (binary writing).

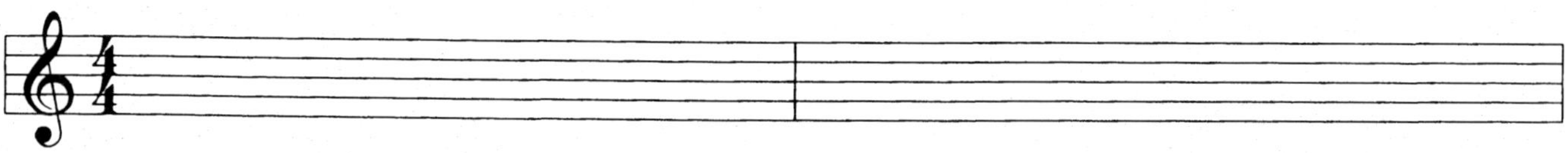

Question 45

worth 8 points

Determine the chords (with basic symbols) that correspond with this improvised phrase:

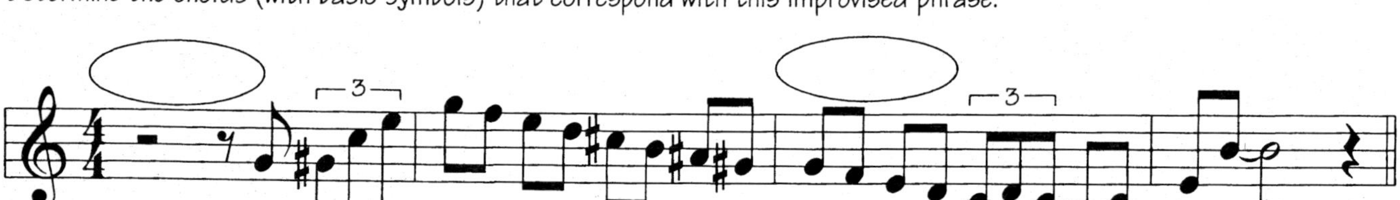

Question 46 worth 8x1 point

With the root note on the bass, write out the following chords:

F7 | Bm7$^{5\flat}$ | Am7^{11} | D♭6

G$^{9}_{6}$ | F dim7 | B♭7$^{5\sharp}$ | D7$^{13\flat}_{9\sharp}$

Question 47 worth 2x4 points

Construct all the inversions of the "Em7(b5)" chord:

Closed position | Drop 2 position

Question 48 worth 4x2 points

Write the arpeggios of the folowing chords:

Fm7 | Am7M

G7 | D dim7

Question 49 worth 8 points

Harmonize with four voices the F#dim7 arpeggio (write the three missing voices underneath voice 1):

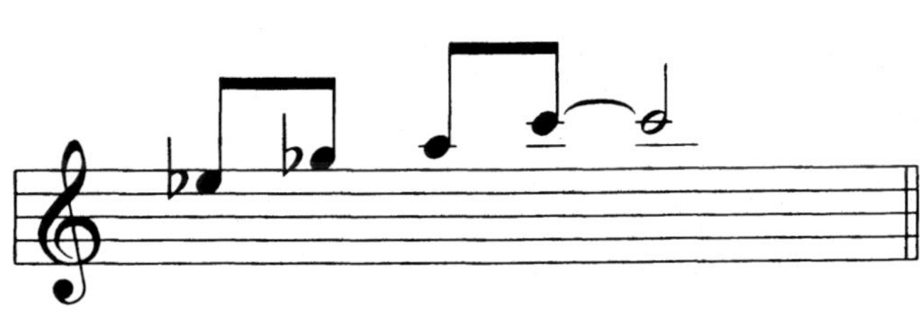

Question 50 worth 8 points

In the three blank measures, write a fourth voice underneath the first three, while using a principle used to harmonize the first fragment of this fourth voice (the measure with the pickup):

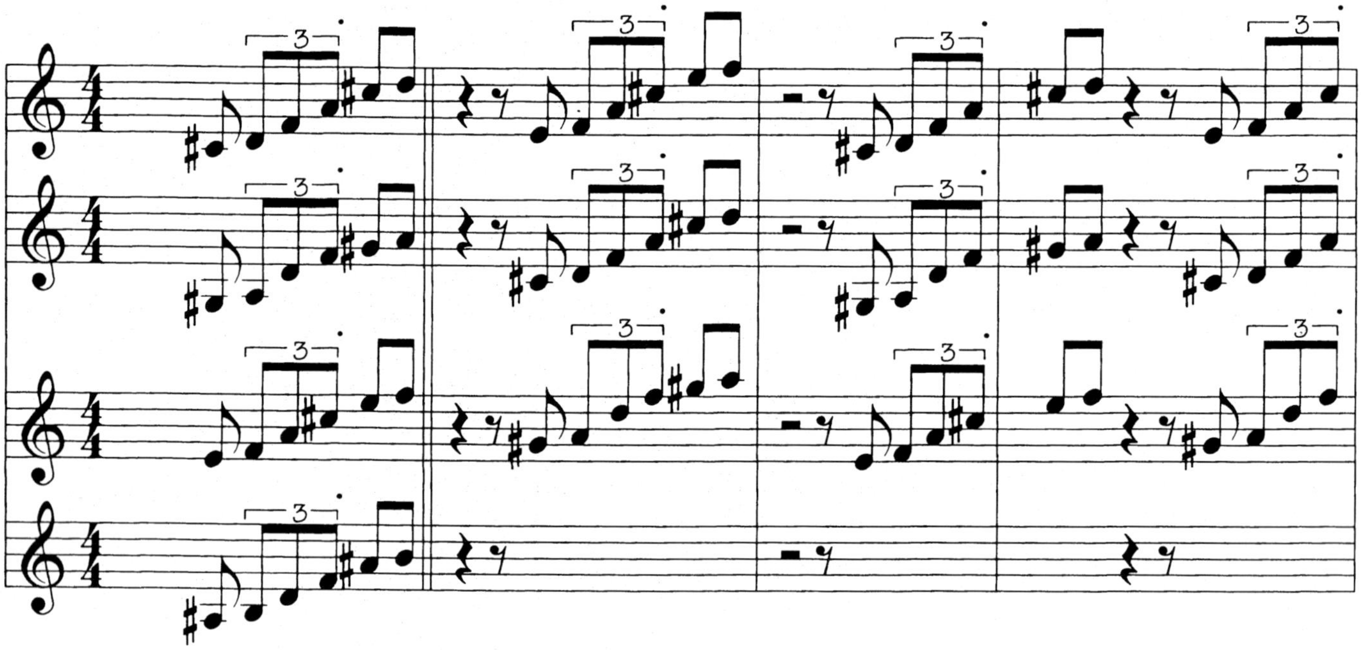

TOTAL POINTS:

.... / 400

SCORES

We have regrouped all the music scores presented in L'Esprit Manouche (the style of Manouche). Use this together with the recordings, however, if it is not available on the MIDI files, you can practice by FOLLOWING THE WRITTEN MUSIC while LISTENING TO IT. This will substantially increase your general understanding of jazz music, and particularly the Manouche style.

#5

Swing For Ninine

— music by ROMANE

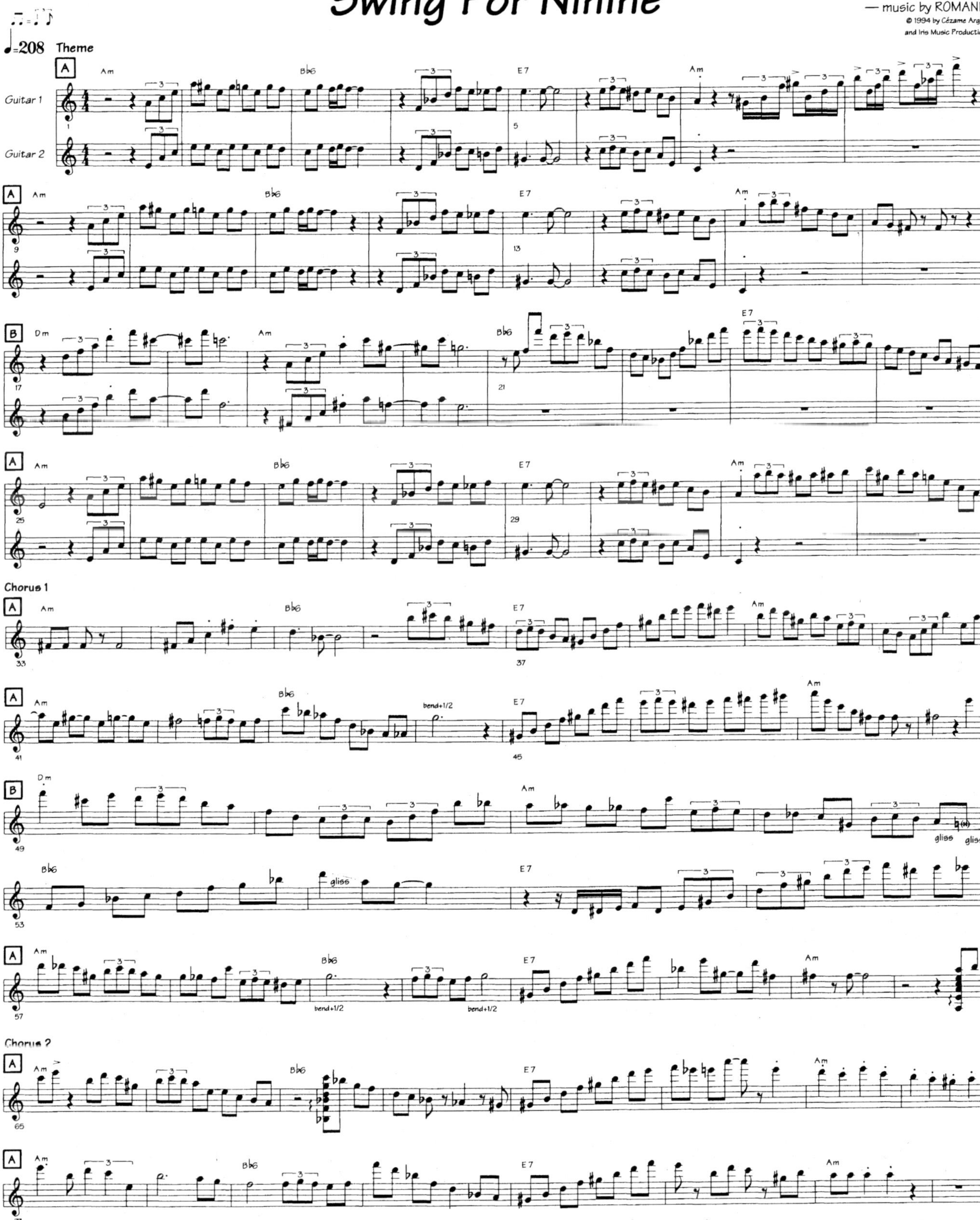

'Swing For Ninine' (continued)

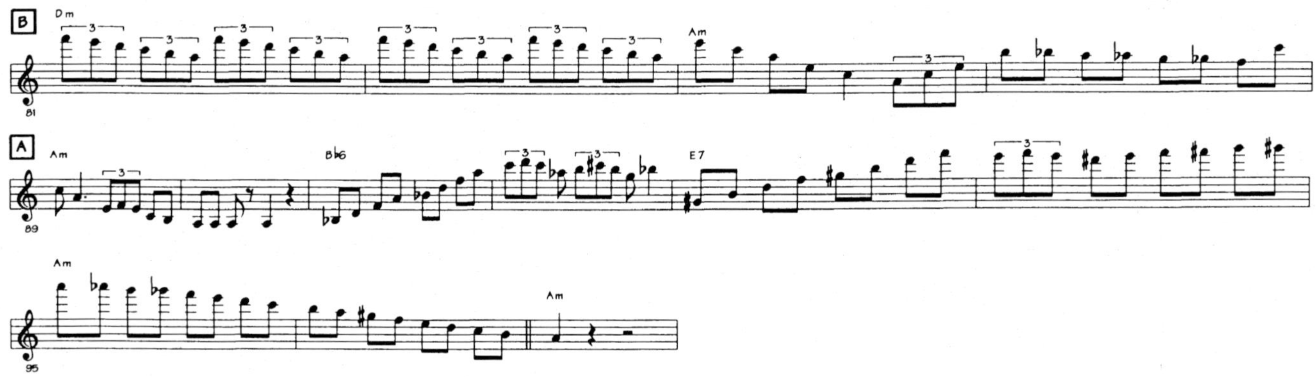

#21

Pour Trois Pas

— music by ROMANE

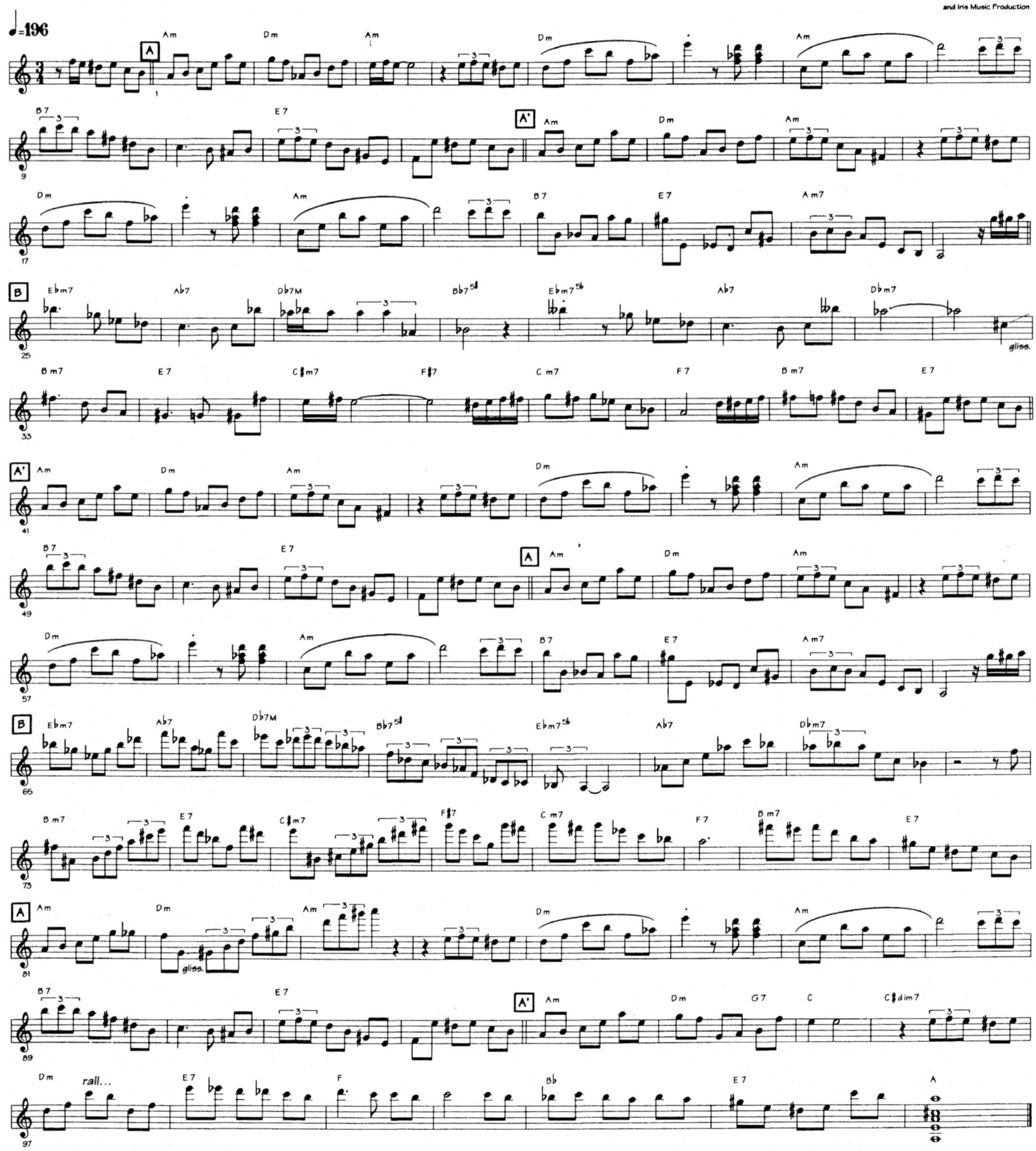

#34 #35 #49

Jo's Remake

— music by ROMANE

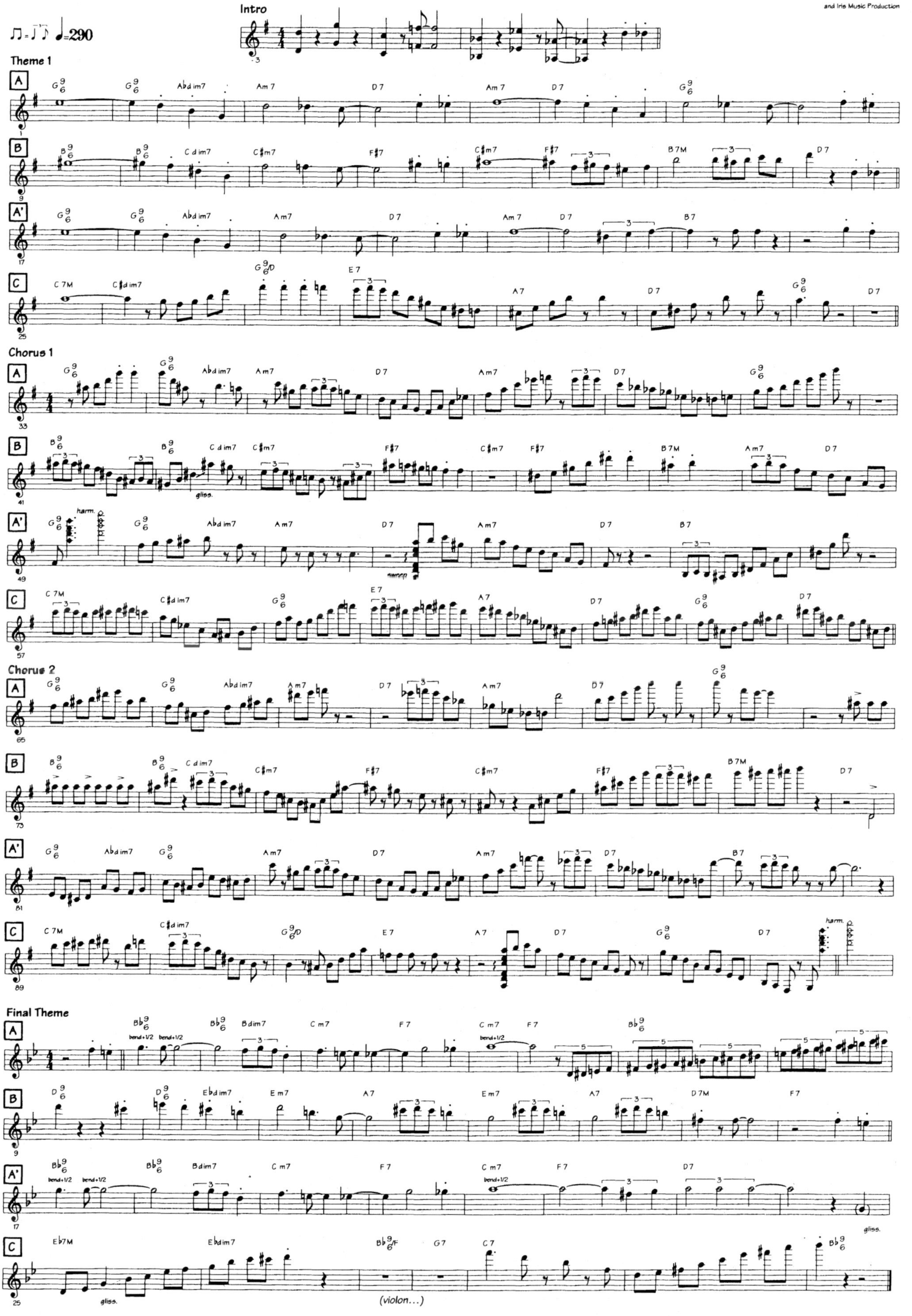

#52

Valse à Patrimonio

— music by ROMANE

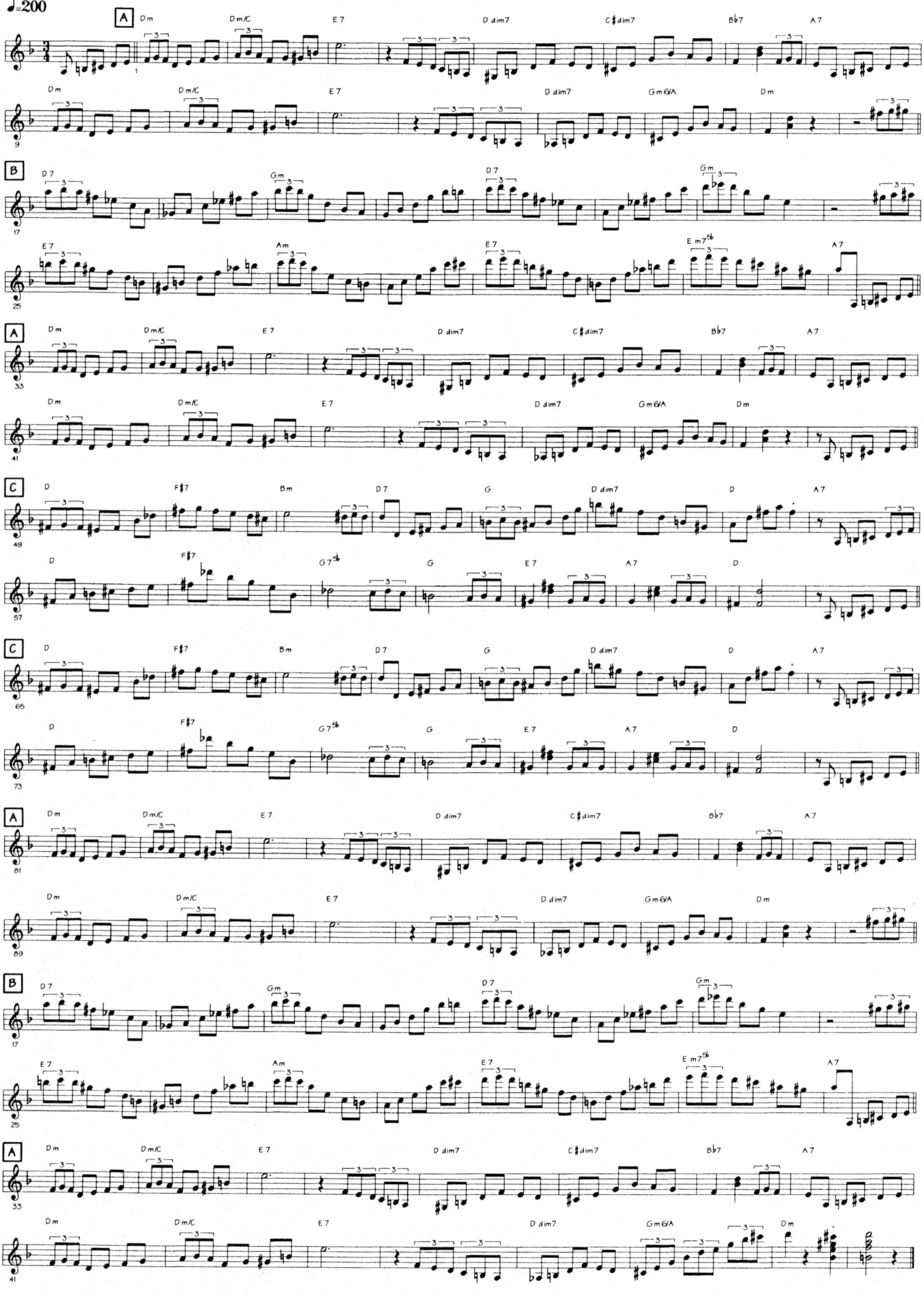

#56

Monticello

— music by ROMANE

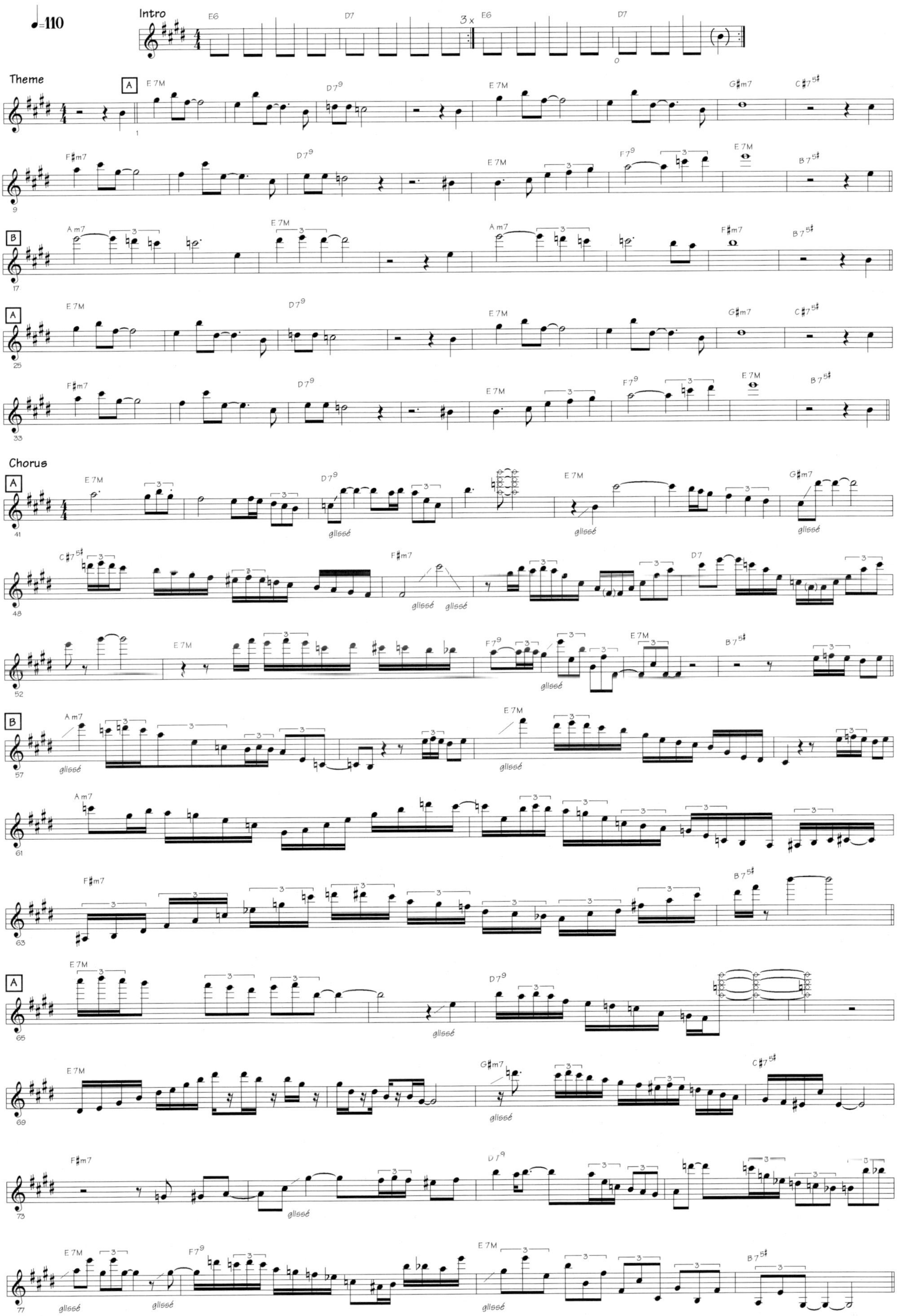

Destinée

#68

♩=240

— music by ROMANE

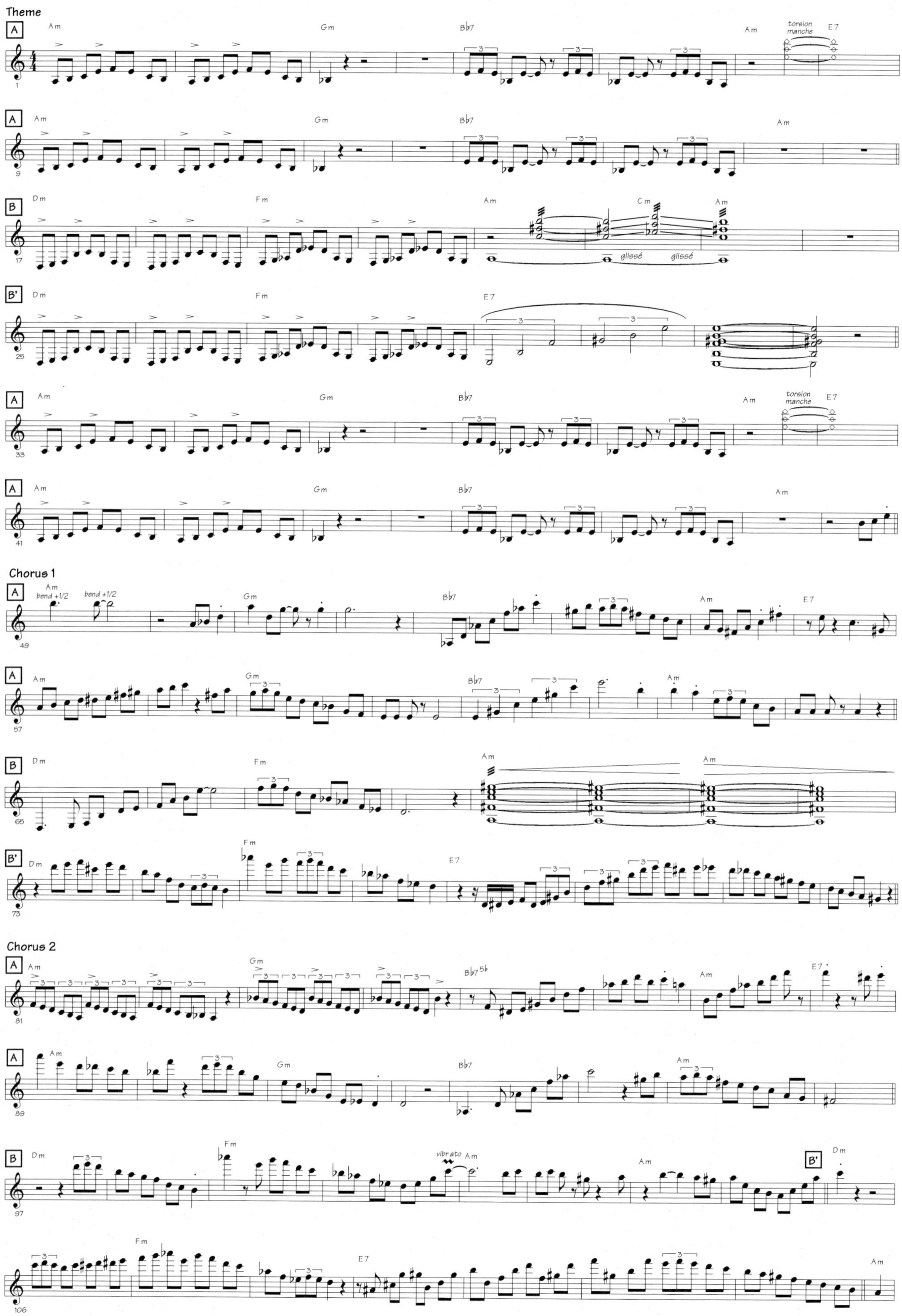

#76

Dans Le Regard De Laura

— music by ROMANE

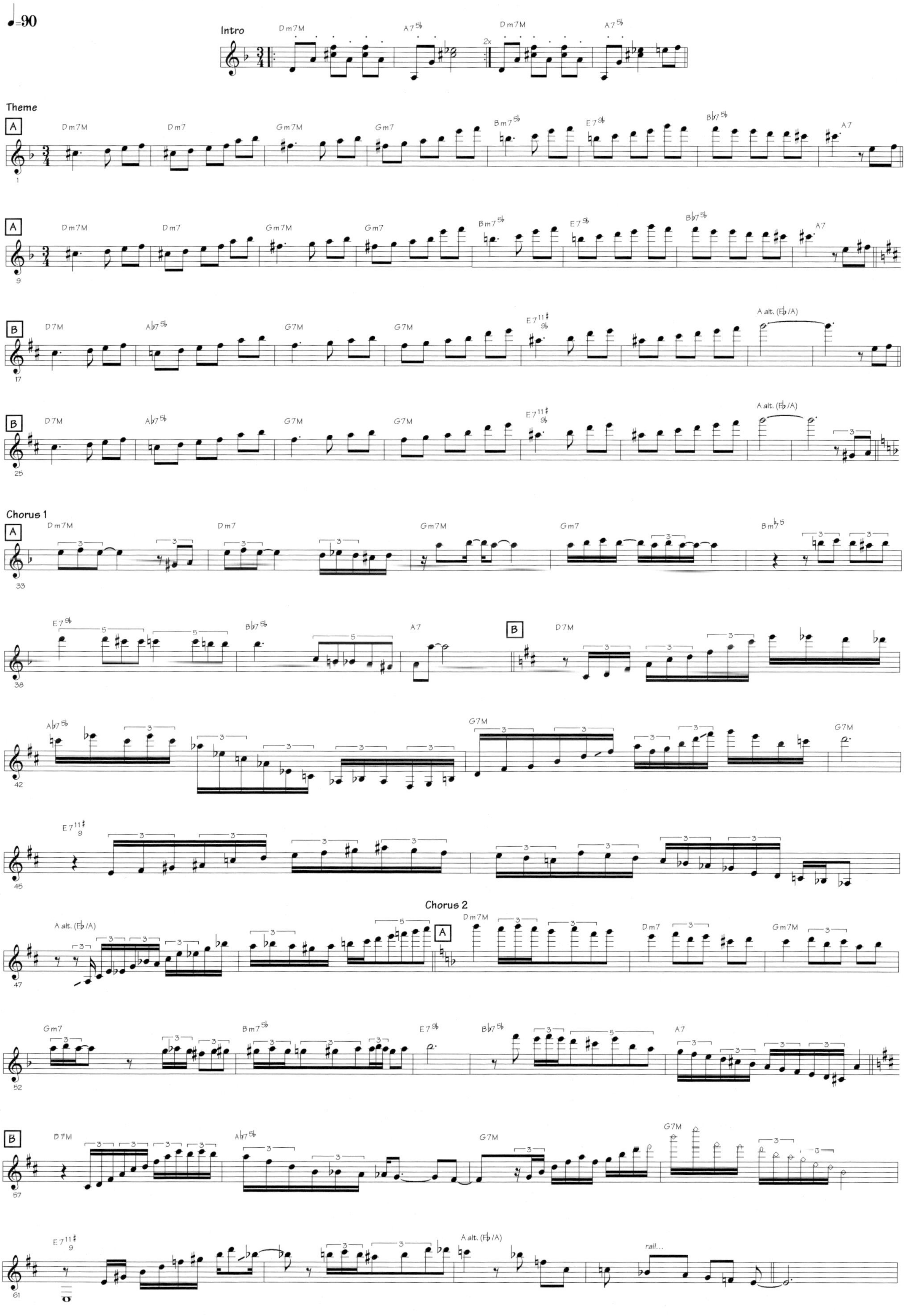

#85

Arc-En-Ciel

— music by ROMANE

Allegro moderato ♩ = 104

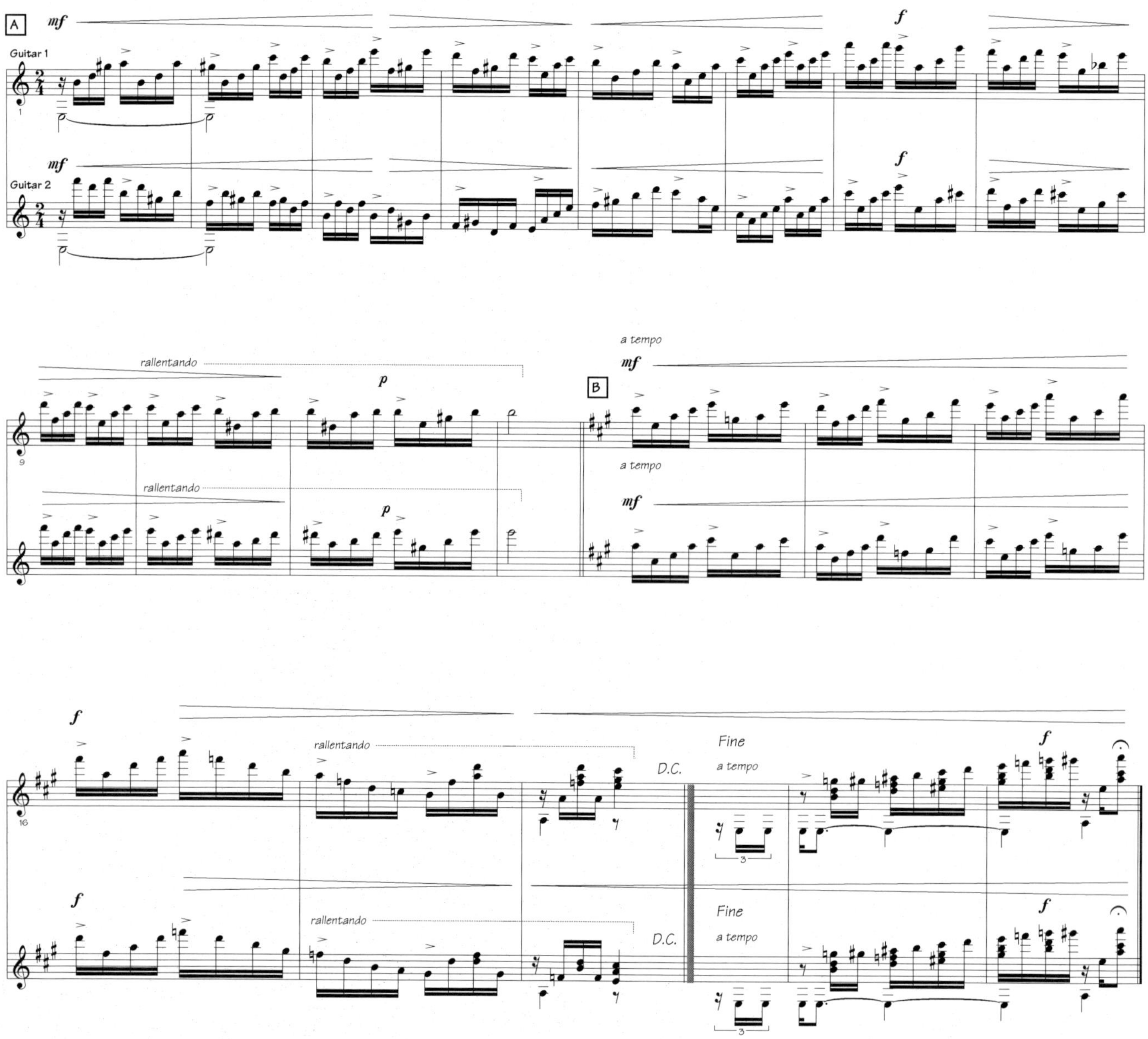

#88

Gypsy Fire

— music by ROMANE

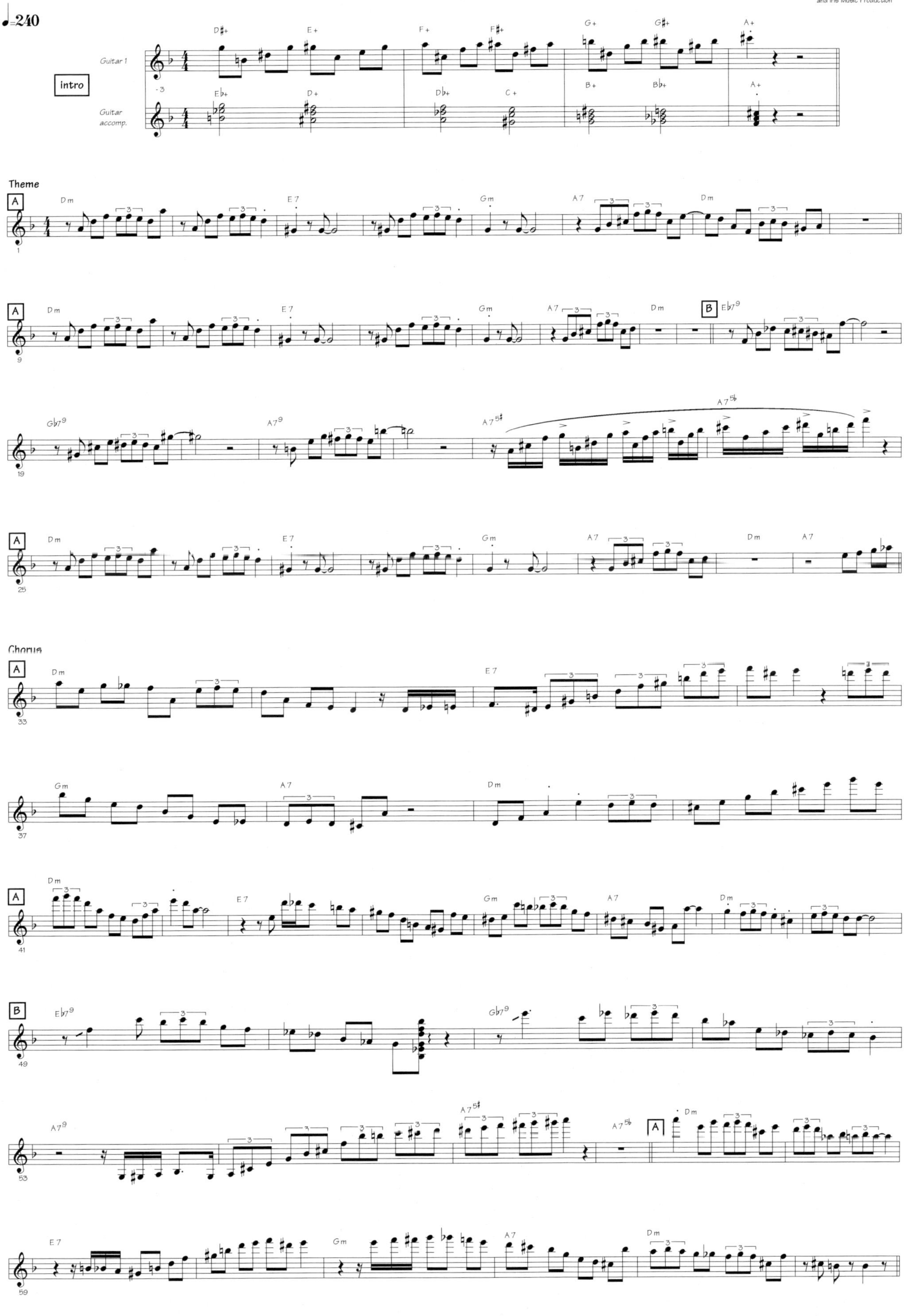

128 AA'AA'BB'BB'AA' #89

Valse à Django

(Montagne Sainte-Geneviève)

— music by Django REINHARDT
arrangement by ROMANE

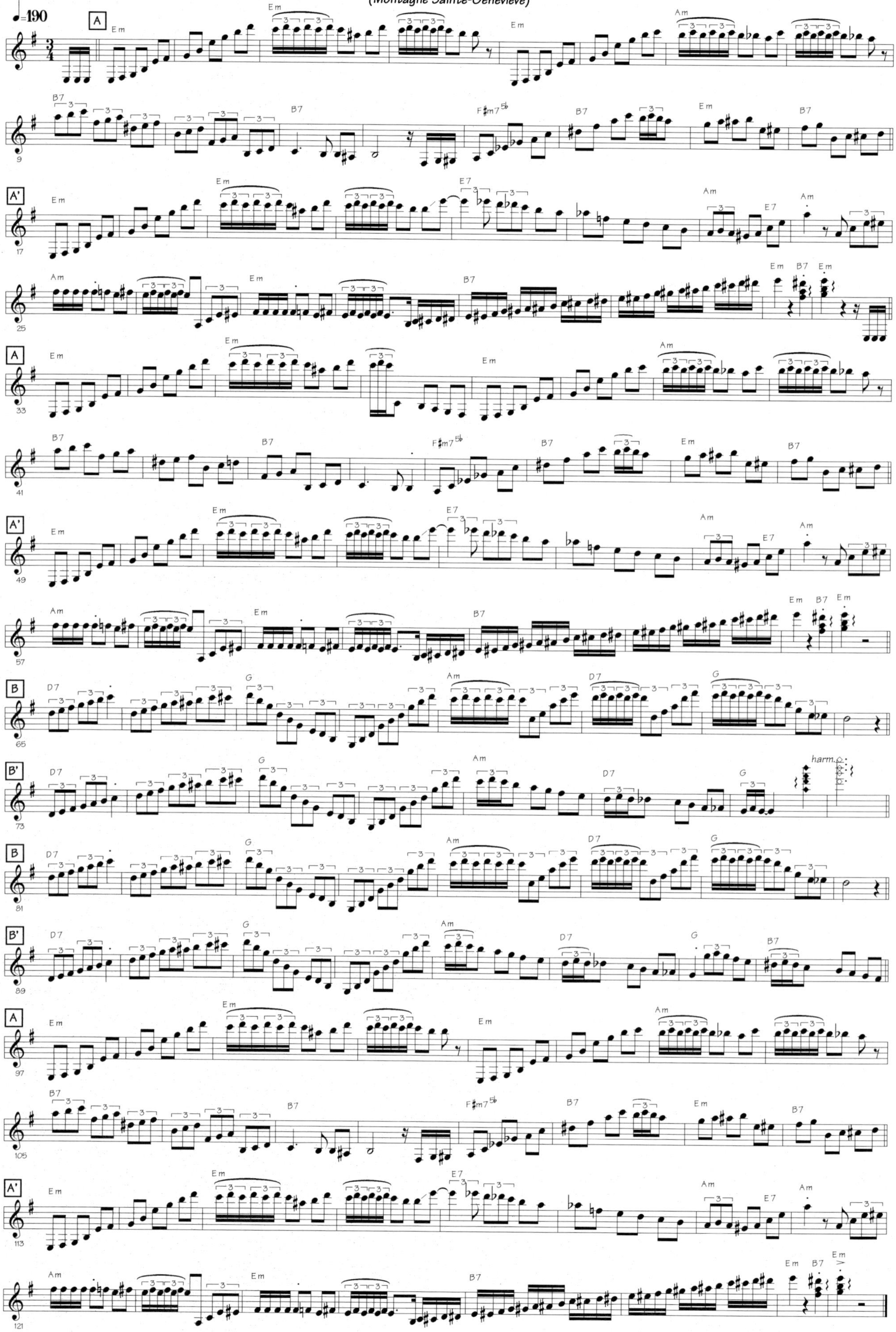

♫ = ♩♪ ♩=250 #90 #91

Manège

— music by ROMANE
© 1996 by Cézame Argile
and Iris Music Production

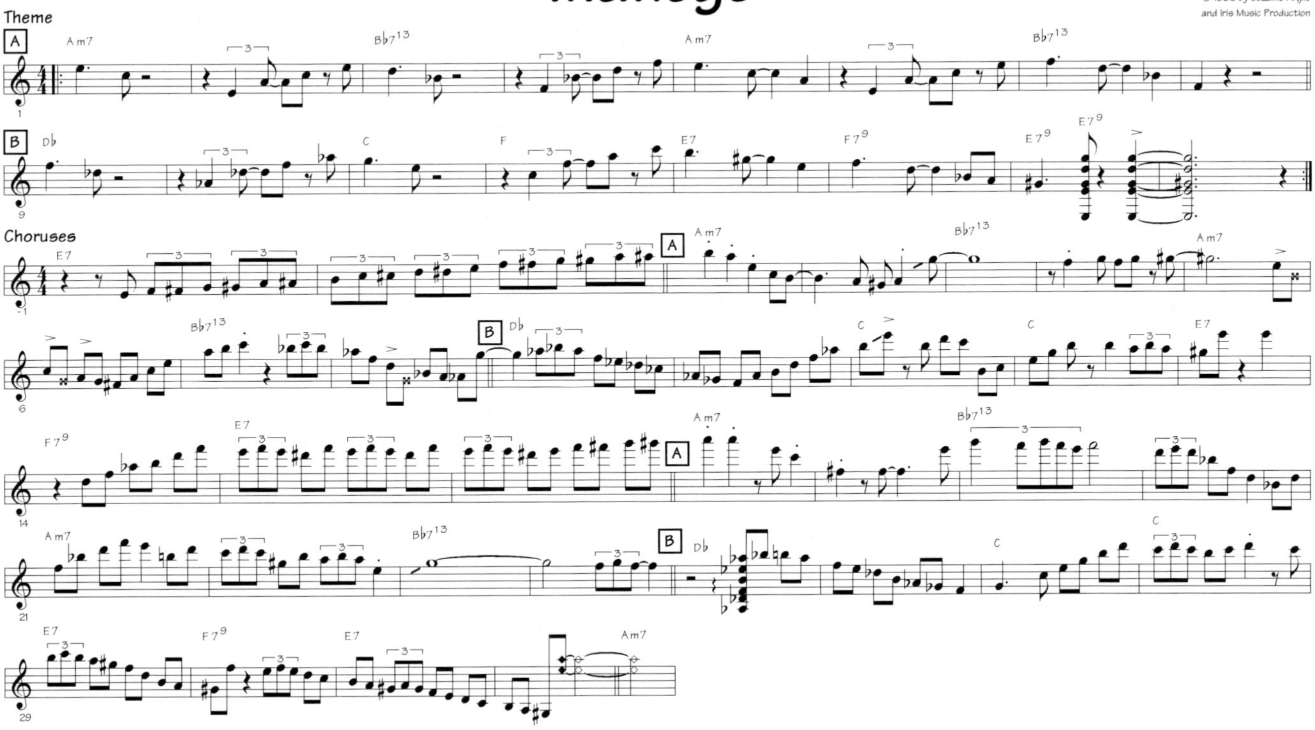

♩ = 240 #93 #94

Ombre

— music by ROMANE
© 1996 by Cézame Argile
and Iris Music Production

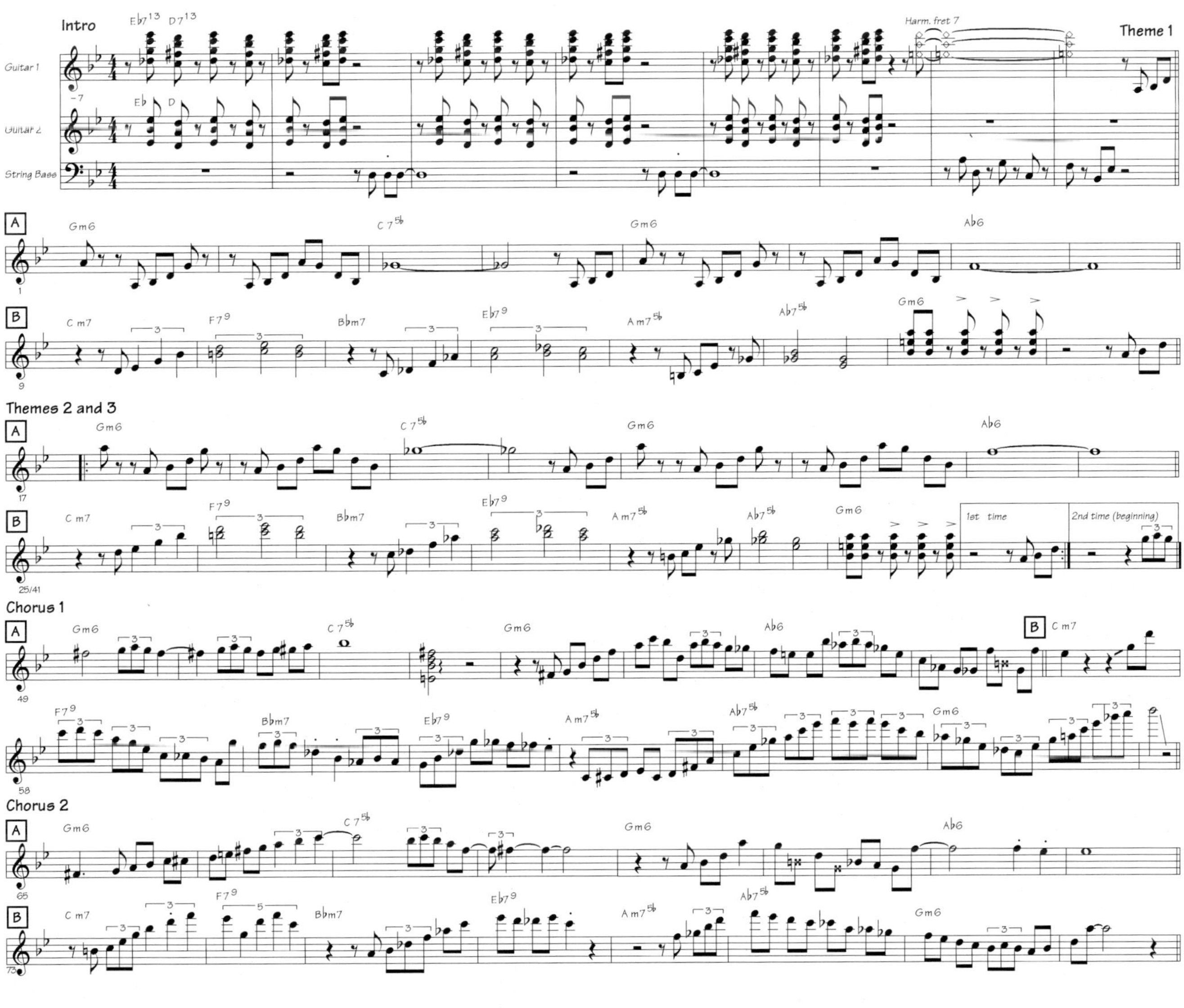

#95

Chassés Croisés

Swing feel

♩=180

— music by Derek SÉBASTIAN

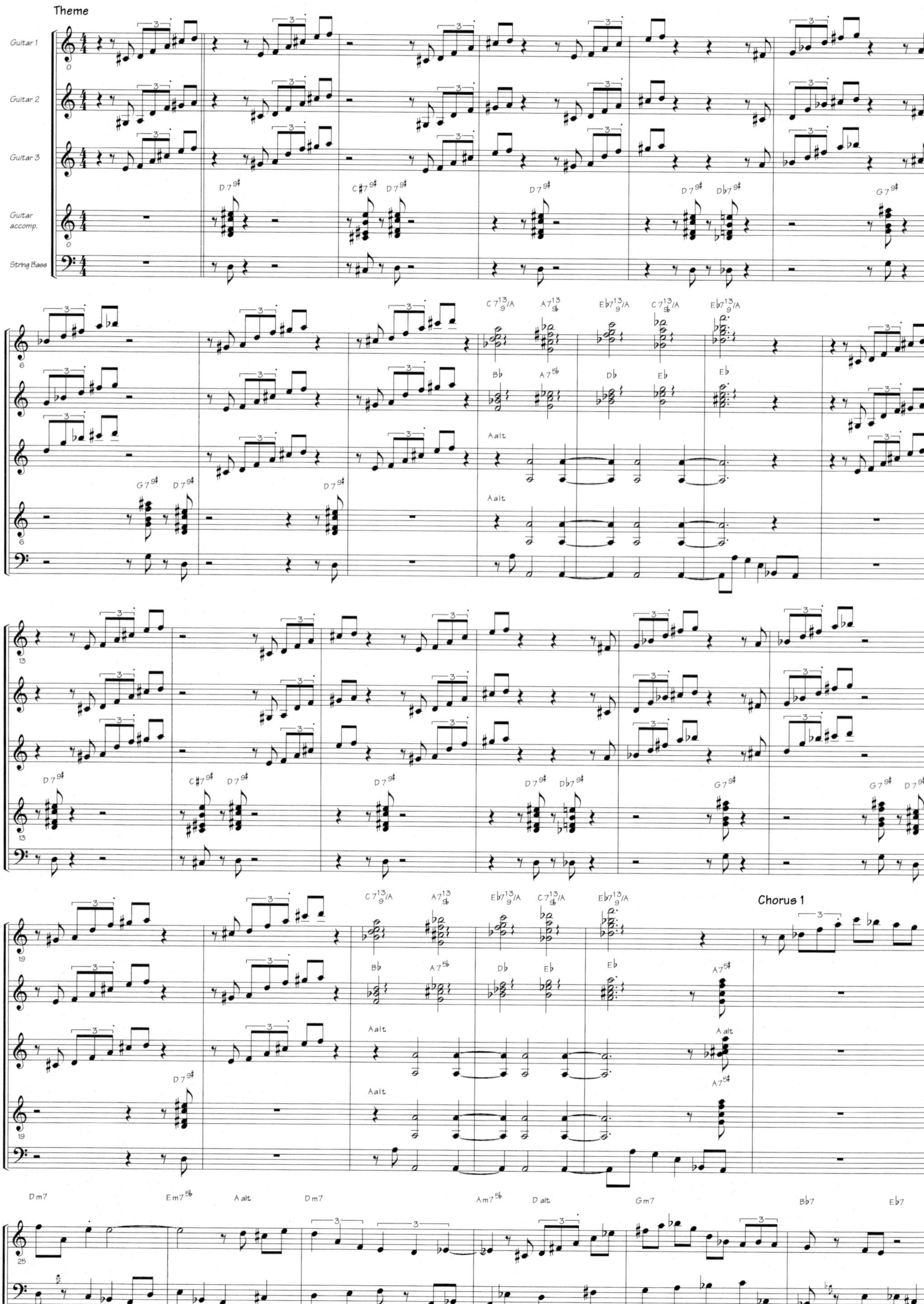

'Chassés Croisés' (continued)

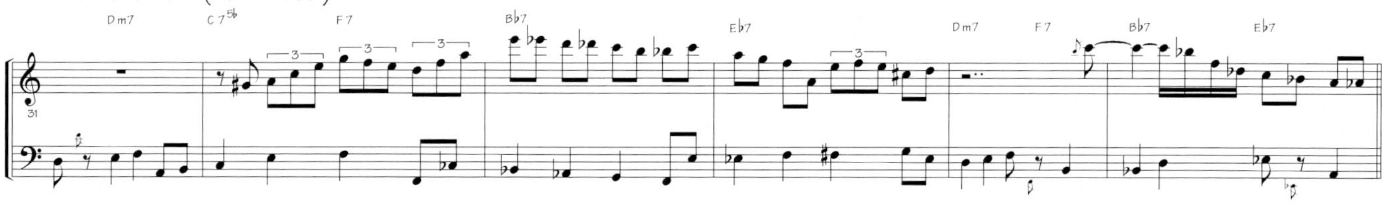

Chorus 2

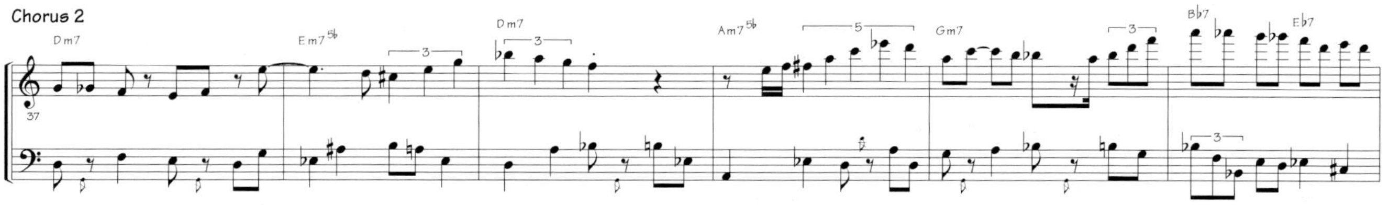

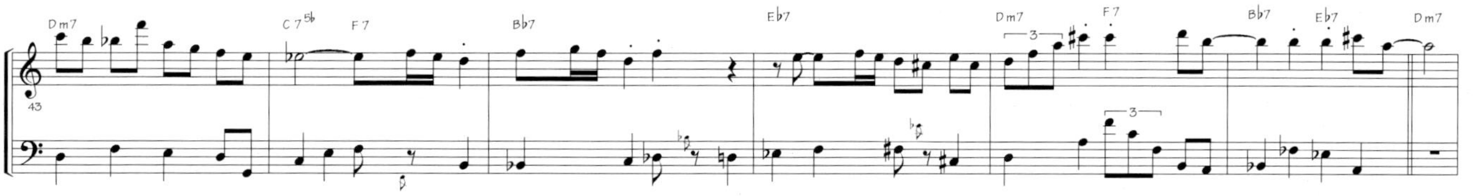

Resume the theme (end of the string-bass in the chorus)

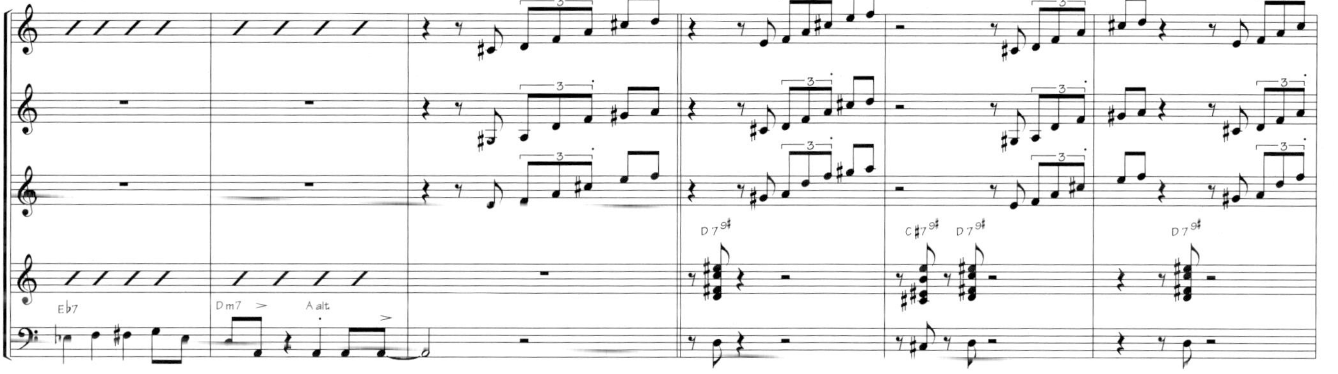

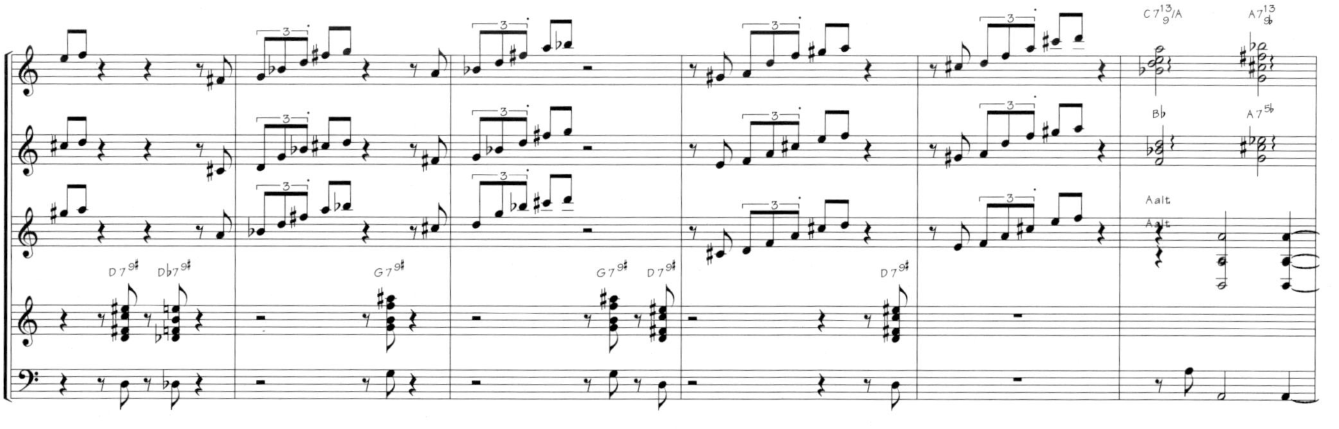

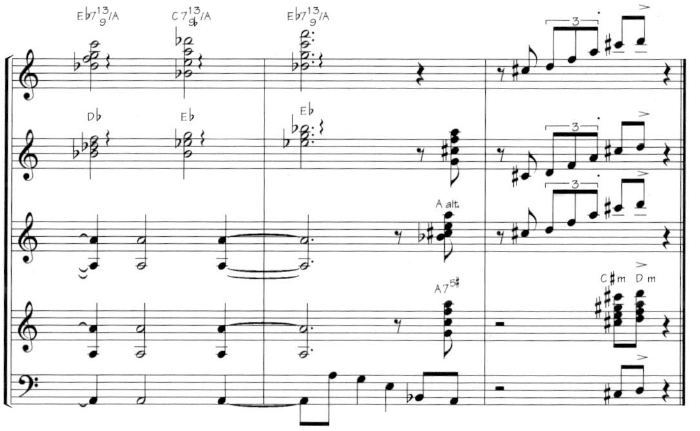

Diagram for the choruses:

Dm7	Em7 5b / A alt.	Dm7	Am7 5b / D alt.
Gm7	Bb7 13 / Eb7 9	Dm7	C7 5b / F7 9
Bb7 13	Eb7 9	Dm7 / F7 9	Bb7 13 / Eb7 9

#97 #98

My Foolish Heart

— Victor YOUNG / Ned WASHINGTON
arr. by ROMANE & Derek SÉBASTIAN

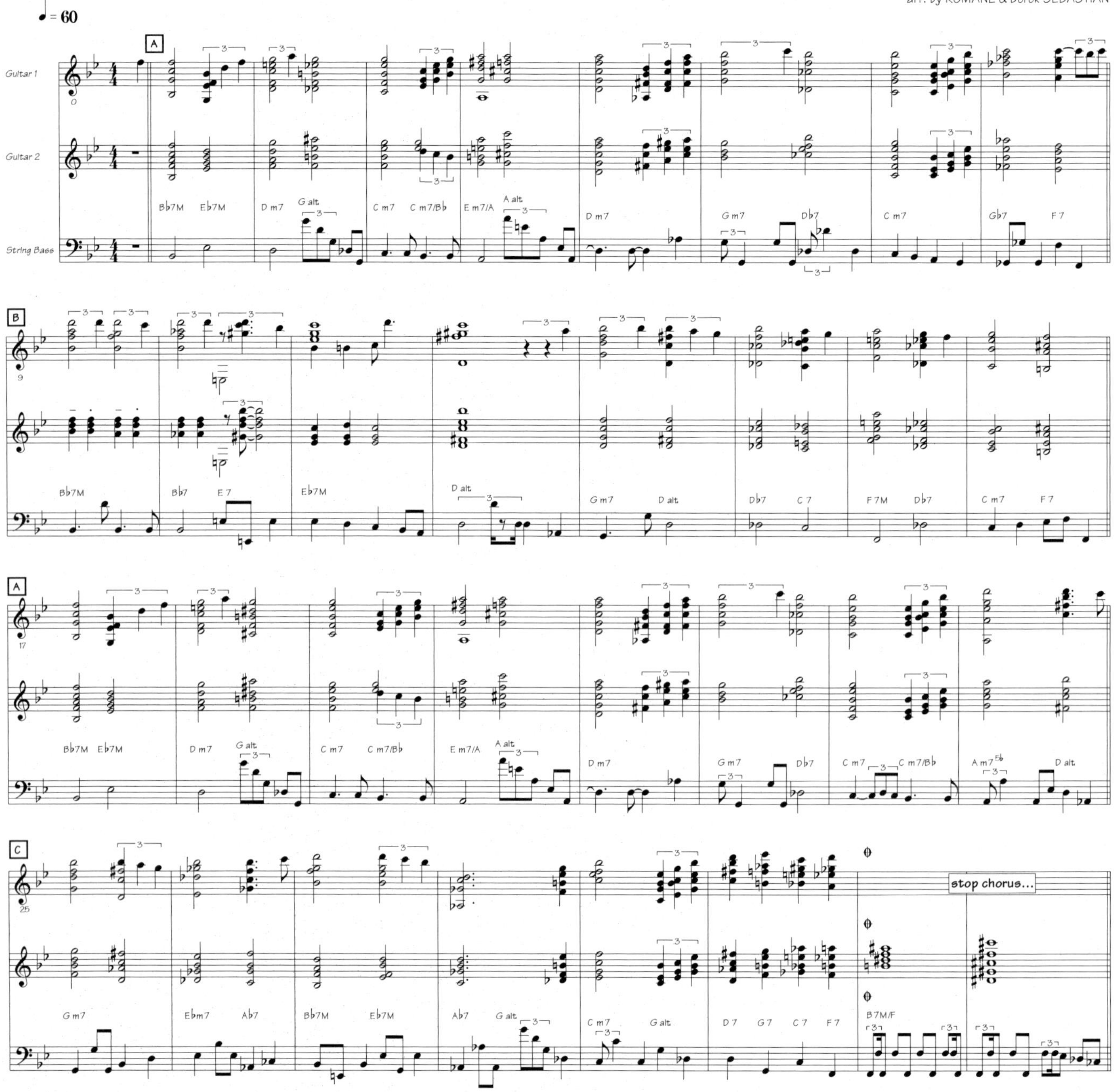

Choruses : split diagram → 1 block = 4/4 doubled diagram → 1 block = 8/4

A	Bb7M / Eb7M	Dm7 / G alt.	Cm7	Em7 / A alt.	Dm7 / D alt.	Gm7 / G alt.	Cm7	Gb7 / F7
B	Bb7M	Bb7	Eb6	Am7b5 / D alt.	Gm7 / D alt.	Db7 / C7	F7M / Db7	Cm7 / F7
A'	7 ⁒							Am7b5 / D alt.
C	Gm7 / D alt.	Ebm7 / Ab7	Bb7M / Eb7M	Ab7 / G alt.	Cm7	D alt. / G alt. / F7 / C7	Bb7M / G alt.	Cm7 / F7

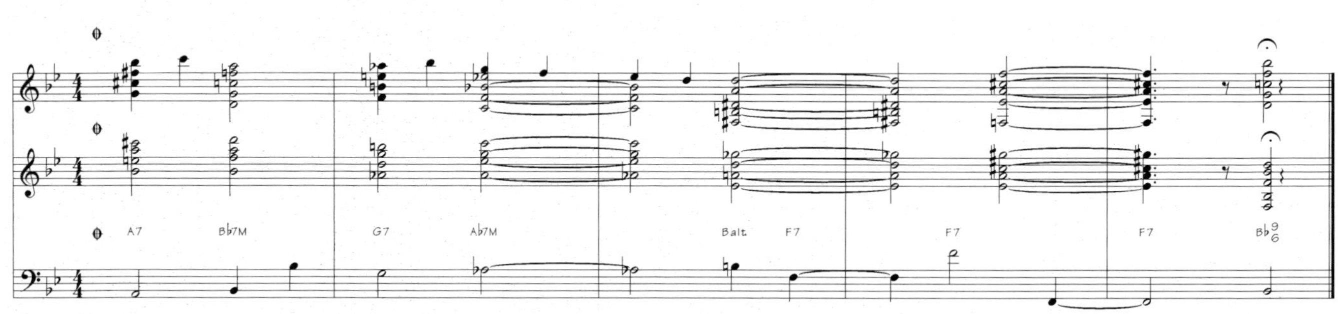

We still have some pages that we will use to give tribute to certain numerous and great musicians who crossed my path during this adventure in these last years. A million pardons to those that cannot be mentioned due to limited space.

– Romane

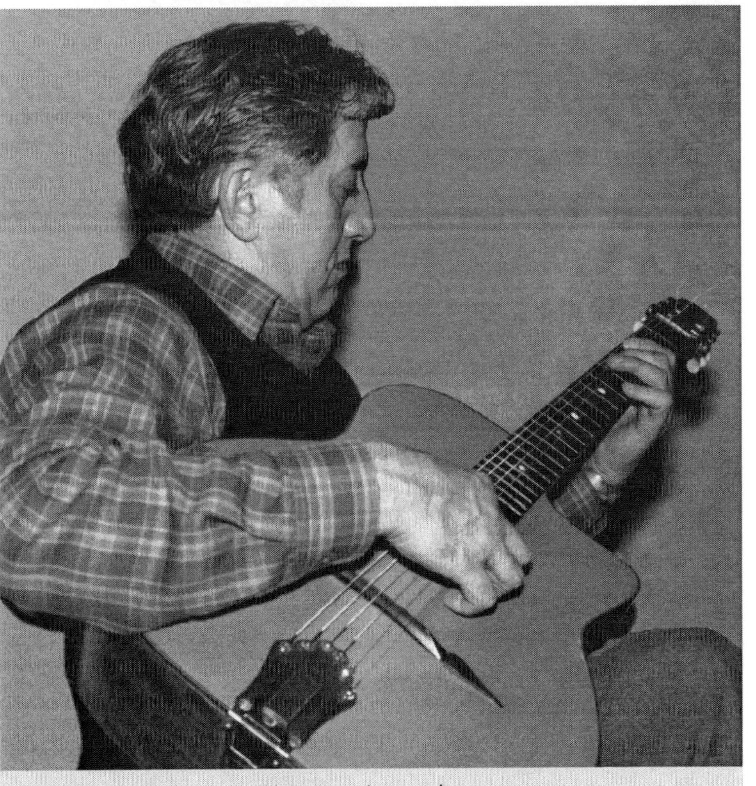

Maurice Leguidcoq

Richard Leguidcoq

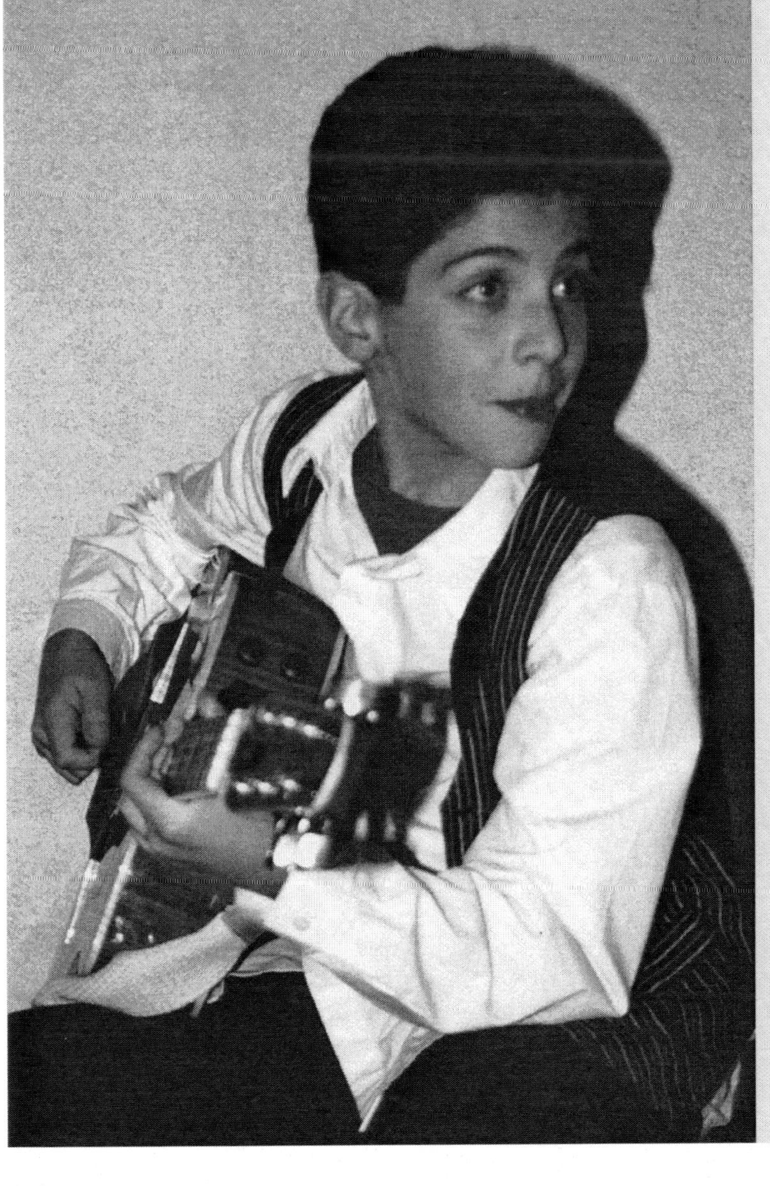

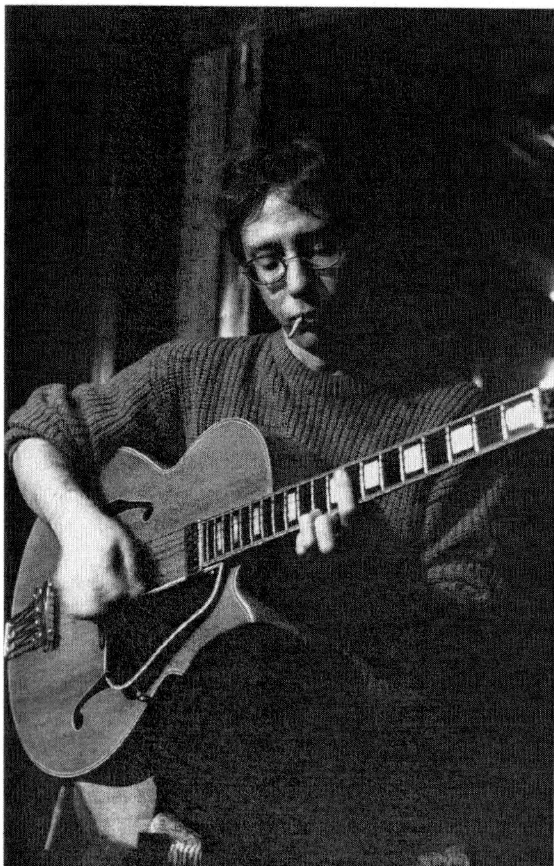

Derek Sébastian

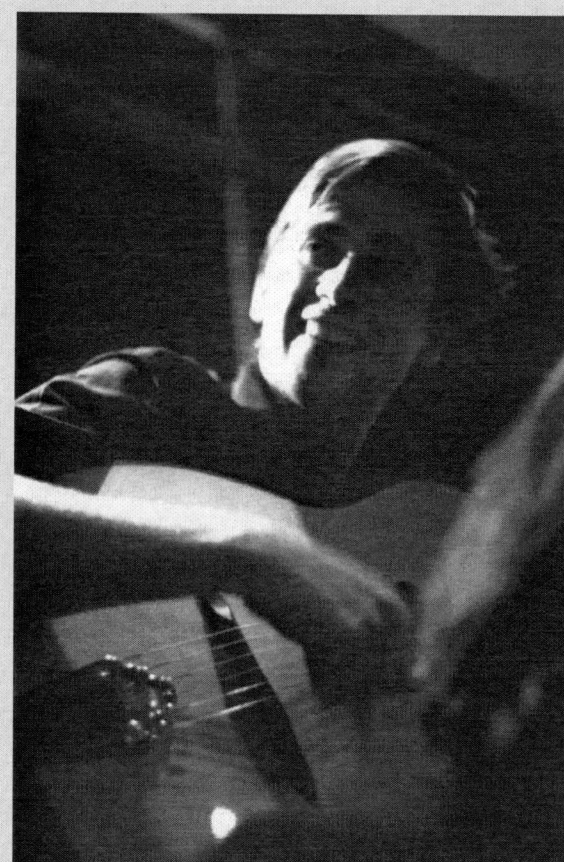

Thomas Dutronc

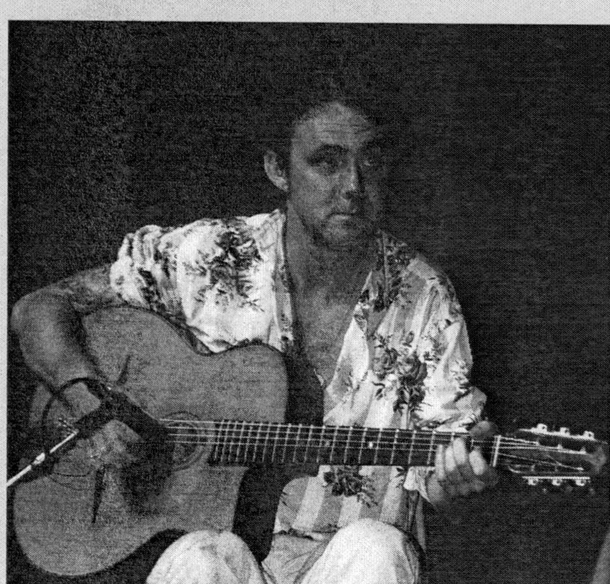

Hervé Legeay

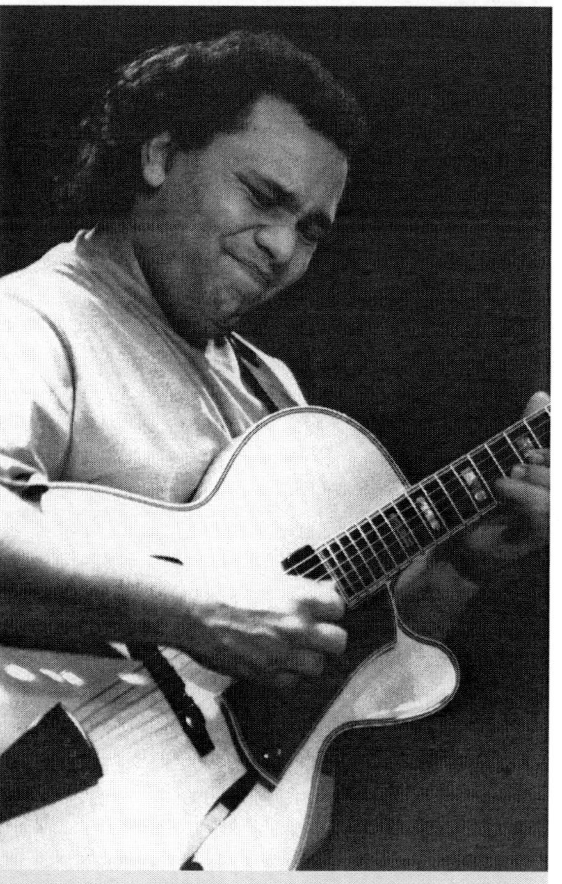

Biréli Lagréne

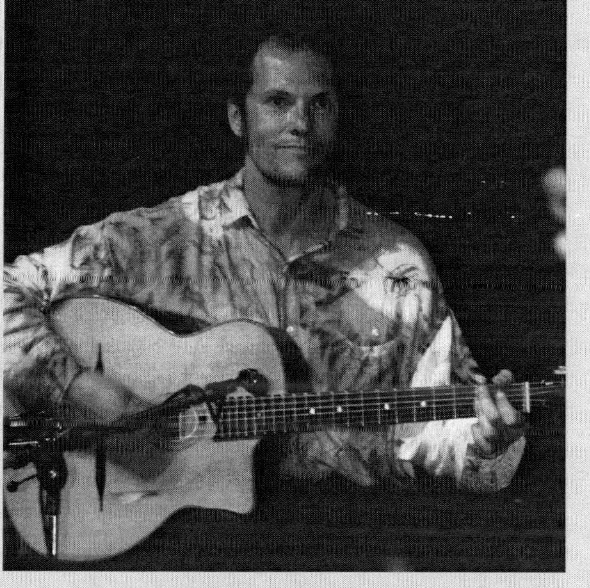

Fred Loizeau

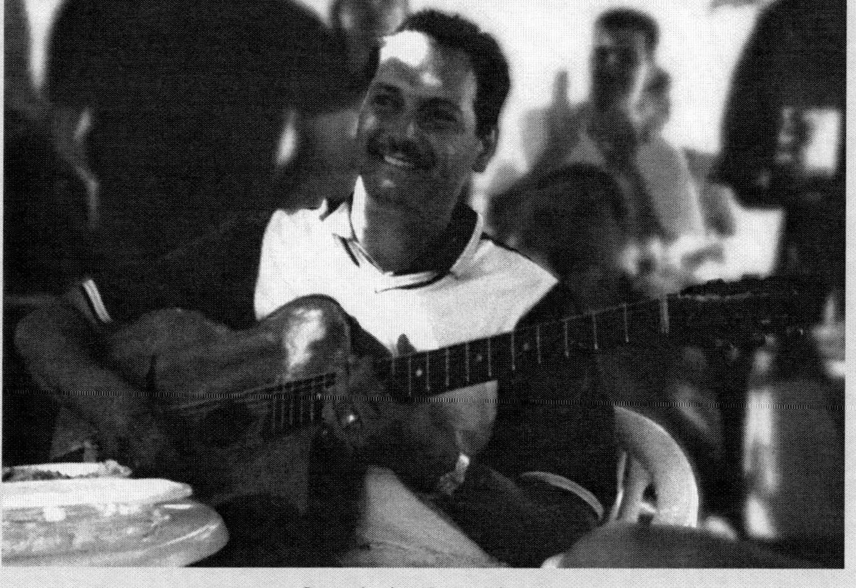

Stochelo Rosenberg

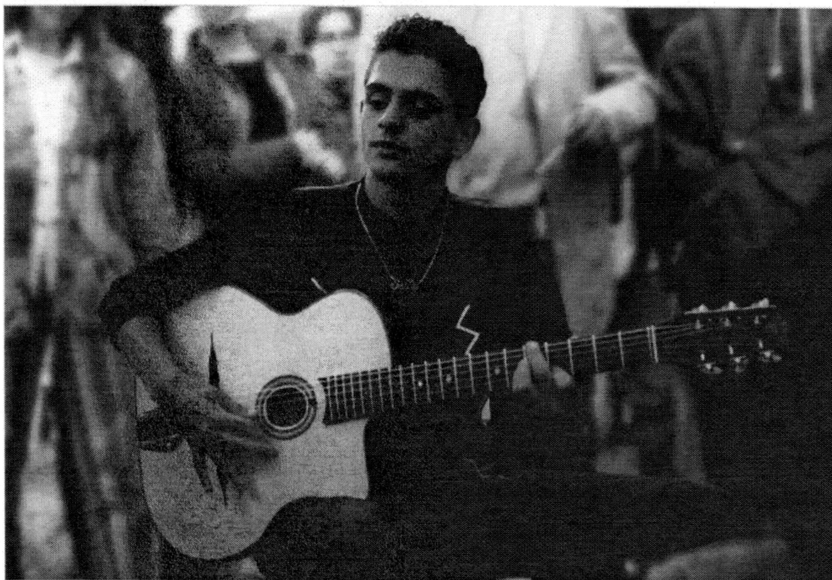

Jimmy Rosenberg

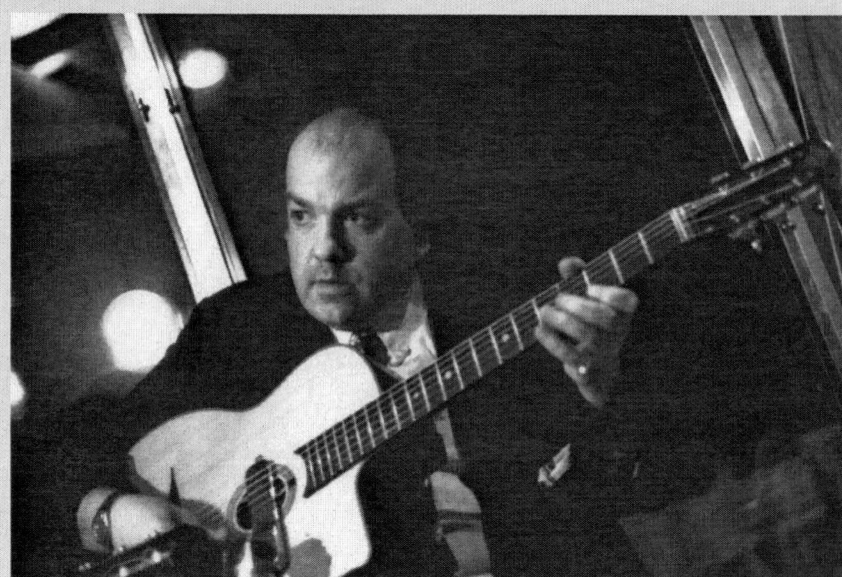

Rodolphe Raffalli

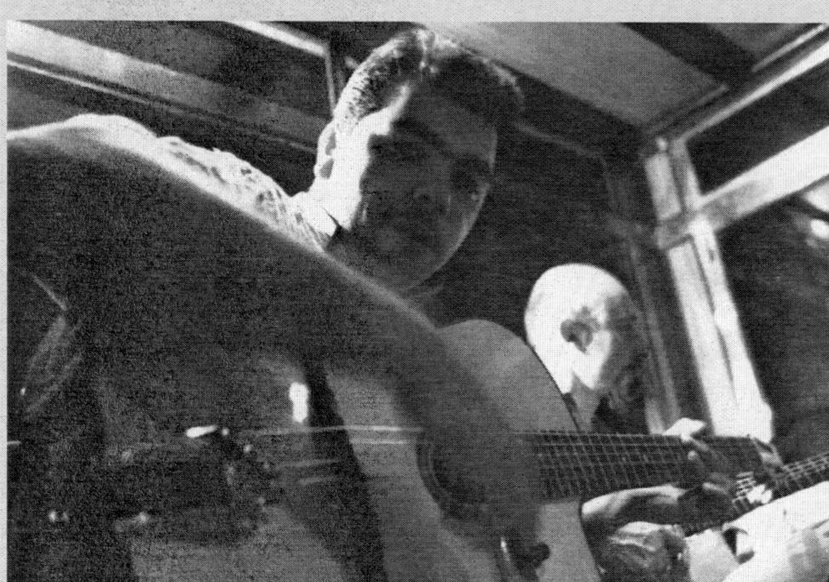

Matcho Weiss

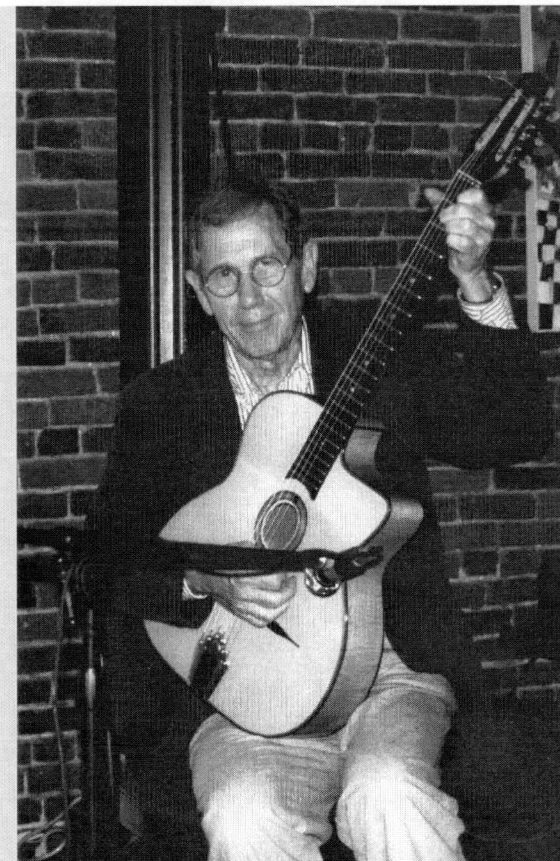

Chet Atkins

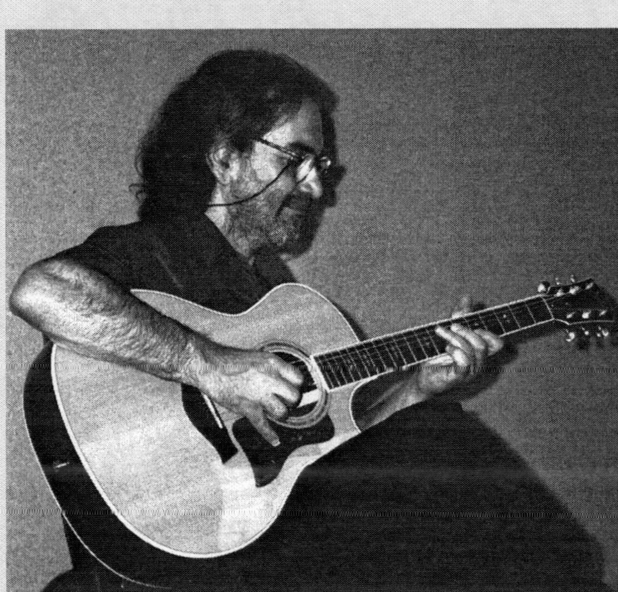

Marcel Dadi

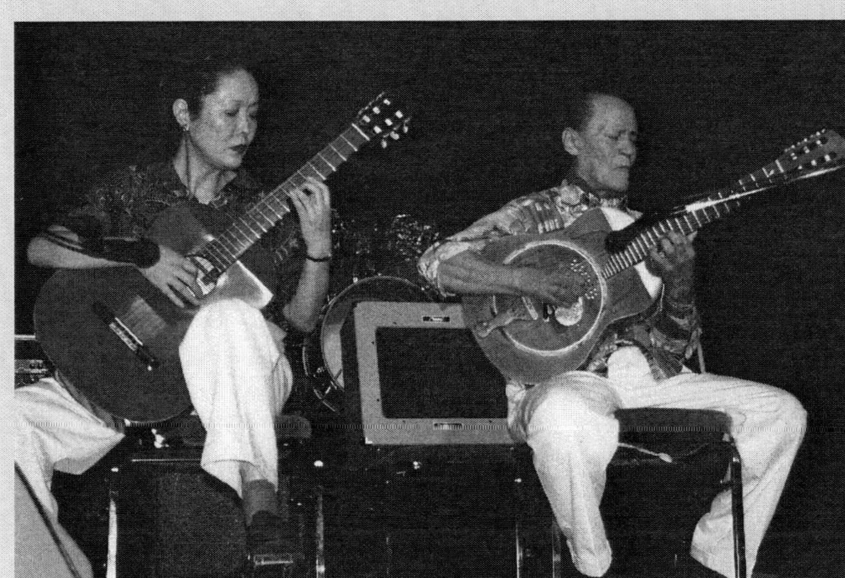

Nato & Michiko Lima (Los Indios Tabajaras)

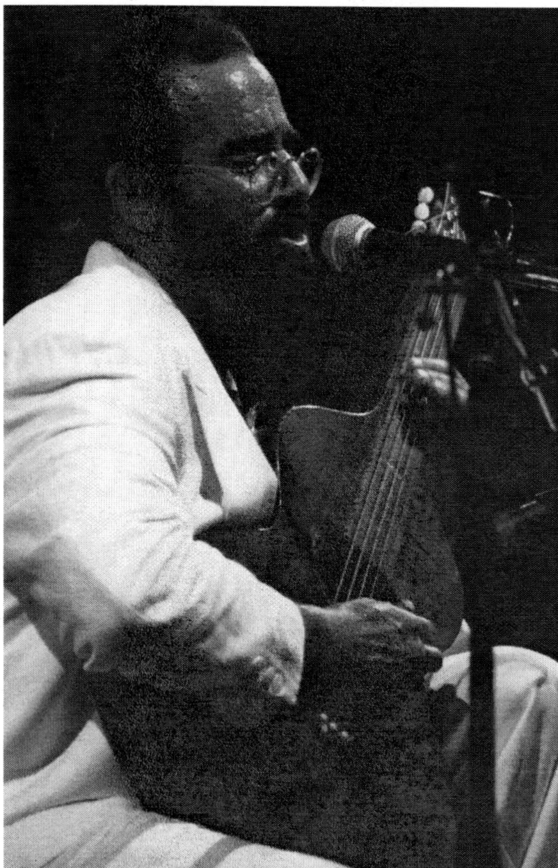

Bob Brozman

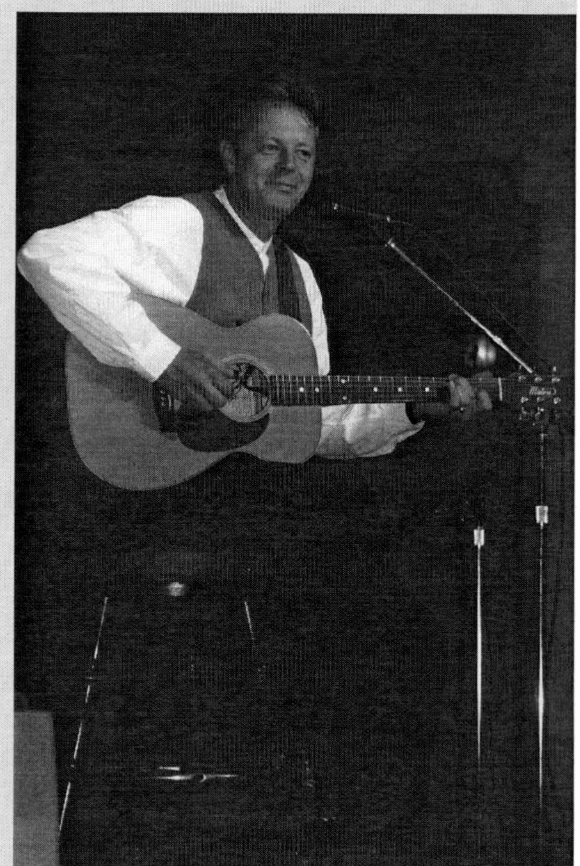

Tommy Emmanuel

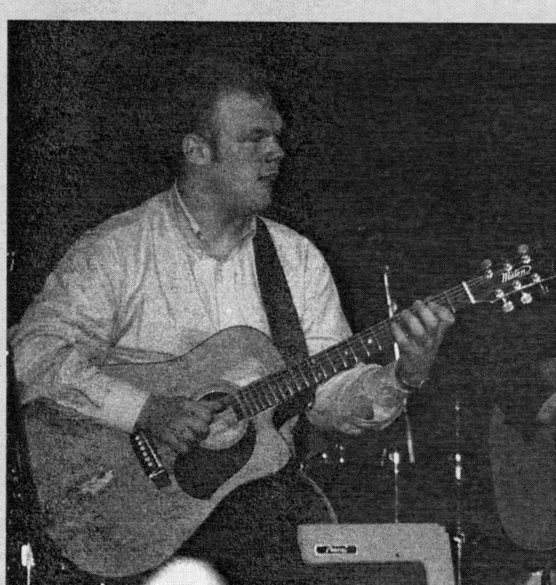

Richard Smith

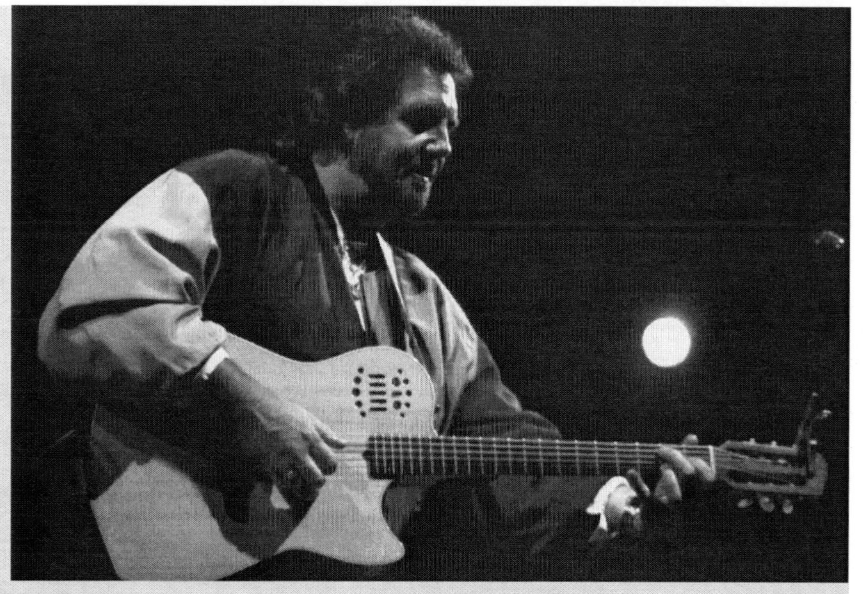

Tom Bresh

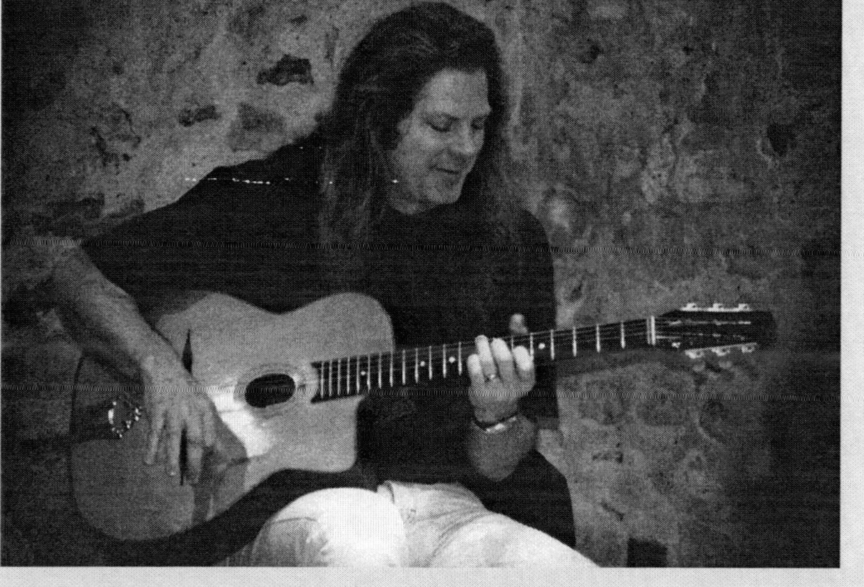

John Jorgenson

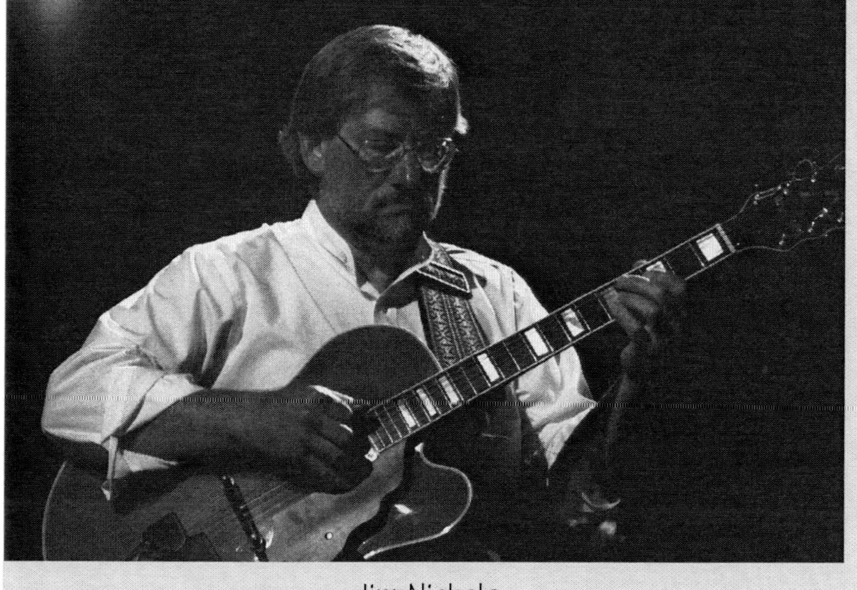

Jim Nichols

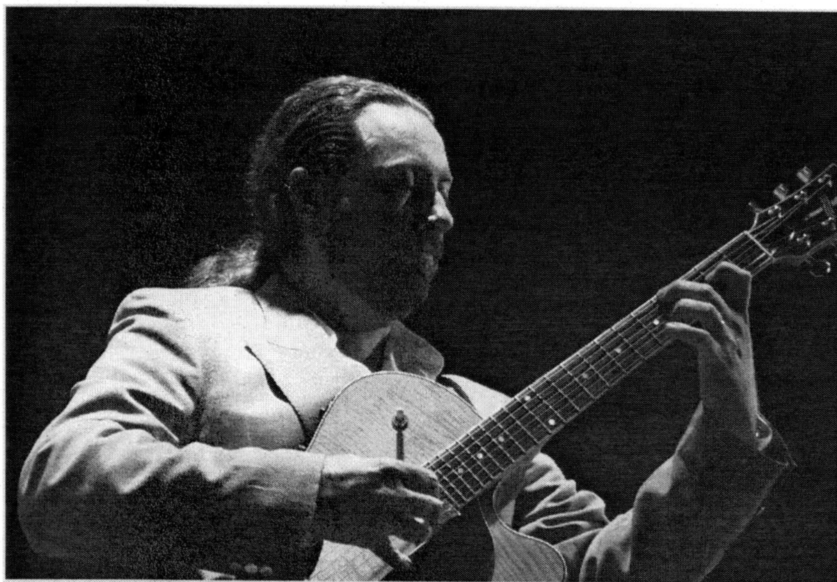

Martin Taylor

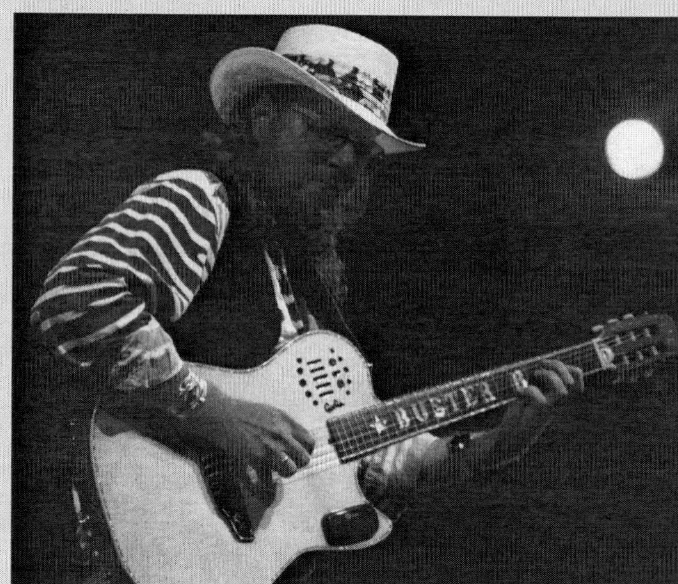

Buster B. Jones

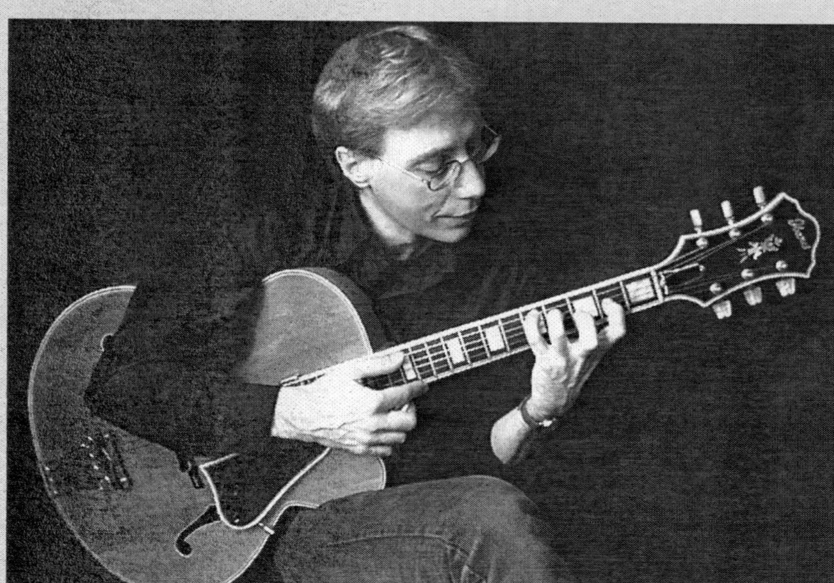

Photo Fabienne Champarnaud

Derek Sébastian

LIST OF M.I.D.I. FILES #00

Much of the CD – ROM (included in this book) is in MS – DOS format (PC and compatibles) rather than Macintosh. You will find the M.I.D.I files that correspond with a specified word list in the order of the pages of this book, The Style of Manouche. If you are lucky enough to have a computer and a sequencer, with authorized software that lets you transfer the M.I.D.I. files, you can listen, at your own leisure. You can practice, with the speed and the instrumental timbre that will suit you!- with the big majority of the exercises the given theory and with the applicable pieces in this book!

001 MID – CHAPTER 01 • Am arpeggio.
002 MID – CHAPTER 01 • Dm arpeggio.
003 MID – CHAPTER 01 • Fdim7 arpeggio.
004 MID – CHAPTER 01 • dim7 with A7 arpeggio.
005 MID – CHAPTER 01 - 02 - 03 - 04 • theme and choruses 1 and 2 of "Swing For Ninine".
006 MID – CHAPTER 02 • exercise 05 • Bb arpeggio.
007 MID – CHAPTER 02 • exercise 06 • E arpeggio.
008 MID – CHAPTER 02 • exercise 07 • A harmonic minor scale.
009 MID – CHAPTER 02 • exercise 07 again • A harmonic minor scale.
010 MID – CHAPTER 02 • harmonization of the A harmonic minor scale with 3, then 4 tones.
011 MID – CHAPTER 02 • inverted dim7 chords + chord substitutions.
012 MID – CHAPTER 03 • exercise 08 • Am6 arpeggio, position 1.
013 MID – CHAPTER 03 • exercise 09 • Am6 arpeggio, position 2.
014 MID – CHAPTER 03 • exercise 10 • Am9 arpeggio, position 1.
015 MID – CHAPTER 03 • exercise 11 • Am9 arpeggio, position 2.
016 MID – CHAPTER 04 • exercise 12 • speed with Am6/9.
017 MID – CHAPTER 04 • exercise 13 • speed with Gm6/9.
018 MID – CHAPTER 04 • exercise 14 • chromatic scale.
019 MID – CHAPTER 05 • exercise 15 • broken Fdim7 arpeggio.
020 MID – CHAPTER 05 • exercise 16 • G7M arpeggio.
021 MID – CHAPTERS 05 - 06 – 07 • theme and choruses of "Pour Trois Pas".
022 MID – CHAPTER 06 • exercise 17 • a sweep/ arpeggio with GM7.
023 MID – CHAPTER 06 • exercise 18 • a sweep/ arpeggio with Am7.
024 MID – CHAPTER 06 • exercise 19 • diagram and designated notes with C6.
025 MID – CHAPTER 07 • exercise 20 • whole tone scale, in descending steps.
026 MID – CHAPTER 07 • exercise 21 • whole tone scale, in ascending steps.
027 MID – CHAPTER 08 • exercise 22 • G Maj. 9 arpeggio.
028 MID – CHAPTER 08 • exercise 23 • dim7 arpeggio with D7.
029 MID – CHAPTER 08 • exercise 24 • continuing the arpeggio with G major.
030 MID – CHAPTER 08 • exercise 25 • diminished scale with a cadence in G major.
031 MID – CHAPTER 08 • exercise 26 • a phrase with G7.
032 MID – CHAPTER 08 • exercise 27 • diagram with G7sus4.
033 MID – CHAPTER 08 • degrees of the major scale linked with descending fifths.
034 MID – CHAPTERS 08 – 09 • theme (first shown) of "Jo's Remake".
035 MID – CHAPTERS 08 – 09 – 10 • choruses 1 and 2 of "Jo's Remake".
036 MID – CHAPTER 09 • exercise 28 • whole tone scale with A7.
037 MID – CHAPTER 09 • exercise 29 • diagram and sweep with G7(b5).
038 MID – CHAPTER 09 • exercise 30 • diagram and sweep with Dm.
039 MID – CHAPTER 10 • exercise 31 • designated notes with G.
040 MID – CHAPTER 10 • exercise 32 • designated notes with G.
041 MID – CHAPTER 10 • exercise 33 • designated notes with Am.
042 MID -- CHAPTER 10 • exercise 34 • designated notes with Am.
043 MID -- CHAPTER 11 • exercise 37 • designated notes with Bb.
044 MID -- CHAPTER 11 • exercise 38 • designated notes with Bb.

045 MID – CHAPTER 11 • exercise 39 • designated notes with Cm.
046 MID – CHAPTER 11 • exercise 40 • designated notes with Cm.
047 MID – CHAPTER 11 • exercise 41 • broken scale of C major.
048 MID – CHAPTER 11 • exercise 42 • broken scale with G major.
049 MID – CHAPTER 11 • final theme/chorus of "Jo's Remake".
050 MID – CHAPTER 12 • exercise 43 • resolution phrase with Am.
051 MID – CHAPTER 12 • exercise 44 • phrase with Am, the Neapolitan minor mode.
052 MID – CHAPTER 12 • "VALSE a PATRIMONIO".
053 MID – CHAPTER 13 • exercise 45 • resolution phrase in C major.
054 MID – CHAPTER 13 • exercise 46 • resolution phrase with II – V – I in C major.
055 MID – CHAPTER 13 • exercise 47 • phrase in A minor.
056 MID – CHAPTERS 13 – 14 – 15 – 16 • theme and choruses of "MONTICELLO".
057 MID – CHAPTER 14 • exercise 48 • half-diminished D scale with D7.
058 MID – CHAPTER 14 • exercise 49 • diminished scale with a G major cadence.
059 MID – CHAPTER 15 • exercise 50 • melodic structure with the diminished scale.
060 MID – CHAPTER 15 • exercise 51 • melodic structure with cadences in fifths.
061 MID – CHAPTER 15 • exercise 52 • syncopated melodic structure with D7.
062 MID – CHAPTER 16 • exercise 53 • resolution tritone phrases with C, triplets.
063 MID – CHAPTER 16 • exercise 54 • resolution tritone phrases with C, sixteenth notes.
064 MID – CHAPTER 16 • exercise 55 • resolution tritone phrase with G.
065 MID – CHAPTER 16 • exercise 56 • resolution tritone phrase with a turnaround in G.
066 MID – CHAPTER 17 • exercise 57 • bi tonal phrase in major triads with D7.
067 MID – CHAPTER 17 • exercise 58 • bi-tonal diagrams in major triads (C and D).
068 MID – CHAPTERS 17 - 18 - 19 • theme and choruses 1 and 2 of "DESTINEE".
069 MID – CHAPTER 18 • exercise • melodic structure with a C major cadence.
070 MID – CHAPTER 18 • VII degree of the melodic minor C scale with 3 to7 sounds.
071 MID – CHAPTER 18 • altered chord developed up to 7 sounds.
072 MID – CHAPTER 19 • exercise 60 • melody with the anatole in C major, diagram 1.
073 MID – CHAPTER 19 • exercise 61 • melodic motive with the anatole in C major, diagram 2.
074 MID – CHAPTER 20 • exercise 62 • melodic motive with the anatole in G major, diagram 1.
075 MID – CHAPTER 20 • exercise 63 • melodic motive with the anatole in G major, diagram 2.
076 MID – CHAPTERS 20 – 21 – 22 • intro, theme and choruses 1 and 2 of "DANS LE REGARD DE LAURA".
077 MID – CHAPTER 21 • exercise 64 • melodic motive harmonized with the anatole in G.
078 MID – CHAPTER 21 • exercise 65 • resolving progression with altered dominant chords.
079 MID – CHAPTER 22 • degrees of he C melodic minor scale having 3, than 4 sounds.
080 MID – CHAPTER 22 • IV degree chord of the C melodic minor scale developed up to 7 sounds.
081 MID – CHAPTER 23 • exercise 70 • skipping intervals with the C major scale.
082 MID – CHAPTER 23 • exercise 71 • skipping intervals with the harmonic minor A scale.
083 MID – CHAPTER 23 • exercise 72 • skipping intervals with the minor harmonic A scale.
084 MID – CHAPTER 23 • exercise 73 • skipping intervals with the minor harmonic A scale.
085 MID – CHAPTERS 23 – 24 • "Arc – En – Ciel".
086 MID – CHAPTER 24 • exercise 74 • classical type arpeggios in the key of G minor.
087 MID – CHAPTER 25 • exercise 75 • introduction of "Gypsy Fire".
088 MID – CHAPTERS 25 – 26 • initial theme, chorus and final theme (CODA) of "Gypsy Fire".
089 MID – CHAPTERS 26 – 27 – 29 – 30 – 31 – 32 • exercise 76 • "Valse a Django".
090 MID – CHAPTER 27 • theme of "Manege".
091 MID – CHAPTER 27 • choruses of "Manege".
092 MID – CHAPTER 28 • the 24 inversions of the C6 chord.
093 MID – CHAPTERS 28 – 29 • intro, theme and chorus 1 of "Ombre".
094 MID – CHAPTER 29 • chorus 2 of "Ombre".
095 MID – CHAPTERS 30 – 31 – 32 • initial theme, choruses and final theme of "Chasses Croises".
096 MID – CHAPTER 33 • original version (theme) of "My Foolish Heart".
097 MID – CHAPTERS 33–34–35 • initial theme (stop chorus) of the "My Foolish Heart" arrangement.
098 MID – CHAPTERS 33-34-35 • final theme (coda) of the "My Foolish Heart" arrangement.

THEMATIC INDEX

Here is the index that we have compiled from the information given in this Style of Manouche book. It is our goal to make it easy for you to search for a theme or a given subject, so that you can use it to practice with it, or to study theory.

HARMONIC PROGRESSION (CONTINUED)

SUBSTITUTIONS

GUITAR TECHNICS

TETRASTRINGS

KEY

TRANSPOSITIONS

TRIADS

THE STYLE OF MANOUCHE

Question 50 worth 8 points

In the three blank measures, write a fourth voice underneath the first three, while using a principle used to harmonize the first fragment of this fourth voice (the measure with the pickup):

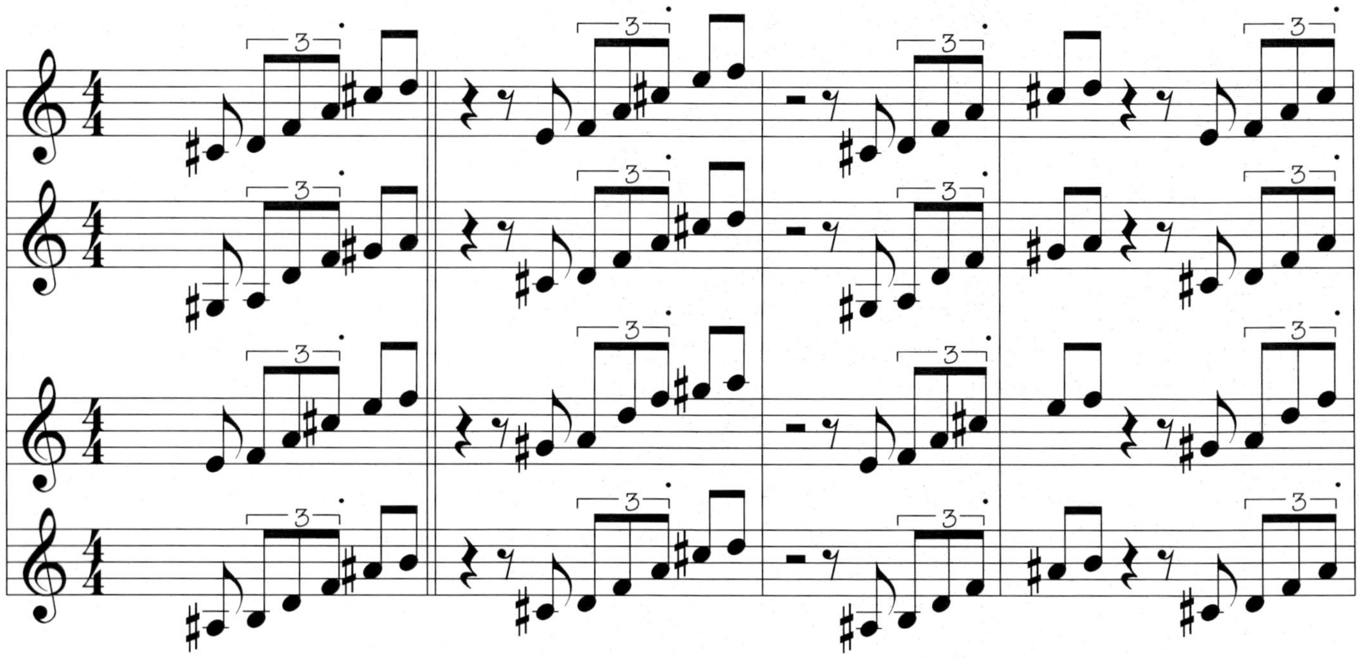

By looking at the measure the anacrouse/pickup as an example, the principle used here is the transposition of the first voice to a one minor third lower position, in the manner to form a vertical Dm6(9) chord that starts with the first note of the triplet (the B-F-A-D notes).

Then we remove the undesirable change, that is to say, the F# note shows up in the last eighth of the triplet. This alteration is undesirable because it is in conflict with the global harmony. It must be a Dm in this measure.

Do the same to harmonize the fourth voice with all the other melodicfragments.

Test answers / page 8

Question 46 worth 8x1 point

With the root note on the bass, write out the following chords:

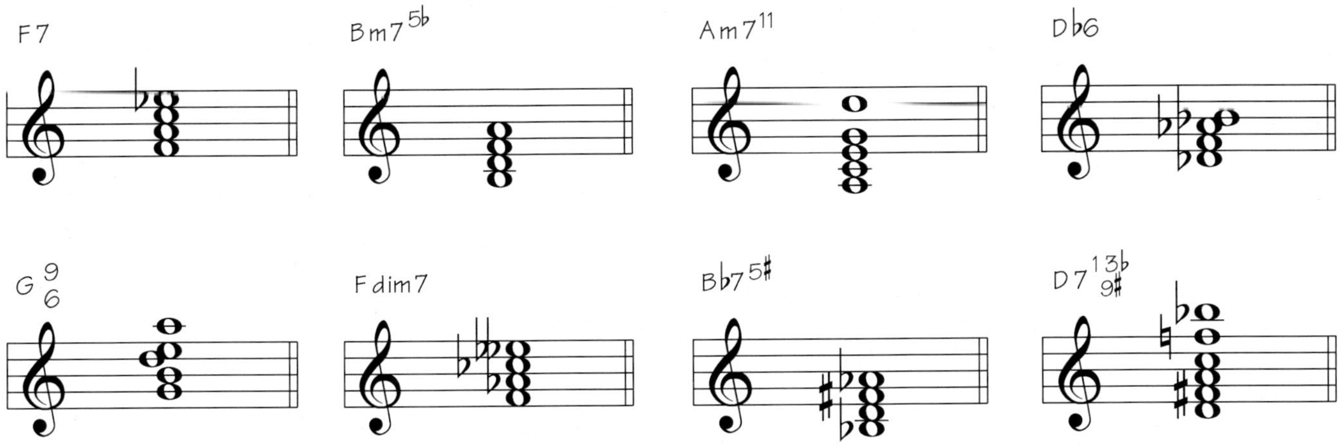

Question 47 worth 2x4 points

Construct all the inversions of the "Em7(b5)" chord:

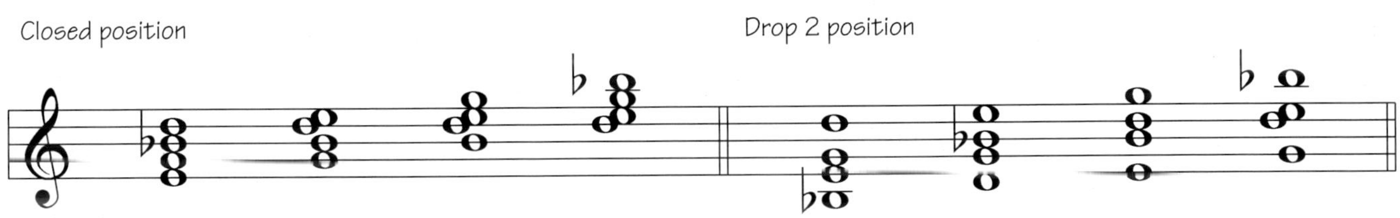

Question 48 worth 4x2 points

Write the arpeggios of the folowing chords:

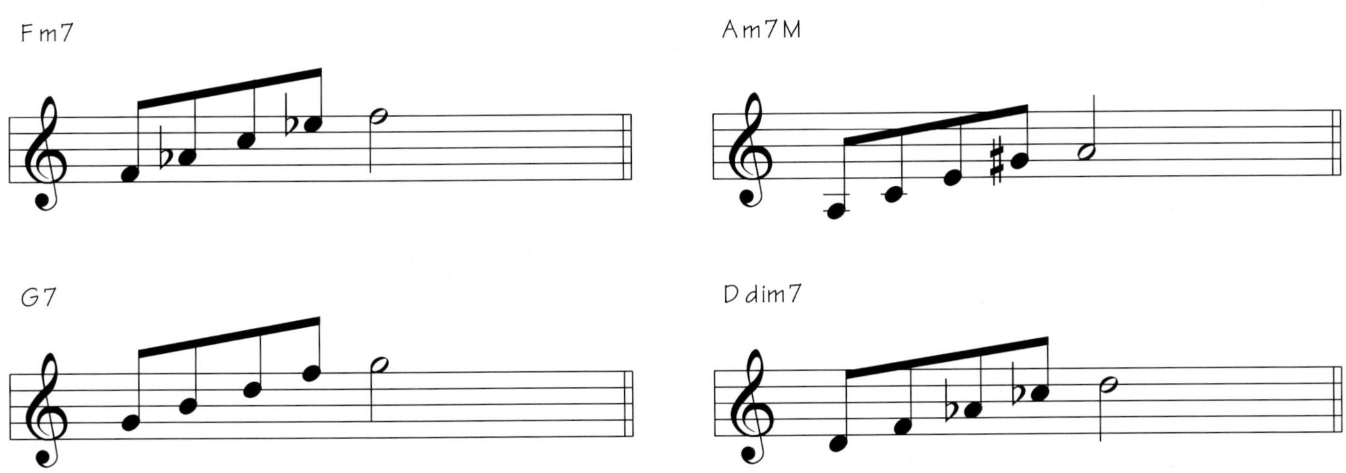

Question 49 worth 8 points

Harmonize with four voices the F#dim7 arpeggio (write the three missing voices underneath voice 1):

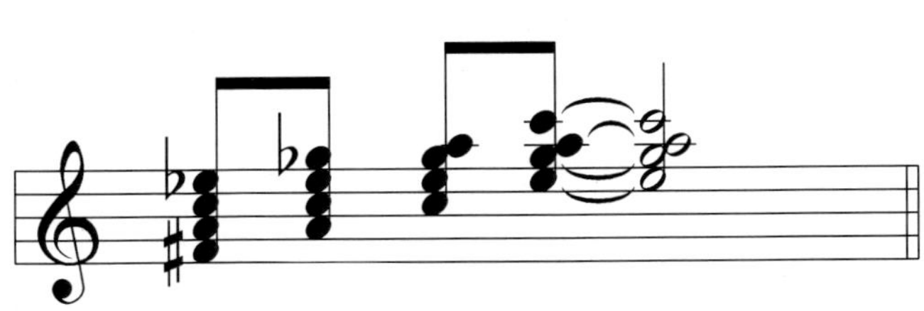

Question 41 continued

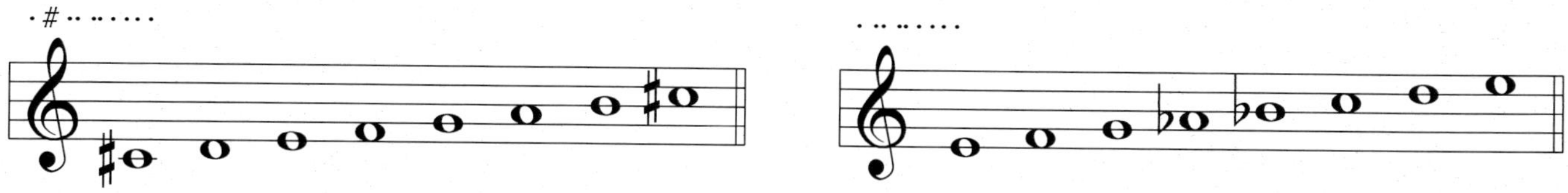

Question 42 — worth 4x2 points

Write one octave of the following scales:

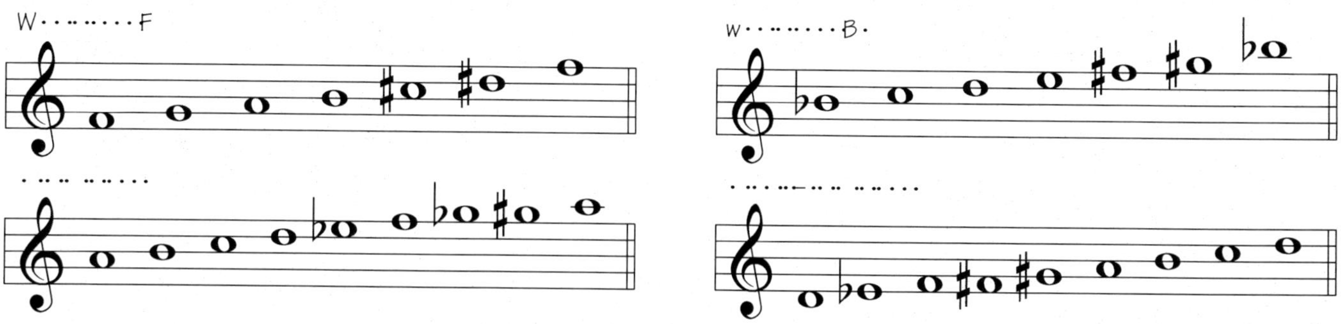

Question 43 — worth 8 points

These four measures are composed by a pianist. On the blank staff, transcribe it for the guitar.

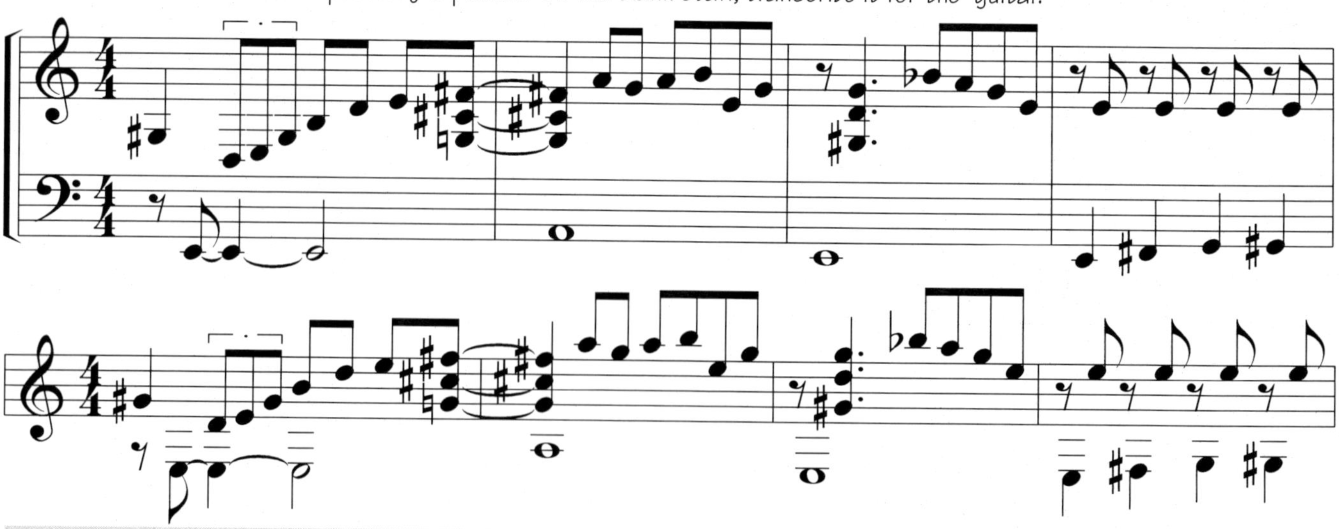

Question 44 — worth 8 points

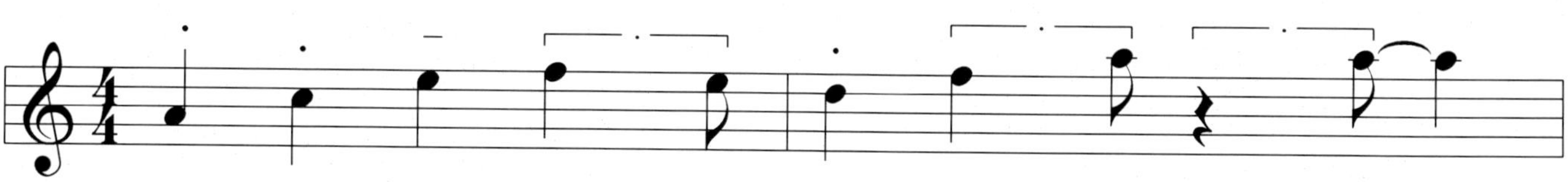

Rewrite the little fragment of the melody above, in the way that a jazzman is accustomed to read it (binary writing).

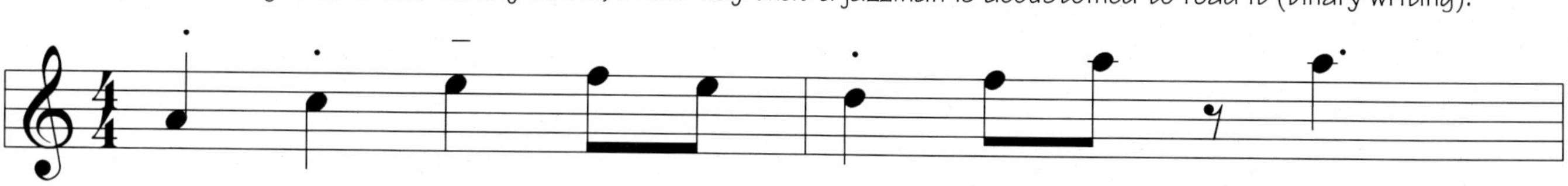

Question 45 — worth 8 points

Determine the chords (with basic symbols) that correspond with this improvised phrase:

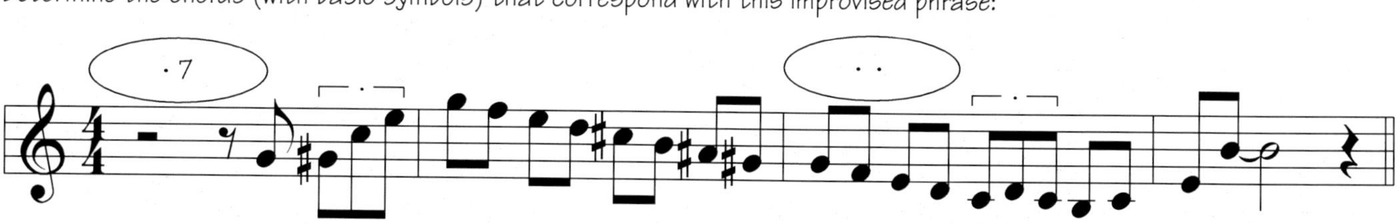

Question 36 worth 8 points

To improvise with the "F7" chord, you could use the F major arpeggio combined with the C# major.

☐ correct ■ incorrect, because, with the F7, we can use the F major arpeggio combined with those that are located one tone higher, which is the G major. Or still yet, the one located that is separated by 3 tones, which is the B major.

Question 37 worth 8 points

The whole "dim7" chord can be put in a relationship with a "7(b9)" type of which the root note is located one minor third lower.

☐ true ■ false, because the root note is located one major third lower. For example as in the case of Gdim7 and E7(9b).

WRITING

Question 38 worth 4x2 points

With the correct key signature, write one octave of the following scales:

E major

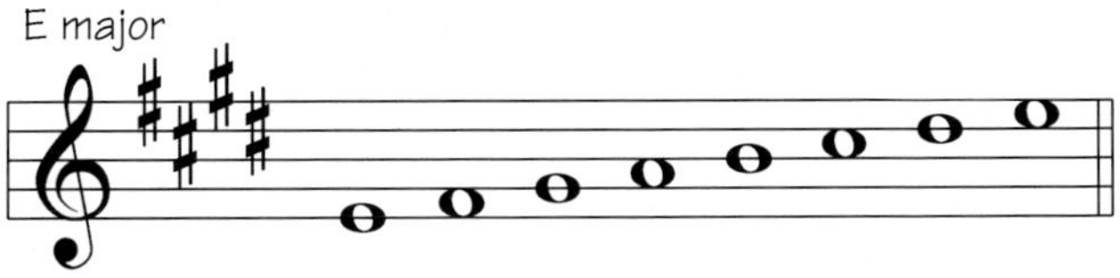

Ab major

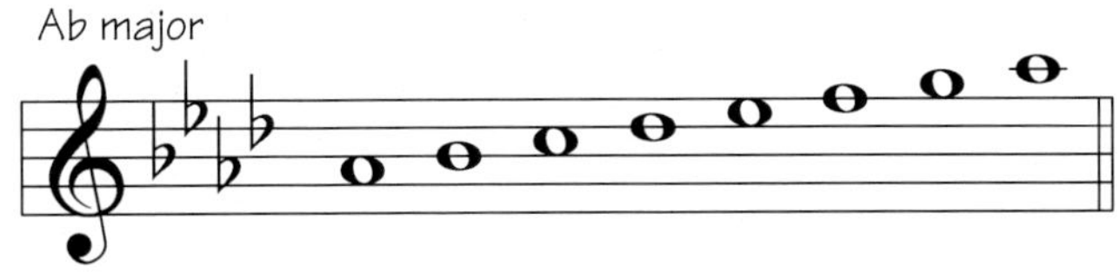

F# major

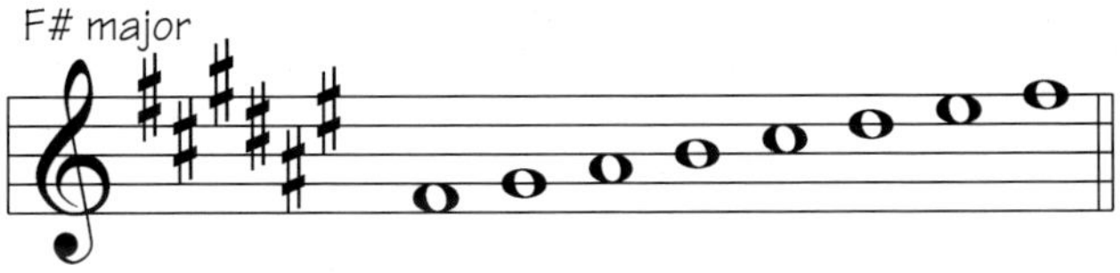

Gb major

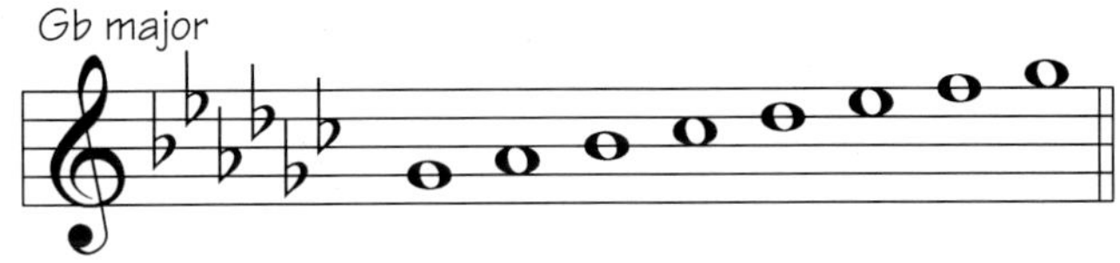

Question 39 worth 4x2 points

With the correct key signature, write one octave of the following scales:

natural minor D

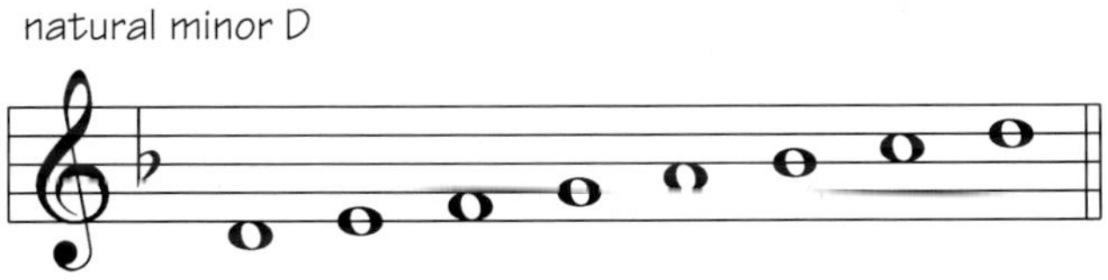

natural minor Eb

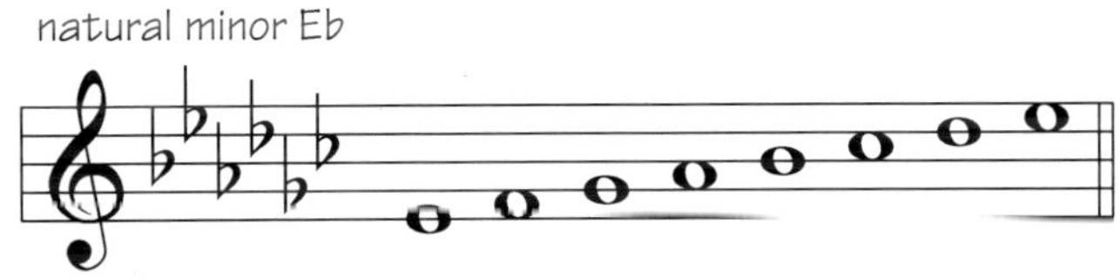

natural minor F#

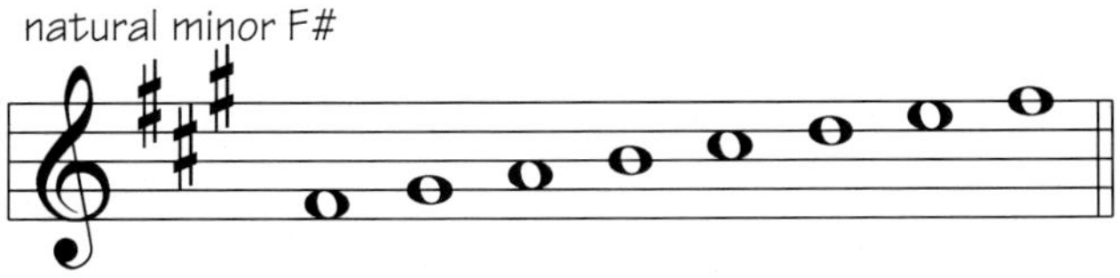

natural minor B

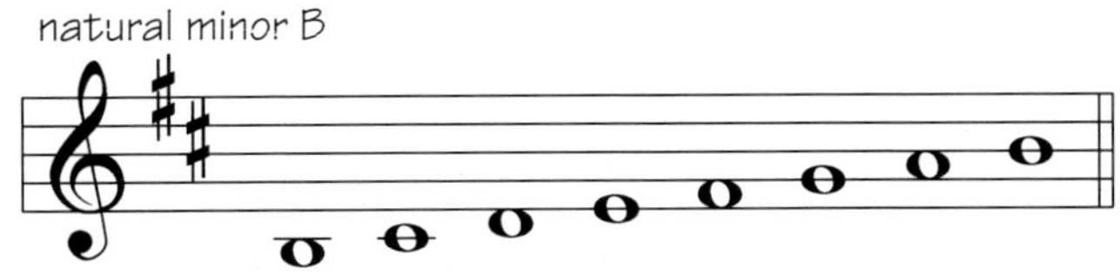

Question 40 worth 4x2 points

Write one octave of the following scales:

harmonic minor D

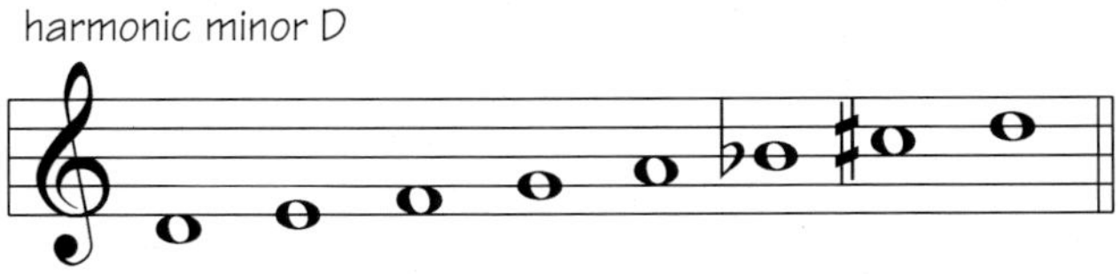

harmonic minor G

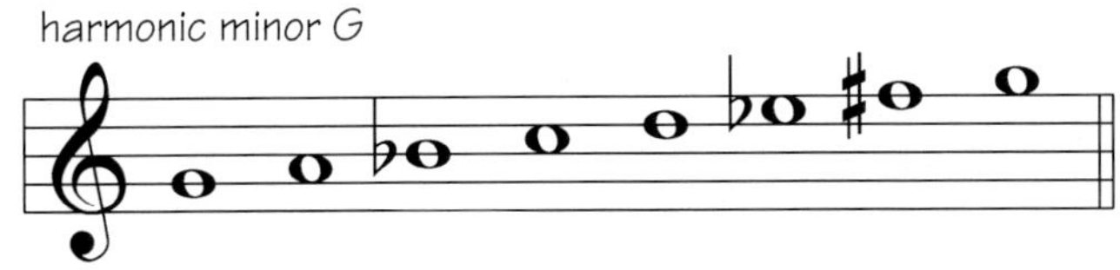

harmonic minor F#

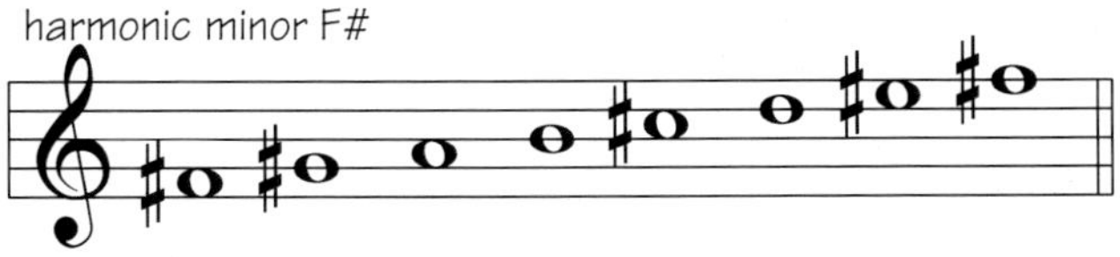

harmonic minor E

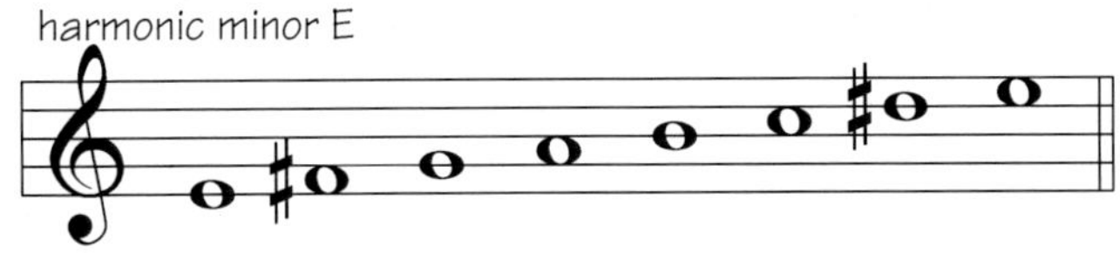

Question 41 worth 4x2 points

Write one octave of the following scales:

melodic minor Bb

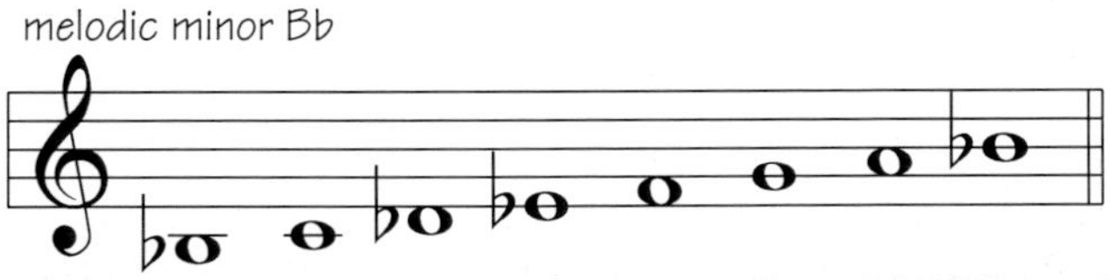

melodic minor G

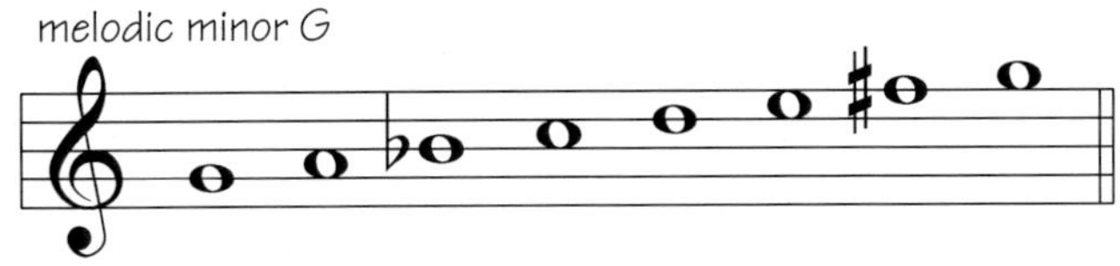

Question 27 worth 8 points

The "AbM7(9, #11)" symbol determines a chord with the following character:

☐ tonal ■ poly tonal, because this chord, formed with the Ab - C - Eb - G - Bb D, is a mixture of Ab major, C minor and G minor triads.

☐ A tonal ☐ tonally ambiguous

Question 28 worth 8 points

a) The harmonic equivalence of "Ebdim7 = F7(b9)" without a root note is:

■ accurate. Eb dim7 = Eb - Gb - A - C, which respectively are the 7 – 9m – 3M – 5 of F7(9b) ☐ not accurate

b) The harmonic equivalence A7(#9, 13) without a root note or without a fifth = Eb7(#9, 13) without a root note or with out a fifth is:

■ accurate. A7(9#,13) = B# -- C# -- F# G, which are respectively the 13M – 7 – 9# -- 3M of Eb7(9#,13). ☐ not accurate

Question 29 worth 2x4 points

a) Which chord is designated as the IV degree of the minor melodic F scale? Bb7

b) Which chord is designated as the V degree of the minor harmonic G scale? D7

Question 30 worth 8 points

Harmonized in four voices, the whole tone scale exclusively generates dominant seventh chords.

■ true ☐ false

Question 31 worth 2x4 points

a) The harmonic equivalency of "Cm6 = Ab7(9)" without a root note is:

☐ accurate ■ not accurate, because Cm6 corresponds with F7(9) without a root note, while Ab7(9) corresponds with Ebm6.

b) the harmonic equivalency of "G7(#9)" without fifth "= Db7(#11, 13)"" without a root note or fifth is:

■ accurate ☐ not accurate

Question 32 worth 8 points

Of the following two types of harmonic progressions, which is called a "be-bop turnaround"?

☐ || DM7 - F7 | Em7 - A7 || ■ || AM7 - C7 | FM7 - Bb7 ||

Question 33 worth 2x4 points

Do the following group of notes specify a "christophe" harmonic progression?

a) || EbM7 - Eb7 - AbM7 – Ab7 - EbM7 | ./. || ■ yes ☐ no

b) || AM7 - A7 - DM7 - Ebdim7 - AM7 | ./. || ■ yes ☐ no

IMPROVISATION

Question 34 worth 8 points

To improvise with the "G7 chord", it is possible to use the "Bdim7" arpeggio.

■ correct ☐ incorrect

Question 35 worth 8 points

Is it possible with the "Eb7" chord to base its improvisation on the "Am7" chord?

☐ correct ■ incorrect, because we consider the Eb7 to be a V degree. It is the II degree of this chord that we can use as a basis, which is the Bbm7 chord.

Question 16 worth 2x4 points

a) What is the tritone substituition of the "Bb7" chord? E7

b) What is the tritone substitution of the "Cb7" chord? F7 (or to be more precise yet, the E#7!).

Question 17 worth 8 points

What are the II - V - I chords in the key of Bb major? Cm7 – F7 – Bb7M

Question 18 worth 8 points

What are the II -V -I chords in the key of D minor? Em7(5B) – A alt. – Dm7

Question 19 worth 8 points

The [Am7 -Ab7 -GM7 -CM7 - F#m7(b5) - B alt. [./.] harmonic progression is in the key of:

☐ A minor ☐ F# minor ☐ C major ■ G major

Question 20 worth 8 points

In the [Bbm7 - A7 - G#m7(b5) - C#alt. - F#m7 [./.] harmonic progression, the A7 chord responds to:

☐ the dominant (A7) → tonic principle ■ the tritone substitution principle

☐ the diatonic progression principle ☐ any of these three principles

Question 21 worth 8 points

All the dominant chords can be used to introduce a major chord with its root note located one tone higher.

■ true, For example, D7 is introducing the E7M (compare the harmonic structure of MONTICELLO). ☐ false

Question 22 worth 8 points

To introduce the "Gm7" chord in a harmonic structure, it is possible to use the following chord:

☐ A7 ☐ B7 ■ D7, being the V degree of Gm7. ☐ E7

Question 23 worth 8 points

To introduce the "Am7" chord in a harmonic structure, it is possible to use the following chord:

☐ C7 ☐ Eb7 ■ Bb7, being the tritonic substitution of the V degree of Am7. ☐ B7

Question 24 worth 4x2 points

Which chords make up the harmonic "anatole" progression of the following keys:

a) G major? G7M (or Bm7) – E7 (or Bb7) – Am7 – D7 (or Ab7) – G7M

b) Bb major? Bb7M (or Dm7) – G7 (or Db7) – Cm7 – F7 (or B7) – Bb7M

c) D major? D7M (or F#m7) – B7 (or F7) -- Em7 – A7 (or Eb7) –D7M

d) Eb major? Eb7M (or Gm7) – C7 (or Gb7) – Fm7 – Bb7 (or E7) – Eb7M

Question 25 worth 8 points

The "D alt." symbol is the same as the "D7(b9, 11)" symbol.

☐ true ■ false, because in each case the "alt." chord doesn't except a perfect eleventh (11). And due to the fact that it gives this particular "D79b,11" coloration, it is a chord that is tonally ambiguous.

Question 26 worth 8 points

Show, in the initial closed order, the notes that make up the "GM7(#11, 13)" chord:

The G -- B -- C# - D - E - F#, that has the respective harmonic functions of F - 3M - 11 #- 5 - 13 - 7M.

Question 8 worth 8 points

A chord with any 4 distinct notes composed with intervals of perfect fourths belongs exclusively to the category of inversions:

☐ closed ■ drop 2, For example, the chord exclusively composed with the notes D-G-C-F notes is in the "drop 2" position, because the D note can placed between the C and F, in a way to make it an initial closed position.

☐ drop 3 ☐ drop 2/4

Question 9 worth 2x4 points

a) As long as we are looking at the melodic concept, at what period in the music history did the diminshed (and/or half-diminished) scale first appear?

During the mid - XXth century (Olivier Messiaen, "Technique De Mon Language Musical", 1944.

b) During what decade of the XXth century did "hard-bebop" first appear in jazz?

In the year 1950

HARMONY

Question 10 worth 2x4 points

a) A "7/9" chord has a root note - M9 - M3 - 7.

■ true ☐ false

b) A "7M13" chord has a Root note - M3 - 5 - M13 - 7.

☐ true ■ false, because the 7M is indispensable (and not the 7).

Question 11 worth 8 points

The harmonic "C alt." symbol is the same as the global "C7(b9, 13)".

☐ true ■ false, because of the 13m(13b) – an "altered" type note - it is indispensable.

Question 12 worth 8 points

The harmonic "E+7" symbol is the same as the "EmM7".

☐ true ■ false, because E+7 is another way to write E7(5#).

Question 13 worth 2x4 points

Are these harmonic symbols likely coherent?

a) CM7(b9, #9) ☐ yes ■ no, there are no alt. ninths in a "7M" chord.

b) C7sus4(9) ■ yes ☐ no

Question 14 worth 2x4 points

a) The "B7" chord is the V degree of which major key? E major

b) The "Cm7" chord is the III degree of which major key? Ab

Question 15 worth 2x4 points

a) The "A7M" chord has the diatonic "F#m7" chord as a substitute.

■ true ☐ false

b) The "Em7(b5)" chord has the diatonic "Bb7" chord as a substitute.

☐ true ■ false, because Em7(5b) = C7(9).

COMPREHENSIVE TEST OF KNOWLEDGE

THEORY AND GENERAL KNOWLEDGE

Question 1 — worth 8 points

A pickup never lasts more than 1 measure.

■ true, The stop-chorus, which can last for 4 measures, is not considered a pickup. ☐ false

Question 2 — worth 8 points

The "𝄎" symbol is a variation of the "𝄍" symbol, and is used the same way.

☐ true ■ false, Because "𝄍" symbol exclusively shows to repeat the immediately preceding measure.

Question 3 — worth 8 points

The notes that form the order of flats in the key signature are separated with intervals of:

☐ an octave ☐ ascending fifths ■ ascending fourth, or descending fifths.

Question 4 — worth 8 points

A natural minor scale is a major scale that starts from its fifth note.

☐ true ■ false, It starts with its sixth note.

Questions 5 — worth 8 points

An ambitus is:

☐ the ability to coordinate the two hands while practicing the guitar.

☐ the ambiguity between two notes of the same pitch but with distinct names.

■ The total distance in intervals between the lowest and highest note of a melody, or part of a melody.

Question 6 — worth 8 points

The melodic "A.L.T" (A Limited Transposition) scale with the following intervals 2M - 2m - 2M - 2m - 2M - 2m - 2M - 2m is called:

■ diminished scale ☐ an augmented scale ☐ a whole tone scale ☐ a half-diminished scale.

Question 7 — worth 2x4 points

a) The chord that has the following notes, from low to high: G - E - B - D is in the position of:

☐ closed ☐ drop 2 ■ drop 3, Because the G note (at the bass of the chord) fits in between the E and B notes.

b) The chord that has the following notes, from low to high: F - A - C - E is in the position of:

Discography

Published with the kind authorization of Editions Cezame Argile & Iris Music Production, the scores in this work and applicable musical extractions correspond with the CD, which is included in this book. These are taken from the following albums:

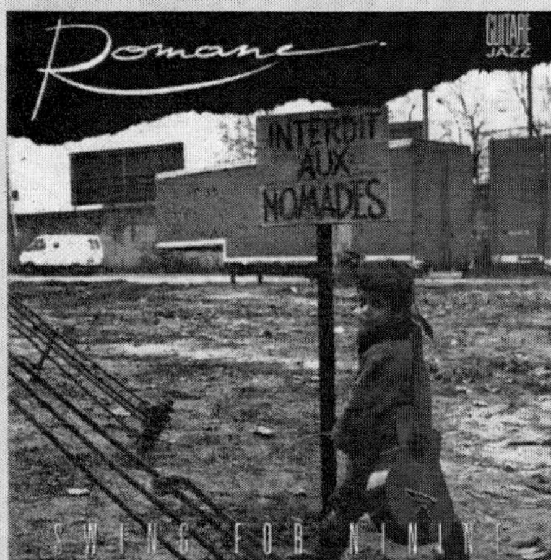

Pour Trois Pas / Arc- En - Ciel

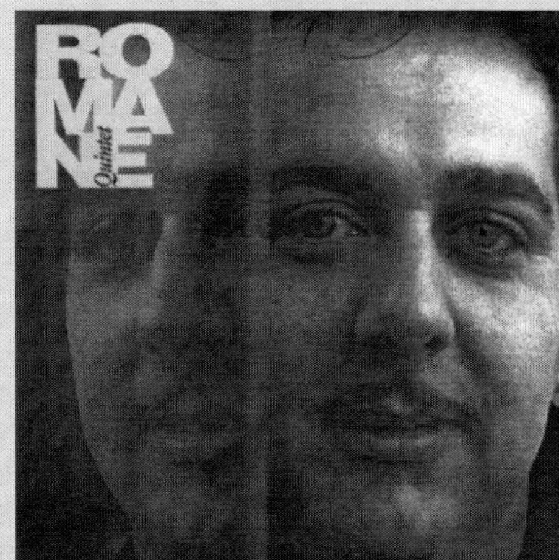

Swing For Ninie / Destinee / Dans Le Regard de Laura

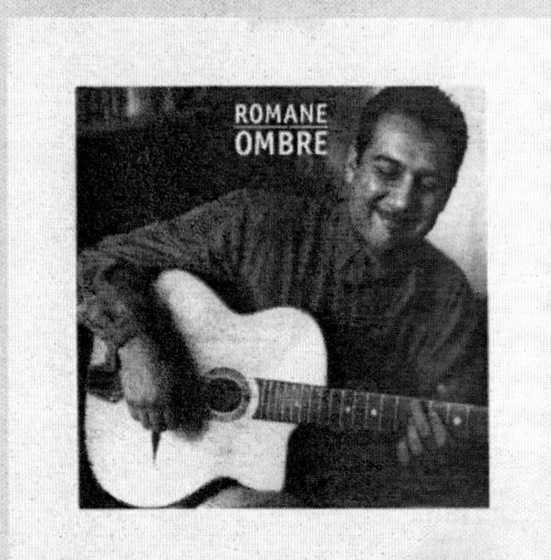

Jo's Remake (Valse a) Patrimonio/ Monticello/ Gypsy Fire/ Manege/Ombre (studio version) /Chasses Croises

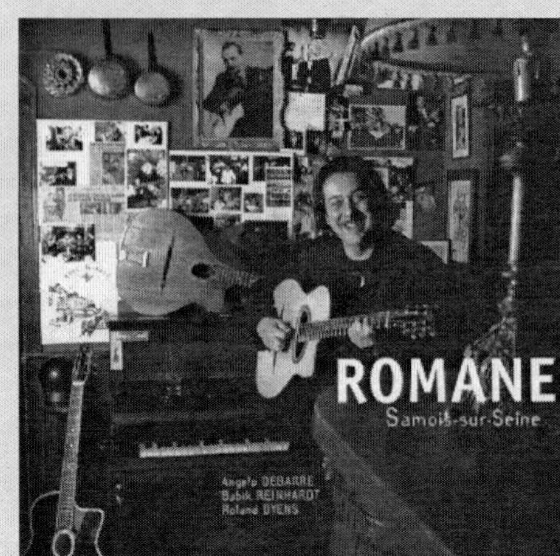

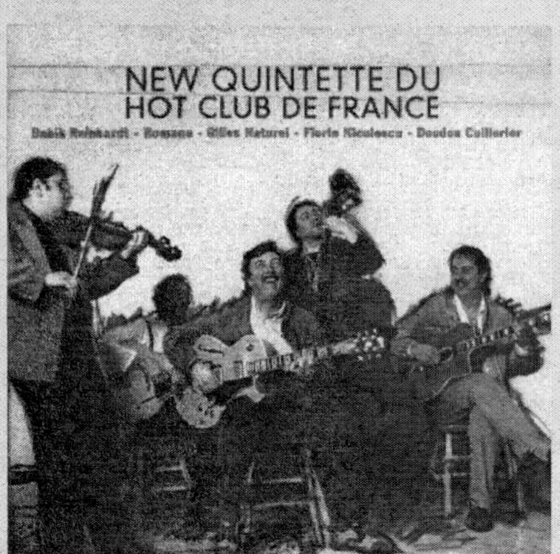

New Quintette du hot club de France (New quintet of France's Hot Club).

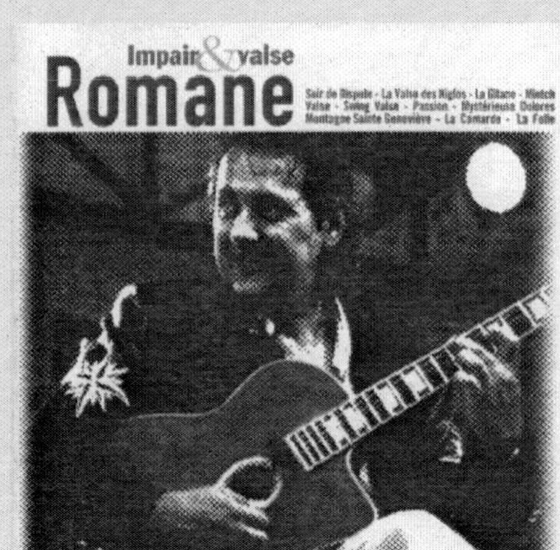

Montagne Sainte- Genevieve (Valse a Django) St. Genevieve Mountain, Waltz of Django.

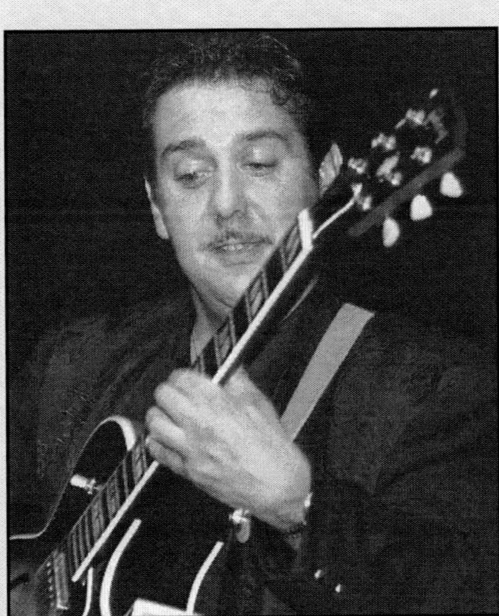

ROMANE

Romane is, in reality and without a doubt, one of the most talented heirs of Django Reinhart's guitar playing style as well as an interpreter of his compositions. When he was twelve yars old, he started to learn the guitar in the company of "gypsies", his adopted brothers who introduced him to gypsy music. From jazz clubs to festivals and concerts, he is part part of our musical landscape of Manouche type jazz. Romane is also successful in the United Sates where he recorded an album in Nashville. With the qualities of a composer and his talented interpretations, we should also mention his meticulous pedagogy, which is the result of this ultimate imposing accompaniment and exhaustive work.

DEREK SEBASTIAN

Derek has been in music for almost thirty years. Today Derek spends his time speaking about the "standards", and visiting his jazz friends and blues men. He is also a music teacher at the ATLA school of Paris, an editor of the French Guitar magazine, and a programmer for the synthesizer. He has created pedagogic musical works. Of these, nearly forty have been published (in the French language), this has gained him quite a solid reputation. He is also involved with the newer type (new age) compositions.

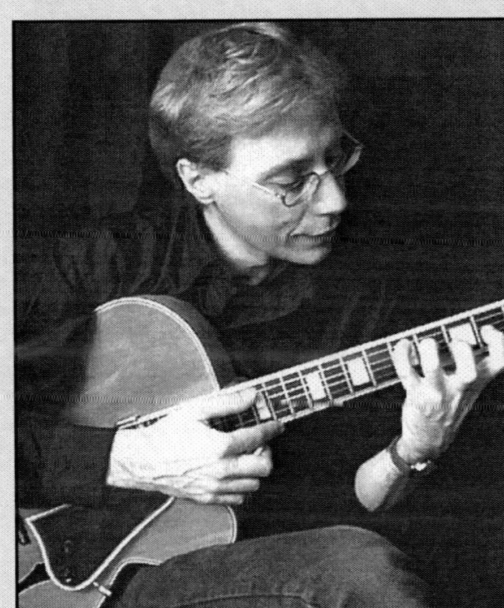

Photo Fabienne Champarnaud

WWW.MELBAY.COM